# AMERICA'S

# 1995

# DIRECTORY

*Major And Minor League*
*Names, Addresses, Schedules,*
*Phone and FAX Numbers:*
*Plus Detailed Information*
*On International, College and*
*Amateur Baseball*

---

**PUBLISHED BY**
**BASEBALL AMERICA**

**EDITOR**
Allan Simpson

**ASSOCIATE EDITOR**
James Bailey

**ASSISTANT EDITOR**
Chris Wright

**GENERAL MANAGER**
Joy C. Tempkins

**PRODUCTION MANAGER**
Janssen Strother

**PUBLISHER**
Dave Chase

**ADVERTISING MANAGER**
Kris Grubbs


Distributed by Simon & Schuster

# 1995 DIRECTORY CONTENTS

## MAJOR LEAGUES



## MINOR LEAGUES



## MISCELLANEOUS

# 1995-1996 CALENDAR

## March, 1995

| Sun | Mon | Tues | Wed | Thur | Fri | Sat |
|---|---|---|---|---|---|---|
| | | | 1 | 2 | 3 | 4 |
| 5 | 6 | 7 | 8 | 9 | 10 | 11 |
| 12 | 13 | 14 | 15 | 16 | 17 | 18 |
| 19 | 20 | 21 | 22 | 23 | 24 | 25 |
| 26 | 27 | 28 | 29 | 30 | 31 | |

## April, 1995

| Sun | Mon | Tues | Wed | Thur | Fri | Sat |
|---|---|---|---|---|---|---|
| | | | | | | 1 |
| 2 | 3 | 4 | 5 | 6 | 7 | 8 |
| 9 | 10 | 11 | 12 | 13 | 14 | 15 |
| 16 | 17 | 18 | 19 | 20 | 21 | 22 |
| 23 | 24 | 25 | 26 | 27 | 28 | 29 |
| 30 | | | | | | |

## May, 1995

| Sun | Mon | Tues | Wed | Thur | Fri | Sat |
|---|---|---|---|---|---|---|
| | 1 | 2 | 3 | 4 | 5 | 6 |
| 7 | 8 | 9 | 10 | 11 | 12 | 13 |
| 14 | 15 | 16 | 17 | 18 | 19 | 20 |
| 21 | 22 | 23 | 24 | 25 | 26 | 27 |
| 28 | 29 | 30 | 31 | | | |

## June, 1995

| Sun | Mon | Tues | Wed | Thur | Fri | Sat |
|---|---|---|---|---|---|---|
| | | | | 1 | 2 | 3 |
| 4 | 5 | 6 | 7 | 8 | 9 | 10 |
| 11 | 12 | 13 | 14 | 15 | 16 | 17 |
| 18 | 19 | 20 | 21 | 22 | 23 | 24 |
| 25 | 26 | 27 | 28 | 29 | 30 | |

## July, 1995

| Sun | Mon | Tues | Wed | Thur | Fri | Sat |
|---|---|---|---|---|---|---|
| | | | | | | 1 |
| 2 | 3 | 4 | 5 | 6 | 7 | 8 |
| 9 | 10 | 11 | 12 | 13 | 14 | 15 |
| 16 | 17 | 18 | 19 | 20 | 21 | 22 |
| 23 | 24 | 25 | 26 | 27 | 28 | 29 |
| 30 | 31 | | | | | |

## August, 1995

| Sun | Mon | Tues | Wed | Thur | Fri | Sat |
|---|---|---|---|---|---|---|
| | | 1 | 2 | 3 | 4 | 5 |
| 6 | 7 | 8 | 9 | 10 | 11 | 12 |
| 13 | 14 | 15 | 16 | 17 | 18 | 19 |
| 20 | 21 | 22 | 23 | 24 | 25 | 26 |
| 27 | 28 | 29 | 30 | 31 | | |

## September, 1995

| Sun | Mon | Tues | Wed | Thur | Fri | Sat |
|---|---|---|---|---|---|---|
| | | | | | 1 | 2 |
| 3 | 4 | 5 | 6 | 7 | 8 | 9 |
| 10 | 11 | 12 | 13 | 14 | 15 | 16 |
| 17 | 18 | 19 | 20 | 21 | 22 | 23 |
| 24 | 25 | 26 | 27 | 28 | 29 | 30 |

## October, 1995

| Sun | Mon | Tues | Wed | Thur | Fri | Sat |
|---|---|---|---|---|---|---|
| 1 | 2 | 3 | 4 | 5 | 6 | 7 |
| 8 | 9 | 10 | 11 | 12 | 13 | 14 |
| 15 | 16 | 17 | 18 | 19 | 20 | 21 |
| 22 | 23 | 24 | 25 | 26 | 27 | 28 |
| 29 | 30 | 31 | | | | |

## November, 1995

| Sun | Mon | Tues | Wed | Thur | Fri | Sat |
|---|---|---|---|---|---|---|
| | | | 1 | 2 | 3 | 4 |
| 5 | 6 | 7 | 8 | 9 | 10 | 11 |
| 12 | 13 | 14 | 15 | 16 | 17 | 18 |
| 19 | 20 | 21 | 22 | 23 | 24 | 25 |
| 26 | 27 | 28 | 29 | 30 | | |

## December, 1995

| Sun | Mon | Tues | Wed | Thur | Fri | Sat |
|---|---|---|---|---|---|---|
| | | | | | 1 | 2 |
| 3 | 4 | 5 | 6 | 7 | 8 | 9 |
| 10 | 11 | 12 | 13 | 14 | 15 | 16 |
| 17 | 18 | 19 | 20 | 21 | 22 | 23 |
| 24 | 25 | 26 | 27 | 28 | 29 | 30 |
| 31 | | | | | | |

## January, 1996

| Sun | Mon | Tues | Wed | Thur | Fri | Sat |
|---|---|---|---|---|---|---|
| | 1 | 2 | 3 | 4 | 5 | 6 |
| 7 | 8 | 9 | 10 | 11 | 12 | 13 |
| 14 | 15 | 16 | 17 | 18 | 19 | 20 |
| 21 | 22 | 23 | 24 | 25 | 26 | 27 |
| 28 | 29 | 30 | 31 | | | |

## February, 1996

| Sun | Mon | Tues | Wed | Thur | Fri | Sat |
|---|---|---|---|---|---|---|
| | | | | 1 | 2 | 3 |
| 4 | 5 | 6 | 7 | 8 | 9 | 10 |
| 11 | 12 | 13 | 14 | 15 | 16 | 17 |
| 18 | 19 | 20 | 21 | 22 | 23 | 24 |
| 25 | 26 | 27 | 28 | 29 | | |

## March, 1996

| Sun | Mon | Tues | Wed | Thur | Fri | Sat |
|---|---|---|---|---|---|---|
| | | | | | 1 | 2 |
| 3 | 4 | 5 | 6 | 7 | 8 | 9 |
| 10 | 11 | 12 | 13 | 14 | 15 | 16 |
| 17 | 18 | 19 | 20 | 21 | 22 | 23 |
| 24 | 25 | 26 | 27 | 28 | 29 | 30 |
| 31 | | | | | | |

## April, 1996

| Sun | Mon | Tues | Wed | Thur | Fri | Sat |
|---|---|---|---|---|---|---|
| | 1 | 2 | 3 | 4 | 5 | 6 |
| 7 | 8 | 9 | 10 | 11 | 12 | 13 |
| 14 | 15 | 16 | 17 | 18 | 19 | 20 |
| 21 | 22 | 23 | 24 | 25 | 26 | 27 |
| 28 | 29 | 30 | | | | |

# EVENTS CALENDAR

## March 1995-February 1996

**March 11-27**—Pan American Games at Mar Del Plata, Argentina.
**March 29**—Opening Day: Mexican League.
**April 2**—Opening Day: National League.
**April 3**—Opening Day: American League.
**April 6**—Opening Day: American Association, International League, Pacific Coast League, Eastern League, Southern League, Texas League, California League, Carolina League, Florida State League, South Atlantic League.
**April 7**—Opening Day: Midwest League.
**May 1**—Major league clubs may resume negotiations with their former players who refused salary arbitration and were unsigned as of Jan. 8.
**May 25-30**—NCAA Division III World Series at Salem, Va.
**May 26-June 1**—NAIA World Series at Sioux City, Ia.
**May 27-June 2**—Junior College World Series at Grand Junction, Colo.
**May 27-June 3**—NCAA Division II World Series at Montgomery, Ala.
**June 1**—Opening Day: Dominican Summer League.
**June 1-3**—Amateur free agent draft.
**June 2-10**—College World Series at Omaha, Neb.
**June 11, 13**—Texas League All-Stars vs. Mexican League All-Stars at El Paso/Torreon, Mexico
**June 15**—Opening Day: New York-Penn League, Northwest League.
**June 17**—Opening Day: Pioneer League.
**June 19**—Opening Day: Appalachian League, Gulf Coast League. South Atlantic League all-star game at Albany, Ga.
**June 20**—Midwest League all-star game at Grand Rapids, Mich. California League all-star game at Lake Elsinore, Calif.
**June 22-25**—Team One National Showcase at Crosley Field, Blue Ash, Ohio.
**June 23-July 2**—World Port Tournament at Rotterdam, Netherlands.
**June 24**—Opening Day: Arizona League. Florida State League all-star game at Port Charlotte, Fla.
**July 7-16**—European Championships at Haarlem, Netherlands.
**July 10**—Double-A all-star game at Shreveport, La.
**July 12**—66th Major League All-Star Game at The Ballpark in Arlington, Texas.
**July 13**—Triple-A all-star game at Scranton/Wilkes-Barre, Pa.
**July 18-26**—U.S. Olympic Festival at Colorado Springs, Colo.
**July 19**—Carolina League all-star game at Lynchburg, Va.
**July 30**—Hall of Fame induction ceremonies at Cooperstown, N.Y.
**July 31**—Hall of Fame Game at Cooperstown, N.Y.
**Aug. 1**—End of major league trading period without waivers.
**Aug. 1-15**—National Baseball Congress World Series at Wichita, Kan.
**Aug. 2-8**—World Children's Baseball Fair at Gifu City, Japan.
**Aug. 11-20**—World Junior Championships at Cape Cod/Boston, Mass.
**Aug. 14-19**—Area Code Games at Long Beach, Calif.
**Aug. 21-26**—Little League World Series at Williamsport, Pa.
**Aug. 25-29**—American Legion World Series at Fargo, N.D.
**Aug. 31**—Postseason major league roster eligibility frozen.
**Sept. 1**—Major league roster limits expanded from 25 to 40.
**Sept. 28-30**—El Paso baseball seminar.
**Oct. 1**—Major league season ends.
**Oct. 2**—Beginning of major league trading period without waivers.
**Oct. 3**—Major league playoffs begin.
**Oct. 10**—Major League Championship Series begin.
**Oct. 21**—World Series begins.
**Oct. 21-Nov. 6**—Intercontinental Cup at Havana, Cuba.
**Oct. 29-Nov. 7**—USA Baseball Fall Trials at Homestead, Fla.
**Nov. TBD**—Re-entry free agent declaration period begins 15 days after World Series ends.
**Nov. 20**—Forty-man major league winter rosters must be filed.
**Dec. 1-3**—National High School Baseball Coaches Association 1995 Convention at Anaheim, Calif.
**Dec. 1-6**—93nd annual Winter Meetings at Los Angeles, Calif.
**Dec. 5**—Rule V draft.
**Jan. 4-7**—American Baseball Coaches Association convention at Nashville, Tenn.
**Feb. 3-8**—Caribbean World Series.

# BASEBALL AMERICA

ESTABLISHED 1981

**PUBLISHER:** Dave Chase

**EDITOR:** Allan Simpson
**MANAGING EDITOR:** Jim Callis
**SENIOR ASSOCIATE EDITOR:** John Royster
**ASSOCIATE EDITOR:** Alan Schwarz
**ASSISTANT EDITOR:** Will Lingo
**ASSISTANT EDITOR:** James Bailey
**EDITORIAL ASSISTANT:** Chris Wright

**GENERAL MANAGER:** Joy C. Tempkins

**PRODUCTION MANAGER:** Janssen Strother
**PRODUCTION ASSISTANT:** Steffanie Woodfin

**BUSINESS MANAGER:** Eric Miller
**FULFILLMENT MANAGER:** Ronnie McCabe
**CUSTOMER SERVICE:** Maxine Tillman, Shirley Carter
**RECEPTIONIST:** Becky Hoskins

**ADVERTISING SALES**
Kris Grubbs, Advertising Manager
Carole Budd, Marketplace Manager
P.O. Box 2089, Durham, NC 27702
Phone (800) 845-2726

Bob Kremer, Bronxville, NY; Phone (914) 793-5026
Ron Keown, Chicago, IL; Phone (312) 822-9100
Jim Forrer, Birmingham, MI; Phone (313) 642 6440

**MEDIA RELATIONS**
Wirz and Associates, Milford, CT; Phone (203) 866-9245.

**NATIONAL NEWSSTAND CONSULTANT**
John Blassingame, Linden, NJ; Phone (201) 862-4651

**BASEBALL AMERICA, Inc.**
**PRESIDENT:** Miles Wolff
P.O. Box 2089, Durham, NC 27702
600 S. Duke St., Durham, NC 27701
Phone: (919) 682-9635
Toll-Free: (800) 845-2726
FAX: (919) 682-2880

# TOLL FREE PHONE NUMBERS

## Airlines

| | |
|---|---|
| Aero Mexico | 800-237-6639 |
| Air Canada | 800-776-3000 |
| Alaska Airlines | 800-426-0333 |
| Aloha Airlines | 800-227-4900 |
| American Airlines | 800-433-7300 |
| Continental Airlines | 800-525-0280 |
| Delta Airlines | 800-221-1212 |
| Northwest Airlines | 800-225-2525 |
| Olympic Airways | 800-223-1226 |
| Qantus Airways | 800-227-4500 |
| Trans World Airlines | 800-221-2000 |
| United Airlines | 800-631-1500 |
| U.S. Air | 800-428-4322 |

## Car Rentals

| | |
|---|---|
| Alamo (except Florida) | 800-327-9633 |
| American International | 800-527-0202 |
| Avis | 800-331-1212 |
| Avis International | 800-331-1084 |
| Budget | 800-527-0700 |
| Dollar | 800-800-4000 |
| Enterprise | 800-325-8007 |
| Hertz | 800-654-3131 |
| Hertz International | 800-654-3001 |
| National | 800-227-7368 |
| Thrifty | 800-367-2277 |

## Hotels/Motels

| | |
|---|---|
| Best Western | 800-528-1234 |
| Choice Hotels | 800-424-6423 |
| Courtyard by Marriott | 800-321-2211 |
| Days Inn | 800-325-2525 |
| Embassy Suites | 800-362-2779 |
| Hampton Inns | 800-426-7866 |
| Hilton Hotels | 800-445-8667 |
| Holiday Inns | 800-465-4329 |
| Howard Johnsons Motor Lodges | 800-654-2000 |
| Hyatt Hotels | 800-228-9000 |
| Marriott Hotels | 800-228-9290 |
| Omni Hotels | 800-843-6664 |
| Radisson Hotels | 800-333-3333 |
| Ramada Inns | 800-228-2828 |
| Red Roof Inns | 800-843-7663 |
| Sheraton Hotels | 800-325-3535 |
| TraveLodge | 800-578-7878 |
| Westin Hotels | 800-228-3000 |

## Rail

| | |
|---|---|
| Amtrak | 800-872-7245 |

# OFFICE OF THE COMMISSIONER

Bud Selig

**Mailing Address:** 350 Park Ave., 17th Floor, New York, NY 10022. **Telephone:** (212) 339-7800. **FAX:** (212) 355-0007.

**Commissioner:** Vacant.

**Chariman, Executive Council:** Allan H. "Bud" Selig.

## Officers and Directors

**Executive Director, Baseball Operations:** Bill Murray. **Supervisors:** Roy Krasik, George Pfister.

**Executive Director, Public Relations:** Richard Levin. **Managers:** Jim Small, Carole Coleman.

**Executive Director, Security/Facility Management:** Kevin Hallinan.

**Chief Financial Officer:** Jeffrey White. **Controller:** Robert Clark.

**General Counsel:** Thomas Ostertag.

**Director, Governmental Relations:** Eugene Callahan.

**Director, Market Development and MLB Charities:** Kathy Francis.

**Director, Minor League Operations:** Jimmie Lee Solomon.

**Director, Special Events:** Carolyn Taylor.

**1995 Major League All-Star Game:** July 11 at The Ballpark in Arlington, Texas.

### MAJOR LEAGUE BASEBALL PLAYER RELATIONS COMMITTEE

**Mailing Address:** 350 Park Ave., New York, NY 10022. **Telephone:** (212) 339-7400. **FAX:** (212) 371-2242.

**General Counsel:** Charles O'Connor.

**Associate Counsel:** John Westhoff, Louis Melendez.

**Contract Administrator:** Barbara Ernst.

### MAJOR LEAGUE BASEBALL PROPERTIES

**Mailing Address:** 350 Park Ave., New York, NY 10022. **Telephone:** (212) 339-7900. **FAX:** (212) 339-7628.

**Vice President, General Counsel:** Don Gibson. **Vice President, Design Services:** Anne Occi. **Director of Publishing:** Michael Bernstein.

### MAJOR LEAGUE BASEBALL INTERNATIONAL

**Mailing Address:** 1301 Avenue of the Americas, 39th Floor, New York, NY 10019. **Telephone:** (212) 977-7301. **FAX:** (212) 977-7309.

**Chief Operating Officer:** Timothy Brosnan.

**Vice President, Market Development:** Steve Baker.

**Director, Market Development:** Paul Archey. **Director, Australia:** Peter Carton. **Game Development Coordinator, Latin America:** George Santiago. **Game Development Coordinator, Europe:** Chris Stuart. **Consultant, Latin America:** Miguel Rodriguez.

# AMERICAN LEAGUE

# AMERICAN LEAGUE

Gene A. Budig

**Mailing Address:** 350 Park Ave., 18th Floor, New York, NY 10022. **Telephone:** (212) 339-7600. **FAX:** (212) 593-7138.

**Board of Directors:** Detroit, Milwaukee, Minnesota, Oakland, Seattle, Toronto.

**President:** Gene A. Budig.

**Vice President:** Gene Autry.

**Executive Director of Umpiring:** Marty Springstead. **Coordinator of Umpire Operations:** Philip Janssen. **Administrator of Umpires/Travel:** Tess Basta.

**Vice President, Administration and Media Affairs:** Phyllis Merhige.

**Director of Waiver and Player Records:** John Ricco.

**Director of Finance:** Derek Irwin.

**Assistant Director of Media Affairs:** Joseph Fitzgerald.

**Administrative Assistant, Secretary to the President:** Carolyn Coen.

**Receptionist:** Nancy Perez.

**Years League Active:** 1901-.

**1995 Opening Date:** April 3. **Closing Date:** Oct. 1.

**No. of Games:** 162.

**Division Structure: East**—Baltimore, Boston, Detroit, New York, Toronto. **Central**—Chicago, Cleveland, Kansas City, Milwaukee, Minnesota. **West**—California, Oakland, Seattle, Texas.

**Roster Limit:** 25, until Aug. 31 when rosters can be expanded to 40.

**Umpires:** Larry Barnett (Prospect, OH), Joe Brinkman (Cocoa, FL), Al Clark (Trenton, NJ), Drew Coble (Graham, NC), Derryl Cousins (Hermosa Beach, CA), Terry Craft (Sarasota, FL), Don Denkinger (Waterloo, IA), Jim Evans (Austin, TX), Dale Ford (Jonesboro, TN), Rich Garcia (Clearwater, FL), Ted Hendry (Phoenix, AZ), John Hirschbeck (Poland, OH), Mark Johnson (Honolulu, HI), Jim Joyce (Beaverton, OR), Ken Kaiser (Rochester, NY), Greg Kosc (Medina, OH), Tim McClelland (West Des Moines, IA), Larry McCoy (Greenway, AR), Jim McKean (St. Petersburg, FL), Chuck Meriwether (Nashville, TN), Durwood Merrill (Hooks, TX), Dan Morrison (Largo, FL), Steve Palermo (Overland Park, KS), Dave Phillips (Lake St. Louis, MO), Rick Reed (Rochester Hills, MI), Mike Reilly (Battle Creek, MI), Rocky Roe (Milford, MI), John Shulock (Vero Beach, FL), Tim Tschida (St. Paul, MN), Vic Voltaggio (Spring Hill, FL), Tim Welke (Kalamazoo, MI), Larry Young (Roscoe, IL). **NOTE:** At press time there were ongoing negotiations for a new agreement between the American and National leagues and the Major League Umpire's Association.

## 1994 Standings

| East | W | L | Pct. | GB |
|---|---|---|---|---|
| New York | 70 | 43 | .619 | — |
| Baltimore | 63 | 49 | .563 | 6½ |
| Toronto | 55 | 60 | .478 | 16 |
| Boston | 54 | 61 | .470 | 17 |
| Detroit | 53 | 62 | .461 | 18 |

| Central | W | L | Pct. | GB |
|---|---|---|---|---|
| Chicago | 67 | 46 | .593 | — |
| Cleveland | 66 | 47 | .584 | 1 |
| Kansas City | 64 | 51 | .557 | 4 |
| Minnesota | 53 | 60 | .469 | 14 |
| Milwaukee | 53 | 62 | .461 | 15 |

| West | W | L | Pct. | GB |
|---|---|---|---|---|
| Texas | 52 | 62 | .456 | — |
| Oakland | 51 | 63 | .447 | 1 |
| Seattle | 49 | 63 | .438 | 2 |
| California | 47 | 68 | .409 | 5½ |

## Stadium Information

| | | Dimensions | | | | |
|---|---|---|---|---|---|---|
| City | Stadium | LF | CF | RF | Capacity | '94 Att. |
| Baltimore | Camden Yards | 335 | 400 | 318 | 48,000 | 2,535,359 |
| Boston | Fenway Park | 315 | 390 | 302 | 34,182 | 1,775,818 |
| California | Anaheim | 333 | 404 | 333 | 64,593 | 1,512,622 |
| Chicago | Comiskey Park | 347 | 400 | 347 | 44,702 | 1,697,398 |
| Cleveland | Jacobs Field | 325 | 405 | 325 | 42,400 | 1,995,174 |
| Detroit | Tiger | 340 | 440 | 325 | 52,416 | 1,184,783 |
| Kansas City | Kauffman | 330 | 410 | 330 | 40,625 | 1,400,494 |
| Milwaukee | County | 315 | 402 | 315 | 53,192 | 1,268,399 |
| Minnesota | HHH Metrodome | 343 | 408 | 327 | 55,883 | 1,398,565 |
| New York | Yankee Stadium | 318 | 408 | 314 | 57,545 | 1,675,556 |
| Oakland | Alameda County | 330 | 400 | 330 | 48,219 | 1,242,692 |
| Seattle | Kingdome | 324 | 410 | 314 | 58,150 | 1,104,206 |
| Texas | Ballpark in Arlington | 334 | 400 | 325 | 48,100 | 2,503,198 |
| Toronto | SkyDome | 330 | 400 | 330 | 50,516 | 2,907,933 |

# BALTIMORE

Peter Angelos

## Telephone, Address

**Office Address:** 333 W. Camden St., Baltimore, MD 21201. **Telephone:** (410) 685-9800. **FAX:** (410) 547-6272.

## Ownership

**Operated by:** The Home Team Limited Partnership.

**Managing General Partner:** Peter Angelos.

**Vice Chairman, Community Projects and Public Affairs:** Tom Clancy.

## BUSINESS OPERATIONS

**Vice Chairman, Business and Finance:** Joe Foss.

**Director of Business Affairs:** Walter Gutowski. **Director of Human Resources:** Martena Wylie Clinton.

**General Counsel:** George Stamas.

## Finance

**Director of Finance:** Robert Ames.

## Marketing, Sales

**Director of Marketing and Advertising:** Scott Nickle. **Assistant Director:** Michael Fiorelli. **Marketing Representative:** Guillermo Lopez. **Marketing Assistant:** Kathy Case. **Director of Sales Operations:** Matt Dryer.

## Public Relations, Communications

**Telephone:** (410) 547-6150. **FAX:** (410) 547-6272.

**Director of Public Relations:** Unavailable. **Assistant Director, Public Relations:** Spiro Alafassos. **Administrative Assistant:** Jennifer Scott. Secretary: Lisa Waskiewicz.

**Director of Community Relations:** Julie Wagner. **Assistant Director of Community Relations:** Stacey Beckwith. **Community Relations Assistant:** Ken Abrams. **Community Relations Administrative Assistant:** Jennifer Ayersman. **Coordinator of Ballpark Entertainment:** Amy Nelson. **Publishing Coordinator:** Stephanie Parrillo.

## Stadium Operations

**Director of Stadium Operations:** Roy Sommerhof. **Assistant Director of Stadium Operations:** Scott Indorf.

**Head Groundskeeper:** Paul Zwaska.

**PA Announcer:** Rex Barney. **Official Scorer:** Bill Stetka.

## Ticketing

**Telephone:** (410) 685-9800. **FAX:** (410) 685-9800.

**Director of Ticket Operations:** Joe Keough. **Ticket Manager:** Audrey Brown. **Assistant Ticket Manager:** Denise Addicks. **Box Office Manager:** Steve Kowalski. **Ticket Distribution Manager:** Baker Koppelman.

## Travel, Clubhouse

**Traveling Secretary:** Phil Itzoe.

**Equipment Manager, Home:** Jim Tyler. **Equipment Manager, Visitors:** Fred Tyler.

## Radio, TV, Media

**Radio Announcers:** Jon Miller, Fred Manfra. **Flagship Station:** WBAL 1090-AM. **No. of Network Stations:** 25.

**TV Announcers:** John Lowenstein, Jim Palmer, Mel Proctor. **Flagship Stations:** WJZ Channel 13, Home Team Sports (regional cable).

**NEWSPAPERS, Daily Coverage:** Baltimore Morning Sun, Baltimore Evening Sun, Washington Post, Washington Times, York (Pa.) Daily Record.

## General Information

**Team Colors:** Orange and black.

**Hometown Dugout:** First Base.

**Stadium Location:** I-95 to exit 52 or 53.

**Standard Games Times:** Day—1:35 p.m. Night—7:35, Sat. 7:05.

**Player Representative:** Mike Mussina.

# ORIOLES

## BASEBALL OPERATIONS

**General Manager:** Roland Hemond.

**Assistant General Manager:** Frank Robinson. **Special Assistants to the General Manager:** Gordon Goldsberry, Fred Uhlman Sr. **Administrative Assistant, Baseball Operations:** Debbie Bent.

Roland Hemond

### Major League Staff

**Manager:** Phil Regan.

**Coaches:** Dugout—Steve Boros; Pitching—Mike Flanagan; Batting—Lee May; First Base—Al Bumbry; Third Base—Chuck Cottier; Bullpen—Elrod Hendricks.

### Medical, Training

**Trainers:** Richard Bancells, Jamie Reed. **Strength and Conditioning Director:** Tim Bishop.

Phil Regan

### Minor Leagues

**Telephone:** (410) 547-6120. **FAX:** (410) 547-6298.

**Director of Player Development:** Syd Thrift. **Assistant Director of Player Development:** Don Buford. **Assistant, Player Development and Scouting:** Lee MacPhail. **Coordinator of Instruction:** David Jauss.

**Roving Instructors:** Bobby Dickerson (infield), Moe Drabowsky (pitching), David Stockstill (hitting), Denny Walling (hitting).

**Head Trainer/Medical Coordinator:** Brian Ebel. **Strength and Conditioning:** Pat Hedge.

### Farm System

| Class | Farm Team | Manager | Bat. Coach | Pitch. Coach |
|---|---|---|---|---|
| AAA | Rochester | Marv Foley | Butch Davis | Claude Osteen |
| AA | Bowie | Bob Miscik | Julio Garcia | Chris Lein |
| A | Frederick | Mike O'Berry | Joe Durham | Larry McCall |
| A | High Desert | Tim Blackwell | Dave Stockstill | Jeff Morris |
| Rookie | Bluefield | Andy Etchebarren | None | Charlie Puleo |
| Rookie | Sarasota | Geno Petralli | Jesus Alfaro | John O'Donoghue |

### Scouting

**Telephone:** (410) 547-6130. **FAX:** (410) 547-6298.

**Director of Scouting:** Gary Nickels (Naperville, IL).

**Advance Scout:** Deacon Jones (Sugar Land, TX).

**Special Assignment Scouts:** Gordon Goldsberry (Lake Forest, CA), Curt Motton (Cockeysville, MD), Fred Uhlman Sr. (Baltimore, MD).

**Scouting Supervisors:** West—John Cox (Redlands, CA); Midwest—Mike Ledna (Buffalo Grove, IL); East—John Stokoe (Bristol, NH).

Gary Nickels

**Scouts:** Rick Arnold (Murrieta, CA), Ray Crone (Waxahachie, TX), Lane Decker (Oklahoma City, OK), Paul Fryer (Calabassas, CA), Jim Gilbert (Hagerstown, MD), John Green (Phoenix, AZ), Jim Howard (Clifton Park, NY), Leo Labossiere (Lincoln, RI), Miguel Machado (Miami, FL), Lamar North (Rossville, GA), Fred Petersen (Lisle, IL), Harry Shelton (Orlando, FL), Ed Sprague (Lodi, CA), Mike Tullier (New Orleans, LA), Earl Winn (Bowling Green, KY), Jerry Zimmerman (Milwaukie, OR).

**International Supervisor:** Manny Estrada (Brandon, FL).

**International Scouts:** Carlos Bernhardt (Dominican Republic), Jesus Halabi (Latin America).

# BOSTON

John Harrington

## Telephone, Address

**Office Address:** Fenway Park, 4 Yawkey Way, Boston, MA 02215. **Telephone:** (617) 267-9440. **FAX:** (617) 236-6797.

## Ownership

**Operated by:** Boston Red Sox Baseball Club.

**General Partner:** Jean R. Yawkey Trust (Trustees: John Harrington, William Gutfarb). **Limited Partners:** H.M. Stevens, Inc.; Dexter Group; Jean R. Yawkey Trust; Dr. Arthur Pappas; Samuel Tamposi; Thomas DiBenedetto; John Harrington.

**Chief Executive Officer:** John Harrington.

# BUSINESS OPERATIONS

**Executive Vice President for Administration:** John Buckley.

## Finance

**Vice President and Chief Financial Officer:** Robert Furbush.

**Controller:** Stanley Tran. **Coordinator of Payroll:** Catherine Fahy. **Coordinator of Central Purchasing:** Eileen Murphy-Tagrin.

## Marketing, Sales

**Vice President, Marketing/Sales:** Larry Cancro.

**Manager of Advertising/Promotions:** Lori McHugh. **Coordinator of Marketing Services:** Susan Pannozzo. **Manager of Corporate Sales:** Robert Capilli. **Director of Food Services:** Patricia Flanagan.

## Public Relations, Communications

**Telephone:** (617) 236-6715. **FAX:** (617) 236-6797.

**Vice President, Public Relations:** Dick Bresciani.

**Manager of Publicity:** Kevin Shea. **Coordinator of Credentials:** Mary Jane Ryan. **Manager of Publications:** Debra Matson. **Manager of Community Relations:** Ronald Burton Jr.

**Vice President, Broadcast Operations:** James Healey. **Manager of Communications:** Jeffrey Goldenberg.

## Stadium Operations

**Vice President, Stadium Operations:** Joseph McDermott.

**Superintendent of Grounds and Maintenance:** Joe Mooney.

**Director of Facilities Management:** Thomas Queenan Jr. **Manager of Property Maintenance:** John Caron.

**PA Announcer:** Leslie Sterling. **Official Scorers:** Charles Scoggins, Ben Ells.

## Ticketing

**Telephone:** (617) 267-1700. **FAX:** (617) 236-6640.

**Director of Ticket Operations:** Joe Helyar. **Manager of Box Office:** Richard Beaton Jr.

## Travel, Clubhouse

**Traveling Secretary:** Steven August.

**Equipment Manager:** Joseph Cochran. **Visiting Clubhouse Operations:** Tom McLaughlin.

## Radio, TV, Media

**Radio Announcers:** Joe Castiglione, Jerry Trupiano. **Flagship Station:** WRKO 680-AM. **No. of Network Stations:** 65.

**TV Announcers:** WSBK—Sean McDonough, Bob Montgomery. NESN—Bob Kurtz, Jerry Remy. **Flagship Stations:** WSBK Channel 38, New England Sports Network (regional cable).

**NEWSPAPERS, Daily Coverage:** Boston Globe, Boston Herald, Patriot Ledger, Providence Journal, Worcester Telegram-Gazette, Hartford Courant.

## General Information

**Team Colors:** Red, white and blue.

**Hometown Dugout:** First Base.

**Standard Games Times:** Day—1:05 p.m. Night—7:05.

**Directions to Stadium:** Massachusetts Turnpike (I-90) to Prudential exit (stay left), right at first set of lights, right on Dalton Street, left on Boylston Street, right on Ipswich Street.

**Player Representative:** Roger Clemens.

# RED SOX

## BASEBALL OPERATIONS

Dan Duquette

**Telephone:** (617) 267-9440. **FAX:** (617) 236-6649.

**Executive Vice President, Baseball Operations:** Lou Gorman.

**Executive Vice President, General Manager:** Dan Duquette.

**Assistant General Managers:** Mike Port, Elaine W. Steward. **Administrative Assistant to General Manager:** Ann Marie Starzyk.

### Major League Staff

**Manager:** Kevin Kennedy.

**Coaches:** Dugout—Tim Johnson; Pitching—Herm Starrette; Batting—Jim Rice; First Base—Frank White; Third Base—Dave Oliver.

### Medical, Training

**Medical Director/Club Physician:** Dr. Arthur Pappas.

Kevin Kennedy

**Trainer:** James Rowe Jr. **Strength and Conditioning Coordinator:** B.J. Baker. **Physical Therapist:** Richard Zawacki.

### Minor Leagues

**Telephone:** (617) 267-9440. **FAX:** (617) 236-6695.

**Director of Player Development and Administration:** Ed Kenney.

**Assistant to Player Development and Scouting:** Erwin Bryant. **Field Coordinator:** Bob Schaefer.

**Roving Instructors:** Dick Berardino (outfield, baserunning), Steve Braun (hitting), Sammy Ellis (pitching).

### Farm System

| Class | Farm Team | Manager | Bat. Coach | Pitch. Coach |
|---|---|---|---|---|
| AAA | Pawtucket | Buddy Bailey | Luis Aguayo | John Cumberland |
| AA | Trenton | Ken Macha | None | Al Nipper |
| A | Sarasota | Tom Barrett | None | Jeff Gray |
| A | Battle Creek | DeMarlo Hale | Darrell Evans | Rick Wise |
| A | Utica | Bob Geren | None | Bill Moloney |
| Rookie | Fort Myers | Felix Maldonado | None | Unavailable |

### Scouting

Wayne Britton

**Scouting Director:** Wayne Britton (Staunton, VA). **Assistant Director, Scouting:** Erwin Bryant.

**Advance Scout:** Unavailable.

**Special Assignment Scouts:** Eddie Haas (Paducah, KY), Frank Malzone (Needham, MA).

**National Crosschecker:** Howard McCullough (Greenville, NC).

**Scouts:** Ray Blanco (Miami, FL), Buzz Bowers (Wayland, MA), Ray Crone Jr. (Waxahachie, TX), Ray Fagnant (Chicopee, MA), Steve McAllister (Chillicothe, IL), Gary Rajsich (Lake Oswego, OR), Mike Rizzo (Rolling Meadows, IL), Phillip Rossi (Archbald, PA), Alex Scott (Mobile, AL), Matt Sczesny (Deer Park, NY), Jerry Stephenson (Fullerton, CA), Fay Thompson (Vallejo, CA), Luke Wrenn (Lakeland, FL), Jeffrey Zona (Mechanicsville, VA).

**Director of International Scouting:** Danny Monzon (Odessa, FL).

**International Scout:** Luis Delgado (Puerto Rico).

# CALIFORNIA

## Telephone, Address

**Office Address:** Anaheim Stadium, 2000 Gene Autry Way, Anaheim, CA 92806. **Mailing Address:** P.O. Box 2000, Anaheim, CA 92803. **Telephone:** (714) 937-7200. **FAX:** (714) 937-7277.

Richard Brown

## Ownership

**Operated by:** Golden West Baseball Company.

**Principal Owners:** Gene Autry, Jackie Autry.

**Chairman of the Board:** Gene Autry.

**Board of Directors:** Gene Autry, Jackie Autry, Richard Brown, Stanley Schneider, John Singleton, Peter Ueberroth.

**President and Chief Executive Officer:** Richard Brown.

**Executive Vice President:** Jackie Autry.

# BUSINESS OPERATIONS

**Vice President/Chief Financial Officer:** Ronald Shirley.

**Director of Human Resources:** Carmen Wesson-Goffney.

**Director, Data Operations:** Andy Roe.

## Finance

**Controller:** Jon Sullivan. **Assistant Controller:** Cristina Fisher. **Staff Accountants:** Doug McKechnie, Jean Ouyang.

## Marketing, Sales

**Vice President, Marketing:** Joe Schrier.

**Director, Marketing:** Craig Gerber. **Assistant Director, Marketing:** Richard McClemmy. **Manager, Publications:** Doug Ward. **Assistant Director, Promotions:** Jann Mueller. **Assistant to Vice President, Marketing:** Jeanne Jernegan. **Marketing Assistant:** Tony Reagins. **Technical Entertainment Coordinator:** Wade Loewe.

**Assistant Vice President, Sales:** Lynn Biggs. **Director, Sales:** Pennie Lundberg. **Manager, Sales:** Marianne Zambrano.

## Public Relations, Communications

**Vice President, Civic Affairs:** Tom Seeberg.

**Assistant Vice President, Media Relations and Broadcasting:** John Sevano. **Director, Baseball Information:** Larry Babcock. **Assistant Director, Baseball Information:** Kraig Kojian. **Assistant, Media Relations:** Carolyn LaPierre. **Club Photographers:** John Cordes, V.J. Lovero.

**Director, Community Relations:** Marie Moreno. **Director, Special Projects:** Corky Lippert. **Administrative Assistant/Speakers Bureau:** Kimberly Andrew.

## Stadium Opertions

**Vice President, Operations:** Kevin Uhlich. **Secretary:** Leslie Flammini.

**PA Announcer:** David Courtney. **Official Scorer:** Ed Munson.

## Ticketing

**Director, Ticketing:** Sheila Brazelton. **Assistant Director, Ticketing:** Susan Weiss. **Administrative Assistants:** Diane Dudaniec, Pat Howell.

## Travel, Clubhouse

**Traveling Secretary:** Frank Sims.

**Equipment Manager:** Ken Higdon. **Visiting Clubhouse:** Brian Harkins.

**Video Coordinator:** Diego Lopez.

## Radio, TV, Media

**Radio Announcers:** Mario Impemba, Bob Starr. **Flagship Station:** KMPC 710-AM.

**TV Announcers:** Ken Brett, Ken Wilson. **Flagship Stations:** KTLA Channel 5, Prime Sports (regional cable).

**NEWSPAPERS, Daily Coverage:** Los Angeles Times, Orange County Register, Long Beach Press-Telegram, Los Angeles Daily News, South Bay Daily Breeze, San Gabriel Valley Tribune, Riverside Press Telegram, Inland Valley Daily Bulletin, San Bernardino Sun, Los Angeles Opinion (Spanish).

## General Information

**Team Colors:** Red, navy blue and silver.

**Hometown Dugout:** Third Base.

**Stadium Location:** Highway 57 (Orange Freeway) to Katella Ave. exit, west on Katella, stadium on west side of Orange Freeway.

**Standard Game Times:** Day—1:05 p.m. Night—7:05.

**Player Representative:** Mark Langston, Gary DiSarcina (alternate).

# ANGELS

## BASEBALL OPERATIONS

**Vice President, General Manager:** Bill Bavasi. **Assistant General Manager:** Tim Mead. **Special Assistants to General Manager:** Preston Gomez, Bob Harrison. **Executive Secretary to General Manager:** Cathy Carey. **Legal Counsel/ Contract Negotiations:** Mark Rosenthal.

**Bill Bavasi**

### Major League Staff

**Manager:** Marcel Lachemann.

**Coaches:** Pitching—Chuck Hernandez; Batting—Rod Carew; Bench—Bobby Knoop; First Base—Joe Maddon; Third Base—Rick Burleson; Bullpen—Bill Lachemann.

### Medical, Training

**Medical Director:** Dr. Lewis Yocum. **Senior Medical Consultant:** Dr. Robert Kerlan.

**Marcel Lachemann**

**Trainers:** Ned Bergert, Rick Smith. **Strength/ Conditioning:** Tom Wilson. **Sports Psychologist:** Ken Ravizza. **Administrative Assistant:** Chris Titchenal.

### Minor Leagues

**Director, Player Development:** Ken Forsch.

**Assistant Director, Scouting/Player Development:** Jeff Parker. **Coordinator of Instruction:** Eddie Rodriguez. **Administrative Assistant, Minor Leagues:** Janet German.

**Roving Instructors:** Bob Clear (general), Mike Couchee (pitching), John McNamara (catching), Gary Pettis (base running), Gene Richards (hitting), Eddie Rodriguez (defense).

### Farm System

| Class | Farm Team | Manager | Bat. Coach | Pitch. Coach |
|---|---|---|---|---|
| AAA | Vancouver | Don Long | John Morris | Gary Ruby |
| AA | Midland | Mario Mendoza | Jeff Barns | Kernan Ronan |
| A | Lake Elsinore | Mitch Seoane | Doug Davis | Howie Gershberg |
| A | Cedar Rapids | Tom Lawless | Charlie Romero | Steve Renko |
| A | Boise | Tom Kotchman | Unavailable | Jim Bennett |
| Rookie | Mesa | Bruce Hines | Orlando Mercado | Zeke Zimmerman |

### Scouting

**Assistant Vice President, Scouting/Player Personnel:** Bob Fontaine Jr.

**Administrative Assistant:** Karen Thomas.

**Major League Scouts:** Dave Garcia (El Cajon, CA), Nick Kamzic (Evergreen Park, IL), Joe McDonald (Lakeland, FL), Rich Schlenker (Walnut Creek, CA), Moose Stubing (Villa Park, CA).

**Advance Scout:** Matt Keough (Cota de Caza, CA).

**Bob Fontaine Jr.**

**Free-Agent Coordinators:** Tom Davis (Livermore, CA), Jay Hankins (Greenwood, MO), Rick Ingalls (Anaheim Hills, CA), Hal Keller (Issaquah, WA), Tim Kelly (Carlsbad, CA), Jon Neiderer (Pittsburgh, PA), Paul Robinson (Fort Worth, TX).

**Free-Agent Supervisors:** Ted Brzenk (Waukesha, WI), John Burden (Fairfield, OH), Tom Burns (Harrisburg, PA), Mike Cadahia (Miami, FL), Red Gaskill (La Marque, TX), Steve Gruwell (West Covina, CA), Kris Kline (Mesa, AZ), Tom Kotchman (Seminole, FL), Tony La Cava (Oakmont, PA), Ron Marigny (Metairie, LA), Jim McLaughlin (Yonkers, NY), Darrell Miller (Yorba Linda, CA), Tom Osowski (Milwaukee, WI), Jerry Streeter (Modesto, CA), Dale Sutherland (La Crescenta, CA), Rip Tutor (Lenoir, NC), Jack Uhey (Vancouver, WA).

**Area Scouts:** Don Archer (Vancouver, B.C.), Fred Hatfield (Tallahassee, FL), Dick Probola (Pittsburgh, PA), Bob Protexter (Sioux City, IA).

**Supervisor, International Scouting:** Lee Sigman. **Administrative Assistant:** Mark Garcia. **Development and Scouting:** Ozzie Virgil.

**International Supervisors:** Marco Davalillo (Venezuela), Pompeyo Davalillo (South America), Leo Figueroa (Mexico, Central America), Wally Komatsubara (Pacific Rim), Duck Lee (Korea, Taiwan), Adrian Meagher (Australia), Jorge Ortiz (Puerto Rico), Eusebio Perez (Mexico, Central America), Reuben Rodriguez (Mexico).

# CHICAGO

Jerry Reinsdorf

## Telephone, Address

**Office Address:** 333 W. 35th St., Chicago, IL 60616. **Telephone:** (312) 924-1000. **FAX:** (312) 451-5116.

## Ownership

**Operated by:** Chicago White Sox, Ltd.

**Chairman:** Jerry Reinsdorf. **Vice Chairman:** Eddie Einhorn.

**Board of Directors:** Fred Brzozowski, Gene Fanning, Jack Gould, Robert Judelson, Judd Malkin, Robert Mazer, Allan Muchin, Jay Pinsky, Larry Pogofsky, Lee Stern, Sanford Takiff, Burton Ury, Charles Walsh.

**General Counsel:** Allan Muchin.

# BUSINESS OPERATIONS

**Executive Vice President:** Howard Pizer.

**Director of Management Information Systems:** Don Brown. **Director of Human Resources:** Moira Foy. **Special Assistant to the Chairman:** Ken Williams.

## Finance

**Vice President, Finance:** Tim Buzard.

**Controller:** Bill Waters. **Accounting Manager:** Julie Knarr.

## Marketing, Sales

**Senior Vice President, Marketing and Broadcasting:** Rob Gallas.

**Director of Marketing and Broadcasting:** Mike Bucek. **Director of Sponsorship Sales and Promotions:** Bob Grim. **Manager of Promotions and Marketing Services:** Sharon Sreniawski. **Manager of Broadcast Operations and Sales:** Jim Muno. **Marketing Account Executives:** Greg Carney, John Browne. **Manager of Scoreboard Operations and Production:** Jeff Szynal.

**Director of Ticket Sales:** Bob Voight. **Manager of Special Sales Programs:** Kevin Spudic.

## Public Relations, Communications

**Telephone:** (312) 451-5300. **FAX:** (312) 451-5116.

**Director of Public Relations:** Doug Abel. **Assistant Director of Public Relations:** Scott Reifert. **Secretary and Credentials Coordinator:** Mary Dosek.

**Coordinator of Publications:** Suzanne Reichart. **Coordinator of Publicity:** Bob Beghtol.

**Director of Community Relations:** Christine Makowski. **Coordinator of Community Relations:** Catherine Brennan.

## Stadium Operations

**Vice President, Stadium Operations:** Terry Savarise.

**Director of Park Operations:** David Schaffer. **Assistant Director of Park Operations:** Dan Polvere. **Manager of Guest Relations:** Julie Taylor.

**Head Groundskeeper:** Roger Bossard.

**PA Announcer:** Gene Honda. **Official Scorer:** Bob Rosenberg.

## Ticketing

**Telephone:** (312) 924-1000. **FAX:** (312) 451-5102.

**Director of Ticket Operations:** Bob Devoy. **Ticket Manager:** Ed Cassin. **Ticket Office Supervisor:** Mike Mazza.

## Travel, Clubhouse

**Traveling Secretary:** Glen Rosenbaum.

**Equipment Manager:** Willie Thompson. **Visiting Clubhouse:** Joe McNamara, Gabe Morell. **Umpires Clubhouse:** Vince Fresso.

## Radio, TV, Media

**Radio Announcers:** John Rooney, Ed Farmer, Ken Korach. **Flagship Station:** WMAQ 670-AM. **No. of Network Stations:** 25.

**TV Announcers:** Ken Harrelson, Tom Paciorek. **Flagship Stations:** WGN TV-9, SportsChannel Chicago (regional cable).

**NEWSPAPERS, Daily Coverage:** Chicago Sun-Times, Chicago Tribune, Arlington Heights Daily Herald, Daily Southtown.

## General Information

**Team Colors:** Silver and black.

**Hometown Dugout:** Third Base.

**Standard Game Times:** Day—1:05 p.m. Night—7:05 p.m.; Sat. 6:05.

**Stadium Location:** 35th Street exit off Dan Ryan Expressway (I-90/94).

**Player Representative:** Mike LaValliere.

# WHITE SOX

## BASEBALL OPERATIONS

Ron Schueler

**Senior Vice President, Major League Operations:** Ron Schueler. **Senior Vice President, Baseball:** Jack Gould. **Vice President, Free Agent and Major League Scouting:** Larry Monroe.

**Director of Baseball Operations:** Dan Evans. **Major League Computer Scouting Analyst:** Mike Maziarka. **Special Projects Analyst for Baseball Operations:** Kim Ng. **Video Coordinator:** Joe Inzerillo.

### Major League Staff

**Manager:** Gene Lamont.

**Coaches:** Dugout—Joe Nossek; Pitching—Jackie Brown; Batting—Walt Hriniak; First Base—Doug Mansolino; Third Base—Terry Bevington; Bullpen—Rick Peterson.

### Medical, Training

**Senior Team Physician:** Dr. James Boscardin.

**Head Trainer:** Herm Schneider. **Assistant Trainer:** Mark Anderson. **Director of Conditioning:** Steve Odgers.

Gene Lamont

### Minor Leagues

**Minor League Development Complex:** 1090 N. Euclid Ave., Sarasota, FL 34237. **Telephone:** (813) 366-8451. **FAX:** (813) 366-6615.

**Director of Minor League Operations:** Steve Noworyta. **Assistant to the Director of Minor League Operations:** Tim Ciombor. **Minor League Administrator:** Judi Miller. **Clubhouse Manager:** Mark Brown. **Receptionist:** Kelly Nance.

**Director of Instruction:** Jim Snyder. **Strength and Conditioning Coordinator:** Vern Gambetta.

**Roving Instructors:** Tony Franklin (infield), Bryan Little (general), Mike Lum (hitting), Dewey Robinson (pitching), Tom Spencer (outfield), Tommy Thompson (catching), Dallas Williams (baserunning).

### Farm System

| Class | Farm Team | Manager | Bat. Coach | Pitch. Coach |
|---|---|---|---|---|
| AAA | Nashville | Rick Renick | Roger LaFrancois | Don Cooper |
| AA | Birmingham | Terry Francona | Mike Barnett | Kirk Champion |
| A | Prince William | Dave Huppert | Jay Ward | Jaime Garcia |
| A | South Bend | Fred Kendall | Mark Haley | Curt Hasler |
| A | Hickory | Mike Rojas | Dave Keller | Bill Ballou |
| Rookie | Bristol | Unavailable | Mark Salas | Unavailable |
| Rookie | Sarasota | Mike Gellinger | Von Joshua | Sean Snedeker |

### Scouting

Duane Shaffer

**Telephone:** (312) 451-5291. **FAX:** (312) 451-5105.

**Director of Scouting:** Duane Shaffer.

**Assistant to the Director of Scouting:** Grace Guerrero Zwit. **Player Development/Scouting Administrator:** Dan Fabian.

**Advance Scouts:** Ed Brinkman (Cincinnati, OH), Bart Johnson (Chicago, IL), Mike Pazik (Bethesda, MD), Dave Yoakum (Orlando, FL).

**National Crosschecker:** George Bradley (Tampa, FL).

**Scouting Supervisors:** East—Mark Bernstein (Great Neck, NY); Midwest—Doug Laumann (Hebron, KY); West—Ed Pebley (Hillsborough, CA).

**Full-Time Scouts:** Steve Arnieri (Chicago, IL), Kevin Burrell (Atlanta, GA), Joseph Butler (East Rancho Dominguez, CA), Scott Cerny (Davis, CA), Alex Cosmidis (Winston-Salem, NC), Larry Grefer (Park Hills, KY), Warren Hughes (Mobile, AL), John Kazanas (Phoenix, AZ), Reggie Lewis (Elkton, MD), Bill Meyer (Sarasota, FL), Jose Ortega (Hialeah, FL), Dave Owen (Arlington, TX), Gary Pellant (Bellevue, WA), Paul Provas (Shawnee Mission, KS), Mike Sgobba (Yorba Linda, CA), Ken Stauffer (Katy, TX), John Tumminia (Newburgh, NY), Ken Williams (Naperville, IL).

**International Scouts:** Juan Bernhardt (Dominican Republic), Hernan Cortes (Venezuela), Miguel Ibarra (Panama).

# CLEVELAND

Richard Jacobs

## Telephone, Address

**Office Address:** Jacobs Field, 2401 Ontario St., Cleveland, OH 44115. **Telephone:** (216) 420-4200. **FAX:** (216) 420-4396.

## Ownership

**Operated by:** The Jacobs Group.

**Chairman of the Board, Chief Executive Officer:** Richard Jacobs.

**Board of Directors:** Richard Jacobs, Martin Cleary, Gary Bryenton.

# BUSINESS OPERATIONS

**Executive Vice President, Business:** Dennis Lehman.

**Manager, Spring Training:** Jerry Crabb.

## Finance

**Vice President, Finance:** Ken Stefanov.

**Controller:** Ron McQuate. **Director, Information Systems:** Dave Powell. **Staff Accountants:** Jim Harrah, Karen Menzing.

## Marketing, Sales

**Vice President, Marketing and Communications:** Jeff Overton.

**Director, Corporate Marketing and Sales:** Jon Starrett. **Corporate Sales Representatives:** Linda Ahern, Scott Bailey. **Manager, Promotion:** Chris Previte.

**Director of Merchandising and Licensing:** Jayne Churchmack.

**Director, Advertising/Publications:** Valerie Arcuri. **Manager, Advertising/Publications:** Kim Carpinello.

**Director, Broadcasting:** Michael Lehr. **Manager, Broadcasting:** Nadine Glinski. **Manager, Scoreboard Operations:** Steve Warren.

## Public Relations, Communications

**Telephone:** (216) 420-4350. **FAX:** (216) 420-4396.

**Vice President, Public Relations:** Bob DiBiasio.

**Manager of Media Relations:** Bart Swain. **Assistant Director of Media Relations:** Susie Gharrity.

**Director of Community Relations:** Allen Davis. **Manager of Community Relations:** Eva Manning.

## Stadium Operations

**Director of Ballpark Operations:** Jim Folk. **Manager, Game Day Staff:** Rodney Lewallen. **Manager, Field Maintenance:** Brandon Koehnke. **Manager, Building Maintenance:** Chris Donahoe.

**PA Announcer:** Mark Tromba. **Official Scorers:** Hank Kosloski, Rick Rembielak.

## Ticketing

**Director, Ticket Sales:** Vic Gregovits. **Manager, Ticket Sales:** Scott Sterneckert. **Manager, Heavy Hitters Club:** Mike Mulhall.

**Director, Ticket Services:** Connie Minadeo. **Manager, Box Office:** Tom McGrane.

## Travel, Clubhouse

**Director, Team Travel:** Mike Seghi.

**Clubhouse Manager:** Stan Hunter. **Equipment Manager:** Jeff Sipos. **Visiting Clubhouse Manager:** Cy Buynak.

**Baseball Video Operations:** Joe Catalioti, Michael Kestner.

## Radio, TV, Media

**Radio Announcers:** Tom Hamilton, Herb Score. **Flagship Station:** WKNR 1220-AM. **No. of Network Stations:** 32.

**TV Announcers:** WUAB—Jack Corrigan, Mike Hegan; SportsChannel—Rick Manning, John Sanders. **Flagship Stations:** WUAB Channel 43, SportsChannel Ohio (regional cable).

**NEWSPAPERS, Daily Coverage:** Cleveland Plain Dealer, Lake County News-Herald, Akron Beacon-Journal.

## General Information

**Team Colors:** Red, white and navy blue.

**Hometown Dugout:** Third Base.

**Standard Game Times:** Day—1:05 p.m.; Night—7:05.

**Stadium Location:** From south—I-77 North to East 9th St. exit, to Ontario Street; From east—I-90/Rt. 2 west to downtown, remain on Rt. 2 to East 9th St., left to stadium.

**Player Representative:** Charles Nagy.

# INDIANS

## BASEBALL OPERATIONS

**Executive Vice President, General Manager:** John Hart.

**Director of Baseball Operations/Assistant General Manager:** Dan O'Dowd. **Administrator, Player Personnel:** Wendy Hoppel.

**Executive Administrative Assistant:** Ethel LaRue. **Assistant, Baseball Operations:** Josh Byrnes. **Administative Assistant:** Barbara Lessman.

John Hart

### Major League Staff

**Manager:** Mike Hargrove.

**Coaches:** Pitching—Mark Wiley; Batting—Charlie Manuel; Dugout/Infield—Buddy Bell; First Base—Dave Nelson; Third Base—Jeff Newman; Bullpen—Luis Isaac.

Mike Hargrove

### Medical, Training

**Medical Director:** Dr. William Wilder.

**Head Trainer:** Jim Warfield. **Assistant Trainer:** Paul Spicuzza. **Strength and Conditioning Coach:** Fernando Montes.

### Minor Leagues

**Director, Minor League Operations:** Mark Shapiro. **Administrative Assistant:** Gordy Gutowsky. **Special Assistant, Baseball Operations:** Johnny Goryl.

**Director of Instruction:** Boyd Coffie.

**Roving Instructors:** Mike Brown (pitching), Scott Hoffman (strength and conditioning), Gordy MacKenzie (outfield), Harry Spilman (hitting).

### Farm System

| Class | Farm Team | Manager | Bat. Coach | Pitch. Coach |
|---|---|---|---|---|
| AAA | Buffalo | Brian Graham | Jack Mull | Dom Chiti |
| AA | Canton-Akron | Ted Kubiak | Joe Mikulik | Greg Booker |
| A | Kinston | Gordy MacKenzie | Dan Williams | Tony Arnold |
| A | Columbus | Jeff Datz | None | Fred Gladding |
| A | Watertown | Joel Skinner | Billy Williams | Ken Rowe |
| Rookie | Burlington | Harry Spilman | Minnie Mendoza | Dave Miller |

### Scouting

**Telephone:** (216) 420-4308. **FAX:** (216) 420-4321.

**Scouting Director:** Jay Robertson. **Assistant, Scouting:** Keith Boeck.

**Major League/Special Assignment Scouts:** Dan Carnevale (Buffalo, NY), Tom Giordano (Amityville, NY), Ted Simmons (Chesterfield, MO), Bill Werle (San Mateo, CA)

**Scouting Supervisors:** West—Jesse Flores (Sacramento, CA), Midwest—Clark Crist (Tucson, AZ), East—Jerry Jordan (Wise, VA).

Dan O'Dowd

**Scouts:** Steve Avila (Olympia, WA), Brad Cameron (Los Alamitos, CA), Paul Cogan (Sacramento, CA), Tom Couston (Chicago, IL), Rene Gayo (El Paso, TX), Mark Germann (Chattanooga, TN), Guy Mader (Tewksbury, MA), Bob Mayer (Somerset, PA), Kasey McKeon (Elon College, NC), Jim Richardson (Marlow, OK), Max Semler (Collierville, TN), Jim Stevenson (Norman, OK), Gene Thompson (Scottsdale, AZ), Gary Tuck (Delray Beach, FL), Craig Wallenbrock (Arcadia, CA), Mark Weidemaier (Tierra Verde, FL).

**International Scouts:** Luis Aponte (Venezuela), Winston Llenas (Domincan Republic).

# DETROIT

John McHale Jr.

## Telephone, Address

**Office Address:** Tiger Stadium, 2121 Trumbull Ave., Detroit, MI 48216. **Telephone:** (313) 962-4000. **FAX:** (313) 962-1128.

## Ownership

**Operated by:** Detroit Tigers, Inc.

**Principal Owners:** Mike Ilitch, Marian Ilitch.

**Chairman of the Board:** Mike Ilitch.

**Board of Directors:** Marian Ilitch, Charles Jones, Jay Bielfield, Denise Ilitch Lites, Ronald Ilitch, Mike Ilitch Jr., Lisa Ilitch Murray, Atanas Ilitch, Christopher Ilitch, Carole Ilitch Trepeck.

**President:** John McHale Jr. **Vice Presidents:** Atanas Ilitch, Christopher Ilitch.

# BUSINESS OPERATIONS

**Chief Executive Officer:** John McHale Jr.

**General Counsel:** Jay Bielfield. **Urban Development:** Emmett Moten.

## Finance

**Controller:** Scott Fisher. **Accounting:** Patricia Kenney, Maureen Kraatz.

## Marketing, Sales

**Director of Marketing:** Michael Dietz. **Assistant Director of Marketing:** Joe Napoli. **Marketing Coordinator:** James Brylewski. **General Sales Manager:** Martin Pawlusiak.

**Season/Group Sales Managers:** Joe Bronzi, Jodi Schroeder. **Telemarketing Manager:** Kevin Marcy.

**Director of Merchandising:** Allan Vella.

## Public Relations, Communications

**Telephone:** (313) 962-4338. **FAX:** (313) 962-1128.

**Senior Director, Public Relations:** Dan Ewald. **Public Relations Manager:** Jill Ulle. **Secretary, Public Relations:** Connie Bell.

**Director of Community Relations:** Kayla French. **Community Relations Coordinator:** Celia Bobrowsky.

**Director of Alumni Relations:** Jim Price.

## Stadium Operations

**Vice President of Stadium Operations:** John Pettit.

**Assistant Director of Operations:** Craig Catallo. **Senior Director, Concessions Operations:** Randy Lippe.

**Head Groundskeepers:** Frank Feneck, Ed Goward.

**PA Announcer:** Jimmy Barrett. **Official Scorer:** Brian Bragg.

## Ticketing

**Director of Ticket Operations:** Ken Marchetti. **Director of Ticket Sales:** Gino D'Ambrosio. **Ticket Operations:** James Cleary, Jean Lakies, Sandra Sobotka.

## Travel, Clubhouse

**Traveling Secretary:** Bill Brown.

**Equipment/Home Clubhouse Manager:** Jim Schmakel. **Visitors Clubhouse:** John Nelson.

## Radio, TV, Media

**Radio Announcer:** Frank Beckmann. **Flagship Station:** WJR 760-AM.

**TV Announcers:** WKBD—George Kell, Al Kaline. PASS—Ernie Harwell, Fred McLeod, Jim Price. **Flagship Stations:** WKBD, PASS (regional cable).

**NEWSPAPERS, Daily Coverage:** Detroit Free Press, The Detroit News, The Oakland Press, Booth Newspaper Group.

## General Information

**Team Colors:** Blue, white and orange.

**Hometown Dugout:** Third Base.

**Standard Game Times:** Day—1:15 p.m. Night—7:05.

**Stadium Directions:** From I-94 West, exit at US 10 South to I-75, to Trumbull Ave. exit, left one block. From I-94 East, exit at I-96 to Lodge Freeway, Rosa Parks Blvd. (Civic Center exit), and take first exit (Rosa Parks Blvd./Tiger Stadium).

**Player Representative:** Mike Henneman.

# TIGERS

## BASEBALL OPERATIONS

**Senior Director, General Manager:** Joe Klein. **Senior Director, Assistant General Manager:** Gary Vitto.

Joe Klein

### Major League Staff

**Manager:** Sparky Anderson.

**Coaches:** Dugout—Billy Consolo; Pitching—Ralph Treuel; Batting—Larry Herndon; First Base—Gene Roof; Third Base—Dick Tracewski; Bullpen—Jeff Jones.

Sparky Anderson

### Medical, Training

**Club Physicians:** Dr. Clarence Livingood, Dr. David Collon, Dr. Terry Lock, Dr. Louis Saco (Florida).

**Head Trainer:** Russ Miller. **Trainer:** Steve Carter. **Strength and Conditioning Coach:** Brad Andress.

### Minor Leagues

**Director of Scouting and Player Development:** Jeff Scott. **Director of Minor League Operations:** David Miller.

**Administrative Assistant, Minor Leagues:** Audrey Zielinski.

**Roving Instructors:** John Lipon (special assignments), Marty Martinez (general), Larry Parrish (hitting).

### Farm System

| Class | Farm Team | Manager | Bat. Coach | Pitch. Coach |
|---|---|---|---|---|
| AAA | Toledo | Tom Runnells | Skeeter Barnes | Rick Adair |
| AA | Jacksonville | Bill Plummer | Mark Meleski | Rich Bombard |
| A | Lakeland | Dave Anderson | Tim Torricelli | Brian Allard |
| A | Fayetteville | Dwight Lowry | Basilio Cabrera | Sid Monge |
| A | Jamestown | Bruce Fields | Juan Lopez | Unavailable |
| Rookie | Lakeland | Kevin Bradshaw | Marty Martinez | Joe Georger |

### Scouting

**Telephone:** (313) 962-4000. **FAX:** (313) 962-4531.

**Director of Scouting:** Jeff Scott. **Administrative Assistant, Scouting:** Gwen Keating.

**Advance Scout:** Jerry Gleaton (Brownwood, TX).

**Special Assignment Scout:** Dick Wiencek (Rancho Mirage, CA).

**National Crosschecker:** Dave Roberts (Portland, OR).

**Scouting Supervisors:** West—Jeff Malinoff (Seattle, WA), East—Don Rowland (Orlando, FL), Midwest—Bill Schudlich (Dearborn, MI).

**Scouts:** Arnie Beyeler (Lakeland, FL), Tom Chandler (Bryan, TX), Nathan Durst (Elmhurst, IL), Andy Hancock (Buford, GA), Jack Hays (Tualatin, OR), Lou Laslo (Pemberville, OH), Joe Lewis (Somerset, MA), Dennis Lieberthal (Westlake, CA), Stan Meek (Norman, OK), John Mirabelli (Cary, NC), Mark Monahan (Ypsilanti, MI), Glenn Murdock (Livonia, MI), Ramon Pena (New York, NY), Steve Souchock (Plantation, FL), Clyde Weir (Mt. Pleasant, MI), Rob Wilfong (West Covina, CA).

**International Scouts:** Liliano Castro (Dominican Republic), Juan Lopez (Puerto Rico), Felix Nivar (Dominican Republic), Ramon Pena (Dominican Republic).

# KANSAS CITY

David Glass

## Telephone, Address

**Office Address:** One Royal Way, Kansas City, MO 64129. **Mailing Address:** P.O. Box 419969, Kansas City, MO 64141. **Telephone:** (816) 921-2200. **FAX:** (816) 921-5775.

## Ownership

**Operated by:** Kansas City Royals Baseball Club, Inc.

**Principal Owner:** Ewing M. Kauffman Trust.

**Chairman of the Board/Chief Executive Officer:** David Glass. **President:** Michael Herman.

**Board of Directors:** David Glass, Michael Herman, Charles Hughes, Muriel Kauffman, Larry Kauffman, Joseph McGuff, Louis Smith.

**Vice President:** Charles Hughes. **Assistant Secretary/General Counsel:** Jennings Newcom.

## BUSINESS OPERATIONS

**Vice President, Administration:** Dennis Cryder.

**Vice President, Government and Consumer Affairs:** Merle Wood.

**Administrative Assistant, Administration:** Louise Adams.

## Finance

**Vice President, Finance:** Dale Rohr.

**Chief Investment Advisor:** Judith Elsea. **Controller:** Patrick Fleischmann. **Director of Benefits and Compensation:** Tom Pfannenstiel. **Director of Lancer Program:** Chris Muehlbach. **Director of Information Services:** Joe Pittelkow. **Director of Information Services/Operations:** Loretta Kratzberg.

## Marketing, Sales

**Director of Marketing:** Mike Behymer.

**Assistant Director of Marketing:** Vernice Givens. **Production Manager:** Larry Magariel. **Marketing Coordinator:** Kim Wollnik.

## Public Relations, Communications

**Telephone:** (816) 921-8154. **FAX:** (816) 921-5775.

**Vice President, Public Relations:** Dean Vogelaar.

**Assistant Directors of Public Relations:** Steve Fink, Barry Holmes. **Administrative Assistant:** Chris Stathos. **Secretary, Public Relations:** Maggie Mistler.

## Stadium Operations

**Director of Stadium Operations:** Tom Folk. **Assistant Director of Stadium Operations:** John Johnson. **Secretary, Stadium Operations:** Judy VanMeter.

**Stadium Engineer:** Duane Robinson. **Assistant Stadium Engineer:** Chris Frank. **Groundskeeper:** Trevor Vance. **Groundskeeper Consultant:** George Toma. **Assistant Groundskeeper:** Bill Butler.

## Ticketing

**Director of Ticket Operations:** Mike Naughton.

**Assistant Director of Ticket Operations:** D'Anne Carnahan. **Director of Season Tickets:** Joe Grigoli. **Group Sales Representative:** Marty Collins. **Ticket Operations Accountant:** Lisa McCoy.

## Travel, Clubhouse

**Traveling Secretary:** Dave Witty. **Equipment Manager:** Mike Burkhalter.

## Radio, TV, Media

**Radio Announcers:** Denny Matthews, Fred White. **Flagship Stations:** WIBW 580-AM, Topeka; KMBZ 980-AM.

**TV Announcers:** Dave Armstrong, Paul Splittorff. **Flagship Station:** KSMO-TV Channel 62.

**NEWSPAPERS, Daily Coverage:** Kansas City Star, Topeka Capital Journal.

## General Information

**Team Colors:** Royal blue and white.

**Hometown Dugout:** First Base.

**Standard Game Times:** Day—1:35 p.m. Night—7:05.

**Stadium Location:** From north or south, take I-435 to stadium exits. From east or west, take I-70 to stadium exits.

**Player Representative:** Jeff Montgomery.

# ROYALS

## BASEBALL OPERATIONS

**Executive Vice President/General Manager:** Herk Robinson.

**Vice President/Baseball Operations:** George Brett.

**Assistant General Manager:** Jay Hinrichs. **Special Assistant to General Manager:** Brian Murphy. **Baseball Operations Assistant:** Dan Glass. **Secretary to the General Manager:** Joanne Snow.

Herk Robinson

### Major League Staff

**Manager:** Bob Boone.

**Coaches:** Bench—Gene Mauch; Pitching—Bruce Kison; Batting—Greg Luzinski; First Base—Mitchell Page; Third Base—Jeff Cox; Bullpen—Jamie Quirk.

### Medical, Training

**Team Physician:** Dr. Steve Joyce.

Bob Boone

**Associate Physicians:** Dr. Mark Bernhardt, Dr. Dan Gurba, Dr. Thomas Phillips, Dr. Charles Rhoades.

**Head Trainer:** Nick Swartz. **Assistant Trainer:** Steve Morrow.

### Minor Leagues

**Director of Minor League Operations:** Bob Hegman. **Administrative Assistant, Minor Leagues:** Muzzy Jackson. **Secretary, Minor Leagues:** Mindy Walker.

**Coordinator of Instuction:** Joe Jones.

**Roving Instructors:** Tom Burgess (hitting), Jerry Cram (pitching), Rich Dauer (infield).

### Farm System

| Class | Farm Team | Manager | Bat. Coach | Pitch. Coach |
|---|---|---|---|---|
| AAA | Omaha | Mike Jirschele | Tom Poquette | Mike Alvarez |
| AA | Memphis | Ron Johnson | U.L. Washington | Gary Lance |
| A | Wilmington | John Mizerock | Sixto Lezcano | Tom Burgmeier |
| A | Springfield | Brian Poldberg | Rafael Santana | Mike Mason |
| A | Spokane | Al Pedrique | Cliff Pastornicky | Theo Shaw |
| Rookie | Fort Myers | Bob Herold | Jose Tartabull | Rick Keeton |

### Scouting

**Telephone:** (816) 921-2200. **FAX:** (816) 921-5775.

**Director of Scouting:** Art Stewart.

**Secretary, Scouting:** Karol Kyte.

**Advance Scout:** Jerry Terrell (Blue Springs, MO).

**Special Assignment Scouts:** Larry Doughty (Pittsburgh, PA), Stan Williams (Lakewood, CA).

**National Crosscheckers:** Allard Baird (Miami Beach, FL), Steve Flores (Temecula, CA), Guy Hansen (Las Vegas, NV), Chuck McMichael (Phoenix, AZ).

Art Stewart

**Scouts:** Frank Baez (Los Angeles, CA), Bob Bishop (San Dimas, CA), Carl Blando (Sarasota, FL), Bob Carter (Chambersburg, PA), Balos Davis (Charlotte, NC), Dave Herrera (Danville, CA), Ray Jackson (Midian, CT), Gary Johnson (Costa Mesa, CA), Al Kubski (Carlsbad, CA), Tony Levato (Peotone, IL), Tom McDevitt (Charleston, IL), Jeff McKay (Springfield, OR), Herb Raybourn (Bradenton, FL), Wil Rutenschroer (Cincinnati, OH), Jerry Stephens (West Bloomfield, MI), Terry Wetzel (Sugar Land, TX), Dennis Woody (Mobile, AL).

**Latin American Supervisor:** Luis Silverio (Dominican Republic).

**International Scout:** Johnny Ramos (Puerto Rico).

# MILWAUKEE

Bud Selig

## Telephone, Address

**Office Address:** Milwaukee County Stadium, 201 S. 46th St., Milwaukee, WI 53214. **Mailing Address:** P.O. Box 3099, Milwaukee, WI 53201. **Telephone:** (414) 933-4114. **FAX:** (414) 933-7323.

## Ownership

**Operated by:** Milwaukee Brewers Baseball Club.

**President, Chief Executive Officer:** Bud Selig.

**Board of Directors:** Bud Selig, Everett Smith, Charles Krause, Bernard Kubale.

## BUSINESS OPERATIONS

**Vice President, General Counsel:** Wendy Selig-Prieb.

**Director of Administration and Human Resources:** Tom Gausden.

**Assistant General Counsel:** Eugene Randolph. **Secretary, Legal and Human Resources:** Mary Burns.

## Finance

**Vice President, Finance:** Dick Hoffmann.

**Assistant Controller:** Paul Baniel. **Director of Management Information Systems:** Dan Krautkramer. **Payroll Coordinator:** Brian Krueger.

## Corporate Affairs

**Vice President, Corporate Affairs:** Laurel Prieb. **Directors of Corporate Affairs:** Jake Frego, Dean Rennicke.

**Vice President, Broadcast Operations:** Bill Haig.

## Public Relations, Communications

**Telephone:** (414) 933-4114. **FAX:** (414) 933-7323.

**Director of Media Relations:** Jon Greenberg. **Director of Publications:** Mario Ziino. **Director of Community Relations:** Michael Downs.

## Stadium Operations

**Vice President, Stadium Operations:** Gabe Paul Jr.

**Director of Stadium Operations:** Chuck Ward.

**Head Groundskeeper:** Gary VandenBerg.

**PA Announcer:** Bob Betts. **Official Scorers:** Tim O'Driscoll, Wayne Franke.

## Ticketing

**Telephone:** (414) 933-9000. **FAX:** (414) 933-3547.

**Vice President, Ticket Sales:** Jeff Eisenberg. **Director of Ticket Operations:** John Barnes. **Manager, Ticket Sales Development:** Jim Bathey. **Director of Brewers Gold Club:** Geoff Campion.

## Travel, Clubhouse

**Traveling Secretary:** Steve Ethier.

**Equipment Manager/Home Clubhouse:** Tony Migliaccio. **Visitors Clubhouse:** Jim Ksicinski.

## Radio, TV, Media

**Radio Announcers:** Pat Hughes, Bob Uecker. **Flagship Station:** WTMJ 620-AM. **No. of Network Stations:** 50.

**TV Announcers:** Unavailable. **Flagship Station:** WVTV Channel 18.

**NEWSPAPERS, Daily Coverage:** Milwaukee Journal, Milwaukee Sentinel.

## General Information

**Team Colors:** Navy, gold and hunter green.

**Hometown Dugout:** First Base.

**Standard Game Times:** Day—1:05 p.m. Night—7:05.

**Stadium Location:** From airport/south, I-94 West to Madison exit, to stadium.

**Player Representative:** B.J. Surhoff.

# BREWERS

## BASEBALL OPERATIONS

**Senior Vice President, Baseball Operations:** Sal Bando.

**Special Assistants to General Manager:** Dee Fondy, Larry Haney, Chuck Tanner.

**Director of Baseball Administration:** Brian Small. **Executive Secretary:** Sandy Ronback.

Sal Bando

### Major League Staff

**Manager:** Phil Garner.

**Coaches:** Pitching—Don Rowe; Batting—Lamar Johnson; First Base—Tim Foli; Third Base—Duffy Dyer; Bullpen—Bill Castro.

### Medical, Training

**Club Physicians:** Dr. Dennis Sullivan, Dr. Drew Palin.

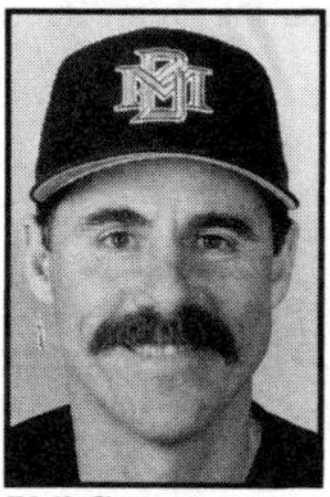

Phil Garner

**Head Trainer:** John Adam. **Assistant Trainer:** Al Price. **Strength and Conditioning Coach:** John Rewolinski.

### Minor Leagues

**Telelphone:** (414) 933-4114. **FAX:** (414) 933-4655.

**Director of Player Development:** Fred Stanley. **Coordinator of Pitching and Player Development:** Bob Humphreys. **Executive Secretary:** Barbara Stark.

**Roving Instructors:** Mick Kelleher (infield), Ed Sedar (outfield), Robbie Wine (catching).

### Farm System

| Class | Farm Team | Manager | Bat. Coach | Pitch. Coach |
|---|---|---|---|---|
| AAA | New Orleans | Chris Bando | Ron Jackson | Bill Campbell |
| AA | El Paso | Tim Ireland | Ken Phelps | Rob Derksen |
| A | Stockton | Bob Mariano | Gus Gil | Mark Littell |
| A | Beloit | Dub Kilgo | Jon Pont | Mike Caldwell |
| Rookie | Helena | Alex Morales | Unavailable | Unavailable |
| Rookie | Chandler | Ralph Dickenson | Luis Salazar | Jim Merrick |

### Scouting

**Telephone:** (414) 933-4114. **FAX:** (414) 933-4655.

**Director of Scouting:** Ken Califano.

**Assistant Director of Scouting:** Scott Martens.

**Major League Scouts:** Harry Dunlop (Elk Grove, CA), Larry Haney (Barboursville, VA), Chuck Tanner (New Castle, PA).

**Special Assignment Scouts:** Roland LeBlanc (La Habra, CA), Walter Youse (Sykesville, MD).

**National Crosscheckers:** East—Ed Durkin (Palm Harbor, FL), West—Lou Snipp (Galveston, TX).

Ken Califano

**Scouting Supervisors:** Midwest—Fred Beene (Oakhurst, TX), Southeast—Russ Bove (Apopka, FL), West Coast—Kevin Christman (San Jose, CA), Northeast—Ron Rizzi (Joppa, MD).

**Scouts:** Jeff Brookens (Chambersburg, PA), Bill Foley (Columbia, SC), Dick Foster (Otis, OR), Danny Garcia (Danbury, CT), Mike Gibbons (West Chester, OH), Ken Houp (Long Beach, CA), Harvey Kuenn Jr. (West Milwaukee, WI), Demie Mainieri (Tamarac, FL), Alex Morales (Boynton Beach, FL), Mike Powers (Galveston, TX), Phil Rizzo (Rolling Meadows, IL), Corey Rodriguez (Sherman Oaks, CA), Bob Sloan (Amarillo, TX), Paul Tretiak (Hannibal, MO), Tom Walsh (Dedham, MA), Red Whitsett (Villa Rica, GA), Ric Wilson (Chandler, AZ), David Young (Kountze, TX).

**International Supervisor:** Felix Delgado (Rio Piedras, PR).

**International Scouts:** Elvio Jimenez (Dominican Republic), John Viney (Australia).

# MINNESOTA

Carl Pohlad

## Telephone, Address

**Office Address:** 501 Chicago Ave. S., Minneapolis, MN 55415. **Telephone:** (612) 375-1366. **FAX:** (612) 375-7473.

## Ownership

**Operated by:** The Minnesota Twins.

**Owner:** Carl Pohlad. **Chairman ot the Board:** Howard Fox Jr.

**Board of Directors:** Donald Benson, Paul Christen, James Pohlad, Robert Pohlad, William Pohlad.

**President:** Jerry Bell.

# BUSINESS OPERATIONS

**Vice President, Operations:** Matt Hoy.

**Administrative Assistant to President, Office Manager:** Joan Boeser.

## Finance

**Vice President, Finance:** Kevin Mather.

**Human Resources Manager:** Raenell Dorn. **Accounting Manager:** Kip Elliott. **Assistant Accounting Manager:** Beth Hahn.

## Marketing, Sales

**Vice President, Sales and Marketing:** Bill Mahre.

**Corporate Sales and Marketing Manager:** Laura Day. **Broadcasting and Advertising Manager:** Wayne Petersen. **Telemarketing Manager:** Paul Foster. **Promotions Manager:** Julie Arndt.

**Sales Managers:** Phil Huebner, Jon Arends.

## Public Relations, Communications

**Telephone:** (612) 375-1366. **FAX:** (612) 375-7473.

**Director of Media Relations:** Rob Antony. **Assistant Director of Media Relations:** Sean Harlin. **Administrative Assistant:** Wendie Erickson.

**Communications Manager:** Dave St. Peter. **Community Relations Manager:** Bobby Van Buren.

## Stadium Operations

**Stadium Operations Manager:** Ric Johnson. **Game Production Manager:** Brian Brantley. **Security Manager:** Doug Will. **Pro Shop Manager:** Mike Stiles. **Operations Coordinator:** Heidi Sammon. **Office Services Coordinator:** Matt Burt.

**Head Groundskeeper:** Dick Ericson. **PA Announcer:** Bob Casey. **Official Scorers:** Tom Mee, Barry Fritz.

## Travel, Clubhouse

**Traveling Secretary:** Remzi Kiratli.

**Equipment/Clubhouse Manager:** Jim Wiesner. **Visitors Clubhouse:** Jim Dunn.

**Internal Video Specialist:** Nyal Peterson.

## Ticketing

**Telephone:** (612) 375-7444. **FAX:** (612) 375-7522.

**Ticket Manager:** Paul Froehle. **Assistant Ticket Manager:** Joe Mee. **Ticket Office Operations Coordinator:** Tracy Nordall.

## Radio, TV, Media

**Radio Announcers:** Herb Carneal, John Gordon. **Flagship Station:** WCCO 830-AM. **No. of Network Stations:** 38.

**TV Announcers:** Dick Bremer, Tommy John. **Flagship Stations:** WCCO Channel 4, Midwest SportsChannel (regional cable).

**NEWSPAPERS, Daily Coverage:** Minneapolis Star-Tribune, St. Paul Pioneer Press.

## General Information

**Team Colors:** Scarlet red, navy blue and white.

**Hometown Dugout:** Third Base.

**Standard Game Times:** Day—12:15 p.m., (weekend) 1:05. Night—7:05.

**Stadium Directions:** I-35W south to Washington Ave. exit or I-35W north to 3rd Street exit. I-94 East to I-35W north to 3rd Street exit or I-4 West to 5th Street exit.

**Player Representative:** Chuck Knoblauch.

# TWINS

## BASEBALL OPERATIONS

**Telephone:** (612) 375-1366. **FAX:** (612) 375-7417.

**Vice President, General Manager:** Terry Ryan.

**Vice President, Assistant General Manager:** Bill Smith. **Administrative Assistant:** Jan Bonneville.

Terry Ryan

### Major League Staff

**Manager:** Tom Kelly.

**Coaches:** Pitching—Dick Such; Batting—Terry Crowley; First Base—Scott Ullger; Third Base—Ron Gardenhire; Bullpen—Rick Stelmaszek.

### Medical, Training

**Club Physicians:** Dr. L.J. Michienzi, Dr. John Steubs.

**Trainer:** Dick Martin. **Assistant Trainer:** Doug Nelson.

Tom Kelly

### Minor Leagues

**Telephone:** (612) 375-1366. **FAX:** (612) 375-7417.

**Director of Minor Leagues:** Jim Rantz. **Assistant Director of Minor Leagues and Scouting:** Jeff Jurgella. **Minor League Field Coordinator:** Larry Corrigan. **Administrative Assistant:** Colleen Schroeder.

**Coordinator of Florida Operations:** Don Leppert.

**Roving Instructor:** Dwight Bernard (pitching).

### Farm System

| Class | Farm Team | Manager | Bat. Coach | Pitch. Coach |
|---|---|---|---|---|
| AAA | Salt Lake | Phil Roof | Steve Liddle | Rick Anderson |
| AA | Hardware City | Sal Butera | Jim Dwyer | Gorman Heimueller |
| A | Fort Myers | Al Newman | Jose Marzan | Rick Tomlin |
| A | Fort Wayne | Dan Rohn | Jose Baez | Stu Cliburn |
| Rookie | Elizabethton | Unavailable | Ray Smith | Jim Shellenback |
| Rookie | Fort Myers | John Russell | Jerry White | Eric Rasmussen |

### Scouting

**Telephone:** (612) 375-7474. **FAX:** (612) 375-7417.

**Scouting Director:** Mike Radcliff.

**Scouting Assistant:** Jeff Jurgella. **Administrative Assistant:** Alison Walk.

**Major League/Advance Scouts:** Ray Coley (Ponte Vedra Beach, FL), Bill Harford (Chicago, IL), Eddie Robinson (Fort Worth, TX).

**Special Assignment Scouts:** Ellsworth Brown (Beason, IL), Cal Ermer (Chattanooga, TN).

**Scouting Supervisors:** West—Vern Followell (Lakewood, CA); Midwest—Mike Ruth (Lee's Summit, MO); East—Earl Frishman (Tampa, FL).

Mike Radcliff

**Full-Time Scouts:** Gene DeBoer (Brandon, WI), Marty Esposito (Hewitt, TX), Scott Groot (Mission Viejo, CA), Deron Johnson (San Francisco, CA), John Leavitt (Shawnee, KS), Joel Lepel (Plato, MN), Bill Lohr (Centralia, WA), Bill Milos (South Holland, IL), Kevin Murphy (Studio City, CA), Tim O'Neil (West Hills, CA), Mark Quimuyog (Dekalb, IL), Clair Rierson (Gilbert, AZ), Ricky Taylor (Hickory, NC), Brad Weitzel (Haines City, FL), John Wilson (West Paterson, NJ).

**International Scouts:** Enrique Brito (Venezuela), Howard Norsetter (Australia, Canada), Edwin Rodriguez (Puerto Rico), Johnny Sierra (Dominican Republic).

# NEW YORK

## Telephone, Address

**Office Address:** Yankee Stadium, Bronx, NY 10451. **Telephone:** (718) 293-4300. **FAX:** (718) 293-8431.

George Steinbrenner

## Ownership

**Operated by:** New York Yankees.

**Principal Owner:** George Steinbrenner. **General Partner:** Joe Molloy.

**Limited Partners:** Harold Bowman, Daniel Crown, James Crown, Lester Crown, Michael Friedman, Marvin Goldklang, Barry Halper, John Henry, Harvey Leighton, Daniel McCarthy, Jessica Molloy, Harry Nederlander, James Nederlander, Robert Nederlander, William Rose Sr., Edward Rosenthal, Jack Satter, Harold Steinbrenner, Henry Steinbrenner, Joan Steinbrenner, Jennifer Swindell, Charlotte Witkind, Richard Witkind.

## BUSINESS OPERATIONS

**Executive Vice President, General Counsel:** David Sussman. **Vice President:** Ed Weaver. **Associate General Counsel:** John Agliano. **Director of Office Administration and Services:** Harvey Winston.

**Director of Florida Operation:** Les Parker. **Director of Administration, Florida Operation:** Rick Onderko.

### Finance

**Vice President/Chief Financial Officer:** Barry Pincus.

**Controller:** Mike Macaluso. **Assistant Controller:** Robert Brown.

### Marketing, Sales

**Director of Marketing:** Debbie Tymon.

**Director of Community Relations:** Brian Smith.

### Public Relations, Communications

**Telephone:** (718) 579-4460. **FAX:** (718) 293-8414.

**Director of Media Relations and Publicity:** Rob Butcher. **Assistant Director of Media Relations and Publicity:** Marty Naughton. **Assistant Director of Public Relations/Special Programs:** Annette Guardabascio.

**Director of Publications:** Tom Bannon. **Assistant Director, Publications:** Gregg Mazzola.

### Stadium Operations

**Director of Stadium Operations:** Sonny Hight. **Manager of Stadium Operations:** Kirk Randazzo. **Director of Customer Services:** Joel White. **Assistant Director of Customer Services:** David Bernstein. **Director of Broadcasting/Video Operations:** John Franzone.

**Head Groundskeeper:** Bob Wilkinson.

**PA Announcer:** Bob Sheppard. **Official Scorers:** Bill Shannon, Red Foley.

### Ticketing

**Vice President, Ticket Operations:** Frank Swaine.

**Executive Director of Ticket Operations:** Jeff Kline. **Ticket Director:** Ken Skrypek. **Director of Group and Season Sales:** Debbie Tymon.

### Travel, Clubhouse

**Traveling Secretary:** David Szen.

**Equipment Manager:** Nick Priore. **Visiting Clubhouse:** Lou Cucuzza.

### Radio, TV, Media

**Radio Announcers:** John Sterling, Michael Kay. **Flagship Station:** WABC 770-AM.

**TV Announcers:** Jim Kaat, David Cohen, Al Trautwig. **Flagship Station:** Madison Square Garden Network (regional cable).

**NEWSPAPERS, Daily Coverage:** New York Daily News, New York Post, New York Times, Newark Star-Ledger, Bergen Record, Newsday, Hartford Courant.

### General Information

**Team Colors:** Blue and white.

**Hometown Dugout:** First Base.

**Standard Game Times:** Day—1:05 p.m., 1:35. Night—7:35.

**Stadium Directions:** I-87 North to 149th or 155th Streets; I-87 South to 161st Street.

**Player Representative:** Steve Howe.

# YANKEES

## BASEBALL OPERATIONS

Gene Michael

**Vice President, General Manager:** Gene Michael.

**Assistant General Manager, Baseball Operations:** Tim McCleary. **Assistant General Manager, Baseball Administration:** Brian Cashman. **Assistant, Baseball Operations:** Thomas May.

**Special Advisor to Owner:** Reggie Jackson.

**Director of Spring Training:** Mark Zettlemeyer. **Spring Training Coordinator:** Marsh Samuel.

### Major League Staff

**Manager:** Buck Showalter.

**Coaches:** Pitching—Billy Connors; Batting—Rick Down; First Base—Brian Butterfield; Third Base—Willie Randolph; Bullpen—Tony Cloninger.

### Medical, Training

**Team Physician:** Dr. Stuart Hershon.

**Head Trainer:** Gene Monahan. **Assistant Trainer:** Steve Donohue. **Strength and Conditioning Coach:** Gary Well.

Buck Showalter

### Minor Leagues

**Florida Complex:** 3102 N. Himes Ave., Tampa, FL 33607. **Telephone:** (813) 875-7753. **FAX:** (813) 877-8505.

**Vice President, Player Development and Scouting:** Bill Livesey.

**Director of Minor League Operations:** Mitch Lukevics. **Assistant Director of Minor League Operations:** Rigo Garcia. **Clubhouse Coordinator/ Equipment Manager:** Dave Hays. **Secretary to Vice President, Player Development and Scouting:** Jackie Williams. **Secretary, Minor Leagues:** Lesa Senker.

**Coordinator of Instruction:** Mark Newman. **Roving Instructors:** Clete Boyer (infield), Nardi Contreras (pitching), Joe Lefebvre (hitting). **Head Trainer:** Mark Littlefield. **Strength and Conditioning Coordinator:** Shawn Powell. **Clubhouse Manager:** Chris Guth.

### Farm System

| Class | Farm Team | Manager | Bat. Coach | Pitch. Coach |
|---|---|---|---|---|
| AAA | Columbus | Bill Evers | Gary Denbo | Dave Schuler |
| AA | Norwich | Jimmy Johnson | Tom Nieto | Juan Nieves |
| A | Tampa | Jake Gibbs | Ken Dominguez | Mark Shiflett |
| A | Greensboro | Trey Hillman | Brian Milner | Pete Filson |
| A | Oneonta | Rob Thomson | Terry Rupp | Tom Filer |
| Rookie | Tampa | Hector Lopez | Rich Arena | Hoyt Wilhelm |

### Scouting

**Vice President, Player Development and Scouting:** Bill Livesey.

**Coordinator of Scouting:** Kevin Elfering. **Assistant Coordinator of Scouting:** Eddie Robinson. **Scouting Secretary:** Debbie Roth.

**Major League/Advance Scouts:** Ron Brand (Roseville, CA), Ron Hansen (Baldwin, MD), Graig Nettles (Del Mar, CA), Ted Uhlaender (McGregor, TX).

**Special Assignment Scouts:** Ket Barber (Ocala, FL), Bill Emslie (Safety Harbor, FL), Clyde King (Goldsboro, NC), Bob Lemon (Long Beach, CA), Dick Williams (Las Vegas, NV).

**National Crosschecker:** Jack Gillis (Sarasota, FL).

**Regional Crosscheckers:** West Coast—Don Lindeberg (Anaheim, CA), Western—Damon Oppenheimer (St. Petersburg, FL), East Coast—Jeff Taylor (Newark, DE), Midwest—Bill Gayton Katy, TX).

**Scouts:** Fernando Arango (Oklahoma City, OK), Mark Batchko (Arlington, TX), Steve Chandler (Lexington, KY), Larry D'Amato (Tualatin, OR), Joe DiCarlo (Ringwood, NJ), Lee Elder (Evans, GA), Paul Faulk (Raleigh, NC), Joel Grampietro (Shrewsbury, MA), Tim Kelly (New Lenox, IL), Greg Orr (Sacramento, CA), Shawn Pender (Drexel Hill, PA), Cesar Presbott (Bronx, NY), Joe Robison (Dayton, TX), Bill Schmidt (Garden Grove, CA), Paul Turco (Sarasota, FL), Leon Wurth (Franklin, TN).

**Coordinator, International Scouting:** Gordon Blakeley (Gilbert, AZ). **Coordinator, Canadian Scouting:** Dick Groch (Marysville, MI). **European Scouting:** Joel Grampietro (Shrewsbury, MA). **Coordinator, Latin American Scouting:** Rudy Santin (Miami, FL).

# OAKLAND

## Telephone, Address

**Office Address:** Oakland-Alameda County Coliseum, Oakland, CA 94621. **Telephone:** (510) 638-4900. **FAX:** (510) 638-4937.

## Ownership

**Operated by:** The Oakland Athletics Baseball Company.

**Owner, Managing General Partner:** Walter A. Haas Jr. (at press time, sale of club to group led by Steve Schott and Ken Hofmann was pending American League approval).

**Chairman, Chief Executive Officer:** Walter J. Haas.

# BUSINESS OPERATIONS

**Vice President, Business Operations:** Alan Ledford.

**Vice President, General Counsel:** George Schell.

## Finance

**Vice President, Finance:** Kathleen Phillips.

**Controller:** Michele Jordan.

## Marketing, Sales

**Promotions Manager:** Susan Bress.

**Director of Broadcast Operations:** Ken Pries.

## Public Relations, Communications

**Telephone:** (510) 638-4900. FAX: (510) 638-4937.

**Director of Public Affairs and Community Relations:** Dave Perron.

**Director of Baseball Information:** Jay Alves. **Director of Media Relations:** Christina Centeno. **Administrative Assistant, Public Affairs and Media Relations:** Doreen Alves.

## Stadium Operations

**Director of Stadium Operations:** David Rinetti.

**Head Groundskeeper:** Clay Wood.

## Ticketing

**Director of Ticket Operations:** Shelley Landeros.

## Travel, Clubhouse

**Director of Team Travel:** Mickey Morabito.

**Clubhouse Manager:** Steve Vucinich. **Visiting Clubhouse Manager:** Mike Thalblum.

## Radio, TV, Media

**Radio Announcers:** Bill King, Lon Simmons, Ray Fosse. **Flagship Station:** KNEW 910-AM.

**TV Announcers:** KRON—Ray Fosse, Dick Stockton; SportsChannel—Ray Fosse, Greg Papa. **Flagship Stations:** KRON Channel 4, SportsChannel (regional cable).

**NEWSPAPERS, Daily Coverage:** San Francisco Chronicle, Oakland Tribune, Contra Costa Times, Sacramento Bee, San Francisco Examiner, San Jose Mercury-News, Hayward Daily Review.

## General Information

**Team Colors:** Green and gold.

**Hometown Dugout:** Third Base.

**Standard Game Times:** Day—1:05 p.m.; weekday, 12:15. Night—7:05.

**Stadium Location:** From San Jose—north on I-880 to Oakland, exit at 66th Ave.; From San Francisco—east on Bay Bridge to I-580 toward Hayward, to downtown Oakland and I-880 south, exit at 66th Avenue; From Sacramento—I-80 west to Oakland, I-580 toward Hayward and I-980 to downtown Oakland, then I-880 South, exit at 66th Avenue.

**Player Representative:** Terry Steinbach.

# ATHLETICS

## BASEBALL OPERATIONS

Sandy Alderson

**President, General Manager:** Sandy Alderson.

**Assistant General Manager:** Billy Beane.

**Special Assistants to the General Manager:** Dick Bogard, Karl Kuehl, Bill Rigney.

**Director of Baseball Administration:** Pamela Pitts. **Baseball Operations Assistant:** David Seifert. **Administrative Assistant:** Betty Shinoda.

### Major League Staff

**Manager:** Tony La Russa.

**Coaches:** Dugout—Carney Lansford; Pitching—Dave Duncan; Hitting—Jim Lefebvre; First Base—Dave McKay; Third Base—Tommie Reynolds; Bullpen—Art Kusnyer.

### Medical, Training

**Medical Director:** Dr. Allan Pont.

**Team Physicians:** Dr. Rick Bost, Dr. Jerrald Goldman.

Tony LaRussa

**Trainer:** Barry Weinberg. **Assistant Trainer:** Larry Davis. **Strength and Conditioning Coach:** Bob Alejo.

### Minor Leagues

**Telephone:** (510) 638-4900. **FAX:** (510) 562-1633.

**Arizona Complex:** Papago Park Baseball Complex, 1802 North 64th St., Phoenix, AZ 85008. **Telephone:** (602) 949-5951. **FAX:** (602) 945-0557.

**Director of Player Development:** Keith Lieppman. **Assistant Director of Player Development:** Brad Fischer.

**Director of Arizona Operations:** Ted Polakowski.

**Roving Instructors:** Bob Cluck (pitching), Brad Fischer (hitting), Ron Plaza (hitting, infield).

### Farm System

| Class | Farm Team | Manager | Bat. Coach | Pitch. Coach |
|---|---|---|---|---|
| AAA | Edmonton | Gary Jones | Orv Franchuk | Pete Richert |
| AA | Huntsville | Dick Scott | None | Glenn Abbott |
| A | Modesto | Casey Parsons | None | Rick Rodriguez |
| A | West Michigan | Jim Colborn | None | Bert Bradley |
| A | So. Oregon | Tony DeFrancesco | None | Unavailable |
| Rookie | Scottsdale | Juan Navarrete | John Kuehl | Gil Patterson |

### Scouting

Grady Fuson

**Director of Scouting:** Grady Fuson.

**Assistant Director of Scouting:** Eric Kubota.

**Special Assignment Scouts:** Dick Bogard (La Palma, CA), J.P. Ricciardi (West Boylston, MA).

**National Crosschecker:** Ron Hopkins (Seattle, WA).

**Scouts:** Tony Arias (Miami Lakes, FL), Steve Bowden (Houston, TX), Ed Crosby (Cypress, CA), Ron Elam (Richmond, VA), Tim Holt (Dallas, TX), John Kuehl (Scottsdale, AZ), Billy Merkel (Columbia, TN), Marty Miller (Chicago, IL), Steve Nichols (Augusta, GA), Chris Pittaro (Trenton, NJ), Joe Robinson (Burlington, IA), Will Schock (San Jose, CA), Ron Vaughn (Corona, CA).

**Director of International Scouting:** Karl Kuehl.

**International Scouts:** Ruben Escalera (Puerto Rico), Ubaldo Heredia (Latin America), Santiago Villalona (Dominican Republic).

# SEATTLE

Chuck Armstrong

## Telephone, Address

**Office Address:** 83 S. King St., Seattle, WA 98104. **Mailing Address:** P.O. Box 4100, Seattle, WA 98104. **Telephone:** (206) 628-3555. **FAX:** (206) 628-3340.

## Ownership

**Operated by:** Baseball Club of Seattle, LP.

**Board of Directors:** John Ellis, Minoru Arakawa, Chris Larson, Howard Lincoln, John McCaw, Frank Shrontz, Craig Watjen.

**Chairman/Chief Executive Officer:** John Ellis.

**President/Chief Operating Officer:** Chuck Armstrong.

# BUSINESS OPERATIONS

**Vice President, Business Development:** Paul Isaki.

**Executive Assistant, Ownership and Business Development:** Janet O'Brien.

## Finance

**Vice President, Finance and Administration:** Brian Beggs.

**Controller:** Denise Podosek. **Financial Analyst:** Kevin Mason. **Manager, Payroll and Benefits Administration:** Shirley Shreve. **Staff Accountant:** Karen Vaughn.

## Marketing, Sales

**Vice President, Sales and Marketing:** Bob Gobrecht.

**Director, Corporate Marketing:** Beth Wojick. **Manager, Corporate Sponsorship Programs:** Robin Karr. **Senior Account Executive:** Al "Moose" Clausen. **Account Executives, Ticket Sales:** Ron Babes, Bob Hellinger, Lyla Smith. **Account Executive, Corporate Marketing:** Ingrid Russell-Narcisse.

## Public Relations, Communications

**Telephone:** (206) 343-4608. **FAX:** (206) 628-3340.

**Vice President, Communications:** Randy Adamack.

**Director of Public Relations:** Dave Aust. **Assistant Director of Public Relations:** Pete Vanderwarker. **Public Relations Assistant:** Tim Hevly. **Manager of Publications:** Allison Mauck.

**Director of Community Relations:** Joe Chard. **Coordinator, Community Relations:** Gina Hasson.

**Manager, Promotions:** Todd Vecchio.

## Ticketing

**Telephone:** (206) 628-3555. **FAX:** (206) 628-3340.

**Manager, Season Ticket Services:** Joan Moeller. **Manager, Ticket Operations:** Connie Zentner. **Coordinators, Ticket Services:** Rob Brautigam, Eric Knutson.

## Stadium Operations

**Director of Stadium Operations:** Tony Pereira.

**Head Groundskeeper:** Wilber Loo.

**PA Announcer:** Tom Hutyler. **Official Scorer:** Harland Beery.

## Travel, Clubhouse

**Traveling Secretary:** Craig Detwiler.

**Equipment Manager:** Henry Genzale. **Video Coordinator:** Carl Hamilton.

## Radio, TV, Media

**Radio Announcers:** Dave Niehaus, Ron Fairly, Ken Levine, Chip Caray. **Flagship Station:** KIRO 710-AM. **No. of Network Stations:** 30.

**TV Announcers:** Dave Niehaus, Chip Caray, Ron Fairly, Ken Levine. **Flagship Station:** KIRO Channel 7, Prime Sports Northwest (regional cable).

**NEWSPAPERS, Daily Coverage:** Seattle Times, Seattle Post-Intelligencer, Tacoma News Tribune, Bellevue Journal American.

## General Information

**Team Colors:** Navy blue, metallic silver and northwest green.

**Hometown Dugout:** Third Base.

**Standard Game Times:** Day—Sun. 1:35 p.m., Wed. 12:35. Night—7:05 p.m., Fri., 7:35.

**Stadium Location:** I-5 or I-90 to Fourth Ave. South exit.

**Player Representative:** Dan Wilson.

# MARINERS

## BASEBALL OPERATIONS

Woody Woodward

**Vice President, Baseball Operations:** Woody Woodward.

**Vice President, Scouting and Player Development:** Roger Jongewaard.

**Assistant to Vice President, Baseball Operations:** George Zuraw. **Director of Baseball Administration:** Lee Pelekoudas. **Administrator, Baseball Operations:** Debbie Larsen.

### Major League Staff

**Manager:** Lou Piniella.

**Coaches:** Bench—John McLaren; Dugout—Lee Elia; Pitching—Bobby Cuellar; First Base—Sam Mejias; Third Base—Sam Perlozzo; Bullpen—Matt Sinatro.

Lou Piniella

### Medical, Training

**Club Physicians:** Dr. Mitch Storey, Dr. Larry Pedegana.

**Head Trainer:** Rick Griffin. **Assistant Trainer:** Tom Newberg.

### Minor Leagues

**Telephone:** (206) 628-3555. **FAX:** (206) 682-4292.

**Director of Player Development:** Jim Beattie. **Assistant Director of Player Development:** Larry Beinfest.

**Coordinator of Instruction:** Jim Skaalen.

### Farm System

| Class | Farm Team | Manager | Bat. Coach | Pitch. Coach |
|---|---|---|---|---|
| AAA | Tacoma | Steve Smith | Ken Griffey Sr. | Jeff Andrews |
| AA | Port City | Dave Myers | Darrin Garner | Ron Romanick |
| A | Riverside | Terry Kennedy | Tom LeVasseur | Juan Eichelberger |
| A | Wisconsin | Mike Goff | Delwyn Young | Unavailable |
| A | Everett | Orlando Gomez | Roger Hansen | Bryan Price |
| Rookie | Peoria | Dave Brundage | Tommy Cruz | Gary Wheelock |

### Scouting

Roger Jongewaard

**Telephone:** (206) 628-3555. **FAX:** (206) 682-4292.

**Director of Scouting:** Roger Jongewaard. **Administrator, Scouting:** Hallie Larson.

**Major League/Special Assignment Scout:** Bill Kearns (Milton, MA).

**National Supervisor/Special Assignment Scout:** Benny Looper (Ada, OK).

**National Crosschecker:** Carroll Sembera (Shiner, TX).

**Scouting Supervisors:** West—Ken Compton (Cypress, CA); Canada—Ken Madeja (Novi, MI); East—Steve Pope (Asheville, NC); Midwest—Dan Jennings (Mobile, AL).

**Area Scouts:** Dave Alexander (Lafayette, IN), Fernando Arguellas (Miami, FL), Al Bundy (Mobile, AL), Kendall Carter (Chandler, AZ), Rodney Davis (Paramount, CA), Larry Harper (Redwood Shores, CA), Tom McNamara (Nanuet, NY), Cotton Nye (Edmond, OK), Don Poplin (Norwood, NC), John Ramey (Lakeland, FL), Chris Smith (The Woodlands, TX), Craig Weissman (San Diego, CA), Bill Young (Melissa, TX).

**International Scouts:** Fernando Arguellas (Latin America).

# TEXAS

## Telephone, Address

**Office Address:** 1000 Ballpark Way, Arlington, TX 76011. **Mailing Address:** P.O. Box 90111, Arlington, TX 76004. **Telephone:** (817) 273-5222. **FAX:** (817) 273-5206.

Tom Schieffer

## Ownership

**Operated by:** Texas Rangers, Ltd.

**General Partners:** Edward "Rusty" Rose, Thomas Schieffer.

**President:** Thomas Schieffer.

# BUSINESS OPERATIONS

**Vice President, Business Operations/Treasurer:** John McMichael.

**Vice President, Administration/Corporate Secretary:** Charles Wangner. **Vice President, Legal Affairs:** Bill Miller.

**Manager, Information Systems:** Nancy Rotonen.

## Finance

**Controller:** Steve McNeill. **Assistant Controller:** Susan Blalock.

## Marketing, Sales

**Vice President, Marketing:** David Dziedzic.

**Director of Corporate Marketing:** Dave Fendrick. **Director of In-Park Entertainment:** Chuck Morgan. **Director of Merchandising:** Nancy McCusker. **Corporate Sales Manager:** Jodi Benefiel. **Promotions Manager:** Chuck Baugh.

**Sales Director:** Ross Scott.

## Public Relations, Communications

**Telephone:** (817) 273-5203. **FAX:** (817) 273-5206.

**Vice President, Public Relations:** John Blake.

**Assistant Director, Public Relations:** John Ralph.

**Director, Publications:** Eric Kolb. **Director, Player Relations:** Taunee Paur-Taylor. **Assistant Director, Player Relations:** Sheila Bolduc. **Administrative Assistant, Public Relations:** Michelle Baugh.

**Director of Spanish Broadcasting, Latin American Liasion:** Luis Mayoral. **Assistant, Special Projects:** Bobby Bragan.

**Vice President, Community Development:** Norman Lyons.

## Stadium Operations

**Vice President, Ballpark Operations:** Jack Hill.

**Chief Engineer:** Kevin Jimison. **Property Manager:** Anita Handy.

**Director, Grounds:** Jim Anglea. **Major League Groundskeeper:** Brad Richards.

**Director, Ballpark Operations:** Kevin Jimison.

**PA Announcer:** Chuck Morgan. **Official Scorers:** Burt Hawkins, Jim Patterson.

## Ticketing

**Telephone:** (817) 273-5100. **FAX:** (817) 273-5190.

**Director, Ticket Operations:** John Schriever. **Assistant Director, Ticket Operations:** Cathy Beatty. **Director, Customer Service:** Jay Miller.

**Group Sales Coordinator:** Lisa Brown. **Season Ticket Coordinator:** Dan Hanrahan.

## Travel, Clubhouse

**Traveling Secretary:** Dan Schimek.

**Equipment Manager:** Zack Minasian. **Visiting Clubhouse:** Joe Macko.

## Radio, TV, Media

**Radio Announcer:** Eric Nadel. **Flagship Station:** KRLD 1080-AM. **No. of Network Stations:** 50.

**TV Announcers:** KTVT—Steve Busby, Jim Sundberg; HSE—Norm Hitzges, Mark Holtz. **Flagship Stations:** KTVT-TV Channel 11, Home Sports Entertainment (regional cable).

**NEWSPAPERS, Daily Coverage:** Dallas Morning News, Fort Worth Star Telegram, Arlington News.

## General Information

**Team Colors:** Red and blue.

**Hometown Dugout:** First Base.

**Game Times:** Day—2:05 p.m. Night—7:05, 7:35.

**Directions to Stadium:** From I-30—Ballpark Way exit, south on Ballpark Way; From Hwy 360—Randol Mill exit, west on Randol Mill.

**Player Representative:** Unavailable.

# RANGERS

## BASEBALL OPERATIONS

**Telephone:** (817) 273-5226. **FAX:** (817) 273-5285.

**Vice President/General Manager:** Doug Melvin. **Assistant General Manager/Player Personnel and Scouting:** Sandy Johnson. **Director of Major League Administration:** Judy Johns. **Administrative Assistant, Baseball Operations:** Bob Garvey.

Doug Melvin

### Major League Staff

**Manager:** Johnny Oates.

**Coaches:** Dugout—Bucky Dent; Pitching—Dick Bosman; Batting—Rudy Jaramillo; First Base—Ed Napoleon; Third Base—Jerry Narron; Bullpen—Larry Hardy.

Johnny Oates

### Medical, Training

**Medical Director:** Dr. Mike Mycoskie. **Club Physician:** Dr. John Conway.

**Head Trainer:** Danny Wheat. **Assistant Trainer:** Ray Ramirez.

### Minor Leagues

**Telephone:** (817) 273-5227. **FAX:** (817) 273-5206.

**Director of Player Development and Minor League Instruction:** Reid Nichols. **Administrative Assistant:** Monty Clegg.

**Roving Instructors:** Perry Hill (infield), Tim Lang (fitness), Jim Lentine (hitting), Steve Luebber (pitching), Bump Willis (infield, baserunning).

### Farm System

| Class | Farm Team | Manager | Bat. Coach | Pitch. Coach |
|---|---|---|---|---|
| AAA | Oklahoma City | Greg Biagini | None | Tom Brown |
| AA | Tulsa | Bobby Jones | None | Jackson Todd |
| A | Charlotte | Butch Wynegar | None | John Tudor |
| A | Charleston | Mike Berger | None | Brad Arnsberg |
| Rookie | Hudson Valley | Bump Wills | None | Steve Foucault |
| Rookie | Port Charlotte | Chino Cadahia | Victor Ramirez | Rick Knapp |

### Scouting

**Telephone:** (817) 273-5227. **FAX:** (817) 273-5206.

**Assistant General Manager, Player Personnel and Scouting:** Sandy Johnson. **Administrative Assistant:** Charlene Homuth.

**Advance Scout:** Mike Paul (Tucson, AZ).

**National Crosschecker:** Bryan Lambe (North Massapequa, NY).

**Scouting Supervisors:** Southeast—Bill Earnhart (Point Clear, AL), West Coast—Len Strelitz (Temple City, CA), Midwest—Rudy Terrasas (Pasadena, TX).

Sandy Johnson

**Scouts:** James Beavers (Atlanta, GA), Joe Branzell (Silver Spring, MD), Mike Daughtry (Elgin, IL), Marc Delpiano (Auburn, NY), Kip Fagg (Murrieta, CA), Jim Fairey (Clemson, SC), Mark Giegler (Howell, MI), Mike Grouse (Lee's Summit, MO), Thomas Gushiken (Pearl City, HI), Tim Hallgren (Clarkston, WA), Larry Izzo (Deer Park, NY), Mike Piatnik (Winter Haven, FL), Alan Regier (Castro Valley, CA), Pat Rigby (Dallas, TX), Randy Taylor (Katy, TX), Mike Toomey (Hyattsville, MD).

**Director of Professional/International Scouting:** Omar Minaya (West New York, NJ).

**International Scouts:** Hector Acevedo (Dominican Republic), Manuel Batista (Puerto Rico), Roney Calderon (Venezuela), Jose Diaz (Venezuela), Cornelio Pena (Dominican Republic), Rodolfo Rosario (Dominican Republic), Danilo Troncoso (Dominican Republic).

# TORONTO

## Telephone, Address

**Office Address:** One Blue Jays Way, Suite 3200, SkyDome, Toronto, Ontario M5V 1J1. **Telephone:** (416) 341-1000. **FAX:** (416) 341-1250.

Paul Beeston

## Ownership

**Operated by:** Toronto Blue Jays Baseball Club.
**Principal Owner:** John Labatt Ltd.
**Chairman:** P.N.T. Widdrington.
**Board of Directors:** Paul Beeston, Peter Bronfman, Gordon Craig, John C. Eaton, N.E. Hardy, Sam Pollock, Hugo Powell, G.W. Radford, Herb Solway, George Taylor, P.N.T. Widdrington.

# BUSINESS OPERATIONS

**President/Chief Executive Officer:** Paul Beeston.
**Executive Administrative Assistant:** Sue Cannell.

## Finance

**Director of Finance:** Susan Quigley. **Manager, Accounting:** Cathy McNamara. **Manager, Information Systems:** Hans Frauenlob. **Manager, Employee Compensation:** Perry Nicoletta.

## Marketing, Sales

**Director of Marketing:** Paul Markle.
**Manager, Promotions and Advertising:** Rick Amos.

## Public Relations, Communications

**Telephone:** (416) 341-1300. **FAX:** (416) 341-1250.
**Director of Public Relations:** Howard Starkman. **Assistant Director of Public Relations:** Mark Leno. **Coordinator of Statistical Information:** Jay Stenhouse. **Administrative Assistant:** Janis Davidson.

## Stadium Operations

**Director of Stadium/Ticket Operations:** George Holm. **Assistant Director and Manager of Field Operations:** Len Frejlich. **Manager of Game Operations:** Mario Coutinho.
**PA Announcer:** Murray Eldon. **Official Scorers:** Neil MacCarl, Joe Sawchuck, Lou Cauz, Doug Hobbs.

## Ticketing

**Telephone:** (416) 341-1234. **FAX:** (416) 341-1177.
**Assistant Director of Ticket Operations, Box Office Manager:** Randy Low. **Manager, Ticket and Group Sales:** Maureen Haffey. **Manager of Ticket Vault Services:** Paul Goodyear. **Manager of Subscriber Services:** Mike Maunder. **Manager of Mail Order Services:** Doug Barr.

## Travel, Clubhouse

**Director of Team Travel:** John Brioux.
**Clubhouse, Equipment Manager:** Jeff Ross. **Visitors Clubhouse:** Ian Duff.

## Radio, TV, Media

**Radio Announcers:** Tom Cheek, Jerry Howarth. **Flagship Station:** THE FAN AM-590. **No. of Network Stations:** 40.
**TV Announcers:** CFTO—Don Chevrier, Tommy Hutton, Fergie Oliver; TSN—Buck Martinez, Dan Shulman; CBC—Tommy Hutton, Brian Williams. **Flagship Stations:** CFTO, CBC, The Sports Network (national cable—Canada).
**NEWSPAPERS, Daily Coverage:** Toronto Globe & Mail, Toronto Sun, Toronto Star, Hamilton Spectator.

## General Information

**Team Colors:** Blue and white.
**Hometown Dugout:** Third Base.
**Standard Game Times:** Day—1:35 p.m. Night—7:35 p.m.
**Player Representative:** Ed Sprague.

# BLUE JAYS

## BASEBALL OPERATIONS

**Vice President/General Manager:** Gord Ash.

**Vice Presidents, Baseball:** Al LaMacchia, Bob Mattick.

**Special Assistant to Vice President:** Al Widmar. **Administrative Assistants, Baseball:** Fran Brown, Heather Connolly, Trina Hiscock.

Gord Ash

### Major League Staff

**Manager:** Cito Gaston.

**Coaches:** Dugout—Gene Tenace; Pitching—Galen Cisco; Batting—Larry Hisle; First Base—Bob Bailor; Third Base—Nick Leyva; Bullpen—Dennis Holmberg.

Cito Gaston

### Medical, Training

**Team Physician:** Dr. Ron Taylor.

**Trainer:** Tommy Craig. **Assistant Trainer:** Brent Andrews. **Strength and Conditioning Coordinator:** Geoffrey Horne.

### Minor Leagues

**Director of Player Development:** Mel Queen. **Administrator, Player Personnel:** Bob Nelson.

**Roving Instructors:** Scott Breeden (pitching), Bill Buckner (hitting), Richie Hebner (hitting), Jim Hoff (infield), Willie Upshaw (hitting).

### Farm System

| Class | Farm Team | Manager | Bat. Coach | Pitch. Coach |
|---|---|---|---|---|
| AAA | Syracuse | Bob Didier | Hector Torres | Bill Monbouquette |
| AA | Knoxville | Garth Iorg | LeRoy Stanton | Mark Connor |
| A | Dunedin | Jim Nettles | Rolando Pino | John Poloni |
| A | Hagerstown | Omar Malave | Scott Miller | Reggie Cleveland |
| A | St. Catharines | J.J. Cannon | Unavailable | Al Widmar |
| Rookie | Medicine Hat | Darren Balsley | Unavailable | Unavailable |
| Rookie | Dunedin | Rocket Wheeler | Randy Phillips | Andre Rabouin |

### Scouting

**Telephone:** (813) 734-5784. **FAX:** (813) 734-0117.

**Director of Scouting:** Bob Engle.

**Administrative Assistant, Scouting:** Donna Kuzoff.

**Advance Scout:** Don Welke (Louisville, KY).

**Special Assignment/Major League Scouts:** Moose Johnson (Arvada, CO), Gordon Lakey (Houston, TX), Duane Larson (Harrisburg, NC), Tim Wilken (Dunedin, FL).

**Western States Supervisor:** Tom Hinkle (Atascadero, CA).

Bob Engle

**Scouting Supervisors:** Dave Blume (Elk Grove, CA), Chris Bourjos (Scottsdale, AZ), Chris Buckley (Temple Terrace, FL), Robert Campbell (Littleton, CO), John Cole (Irvine, CA), Ellis Dungan (Pensacola, FL), Joe Ford (Yukon, OK), Jim Hughes (McKinney, TX), Ted Lekas (Worcester, MA), Ben McLure (Palmyra, PA), Bill Moore (Ontario, CA), Andy Pienovi (Portland, OR), Alvin Rittman (Memphis, TN), Jorge Rivera (Puerto Nuevo, PR), Mike Russell (Raleigh, NC), Joseph Siers (Lexington, KY), Mark Snipp (Fort Worth, TX), Neil Summers (Dix Hills, NY), Ron Tostenson (Issaquah, WA).

**Scouts:** Don Hara (Long Beach, CA), Tim Hewes (Bakersfield, CA), Jerry Sobeck (San Jose, CA).

**Director of Canadian Scouting:** Bill Byckowski.

**Director of International Scouting:** Wayne Morgan (Morgan Hill, CA). **Latin America Coordinator:** Epy Guerrero (Dominican Republic).

**International Scouts:** Domingo Carrasquel (Venezuela), Armando Chacon (Aruba), Wayne Durbidge (Australia), Paul Elliott (Australia), Juan Escobar (Venezuela), John Galloway (Australia), Bob Goodin (Australia), Ignacio Javier (Dominican Republic), Jaime Pena (Dominican Republic), Roberto Pineyro (Dominican Republic), Thomas Santana (Dominican Republic), Jose Tamarez (Dominican Republic), Greg Wade (Australia).

# NATIONAL LEAGUE

# NATIONAL LEAGUE

Leonard Coleman

**Mailing Address:** 350 Park Ave., New York, NY 10022. **Telephone:** (212) 339-7700. **FAX:** (212) 935-5069.

**Executive Committee:** Chicago, Cincinnati, Los Angeles.

**President and Treasurer:** Leonard Coleman.

**Senior Vice President and Secretary:** Katy Feeney.

**Director of Umpire Supervision:** Ed Vargo.

**Executive Director, Public Relations:** Ricky Clemons.

**Executive Secretary:** Rita Aughavin. **Executive Director, Player Records and Assistant Secretary:** Nancy Crofts. **Assistant, Media Relations and Player Records:** Glenn Wilburn.

**Administrative Assistant/Umpires:** Cathy Davis.

**Years League Active:** 1876-.

**1995 Opening Date:** April 2. **Closing Date:** Oct. 1.

**No. of Games:** 162.

**Division Structure: East**—Atlanta, Florida, Montreal, New York, Philadelphia. **Central**—Chicago, Cincinnati, Houston, Pittsburgh, St. Louis. **West**—Colorado, Los Angeles, San Diego, San Francisco.

**Roster Limit:** 25, until Aug. 31 when roster can be expanded to 40.

**Umpires:** Wally Bell (Youngstown, OH), Greg Bonin (Lafayette, LA), Gerry Crawford (Havertown, PA), Gary Darling (Gilbert, AZ), Bob Davidson (Littleton, CO), Gerry Davis (Appleton, WI), Dana DeMuth (Gilbert, AZ), Bruce Froemming (Vero Beach, FL), Brian Gorman (Glendale, CA), Eric Gregg (Philadelphia, PA), Tom Hallion (Louisville, KY), Angel Hernandez (Pembroke Pines, FL), Mark Hirschbeck (Stratford, CT), Bill Hohn (Collegeville, PA), Jeff Kellogg (Dearborn Heights, MI), Jerry Layne (Winter Haven, FL), Randy Marsh (Edgewood, KY), John McSherry (Dobbs Ferry, NY), Ed Montague (San Mateo, CA), Larry Poncino (San Clemente, CA), Frank Pulli (Palm Harbor, FL), Jim Quick (Incline Village, CA), Ed Rapuano (North Haven, CT), Charlie Reliford (Imperial, PA), Steve Rippley (Seminole, FL), Paul Runge (El Cajon, CA), Terry Tata (Cheshire, CT), Larry Vanover (Antioch, TN), Harry Wendelstedt (Ormond Beach, FL), Joe West (Kilby Island, NC), Charlie Williams (Chicago, IL), Mike Winters (San Diego, CA).

## 1994 Standings

| East | W | L | Pct. | GB | Central | W | L | Pct. | GB |
|---|---|---|---|---|---|---|---|---|---|
| Montreal | 74 | 40 | .649 | — | Cincinnati | 66 | 48 | .579 | — |
| Atlanta | 68 | 46 | .596 | 6 | Houston | 66 | 49 | .574 | ½ |
| New York | 55 | 58 | .487 | 18½ | Pittsburgh | 53 | 61 | .465 | 13 |
| Philadelphia | 54 | 61 | .470 | 20½ | St. Louis | 53 | 61 | .463 | 13 |
| Florida | 51 | 64 | .443 | 23½ | Chicago | 49 | 64 | .434 | 16½ |
| **West** | **W** | **L** | **Pct.** | **GB** | **West** | **W** | **L** | **Pct.** | **GB** |
| Los Angeles | 58 | 56 | .509 | — | Colorado | 53 | 64 | .453 | 6½ |
| San Francisco | 55 | 60 | .478 | 3½ | San Diego | 47 | 70 | .402 | 12½ |

## Stadium Information

| | | Dimensions | | | | |
|---|---|---|---|---|---|---|
| City | Stadium | LF | CF | RF | Capacity | '94 Att. |
| Atlanta | Fulton County | 330 | 402 | 330 | 52,007 | 2,539,240 |
| Chicago | Wrigley Field | 355 | 400 | 353 | 38,710 | 1,845,208 |
| Cincinnati | Riverfront | 330 | 404 | 330 | 52,392 | 1,897,691 |
| Colorado | Coors Field | 347 | 424 | 350 | 50,000 | 3,281,511 |
| Florida | Joe Robbie | 335 | 410 | 345 | 46,500 | 1,937,467 |
| Houston | Astrodome | 330 | 400 | 330 | 54,816 | 1,561,136 |
| Los Angeles | Dodger | 330 | 400 | 330 | 56,000 | 2,279,421 |
| Montreal | Olympic | 325 | 404 | 325 | 43,739 | 1,276,250 |
| New York | Shea | 338 | 410 | 338 | 55,601 | 1,151,471 |
| Philadelphia | Veterans | 330 | 408 | 330 | 62,382 | 2,290,971 |
| Pittsburgh | Three Rivers | 335 | 400 | 335 | 47,972 | 1,222,517 |
| St. Louis | Busch | 330 | 402 | 330 | 54,224 | 1,866,544 |
| San Diego | SD Jack Murphy | 327 | 405 | 327 | 59,022 | 953,857 |
| San Francisco | Candlestick Park | 335 | 400 | 335 | 58,000 | 1,704,614 |

# ATLANTA

Stan Kasten

## Telephone, Address

**Office Address:** 521 Capitol Ave. SW, Atlanta, GA 30312. **Mailing Address:** P.O. Box 4064, Atlanta, GA 30302. **Telephone:** (404) 522-7630. **FAX:** (404) 614-1391.

## Ownership

**Operated by:** Atlanta National Baseball Club, Inc.

**Principal Owner:** Ted Turner.

**Chairman of the Board:** Bill Bartholomay.

**Board of Directors:** Henry Aaron, Bill Bartholomay, Bobby Cox, Stan Kasten, Rubye Lucas, Terence McGuirk, John Schuerholz, M.B. Seretean, Ted Turner.

**President:** Stan Kasten.

**Senior Vice President and Assistant to the President:** Hank Aaron.

# BUSINESS OPERATIONS

**Senior Vice President, Administration:** Bob Wolfe.

**Administrative Services Manager:** Linda Miller. **Director of Human Resources:** Liza Stricklin.

## Finance

**Controller:** Chip Moore.

## Marketing, Sales

**Vice President/Marketing and Broadcasting:** Wayne Long.

**Senior Director of Promotions and Civic Affairs:** Miles McRea. **Director of Ticket Sales:** Paul Adams. **Director of Merchandising:** Bob Hope. **Director of Advertising:** Amy Richter. **Director of Braves Foundation:** Danny Goodwin. **Director of Multicultural Marketing:** Peter Serrano.

## Public Relations, Communications

**Telephone:** (404) 522-7630. **FAX:** (404) 614-1391.

**Director of Public Relations:** Jim Schultz.

**Media Relations Managers:** Phil Civins, Glen Serra. **Publications Manager:** Mike Ringering. **Director of Community Relations:** Dexter Santos.

## Stadium Operations

**Director of Stadium Operations:** Larry Bowman. **Operations Manager:** George McClendon. **Security Manager:** Jan Freund.

**Field Director:** Ed Mangan.

**PA Announcer:** Marshall Mann. **Official Scorers:** Mark Frederickson, Paul Newberry.

## Ticketing

**Telephone:** (800) 326-4000. **FAX:** (404) 614-1391.

**Director of Ticket Operations:** Ed Newman. **Assistant Director of Ticket Operations:** Sam Williams. **Director of Ticket Sales:** Paul Adams.

## Travel, Clubhouse

**Director of Team Travel and Equipment Manager:** Bill Acree.

**Visiting Clubhouse Manager:** John Holland. **Assistant Equipment Manager:** Casey Stevenson.

## Radio, TV, Media

**Radio Announcers:** Skip Caray, Pete Van Wieren, Don Sutton, Joe Simpson. **Flagship Station:** WSB 750-AM. **No. of Network Stations:** 75.

**TV Announcers:** Skip Caray, Pete Van Wieren, Don Sutton, Joe Simpson, Tim Brando, Ernie Johnson. **Flagship Stations:** WTBS Channel 17, SportSouth (regional cable).

**NEWSPAPERS, Daily Coverage:** Atlanta Journal-Constitution, Morris News Service.

## General Information

**Team Colors:** Red, white and blue.

**Hometown Dugout:** First Base.

**Standard Game Times:** Day—1:10 p.m. Night—7:40, Sat. 7:10.

**Directions to Stadium:** I-75/85 northbound, take exit 90; I-75/85 southbound, take exit 91; I-20 westbound, take exit 24; I-20 eastbound, take exit 22.

**Player Representative:** Tom Glavine.

# BRAVES

## BASEBALL OPERATIONS

**Executive Vice President and General Manager:** John Schuerholz.

**Assistant General Manager:** Dean Taylor. **Special Assistants to General Manager:** Bill Lajoie, Paul Snyder. **Baseball Operations Assistant:** Dave Wilder.

John Schuerholz

### Major League Staff

**Manager:** Bobby Cox.

**Coaches:** Dugout—Jim Beauchamp; Pitching—Leo Mazzone; Batting—Clarence Jones; First Base—Pat Corrales; Third Base—Jimy Williams; Bullpen—Ned Yost.

Bobby Cox

### Medical, Training

**Team Physician:** Dr. David Watson.

**Trainer:** Dave Pursley. **Assistant Trainer:** Jeff Porter. **Strength and Conditioning Director:** Frank Fultz.

### Minor Leagues

**Assistant General Manager/Player Personnel:** Chuck LaMar.

**Assistant Director of Player Development:** Rod Gilbreath. **Administrative Assistant, Minor Leagues:** Bobbie Cranford.

**Special Assistants, Player Personnel:** Jose Martinez, Willie Stargell.

**Field Coordinator:** Bobby Dews.

**Roving Instructors:** Ken Crenshaw (strength and conditioning), Leon Roberts (hitting), Joe Szekely (catching), Dave Tomlin (pitching).

### Farm System

| Class | Farm Team | Manager | Bat. Coach | Pitch. Coach |
|---|---|---|---|---|
| AAA | Richmond | Grady Little | Glenn Hubbard | Bill Fischer |
| AA | Greenville | Bruce Benedict | Randy Ingle | Bruce Dal Canton |
| A | Durham | Matt West | Brian Snitker | Bill Slack |
| A | Macon | Nelson Norman | Dave Hilton | Larry Jaster |
| A | Eugene | Paul Runge | Wallace Johnson | Jerry Nyman |
| Rookie | Danville | Max Venable | Angel Morris | Mark Ross |
| Rookie | W. Palm Beach | Jim Saul | Sonny Jackson | Eddie Watt |

### Scouting

**Director of Scouting:** Chuck Lamar.

**Assistant Director of Scouting:** Don Mitchell. **Scouting and Player Development Assistant:** Scott Proefrock. **Administrative Assistant, Scouting:** Linda Smith.

**Major League/Advance Scouts:** Scott Nethery (Atlanta, GA), Fred Shaffer (New Castle, PA), John Van Ornum (North Fork, CA), Bill Wight (Carmichael, CA), Don Williams (Paragould, AR).

**National Supervisors:** Bart Braun (Vallejo, CA), Don Mitchell (Marietta, GA).

Chuck LaMar

**Regional Supervisors:** Roy Clark (Martinsville, VA), John Flannery (Austin, TX), Deric Ladnier (Cantonment, FL), David Wilder (Berkeley, CA).

**Area Scouts:** Mack Babitt (Richmond, CA), Butch Baccala (Sherwood, OR), Doug Baker (Encinitas, CA), Stu Cann (Bradley, IL), Ray Corbett (College Station, TX), Hep Cronin (Cincinnati, OH), Tom Ealy (Phoenix, AZ), Rob English (Duluth, GA), Steve Givens (Tallahassee, FL), John Hagemann (Staten Island, NY), Steve Jongewaard (Huntington Beach, CA), Brian Kohlscheen (York, NE), Scott Littlefield (Brandon, FL), Jim Martz (Lima, OH), Drayton Moore (Herndon, VA), Marco Paddy (Columbus, GA), Julian Perez (Levittown, PR), Mac Seibert (Molino, FL), John Stewart (Granville, NY), Junior Vizcaino (Durham, NC), Bob Wadsworth (Westminster, CA).

**Scouts:** Joe Caputo (Royersford, PA), Robert Dunning (Phoenix, AZ), Jerry Gardner (Los Alamitos, CA), Ralph Garr (Missouri City, TX), Jim Guinn (Fairfield, CA), Bob Irwin (Seal Beach, CA), Robert Lucas (East Point, GA), Ernie Pederson (Tinley Park, IL), Jack Powell (Sweetwater, TN), Charlie Smith (Austin, TX), Bob Turzilli (Kinnelon, NJ).

**International Supervisor:** Bill Clark (Columbia, MO). **Latin American Supervisor:** Carlos Rios (Lantana, FL).

# CHICAGO

## Telephone, Address

**Office Address:** Wrigley Field, 1060 West Addison St., Chicago, IL 60613. **Telephone:** (312) 404-2827. **FAX:** (312) 404-4129.

Andy MacPhail

## Ownership

**Operated by:** Chicago National League Ball Club, Inc.

**Owner:** Tribune Company.

**Board of Directors:** James Dowdle, Andy MacPhail, Andrew McKenna.

**President/Chief Executive Officer:** Andy MacPhail.

# BUSINESS OPERATIONS

**Executive Vice President, Business Operations:** Mark McGuire.

**Senior Legal Counsel:** Donn Davis. **Legal Counsel:** Crane Kenney. **Corporate Secretary:** Stanley Gradowski. **Executive Secretary, Business Operations:** Annette Hannah.

**Director, Human Resources:** Wendy Lewis. **Human Resources Representative:** Desiree Brazelton. **Human Resources Specialist:** Mary Donnawell.

## Finance

**Director, Planning and Control:** Margaret Durkin. **Manager, Accounting:** Jodi Norman. **Manager, Information Systems:** Carl Rice. **Accountant:** Rick Grember.

## Marketing, Sales

**Vice President, Marketing and Broadcasting:** John McDonough.

**Manager, Sponsorship/Advertising:** Jay Blunk. **Manager, Broadcasting/Special Events:** Phil Bedella. **Manager, Cubs Care/Community Relations:** Rebecca Polihronis. **Senior Account Executive:** Sam Riber. **Account Executive:** Susan Otolski.

## Public Relations, Communications

**Telephone:** (312) 404-4191. **FAX:** (312) 404-4129.

**Director, Media Relations:** Sharon Pannozzo. **Media Information Coordinator:** Chuck Wasserstrom. **Media Relations Assistant:** Wanda Taylor.

**Director of Publications/Special Projects:** Ernie Roth. **Manager, Publications:** Ed McGregor. **Photographer:** Stephen Green.

## Stadium Operations

**Director, Stadium Operations:** Tom Cooper. **Assistant Director, Stadium Operations:** Paul Rathje.

**Manager, Event Operations/Security:** Mike Hill. **Facility Supervisor:** Frank Capparelli.

**PA Announcer:** Wayne Messmer. **Official Scorers:** Bob Rosenberg, Don Friske.

## Ticketing

**Telephone:** (312) 404-2827. **FAX:** (312) 404-4014.

**Director, Ticket Operations**: Frank Maloney. **Assistant Director, Ticket Sales:** Jim Coffey. **Assistant Director, Ticket Services:** Joe Kirchen.

## Travel, Clubhouse

**Traveling Secretary:** Jimmy Bank.

**Equipment Manager:** Yosh Kawano. **Assistant Equipment Manager:** Dana Noeltner. **Visiting Clubhouse Manager:** Tom Hellmann.

**Video Systems Coordinator:** Jerry Cell.

## Radio, TV, Media

**Radio Announcers:** Thom Brennaman, Harry Caray, Ron Santo. **Flagship Station:** WGN 720-AM.

**TV Announcers:** Thom Brennaman, Harry Caray, Steve Stone. **Flagship Stations:** WGN Channel 9, ChicagoLand (regional cable).

**NEWSPAPERS, Daily Coverage:** Chicago Sun-Times, Chicago Tribune, Arlington Heights Daily Herald.

## General Information

**Team Colors:** Royal blue and white.

**Hometown Dugout:** Third Base.

**Standard Game Times:** Day—1:20 p.m., 2:20. Night—7:05.

**Stadium Location:** Five miles along Addison Street East exit off I-90/I-94.

**Player Representative:** Randy Myers.

# CUBS

## BASEBALL OPERATIONS

**Telephone:** (312) 404-2827. **FAX:** (312) 404-4111.

**General Manager:** Ed Lynch.

**Director of Baseball Administration:** Scott Nelson. **Special Assistant to the General Manager:** John Young.

**Director, Arizona Operations/Special Assignment Scout:** Larry Himes. **Special Player Consultant:** Hugh Alexander.

**Executive Secretary, Major League Operations:** Arlene Gill. **Baseball Operations Assistant:** Michelle Blanco.

**Ed Lynch**

### Major League Staff

**Manager:** Jim Riggleman.

**Coaches:** Bench—Max Oliveras; Pitching—Ferguson Jenkins; Hitting—Billy Williams; First Base—Dan Radison; Third Base—Tony Muser; Bullpen—Dave Bialas.

**Jim Riggleman**

### Medical, Training

**Team Physicians:** Dr. John Marquardt, Dr. Michael Schafer.

**Head Trainer:** John Fierro. **Assistant Trainer:** Brian McCann. **Physical Development Coordinator:** Garrett Giemont.

### Minor Leagues

**Telephone:** (312) 404-2827. **FAX:** (312) 404-4147.

**Director, Player Development:** Jim Hendry.

**Director, Minor League Business Operations:** Connie Kowal. **Minor League Operations Assistant:** Patti Kargakis.

**Coordinator of Instruction:** Tom Gamboa.

**Roving Instructors:** Bruce Hammel (physical development), Rick Kranitz (pitching), Gary Matthews (hitting), Jimmy Piersall (outfield). **Strength Coordinator:** Bruce Hammel.

**Equipment Manager:** Michael Burkhart.

### Farm System

| Class | Farm Team | Manager | Bat. Coach | Pitch. Coach |
|---|---|---|---|---|
| AAA | Iowa | Ron Clark | Glenn Adams | Bill Earley |
| AA | Orlando | Bruce Kimm | Chris Speier | Marty DeMerritt |
| A | Daytona | Dave Trembley | Richie Zisk | Gary Lucas |
| A | Rockford | Steve Roadcap | Steve Dillard | Alan Dunn |
| A | Williamsport | Oneri Fleita | Moe Hill | Scott May |
| Rookie | Fort Myers | Sandy Alomar | Unavailable | Oscar Acosta |

### Scouting

**Director of Scouting:** Al Goldis (Sarasota, FL).

**Scouting Consultant:** Vedie Himsl (Chicago, IL). **Scouting Secretary:** Patricia Honzik.

**Advance Scout:** Keith Champion (Ballwin, MO).

**Regional Supervisors:** Northeast—Billy Blitzer (Brooklyn, NY), Central—John Stockstill (San Ramon, CA), West—Larry Maxie (Upland, CA), Southeast/International—Tony DeMacio (Chamblee, GA).

**Al Goldis**

**Scouts:** Tom Bourque (Cambridge, MA), Mike Bricker (Columbia, SC), Bill Capps (Arlington, TX), Jim Crawford (Chattanooga, TN), Frank DeMoss (Fairmont, WV), Preston Douglas (St. Augustine, FL), Ed Ford (Jersey City, NJ), Steve Fuller (Brea, CA), Doug Gassaway (Blum, TX), Al Geddes (Canby, OR), John Gracio (Chandler, AZ), Gene Handley (Huntington Beach, CA), Joe Housey (Hollywood, FL), Toney Howell (Chicago, IL), Spider Jorgensen (Cucamonga, CA), Buzzy Keller (Seguin, TX), Buddy Mercado (Maumelle, AR), Bob Steinkamp (Beatrice, NE), Billy Swoope (Richmond, VA).

**International Scouts:** Alberto Rondon (Venezuela), Fermin Ubri (Dominican Republic).

# CINCINNATI

## Telephone, Address

**Office Address:** 100 Riverfront Stadium, Cincinnati, OH 45202. **Telephone:** (513) 421-4510. **FAX:** (513) 421-7342.

Marge Schott

## Ownership

**Operated by:** The Cincinnati Reds, Inc.

**Principal Owner/General Partner:** Marge Schott.

**Limited Partners:** Frisch's Restaurants, Inc.; Carl Kroch; Carl Lindner; Multimedia, Inc.; Mrs. Louis Nippert; William Reik Jr.; George Strike.

# BUSINESS OPERATIONS

**Administrative Assistant:** Joyce Pfarr.

## Finance

**Controller:** Kevin Krietzer.

**Payroll Supervisor:** Cathy Secor.

## Marketing, Sales

**Director of Marketing:** Chip Baker. **Director of Season Ticket Sales:** Pat McCaffrey. **Director of Group Sales:** Barb McManus.

## Public Relations, Communications

**Telephone:** (513) 421-4510, ext. 250. **FAX:** (513) 421-7342.

**Director, Public Relations:** Jon Braude. **Assistant Director, Public Relations:** Joe Kelley.

## Stadium Operations

**Director of Stadium Operations:** Joanne Pettyjohn.

**Head Groundskeeper:** Gary Wahoff.

**PA Announcer:** Jon Braude. **Official Scorer:** Glenn Sample.

## Ticketing

**Telephone:** (513) 421-4510, ext. 300. **FAX:** (513) 421-7342.

**Director of Ticket Operations:** John O'Brien. **Assistant Ticket Director:** Ken Ayer.

## Travel, Clubhouse

**Traveling Secretary:** Joel Pieper.

**Equipment Manager:** Bernie Stowe. **Home Clubhouse:** Mark Stowe, Rick Stowe. **Visitors Clubhouse:** Ernie Britton.

## Radio, TV, Media

**Radio Announcers:** Marty Brennaman, Joe Nuxhall. **Flagship Station:** WLW 700-AM.

**TV Announcers:** Marty Brennaman, George Grande, Chris Welsh. **Flagship Stations:** WLWT Channel 5, SportsChannel Ohio (regional cable).

**NEWSPAPERS, Daily Coverage:** Cincinnati Enquirer, Cincinnati Post, Dayton Daily News, Columbus Dispatch.

## General Information

**Team Colors:** Red and white.

**Hometown Dugout:** First Base.

**Standard Game Times:** Day—2:15 p.m.; Night—7:35, Sat. 7:05.

**Stadium Location:** From north, take I-75 South, follow downtown signs and exit on Pete Rose Way. From Kentucky, take I-75 North, follow north I-71 sign to Pete Rose Way.

**Player Representative:** Hal Morris.

# REDS

## BASEBALL OPERATIONS

**Telephone:** (513) 421-4510, ext. 200. **FAX:** (513) 421-7342.

**General Manager:** Jim Bowden.

**Senior Advisor, Baseball Operations:** Larry Barton Jr. (Fontana, CA). **Special Assistant to General Manager:** Gene Bennett. **Senior Advisor, Player Personnel:** Jack McKeon.

Jim Bowden

### Major League Staff

**Manager:** Davey Johnson. **Assistant Manager:** Ray Knight.

**Coaches:** Dugout/Hitting—Hal McRae; Pitching—Don Gullett; Hitting/Third Base—Ray Knight; First Base—Joel Youngblood; Bullpen—Grant Jackson.

Davey Johnson

### Medical, Training

**Club Physician:** Dr. Scott Jolson.

**Head Trainer:** Greg Lynn. **Assistant Trainer:** Unavailable.

### Minor Leagues

**Telephone:** (513) 421-4510, ext. 239. **FAX:** (513) 421-7342.

**Director of Player Development:** Chief Bender. **Assistant, Baseball Operations:** Darrell "Doc" Rodgers. **Administrative Assistant, Player Development:** Lois Schneider.

**Field Coordinator:** Jim Lett. **Roving Instructor:** Jim Hickman (hitting).

### Farm System

| Class | Farm Team | Manager | Bat. Coach | Pitch. Coach |
|---|---|---|---|---|
| AAA | Indianapolis | Marc Bombard | Jim Thrift | Mike Griffin |
| AA | Chattanooga | Dave Miley | None | Terry Abbott |
| A | Winston-Salem | Mark Berry | None | Derek Botelho |
| A | Charleston, W.Va. | Razor Shines | None | Mack Jenkins |
| Rookie | Billings | Donnie Scott | None | Steve Oliverio |
| Rookie | Princeton | John Stearns | None | Brad Kelley |

### Scouting

**Director of Scouting:** Julian Mock (Fayetteville, GA).

**Administrative Assistant, Scouting:** Wilma Mann. **Secretary, Player Development and Scouting:** Lois Hudson.

**Advance Scout:** John Stearns (Boulder, CO).

**National Crosscheckers:** Jeff Barton (Gilbert, AZ), Clay Daniel (Clermont, FL), Thomas Wilson (Tuscaloosa, AL).

Julian Mock

**Scouting Supervisors:** Johnny Almaraz (Spring Branch, TX), Ray Bellino (Jersey City, NJ), George Brill (Tigard, OR), Robby Corsaro (Adelanto, CA), Robert Filotei (Wilmer, AL), Les Houser (Gilbert, AZ), David Jennings (St. Charles, MO), Steve Kring (Charlotte, NC), John Luedtke (Fayetteville, AR), Mike Mangan (Clermont, FL), Tom Severtson (Denver, CO), Bob Szymkowski (Riverdale, IL), Marion Trumbo (Bluemont, VA), Mike Wallace (Escondido, CA), Jeff Zimmerman (Rancho Cordova, CA).

**Scouts:** Fred Blair (Springfield, OH), Jim Connor (Florence, KY), Jim Grief (Paducah, KY), Don Gust (West Jordan, UT), Fred Hayes (Battle Creek, MI), Fred Leone (Pelham Manor, NY), Dion Lowe (Decatur, GA), Jerry Raddatz (Winona, MN), Doug Stuart (Brentwood, TN), Lee Toole (Council Bluffs, IA), Jim Vennari (Pomeroy, OH), John Walsh (Windsor, CT), Murray Zuk (Souris, Manitoba).

**International Scouts:** Jose Moreno (Dominican Republic), Miguel Nava (Venezuela).

# COLORADO

Jerry McMorris

## Telephone, Address

**Office Address:** 2001 Blake St., Denver, CO 80205. **Telephone:** (303) 292-0200. **FAX:** (303) 312-2319.

## Ownership

**Operated by:** Colorado Baseball Partnership 1993, Ltd.

**Principal Owners/Board of Directors:** Jerry McMorris, Oren Benton, Charles Monfort.

**Chairman:** Jerry McMorris.

## BUSINESS OPERATIONS

**Senior Vice President/Secretary and Corporate Counsel:** Clark Weaver.

**Vice President, Operations:** Keli McGregor.

**Director of Human Resources:** Liz Stecklein.

## Finance

**Senior Vice President, Chief Financial Officer:** Harold Roth.

**Vice President, Finance:** Michael Kent.

**Director of Management Information Systems:** Mary Burns. **Senior Staff Accountant:** Gary Lawrence. **Staff Accountant:** Phil Emerson.

## Marketing, Sales

**Vice President, Sales and Marketing:** David Glazier.

**Director of Corporate Sales:** Marcy English. **Director of Corporate Marketing:** Mike Arthur. **Manager of Promotions:** Alan Bossart.

**Manager of Season Ticket Sales:** Jeff Benner. **Supervisor of Group Sales:** Erin Weiss.

**Director of Broadcast Operations:** Eric Brummond.

## Public Relations, Communications

**Telephone:** (303) 292-0200. **FAX:** (303) 830-8977.

**Director of Public Relations:** Mike Swanson. **Assistant Director of Public Relations:** Coley Brannon. **Staff Assistants:** John Kehl, Raili Mood.

**Director of Publications:** Jimmy Oldham.

**Manager of Player Relations:** Karin Bearnarth. **Coordinator of Player Relations:** Mike Thumin.

**Director of Community Affairs:** Roger Kinney. **Manager of Community Services:** Barb Maniscalco.

## Stadium Operations

**Director of Stadium Services:** Kevin Kahn. **Assistant Director of Stadium Services:** Steve Mikolajczak.

**Head Groundskeeper:** Mark Razum.

**PA Announcer:** Kelly Burnham. **Official Scorers:** Frank Haraway, Dave Einspar, Jack Rose.

## Ticketing

**Assistant Vice President, Ticket Operations:** Sue Ann McClaren. **Director of Ticket Operations:** Chuck Javernick. **Assistant Director of Ticket Operations:** Kevin Fenton. **Vault Manager:** T. Robinson. **Manager of Ticket Processing:** Eric O'Leary.

## Travel, Clubhouse

**Director of Team Travel:** Peter Durso.

**Assistant to Director, Team Travel:** Adele Armagost.

**Equipment Manager:** Dan McGinn. **Visitors Clubhouse:** Keith Schultz.

## Radio, TV, Media

**Radio Announcers:** Wayne Hagin, Jeff Kingery. **Flagship Station:** KOA 850-AM. **No. of Network Stations:** 42.

**TV Announcers:** Dave Campbell, Charlie Jones. **Flagship Station:** KWGN Channel 2.

**NEWSPAPERS, Daily Coverage:** Rocky Mountain News, Denver Post.

## General Information

**Team Colors:** Purple, black and silver.

**Hometown Dugout:** First Base.

**Standard Game Times:** Day—1:05 p.m., 3:05; Night—7:05, Sat. 6:05.

**Stadium Location:** From airport, I-70 West to I-25 South to 19th Street, exit to right.

**Player Representative:** Joe Girardi.

# ROCKIES

## BASEBALL OPERATIONS

**Telephone:** (303) 312-2312. **FAX:** (303) 312-2320.

**Senior Vice President/General Manager:** Bob Gebhard. **Assistant General Manager:** Tony Siegle. **Administrative Assistant:** Chris Rice.

Bob Gebhard

### Major League Staff

**Manager:** Don Baylor.

**Coaches:** Dugout—Don Zimmer; Pitching—Larry Bearnarth; Batting/First Base—Art Howe; Third Base—Ron Hassey; Bullpen—Rick Mathews.

### Medical, Training

**Club Physicians:** Dr. Wayne Gersoff, Dr. Allen Schreiber.

Don Baylor

**Head Trainer:** Dave Cilladi. **Assistant Trainer:** Tom Probst. **Strength and Conditioning Director:** Mark Wilbert.

### Minor Leagues

**Telephone:** (303) 312-2313. **FAX:** (303) 312-2319.

**Vice President, Player Personnel:** Dick Balderson. **Assistant Director of Player Personnel:** Paul Egins. **Administrative Assistant:** Jill Darnell.

**Coordinator of Instruction:** Gene Glynn.

**Roving Instructor:** Clint Hurdle (hitting).

### Farm System

| Class | Farm Team | Manager | Bat. Coach | Pitch. Coach |
|---|---|---|---|---|
| AAA | Colo. Springs | Brad Mills | Amos Otis | Frank Funk |
| AA | New Haven | Paul Zuvella | Greg Gross | Chuck Estrada |
| A | Salem | Bill Hayes | Tony Torchia | Billy Champion |
| A | Asheville | Bill McGuire | Joe Marchese | Jack Lamabe |
| A | Portland | P.J. Carey | Al Bleser | Stan Kyles |
| Rookie | Chandler | Jim Eppard | Rolando Fernandez | Mike Ericson |

### Scouting

**Telephone:** (303) 292-0200. **FAX:** (303) 312-2319.

**Director of Scouting:** Pat Daugherty.

**Assistant Director of Scouting:** Jay Darnell. **Administrative Assistant:** Penny Biever.

**Major League Advance Scout:** Pat Dobson (Cape Coral, FL).

**Major League Scouts:** Gary Blaylock (Malden, MO), Jack Bloomfield (McAllen, TX), Jim Fanning (Pointe Claire, Quebec), Bill Harford (Chicago, IL), Mel Nelson (Highland, CA).

Pat Daugherty

**National Crosscheckers:** Herb Hippauf (Sunnyvale, CA), Jeff Schugel (Winter Haven, FL).

**Regional Crosscheckers:** West—Bruce Andrew (Northridge, CA), Midwest—Dave Holliday (Coalgate, OK), East—Robyn Lynch (Safety Harbor, FL).

**Full-Time Scouts:** Mark Corey (Kenner, LA), Ty Coslow (Louisville, KY), Dar Cox (Red Oak, TX), Abe Flores (Huntington Beach, CA), Mike Garlatti (Edison, NJ), Larry High (Mesa, AZ), Bert Holt (Visalia, CA), Greg Hopkins (Portland, OR), Pat Jones (Davie, FL), Jimmy Lester (Columbus, GA), Frank Mattox (Los Angeles, CA), Danny Montgomery (Charlotte, NC), Steve Murray (Paradise Valley, AZ), Lance Nichols (Dodge City, KS), Art Pontarelli (Cranston, RI), Ed Santa (Columbus, OH), Nick Venuto (Crown Pointe, IN), Tom Wheeler (Pleasant Hill, CA).

**International Scouts:** Bill MacKenzie (Canada), Jorge Posada (Puerto Rico).

# FLORIDA

Wayne Huizenga

## Telephone, Address

**Office Address:** Joe Robbie Stadium, 2267 NW 199th St., Miami, FL 33056. **Telephone:** (305) 626-7400. **FAX:** (305) 626-7302.

## Ownership

**Operated by:** Florida Marlins Baseball Club, Inc.

**Principal Owner/Chairman:** Wayne Huizenga.

**Partners:** Steven Berrard, Harris Hudson, Harry Huizenga, Wayne Huizenga Jr.

**Special Counsel:** James Blosser. **Special Consulant:** Richard Rochon.

**President:** Donald Smiley.

# BUSINESS OPERATIONS

**Vice President, Operations:** Richard Andersen. **Executive Secretary:** Eileen Parsons.

## Finance

**Vice President, Finance and Administration:** Jonathan Mariner.

**Accounting Manager:** Susan Jaison. **Senior Staff Accountant:** David Kuan. **Staff Accountants:** Donna Hancock, Nancy Hernandez.

## Marketing, Sales

**Vice President, Sales and Advertising:** Bob Kramm. **Director of Season and Group Sales:** Frank Gernert. **Director of Corporate Sponsorships and Promotions:** Neal Bendesky. **Corporate Sales Manager:** Ben Creed. **Sales Managers:** Patrick McNamara, Mike Stanfield, Jeff Sturgis.

## Public Relations, Communications

**Telephone:** (305) 626-7429. **FAX:** (305) 626-7403.

**Vice President, Broadcasting:** Dean Jordan.

**Director of Media Relations:** Chuck Pool. **Assistant Directors of Media Relations:** Mark Geddis, Adolfo Salgueiro. **Media Relations Assistant:** Margo Malone.

**Publications Manager:** Leslie Riguero.

**Director of Community Relations:** Jorge Arrizurieta. **Director of International Relations:** Tony Perez.

## Stadium Operations

**Facility Operations Manager:** Martin Becker.

**Director, Brevard County Operations:** Ken Lehner. **Assistant Director, Brevard Operations:** Russ Brandon.

**PA Announcer:** Jay Rokeach. **Official Scorers:** Harvey Greene, Sonny Hirsch, Doug Pett.

## Ticketing

**Telephone:** (305) 620-2578. **FAX:** (305) 626-7432.

**Director of Ticket Operations:** Bill Galante. **Ticket Operations Manager:** Steven Froot. **Ticket Services Manager:** Andy Major.

## Travel, Clubhouse

**Director of Team Travel:** Bill Beck.

**Equipment Manager:** Mike Wallace. **Assistant Equipment Manager:** Matt Rosenthal. **Visitors Clubhouse:** Carlos Ledezma.

**Video Coordinator:** Mike Carr.

## Radio, TV, Media

**Radio Announcers:** English—Joe Angel, Dave O'Brien. Spanish—Felo Ramirez, Manolo Alvarez. **Flagship Stations:** English—WQAM 560-AM; Spanish—WCMQ 1210-AM.

**TV Announcers:** Jay Randolph, Gary Carter. **Flagship Stations:** WBFS Channel 33, Sunshine Network (regional cable).

**NEWSPAPERS, Daily Coverage:** Miami Herald, Fort Lauderdale Sun-Sentinel, Palm Beach Post, Florida Today. Spanish—El Nuevo Herald.

## General Information

**Team Colors:** Teal, black and silver.

**Hometown Dugout:** First Base.

**Standard Game Times:** Day—1:35 p.m. Night—7:35; Sat., 7:05; Sun. (June-August), 6:05.

**Stadium Location:** From south—Florida Turnpike to stadium exit; From north—I-95 to I-595 to Florida Turnpike to stadium exit; From west—I-75 to I-595 to Florida Turnpike to stadium exit.

**Player Representative:** Bryan Harvey.

# MARLINS

## BASEBALL OPERATIONS

**Executive Vice President, General Manager:** Dave Dombrowski.

**Assistant General Manager:** Frank Wren. **Special Assistants to the General Manager:** Gary Hughes, John Boles. **Senior Advisor, Player Personnel:** Whitey Lockman. **Director, Latin American Operations:** Al Avila. **Assistant, Baseball Operations:** DeJon Watson.

Dave Dombrowski

### Major League Staff

**Manager:** Rene Lachemann.

**Coaches:** Pitching—Larry Rothschild; Batting—Jose Morales; First Base—Rusty Kuntz; Third Base—Cookie Rojas; Bullpen—Rick Williams.

### Medical, Training

**Club Physician:** Dr. Dan Kanell.

**Head Trainer:** Larry Starr. **Assistant Trainer:** Kevin Rand. **Strength and Conditioning Director:** Rick Slate.

Rene Lachemann

### Minor Leagues

**Telephone:** (407) 633-8119. **FAX:** (407) 633-9216.

**Director of Player Development:** John Boles. **Director of Minor League Administration:** Dan Lunetta. **Administrative Assistants:** Kim-Lee Carkeek, Laurie Soltman.

**Coordinator of Trainers and Equipment:** John Spinosa.

**Roving Instructors:** Lorenzo Bundy (outfield/base running), Rich Dubee (pitching), Jack Maloof (hitting), Toby Oldham (strength/fitness), Tony Taylor (infield).

### Farm System

| Class | Farm Team | Manager | Bat. Coach | Pitch. Coach |
|---|---|---|---|---|
| AAA | Charlotte | Sal Rende | Adrian Garrett | Mike Parrott |
| AA | Portland | Carlos Tosca | Jeff Pentland | Rich Gale |
| A | Brevard County | Fredi Gonzalez | Jose Castro | Britt Burns |
| A | Kane County | Lynn Jones | Rod Allen | Brian Peterson |
| A | Elmira | Paul Kirsch | Steve McFarland | Bill Long |
| Rookie | Melbourne | Juan Bustabad | Jon Deeble | Randy Hennis |

### Scouting

**Telephone:** (305) 626-7217. **FAX:** (305) 626-7433.

**Director of Scouting:** Gary Hughes.

**Associate Director of Scouting/Director of International Operations:** Orrin Freeman. **Administrative Assistant:** Cheryl Evans.

**Advance Scout:** Ken Kravec (Sarasota, FL).

**Special Assignment Scouts:** Whitey Lockman (Scottsdale, AZ), Scott Reid (Phoenix, AZ).

**National Crosscheckers:** Orrin Freeman (La Jolla, CA), Jax Robertson (Cary, NC).

**Regional Crosscheckers:** Central—Murray Cook (Cincinnati, OH); West—Dick Egan (Phoenix, AZ); East—Greg Zunino (Cape Coral, FL).

Gary Hughes

**Full-Time Scouts:** Rich Bordi (Vancouver, WA), Ty Brown (Ruther Glen, VA), John Castleberry (High Point, NC), David Chadd (Manhattan, KS), Brad Del Barba (Taylor Mill, KY), Will George (Pennsauken, NJ), Bob Laurie (Plano, TX), Grady Mack (Hermosa Beach, CA), Steve McFarland (Scottsdale, AZ), Steve Minor (Long Beach, CA), Stan Saleski (Dayton, OH), Bill Scherrer (Buffalo, NY), Tim Schmidt (San Bernardino, CA), Bill Singer (Decatur, AL), Keith Snider (Stockton, CA), DeJon Watson (Hollywood, FL), Jeff Wren (St. Petersburg, FL), Stan Zielinski (Winfield, IL).

**International Scouts:** Jon Deeble (Australia), Cucho Rodriguez (Puerto Rico).

# HOUSTON

Drayton McLane

## Telephone, Address

**Office Address:** 8400 Kirby Dr., Houston, TX 77054. **Mailing Address:** P.O. Box 288, Houston, TX 77001. **Telephone:** (713) 799-9500. **FAX:** (713) 799-9562.

## Ownership

**Operated by:** McLane Group, LP.

**Principal Owner/Chairman of the Board:** Drayton McLane Jr.

**Directors:** Drayton McLane Jr., Sandy Sanford, Bob McClaren.

# BUSINESS OPERATIONS

**Senior Vice President, Business Operations:** Bob McClaren.

**Vice President, Human Resources:** Mike Anders.

## Finance

**Controller:** Robert McBurnett.

**Accounts Receivable:** Mary Ann Bell. **Accounts Payable:** Irene Dumenil. **General Accounting:** Mary Duvernay, Rita Suchma. **Payroll:** Marla Rodgers.

## Marketing, Sales

**Director of Marketing:** Pam Gardner. **Director of Telemarketing:** Matt Kastel. **Program Manager, Premium Sales:** John Sorrentino.

**Director of Advertising:** Amy Kress. **Assistant Director of Advertising:** Trey Wilkinson. **Advertising Sales:** Rachel Mujica. **Assistant, Advertising Sales:** Marian Harper.

**Director of Broadcasting/Promotions:** Jamie Hildreth. **Administrative Assistant, Broadcasting:** Anna Cardinale.

**Youth Programs Coordinator:** Heather Cox.

## Public Relations, Communications

**Telephone:** (713) 799-9600. **FAX:** (713) 799-9562.

**Director of Media Relations:** Rob Matwick. **Assistant Director of Media Relations:** Tyler Barnes.

**Director of Community Development:** Gene Pemberton. **Program Executive, Community Outreach:** Robert Reid. **Administrative Assistant, Community Development:** Lisa O'Rourke.

**Mascot Program Coordinator:** Steve Amaya.

## Stadium Operations

**Director of Stadium Operations:** Gary Cavey.

**Head Groundskeeper:** Willie Berry.

**PA Announcer:** Bob Ford. **Official Scorers:** Fred Duckett, Ivy McLemore, Rick Blount.

## Ticketing

**Telephone:** (713) 6-ASTROS. **FAX:** (713) 799-9525.

**Director of Ticket Sales and Services:** Rich Fromstein.

**Program Manager, Premium Sales:** John Sorrentino. **Director of Telemarketing:** Matt Kastel.

## Travel, Clubhouse

**Traveling Secretary:** Barry Waters.

**Equipment Manager:** Dennis Liborio. **Visiting Clubhouse Manager:** Steve Perry.

## Radio, TV, Media

**Radio Announcers:** Milo Hamilton, Larry Dierker, Bill Brown, Vince Cotroneo. **Flagship Station:** KPRC 950-AM. **No. of Network Stations:** 50.

**Television Announcers:** Bill Brown, Milo Hamilton, Larry Dierker, Bill Worrell. **Flagship Stations:** KTXH Channel 20, Home Sports Entertainment (regional cable).

**NEWSPAPERS, Daily Coverage:** Houston Chronicle, Houston Post.

## General Information

**Team Colors:** Navy and metallic gold.

**Hometown Dugout:** First Base.

**Standard Game Times:** Day—1:35 p.m. Night—7:05.

**Stadium Location:** Located at Loop 610 south and Kirby Drive exit.

**Player Representative:** Chris Donnels.

# ASTROS

## BASEBALL OPERATIONS

**President:** Tal Smith.

**General Manager:** Bob Watson.

**Director of Baseball Administration:** Barry Waters. **Administrative Assistant, Major League Operations:** Beverly Rains.

Bob Watson

### Major League Staff

**Manager:** Terry Collins.

**Coaches:** Pitching—Mel Stottlemyre; Batting—Steve Henderson; First Base/Outfield—Jesse Barfield; Third Base—Matt Galante; Bullpen—Julio Linares.

Terry Collins

### Medical, Training

**Team Physician:** Dr. Bill Bryan.

**Head Trainer:** Dave Labossiere. **Assistant Trainer:** Rex Jones. **Strength and Conditioning Coach** Gene Coleman.

### Minor Leagues

**Telephone:** (713) 799-9867. **FAX:** (713) 799-9562.

**Director of Player Development:** Fred Nelson.

**Director of Major and Minor League Player Relations:** Tim Purpura. **Administrative Assistant, Minor League Operations:** Carol Wogsland.

**Coordinator of Instruction:** Tom Wiedenbauer.

**Roving Instructor:** Dave Hudgens (hitting).

### Farm System

| Class | Farm Team | Manager | Bat. Coach | Pitch. Coach |
|---|---|---|---|---|
| AAA | Tucson | Rick Sweet | Don Reynolds | Brent Strom |
| AA | Jackson | Tim Tolman | None | Charlie Taylor |
| A | Kissimmee | Dave Engle | Ivan DeJesus | Jack Billingham |
| A | Quad City | Jim Pankovits | None | Jim Hickey |
| A | Auburn | Manny Acta | None | Don Alexander |
| Rookie | Kissimmee | Bobby Ramos | None | Stan Boroski |

### Scouting

**Telephone:** (713) 799-9616. **FAX:** (713) 799-9562.

**Director of Scouting:** Dan O'Brien.

**Assistant Director of Scouting/Director of International Development:** David Rawnsley.

**Advance Scout:** Dick Hager (Sunnyvale, CA). **Major League Scouts:** George Brophy (Minneapolis, MN), Bob Skinner (San Diego, CA).

**National Crosscheckers:** David Lakey (Austin, TX), Paul Weaver (Carpinteria, CA).

Dan O'Brien

**Regional Supervisors:** Northeast—Gerry Craft (St. Clairsville, OH); Central—Bill Kelso (Kansas City, MO); West Coast—Bob King (La Mesa, CA); West—Walt Matthews (Texarkana, TX); Southeast—Lynwood Stallings (Kingsport, TN).

**Scouts:** Stan Boroski (Kissimmee, FL), Ralph Bratton (Dripping Springs, TX), Jug DeFord (Manchester, TN), Doug Deutsch (Costa Mesa, CA), Chuck Edmondson (Texarkana, AR), Orlando Estevez (Miami, FL), Brian Granger (Dickson, TN), Dan Huston (Bellevue, WA), Mike Maggart (Penn Yan, NY), Tom Mooney (Pittsfield, MA), Joe Pittman (Columbus, GA), Jim Pransky (Urbana, IL), Deron Rombach (Escondido, CA), Nelson Rood (Scottsdale, AZ), Rick Schroeder (San Jose, CA), Mark Servais (LaCrosse, WI), Tad Slowik (Niles, IL), Kevin Stein (Blacklick, OH), Greg Whitworth (Canyon Country, CA).

**Latin American Supervisor:** Julio Linares (Dominican Republic).

**International Scouts:** Ricardo Aponte (Dominican Republic), Domingo Mercedes (Dominican Republic), Jim Pransky (Canada), Andres Reiner (Venezuela), Anibal Reluz (Panama), Adriano Rodriguez (Dominican Republic), Frankie Thon (Puerto Rico), Pablo Torrealba (Venezuela), Grant Weir (Australia).

# LOS ANGELES

Peter O'Malley

## Telephone, Address

**Office Address:** 1000 Elysian Park Ave., Los Angeles, CA 90012. **Telephone:** (213) 224-1500. **FAX:** (213) 224-1269.

## Ownership

**Operated by:** Los Angeles Dodgers, Inc.

**Principal Owner/Chairman:** Peter O'Malley.

**Board of Directors:** Harry Bardt, Roland Seidler, Terry Seidler.

**Vice President/Treasurer:** Roland Seidler.

**Vice President, Campo las Palmas complex (Dominican Republic):** Ralph Avila.

# BUSINESS OPERATIONS

**Director, Human Resources and Administration:** Irene Tanji. **Human Resources Administrator:** Sandy Yonemoto.

**Supervisor, Administrative Services:** Linda Cohen.

**Managing Director, Dodgertown:** Craig Callan.

## Finance

**Vice President, Finance:** Bob Graziano.

**Director of Management Information Systems:** Mike Mularky. **Director of Accounting and Finance:** Bill Foltz.

## Marketing, Sales

**Vice President, Marketing:** Barry Stockhamer.

**Director, Advertising and Special Events:** Paul Kalil. **Director, Ticket Marketing:** Allan Erselius. **Supervisor, Group Sales:** Steve Everett. **Special Projects Coordinator:** Monique LaVeau-Brennan.

**Director, Broadcast and Publications:** Brent Shyer. **Supervisor, Broadcast and Publications:** Paul Gomez.

## Public Relations, Communications

**Telephone:** (213) 224-1301. **FAX:** (213) 224-1459.

**Vice President, Communications:** Tommy Hawkins.

**Director of Publicity:** Jay Lucas. **Assistant Publicity Director:** Derrick Hall. **Administrative Assistant, Publicity:** Barbara Conway.

**Assistant, Baseball Information:** Dave Tuttle. **Assistant, Media and International Relations:** Annette Bagley. **Archivist:** John Olguin.

**Director of Community Relations:** Don Newcombe.

## Stadium Operations

**Director of Stadium Operations:** Doug Duennes **Assistant, Stadium Operations:** Vicki Johnson.

**Head Groundskeeper:** Al Meyers.

**PA Announcer:** Mike Carlucci. **Official Scorers:** Terry Bales, Larry Kahn.

## Ticketing

**Telephone:** (213) 224-1471. **FAX:** (213) 224-1269.

**Director of Ticket Operations:** Debra Duncan. **Ticket Manager:** Gary Barbee. **Manager, Game Day Sales:** Billy Hunter.

## Travel, Clubhouse

**Traveling Secretary:** Billy DeLury.

**Dodger Clubhouse Manager:** Dave Wright. **Visiting Clubhouse Manager:** Jerry Turner.

## Radio, TV, Media

**Radio Announcers:** English—Vin Scully, Rick Monday, Ross Porter. Spanish—Jaime Jarrin, Rene Cardenas. **Flagship Stations:** English—KABC 790-AM. Spanish—KWKW 1330-AM.

**TV Announcers:** Vin Scully, Rick Monday, Ross Porter. **Flagship Station:** KTLA Channel 5.

**NEWSPAPERS, Daily Coverage:** Los Angeles Times, South Bay Daily Breeze, Los Angeles Daily News, Long Beach Press-Telegram, Pasadena Star News, Orange County Register, San Bernardino Sun.

## General Information

**Team Colors:** Dodger blue and white.

**Hometown Dugout:** Third Base.

**Stadium Location:** I-5 to Stadium Way exit, left on Stadium Way, right on Academy Road, left to Stadium Way to Elysian Park Ave.

**Standard Game Times:** Day—1:05 p.m. Night—7:05, Wed. 7:35.

**Player Representative:** Brett Butler.

# DODGERS

## BASEBALL OPERATIONS

**Executive Vice President, Player Personnel:** Fred Claire.

**Administrator, Baseball Operations:** Robert Schweppe. **Secretary to Executive Vice President:** Rosalyn Gutierrez.

Fred Claire

### Major League Staff

**Manager:** Tommy Lasorda.

**Coaches:** Dugout—Bill Russell; Pitching—Dave Wallace; Batting/First Base—Reggie Smith; Third Base—Joe Amalfitano; Bullpen—Mark Cresse.

### Medical, Training

**Team Physicians:** Dr. Frank Jobe, Dr. Michael Mellman, Dr. Herndon Harding.

**Head Trainer:** Bill Buhler. **Assistant Trainer:** Charlie Strasser. **Physical Therapist:** Pat Screnar.

Tom Lasorda

### Minor Leagues

**Telephone:** (213) 224-1431. **FAX:** (213) 224-1359.

**Director of Minor League Operations:** Charlie Blaney. **Administrative Assistant, Minor Leagues:** Luchy Guerra. **Secretary, Minor Leagues:** Lucy Valdez. **Data Entry Operator:** John Hesket.

**Field Coordinator:** Glenn Hoffman.

**Roving Instructors:** Tom Beyers (hitting), Tim Day (physical therapist), Chico Fernandez (infield), Goose Gregson (pitching), Leo Posada (hitting), Mike Scioscia (catching), Joe Vavra (baserunning).

### Farm System

| Class | Farm Team | Manager | Bat. Coach | Pitch. Coach |
|---|---|---|---|---|
| AAA | Albuquerque | Rick Dempsey | Dick McLaughlin | Burt Hooton |
| AA | San Antonio | John Shelby | Nate Oliver | Luis Tiant |
| A | Vero Beach | Jon Debus | Tony Harris | Guy Conti |
| A | San Bernardino | Ron Roenicke | Dino Ebel | Dennis Lewallyn |
| A | Yakima | Joe Vavra | Brett Magnusson | Mark Brewer |
| Rookie | Great Falls | John Shoemaker | Mickey Hatcher | Edwin Correa |

### Scouting

**Telephone:** (213) 224-1437. **FAX:** (213) 224-1359.

**Director, Scouting:** Terry Reynolds.

**Special Assignment Scouts:** Mel Didier (Arlington, TX), Gary Sutherland (Monrovia, CA), Tim Thompson (Lewistown, PA).

**National Crosscheckers:** Eddie Bane (Phoenix, AZ), Tommy Mixon (Macon, GA).

**Regional Supervisors:** West—Gib Bodet (San Clemente, CA); Midwest—John Keenan (Great Bend, KS); East—Gary LaRocque (Greensboro, NC).

Terry Reynolds

**Scouts:** Bill Barkley (Waco, TX), Joe Campbell (Leeds, AL), Bobby Darwin (Cerritos, CA), Joe Ferrone (Sherman Oaks, CA), Mike Hankins (Summit, MO), Dick Hanlon (Millbrae, CA), Dennis Haren (San Diego, CA), Hank Jones (Vancouver, WA), Lon Joyce (Spartanburg, SC), Gene Kerns (Hagerstown, MD), John Kosciak (Milford, MA), Mike Leuzinger (Grand Prairie, TX), Carl Loewenstine (Hamilton, OH), Dale McReynolds (Walworth, WI), Camilo Pascual (Miami, FL), Bill Pleis (Parrish, FL), Ross Sapp (Moreno Valley, CA), Mark Sheehy (Sacramento, CA), Tom Thomas (Phoenix, AZ), Glen VanProyen (West Chicago, IL).

**International Supervisors:** Eddie Rodriguez (Puerto Rico), Jim Stoeckel (Europe, Asia, Australia).

# MONTREAL

Claude Brochu

## Telephone, Address

**Office Address:** 4549 Pierre-de-Coubertin Ave., Montreal, Quebec H1V 3N7. **Mailing Address:** P.O. Box 500, Station M, Montreal, Quebec H1V 3P2. **Telephone:** (514) 253-3434. **FAX:** (514) 253-8282.

## Ownership

**Operated by:** Montreal Baseball Club, Inc.

**President and General Partner:** Claude Brochu.

**Chairman of the Partnership Committee:** Jacques Menard. **Vice Chairmen of the Partnership Committee:** Claude Blanchet, Jocelyn Proteau, Louis Tanguay.

# BUSINESS OPERATIONS

## Finance

**Vice President, Finance:** Laurier Carpentier.

**Director, Financial Planning and Administration:** Michel Bussiere. **Director, Accounting Services:** Constance Jodoin.

## Marketing, Sales

**Vice President, Marketing and Communications:** Richard Morency.

**Director, Corporate Sales:** John DiTerlizzi. **Director of Special Events:** Claudine Cook. **Director of Promotions:** Luigi Carolo. **Director, Advertising:** Johanne Heroux. **Director, Merchandising:** Susan LeBlanc.

## Public Relations, Communications

**Director, Media Services:** Monique Giroux. **Director of Media Operations:** P.J. Loyello.

## Stadium Operations

**Vice President, Stadium Operations:** Claude Delorme.

**Director of Stadium Operations:** Pierre Touzin.

**Head Groundskeeper:** Jean-Claude Beaudoin.

**PA Announcer:** Alain Rouleau. **Official Scorers:** Michel Spinelli, Bob Mann.

## Ticketing

**Director, Season Ticket Sales:** Claude Chabot. **Director, Ticket Office:** Chantal Dalpe. **Director, Group Sales:** Ronald Martineau. **Manager, Group Sales:** Suzanne Lemoignan.

## Clubhouse

**Equipment Manager:** John Silverman. **Visiting Clubhouse:** Bryan Greenberg.

## Radio, TV, Media

**Radio Announcers:** CKAC/French—Jacques Doucet, Rodger Brulotte, Alain Chantelois. CIQC/English—Dave Van Horne, Ken Singleton, Elliott Price. **Flagship Stations:** French—CKAC 730-AM. English—CIQC 600-AM.

**TV Announcers:** SRC/French—Camille Dube, Claude Raymond. TSN/English—Dave Van Horne, Ken Singleton. **Flagship Stations:** French—Societe Radio Canada. English—The Sports Network (national cable).

**NEWSPAPERS, Daily Coverage:** French—La Presse, Le Journal de Montreal, La Presse Canadienne. English—Montreal Gazette.

## General Information

**Team Colors:** Blue, white and red.

**Hometown Dugout:** Third Base.

**Standard Game Times:** Day—1:35 p.m.; Night—7:35 p.m.

**Stadium Location:** From New England, take I-87 North from Vermont to Quebec Highway 15 to the Jacques Cartier Bridge, exit left, right on Sherbrooke. From upstate New York, take I-81 North to Canada's Highway 401, east to Quebec Highway 20, north to Highway 40 to the Boulevard Pie IX exit south to stadium. Access by subway from downtown Montreal to Pie IX Metro station.

**Player Representative:** John Wetteland.

# EXPOS

## BASEBALL OPERATIONS

**Vice President/General Manager:** Kevin Malone.

**Vice President/Baseball Operations:** Bill Stoneman.

**General Manager, West Palm Beach Operations:** Rob Rabenecker.

Kevin Malone

### Major League Staff

**Manager:** Felipe Alou.

**Coaches:** Dugout—Jim Tracy; Pitching—Joe Kerrigan; Batting/First Base—Tommy Harper; Third Base—Jerry Manuel; Bullpen—Pierre Arsenault.

### Medical, Training

**Team Orthopedist:** Dr. Larry Coughlin.

**Head Trainer:** Ron McClain. **Assistant Trainer:** Mike Kozak.

Felipe Alou

### Minor Leagues

**Office Address:** Municipal Stadium, 715 Hank Aaron Dr., West Palm Beach, FL 33401.

**Telephone:** (407) 684-6801. **FAX:** (407) 681-4876.

**Director, Player Development:** Bill Geivett. **Assistant Director, Player Development:** Neal Huntington. **Secretary, Minor Leagues:** Melissa Emery.

**Coordinator of Minor League Field Operations:** Dave Machemer.

**Roving Instructors:** Jim Benedict (pitching), Sean Cunningham (conditioning and rehabilitation), Dave Machemer (infield), Pat Roessler (hitting).

### Farm System

| Class | Farm Team | Manager | Bat. Coach | Pitch. Coach |
|---|---|---|---|---|
| AAA | Ottawa | Pete Mackanin | None | Chuck Kniffin |
| AA | Harrisburg | Pat Kelly | None | Bo McLaughlin |
| A | West Palm Beach | Gomer Hodge | None | Jeff Fischer |
| A | Albany | Doug Sisson | Angel Salazar | Stan Fansler |
| A | Vermont | Jim Gabella | None | Butch Hughes |
| Rookie | West Palm Beach | Rick Sofield | Luis Dorante | Mitch Zwolensky |

### Scouting

**Office Address:** Expos Minor League Development Center, 6850 Lawrence Rd., Lantana, FL 33462. **Mailing Address:** P.O. Box 6808, Lake Worth, FL 33466. **Telephone:** (407) 433-1990. **FAX:** (407) 433-3481.

**Director of Scouting:** Ed Creech (Moultrie, GA).

**Assistant Scouting Director:** Gregg Leonard. **Secretary, Scouting:** Jennifer Shaler.

**Major League Scout:** Eddie Haas (Paducah, KY).

**Regional Supervisors:** West—Jim Fleming (Norman, OK). East—David Littlefield (Delafield, WI).

Ed Creech

**Scouts:** Mark Baca (Seattle, WA), Dennis Cardoza (Norman, OK), Doug Carpenter (Boca Raton, FL), Phil Favia (Phoenix, AZ), Dan Freed (Bloomington, IL), Jim Gabella (Cleveland, OH), John Hughes (San Francisco, CA), Bob Johnson (Rockaway, NJ), Jeff Kahn (Mobile, AL), Dave Malpass (Cary, NC), Roy McMillan (Bonham, TX), Bob Oldis (Iowa City, IA), Hank Sargent (Lakeland, FL), Scott Stanley (Los Angeles, CA).

**Director, International Operations:** Fred Ferreira (Fort Lauderdale, FL).

**International Scouts:** Emilio Carrasquel (Venezuela), Arturo DeFreites (Dominican Republic), Juan Loyola (Puerto Rico), Carlos Moreno (Venezuela), Tomas Morales (Mexico), Rene Picota (Panama).

# NEW YORK

Fred Wilpon

## Telephone, Address

**Office Address:** Shea Stadium, 126th St. and Roosevelt Ave., Flushing, NY 11368. **Telephone:** (718) 507-6387. **FAX:** (718) 565-4382.

## Ownership

**Operated by:** Metropolitan Baseball Club, Inc.
**Chairman of the Board:** Nelson Doubleday.
**President:** Fred Wilpon.
**Board of Directors:** Nelson Doubleday, Fred Wilpon, Saul Katz, Joe McIlvaine, Marvin Tepper, Richard Cummins.

# BUSINESS OPERATIONS

**Chief Executive Officer:** Fred Wilpon.
**Vice President, Business Affairs and General Counsel:** David Howard.

## Finance

**Senior Vice President, Treasurer:** Harry O'Shaughnessy.
**Senior Staff Accountants:** Audrey Dussard, Alan Kindler. **Director, Administration and Data Processing:** Russell Richardson.

## Marketing, Sales

**Vice President, Marketing:** Mark Bingham.
**Director of Community Outreach:** Jill Knee.
**Director of Promotions:** James Plummer.
**Season Ticket Manager:** Marie Melluso. **Ticket Sales Audit Manager:** Toni Giordano. **Computer Ticket Operations:** John Giglio.

## Public Relations, Communications

**Telephone:** (718) 565-4330. **FAX:** (718) 565-4382.
**Director of Media Relations:** Jay Horwitz. **Administrative Assistant:** Stella Fiore.

## Stadium Operations

**Vice President, Stadium Operations:** Bob Mandt.
**Stadium Manager:** John McCarthy.
**Head Groundskeeper:** Pete Flynn.
**PA Announcer:** Unavailable. **Official Scorers:** Red Foley, Bill Shannon.

## Ticketing

**Telephone:** (718) 507-8499. **FAX:** (718) 507-6396.
**Vice President, Ticket Sales and Services:** Bill Ianniciello.
**Director, Ticket Operations:** Dan DeMato. **Manager, Customer Relations:** Joann Galardy.

## Travel, Clubhouse

**Traveling Secretary:** Unavailable.
**Equipment Manager/Clubhouse Operations:** Charlie Samuels. **Visiting Clubhouse Manager:** Tony Carullo.

## Radio, TV, Media

**Radio Announcers:** Bob Murphy, Gary Cohen. **Flagship Station:** WFAN 660-AM. **No. of Stations on Network:** 10.
**TV Announcers:** WWOR—Ralph Kiner, Tim McCarver, Rusty Staub. SportsChannel— Fran Healy, Gary Thorne. **Flagship Stations:** WWOR Channel 9, SportsChannel America (regional cable).
**NEWSPAPERS, Daily Coverage:** New York Times, New York Daily News, New York Post, Newsday, Newark Star-Ledger, The Bergen Record, Gannett-Westchester.

## General Information

**Team Colors:** Blue and orange.
**Hometown Dugout:** First Base.
**Standard Game Times:** Day—1:40 p.m. Night—7:40; Sat., 7:10.
**Stadium Location:** From the Bronx and Westchester, take Cross Bronx Expressway to the Bronx-Whitestone Bridge, then take bridge to the Whitestone Expressway to the Northern Boulevard/Shea Stadium exit.
**Player Representative:** Bobby Bonilla.

# METS

## BASEBALL OPERATIONS

Joe McIlvaine

**Telephone:** (718) 565-4302. **FAX:** (718) 507-6391.

**Executive Vice President, Baseball Operations:** Joe McIlvaine.

**Assistant Vice President, Baseball Operations:** Gerry Hunsicker. **Baseball Administrator:** Maureen Cooke. **Secretary:** Lynne Daly. **Baseball Data Analyst:** Drew Marino.

### Major League Staff

**Manager:** Dallas Green.

**Coaches:** Dugout—Bobby Wine; Pitching—Greg Pavlick; Batting—Tom McCraw; First Base—Frank Howard; Third Base—Mike Cubbage; Bullpen—Steve Swisher.

### Medical, Training

**Team Physician:** Dr. David Altchek. **Associate Team Physician:** Dr. David Dines.

**Trainer:** Fred Hina. **Assistant Trainer:** Sam McCrary. **Strength and Conditioning Coordinator:** Jeff Mangold.

Dallas Green

### Minor Leagues

**Office Address:** 525 NW Peacock Blvd., Port St. Lucie, FL 34986. **Telephone:** (407) 871-2132. **FAX:** (407) 871-2181.

**Director, Minor League Operations:** Steve Phillips. **Assistant Director, Minor League Operations:** Jim Duquette. **Administrator, Minor Leagues:** Debbie Pulaski.

**Coordinator of Instruction:** Bobby Floyd. **Assistant Coordinator of Instruction:** Chuck Hiller.

**Roving Instructors:** Ken Berry (hitting), Al Jackson (pitching), Rick Miller (outfield, baserunning), Mookie Wilson (outfield, baserunning).

### Farm System

| Class | Farm Team | Manager | Bat. Coach | Pitch. Coach |
|---|---|---|---|---|
| AAA | Norfolk | Toby Harrah | Ron Washington | Bob Apodaca |
| AA | Binghamton | John Tamargo | None | Bill Latham |
| A | St. Lucie | Rafael Landestoy | None | Randy Niemann |
| A | Columbia | Howie Freiling | None | Ray Rippelmeyer |
| A | Pittsfield | Ron Gideon | None | Dave LaRoche |
| Rookie | Kingsport | John Gibbons | None | Dave Jorn |
| Rookie | St. Lucie | John Stephenson | Felix Millan | None |

### Scouting

John Barr

**Office Address:** 525 NW Peacock Blvd., Port St. Lucie, FL 34986. **Telephone:** (407) 871-2132. **FAX:** (407) 871-2181.

**Director of Scouting:** John Barr.

**Assistant Director, Scouting:** Jim Duquette. **Administrative Assistant, Scouting:** Tom Allison.

**Advance Scout:** Dick Gernert (Reading, PA).

**Major League Scouts:** Carmen Fusco (Camp Hill, PA), Harry Minor (Long Beach, CA).

**Special Assignment Scouts:** Darrell Johnson (Ord, NE), Buddy Kerr (Oradell, NJ).

**National Crosscheckers:** Paul Ricciarini (Pittsfield, MA), Jack Zduriencik (Pittsburgh, PA).

**Regional Scouting Directors:** Northern states, Latin America, Texas—Roland Johnson (Newington, CT); South—Joe Mason (Millbrook, AL); West—Bob Minor (Long Beach, CA).

**Area Supervisors:** Paul Baretta (Kensington, CT), Larry Chase (Pearcy, AR), Lin Garrett (Wesley Chapel, FL), Rob Guzik (Latrobe, PA), R.J. Harrison (Phoenix, AZ), Dave Lottsfeldt (Garland, TN), Lee May Jr. (Cincinnati, OH), Marlin McPhail (Irmo, SC), Jim Miller (San Jose, CA), Joe Nigro (Staten Island, NY), Mark Ralston (Chatsworth, CA), Jim Reeves (Milwaukie, OR), Bob Rossi (Baton Rouge, LA), Terry Tripp (Harrisburg, IL), Greg Tubbs (Cookeville, TN), Jim Woodward (La Mirada, CA).

**International Scouts:** Carlos Pascual (Latin America), Junior Roman (Puerto Rico), Eddy Toledo (Dominican Republic).

# PHILADELPHIA

## Telephone, Address

**Office Address:** Veterans Stadium, 3501 S. Broad St., Philadelphia, PA 19148. **Mailing Address:** P.O. Box 7575, Philadelphia, PA 19101. **Telephone:** (215) 463-6000. **FAX:** (215) 389-3050.

**Bill Giles**

## Ownership

**Operated by:** The Phillies.

**President, Managing General Partner:** Bill Giles. **Co-General Partner:** David Montgomery.

**Partners:** Claire Betz, Fitz Eugene Dixon Jr., Double Play, Inc. (Herbert Middleton Jr.), Tri-Play Associates (Alexander Buck, Mahlon Buck Jr., William Buck).

# BUSINESS OPERATIONS

**Chief Executive Officer:** Bill Giles. **Executive Vice President/Chief Operating Officer:** David Montgomery.

**Secretary and General Counsel:** Bill Webb. **Executive Secretary:** Nancy Nolan. **Director, Planning/Development:** Tom Hudson. **Director, Business Development:** Joseph Giles.

## Finance

**Senior Vice President, Finance and Planning:** Jerry Clothier.

**Secretary, Finance:** JoAnn Marano. **Controller:** Lou Perez.

**Director, Information Systems:** Brian Lamoreaux.

## Marketing, Promotions

**Vice President, Marketing:** Dennis Mannion.

**Manager, Marketing Services:** Kurt Funk. **Manager, Advertising and Broadcasting:** JoAnne Levy-Lamoreaux.

**Manager, Corporate Marketing:** Dave Buck.

**Manager, Entertainment:** Chris Legault. **Manager, Fan Development:** Rob Holiday. **Manager, Merchandising:** Mike Connor.

## Public Relations, Communications

**Vice President, Public Relations:** Larry Shenk.

**Manager, Print/Creative Services:** Tina Urban. **Manager, Publicity:** Leigh Tobin. **Manager, Media Relations:** Gene Dias. **Administrator, Public Relations:** Karen Nocella.

**Director, Community Relations:** Regina Castellani.

## Stadium Operations

**Director, Stadium Operations:** Mike DiMuzio. **Secretary, Stadium Operations:** Bernie Mansi.

**Supervisor, Field and Maintenance Operations:** Ralph Frangipani.

**PA Announcer:** Dan Baker. **Official Scorer:** Unavailable.

## Ticketing

**Telephone:** (215) 463-1000. **FAX:** (215) 463-6025.

**Vice President, Ticket Operations:** Richard Deats.

**Director, Sales:** Rory McNeil. **Director, Ticket Department:** Dan Goroff. **Director, Sales Operations:** John Weber. **Director, Group Sales:** Kathy Killian.

## Travel, Clubhouse

**Traveling Secretary:** Eddie Ferenz.

**Manager, Equipment and Home Clubhouse:** Frank Coppenbarger. **Assistant Equipment Manager:** Joe Dunn. **Manager, Visiting Clubhouse:** Kevin Steinhour.

## Radio, TV, Media

**Radio Announcers:** Harry Kalas, Richie Ashburn, Andy Musser, Chris Wheeler. **Flagship Station:** WGMP 1210-AM.

**TV Announcers:** Harry Kalas, Richie Ashburn, Andy Musser, Chris Wheeler; Todd Kalas, Garry Maddox. **Flagship Stations:** WPHL Channel 17, PRISM, SportsChannel Philadelphia.

**NEWSPAPERS, Daily Coverage:** Philadelphia Inquirer, Philadelphia Daily News, Camden Courier-Post, Wilmington News-Journal, Delaware County Times, Trentonian.

## General Information

**Team Colors:** Red and white.

**Hometown Dugout:** First Base.

**Game Times:** Day—1:35 p.m. Night—7:35, Sat, 7:05.

**Stadium Location:** I-95 or I-76 West to Broad Street exit.

**Player Representative:** Darren Daulton.

# PHILLIES

## BASEBALL OPERATIONS

**Telephone:** (215) 463-6000. **FAX:** (215) 755-9324.

**Senior Vice President, General Manager:** Lee Thomas. **Assistant General Manager:** Ed Wade.

**Assistant to the President:** Paul Owens.

**Administrator, Baseball Operations:** Susan Ingersoll.

Lee Thomas

### Major League Staff

**Manager:** Jim Fregosi.

**Coaches:** Dugout—John Vukovich; Pitching—Johnny Podres; Batting—Denis Menke; First Base—Mel Roberts; Third Base—Larry Bowa; Bullpen—Mike Ryan.

### Medical, Training

**Team Physician:** Dr. Phillip Marone.

**Head Trainer:** Jeff Cooper. **Assistant Trainer:** Mark Andersen. **EAP Coordinator:** Dr. William O'Brien.

Jim Fregosi

### Minor Leagues

**Telephone:** (215) 952-8225. **FAX:** (215) 755-9324.

**Director of Player Development:** Del Unser. **Director of Florida Operations:** John Timberlake. **Secretary, Minor Leagues and Scouting:** Maryann Skedzielewski. **Computer Analyst:** Jay McLaughlin.

**Coordinator of Instruction:** Don Blasingame.

**Roving Instructors:** Ramon Aviles (infield), Glenn Brummer (catching), George Culver (pitching), Billy DeMars (hitting), Jerry Martin (hitting), Hap Hudson (rehabilitation).

### Farm System

| Class | Farm Team | Manager | Bat. Coach | Pitch. Coach |
|---|---|---|---|---|
| AAA | Scranton/W-B | Mike Quade | Dave Cash | Jim Wright |
| AA | Reading | Bill Dancy | Bill Robinson | None |
| A | Clearwater | Don McCormack | Greg Legg | Darold Knowles |
| A | Piedmont | Roy Majtyka | Tony Scott | John Martin |
| A | Batavia | Al LeBoeuf | Floyd Rayford | Ken Westray |
| Rookie | Martinsville | Ramon Henderson | Kelly Heath | Carlos Arroyo |

### Scouting

**Telephone:** (215) 952-8225. **FAX:** (215) 755-9324.

**Director of Scouting:** Mike Arbuckle.

**Advance Scout:** Hank King (Limerick, PA).

**Major League Coverage:** Ray Shore (Tarpon Springs, FL), Jimmy Stewart (Odessa, FL).

**Professional Coverage:** Bing Devine (St. Louis, MO), Buck Rodgers (Yorba Linda, CA), Larry Rojas (Clearwater, FL).

**National Supervisor:** Marti Wolever (Papillon, NE).

Mike Arbuckle

**Regional Supervisors:** Central—Sonny Bowers (Waco, TX), West—Dean Jongwaard (Fountain Valley, CA), East—Dick Lawlor (Windsor, CT).

**Scouts:** Sal Agostinelli (Nesconset, NY), Emil Belich (West Allis, WI), Tommy Ferguson (Santa Ana, CA), Eli Grba (Elkmont, AL), Bill Harper (Corvallis, OR), Ken Hultzapple (Newport, PA), John Kennedy (Peabody, MA), Jerry Lafferty (Trenton, MO), Terry Logan (Brenham, TX), Fred Mazuca (Orange, CA), Lloyd Merritt (Allison Park, PA), Art Parrack (Goldenrod, FL), Bob Poole (Redwood City, CA), Dave Sirak (Camarillo, CA), Mitch Sokol (Phoenix, AZ), Roy Tanner (Charleston, SC), Scott Trcka (Hobart, IN).

**Latin American Supervisor:** George Lauzerique (West Palm Beach, FL).

**International Scouts:** Jose Leiva (Venezuela), Willie Montanez (Puerto Rico).

# PITTSBURGH

Mark Sauer

## Telephone, Address

**Office Address:** 600 Stadium Circle, Pittsburgh, PA 15212. **Mailing Address:** P.O. Box 7000, Pittsburgh, PA 15212. **Telephone:** (412) 323-5000. **FAX:** (412) 323-1724.

## Ownership

**Operated by:** Pittsburgh Associates.

**Chairman of the Board:** Vincent Sarni.

**Board of Directors:** Joe L. Brown, Frank Cahouet, Richard Cyert, Douglas Danforth, Robert Hernandez, Eugene Litman, John McConnell, Thomas Murphy Jr., Thomas O'Brien, Paul H. O'Neill, Frederic Reynolds, Vincent Sarni, Mark Sauer, Harvey Walken.

# BUSINESS OPERATIONS

**President and Chief Executive Officer:** Mark Sauer.

## Finance

**Vice President, Finance and Administration:** Kenneth Curcio.

**Assistant Vice President, Finance:** Patti Mistick. **Director of Finance:** Jim Plake. **Director of Information Systems:** Sanjay Chakrabarty.

## Marketing, Sales

**Vice President, Marketing and Operations:** Steven Greenberg.

**Vice President, Broadcasting and Advertising Sales:** Mark Driscoll.

**Senior Director, Sales and Marketing:** Robert Derda Jr. **Sales Manager, Broadcasting and Promotions:** Mark Ferraco. **Director of Community Relations, Special Events:** Kathy Guy. **Director of Community Service, Sales:** Alexander Gordon. **Director of Corporate Relations:** Nelson Briles. **Broadcasting Coordinator:** Jon Mercurio.

## Public Relations, Communications

**Telephone:** (412) 323-5031. **FAX:** (412) 323-9133.

**Director of Media Relations:** Jim Trdinich. **Assistant Director of Media Relations:** Sally O'Leary.

**Director of In-Game Entertainment:** Michael Gordon.

## Stadium Operations

**Director of Operations:** Dennis DaPra. **Director of Merchandising:** Joe Billetdeaux. **Director of Bradenton Baseball Operations:** Jeff Podobnik.

**PA Announcer:** Tim DeBacco. **Official Scorers:** Bob Webb, Tony Krizmanich, Evan Pattak.

## Ticketing

**Telephone:** 1-800-BUY-BUCS. **FAX:** (412) 323-5388.

**Director of Ticket Operations:** Gary Remlinger. **Ticket Services Coordinator:** Dave Wysocki.

## Travel, Clubhouse

**Traveling Secretary:** Greg Johnson.

**Equipment Manager:** Roger Wilson. **Visitors Clubhouse:** John Bucci.

## Radio, TV, Media

**Radio Announcers:** Lanny Frattare, Steve Blass, Greg Brown, Bob Walk. **Flagship Station:** KDKA 1020-AM. **No. of Network Stations:** 53.

**TV Announcers:** Lanny Frattare, Steve Blass, Greg Brown, Bob Walk. **Flagship Station:** Unavailable.

**NEWSPAPERS, Daily Coverage:** Pittsburgh Post-Gazette, Pittsburgh Tribune-Review, Beaver Valley Times, McKeesport Daily News, North Hills News Record, Valley News Dispatch, Washington Observer-Reporter.

## General Information

**Team Colors:** Black and gold.

**Hometown Dugout:** First Base.

**Standard Game Times:** Day—3:05 p.m. Night—7:35, Sat.—7:05, Sun.—1:35.

**Stadium Directions:** From south—I-279 through Fort Pitt Tunnel, across Fort Pitt Bridge and take stadium exit (left lane), cross Fort Duquesne Bridge, exit left to stadium. From north—I-279 to Three Rivers Stadium exit (left lane). From east—I-376 to exit 1 (north side), cross Fort Duquesne Bridge, exit left ramp to stadium.

**Player Representative:** Al Martin.

# PIRATES

## BASEBALL OPERATIONS

**Senior Vice President/General Manager:** Cam Bonifay.

**Director of Major League Administration:** John Sirignano. **Special Assistants to General Manager:** Leland Maddox, Ken Parker, Peter Vuckovich, Lenny Yochim.

Cam Bonifay

### Major League Staff

**Manager:** Jim Leyland.

**Coaches:** Dugout—Bill Virdon; Pitching—Ray Miller; Batting—Milt May; First Base—Tommy Sandt; Third Base—Rich Donnelly; Bullpen—Spin Williams.

### Medical, Training

**Team Physician:** Dr. Joe Coroso. **Team Orthopedist:** Dr. Jack Failla. **Head Trainer:** Kent Biggerstaff. **Assistant Trainer:** Dave Tumbas. **Strength and Conditioning Coach:** Dr. Warren Sipp.

Jim Leyland

### Minor Leagues

**Telephone:** (412) 323-5033. **FAX:** (412) 323-5024.

**Director of Minor Leagues:** Chet Montgomery. **Secretary, Minor Leagues:** Diane Grimaldi.

**Field Coordinator:** Jack Lind. **Pitching Coordinator:** Tom Dettore.

**Roving Instructors:** Rocky Bridges (infield), Bill Henry (fitness), Joe Lonnett (catching), Jay Loviglio (baserunning), Theron Todd (hitting).

### Farm System

| Class | Farm Team | Manager | Bat. Coach | Pitch. Coach |
|---|---|---|---|---|
| AAA | Calgary | Bobby Meacham | Ben Oglivie | Wayne Garland |
| AA | Carolina | Trent Jewett | Don Werner | Dave Rajsich |
| A | Lynchburg | Marc Hill | None | Jim Bibby |
| A | Augusta | Jeff Banister | None | Bruce Tanner |
| A | Erie | Scott Little | None | Larry Smith |
| Rookie | Bradenton | Woody Huyke | None | Steve Watson |

### Scouting

**Telephone:** (412) 323-5035. **FAX:** (412) 323-5024.

**Director of Scouting:** Paul Tinnell.

**Administrative Assistant, Scouting:** Sandy Deutsch.

**Scouting Coordinators:** Ron King (Sacramento, CA), Fred Wright (Charlotte, NC).

**Special Assignment Scouts:** Bill Bryk (Dolton, IL), Angel Figueroa (Cave Creek, AZ).

Paul Tinnell

**Scouting Supervisors:** Tom Barnard (Houston, TX), Grant Brittain (Oklahoma City, OK), Dana Brown (Somerset, NJ), Steve Demeter (Cleveland, OH), Steve Fleming (Matoaca, PA), Dave Klipstein (Eupora, MS), Scott Lovecamp (St. Petersburg, FL), Boyd Odom (Cumming, GA), Ed Roebuck (Lakewood, CA), Roy Smith (Scottsdale, AZ), George Swain (Raleigh, NC), Douglas Takaragawa (Fountain Valley, CA), Mike Williams (Oakland, CA).

**Scouts:** Kidd Carr (Roanoke, VA), Alex Dupaty (Sacramento, CA), John Fedders (Naticoke, PA), Fred Garcia (Littleton, CO), Elmer Gray (Pittsburgh, PA), Roger Janeway (Huber Heights, OH), Hank Krause (Akron, IA), Buddy Paine (Harrison, NY), Steve Riha (Houston, TX), Tom Rogers (Apopka, FL), Jerry Sanders (Thibodaux, LA), Tom Tornincasa (Crown Point, IN).

**Latin American Coordinators:** Pablo Cruz (Dominican Republic), Jose Luna (Puerto Rico).

**International Scouts:** Ismael Cruz (Colombia), Pablo Cruz (Dominican Republic), Luis Gonzalez (Dominican Republic), Pastor Melendez (Venezuela), Steve Oleschuk (Canada), Delvy Santiago (Puerto Rico), Alex Zapata (Panama).

# ST. LOUIS

August Busch

## Telephone, Address

**Office Address:** 250 Stadium Plaza, St. Louis, MO 63102. **Telephone:** (314) 421-3060. **FAX:** (314) 425-0640.

## Ownership

**Operated by:** Civic Center Corp.
**Principal Owner:** Anheuser-Busch, Inc.
**Chairman of the Board:** August A. Busch III.
**President:** Mark Lamping.
**Vice Chairmen:** Fred Kuhlmann, Stuart Meyer.
**Senior Vice President:** Stan Musial.

## BUSINESS OPERATIONS

**Vice President, Business Operations:** Mark Gorris.

**Director of Human Resources:** Mariam Rhodes.

**Senior Administrative Assistant to President:** Elaine Milo. **Senior Administrative Assistant to Vice Chairmen:** Pat Larson. **Administrative Assistant to Vice President, Business Operations:** Renee Garrett.

**Manager, Office Services:** Patti McCormick.

## Finance

**Controller:** Brad Wood.

**Director, Management Information Services:** Sally Lemons. **Senior Staff Accountant:** Natalie Boyd.

## Marketing, Sales

**Vice President, Marketing:** Marty Hendin.

**Director of Target Marketing:** Ted Savage. **Director of Promotions:** Nancy Trammell. **Director of Season Ticket Sales:** Kevin Wade. **Director of Group Sales:** Joe Strohm. **Director of Broadcast Operations:** Dan Farrell. **Administrative Assistant, Marketing:** Mary Ellen Edmiston.

## Public Relations, Communications

**Telephone:** (314) 425-0626. **FAX:** (314) 982-7399.

**Director of Public Relations:** Brian Bartow. **Public Relations Assistant:** Mary Ford.

## Stadium Operations

**Head Groundskeeper:** Jim Fortel.

**PA Announcer:** John Ulett. **Official Scorers:** Jack Herman, Mike Eisenbath.

## Ticketing

**Telephone:** (314) 421-2400. **FAX:** (314) 425-0649.

**Director of Ticket Operations:** Josephine Arnold. **Manager, Ticket Sales/Services:** Chris Scherting.

## Travel, Clubhouse

**Traveling Secretary:** C.J. Cherre.

**Equipment Manager:** Buddy Bates. **Assistant Equipment Manager:** Rip Rowan. **Visiting Clubhouse Manager:** Jerry Risch.

## Radio, TV, Media

**Radio Announcers:** Jack Buck, Joe Buck, Bob Carpenter, Mike Shannon. **Flagship Station:** KMOX 1120-AM.

**TV Announcers:** Jack Buck, Joe Buck, Bob Carpenter, Mike Shannon. **Flagship Station:** KPLR Channel 11.

**NEWSPAPER, Daily Coverage:** St. Louis Post-Dispatch.

## General Information

**Team Colors:** Red, white and navy blue.

**Hometown Dugout:** First Base.

**Standard Game Times:** Weekdays—12:35 p.m., 7:05, 7:35; Sat.-Sun..—1:15, 7:05.

**Stadium Directions:** From Illinois, take I-55 South, I-64 West, I-70 West or US 40 West across the Mississippi River (Poplar Street Bridge) to Busch Stadium exit. In Missouri, take I-55 North, I-64 East, I-70 East, I-44 East or US 40 East to downtown St. Louis and Busch Stadium exit.

**Player Representative:** Todd Zeile.

# CARDINALS

## BASEBALL OPERATIONS

**Telephone:** (314) 425-0687. **Fax:** (314) 425-0648.

**Vice President, General Manager:** Walt Jocketty. **Director, Major League Player Personnel:** Jerry Walker. **Senior Administrative Assistant:** Judy Carpenter-Barada.

Walt Jocketty

### Major League Staff

**Manager:** Joe Torre.

**Coaches:** Dugout—Red Schoendienst; Pitching—Mark Riggins; Batting—Chris Chambliss; First Base—Jose Cardenal; Third Base—Gaylen Pitts; Bullpen—Bob Gibson.

### Medical, Training

**Team Doctor:** Dr. Stan London.

Joe Torre

**Head Trainer:** Gene Gieselmann. **Assistant Trainer:** Brad Henderson.

### Minor Leagues

**Telephone:** (314) 421-3060. **FAX:** (314) 425-0638.

**Director of Player Development:** Mike Jorgensen. **Assistant Director, Player Development:** Scott Smulczenski. **Baseball Operations/Computer Analyst:** John Vuch. **Administrative Assistant, Minor Leagues:** Judy Francis.

**Senior Field Coordinator:** George Kissell. **Assistant Field Coordinator:** Mark DeJohn.

**Roving Instructors:** George Hendrick (hitting/outfield), Rick Mahler (pitching).

### Farm System

| Class | Farm Team | Manager | Bat. Coach | Pitch. Coach |
|---|---|---|---|---|
| AAA | Louisville | Joe Pettini | Joe Cunningham | Dyar Miller |
| AA | Arkansas | Mike Ramsey | Jeff Shireman | Marty Mason |
| A | St. Petersburg | Chris Maloney | John Lewis | Rich Folkers |
| A | Peoria | Roy Silver | Keith Smith | Ray Searage |
| A | Savannah | Scott Melvin | Mauricio Nunez | Dave Ricketts |
| A | New Jersey | Luis Melendez | Tim Redman | Hub Kittle |
| Rookie | Johnson City | Steve Turco | Ramon Ortiz | Bob Milliken |

### Scouting

**Telephone:** (314) 421-3060. **FAX:** (314) 425-0640.

**Director of Scouting:** Marty Maier (Oakland, CA).

**Advance Scout:** Jack Hubbard (Safety Harbor, FL).

**Special Assignment Scouts:** Fred McAlister (Clearwater, FL), Mike Squires (Kalamazoo, MI), Bill Harford (Chicago, IL).

**National Crosscheckers:** Marty Keough (Irvine, CA), Fred McAlister (Clearwater, FL).

Marty Maier

**Scouts:** Jim Bayens (Richmond Hill, GA), Jim Belz (Springfield, IL), Randy Benson (Salisbury, NC), Tim Conroy (Victorville, GA), John DiPuglia (Miami, FL), Chuck Fick (Newbury Park, CA), Manny Guerra (North Las Vegas, NV), Mike Harris (Houston, TX), Tom McCormack (University City, MO), Joe Morlan (New Albany, OH), Scott Nichols (Wheeling, WV), Jay North (Vacaville, CA), Joe Rigoli (Parsippany, NJ), Mike Roberts (Overland Park, KS), Hal Smith (Hilltop Lakes, TX), Roger Smith (Eastman, GA).

**International Supervisors:** Jorge Aranzamendi (Puerto Rico), Roberto Diaz (Dominican Republic).

# SAN DIEGO

Larry Lucchino

## Telephone, Address

**Office Address:** Jack Murphy Stadium, 9449 Friars Rd., San Diego, CA 92108. **Mailing Address:** P.O. Box 2000, San Diego, CA 92112. **Telephone:** (619) 283-4494. **FAX:** (619) 282-2228.

## Ownership

**Operated by:** Padres, LP.

**Principal Owners:** John Moores, Larry Lucchino.

**Chairman of the Board:** John Moores.

**President:** Dick Freeman.

## BUSINESS OPERATIONS

**Chief Executive Officer:** Larry Lucchino.

**Executive Vice President:** Bill Adams. **Director of Administrative Services:** Lucy Freeman.

**Executive Assistant to the President:** Arlene Billings.

## Finance

**Vice President, Finance:** Bob Wells.

## Marketing, Sales

**Vice President, Marketing:** Don Johnson.

**Sales Manager:** Brent Haines. **Director of Merchandising:** Michael Babida.

## Media Relations

**Telephone:** (619) 584-7210. **FAX:** (619) 282-8886.

**Vice President, Public Affairs:** Charles Steinberg.

**Director of Media Relations:** Roger Riley. **Assistant Director of Media Relations:** Dennis Smythe.

## Stadium Operations

**Vice President, Game Operations and Special Projects:** Andy Strasberg. **Director of Video Operations:** Mark Guglielmo.

**Director of Stadium Operations:** Unavailable. **Assistant Director of Stadium Operations:** Chris Fighera.

**Head Groundskeeper:** Steve Wightman.

**PA Announcer:** Bruce Binkowski. **Official Scorers:** Phil Collier, Bill Zavestoski.

## Ticketing

**Telephone:** (619) 283-4494. **FAX:** (619) 280-6239.

**Director of Ticket Operations:** Dave Gilmore. **Director of Ticket Sales:** Jack Autry. **Assistant Director of Ticket Services:** Bill Risser.

## Travel, Clubhouse

**Traveling Secretary:** Roger Riley.

**Equipment Manager:** Brian Prilaman. **Visiting Clubhouse:** Bob Doty.

## Radio, TV, Media

**Radio Announcers:** Jerry Coleman, Ted Leitner. **Flagship Stations:** KFMB 760-AM.

**TV Announcers:** Jerry Coleman, Bob Chandler, Ted Leitner. **Flagship Stations:** KFMB-TV, Prime Ticket Network (regional cable).

**NEWSPAPERS, Daily Coverage:** San Diego Union-Tribune, Escondido Times-Advocate, North County Blade-Citizen, Daily Californian.

## General Information

**Team Colors:** Navy blue and orange.

**Hometown Dugout:** First Base.

**Standard Game Times:** 7:05 p.m.; Sun. 1:05.

**Stadium Location:** From downtown—take Rt. 163 North to Friars Road, east to stadium. From north—take I-15 South to Friars Road, west to stadium, or I-805 South to Rt. 163 South to Friars Road, west to stadium. From east—take I-8 West to I-15 North to Friars Road, west to stadium. From west—take I-8 East to Rt. 163 North to Friars Road, east to stadium.

**Player Representative:** Unavailable.

# PADRES

## BASEBALL OPERATIONS

**Vice President/Baseball Operations and General Manager:** Randy Smith.

**Assistant General Manager:** Steve Lubratich. **Executive Assistant to General Manager:** Linda Barron.

Randy Smith

### Major League Staff

**Manager:** Bruce Bochy.

**Coaches:** Dugout—Rob Picciolo; Pitching—Sonny Siebert; Batting—Merv Rettenmund; First Base—Davey Lopes; Third Base—Graig Nettles; Bullpen—Tye Waller.

### Medical, Training

**Club Physician:** Scripps Clinic Medical Staff.

Bruce Bochy

**Head Trainer:** Larry Duensing. **Assistant Trainer:** Todd Hutcheson. **Strength and Conditioning Director:** Dean Armitage.

### Minor Leagues

**Telephone:** (619) 283-4494. **FAX:** (619) 282-2228.

**Director of Minor League Operations:** Priscilla Oppenheimer. **Secretary, Minor Leagues:** Earleen Bender.

**Coordinator of Instruction:** Russ Nixon.

**Roving Instructors:** Duane Espy (hitting), Bobby Mitchell (outfield, baserunning), Garry Templeton (infield), Dan Warthen (pitching).

### Farm System

| Class | Farm Team | Manager | Bat. Coach | Pitch. Coach |
|---|---|---|---|---|
| AAA | Las Vegas | Tim Flannery | None | Jon Matlack |
| AA | Memphis | Jerry Royster | None | Dean Treanor |
| A | Rancho Cuca. | Marty Barrett | None | Dave Smith |
| A | Clinton | Ed Romero | None | Saul Soltero |
| Rookie | Idaho Falls | Mike Basso | Gary Roenicke | Scipio Spinks |
| Rookie | Peoria | Unavailable | Manny Lantigua | Al Hargesheimer |

### Scouting

**Telephone:** (619) 584-7232. **FAX:** (619) 282-2228.

**Director of Scouting:** Kevin Towers.

**Secretary, Scouting:** Herta Bingham.

**Major League Scouts:** Ken Bracey (Morton, IL), Randy Johnson (Escondido, CA).

**National Crosschecker:** Brad Sloan (Brimfield, IL).

**Regional Supervisors:** East—Bob Cummings (Oaklawn, IL), West—Logan White (Chandler, AZ).

**Special Assignment Scout:** Al Hargesheimer (Arlington Heights, IL).

Kevin Towers

**Full-Time Scouts:** Howard Bowens (Tacoma, WA), Eddie Dixon (Sasser, GA), Jimmy Dreyer (Bedford, TX), Denny Galehouse (Doylestown, OH), Donnie Lyle (Sacramento, CA), Jim Marshall (Clearwater, FL), Tim McWilliam (Tucson, AZ), Rene Mons (Manchester, NH), Pat Murtaugh (Lafayette, IN), Gary Roenicke (Franktown, CO), Bruce Seid (Studio City, CA), Greg Smith (Antioch, TN), Van Smith (Belleville, IL), Jeff Wetherby (Pensacola, FL).

**Part-Time Scouts:** Mike Becker (Flushing, NY), Robert Gutierrez (Carol City, FL), Bill Killian (Stanwood, MI), Rick Magnante (Van Nuys, CA), Darryl Milne (Denver, CO), Chuck Pierce (Bakersfield, CA).

**International Scouts:** Pedro Avila (Venezuela), Julio Coronado (Dominican Republic), Ronquito Garcia (Puerto Rico), Tim Harkness (Canada), Juan Melo (Dominican Republic).

# SAN FRANCISCO

Peter Magowan

## Telephone, Address

**Office Address:** Candlestick Park, San Francisco, CA 94124. **Telephone:** (415) 468-3700. **FAX:** (415) 467-0485.

## Ownership

**Operated by:** San Francisco Baseball Associates, LP.

**Managing General Partner:** Peter Magowan.

## BUSINESS OPERATIONS

**Executive Vice President:** Larry Baer.

**Senior Vice President, Business Operations:** Patrick Gallagher.

**Director of Legal and Governmental Affairs:** Jack Bair. **Human Resources Manager:** Moira McNamara.

## Finance

**Vice President and Chief Financial Officer:** John Yee.

**Controller:** Larry Dodd. **Assistant Controller:** Norma Edar.

**Director of Management Information Systems:** Jerry Drobny.

## Marketing, Sales

**Director of Marketing/Sales:** Mario Alioto.

**Promotions Manager:** Valerie McGuire. **General Manager, Retail:** Connie Kullberg.

## Public Relations, Communications

**Telephone:** (415) 330-2448. **FAX:** (415) 467-0485.

**Director of Public Relations/Community Development:** Bob Rose.

**Media Relations Manager:** Jim Moorehead. **Media Relations Assistant/Broadcast Coordinator:** Maria Jacinto. **Media Relations Assistant:** Blake Rhodes. **Publications Manager:** Nancy Donati. **Program Coordinator, Community Development:** Dave Craig.

## Stadium Operations

**Vice President, Stadium Operations and Security:** Jorge Costa.

**Director of Stadium Operations:** Gene Telucci. **Director of Event Personnel:** Deborah Houston.

**PA Announcer:** Sherry Davis. **Official Scorers:** Dick O'Connor, Bob Stevens.

## Ticketing

**Telephone:** (415) 467-8000. **FAX:** (415) 467-3803.

**Director of Ticket Services:** Russ Stanley. **Ticket Services Manager:** Bob Bisio. **Ticket Sales Manager:** Craig Hedrick.

## Travel, Clubhouse

**Traveling Secretary:** Reggie Younger Jr.

**Equipment Manager:** Mike Murphy. **Visitors Clubhouse:** Harvey Hodgerney. **Clubhouse Assistants:** David Loewenstein, Dennis Parry.

## Radio, TV, Media

**Radio Announcers:** Hank Greenwald, Mike Krukow, Ted Robinson. **Flagship Station:** KNBR 680-AM. **No. of Network Stations:** 16.

**TV Announcers:** KTVU—Mike Krukow, Ted Robinson; SportsChannel—Duane Kuiper, Mike Krukow. **Flagship Stations:** KTVU Channel 2, SportsChannel Pacific (regional cable).

**NEWSPAPERS, Daily Coverage:** San Francisco Chronicle, San Francisco Examiner, San Jose Mercury News, Contra Costa Times, Sacramento Bee, Oakland Tribune.

## General Information

**Team Colors:** Orange and black

**Hometown Dugout:** First Base.

**Standard Game Times:** Day—12:35 p.m., 1:05. Night—7:05, 7:35.

**Stadium Location:** Highway 101 to Candlestick Park exit.

**Player Representative:** Unavailable.

# GIANTS

## BASEBALL OPERATIONS

Bob Quinn

**Telephone:** (415) 330-2507. **FAX:** (415) 467-0485.

**Senior Vice President, General Manager:** Bob Quinn.

**Assistant to the General Manager/Vice President of Scouting and Player Personnel:** Brian Sabean. **Special Consultant, Baseball Operations and Administration:** Ned Colletti. **Executive Assistant:** Jamie Gaines. **Administrative Assistant:** Karen Sweeney.

### Major League Staff

**Manager:** Dusty Baker.

**Coaches:** Dugout—Bob Lillis; Pitching—Dick Pole; Batting/First Base—Bobby Bonds; Third Base—Wendell Kim; Bullpen—Bob Brenly.

Dusty Baker

### Medical, Training

**Team Physicians:** Dr. Gordon Campbell, Dr. Warren King, Dr. William Straw.

**Head Trainer:** Mark Letendre. **Assistant Trainer:** Barney Nugent. **Rehabilitation Coordinator:** Stan Conte.

### Minor Leagues

**Director of Player Development:** Jack Hiatt. **Assistant Director of Player Development:** Bobby Evans.

**Coordinator of Latin American Instruction:** Carlos Alfonso.

**Roving Instructors:** Gene Clines (hitting), Harry Marra (conditioning), Les Moss (pitching), Ron Perranoski (pitching).

### Farm System

| Class | Farm Team | Manager | Bat. Coach | Pitch. Coach |
|---|---|---|---|---|
| AAA | Phoenix | Keith Bodie | Unavailable | Steve Cline |
| AA | Shreveport | Ron Wotus | Frank Cacciatore | Joel Horlen |
| A | San Jose | Carlos Lezcano | Jim Davenport | Todd Oakes |
| A | Burlington | Mike Hart | Mickey Brantley | Keith Comstock |
| A | Bellingham | Glenn Tufts | Juan Lopez | Elias Sosa |

### Scouting

Brian Sabean

**Telephone:** (415) 330-2538. **FAX:** (415) 330-2691.

**Coordinator of Scouting:** Bob Hartsfield (Woodstock, GA).

**Assistant Coordinator of Scouting:** Matt Nerland.

**Major League Scouts:** Cal Emery (Lake Forest, CA), Dick Tidrow (Lee's Summit, MO).

**National Crosschecker:** Randy Waddill (Valrico, FL).

**Regional Crosscheckers:** North—Jack Bowen (Bethel Park, PA); West—Doug Mapson (Phoenix, AZ); South—Larry Osborne (Atlanta, GA).

**Scouts:** Dick Cole (Costa Mesa, CA), Bob Gardner (Oviedo, FL), Chuck Hensley (Bakersfield, CA), Mike Keenan (Manhattan, KS), Tom Korenek (Houston, TX), Jerry Marik (Chicago, IL), Alan Marr (Bellmore, NY), Doug McMillan (Shingle Springs, CA), Tony Michalak (Covington, KY), Bobby Myrick (Colonial Heights, VA), Rick Ragazzo (Tustin, CA), John Shafer (Portland, OR), Joe Strain (Englewood, CO), Todd Thomas (St. Louis, MO), Elanis Westbrooks (Birmingham, AL), Tom Zimmer (St. Petersburg, FL).

**Coordinator of Latin American Operations:** Luis Rosa (Puerto Rico). **Dominican Republic Supervisor:** Matty Alou (Dominican Republic).

**International Scouts:** Claudio Brito (Dominican Republic), Jose Cassino (Panama), Pedro De la Paz (Dominican Republic), Pablo Delgado (Puerto Rico), Diego Herrera (Venezuela), Ramon Linares (Dominican Republic), Jose Marcano (Puerto Rico), Abraham Martinez (Puerto Rico), Hector Rivera (Puerto Rico), Jorge Urribarri (Venezuela).

# MAJOR LEAGUE SCHEDULES

# AMERICAN LEAGUE

## BALTIMORE ORIOLES
### Oriole Park at Camden Yards

**APRIL**
**3**-5-**6** ... Chicago
7-**8**-**9** ... Texas
10-12 ... at Chicago
13-14-15-**16** ... at Texas
18-19 ... Kansas City
21-**22**-**23** ... Minnesota
24-25-26 at Kansas City
27-28-29-**30** ... at Minn.
**MAY**
2-3-**4** ... Milwaukee
5-**6**-**7** ... Toronto
8-9-10-11 ... at Boston
12-**13**-**14** ... Cleveland
16-17-18 ... Detroit
19-**20**-**21** ... at New York
23-24-**25** ... at Oakland
26-27-**28** ... at Seattle
29-30-31 ... at California
**JUNE**
2-**3**-4 ... Oakland
5-6-7-**8** ... Seattle
9-10-**11** ... California
12-13-14 ... at Cleveland
16-17-**18** ... at Detroit
19-20-21 ... New York
23-24-**25** ... Boston
26-27-**28** ... at Milwaukee
29-30 ... at Toronto
**JULY**
**1**-**2** ... at Toronto
3-**4**-5 ... Minnesota
6-7-8-**9** ... at Chicago
13-14-15-**16** ... K.C.
17-18 ... at Texas
19-**20** ... at Minnesota
21-22-23 at Kansas City
25-26-27 ... Texas
28-29-**30** ... Chicago
31 ... Toronto
**AUGUST**
1-2-3 ... Toronto
4-5-**6** ... Milwaukee
7-8-**9** ... at New York
11-12-**13** ... at Boston
14-15-**16** ... Cleveland
18-19-**20** ... at Oakland
21-22-23 ... at Seattle
24-25-26-**27** ... at Calif.
29-30-31 ... Oakland
**SEPTEMBER**
1-2-**3** ... Seattle
**4**-5-6 ... California
8-**9**-**10** ... at Cleveland
11-12-13 ... Boston
14-15-16-**17** ... New York
18-**19**-**20**-**21** ... at Detroit
22-23-**24** ... at Milwaukee
26-27 ... at Toronto
29-**30** ... Detroit
**OCTOBER**
**1** ... Detroit

## BOSTON RED SOX
### Fenway Park

**APRIL**
4-5 ... at Minnesota
**7**-**8**-**9** ... at Kansas City
**10**-**12** ... Texas
14-**15**-**16**-**17** ... K.C.
18-19-20 ... at Texas
21-22-**23**-24 . at Chicago
25-26 ... Minnesota
28-**29**-**30** ... Chicago
**MAY**
1-2-3-4 ... at New York
5-**6**-**7** ... at Detroit
8-9-10-11 ... Baltimore
12-**13**-**14** ... New York
16-**17** ... at Milwaukee
18-19-**20**-**21** .. Cleveland
23-24-**25** ... at Seattle
26-27-**28** ... at California
**29**-30-**31** ... at Oakland
**JUNE**
2-**3**-**4** ... Seattle
5-6-7-8 ... California
9-**10**-**11** ... Oakland
12-13-14 ... at Toronto
16-**17**-**18** ... Milwaukee
19-20-21 ... at Cleveland
23-24-**25** ... at Baltimore
26-27-28 ... Toronto
**29**-30 ... Detroit
**JULY**
**1**-**2** ... Detroit
3-4-5 ... at Kansas City
6-7-8-**9** ... at Minnesota
13-14-15-16 ... Texas
17-**18** ... Kansas City
19-20 ... at Chicago
21-**22**-**23**-**24** .. Minnesota
25-26-**27** ... Chicago
28-29-**30** ... at Texas
**AUGUST**
1-2-3 ... at Detroit
4-5-**6**-**7** ... at Toronto
8-9 ... Cleveland
11-12-**13** ... Baltimore
14-15-**16** ... New York
18-19-**20** ... at Seattle
21-22-23 ... at California
24-25-**26**-**27**. at Oakland
29-30-31 ... Seattle
**SEPTEMBER**
1-**2**-**3** ... California
**4**-5-6 ... Oakland
8-**9**-10 ... at New York
11-12-13 ... at Baltimore
15-**16**-**17** ... at Cleveland
18-19-20 ... Milwaukee
22-**23**-**24** ... Toronto
25-26-27 ... Detroit
28-29-**30** ... at Milwaukee
**OCTOBER**
**1** ... at Milwaukee

## CALIFORNIA ANGELS
### Anaheim Stadium

**APRIL**
**4**-5-6 ... Milwaukee
7-8-**9** ... Cleveland
**10**-**12** ... at Milwaukee
14-**15**-**16**-**17** ... at Cleve.
**18**-**19** ... at Detroit
21-22-**23** ... Toronto
24-25-26 ... Detroit
28-**29**-**30** ... at Toronto
**MAY**
**1** ... at Toronto
2-3-4 ... Oakland
5-6-**7** ... Seattle
9-10-**11** ... Texas
12-13-**14** at Kansas City
15-16-17-**18** ... at Minn.
19-20-**21** ... at Chicago
23-24-25 ... New York
26-27-**28** ... Boston
29-30-31 ... Baltimore
**JUNE**
2-**3**-**4** ... at New York
5-6-7-8 ... at Boston
9-10-**11** ... at Baltimore
12-13-14 ... Minnesota
15-16-17-**18** ... Chicago
19-20-21 ... Kansas City
23-24-**25**-26 ... at Seattle
27-28-29 ... at Texas
30 ... at Oakland
**JULY**
**1**-**2** ... at Oakland
4-5-6 ... Toronto
7-8-**9** ... Milwaukee
13-14-15-**16** ... at Detroit
17-18 ... at Cleveland
19-20 ... at Toronto
21-22-**23** ... Detroit
24-25-**26** ... Cleveland
27-28-29-**30** ... at Mil.
**AUGUST**
1-2-3 ... Seattle
4-5-**6**-**7** ... Texas
8-9-**10** ... at Kansas City
11-12-**13** ... at Minnesota
14-15-**16** ... at Chicago
18-19-**20** ... New York
21-22-23 ... Boston
24-25-26-**27** ... Baltimore
29-**30**-31 ... at New York
**SEPTEMBER**
1-**2**-**3** ... at Boston
**4**-5-6 ... at Baltimore
8-9-**10** ... Minnesota
12-13 ... Chicago
15-16-**17** ... Kansas City
18-19-**20** ... at Oakland
22-23-**24** ... at Texas
25-26-27 ... at Seattle
28-29-30 ... Oakland
**OCTOBER**
**1** ... Oakland

# CHICAGO WHITE SOX
## Comiskey Park

**APRIL**
3-5-**6** .......... at Baltimore
**7-8-9** .......... New York
10-12 .......... Baltimore
13-**14-15-16** ....... at N.Y.
17-18-19-20 . Milwaukee
21-22-**23**-24 ....... Boston
25-**26** ....... at Milwaukee
28-**29-30** ........ at Boston

**MAY**
2-3 .............. at Toronto
5-6-**7** .......... Kansas City
8-9-10 .......... Minnesota
12-13-**14** ........ at Seattle
16-17-**18** .......... Oakland
19-20-**21** ........ California
23-**24** .................. Texas
26-**27-28** .......... at Detroit
**29**-30-31 .... at Cleveland

**JUNE**
1 ............... at Cleveland
2-3-**4** .................. Detroit
5-6-7 ................ Toronto
9-10-11 ........... at Texas
**12**-13-14 ...... at Oakland
15-16-17-**18** ...... at Calif.
19-20-21-**22** ....... Seattle
23-24-**25** ........ Cleveland
26-27-**28** ... at Minnesota
30 .......... at Kansas City

**JULY**
1-**2** ......... at Kansas City
3-**4**-5 ............. New York
6-7-8-**9** ........... Baltimore
13-14-15-**16** ......... at Mil.
17-18 ......... at New York
19-20 ................. Boston
21-22-**23** ....... Milwaukee
25-26-**27** ........ at Boston
28-29-**30** .... at Baltimore
31 .............. Kansas City

**AUGUST**
1-2-**3** ......... Kansas City
4-5-**6** ......... at Cleveland
7-8-9 ............. at Seattle
11-12-**13** .......... Oakland
14-15-**16** ........ California
17-18-19-**20** ......... Texas
21-22-**23** ......... at Detroit
24-25-**26-27** .. at Toronto
29-30-**31** ............. Detroit

**SEPTEMBER**
1-2-3 ................ Toronto
4-5-6-7 ............. at Texas
8-**9-10** .......... at Oakland
12-13 .......... at California
15-16-**17** ............ Seattle
18-19-20 ........ Cleveland
22-23-**24**-25 ...... at Minn.
26-27-28 at Kansas City
29-30 ............ Minnesota

**OCTOBER**
**1** .................. Minnesota

# CLEVELAND INDIANS
## Jacobs Field

**APRIL**
**3**-4-5 ............ at Oakland
7-8-**9** .......... at California
**11**-12 ............. Oakland
14-**15-16-17** ... California
18-19 ................. Seattle
21-**22-23-24** ......... Texas
25-26 ............. at Seattle
27-28-29-**30** ..... at Texas

**MAY**
2-3-**4** .............. at Detroit
5-**6-7** ............. Minnesota
8-9-10 ........ Kansas City
12-**13-14** .... at Baltimore
16-17 ........ at New York
18-19-**20-21** ... at Boston
22-23-24 ....... Milwaukee
26-**27-28** ....... at Toronto
**29**-30-31 .......... Chicago

**JUNE**
1 ....................... Chicago
2-**3-4** ................ Toronto
5-6-7 .................. Detroit
8-9-10-**11** . at Milwaukee
12-13-14 ........ Baltimore
16-**17**-18 ........ New York
19-20-21 ............ Boston
23-24-**25** ...... at Chicago
26-27-**28** at Kansas City
29-30 ........ at Minnesota

**JULY**
1-**2** ........... at Minnesota
**4**-5 ..................... Texas
6-7-**8-9** ............... Seattle
13-14-15-**16** ..... Oakland
17-18 ............. California
19-**20** ............... at Texas
21-**22-23** ...... at Oakland
24-25-**26** .... at California
27-28-29-**30** ... at Seattle

**AUGUST**
1-2-3 ............ Minnesota
4-5-**6** ................ Chicago
8-9 ................. at Boston
10-11-12-**13** ....... at N.Y.
14-15-**16** .... at Baltimore
17-18-19-**20** . Milwaukee
21-22-23 ....... at Toronto
25-**26-27** ............ Detroit
28-29-30-31 ...... Toronto

**SEPTEMBER**
1-2-**3-4** ............at Detroit
5-6 ........... at Milwaukee
8-**9-10** ........... Baltimore
11-12-13 ........ New York
15-**16-17** ........... Boston
18-19-20 ...... at Chicago
22-23-**24**-25 ....... at K.C.
26-27-**28** ... at Minnesota
29-**30** .......... Kansas City

**OCTOBER**
**1** ................ Kansas City

# DETROIT TIGERS
## Tiger Stadium

**APRIL**
**3-5** ............. Kansas City
6-7-**8-9** ......... at Oakland
10-11-12 at Kansas City
14-**15-16** .......... Oakland
**18-19** .............. California
**20**-21-**22-23** ....... Seattle
24-25-26 .... at California
27-28-29-**30** ... at Seattle

**MAY**
2-3-**4** ............. Cleveland
5-**6-7** .................. Boston
9-10-**11** ..... at Milwaukee
12-13-**14** .......... at Texas
16-17-18 .... at Baltimore
19-**20-21** ........... Toronto
23-24-**25** ....... Minnesota
26-**27-28** .......... Chicago
29-30-**31** ....... at Toronto

**JUNE**
2-3-**4** ........... at Chicago
5-6-7 ......... at Cleveland
8-9-10-**11** .. at Minnesota
12-13-14-15 ... New York
16-17-**18** ........ Baltimore
19-20-21 ............. Texas
23-24-**25** ....... Milwaukee
26-27-**28** .... at New York
**29**-30 ............. at Boston

**JULY**
**1-2** .................. at Boston
**4-5** ..................... Seattle
6-7-8-**9** ....... Kansas City
13-14-15-**16** ... California
17-**18** ............. at Seattle
19-**20** ............ at Oakland
21-22-**23** .... at California
25-26-**27** .......... Oakland
28-29-**30** at Kansas City

**AUGUST**
1-2-3 .................. Boston
4-5-**6** ............. New York
8-9-10 .............. at Texas
11-12-**13**-14 ......... at Mil.
15-16-17 ........... Toronto
18-19-**20** ........ Minnesota
21-22-**23** ........... Chicago
25-**26-27** ....... at Cleveland
29-30-31 ...... at Chicago

**SEPTEMBER**
1-2-**3-4** .......... Cleveland
**5-6** ........... at Minnesota
8-**9-10**-11 ...... at Toronto
12-**13-14** ....... Milwaukee
15-16-**17** ............. Texas
18-**19-20-21** ...... Baltimore
22-**23-24** .... at New York
25-26-27 ........ at Boston
29-**30** .......... at Baltimore

**OCTOBER**
**1** ................. at Baltimore

# KANSAS CITY ROYALS
## Kauffman Stadium

**APRIL**
**3-5** ... at Detroit
**7-8-9** ... Boston
10-11-12 ... Detroit
14-**15-16-17** ... at Boston
18-19 ... at Baltimore
20-21-**22-23** ... at N.Y.
24-25-26 ... Baltimore
28-**29-30** ... New York

**MAY**
2-3-**4** ... at Minnesota
5-6-**7** ... at Chicago
8-9-10 ... at Cleveland
12-13-**14** ... California
16-17-18 ... Seattle
19-20-**21** ... Oakland
**22**-23-24 ... at Toronto
25-26-27-**28** ... at Mil.
29-30-31 ... Texas

**JUNE**
2-3-**4** ... Milwaukee
5-6-7 ... at Texas
9-10-**11** ... Toronto
12-13-**14** ... at Seattle
**15-16-17-18** ... at Oakland
19-20-21 ... at California
23-24-**25** ... Minnesota
26-27-**28** ... Cleveland
30 ... Chicago

**JULY**
1-**2** ... Chicago
3-4-5 ... Boston
6-7-8-**9** ... at Detroit
13-14-15-**16** ... at Balt.
17-**18** ... at Boston
**19**-20 ... at New York
21-22-23 ... Baltimore
25-26-**27** ... New York
28-29-**30** ... Detroit
31 ... at Chicago

**AUGUST**
1-2-**3** ... at Chicago
4-5-**6** ... at Minnesota
8-9-**10** ... California
11-12-**13** ... Seattle
14-15-16 ... Oakland
18-19-**20** ... at Toronto
21-22-**23** ... at Milwaukee
24-25-26-**27** ... Texas
29-30-31 ... Milwaukee

**SEPTEMBER**
1-2-3 ... at Texas
4-5-6 ... Toronto
8-9-**10** ... at Seattle
12-**13-14** ... at Oakland
15-16-**17** ... at California
18-19-20-21 ... Minnesota
22-23-**24**-25 ... Cleveland
26-27-28 ... Chicago
29-**30** ... at Cleveland

**OCTOBER**
**1** ... at Cleveland

# MILWAUKEE BREWERS
## County Stadium

**APRIL**
**4**-5-6 ... at California
7-8-**9** ... at Seattle
**10-12** ... California
13-**14-15-16** ... Seattle
17-18-19-20 ... at Chicago
21-**22-23** ... at Oakland
25-**26** ... Chicago
28-**29-30** ... Oakland

**MAY**
**1** ... Oakland
2-3-**4** ... at Baltimore
5-**6-7** ... at New York
9-10-**11** ... Detroit
12-**13-14** ... Toronto
16-**17** ... Boston
18-19-20-**21** ... at Texas
22-23-24 ... at Cleveland
25-26-27-**28** ... K.C.
**29**-30-**31** ... Minnesota

**JUNE**
2-3-**4** ... at Kansas City
6-7 ... at Minnesota
8-9-10-**11** ... Cleveland
12-13-**14** ... Texas
16-**17-18** ... at Boston
19-20-21-**22** ... at Toronto
23-24-**25** ... at Detroit
26-27-**28** ... Baltimore
29-30 ... New York

**JULY**
1-**2** ... New York
4-5-**6** ... at Oakland
7-8-**9** ... at California
13-14-15-**16** ... Chicago
17-18 ... Oakland
19-**20** ... Seattle
21-22-**23** ... at Chicago
24-25-**26** ... at Seattle
27-28-29-**30** ... California

**AUGUST**
1-**2**-3 ... at New York
4-5-**6** ... at Baltimore
8-9-**10** ... Toronto
11-12-**13**-14 ... Detroit
15-16 ... at Texas
17-18-19-**20** ... at Cleve.
21-22-**23** ... Kansas City
24-25-26-**27** ... Minnesota
29-30-31 at Kansas City

**SEPTEMBER**
1-2-**3-4** ... at Minnesota
5-6 ... Cleveland
8-9-**10** ... Texas
12-**13-14** ... at Detroit
15-**16-17** ... at Toronto
18-19-20 ... at Boston
22-23-**24** ... Baltimore
26-**27** ... New York
28-29-**30** ... Boston

**OCTOBER**
**1** ... Boston

# MINNESOTA TWINS
## Hubert H. Humphrey Metrodome

**APRIL**
4-5 ... Boston
6-7-8-**9** ... Toronto
10-12 ... at New York
**14-15-16** ... at Toronto
17-18-**19** ... New York
21-**22-23** ... at Baltimore
25-26 ... at Boston
27-28-29-**30** ... Baltimore

**MAY**
2-3-4 ... Kansas City
5-**6-7** ... at Cleveland
8-9-10 ... at Chicago
12-13-**14** ... Oakland
15-16-17-**18** ... California
19-20-**21** ... Seattle
23-24-**25** ... at Detroit
26-27-**28** ... Texas
**29**-30-31 ... at Milwaukee

**JUNE**
1-2-3-**4** ... at Texas
6-7 ... Milwaukee
8-9-10-**11** ... Detroit
12-13-14 ... at California
16-17-**18** ... at Seattle
19-20-21 ... at Oakland
23-24-**25** at Kansas City
26-27-**28** ... Chicago
29-30 ... Cleveland

**JULY**
1-**2** ... Cleveland
3-**4**-5 ... at Baltimore
6-7-8-**9** ... Boston
13-14-15-**16** ... at N.Y.
17-18 ... Toronto
19-**20** ... Baltimore
21-**22-23**-24 ... at Boston
25-26-**27** ... at Toronto
28-29-**30** ... New York

**AUGUST**
1-2-3 ... at Cleveland
4-5-**6** ... Kansas City
7-8-9 ... Oakland
11-12-**13** ... California
14-15-16 ... Seattle
18-19-**20** ... at Detroit
21-22-23 ... at Texas
24-25-26-**27** ... at Mil.
28-29-**30** ... Texas

**SEPTEMBER**
1-2-**3-4** ... Milwaukee
5-**6** ... Detroit
8-9-**10** ... at California
11-12-13 ... at Seattle
15-16-**17** ... at Oakland
18-19-20-21 ... at K.C.
22-23-**24**-25 ... Chicago
26-27-**28** ... Cleveland
29-30 ... at Chicago

**OCTOBER**
**1** ... at Chicago

# NEW YORK YANKEES
## Yankee Stadium

**APRIL**

**3**-5 ........ at Texas
**7**-**8**-**9** ........ at Chicago
**10**-**12** ........ Minnesota
13-**14**-**15**-**16** ..... Chicago
17-18-**19** ... at Minnesota
20-21-**22**-**23** ........ K.C.
25-26 ........ Texas
28-**29**-**30** at Kansas City

**MAY**

1-2-3-4 ........ Boston
5-**6**-**7** ........ Milwaukee
9-10-11 ........ at Toronto
12-**13**-**14** ........ at Boston
16-17 ........ Cleveland
19-**20**-**21** ........ Baltimore
23-24-25 .... at California
26-**27**-**28** ...... at Oakland
**29**-30-31 ....... at Seattle

**JUNE**

2-**3**-**4** ........ California
5-6-7-8 ........ Oakland
9-**10**-**11** ........ Seattle
12-13-14-15 .... at Detroit
16-**17**-18 .... at Cleveland
19-20-21 .... at Baltimore
23-**24**-**25** ........ Toronto
26-**27**-**28** ........ Detroit
29-30 ........ at Milwaukee

**JULY**

**1**-**2** ........ at Milwaukee
3-4-5 ........ at Chicago
6-7-8-**9** ........ at Texas
13-14-15-**16** .. Minnesota
17-18 ........ Chicago
**19**-20 ........ Kansas City
21-**22**-**23**-24 ........ Texas
25-26-27 at Kansas City
28-29-**30** ... at Minnesota

**AUGUST**

1-**2**-3 ........ Milwaukee
4-5-**6** ........ at Detroit
7-8-**9** ........ Baltimore
10-11-12-**13** .. Cleveland
14-15-**16** ........ at Boston
18-19-**20** .... at California
21-**22**-**23** ...... at Oakland
24-25-26-**27** ... at Seattle
29-**30**-31 ........ California

**SEPTEMBER**

1-**2**-**3** ........ Oakland
**4**-5-6 ........ Seattle
8-**9**-10 ........ Boston
11-12-13.... at Cleveland
14-15-16-**17** ....... at Balt.
18-19-20-21 ...... Toronto
22-**23**-**24** ........ Detroit
26-27 ........ at Milwaukee
29-**30** ........ at Toronto

**OCTOBER**

**1** ........ at Toronto

# OAKLAND ATHLETICS
## Oakland-Alameda County Coliseum

**APRIL**

**3**-4-5 ........ Cleveland
**6**-7-**8**-**9** ........ Detroit
**11**-12 ........ at Cleveland
14-15-**16** ........ at Detroit
18-19-**20** ........ Toronto
21-**22**-**23** ....... Milwaukee
25-26-**27** ....... at Toronto
28-**29**-**30**... at Milwaukee

**MAY**

**1** ........ at Milwaukee
2-3-4 ........ at California
5-**6**-**7**-8 ........ Texas
9-10-**11** ........ Seattle
12-13-**14**... at Minnesota
16-17-**18** ...... at Chicago
19-20-**21** at Kansas City
23-24-**25** ........ Baltimore
26-**27**-**28** ........ New York
**29**-30-31 ........ Boston

**JUNE**

2-**3**-4 ........ at Baltimore
5-6-7-8....... at New York
9-**10**-**11** ........ at Boston
12-**13**-14 ........ Chicago
15-16-**17**-18 ........ K.C.
19-**20**-21 ....... Minnesota
23-24-**25**-26..... at Texas
27-28-**29** ........ at Seattle
30 ........ California

**JULY**

**1**-**2** ........ California
4-5-**6** ........ Milwaukee
7-**8**-**9** ........ Toronto
13-14-15-**16** .... at Cleve.
17-18 ........ at Milwaukee
19-**20** ........ Detroit
21-**22**-**23** ........ Cleveland
25-26-**27** ........ at Detroit
28-**29**-**30** ....... at Toronto

**AUGUST**

1-**2**-**3** ........ Texas
4-5-**6** ........ Seattle
7-8-9 ........ at Minnesota
11-12-**13** ...... at Chicago
14-15-16 at Kansas City
18-19-**20** ........ Baltimore
21-**22**-**23** ........ New York
24-25-**26**-**27** ....... Boston
29-30-31 .... at Baltimore

**SEPTEMBER**

1-2-**3** ........ at New York
**4**-5-6 ........ at Boston
8-**9**-**10** ........ Chicago
12-**13**-**14** .... Kansas City
15-**16**-**17** ....... Minnesota
18-19-**20** ........ California
**21**-22-23-**24** ... at Seattle
26-**27** ........ at Texas
28-29-**30** .... at California

**OCTOBER**

**1** ........ at California

# SEATTLE MARINERS
## Kingdome

**APRIL**

**3**-4-5 ........ at Toronto
7-8-**9** ........ Milwaukee
11-**12** ........ Toronto
13-**14**-**15**-**16** ........ at Mil.
17-18 ........ at Cleveland
**20**-21-**22**-**23**.... at Detroit
25-26 ........ Cleveland
27-28-29-30 ........ Detroit

**MAY**

1-2-3 ........ at Texas
5-6-**7** ........ at California
9-10-**11** ........ at Oakland
12-13-**14** ........ Chicago
16-17-18 at Kansas City
19-20-**21** ... at Minnesota
23-24-**25** ........ Boston
26-27-**28** ........ Baltimore
**29**-30-31 ....... New York

**JUNE**

2-**3**-**4** ........ at Boston
5-6-7-**8** ....... at Baltimore
9-**10**-**11** ...... at New York
12-13-**14** .... Kansas City
16-17-**18** ....... Minnesota
19-20-21-**22** . at Chicago
23-24-**25**-26 ... California
27-28-**29** ........ Oakland
30 ........ Texas

**JULY**

**1**-**2** ........ Texas
4-**5** ........ at Detroit
6-7-**8**-**9** ...... at Cleveland
13-14-15-**16** ...... Toronto
17-**18** ........ Detroit
19-**20** ........ at Milwaukee
21-**22**-**23** ....... at Toronto
24-25-**26** ....... Milwaukee
27-28-29-**30** .. Cleveland

**AUGUST**

1-2-3 ........ at California
4-5-**6** ........ at Oakland
7-8-9 ........ Chicago
11-12-**13** at Kansas City
14-15-16 ... at Minnesota
18-19-**20** ........ Boston
21-22-23 ........ Baltimore
**24**-25-26-**27** ... New York
29-30-31 ........ at Boston

**SEPTEMBER**

1-2-**3** ........ at Baltimore
**4**-5-6 ........ at New York
8-9-**10** ........ Kansas City
11-12-13 ....... Minnesota
15-16-**17** ...... at Chicago
18-19-20 ........ Texas
**21**-22-23-**24** ..... Oakland
25-26-27 ........ California
28-29-30 ........ at Texas

**OCTOBER**

**1** ........ at Texas

# TEXAS RANGERS
## Ballpark in Arlington

### APRIL
**3**-5 ... New York
7-**8**-**9** ... at Baltimore
**10**-**12** ... at Boston
13-14-15-**16** ... Baltimore
18-19-20 ... Boston
21-**22**-**23**-**24** ... at Cleve.
25-26 ... at New York
27-28-29-**30** ... Cleveland

### MAY
1-2-3 ... Seattle
5-**6**-**7**-8 ... at Oakland
9-10-**11** ... at California
12-13-**14** ... Detroit
15-16-17 ... Toronto
18-19-20-**21** ... Milwaukee
23-24 ... at Chicago
26-27-**28** ... at Minnesota
29-30-31 at Kansas City

### JUNE
1-2-3-**4** ... Minnesota
5-6-7 ... Kansas City
9-10-11 ... Chicago
12-13-**14** ... at Milwaukee
16-**17**-**18** ... at Toronto
19-20-21 ... at Detroit
23-24-25-26 ... Oakland
27-28-29 ... California
30 ... at Seattle

### JULY
1-**2** ... at Seattle
**4**-5 ... at Cleveland
6-7-8-**9** ... New York
13-14-15-16 ... at Boston
17-18 ... Baltimore
19-**20** ... Cleveland
21-22-**23**-24 ... at N.Y.
25-26-27 ... at Baltimore
28-29-30 ... Boston

### AUGUST
1-**2**-**3** ... at Oakland
4-5-**6**-**7** ... at California
8-9-10 ... Detroit
11-12-13 ... Toronto
15-16 ... Milwaukee
17-18-19-**20** ... at Chicago
21-22-23 ... Minnesota
24-25-26-**27** ... at K.C.
28-29-**30** ... at Minnesota

### SEPTEMBER
1-2-3 ... Kansas City
4-5-6-7 ... Chicago
8-9-**10** ... at Milwaukee
12-13-14 ... at Toronto
15-16-**17** ... at Detroit
18-19-20 ... at Seattle
22-23-**24** ... California
26-27 ... Oakland
28-29-30 ... Seattle

### OCTOBER
**1** ... Seattle

# TORONTO BLUE JAYS
## SkyDome

### APRIL
**3**-4-5 ... Seattle
6-7-8-**9** ... at Minnesota
11-**12** ... at Seattle
**14**-**15**-**16** ... Minnesota
18-19-**20** ... at Oakland
21-22-**23** ... at California
25-26-**27** ... Oakland
28-**29**-**30** ... California

### MAY
**1** ... California
2-3 ... Chicago
5-**6**-**7** ... at Baltimore
9-10-11 ... New York
12-**13**-**14** ... at Milwaukee
15-16-17 ... at Texas
19-**20**-**21** ... at Detroit
**22**-23-24 ... Kansas City
26-**27**-**28** ... Cleveland
29-30-**31** ... Detroit

### JUNE
2-**3**-**4** ... at Cleveland
5-6-7 ... at Chicago
9-10-**11** ... at Kansas City
12-13-14 ... Boston
16-**17**-**18** ... Texas
19-20-21-**22** ... Milwaukee
23-**24**-**25** ... at New York
26-27-28 ... at Boston
29-30 ... Baltimore

### JULY
**1**-**2** ... Baltimore
4-5-6 ... at California
7-**8**-**9** ... at Oakland
13-14-15-**16** ... at Seattle
17-**18** ... at Minnesota
19-20 ... California
21-**22**-**23** ... Seattle
25-26-**27** ... Minnesota
28-**29**-**30** ... Oakland
31 ... at Baltimore

### AUGUST
1-2-3 ... at Baltimore
4-5-6-7 ... Boston
8-9-**10** ... at Milwaukee
11-12-13 ... at Texas
15-16-17 ... at Detroit
18-19-**20** ... Kansas City
21-22-23 ... Cleveland
24-25-**26**-**27** ... Chicago
28-29-30-31 ... at Cleve.

### SEPTEMBER
1-2-3 ... at Chicago
4-5-6 ... at Kansas City
8-**9**-**10**-11 ... Detroit
12-13-14 ... Texas
15-**16**-**17** ... Milwaukee
18-19-20-21 ... at N.Y.
**22**-**23**-**24** ... at Boston
26-27 ... Baltimore
29-**30** ... New York

### OCTOBER
**1** ... New York

**NOTE:** Dates in **bold** indicate afternoon games.

# NATIONAL LEAGUE

## ATLANTA BRAVES
### Atlanta-Fulton County Stadium

**APRIL**
4-**5** ........... at San Diego
7-8-**9** ............. Pittsburgh
11-12-**13** ....... San Diego
14-**15**-**16**-**17** ...... at Pitts.
18-19-20. San Francisco
21-22-**23** .... Los Angeles
24-**25**-**26** ............ at S.F.
27-28-29-**30** ........ at L.A.

**MAY**
2-3-4 .............. at Florida
5-6-7-8 ....... Philadelphia
9-10-11 ...... at New York
12-13-**14** ........ Cincinnati
15-16-17-18 .... Colorado
19-20-**21** ............ Florida
23-24-**25** ...... at St. Louis
26-27-**28** ...... at Houston
**29**-**31** ........... at Chicago

**JUNE**
2-3-**4** ............... Houston
5-6-7 ................ Chicago
9-10-**11** ............ St. Louis
13-14-15 ...... at Montreal
16-17-**18** ..... at Colorado
19-20-21-**22** ...... at Cinc.
23-24-**25** ........ New York
26-27-**28** ......... Montreal
30 ........ at Philadelphia

**JULY**
1-**2**-3 ....... at Philadelphia
4-5-6 .......... Los Angeles
7-8-9 ....... San Francisco
13-14-15-**16** ...... at S.D.
18-19-20 ....... Pittsburgh
21-22-**23** ....... San Diego
24-**25** ......... at Pittsburgh
26-27 ..... at Los Angeles
28-**29**-**30** ...... at San S.F.

**AUGUST**
1-2-3 .......... Philadelphia
4-5-**6**-**7** ......... at Montreal
8-9-10 ........... Cincinnati
11-12-**13** ........ Colorado
14-15-16 ............ Florida
18-19-**20** ...... at St. Louis
21-22-23 ...... at Houston
**25**-**26**-**27**-**28** . at Chicago
29-30-31 .......... Houston

**SEPTEMBER**
1-2-**3** ............... Chicago
4-5-**6** ................ St. Louis
7-8-9-**10** .......... at Florida
11-12-**13** ..... at Colorado
15-**16**-17 .... at Cincinnati
18-19-20-21 ... New York
22-23-**24** .......... Montreal
26-27 ..... at Philadelphia
29-**30** ......... at New York

**OCTOBER**
**1** ............... at New York

## CHICAGO CUBS
### Wrigley Field

**APRIL**
3-4-5-**6** ....... at Cincinnati
7-**8**-**9** .......... at New York
**11**-**12** ............ Cincinnati
**13**-**14**-**15**-**16** ... New York
17-18-**19** ............ at Phil.
20-21-**22**-**23** at Montreal
24-25-**26** .... Philadelphia
**27**-**28**-**29**-**30** .... Montreal

**MAY**
2-**3** .................. Houston
5-6-**7** ......... at Pittsburgh
8-9-10 .......... at St. Louis
**12**-**13**-**14** ....... San Diego
**15**-**16**-**17** ............ at S.F.
19-20-**21** ............ at L.A.
22-23-**24** ..... at Colorado
**26**-**27**-**28** ............ Florida
**29**-**31** ................. Atlanta

**JUNE**
2-3-**4** .............. at Florida
5-6-**7** .............. at Atlanta
8-**9**-**10**-**11** ........ Colorado
13-**14**-**15**. San Francisco
**16**-**17**-**18** .... Los Angeles
19-20-**21** ... at San Diego
22-23-24-**25**. at Houston
26-27-**28** ....... Pittsburgh
**29**-**30** .............. St. Louis

**JULY**
**1**-2 .................. St. Louis
4-5-**6** .......... at New York
7-8-**9** ...... at Philadelphia
**13**-**14**-15-**16** ... Cincinnati
17-**18** ............ New York
19-20 ........... at Montreal
21-22-**23** ..... at Cincinnati
24-**25**-**26** .......... Montreal
**28**-**29**-**30** .... Philadelphia

**AUGUST**
1-2-3 ........ at Pittsburgh
4-5-**6** ........... at St. Louis
8-**9**-**10** ........... San Diego
11-12-**13** ............ at S.F.
14-15-**16** ............ at L.A.
17-18-19-**20** ...... at Colo.
22-**23**-**24** ............ Florida
**25**-**26**-**27**-**28** ....... Atlanta
29-30-31 ......... at Florida

**SEPTEMBER**
1-2-**3** ............. at Atlanta
**4**-**6** .................. Colorado
**8**-**9**-**10** ..... San Francisco
11-12-**13** .... Los Angeles
15-16-**17** ... at San Diego
18-19-20 ...... at Houston
21-**22**-**23**-**24** .. Pittsburgh
25-26-27 .......... St. Louis
**28**-**29**-**30** .......... Houston

**OCTOBER**
**1** ....................... Houston

## CINCINNATI REDS
### Riverfront Stadium

**APRIL**
**3**-4-5-**6** ............ Chicago
7-**8**-**9**-**10** ........ San Diego
**11**-**12** ............ at Chicago
**13**-14-**15**-**16** ........ at S.F.
18-19-20 .... Los Angeles
21-**22**-**23**. San Francisco
24-25-26 at Los Angeles
27-28-29-**30** ....... at S.D.

**MAY**
2-3-4 .......... Philadelphia
5-**6**-**7** .............. New York
9-10-11 .......... at Florida
12-13-**14** ........ at Atlanta
16-17 ........... at Montreal
19-20-**21** ......... Colorado
22-23-24 .......... Houston
26-27-**28** ...... at St. Louis
30-31 ......... at Pittsburgh

**JUNE**
1 ................ at Pittsburgh
2-3-**4** ................ St. Louis
5-6-**7** ............... Pittsburgh
8-9-10-**11** ..... at Houston
12-13-**14** ..... at Colorado
16-17-**18** .......... Montreal
19-20-21-**22** ....... Atlanta
23-24-**25** ............ Florida
27-28-**29** ............ at Phil.
30 ............. at New York

**JULY**
**1**-**2** ............ at New York
4-5-6 ....... San Francisco
7-8-**9** .......... Los Angeles
**13**-**14**-15-**16** . at Chicago
17-18-19 ... at San Diego
21-22-**23** .......... Chicago
24-**25** ............ San Diego
26-27 .. at San Francisco
28-29-**30** ............ at L.A.

**AUGUST**
1-2-3 ............. New York
4-5-**6** .......... Philadelphia
8-9-10 ............ at Atlanta
11-12-**13** ......... at Florida
14-15-**16** ......... Colorado
18-19-**20** .......... Houston
21-22-23-**24** at St. Louis
25-26-**27** ... at Pittsburgh
28-29-30 .......... St. Louis
31 .................. Pittsburgh

**SEPTEMBER**
1-2-**3** ............. Pittsburgh
**4**-5-6 ............ at Houston
8-**9**-**10** ......... at Colorado
11-12-13 ............. Florida
15-**16**-17 ............ Atlanta
18-19-**20** .......... Montreal
22-23-**24** at Philadelphia
25-26-27 .... at New York
28-29-**30** ...... at Montreal

**OCTOBER**
**1** .................. at Montreal

# COLORADO ROCKIES
## Coors Field

**APRIL**
- **4-6** ... at New York
- **7-8-9** ... Philadelphia
- 10-**11** ... Montreal
- 13-14-15-**16** ... at Phil.
- **17**-18 ... at Montreal
- 20-21-**22**-23 ... Houston
- 24-25-**26** ... New York
- 27-28-29-**30**. at Houston

**MAY**
- 1-2-**3** ... San Diego
- 5-**6-7** ... Los Angeles
- 9-10-**11** ... San Francisco
- 12-13-14 ... at Florida
- 15-16-17-18 ... at Atlanta
- 19-20-**21** ... at Cincinnati
- 22-23-**24** ... Chicago
- 26-27-**28** ... at Pittsburgh
- **29**-30-31 ... at St. Louis

**JUNE**
- 2-3-**4** ... Pittsburgh
- 5-6-**7** ... St. Louis
- 8-**9-10-11** ... at Chicago
- 12-13-**14** ... Cincinnati
- 16-17-**18** ... Atlanta
- 19-20-**21** ... Florida
- **22-23-24-25** ... at S.D.
- **27-28** .. at San Francisco
- 29-30 ... at Los Angeles

**JULY**
- 1-**2** ... at Los Angeles
- 3-4-5 ... Houston
- 6-7-8-**9** ... Montreal
- 13-14-15-**16** ... at N.Y.
- 17-18-**19** ... Philadelphia
- 21-22-**23** ... New York
- 24-25 ... at Philadelphia
- 26-**27** ... at Houston
- 28-29-**30-31** at Montreal

**AUGUST**
- 1-2-**3** ... Los Angeles
- 4-5-**6** ... San Diego
- 8-9-**10** ... at Florida
- 11-12-**13** ... at Atlanta
- 14-15-**16** ... at Cincinnati
- 17-18-19-**20** ... Chicago
- 22-23-**24** ... Pittsburgh
- 25-26-**27** ... St. Louis
- 28-29-30 ... at Pittsburgh

**SEPTEMBER**
- 1-2-**3** ... at St. Louis
- **4-6** ... at Chicago
- 8-**9-10** ... Cincinnati
- 11-12-**13** ... Atlanta
- 15-**16-17** ... Florida
- 18-19-20 ... at San Diego
- 21-22-**23-24** ... at S.F.
- 25-26-27 at Los Angeles
- 28-29-**30**. San Francisco

**OCTOBER**
- **1** ... San Francisco

# FLORIDA MARLINS
## Joe Robbie Stadium

**APRIL**
- 2 ... New York
- 3-4-5 ... Los Angeles
- 6-7-8-**9** ... San Francisco
- **11**-12 ... at Los Angeles
- 14-15-**16** ... at San Diego
- 18-19 ... St. Louis
- 20-21-22-**23** .. San Diego
- 25-**26** ... at St. Louis
- **27**-28-**29-30** ... at S.F.

**MAY**
- 2-3-4 ... Atlanta
- 5-**6-7**-8 ... at Montreal
- 9-10-11 ... Cincinnati
- 12-13-14 ... Colorado
- 15-16-17 ... Philadelphia
- 19-20-**21** ... at Atlanta
- 23-24-25 ... at Pittsburgh
- **26-27-28** ... at Chicago
- **29**-31 ... Houston

**JUNE**
- 2-3-4 ... Chicago
- 5-6-**7** ... at Houston
- 8-9-10-11 ... Pittsburgh
- 13-14-15 ... at New York
- 16-17-**18** at Philadelphia
- 19-20-**21** ... at Colorado
- 23-24-**25** ... at Cincinnati
- 27-28 ... New York
- 29-30 ... Montreal

**JULY**
- 1-**2** ... Montreal
- 3-4-**5** ... at San Diego
- 6-7-8-**9** ... at St. Louis
- 13-14-15-**16** ... at L.A.
- 17-**18** .. at San Francisco
- 20-21-22-23 ... L.A.
- 24-**25** ... San Francisco
- 26-**27** ... San Diego
- 28-29-30-31 ... St. Louis

**AUGUST**
- 1-2 ... at Montreal
- 4-5-**6**-7 ... at New York
- 8-9-10 ... Colorado
- 11-12-**13** ... Cincinnati
- 14-15-16 ... at Atlanta
- 18-19-**20**-21 ... at Pitts.
- 22-**23-24** ... at Chicago
- 25-26-27-28 ... Houston
- 29-30-31 ... Chicago

**SEPTEMBER**
- 1-2-**3** ... at Houston
- 4-6 ... Pittsburgh
- 7-8-9-10 ... Atlanta
- 11-12-13 ... at Cincinnati
- 15-**16-17** ... at Colorado
- 18-19-20-21 ... at Phil.
- 22-23-**24** ... New York
- 25-26-27 ... Montreal
- 29-30 ... Philadelphia

**OCTOBER**
- **1** ... Philadelphia

# HOUSTON ASTROS
## Astrodome

**APRIL**
- 4-5 ... San Francisco
- 6-7-8-**9** ... Los Angeles
- **11**-12 .. at San Francisco
- 13-14-15-**16** ... at L.A.
- 17-18-**19** ... San Diego
- 20-21-**22**-23 at Colorado
- 25-**26** ... at San Diego
- 27-28-29-**30** ... Colorado

**MAY**
- 2-**3** ... at Chicago
- 4-5-6-7 ... at St. Louis
- **8**-9-10-**11** .. at Pittsburgh
- 12-13-**14** ... Philadelphia
- 16-17-18 ... New York
- 19-20-**21** ... Montreal
- 22-23-24 ... at Cincinnati
- 26-27-**28** ... Atlanta
- **29**-31 ... at Florida

**JUNE**
- 2-3-**4** ... at Atlanta
- 5-6-**7** ... Florida
- 8-9-10-**11** ... Cincinnati
- 13-14-15 at Philadelphia
- 16-**17-18** ... at New York
- 19-20-21 ... at Montreal
- 22-23-24-**25** ... Chicago
- 26-27-**28** ... St. Louis
- 30 ... Pittsburgh

**JULY**
- 1-**2** ... Pittsburgh
- 3-4-5 ... at Colorado
- 6-7-8-**9** ... San Diego
- **13**-14-15-**16** ... at S.F.
- 17-**18** ... at Los Angeles
- 20-21-22-**23** ... S.F.
- 24-25 ... Los Angeles
- 26-**27** ... Colorado
- 28-29-**30-31** ... at S.D.

**AUGUST**
- 1-2-3 ... at St. Louis
- 4-5-**6** ... at Pittsburgh
- 8-9-10 ... Montreal
- 11-12-13 ... New York
- 15-16-**17** ... Philadelphia
- 18-19-**20** ... at Cincinnati
- 21-22-23 ... Atlanta
- 25-26-27-28 ... at Florida
- 29-30-31 ... at Atlanta

**SEPTEMBER**
- 1-2-**3** ... Florida
- **4**-5-6 ... Cincinnati
- 8-9-**10** ... at Philadelphia
- 12-13-14 ... at New York
- 15-**16-17** ... at Montreal
- 18-19-20 ... Chicago
- 22-23-**24** ... St. Louis
- 25-26-**27** ... Pittsburgh
- **28-29-30** ... at Chicago

**OCTOBER**
- **1** ... at Chicago

# LOS ANGELES DODGERS
## Dodger Stadium

**APRIL**
4-5-6.............. at Florida
6-7-8-**9**......... at Houston
**11**-12................. Florida
13-14-15-**16**..... Houston
18-19-20.... at Cincinnati
21-22-**23**........ at Atlanta
24-25-26........ Cincinnati
27-28-29-**30**....... Atlanta

**MAY**
**1**-**2**-3... at San Francisco
5-**6**-**7**........... at Colorado
8-9-**10**....... at San Diego
12-13-**14**.......... St. Louis
15-16-17-18 .. Pittsburgh
19-20-**21**.......... Chicago
23-24-25.... at New York
26-**27**-28...... at Montreal
29-30-31 at Philadelphia

**JUNE**
2-3-**4**............. New York
5-6-7................ Montreal
9-10-**11**...... Philadelphia
13-14-15 ... at Pittsburgh
**16**-**17**-**18**...... at Chicago
19-20-**21**...... at St. Louis
22-23-24-25........... S.F.
26-27-28....... San Diego
29-30............. Colorado

**JULY**
1-**2**................. Colorado
4-5-6............. at Atlanta
7-8-**9**.......... at Cincinnati
13-14-15-**16**....... Florida
17-**18**.............. Houston
20-21-22-23 ... at Florida
24-25.......... at Houston
26-27................. Atlanta
28-29-**30**........ Cincinnati

**AUGUST**
1-2-**3**.......... at Colorado
4-5-**6**-**7**................ at S.F.
8-9-10............. St. Louis
11-12-**13**....... Pittsburgh
14-15-**16**.......... Chicago
18-19-**20**.... at New York
21-22-23...... at Montreal
24-25-26-27....... at Phil.
29-30-31........ New York

**SEPTEMBER**
1-2-**3**............... Montreal
4-5-6.......... Philadelphia
8-9-**10**....... at Pittsburgh
11-12-**13**...... at Chicago
15-16-**17**...... at St. Louis
19-20...... San Francisco
21-22-23-**24**.. San Diego
25-26-27......... Colorado
29-30........ at San Diego

**OCTOBER**
**1**.............. at San Diego

# MONTREAL EXPOS
## Olympic Stadium

**APRIL**
3-**5**-**6**......... at Pittsburgh
7-8-**9**........... at St. Louis
10-**11**.......... at Colorado
**13**-**14**-**15**-**16**.... St. Louis
**17**-18.............. Colorado
20-21-**22**-**23**..... Chicago
24-25-**26**....... Pittsburgh
**27**-**28**-**29**-**30**. at Chicago

**MAY**
2-3-4.............. New York
5-**6**-**7**-8............... Florida
9-10-**11** .. at Philadelphia
12-**13**-14-15....... at N.Y.
16-17............ Cincinnati
19-20-**21**...... at Houston
23-24-25....... San Diego
26-**27**-**28**.... Los Angeles
29-30-31. San Francisco

**JUNE**
2-3-**4**......... at San Diego
5-6-7...... at Los Angeles
9-**10**-**11**............... at S.F.
13-14-15............ Atlanta
16-17-**18**.... at Cincinnati
19-20-21.......... Houston
23-24-**25**....... Pittsburgh
26-27-**28**........ at Atlanta
29-30.............. at Florida

**JULY**
1-**2**.................. at Florida
3-**4**-5............ at St. Louis
6-7-8-**9**........ at Colorado
13-14-15-**16**........... Phil.
17-18............... St. Louis
19-20................ Chicago
21-22-**23** ... at Pittsburgh
24-**25**-**26**...... at Chicago
28-29-**30**-**31**.... Colorado

**AUGUST**
1-2...................... Florida
4-5-**6**-**7**................ Atlanta
8-9-10.......... at Houston
11-12-**13**-**14**....... at Phil.
15-16......... at New York
18-19-**20**....... San Diego
21-22-23.... Los Angeles
24-25-26-**27**.......... S.F.
29-30-**31**... at San Diego

**SEPTEMBER**
1-2-**3**...... at Los Angeles
**4**-5-**6**... at San Francisco
8-**9**-**10**-11....... New York
12-13......... Philadelphia
15-**16**-**17**.......... Houston
18-19-**20**.... at Cincinnati
22-23-**24**........ at Atlanta
25-26-27......... at Florida
28-29-**30**........ Cincinnati

**OCTOBER**
**1**.................... Cincinnati

# NEW YORK METS
## Shea Stadium

**APRIL**
2..................... at Florida
**4**-**6**.................. Colorado
7-**8**-**9**................ Chicago
10-11-**12**... at Pittsburgh
**13**-**14**-**15**-**16**. at Chicago
**18**-**19**............ Pittsburgh
20-21-22-**23** at St. Louis
24-25-**26**..... at Colorado
28-**29**-**30**.......... St. Louis

**MAY**
2-3-4............ at Montreal
5-**6**-**7**.......... at Cincinnati
9-10-11............. Atlanta
12-**13**-14-15.... Montreal
16-17-18...... at Houston
19-20-**21** at Philadelphia
23-24-25.... Los Angeles
26-**27**-**28**. San Francisco
**29**-30-31....... San Diego

**JUNE**
2-3-**4**...... at Los Angeles
**5**-**6**-7-**8**................ at S.F.
9-10-**11**..... at San Diego
13-14-15............. Florida
16-**17**-**18**.......... Houston
19-20-21-22........... Phil.
23-24-**25**........ at Atlanta
27-28.............. at Florida
30.................. Cincinnati

**JULY**
1-**2**................ Cincinnati
4-5-6................ Chicago
7-8-**9**......... at Pittsburgh
13-14-15-**16**.... Colorado
17-**18**............ at Chicago
19-20........... at St. Louis
21-22-**23**..... at Colorado
25-26-**27**.......... St. Louis
28-29-**30**-31 .. Pittsburgh

**AUGUST**
1-2-3......... at Cincinnati
4-5-**6**-7............... Florida
8-9-10.... at Philadelphia
11-12-**13**...... at Houston
15-16............... Montreal
18-19-**20**.... Los Angeles
21-22-**23**. San Francisco
24-25-26-**27**.. San Diego
29-30-31............ at L.A.

**SEPTEMBER**
1-**2**-**3**... at San Francisco
4-5-6......... at San Diego
8-**9**-**10**-11.... at Montreal
12-13-14.......... Houston
15-**16**-**17**.... Philadelphia
18-19-20-21 ... at Atlanta
22-23-**24**......... at Florida
25-26-27........ Cincinnati
29-**30**.................. Atlanta

**OCTOBER**
**1**......................... Atlanta

## PHILADELPHIA PHILLIES
**Veterans Stadium**

### APRIL
**3**-4-5-**6** ... at St. Louis
**7-8-9** ... at Colorado
**10**-11-**12** ... St. Louis
13-14-15-**16** ... Colorado
17-18-**19** ... Chicago
21-22-**23** ... at Pittsburgh
24-25-**26** ... at Chicago
27-28-29-**30** ... Pittsburgh

### MAY
2-3-4 ... at Cincinnati
5-6-**7**-8 ... at Atlanta
9-10-**11** ... Montreal
12-13-**14** ... at Houston
15-16-17 ... at Florida
19-20-**21** ... New York
23-24-25. San Francisco
26-27-**28** ... San Diego
29-30-31 ... Los Angeles

### JUNE
2-**3**-**4** ... at San Francisco
5-6-**7** ... at San Diego
9-10-**11** ... at Los Angeles
13-14-15 ... Houston
16-17-**18** ... Florida
19-20-21-22 ... at N.Y.
22-**24**-**25** ... at St. Louis
27-28-**29** ... Cincinnati
30 ... Atlanta

### JULY
1-**2**-3 ... Atlanta
**4**-5-6 ... at Pittsburgh
7-8-**9** ... Chicago
13-14-15-**16** at Montreal
17-18-**19** ... at Colorado
21-22-**23** ... St. Louis
24-25 ... Colorado
26-**27** ... Pittsburgh
**28-29-30** ... at Chicago

### AUGUST
1-2-3 ... at Atlanta
4-5-**6** ... at Cincinnati
8-9-10 ... New York
11-12-**13-14** ... Montreal
15-16-**17** ... at Houston
18-19-**20**. San Francisco
21-22-23 ... San Diego
24-25-26-27 ... L.A.
**29-30-31** ... at S.F.

### SEPTEMBER
1-2-**3** ... at San Diego
4-5-6 ... at Los Angeles
8-9-**10** ... Houston
12-13 ... at Montreal
15-**16-17** ... at New York
18-19-20-21 ... Florida
22-23-**24** ... Cincinnati
26-27 ... Atlanta
29-30 ... at Florida

### OCTOBER
**1** ... at Florida

## PITTSBURGH PIRATES
**Three Rivers Stadium**

### APRIL
3-**5-6** ... Montreal
7-8-**9** ... at Atlanta
10-11-**12** ... New York
14-15-**16**-17 ... Atlanta
**18-19** ... at New York
21-22-**23** ... Philadelphia
24-25-**26** ... at Montreal
27-28-29-**30** ... at Phil.

### MAY
1-2-**3** ... at St. Louis
5-6-**7** ... Chicago
**8**-9-10-**11** ... Houston
12-**13-14** ... at S.F.
15-16-17-18 ... at L.A.
19-20-**21** ... at San Diego
23-24-25 ... Florida
26-27-**28** ... Colorado
30-31 ... Cincinnati

### JUNE
1 ... Cincinnati
2-3-**4** ... at Colorado
5-6-**7** ... at Cincinnati
8-9-10-**11** ... at Florida
13-14-15 ... L.A.
16-17-**18** ... San Diego
19-20-**21**. San Francisco
23-24-**25** ... at Montreal
26-27-**28** ... at Chicago
30 ... at Houston

### JULY
1-**2** ... at Houston
**4**-5-6 ... Philadelphia
7-8-**9** ... New York
13-14-15-**16** ... St. Louis
18-19-20 ... at Atlanta
21-22-**23** ... Montreal
24-**25** ... Atlanta
26-**27** ... at Philadelphia
28-29-**30**-31 ... at N.Y.

### AUGUST
1-2-3 ... Chicago
4-5-**6** ... Houston
8-9-10. at San Francisco
11-12-**13** ... at L.A.
14-15-16 ... at San Diego
18-19-**20**-21 ... Florida
22-23-**24** ... at Colorado
25-26-**27** ... Cincinnati
28-29-30 ... Colorado
31 ... at Cincinnati

### SEPTEMBER
1-2-**3** ... at Cincinnati
4-**6** ... at Florida
8-9-**10** ... Los Angeles
11-12-13 ... San Diego
15-16-**17**. San Francisco
18-19-20 ... St. Louis
21-**22-23-24** . at Chicago
25-26-**27** ... at Houston
29-**30** ... at St. Louis

### OCTOBER
**1** ... at St. Louis

## ST. LOUIS CARDINALS
**Busch Stadium**

### APRIL
**3**-4-5-**6** ... Philadelphia
7-8-**9** ... Montreal
**10**-11-**12** ... at Phil.
**13-14-15-16** at Montreal
18-19 ... at Florida
20-21-22-**23** ... New York
25-**26** ... Florida
28-**29-30** ... at New York

### MAY
1-2-**3** ... Pittsburgh
4-5-6-**7** ... Houston
8-9-10 ... Chicago
12-13-**14** ... at L.A.
15-16-17 ... at San Diego
**18-19**-20-**21** ... at S.F.
23-24-**25** ... Atlanta
26-27-**28** ... Cincinnati
**29**-30-31 ... Colorado

### JUNE
2-3-**4** ... at Cincinnati
5-6-**7** ... at Colorado
9-10-**11** ... at Atlanta
13-14-15 ... San Diego
16-17-**18**. San Francisco
19-20-**21** ... Los Angeles
23-**24-25** ... Philadelphia
26-27-**28** ... at Houston
**29-30** ... at Chicago

### JULY
**1**-2 ... at Chicago
3-**4**-5 ... Montreal
6-7-8-**9** ... Florida
13-14-15-**16** ... at Pitts.
17-18 ... at Montreal
19-20 ... New York
21-22-**23** at Philadelphia
25-26-**27** ... at New York
28-29-30-31 ... at Florida

### AUGUST
**1**-2-3 ... Houston
**4**-5-**6** ... Chicago
8-9-10 ... at Los Angeles
11-11-**13** ... at San Diego
**14-15**-16 ... at S.F.
18-19-20 ... Atlanta
21-22-23-**24** ... Cincinnati
25-26-**27** ... at Colorado
28-29-30 ... at Cincinnati

### SEPTEMBER
1-2-**3** ... Colorado
4-5-**6** ... at Atlanta
8-9-**10** ... San Diego
11-12-13 ... S.F.
15-16-**17** ... Los Angeles
18-19-20 ... at Pittsburgh
22-23-**24** ... at Houston
25-26-**27** ... at Chicago
29-**30** ... Pittsburgh

### OCTOBER
**1** ... Pittsburgh

# SAN DIEGO PADRES
## Jack Murphy Stadium

### APRIL
4-**5**........................ Atlanta
7-**8-9-10**..... at Cincinnati
11-12-**13**........ at Atlanta
14-15-**16**............. Florida
17-18-**19**...... at Houston
20-21-22-**23** ... at Florida
25-**26**............... Houston
27-28-29-**30**... Cincinnati

### MAY
1-2-**3**........... at Colorado
**4**-5-6-**7** ... San Francisco
8-9-**10**........ Los Angeles
**12-13-14**...... at Chicago
15-16-17.......... St. Louis
19-20-**21**....... Pittsburgh
23-24-25..... at Montreal
26-27-**28** at Philadelphia
**29**-30-**31**.... at New York

### JUNE
2-3-**4**................ Montreal
5-6-**7**.......... Philadelphia
9-10-**11**.......... New York
13-14-15...... at St. Louis
16-17-**18** ... at Pittsburgh
19-20-**21**.......... Chicago
**22**-23-24-**25**.... Colorado
26-27-28............. at L.A.
30....... at San Francisco

### JULY
**1**-2...... at San Francisco
3-4-**5**.................... Florida
6-7-8-**9**......... at Houston
**13**-14-15-**16**....... Atlanta
17-18-19........ Cincinnati
21-22-**23**........ at Atlanta
24-25......... at Cincinnati
26-**27**.............. at Florida
28-29-**30-31**..... Houston

### AUGUST
1-2-**3**...... San Francisco
4-5-**6**.......... at Colorado
8-9-10.......... at Chicago
11-11-**13**.......... St. Louis
14-15-16....... Pittsburgh
18-19-**20**...... at Montreal
21-22-23 at Philadelphia
24-25-26-**27**....... at N.Y.
29-30-**31**.......... Montreal

### SEPTEMBER
1-2-**3**......... Philadelphia
4-5-6............. New York
8-9-**10**.......... at St. Louis
11-12-13 ... at Pittsburgh
15-16-**17**.......... Chicago
18-19-20......... Colorado
21-22-23-**24**........ at L.A.
25-26-**27**............. at S.F.
29-30......... Los Angeles

### OCTOBER
**1**............... Los Angeles

# SAN FRANCISCO GIANTS
## Candlestick Park

### APRIL
4-5............... at Houston
6-7-8-9........... at Florida
**11**-12............... Houston
**13**-14-**15**-16... Cincinnati
18-19-20........ at Atlanta
21-**22-23**.... at Cincinnati
24-**25-26**............ Atlanta
**27**-28-**29-30**........Florida

### MAY
**1-2**-3.......... Los Angeles
4-5-6-**7**...... at San Diego
9-10-**11**....... at Colorado
12-**13-14**....... Pittsburgh
**15-16-17**.......... Chicago
**18**-19-**20-21**.... St. Louis
23-24-25 at Philadelphia
26-**27-28**.... at New York
29-30-31...... at Montreal

### JUNE
2-**3-4**.......... Philadelphia
**5-6**-7-**8**........... New York
9-**10-11**............ Montreal
13-**14-15**...... at Chicago
16-17-**18**...... at St. Louis
19-20-**21** ... at Pittsburgh
22-23-24-**25**........ at L.A.
**27-28**.............. Colorado
30................. San Diego

### JULY
**1-2**................ San Diego
4-5-6.......... at Cincinnati
7-8-9.............. at Atlanta
**13**-14-15-**16**..... Houston
17-**18**.................. Florida
20-21-22-**23**. at Houston
24-**25**.............. at Florida
26-**27**............. Cincinnati
28-**29-30**............ Atlanta

### AUGUST
1-2-**3**......... at San Diego
4-5-**6-7**....... Los Angeles
**8-9-10**........... Pittsburgh
11-12-**13**.......... Chicago
**14-15**-16.......... St. Louis
18-19-**20** at Philadelphia
21-22-**23**.... at New York
24-25-26-**27** at Montreal
**29-30-31**.... Philadelphia

### SEPTEMBER
1-**2-3**...............New York
**4**-5-6................ Montreal
**8-9-10**.......... at Chicago
11-12-13...... at St. Louis
15-16-**17** ... at Pittsburgh
19-20..... at Los Angeles
21-22-**23-24**.... Colorado
25-26-**27**....... San Diego
28-29-**30**......at Colorado

### OCTOBER
**1**................. at Colorado

**NOTE:** Dates in **bold** indicate afternoon games.

# SPRING TRAINING

## AMERICAN LEAGUE

### BALTIMORE ORIOLES

**Major League Club**

**Hotel Address:** Training—Inn of Osprey, 1660 S. Tamiami Trail, Osprey, FL 34229. Telephone: (813) 966-2121. Games—Hilton and Towers, 333 First St. S., St. Petersburg, FL 33701. Telephone: (813) 894-5000. FAX: (813) 922-3751. **Complex Address:** Training—Twin Lakes Park, 6700 Clark Road, Sarasota, FL 34241. Telephone: (813) 923-1996. Games—Huggins-Stengel Complex, 1320 Fifth St. N., St. Petersburg, FL 33701. Telephone: (813) 892-5971.

**Minor League Clubs**

**Hotel Address:** Knight's Inn, 668 67th St. Circle E, Bradenton, FL 34208. Telephone: (813) 745-1876. **Complex Address:** Twin Lakes Park, 6700 Clark Road, Sarasota, FL 34241. Telephone: (813) 923-1996.

### BOSTON RED SOX

**Major League Club**

**Hotel Address:** Sheraton Harbor Place, 2500 Edwards Dr., Fort Myers, FL 33901. Telephone: (813) 337-0300. FAX: (813) 334-6835. **Complex Address:** City of Palms Park, 2201 Edison Ave., Fort Myers, FL 33901. Telephone: (813) 334-4799. FAX: (813) 332-8105.

**Minor League Clubs**

**Hotel Address:** Sheraton HarborPlace, 2500 Edwards Dr., Fort Myers, FL 33901. Telephone: (813) 337-0300. FAX: (813) 334-6835. **Complex Address:** Red Sox Minor League Complex, 4301 Edison Ave., Fort Myers, FL 33916. Telephone: (813) 332-8106. FAX: (813) 332-8107.

### CALIFORNIA ANGELS

**Major League Club**

**Hotel Address:** Fiesta Inn, 2100 S. Priest Dr., Tempe, AZ 85282. Telephone: (602) 967-1441. **Complex Address:** Tempe Diablo Stadium, 2200 W. Alameda, Tempe, AZ 85282. Telephone: (602) 438-4300.

**Minor League Clubs**

**Hotel Address:** Mesa Hilton Pavillion, 1011 W. Holmes Ave., Mesa, AZ 85210. Telephone: (602) 833-5555. **Complex Address:** Gene Autry Park, 4125 E. McKellips, Mesa, AZ 85205. Telephone: (602) 830-4137. FAX: (602) 830-5212.

### CHICAGO WHITE SOX

**Major League Club**

**Hotel Address:** Sleep Inn, 900 University Parkway, Sarasota, FL 34234. Telephone: (813) 359-8558. **Complex Address:** Ed Smith Stadium, 1090 N. Euclid Ave., Sarasota, FL 34237. Telephone: (813) 366-8451. FAX: (813) 366-6615.

**Minor League Clubs**

**Hotel Address:** Bradenton Inn, 2303 First St. E. (U.S. 41), Bradenton, FL 34208. Telephone: (813) 747-6465. **Complex Address:** Same as major league club.

### CLEVELAND INDIANS

**Major League Club**

**Hotel Address:** Holiday Inn, 1150 Third St. SW, Winter Haven, FL 33880. Telephone: (813) 294-4451. FAX: (813) 293-9829. **Complex Address:** Chain of Lakes Park, Cypress Gardens Blvd. and US 17, Winter Haven, FL 33880. Telephone: (813) 291-5803 or 293-5405. FAX: (813) 291-4491.

**Minor League Clubs**

**Hotel, Complex Address:** Same as major league club.

### DETROIT TIGERS

**Major League Club**

**Hotel Address:** Hoilday Inn-South, 3405 S, Florida Ave., Lakeland, FL 33803. Telephone: (813) 646-5731. FAX: (813) 646-5215. **Complex Address:** Tigertown, P.O. Box 90187, Lakeland, FL 33804. Telephone: (813) 686-8075. FAX: (813) 688-9589.

**Minor League Clubs**

**Hotel, Complex Address:** Tigertown, P.O. Box 90187, Lakeland, FL 33804. Telephone: (813) 686-8075. FAX: (813) 688-9589.

### KANSAS CITY ROYALS

**Major League Club**

**Hotel Address:** Holiday Inn, I-4 and US 27, Haines City, FL 33845. Telephone: (813) 424-2211. **Complex Address:** Baseball City Stadium, 300 Stadium Way, Davenport, FL 33837. Telephone: (813) 424-7211. FAX: (813) 424-5611.

**Minor League Clubs**

**Hotel, Complex Address:** Same as major league club.

## MILWAUKEE BREWERS

**Major League Club**

**Hotel Address:** The Dobson Ranch Inn, 1666 S. Dobson Road, Mesa, AZ 85202. Telephone: (602) 831-7000. **Complex Address:** Compadre Stadium, 4001 S. Alma School Road, Chandler, AZ 85248. Mailing Address: P.O. Box 2650, Chandler, AZ 85244. Telephone: (602) 895-6000. FAX: (602) 895-2649.

**Minor League Clubs**

**Hotel Address:** Quality Inn Phoenix Southeast, 5121 E. LaPuente Ave., Phoenix, AZ 85044. Telephone: (602) 893-3900. **Complex Address:** Chandler Complex, 4500 S. Alma School Road, Chandler, AZ 85248. Telephone: (602) 895-1412. FAX: (602) 895-1414.

## MINNESOTA TWINS

**Major League Club**

**Hotel Address:** Holiday Inn Bell Tower, 13051 Bell Tower Dr., Ft. Myers, FL 33907. Telephone: (813) 482-2900. **Complex Address:** Lee County Sports Complex, 14100 Six Mile Cypress Pkwy., Ft. Myers, FL 33912. Telephone: (813) 768-4200. FAX: (813) 768-4207.

**Minor League Clubs**

**Hotel Address:** Radisson Inn,12635 Cleveland Ave. (US 41), Ft. Myers, FL 33907. Telephone: (813) 936-4300. FAX: (813) 936-2058. **Complex Address:** Lee County Sports Complex, 14200 Six Mile Cypress Pkwy., Ft. Myers, FL 33912. Telephone: (813) 768-4280. FAX: (813) 768-4211.

## NEW YORK YANKEES

**Major League Club**

**Hotel Address:** Palm-Aire Spa Resort, 2501 Palm-Aire Drive N., Pompano Beach, FL 33069. Telephone: (305) 972-3300. **Complex Address:** Fort Lauderdale Stadium, 5301 NW 12th Ave., Fort Lauderdale, FL 33309. Telephone: (305) 776-1921.

**Minor League Clubs**

**Hotel Address:** Holiday Inn, 4732 N. Dale Mabry, Tampa, FL 33614. Telephone: (813) 877-6061. **Complex Address:** Tampa Complex, 3102 N. Himes Ave., Tampa, FL 33607. Telephone: (813) 875-7753.

## OAKLAND ATHLETICS

**Major League Club**

**Hotel Address:** Doubletree Suites, 320 North 44th St., Phoenix, AZ 85008. Telephone: (602) 225-0500. **Complex Address:** Phoenix Municipal Stadium, 5999 East Van Buren, Phoenix, AZ 85008. Telephone: (602) 392-0217.

**Minor League Clubs**

**Hotel Address:** Days Inn Scottsdale Resort, 4710 North Scottsdale Road, Scottsdale, AZ 85251. Telephone: (602) 947-5411. **Complex Address:** Papago Park Baseball Complex, 1802 N. 64th St., Phoenix, AZ 85004. Telephone: (602) 949-5951. FAX: (602) 949-0557.

## SEATTLE MARINERS

**Major League Club**

**Hotel Address:** Pointe Hilton at Squaw Peak, 7677 N. 16th St., Phoenix, AZ 85020. Telephone: (602) 997-2626. **Complex Address:** Peoria Sports Complex, 15707 N. 83rd Ave., Peoria, AZ 85382. Telephone: (602) 412-9000. FAX: (602) 412-7888.

**Minor League Clubs**

**Hotel Address:** Comfort Inn-Turf Paradise, 1711 W. Bell Rd., Phoenix, AZ 85023. Telephone: (602) 866-2089. **Complex Address:** Same as major league club.

## TEXAS RANGERS

**Major League Club**

**Hotel Address:** Days Inn Murdock, 1941 Tamiami Trail, Murdock, FL 33938. Telephone: (813) 627-8900. FAX: (813) 743-8503. **Stadium Address:** Charlotte County Stadium, 3609 El Jobean Road, Port Charlotte, FL 33948. Telephone: (813) 625-9500. FAX: (813) 624-5168.

**Minor League Clubs**

**Hotel, Complex Address:** Same as major league club.

## TORONTO BLUE JAYS

**Major League Club**

**Hotel:** None. **Stadium Address:** Dunedin Stadium, 311 Douglas Ave., Dunedin, FL 34698. Telephone: (813) 733-9302.

**Minor League Clubs**

**Hotel Address:** Comfort Inn, 27988 U.S. 19 North, Clearwater, FL 34621. Telephone: (813) 796-1234. **Complex Address:** Cecil P. Englebert Complex, 1700 Solon Ave., Dunedin, FL 34697. Telephone: (813) 733 9302. FAX: (813) 733-9389.

# NATIONAL LEAGUE

## ATLANTA BRAVES

### Major League Club

**Hotel Address:** Palm Beach Gardens Marriott, 4000 RCA Blvd., Palm Beach Gardens, FL 33410. Telephone: (407) 622-8888. FAX: (407) 622-0052. **Stadium Address:** Municipal Stadium, 715 Hank Aaron Dr., West Palm Beach, FL 33401. Telephone: (407) 471-3600. FAX: (407) 689-2334.

### Minor League Clubs

**Hotel Address:** Ramada Inn Hotel, 630 Clearwater Park Road, West Palm Beach, FL 33401. Telephone: (407) 833-1234. **Complex Address:** Municipal Stadium, 715 Hank Aaron Dr., West Palm Beach, FL 33401. Telephone: (407) 471-3620.

## CHICAGO CUBS

### Major League Club

**Hotel Address:** Mezona Motor Inn, 250 W. Main St., Mesa, AZ 85202. Telephone: (602) 834-9233. **Complex Address:** HoHoKam Park, 1235 N. Center St., Mesa, AZ 85201. Telephone: (602) 461-8010. FAX: (602) 461-0673.

### Minor League Clubs

**Hotel Address:** Maricopa Motor Inn, 3 E. Main St., Mesa, AZ 85202. Telephone: (602) 834-6060. **Complex Address:** Fitch Park, 655 N. Center St., Mesa, AZ 85201. Telephone: (602) 844-2391.

## CINCINNATI REDS

### Major League Club

**Hotel Address:** Holiday Inn-Plant City, I-4 at exit 11, Plant City, FL 33566. Telephone: (813) 752-3141. FAX: (813) 754-5657. **Complex Address:** Plant City Stadium, 1900 S. Park Road, Plant City, FL 33566. Telephone: (813) 752-1878. FAX: (813) 757-6351.

### Minor League Clubs

**Hotel, Complex Address:** Same as major league club.

## COLORADO ROCKIES

### Major League Club

**Hotel Address:** Viscount Suites, 4855 E. Broadway, Tucson, AZ 85716. Telephone: (602) 745-6500. FAX: (602) 790-5114. **Complex Address:** Hi Corbett Field, 3400 E. Camino Campestre, Tucson, AZ 85716. Telephone: (602) 322-4549. FAX: (602) 322-4545.

### Minor League Clubs

**Hotel Address:** Aztec Inn Suites, 102 N. Alvernon Way, Tucson, AZ 85711. Telephone: (602) 795-0330. FAX: (602) 326-2111. **Complex Address:** Same as major league club.

## FLORIDA MARLINS

### Major League Club

**Hotel Address:** Melbourne Hilton, 200 Rialto Place, Melbourne, FL 32901. Telephone: (407) 768-0200. **Complex Address:** Space Coast Stadium, 5600 Stadium Pkwy., Melbourne, FL 32940. Telephone: (407) 633-9200.

### Minor League Clubs

**Hotel Address:** Holiday Inn Oceanside, 1300 N. Atlantic Ave., Cocoa Beach, FL. Telephone: (407) 783-2271. FAX: (407) 784-8878. **Complex Address:** Carl Barger Baseball Complex, 5600 Stadium Pkwy., Melbourne, FL 32940. Telephone: (407) 633-9200.

## HOUSTON ASTROS

### Major League Club

**Hotel Address:** Sol Orlando Village Resort Hotel, 4787 W. Irlo Bronson Memorial Hwy., Kissimmee, FL 34746. Telephone: (407) 397-0555. FAX: (407) 397-0553. **Complex Address:** Osceola County Stadium, 1000 Bill Beck Blvd., Kissimmee, FL 34744. Telephone: (407) 933-6500. FAX: (407) 397-0553.

### Minor League Clubs

**Hotel Address:** Holiday Inn-Kissimmee, 2009 W. Vine St. (US 192), Kissimmee, FL 34741. Telephone: (407) 846-2713. FAX: (407) 846-8695. **Complex Address:** Same as major league club.

## LOS ANGELES DODGERS

### Major League Club

**Hotel Address:** Dodgertown, 4001 26th St., Vero Beach, FL 32961. Telephone: (407) 569-4900. **Complex Address:** Same.

### Minor League Clubs

**Hotel, Complex Address:** Same as major league club.

## MONTREAL EXPOS

### Major League Club

**Hotel Address:** Comfort Inn, 1901 Palm Beach Lakes Blvd., West Palm Beach, FL 33409. Telephone: (407) 689-6100. **Complex Address:** West Palm Beach Municipal Stadium, 715 Hank Aaron Dr., West Palm Beach, FL 33401. Telephone: (407) 684-6801. FAX: (407) 681-4876.

### Minor League Clubs

**Hotel Address:** Comfort Inn, 1901 Palm Beach Lakes Blvd., West Palm

Beach, FL 33409. Telephone: (407) 689-6100. **Complex Address:** Expos Minor League Development Center, Santaluces High School, 6850 Lawrence Road, Lantana, FL 33462. Telephone: (407) 433-1990. FAX: (407) 433-3481.

## NEW YORK METS

### Major League Club

**Hotel Address:** Holiday Inn, 10120 S. Federal Hwy., Port St. Lucie, FL 34986. Telephone: (407) 337-2200. FAX: (407) 335-7872. **Complex Address:** St. Lucie County Sports Complex, 525 NW Peacock Blvd., Port St. Lucie, FL 34986. Telephone: (407) 871-2100. FAX: (407) 878-9802.

### Minor League Clubs

**Hotel Address:** Same as major league club. **Complex Address:** Mets Minor League Complex, 525 NW Peacock Blvd., Port St. Lucie, FL 34986. Telephone: (407) 871-2132. FAX: (407) 871-2181.

## PHILADELPHIA PHILLIES

### Major League Club

**Hotel:** None. **Complex Address:** Jack Russell Memorial Stadium, 800 Phillies Dr., Clearwater, FL 34615. Telephone: (813) 441-9943. FAX: (813) 461-7768.

### Minor League Clubs

**Hotel Address:** Best Western, 120 US Hwy. 19 N., Clearwater, FL 34625. Telephone: (813) 799-1565.; Holiday Inn, 21030 US Hwy. 19 N., Clearwater, FL 34625. Telephone: (813) 797-8173. **Complex Address:** Carpenter Complex, 651 Old Coachman Road, Clearwater, FL 34625. Telephone: (813) 799-0503. FAX: (813) 726-1793.

## PITTSBURGH PIRATES

### Major League Club

**Hotel Address:** Pirate City, 1701 Roberto Clemente Memorial Dr. (27th St. E.), Bradenton, FL 34208. Telephone: (813) 747-3031. FAX: (813) 747-9549. **Complex Address:** Same.

### Minor League Clubs

**Hotel, Complex Address:** Same as major league club.

## ST. LOUIS CARDINALS

### Major League Club

**Hotel Address:** St. Petersburg Hilton Towers, 333 1st St. South, St. Petersburg, FL 33701. Telephone: (813) 894-5000. **Complex Address:** Al Lang Stadium, 180 Second Ave. SE, St. Petersburg, FL 33701. Telephone: (813) 896-4641.

### Minor League Clubs

**Hotel Address:** The Best Western Mirage, 5005 34th St. N., St. Petersburg, FL 33714. Telephone: (813) 525-1181. **Complex Address:** Busch Complex, 7901 30th Ave. N., St. Petersburg, FL 33733. Telephone: (813) 345-5300.

## SAN DIEGO PADRES

### Major League Club

**Hotel Address:** Players—Holiday Inn Corporate Center Hotel, 2532 W. Peoria Ave., Phoenix, AZ 85029. Telephone: (602) 943-2341. Staff—Fountain Suites, 2577 W. Greenway Road, Phoenix, AZ 85023. Telephone: (602) 375-1777. **Complex Address:** Peoria Sports Complex, 8131 W. Paradise Lane, Peoria, AZ 85382. Telephone: (602) 486-7000. FAX: (602) 486-9341.

### Minor League Clubs

**Hotel Address:** Premier Inn at Metro Center, 10402 Black Canyon Highway, Phoenix, AZ 85051. Telephone: (602) 943-2371. **Complex Address:** Same as major league club.

## SAN FRANCISCO GIANTS

### Major League Club

**Hotel Address:** Scottsdale Plaza Resort, 7200 N. Scottsdale Road, Scottsdale, AZ 85253. Telephone: (602) 948-5000. FAX: (602) 998-5971. **Complex Address:** Scottsdale Stadium, 7408 E. Osborn Road., Scottsdale, AZ 85251. Telephone: (602) 990-7972. FAX: (602) 990-2643.

### Minor League Clubs

**Hotel Address:** Ramada Inn Suites, 1635 N. Scottsdale Road, Tempe, AZ 85281. Telephone: (602) 947-3711. FAX: (602) 949-7902. **Complex Address:** Indian School Park, 4415 N. Hayden Road, Scottsdale, AZ 85251. Telephone: (602) 990-0052. FAX: (602) 990-2349.

# MAJORS
# OTHER INFORMATION

## THE BASEBALL NETWORK

**Mailing Address:** 1301 Sixth Ave., 39th Floor, New York, NY 10019. **Telephone:** (212) 977-7300. **FAX:** (212) 977-7977.

**President, Chief Executive Officer:** Ken Schanzer.

**Executive Vice President, Sales and Marketing:** Mike Trager. **Vice President, Business Affairs:** Jon Litner.

**Controller:** Megan O'Donnell.

**Coordinating Producer:** John Fillipelli. **Vice President, Production and Operations:** Dave Alworth. **Director of Operations:** Ed Delaney.

## MAJOR LEAGUE BASEBALL PRODUCTIONS
## THE PHOENIX COMMUNICATIONS GROUP, INC.

**Mailing Address:** 3 Empire Blvd., South Hackensack, NJ 07606. **Telephone:** (201) 807-0888. **FAX:** (201) 807-0272.

**Chairman:** Joe Podesta. **President:** James Holland. **Senior Vice President, Executive Producer:** Geoff Belinfante. **Vice President, Director of Baseball Programming:** Mike Kostel.

## MAJOR LEAGUE PLAYERS ASSOCIATION

**Mailing Address:** 12 E. 49th St., 24th Floor, New York, NY 10017. **Telephone:** (212) 826-0808. **FAX:** (212) 752-3649.

**Executive Director and General Counsel:** Donald Fehr.

**Special Assistants:** Mark Belanger, Tony Bernazard.

**Associate General Counsel:** Eugene Orza. **Assistant General Counsel:** Lauren Rich, Doyle Pryor. **Counsel:** Arthur Schack.

**Director of Licensing:** Judy Heeter. **Manager, Marketing Services:** Allyne Price. **Manager, Retail Licensing:** Tina Morris.

**Executive Board:** Player representatives of the 28 major league clubs.

**League Representatives:** Terry Steinbach (American League), Jay Bell (National League).

## MAJOR LEAGUE SCOUTING BUREAU

**Mailing Address:** 23712 Birtcher Dr., Suite A, Lake Forest, CA 92630. **Telephone:** (714) 458-7600. **FAX:** (714) 458-9454.

**Director:** Don Pries.

**Assistant Director:** Frank Marcos. **Administrator:** RoseMary Durgin. **Computer Operations Administrator:** Mike Wilson. **Secretary:** Rease Leverenz.

**Board of Directors:** Bill Murray, chairman; Sandy Alderson (Athletics), Dan Duquette (Red Sox), Bob Gebhard (Rockies), Lou Gorman (Red Sox), Roland Hemond (Orioles), Joe Klein (Tigers), Joe McIlvaine (Mets), Art Stewart (Royals), Don Pries.

**Scouts:** Brannon Bonifay (Okeechobee, FL), Dick Colpaert (Utica, MI), Jeff Cornell (Lee's Summit, MO), Whitey DeHart (Molalla, OR), Dan Dixon (San Diego, CA), Art Gardner (Walnut Grove, MS), Rusty Gerhardt (Arlington, TX), Todd Guggiana (Sunset Beach, CA), Mike Hamilton (Arlington, TX), Doug Horning (Schererville, IN), Bill Jackson (Peoria, AZ), Brad Kohler (Easton, PA), Don Kohler (Plainfield, NJ), Mike Larson (Waseca, MN), Jethro McIntyre (Pittsburg, CA), John McMichen (Cincinnati, OH), Lenny Merullo (Reading, MA), Paul Mirocke (Lutz, FL), Rick Oliver (LaVerne, CA), Tim Osborne (Marietta, GA), Bud Pritchard (Fullerton, CA), Gary Randall (Nashville, TN), Al Ronning (Sunnyvale, CA), Kevin Saucier (Pensacola, FL), Pat Shortt (Rockville Centre, NY), Craig Smajstrla (Pearland, TX), Ed Sukla (Irvine, CA), Jim Walton (Shattuck, OK).

**Canadian Scouts:** Jim Baba (Saskatoon, Saskatchewan), Ron Betts (Edmonton, Alberta), Kevin Bly (Thornhill, Ontario), Walt Burrows (Brentwood Bay, B.C.), Bob Cohen (North York, Ontario), John Dunsford (Charlottetown, P.E.I.), Gerry Falk (Carman, Manitoba), Bill Green (Vancouver, B.C.), Sean Gulliver (St. John's, Newfoundland), Ian Jordan (Chomedey, Quebec), Mick Kozlowski (Kitchener, Ontario), Glen Matheson (Truro, Nova Scotia), Dave McManus (Fredericton, New Brunswick), Jean Mercier (Charlesbourg, Quebec), Tom Valcke (Windsor, Ontario).

**Puerto Rican Scout:** Pepito Centeno (Bayamon).

## MAJOR LEAGUE UMPIRES ASSOCIATION

**Mailing Address:** 1735 Market St., Suite 3420, Philadelphia, PA 19103. **Telephone:** (215) 979-3200.

**General Counsel:** Richie Phillips.

## MLB UMPIRE DEVELOPMENT PROGRAM

**Mailing Address:** P.O. Box A, St. Petersburg, FL 33731. **Telephone:** (813) 823-1286. **FAX:** (813) 823-7212.

**Executive Director:** Edwin Lawrence.

**Administrative Assistant:** Barbara Douglas. **Bookkeeper:** Lillian Patterson.

**Director of Field Supervision:** Mike Fitzpatrick (Kalamazoo, MI).

**Supervisors:** Dennis Cregg (Webster, MA), Tom Lepperd (Des Moines, IA), Dick Nelson (Maumelle, AR).

**Area Observers:** Joe Linsalata (Hollywood, FL), Jerry Neudecker (Mary Esther, FL).

## NATIONAL BASEBALL HALL OF FAME AND MUSEUM

**Mailing Address:** P.O. Box 590, Cooperstown, NY 13326. **Telephone:** (607) 547-7200. **FAX:** (607) 547-2044.

**Chairman:** Ed Stack. **President:** Don Marr. **Vice President:** Bill Guilfoile. **Vice President:** Frank Simio. **Controller:** Fran Althiser. **Registrar:** Peter Clark. **Director of Public Relations:** Jeff Idelson. **Director of Retail Marketing:** David Reed. **Curator:** William Spencer.

**1995 Hall of Fame Induction Ceremonies:** July 30, Cooperstown, NY. **Hall of Fame Game:** July 31.

## ALUMNI ASSOCIATIONS

### MLB Players Alumni Association

**Mailing Address, National Headquarters:** 3637 4th St. N., Suite 480, St. Petersburg, FL 33704. **Telephone:** (813) 822-3399. **FAX:** (813) 822-6300.

**Mailing Address, Corporate Marketing:** 381 Mansfield Ave., Suite 115, Pittsburgh, PA 15220. **Telephone:** (412) 928-0885. **FAX:** (412) 928-9720.

**President:** Brooks Robinson.

**Vice Presidents:** Bob Boone, Carl Erskine, Mike Hegan, Chuck Hinton, Al Kaline, Billy Williams, Mike Schmidt, Rusty Staub, Billy Williams.

**Secretary/Treasurer:** Fred Valentine.

**Board of Directors:** George Brett, Nelson Briles, Darrel Chaney, Denny Doyle, Jim "Mudcat" Grant, Rich Hand, Jim Hannan, Tug McGraw, Bob Miller, Jerry Moses, Dick Radatz, Brooks Robinson, Eddie Robinson, Ken Sanders, Fred Valentine, Carl Warwick, Robin Yount.

**Director Emeritus:** Bob Allison.

**Executive Vice President:** Dan Foster. **General Counsel:** Sam Moore. **Director of Member Services:** Peggy McKenna. **Director of Special Events:** Chris Torgusen. **Manager of Special Events:** Jon Grove. **Special Events Coordinator:** Ben Taft.

### Association of Professional Baseball Players of America

**Mailing Address:** 12062 Valley View St., Suite 211, Garden Grove, CA 92645. **Telephone:** (714) 892-9900. **FAX:** (714) 897-0233.

**President:** John McHale.

**Secretary-Treasurer:** Chuck Stevens.

**1st Vice President:** Joe DiMaggio. **2nd Vice President:** Arthur Richman. **3rd Vice President:** Bob Kennedy.

**Advisory Council:** Calvin Griffith, Eddie Sawyer.

### Baseball Assistance Team (BAT)

**Mailing Address:** 350 Park Ave., New York, NY 10022. **Telephone:** (212) 339-7884. **FAX:** (212) 888-8632.

**Chairman:** Ralph Branca. **President:** Joe Garagiola. **Vice Presidents:** Joe Black, Earl Wilson. **Executive Director:** Frank Slocum. **Secretary and Treasurer:** Tom Ostertag. **Administrator:** Eleanor Mieszerski.

## BASEBALL CHAPEL

**Mailing Address:** P.O. Box 300, Bloomingdale, NJ 07403. **Telephone:** (201) 838-8111. **FAX:** (201) 838-1145.

**President:** Gary Carter.

**Executive Director:** Dave Swanson.

**Area Representatives:** David Fisher (Toronto, Ontario), Dave Krueger (Ellicott City, MD), Bruce Reynolds (Clearwater, FL), Jeff Totten (Birmingham, MI), John Werhas (Anaheim Hills, CA).

**Minor League Coordinator:** Rip Kirby (Phoenix, AZ). Telephone: (602) 996-7777.

**Latin America Coordinator:** Carlos Rios (Lantana, FL).

## THE BASEBALL TRADE SHOW

**Mailing Address:** P.O. Box A, St. Petersburg, FL 33731. **Telephone:** (813) 823-4050, ext. 102. **FAX:** (813) 821-5819.

**Show Director:** Larry Wiederecht.

## PROFESSIONAL BASEBALL EMPLOYMENT OPPORTUNITIES

**Mailing Address:** P.O. Box 310, Old Fort, NC 28762. **Telephone:** (800) 842-5618. **FAX:** (704) 668-4762.

**Director:** Ann Perkins.

# MEDIA INFORMATION

## BASEBALL STATISTICS, RESEARCH

### ELIAS SPORTS BUREAU, INC.

Official Major League Statistician

**Mailing Address:** 500 Fifth Ave., New York, NY 10110. **Telephone:** (212) 869-1530. **FAX:** (212) 354-0980.

**General Manager:** Seymour Siwoff.

### HOWE SPORTSDATA INTERNATIONAL, INC.

Official Minor League Statistician

**Mailing Address:** Boston Fish Pier, West Bldg. #2, Suite 306, Boston, MA 02210. **Telephone:** (617) 951-0070. **Stats Service:** (617) 951-1379. **FAX:** (617) 737-9960.

**President:** Jay Virshbo. **Vice President/Product Development:** Jim Keller. **Vice President/Administration:** Mike Walczak. **Director of Client Services:** Tom Graham. **Operations Manager:** Chris Pollari. **Communications Manager:** John Foley. **Records Manager:** Bob Townsend. **Data Processing Manager:** Wally Kent. **Manager, Night Operations:** Vin Vitro. **Assistant Manager, Night Operations:** Paul LaRocca. **Statistician/Marketing Coordinator:** Brian Joura. **Statisticians:** Bob Chaban, Dan Landesman.

**West Coast Office:** P.O. Box 5061, San Mateo, CA 94402. **Telephone:** (415) 345-2907. **FAX:** (415) 571-1217. **Executive Vice President:** Bill Weiss.

### STATS, INC.

**Mailing Address:** 8131 N. Monticello, Skokie, IL 60076. **Telephone:** (708) 676-3322. **FAX:** (708) 676-0821.

**President and Chief Executive Officer:** John Dewan. **Vice Presidents:** Susan Dewan, Arthur Ashley, Bob Meyerhoff, Bryan Burns. **Director of Marketing:** Ross Schaufelberger. **Analysts:** David Pinto, Robert Mecca. **Director of Team Operations:** Steve Moyer. **Director of Major League Operations:** Craig Wright. **Director of Publications:** Don Zmenda.

### SOCIETY FOR AMERICAN BASEBALL RESEARCH

**Mailing Address:** P.O. Box 93183, Cleveland, OH 44101. **Telephone:** (216) 575-0500. **FAX:** (216) 575-0502.

**President:** David Pietrusza (Scotia, NY). **Vice President:** Claudia Perry (Houston, TX). **Secretary:** Bob Ruland (Southfield, MI). **Treasurer:** Norman Macht (Baltimore, MD). **Directors:** Frederick Ivor-Campbell, Mark Rucker, Larry Gerlach, David Vincent.

**Executive Director:** Morris Eckhouse. **Office Manager:** John Zajc.

**Publications Director:** Mark Alvarez.

## TELEVISION

### ESPN

**Mailing Address: Bristol Office**—ESPN Plaza, Bristol, CT 06010. **Telephone:** (203) 585-2000. **FAX:** (203) 585-2422. **New York Office**—605 Third Ave., New York, NY 10158. **Telephone:** (212) 916-9200.

**President and Chief Executive Officer:** Steve Bornstein.

**Director, Communications:** Mike Soltys. **Manager, Programming Information:** Diane Lamb. **Communications Coordinator:** Rob Tobias.

**Senior Vice President, Production:** Howard Katz. **Senior Vice President, Programming:** John Wildhack. **Senior Coordinating Producer:** Jed Drake. **Executive Editor:** John Walsh. **Senior Vice President, Remote Productions:** Steve Anderson. **Managing Editor:** Bob Eaton. **Coordinating Producer, Baseball Tonight:** Jeff Schneider.

**Sunday Night Telecasts:** Play-by-play—Jon Miller. Analyst—Joe Morgan.

**Studio Hosts:** Chris Berman, Gary Miller.

**Play-by-Play Announcers:** Unavailable.

**Analyst:** Peter Gammons.

### THE BASEBALL NETWORK

**Mailing Address:** 1301 Sixth Ave., 39th Floor, New York, NY 10019. **Telephone:** (212) 977-7300. **FAX:** (212) 977-7977.

### NBC

**Mailing Address:** 30 Rockefeller Plaza, Suite 1415, New York, NY 10112. **Telephone:** (212) 664-4444. **FAX:** (212) 664-6365.

**President, NBC Sports:** Dick Ebersol.

**Vice President, Sports Information and Special Projects:** Ed Markey.

**Play-by-Play Announcers:** Bob Costas, Dick Enberg, Joe Morgan, Bob Uecker.

## ABC

**Mailing Address:** 47 West 66th St., New York, NY 10023. **Telephone:** (212) 456-7777.

**President, ABC Sports:** Dennis Swanson.

**Director of Sports Information:** Mark Mandel.

**Play-by-Play Announcers:** Tim McCarver, Al Michaels, Brent Musberger, Jim Palmer.

## CTV (Canada)

**Mailing Address:** 250 Yonge St., Suite 1800, Toronto, Ontario M5B 2N8. **Telephone:** (416) 595-4100. **FAX:** (416) 595-5998.

## THE SPORTS NETWORK (Canada)

**Mailing Address:** 2225 Sheppard Ave. East, Suite 10, North York, Ontario M2J 5C2. **Telephone:** (416) 494-1212. **FAX:** (416) 490-7010.

## SUPER STATIONS

### WGN, Chicago (Chicago Cubs, Chicago White Sox)

**Mailing Address:** 2501 Bradley Place, Chicago, IL 60618. **Telephone:** (312) 528-2311.

### WTBS, Atlanta (Atlanta Braves)

**Mailing Address:** One CNN Center, P.O. Box 105366, Atlanta, GA 30348. **Telephone:** (404) 827-1700. **FAX:** (404) 827-1593.

### WWOR, New York (New York Mets)

**Mailing Address:** 9 Broadcast Plaza, Secaucus, NJ 07096. **Telephone:** (201) 330-2246. **FAX:** (201) 330-3844.

# RADIO

## ESPN

**Mailing Address:** ESPN Plaza, Bristol, CT 06010. **Telephone:** (203) 585-2661. **FAX:** (203) 589-5523.

**General Manager:** Mark Mason. **Executive Producer:** John Martin. **Program Director:** Len Weiner.

## CBS

**Mailing Address:** 51 W. 52nd St., New York, NY 10019. **Telephone:** (212) 975-4321. **FAX:** (212) 975-3515.

**Vice President, Executive Producer:** Frank Murphy. **Director, Sports and Features:** David Kurman. **Vice President, Communications:** Helene Blieberg.

# PRESS ASSOCIATIONS

## ASSOCIATED PRESS

**Mailing Address:** 50 Rockefeller Plaza, New York, NY 10020. **Telephone:** (212) 621-1630. **FAX:** (212) 621-1639.

**Sports Editor:** Terry Taylor.

## CANADIAN PRESS

**Mailing Address:** National Office—36 King St. E., Toronto, Ontario M5C 2L9. **Telephone:** (416) 594-2154.

**Sports Editor:** Ross Hopkins. **Baseball Writer:** Doug Smith.

## BASEBALL WRITERS ASSOCIATION OF AMERICA

**Mailing Address:** 78 Olive St., Grove, NY 11755. **Telephone:** (516) 981-7938.

**President:** Paul Meyer (Pittsburgh Post Gazette).

**Vice President:** Jerome Holtzman (Chicago Tribune).

**Board of Directors:** Paul Hagen (Philadephia Daily News), Rick Hummel (St. Louis Post Dispatch), Serge Touchette (Journal de Montreal), Nick Peters (Sacramento Bee).

**Secretary-Treasurer:** Jack O'Connell (Hartford Courant).

## NATIONAL ASSOCIATION OF BASEBALL WRITERS & BROADCASTERS

**Mailing Address:** P.O. Box A, St. Petersburg, FL 33731. **Telephone:** (813) 823-4050. **FAX:** (813) 821-5819.

**Secretary-Treasurer:** Bob Sparks (National Association).

## NATIONAL COLLEGIATE BASEBALL WRITERS ASSOCIATION

**Mailing Address:** P.O. Box 14485, UF Station, Gainesville, FL 32604. **Telephone:** (904) 375-4683, ext. 6102. **FAX:** (904) 375-4809.

**President:** Shelley Poe (West Virginia). **First Vice President:** Bob Brendel (Missouri). **Secretary-Treasurer:** Steve McClain (Florida). **Newsletter Editor:** Mike Stamus (Georgia Tech).

# BASEBALL TICKERS

## SPORTSTICKER

**Mailing Address:** Harborside Financial Center, 600 Plaza Two, Jersey City, NJ 07311. **Telephone:** (201) 309-1200. **FAX:** (201) 860-9742.

**President:** Peter Bavasi. **Vice President:** Rick Alessandri. **General Manager:** John Mastroberardino. **Managing Editor:** Joe Carnicelli. **Administrator, News Operations:** Jim Morganthaler.

# NEWSPAPERS/PERIODICALS

## USA TODAY

**Mailing Address:** 1000 Wilson Blvd., Arlington, VA 22229. **Telephone/Baseball Desk:** (703) 276-3762. **FAX:** (703) 558-3988.

**Baseball Editors:** Bob Velin, Karen Allen. **Baseball Columnist:** Hal Bodley. **Major League Beat Writers:** Rod Beaton (NL), Mel Antonen (AL). **Baseball Reporters:** Chuck Johnson, Mike Dodd. **Agate:** Matt Seaman.

## USA TODAY BASEBALL WEEKLY

**Mailing Address:** 1000 Wilson Blvd., 21st floor, Arlington, VA 22229. **Telephone:** (703) 558-5630. **FAX:** (703) 558-4678.

**Publisher:** Keith Cutler. **Executive Editor:** Lee Ivory. **Editor:** Paul White. **National Sales Manager:** Jim Schiekofer. **Classified Sales Manager:** Lynn Busby.

## THE SPORTING NEWS

**Mailing Address:** 1212 N. Lindbergh Blvd., St. Louis, MO 63132. **Telephone:** (314) 997-7111. **FAX:** (314) 993-7723.

**Editor:** John Rawlings. **Executive Editor:** Steve Meyerhoff.

**Books/Yearbooks:** Mike Nahrstedt (Managing Editor), Mike Huguenin (Assistant Managing Editor).

## SPORTS ILLUSTRATED

**Mailing Address:** Time & Life Building, 1271 Ave. of the Americas, New York, NY 10020. **Telephone:** (212) 522-1212. **FAX, Editorial:** (212) 522-4543. **FAX, Public Relations:** (212) 522-0610.

**Managing Editor:** Mark Mulvoy. **Senior Editor, Baseball:** Mike Bevans. **Writers:** Tim Kurkjian, Steve Rushin, Tom Verducci. **Reporters:** Kostyn Kennedy, Mark McClusky, Damian Slattery.

**Director of Communications:** Art Berke. **Publicity Director:** Roger Jackson.

## BASEBALL DIGEST

**Mailing Address:** 990 Grove St., Evanston, IL 60201. **Telephone:** (708) 491-6440. **FAX:** (708) 491-0867.

**Editor:** John Kuenster. **Managing Editor:** Bob Kuenster.

## STREET AND SMITH'S BASEBALL

**Mailing Address:** 140 East 45th St., New York, NY 10017. **Telephone:** (212) 880-8698. **FAX:** (212) 880-4347.

**Publisher:** Sal Schiliro. **Editor:** Gerard Kavanagh. **Advertising Director:** Angelo Kalogiannis.

## SPRING TRAINING BASEBALL YEARBOOK

**Mailing Address:** P.O. Box 667, Chapel Hill, NC 27514. **Telephone:** (919) 967-2420. **FAX:** (919) 967-6294.

**Publisher:** Merle Thorpe. **Editor:** Myles Friedman.

## COLLEGIATE BASEBALL

**Mailing Address:** P.O. Box 50566, Tucson, AZ 85703. **Telephone:** (602) 623-4530. **FAX:** (602) 624-5501.

**Publisher:** Lou Pavlovich. **Editor:** Lou Pavlovich Jr.

## INTERNATIONAL BASEBALL RUNDOWN

**Mailing Address:** P.O. Box 608, Glen Ellyn, IL 60138. **Telephone:** (708) 668-8341. **FAX:** (708) 668-2148.

**Editor:** Jeff Elijah.

## BASEBALL BUSINESS JOURNAL

**Mailing Address:** P.O. Box 218, Atlantic, VA 23303. **Telephone/FAX:** (804) 824-3942.

**Publisher:** Sports Vue, Inc. **Managing Editor:** Charles Cuttone. **Editor:** Linda Powell Cuttone.

# HOBBY PUBLICATIONS

## BECKETT PUBLICATIONS

**Mailing Address:** 15850 Dallas Parkway, Dallas, TX 75248. **Telephone:** (214) 991-6657. **FAX:** (214) 991-8930.

**Managing Editor:** Pepper Hastings. **Associate Editor, Beckett Baseball Card Monthly:** Mike Payne. **Associate Editor, Focus on Future Stars:** Patrick Wascovich.

## KRAUSE PUBLICATIONS

**Mailing Address:** 700 E. State St., Iola, WI 54990. **Telephone:** (715) 445-2214. **FAX:** (715) 445-4087.

**Publisher:** Hugh McAloon.

**Editor, Fantasy Baseball:** Greg Ambrosius. **Editor, Baseball Cards Magazine:** Greg Ambrosius. **Editor, Sports Collectors Digest:** Tom Mortenson.

## BASEBALL CARD UPDATE

**Mailing Address:** P.O. Box 467, East Haven, CT 06512. **Telephone:** (203) 468-2742.

**Editor:** Mike Brochin.

## TUFF STUFF/TUFF STUFF'S COLLECT!

**Mailing Address:** 1934 East Parham Rd., Richmond, VA 23228.

**Telephone:** (800) 899-8833.

**Editor:** Larry Canale. **News Editor:** Michael Litos.

# TEAM PUBLICATIONS

### COMAN PUBLISHING, INC.

(Atlanta Braves, Boston Red Sox, Cincinnati Reds, New York Mets)

**Mailing Address:** P.O. Box 2331, Durham, NC 27702. **Telephone:** 800-421-7751; (919) 688-0218. **FAX:** (919) 682-1532.

**Publisher:** Stuart Coman.

**Editor, Tomahawk** (Atlanta Braves): Bill Ballew. **Managing Editor, New York Mets Inside Pitch**: Todd McGee. **Editor, Diehard** (Boston Red Sox): George Whitney. **Editor, Reds Report:** Mark Schmetzer.

### JET MEDIA

(Indians Ink)

**Mailing Address:** P.O. Box 1847, Stow, OH 44224. **Telephone:** (216) 953-2200. **FAX:** (216) 953-2202.

**Editor:** Frank Derry.

### PHILLIES REPORT

(Philadelphia Phillies)

**Mailing Address:** P.O. Box 157, Springfield, PA 19064. **Telephone:** (610) 543-4077.

**Editor:** Rich Westcott.

### VINE LINE

(Chicago Cubs)

**Mailing Address:** 1060 W. Addison St., Chicago, IL 60613. **Telephone:** (312) 404-2827.

**Managing Editor:** Ernie Roth. **Editor:** Ed McGregor.

### YANKEES MAGAZINE

(New York Yankees)

**Mailing Address:** Yankee Stadium, Bronx, NY 10451. **Telephone:** (718) 579-4495.

**Publisher:** Tom Bannon. **Editor:** Gregg Mazzola.

# BASEBALL CARD MANUFACTURERS

### DONRUSS TRADING CARDS

**Mailing Address:** 500 N. Field Dr., Lake Forest IL 60045. **Telephone:** (708) 735-7500.

### FLEER

**Mailing Address:** Executive Plaza, 1120 Route 73, Mt. Laurel, NJ 08054. **Telephone:** (609) 231-6200. **FAX:** (609) 727-9460.

### PACIFIC TRADING CARDS

**Mailing Address:** 18424 Hwy. 99, Lynnwood, WA 98037. **Telephone:** (800) 551-2002.

### PINNACLE BRANDS

**Mailing Address:** 924 Avenue J East, Grand Prairie, TX 75050. **Telephone:** (214) 601-7000. **FAX:** (214) 601-7093.

### SCOREBOARD/CLASSIC

**Mailing Address:** 1951 Old Cuthbert Rd., Cherry Hill, NJ 08034. **Telephone:** (609) 354-9000. **FAX:** (609) 427 3565.

### SIGNATURE ROOKIES

**Mailing Address:** P.O. Box 406, Factoryville, PA 18419. **Telephone:** (717) 945-7753. **FAX:** (717) 945-7803.

### TOPPS

**Mailing Address:** One Whitehall St., New York, NY 10004. **Telephone:** (212) 376-0300. **FAX:** (212) 376-0573.

### UPPER DECK

**Mailing Address:** 5909 Sea Otter Place, Carlsbad, CA 92008. **Telephone:** (619) 929-6500.

# MINOR LEAGUES

# NATIONAL ASSOCIATION

Mike Moore

**Office Address:** 201 Bayshore Dr. SE, St. Petersburg, FL 33701. **Mailing Address:** P.O. Box A, St. Petersburg, FL 33731. **Telephone:** (813) 822-6937. **FAX:** (813) 821-5819.

**Founded:** 1901.

**President:** Mike Moore.

**Vice President:** Stan Brand (Washington, DC).

**Chief Operating Officer:** Pat O'Conner.

**General Counsel:** Ben Hayes. **Special Counsel:** George Yund (Cincinnati, OH).

**Executive Director/Special Events, Projects:** Bob Sparks. **Executive Director/ Business, Finance:** Bob Miller. **Director of Marketing and Public Relations:** Ron Myers. **Director of Licensing:** Misann Ellmaker. **Director of Information:** Larry Wiederecht. **Manager, Trademark Services:** Brian Warnock. **Manager of Sales and Marketing/Coordinator of Facilities:** Tim Brunswick.

**Assistant to the President:** Janet Swengros. **Assistant to the Chief Operating Officer/Marketing:** Kelly Butler. **Assistant to Special Events/ Director of Winter Meetings Registration:** Carolyn Ashe. **Assistant to Licensing/Marketing:** Lori Ann Whitson.

**1995 WINTER MEETINGS:** Dec. 1-7, Los Angeles, CA.

## Affiliated Members/Council of League Presidents

### Class AAA

| League | President | Telephone | FAX Number |
|---|---|---|---|
| American Assn. | Branch Rickey | (513) 271-4800 | (513) 271-7887 |
| International | Randy Mobley | (614) 791-9300 | (614) 791-9009 |
| Mexican | Pedro Treto Cisneros | (525) 557-1007 | (525) 395-2454 |
| Pacific Coast | Bill Cutler | (602) 838-2171 | (602) 838-2741 |

### Class AA

| League | President | Telephone | FAX Number |
|---|---|---|---|
| Eastern | John Levenda | (717) 233-4909 | — |
| Southern | Arnold Fielkow | (404) 428-4749 | (404) 428-4849 |
| Texas | Tom Kayser | (210) 545-5297 | (210) 545-5298 |

### Class A Advanced

| League | President | Telephone | FAX Number |
|---|---|---|---|
| California | Joe Gagliardi | (408) 369-8038 | (408) 369-1409 |
| Carolina | John Hopkins | (910) 691-9030 | (910) 691-9070 |
| Florida State | Chuck Murphy | (904) 252-7479 | (904) 252-7495 |

### Class A

| League | President | Telephone | FAX Number |
|---|---|---|---|
| Midwest | George Spelius | (608) 364-1188 | (608) 364-1913 |
| South Atlantic | John Moss | (704) 739-3466 | (704) 739-1974 |

### Short-Season Class A

| League | President | Telephone | FAX Number |
|---|---|---|---|
| New York-Penn | Bob Julian | (315) 733-8036 | (315) 733-8036 |
| Northwest | Bob Richmond | (503) 686-5412 | (503) 484-7672 |

### Rookie Advanced

| League | President | Telephone | FAX Number |
|---|---|---|---|
| Appalachian | Bill Halstead | (703) 669-3644 | (703) 669-2618 |
| Pioneer | Jim McCurdy | (509) 456-7615 | (509) 456-0136 |

### Rookie

| League | President | Telephone | FAX Number |
|---|---|---|---|
| Arizona | Bob Richmond | (602) 483-8224 | (602) 443-3450 |
| Dominican Summer | Freddy Jana | (809) 565-0714 | — |
| Gulf Coast | Tom Saffell | (813) 966-6407 | (813) 966-6872 |

## National Association Board of Trustees

**American Association**—Dan Ulmer (Louisville). **International League**—Mike Tamburro (Pawtucket). **Pacific Coast League**—Richard Holtzman (Tucson). **Eastern League**—Peter Kirk, vice-chairman (Bowie). **Southern League**—Steve Bryant (Carolina). **Texas League**—Miles Prentice (Midland). **California League**—Lowell Patton (Bakersfield). **Carolina League**—Calvin Falwell (Lynchburg). **Florida State League**—Ken Carson, secretary (Dunedin). **Midwest League**—Dave Walker (Burlington). **South Atlantic League**—Winston Blenckstone (Hagerstown). **New York-Penn League**— Bob Fowler, chairman (Utica). **Northwest League**—Bob Beban (Eugene). **Appalachian League**—Bill Smith (Elizabethton). **Pioneer League**—Bob Wilson (Billings). **Gulf Coast League**—Cam Bonifay (Pirates).

# AMERICAN ASSOCIATION

## Class AAA

**Office Address:** 6801 Miami Ave., Suite 3, Cincinnati, OH 45243. **Telephone:** (513) 271-4800. **FAX:** (513) 271-7887.

**President/Treasurer:** Branch B. Rickey.

**Vice President:** Ken Grandquist. **Secretary:** Max Schumacher.

**Directors:** Joe Adams (Omaha), Clayton Bennett (Oklahoma City), John Dikeou (New Orleans), Ken Grandquist (Iowa), Robert Rich Jr. (Buffalo), Larry Schmittou (Nashville), Max Schumacher (Indianapolis), Dan Ulmer (Louisville).

**Administrative Assistants:** Diane Rickey, Laurie Duncan.

**Years League Active:** 1902-1962, 1969-.

**1995 Opening Date:** April 6. **Closing Date:** Sept. 4.

Branch Rickey

**Member Clubs:** Buffalo, Indianapolis, Iowa, Louisville, Nashville, New Orleans, Oklahoma City, Omaha.

**Playoff Format:** Top four teams qualify. First-place team meets fourth-place team, and second-place team meets third-place team in best-of-5 semifinals. Winners meet in best-of-5 series for league championship.

**No. of Games:** 144.

**All-Star Game:** July 12 at Scranton/Wilkes-Barre (joint Triple-A game).

**Roster Limit:** 23 active, until midnight Aug. 10 when roster can be expanded to 25. **Player Eligibility Rule:** No restrictions.

**Brand of Baseball:** Rawlings.

**Statistician:** Howe Sportsdata International, Boston Fish Pier, West Bldg. #2, Suite 306, Boston MA 02210.

**Umpires:** Mark Barron (Lilburn, GA), Gary Cederstrom (Minot, ND), Chuck Clabough (Ellisville, MO), Eric Cooper (Des Moines, IA), Chris Jones (Wheatridge, CO), Matt Malone (Birmingham, AL), Vince Rainforth (Lincoln, IL), Tony Randazzo (Bloomingdale, IL), Rich Rieker (St. Louis, MO), Richard Roder (Ramsen, IA), Scott Simonides (Lakeland, FL), Bennie Walton (Lake Worth, FL).

### 1994 Standings (Overall)

| Club (Affiliate) | W | L | Pct. | GB | '94 Manager |
|---|---|---|---|---|---|
| *Indianapolis (Reds) | 86 | 57 | .601 | — | Marc Bombard |
| Nashville (White Sox) | 83 | 61 | .576 | 3½ | Rick Renick |
| New Orleans (Brewers) | 78 | 66 | .542 | 8½ | Chris Bando |
| Louisville (Cardinals) | 74 | 68 | .521 | 11½ | Joe Pettini |
| Iowa (Cubs) | 69 | 74 | .483 | 17 | Rick Patterson |
| Omaha (Royals) | 68 | 76 | .472 | 18½ | Jeff Cox |
| Oklahoma City (Rangers) | 61 | 83 | .424 | 25½ | Bobby Jones |
| Buffalo (Pirates) | 55 | 89 | .382 | 31½ | Doc Edwards |

*Won playoffs.

### Stadium Information

| | | Dimensions | | | | |
|---|---|---|---|---|---|---|
| Club | Stadium | LF | CF | RF | Capacity | '94 Att. |
| Buffalo | Pilot Field | 325 | 410 | 325 | 20,900 | 982,493 |
| Indianapolis | Owen J. Bush | 335 | 395 | 335 | 12,934 | 339,208 |
| Iowa | Sec Taylor | 335 | 400 | 335 | 10,500 | 485,734 |
| Louisville | Cardinal* | 360 | 405 | 312 | 33,500 | 573,174 |
| Nashville | Herschel Greer | 327 | 400 | 327 | 17,000 | 300,827 |
| New Orleans | Privateer Park | 330 | 400 | 330 | 4,700 | 186,806 |
| Okla. City | All Sports | 340 | 415 | 340 | 15,000 | 327,044 |
| Omaha | Rosenblatt | 332 | 408 | 332 | 23,000 | 439,277 |

*Artificial Turf playing surface

## BUFFALO
## *BISONS*

**Office Address:** 275 Washington St., Buffalo, NY 14203. **Mailing Address:** P.O. Box 450, Buffalo, NY 14205. **Telephone:** (716) 846-2000. **FAX:** (716) 852-6530.

**Affiliation (first year):** Cleveland Indians (1995). **Years in League:** 1985-.

**Team Colors:** Red, white and blue.

### Ownership, Management

**Operated by:** Bison Baseball, Inc.

**Principal Owner/President:** Robert E. Rich Jr.

**Chairman of the Board:** Robert E. Rich Sr.

**Executive Vice President:** Melinda Rich. **Vice President/Secretary:** William Gisel Jr. **Vice President/Treasurer:** David Rich.

**Vice President/Baseball Operations:** Mike Billoni. **Vice President/ Stadium Services:** Jonathan Dandes. **Vice President/Sales and Marketing:** Marta Hiczewski.

**General Manager:** Mike Buczkowski. **Controller:** John Dougherty. **Head Groundskeeper:** Jim Hornung. **Director of Media Relations:** John Isherwood. **Director of Marketing:** Rick Orienza. **Director of Sales:** Wayne Davis. **Director of Community Relations:** John Wiedeman. **Director of Ticket Sales:** Mike Poreda. **Director of Merchandising:** Nancy Martin. **Marketing Research:** Todd Mazurek. **Baseball Operations:** Bradley Owen. **Office Manager:** Margaret Russo. **Director of Clubhouse Operations:** Ronald Krauza.

### Field Staff

**Manager:** Brian Graham. **Coaches:** Dom Chiti (pitching), Jack Mull.

**Trainer:** Lee Kuntz.

### Game Information

**Radio Announcers:** Pete Weber, Darrian Chapman. **No. of Games Broadcast:** Home-72, Away-72. **Flagship Station:** WGR 550-AM.

**PA Announcer:** Duke McGuire. **Official Scorers:** Kevin Lester, Mike Kelly.

**Stadium Name:** Pilot Field. **Location:** I-190 to Elm Street exit, left on Swan Street. **Standard Game Times:** 7:05 p.m.; Sun. 2:05.

**Visiting Club Hotel:** Buffalo Downtown Holiday Inn, 620 Delaware Ave., Buffalo, NY 14202. Telephone: (716) 886-2121.

## INDIANAPOLIS
## *INDIANS*

**Office Address:** 1501 W. 16th St., Indianapolis, IN 46202. **Telephone:** (317) 269-3545. **FAX:** (317) 269-3541.

**Affiliation (first year):** Cincinnati Reds (1993). **Years in League:** 1902-62, 1969-.

**Team Colors:** Red and black.

### Ownership, Management

**Operated by:** Indianapolis Indians, Inc.

**Chairman of the Board:** Henry Warren.

**President/General Manager:** Max Schumacher. **Assistant General Manager/Director of Sales and Marketing:** Cal Burleson. **Director of Business Operations**: Scott Doehrman. **Senior Account Representatives:** Melinda Doehrman, Howard Kellman. **Director of Stadium Operations:** Dan Madden. **Director of Media Relations:** Mark Walpole. **Publications Editor:** Tim Harms. **Director of Community Relations:** Kenny Roll. **Director of Promotions:** Daryle Keith. **Director of Ticket Sales:** Mike Schneider. **Director of Group Sales:** Randy Lewandowski. **Ticket Office:** Chris Herndon. **Director of Special Projects:** Bruce Schumacher. **Director of Clubhouse Operations:** Bobby Smith. **Office Manager:** Brad Morris.

### Field Staff

**Manager:** Marc Bombard. **Coaches:** Mike Griffin (pitching), Jim Thrift.

**Trainer:** John Young.

### Game Information

**Radio Announcers:** Tim Akins, Brian Giffin, Howard Kellman. **No. of Games Broadcast:** Home-72, Away-72. **Flagship Stations:** WNDE 1260-AM, WIRE 100.9-FM.

**PA Announcer:** Bruce Schumacher. **Official Scorer:** Ron Schludecker.

**Stadium Name:** Owen J. Bush Stadium. **Location:** From east—70

West to 65 North to Meridian Street exit, right to 16th Street, left on 16th Street; From south—65 North to Meridian Street exit; From west—465 North/South to Crawfordsville Road, to 16th Street, right on 16th; From north—Meridian Street South to 16th Street, right on 16th. **Standard Game Times:** 7:15 p.m.; Sun. (April-June) 2, (July-Sept.) 6.

**Visiting Club Hotel:** Ramada Inn South, 4514 S. Emerson Ave., Indianapolis, IN 46203. Telephone: (317) 787-3344.

# IOWA
## *CUBS*

**Office Address:** 350 SW 1st St., Des Moines, IA 50309. **Telephone:** (515) 243-6111. **FAX:** (515) 243-5152.

**Affiliation (first year):** Chicago Cubs (1981). **Years in League:** 1969-.

**Team Colors:** Blue and red.

### Ownership, Management

**Operated by:** Greater Des Moines Baseball Co., Inc.

**Principal Owners:** Ken Grandquist, Dick Easter.

**President:** Ken Grandquist. **Secretary/Treasurer:** Dick Easter.

**General Manager:** Sam Bernabe. **Assistant General Manager:** Todd Guske. **Controller:** Sue Tollefson. **Director of Stadium Operations:** Steve Heimbach. **Head Groundskeeper:** Mike Andresen. **Director of Public Relations:** Rick Rungaitis. **Director of Sales/Marketing:** Kelly Liber. **Account Executives:** Todd Kirke, Jim Nahas. **Director of Group Sales:** Nick Willey. **Office Manager:** Stacy Butcher.

### Field Staff

**Manager:** Ron Clark. **Coaches:** Glenn Adams, Bill Earley (pitching).

**Trainer:** Bob Grimes.

### Game Information

**Radio Announcer:** Deene Ehlis. **No. of Games Broadcast:** Home-72, Away-72. **Flagship Station:** KIOA 940-AM.

**PA Announcer:** Glen Norman, Chuck Shockley. **Official Scorer:** Dick McDonald.

**Stadium Name:** Sec Taylor Stadium. **Location:** I-235 to 3rd Street exit, south on 3rd Street to Court Ave., left to 2nd Street, right on 2nd. **Standard Game Times:** 7:15 p.m.; Sun. (April-May) 2:05, (June-Sept.) 6:05.

**Visiting Club Hotel:** Hotel Savery & Spa, 401 Locust St., Des Moines, IA 50309. Telephone: (800) 798-2151.

# LOUISVILLE
## *REDBIRDS*

**Office Address:** Cardinal Stadium, Phillips Lane and Freedom Way, Louisville, KY 40213.

**Mailing Address:** P.O. Box 36407, Louisville, KY 40233. **Telephone:** (502) 367-9121. **FAX:** (502) 368-5120.

**Affiliation (first year):** St. Louis Cardinals (1982). **Years in League:** 1902-62, 1982-.

**Team Colors:** Red, white and royal blue.

### Ownership, Management

**Operated by:** Louisville Baseball Club, Inc.

**Principal Owners:** Dan Ulmer, John Hillerich III, Dale Owens, Edward Glasscock, Jim Morrissey, Tom Musselman, Bob Stallings, Gary Ulmer.

**Chairman of the Board:** Dan Ulmer. **Corporation President:** John Hillerich III. **Club President:** Gary Ulmer.

**Vice President/General Manager:** Dale Owens. **Assistant General Manager/Director of Marketing and Public Relations:** Tab Brockman. **Assistant General Manager/Director of Sales:** Greg Galiette. **Bookkeeper:** Jane Hoben. **Director of Baseball Operations:** Mary Barney. **Director of Broadcast Operations:** Jim Kelch. **Director of Group Sales:** Tracy Harper. **Director of Stadium Operations:** Howard Dorland. **Director of Stadium Promotions:** Dave Allen. **Ticket Manager:** Dave Arnold.

### Field Staff

**Manager:** Joe Pettini. **Coaches:** Joe Cunningham, Dyar Miller (pitching).

**Trainer:** Mark O'Neal.

### Game Information

**Radio Announcers:** Jim Kelch, Dave Wilson. **No. of Games Broadcast:** Home-72, Away-72. **Flagship Station:** WAVE 970-AM.

**PA Announcer:** Joe Arnold. **Official Scorer:** Ed Peak.

**Stadium Name:** Cardinal Stadium. **Location:** Intersection of I-65 and I-264 at Kentucky Fair and Expo Center. **Standard Game Times:** 7:05 p.m.; Sun. 1:30.

**Visiting Club Hotels:** Executive Inn, 978 Phillips Lane, Louisville, KY 40213. Telephone: (502) 367-9121; Days Inn, 101 E. Jefferson St., Louisville, KY 40202. Telephone: (502) 585-2200.

# NASHVILLE *SOUNDS*

**Office Address:** 534 Chestnut St., Nashville, TN 37203. **Mailing Address:** P.O. Box 23290, Nashville, TN 37202. **Telephone:** (615) 242-4371. **FAX:** (615) 256-5684.

**Affiliation (first year):** Chicago White Sox (1993). **Years in League:** 1985-.

**Team Colors:** Royal blue and red.

## Ownership, Management

**Operated by:** Nashville Sounds Baseball Club, Ltd.

**Principal Owner/President, General Manager:** Larry Schmittou. **Director of Sales/Marketing, Business Operations:** Ron Schmittou. **Director of Stadium Operations:** Brad Dennis. **Assistant Director of Stadium Operations:** Brad Meyers. **Head Groundskeeper:** Dave Nasypany. **Director of Media Relations:** Robbie Bohren. **Director of Promotions/Souvenirs:** Mike Schmittou. **Director of Ticket Sales:** Dot Cloud. **Director of Group Sales:** D Smith. **Director of Concessions:** Walt Mehlenbacher. **Office Manager:** Sharon Carson.

## Field Staff

**Manager:** Rick Renick. **Coaches:** Don Cooper (pitching), Roger LaFrancois.

**Trainer:** Greg Latta.

## Game Information

**Radio Announcer:** Steve Carroll. **No. of Games Broadcast:** Home-72, Away-72. **Flagship Station:** WWTN 99.7-FM.

**PA Announcer:** Harvey Magee. **Official Scorer:** Randy Guiler.

**Stadium Name:** Herschel Greer Stadium. **Location:** I-65 to Wedgewood exit. **Standard Game Times:** 7:15 p.m.; Sun. (April-May) 2:05, (June-Sept.) 7:15.

**Visiting Club Hotel:** Quality Inn-Hall of Fame, 1407 Division St., Nashville, TN 37203. **Telephone:** (615) 242-1631.

# NEW ORLEANS *ZEPHYRS*

**Office Address:** 139 Robert E. Lee Blvd., New Orleans, LA 70124. **Mailing Address:** P.O. Box 24672, New Orleans, LA 70184. **Telephone:** (504) 282-6777. **FAX:** (504) 282-9821.

**Affiliation (first year):** Milwaukee Brewers (1993). **Years in League:** 1977, 1993-.

**Team Colors:** Blue and green.

## Ownership, Management

**Operated by:** Dikeou Enterprises.

**Principal Owner/President:** John Dikeou (pending sale of club to Rob Couhig).

**General Manager:** Unavailable. **Controller:** Ira Brenner. **Director of Operations:** Chris Sinatra. **Head Groundskeeper:** Tom Schwaner. **Director of Media/Public Relations:** Les East. **Director of Sales/Marketing:** Carol Asher. **Director of Ticket Sales:** Steve Gibson. **Clubhouse Operations:** Richard Runnels.

## Field Staff

**Manager:** Chris Bando. **Coaches:** Bill Campbell (pitching), Ron Jackson.

**Trainer:** Peter Kolb.

## Game Information

**Radio Announcer:** Ken Trahan. **No. of Games Broadcast:** Home-72, Away-72. **Flagship Stations:** WWL 870-AM, WSMB 1350-AM.

**PA Announcer:** Unavailable. **Official Scorer:** J.L. Vangilder.

**Stadium Name:** Privateer Park. **Location:** I-10 to I-610, Franklin exit lakebound, right on Leon C. Simon Blvd., left on Press Drive. **Standard Game Times:** 7:05 p.m.; Sun. 6:05.

**Visiting Club Hotel:** Avenue Plaza Suites, 2111 St. Charles Ave., New Orleans, LA 70170. Telephone: (504) 566-1212.

## OKLAHOMA CITY
*89ers*

**Office Address:** State Fairgrounds, 89er Drive, Oklahoma City, OK 73107. **Mailing Address:** P.O. Box 75089, Oklahoma City, OK 73147. **Telephone:** (405) 946-8989. **FAX:** (405) 942-4198.

**Affiliation (first year):** Texas Rangers (1983). **Years in League:** 1962, 1969-.

**Team Colors:** Blue, red and white.

### Ownership, Management

**Operated by:** Oklahoma City Athletic Club, Inc.

**President:** Clayton Bennett. **Vice Presidents:** Larry Mathis, Bill Mathis. **Secretary/Treasurer:** John Perri.

**Assistant General Managers:** Joe Holt, Dorsena Picknell. **Director of Public Relations/Marketing:** John Allgood. **Sales Director:** Brad Tammen. **Assistant Sales Directors:** Geoff Dulaney, Michael Morey. **Account Executives:** Jeff Brown, Rob Day, Brian McPherson, Nancy Mullins, Stephanie Requa. **Head Groundskeeper:** Russell Brown. **Operations Assistants:** Dee Hood, Andrew Putnam. **Administrative Assistant:** Sandy Candler.

### Field Staff

**Manager:** Greg Biagini. **Coach:** Tom Brown (pitching).

**Trainer:** Greg Harrel.

### Game Information

**Radio Announcer:** Brian Barnhart. **No. of Games Broadcast:** Home-72, Away-72. **Flagship Station:** WKY 930-AM.

**PA Announcer:** Unavailable. **Official Scorer:** Volney Meece.

**Stadium Name:** All Sports Stadium. **Location:** I-44 West to NW 10th Street, east to 89er Drive on the State Fairgrounds. **Standard Game Times:** April-May 6:35 p.m., June-Aug. 7:05; Sun. 1:35.

**Visiting Club Hotel:** Holiday Inn Northwest, 3535 NW 39th Expressway, Oklahoma City, OK 73147. Telephone: (405) 947-2351.

## OMAHA
*ROYALS*

**Office Address:** 1202 Bert Murphy Ave., Omaha, NE 68107. **Mailing Address:** P.O. Box 3665, Omaha, NE 68103. **Telephone:** (402) 734-2550. **FAX:** (402) 734-7166.

**Affiliation (first year):** Kansas City Royals (1969). **Years in League:** 1955-59, 1961-62, 1969-.

### Ownership, Management

**Operated by:** Omaha Royals, LP.

**Principal Owners:** Union Pacific Railroad, Warren Buffett, Walter Scott Jr.

**President:** Joe Adams.

**Vice President/General Manager:** Bill Gorman. **Assistant General Manager:** Terry Wendlandt. **Director of Marketing and Public Relations:** Rob Goodman. **Ticket Manager:** Mark Morris. **Administrative Assistant:** Kay Besta. **Controller:** Jessica Graner. **Comptroller:** Sue Nicholson. **Account Representatives:** Mike Mashanic, Mike Stephens. **Administrative Receptionist:** Marlene Lee. **General Manager, Concessions:** Bill Greathouse. **Stadium Superintendent:** Jesse Cuevas.

### Field Staff

**Manager:** Mike Jirschele. **Coaches:** Mike Alvarez (pitching), Tom Poquette.

**Trainer:** Mark Farnsworth.

### Game Information

**Radio Announcers:** Frank Adkisson, Kevin McNabb. **No. of Games Broadcast:** Home-72, Away-72. **Flagship Station:** KEZO 1490-AM.

**PA Announcer:** Unavailable. **Official Scorer:** Howard Brantz.

**Stadium Name:** Rosenblatt Stadium. **Location:** I-80 to 13th Street South exit, south one block. **Standard Game Times:** 7:05 p.m.; Wed. 12:05; Sun. 2:05.

**Visiting Club Hotel:** Ramada Inn Central, 7007 Grover St., Omaha, NE 68106. Telephone: (402) 397-7030.

# INTERNATIONAL LEAGUE

## Class AAA

Randy Mobley

**Office Address:** 55 South High St., Suite 202, Dublin, OH 43017. **Telephone:** (614) 791-9300. **FAX:** (614) 791-9009.

**President/Treasurer:** Randy Mobley.

**Vice Presidents:** Harold Cooper, Dave Rosenfield, George Sisler. **Corporate Secretary:** Richard Davis.

**Directors:** Bruce Baldwin (Richmond), Gene Cook (Toledo), Howard Darwin (Ottawa), Dave Rosenfield (Norfolk), Ken Schnacke (Columbus), Naomi Silver (Rochester), Tex Simone (Syracuse), Spencer Stolpen (Charlotte), Mike Tamburro (Pawtucket), Bill Terlecky (Scranton/Wilkes-Barre).

**Office Secretary:** Marcia Willison.

**Years League Active:** 1884-.

**Division Structure: East**—Ottawa, Pawtucket, Rochester, Scranton/Wilkes-Barre, Syracuse. **West**—Charlotte, Columbus, Norfolk, Richmond, Toledo.

**1995 Opening Date:** April 6. **Closing Date:** Sept. 2.

**No. of Games:** 142.

**Playoff Format:** First-place teams in each division play second-place teams in best-of-5 series. Winners meet in best-of-5 series for league championship.

**All-Star Game:** July 12 at Scranton/Wilkes-Barre (joint Triple-A game).

**Roster Limit:** 23 active, until midnight Aug. 10 when roster can be expanded to 25. **Player Eligibility Rule:** No restrictions.

**Brand of Baseball:** Rawlings ROM-INT.

**Statistician:** Howe Sportsdata International, Boston Fish Pier, West Bldg. #2—Suite 306, Boston MA 02210.

**Umpires:** C.B. Bucknor (Brooklyn, N.Y.), Pete Celestino (Lindenhurst, N.Y.), Pat Connors (Berlin, WI), Lazaro Diaz (Miami, FL), Bruce Dreckman (Marcus, IA), Doug Eddings (Las Cruces, NM), Brian Gibbons (South Bend, IN), Ed Hickox (DeLand, FL), Gerald Meals (Salem, OH), Paul Nauert (Norcross, GA), Brian O'Nora (Youngstown, OH), Scott Potter (Holly Hill, FL), Greg Street (Wendell, NC), Jim Wheeler (Little Rock, AR), Matt Winnans (Watertown, CT).

### 1994 Standings (Overall)

| Club (Affiliate) | W | L | Pct. | GB | '94 Manager(s) |
|---|---|---|---|---|---|
| *#Richmond (Braves) | 80 | 61 | .567 | — | Grady Little |
| #Pawtucket (Red Sox) | 78 | 64 | .549 | 2½ | Buddy Bailey |
| Charlotte (Indians) | 77 | 65 | .542 | 3½ | Brian Graham |
| Columbus (Yankees) | 74 | 68 | .521 | 6½ | Stump Merrill |
| Syracuse (Blue Jays) | 71 | 71 | .500 | 9½ | Bob Didier |
| Ottawa (Expos) | 70 | 72 | .493 | 10½ | Jim Tracy |
| Rochester (Orioles) | 67 | 74 | .475 | 13 | Bob Miscik |
| Norfolk (Mets) | 67 | 75 | .472 | 13½ | Bobby Valentine |
| Toledo (Tigers) | 63 | 79 | .444 | 17½ | Joe Sparks, Larry Parrish |
| Scranton/W-B (Phillies) | 62 | 80 | .437 | 18½ | Mike Quade |

*Won playoffs #Won division title.

### Stadium Information

| | | Dimensions | | | | |
|---|---|---|---|---|---|---|
| Club | Stadium | LF | CF | RF | Capacity | '94 Att. |
| Charlotte | Knights Castle | 325 | 400 | 325 | 10,002 | 391,730 |
| Columbus | Cooper* | 355 | 400 | 330 | 15,000 | 535,145 |
| Norfolk | Harbor Park | 333 | 410 | 338 | 12,057 | 546,826 |
| Ottawa | Ottawa | 325 | 404 | 325 | 10,332 | 596,858 |
| Pawtucket | McCoy | 325 | 380 | 325 | 6,010 | 469,029 |
| Richmond | The Diamond | 330 | 402 | 330 | 12,146 | 507,322 |
| Rochester | Silver | 320 | 415 | 315 | 11,000 | 364,188 |
| Scranton | Lackawanna County* | 330 | 408 | 330 | 10,800 | 476,053 |
| Syracuse | MacArthur | 320 | 434 | 320 | 8,416 | 329,594 |
| Toledo | Ned Skeldon | 325 | 410 | 325 | 10,025 | 293,124 |

*Artificial Turf playing surface

## CHARLOTTE *KNIGHTS*

**Office Address:** 2280 Deerfield Dr., Fort Mill, SC 29716. **Mailing Address:** P.O. Box 1207, Fort Mill, SC 29716. **Telephone:** (803) 548-8050 or (704) 357-8071. **FAX:** (803) 548-8055.

**Affiliation (first year):** Florida Marlins (1995). **Years in League:** 1993-.
**Team Colors:** Teal and purple.

### Ownership, Management

**Operated by:** Charlotte Baseball Inc.
**Principal Owner/Chairman of the Board:** George Shinn.
**President:** Spencer Stolpen.
**Vice President/Business Operations:** Sam Russo.

**General Manager:** Pete Moore. **Controller:** Lisa Barnette. **Director of Stadium Operations:** Marc Farha. **Director of Media Relations:** Karl Lyles. **Director of Sales/Marketing:** Julie Sigmon. **Account Representatives:** Chad Bolen, Scott Graham, Jeff Griggs, Alfred Hamilton, Jon Percival. **Director of Community Relations:** Lin Pugh. **Director of Promotions:** Lisa Chico. **Director of Ticket Sales:** Chris Carroll. **Director of Group Sales:** Dwayne Coulter. **Head Groundskeeper:** Larry Rhodes. **Clubhouse Operations:** Jody Pucello. **Office Manager:** Susan Buff. **Receptionist:** Felicia Hill. **Accountant:** Lee Nunnally.

### Field Staff

**Manager:** Sal Rende. **Coaches:** Adrian Garrett, Mike Parrott (pitching). **Trainer:** Mike Leon.

### Game Information

**Radio Announcer:** Pat McConnell. **No. of Games Broadcast:** Home-71, Away-71. **Flagship Station:** WFOX 610-AM.

**PA Announcer:** Unavailable. **Official Scorers:** Sam Copeland, Ed Walton.

**Stadium Name:** Knights Castle. **Location:** Exit 88 off I-77, Gold Hill Road to Deerfield Drive. **Standard Game Times:** 7:05 p.m.; Sun. (April-May) 2:05, (June-Sept.) 6:05.

**Visiting Club Hotel:** Charlotte Marriott Executive Park, 5700 Westpark Dr., Charlotte, NC 28217. Telephone: (704) 527-9650.

## COLUMBUS *CLIPPERS*

**Office Address:** 1155 W. Mound St., Columbus, OH 43223. **Telephone:** (614) 462-5250. **FAX:** (614) 462-3271.

**Affiliation (first year):** New York Yankees (1979). **Years in League:** 1955-70, 1977-.

**Team Colors:** Red, white and blue.

### Ownership, Management

**Operated by:** Columbus Baseball Team, Inc.
**Principal Owner:** Franklin County, Ohio.
**Chairman:** Donald Borror. **President:** Richard Smith.

**General Manager:** Ken Schnacke. **Assistant General Manager/Park Supervisor, Concessions:** Dick Fitzpatrick. **Assistant General Manager/ Marketing, Advertising:** Mark Warren. **Director of Business Operations:** John Allen. **Director of Stadium Operations:** Steve Dalin. **Director of Media Relations:** Brad Kullman. **Director of Merchandising:** Gregg Kaye. **Director of Group Sales:** Mark Galuska. **Assistant Director of Marketing:** Jim Coverstone. **Assistant Director of Advertising:** Chad Ogden. **Assistant Sales Director:** Keif Fetch. **Director of Ticket Operations:** Scott Ziegler. **Clubhouse Operations:** Tom Graney. **Assistant to General Manager:** Judi Timmons. **Secretary:** Jessica Sopko.

### Field Staff

**Manager:** Bill Evers. **Coaches:** Hop Cassady, Gary Denbo, Dave Schuler (pitching). **Trainer:** Darren London.

### Game Information

**Radio Announcer:** Terry Smith. **No. of Games Broadcast:** Home-70, Away-71. **Flagship Station:** WBNS 1460-AM.

**PA Announcers:** Dan Donovan, Skip Mosic, John Ross. **Official Scorers:** Chuck Emmerling, Randy Parker, Jeff Rapp.

**Stadium Name:** Cooper Stadium. **Location:** I-70 West to Mound Street exit (98B), left to stadium; I-70 East to Broad Street exit (97), left on Broad, right on Glenwood. **Standard Game Times:** 7:05 p.m.; Sat. 6:05; Sun.

(April-June) 2:05, (July-Sept.) 6:05.

**Visiting Club Hotel:** Best Western-Columbus North, 888 E. Dublin-Granville Rd., Columbus, OH 43229. Telephone: (614) 888-8230.

# NORFOLK *TIDES*

**Office Address:** 150 Park Ave., Norfolk, VA 23510. **Telephone:** (804) 622-2222. **FAX:** (804) 624-9090.

**Affiliation (first year):** New York Mets (1969). **Years in League:** 1969-.

**Team Colors:** Blue, white and silver.

## Ownership, Management

**Operated by:** Tides Baseball Club, LP.

**President:** Kenneth Young.

**General Manager:** Dave Rosenfield. **Director of Sales:** Ed Nagourney. **Director of Stadium Operations:** Joe Gorza. **Director of Media Relations:** Shon Sbarra. **Director of Ticket Operations:** Ted Hawver. **Ticket Manager:** Linda Waisanen. **Community Relations Manager:** Mike Dotts. **Promotions/Merchandise Coordinator:** Jay Richardson. **Business Manager:** David Hall. **Receptionist:** Mildred Ealy. **Equipment/Clubhouse Manager:** Kevin Kierst. **Head Groundskeeper:** Ken Magner. **Assistant Groundskeeper:** Marc Rosenfield.

## Field Staff

**Manager:** Toby Harrah. **Coaches:** Bob Apodaca (pitching), Ron Washington.

**Trainer:** Joe Hawkins.

## Game Information

**Radio Announcers:** Jack Ankerson, Rob Evans. **No. of Games Broadcast:** Home-71, Away-71. **Flagship Station:** WTAR 790-AM.

**PA Announcer:** Frank Bennett. **Official Scorer:** Bob Moskowitz.

**Stadium Name:** Harbor Park. **Location:** Exit 9 (11A or 11B) off I-264, adjacent to the Elizabeth River. **Standard Game Times:** 7:15 p.m.; Sun. (April-June, Aug.) 1:15, (July) 6:15.

**Visiting Club Hotel:** Omni Norfolk, 777 Waterside Dr., Norfolk, VA 23510. Telephone: (804) 622-6664.

# OTTAWA *LYNX*

**Office Address:** 300 Coventry Road, Ottawa, Ontario K1K 4P5. **Telephone:** (613) 747-5969. **FAX:** (613) 747-0003.

**Affiliation (first year):** Montreal Expos (1993). **Years in League:** 1993-.

**Team Colors:** Black and silver.

## Ownership, Management

**Operated By:** Ottawa Triple-A Baseball.

**Principal Owner/President:** Howard Darwin.

**General Manager:** Joe Bohringer. **Controller:** Ruth Saunders. **Director of Stadium Operations:** Jack Darwin. **Head Groundskeeper:** Al Dungey. **Director of Sales/ Marketing:** Murray Wilson. **Senior Account Representative:** Don Charette. **Assistant Marketing Director:** Sharon Holzman. **Director of Ticket Sales:** Joe Fagan. **Director of Media/Public Relations:** Morgan Quarry. **Director of Special Projects:** Mark McKenna. **Clubhouse Operations:** John Bryk. **Office Manager:** Rupert Darwin. **Merchandise Manager:** Nancy Darwin. **Receptionists:** Heather Gale, Julie Wolff.

## Field Staff

**Manager:** Pete Mackanin. **Coach:** Chuck Kniffin (pitching).

**Trainer:** Jim Young.

## Game Information

**Radio Announcer:** Mark Sutcliffe. **No. of Games Broadcast:** Home-20, Away-0. **Flagship Station:** CFRA 580-AM.

**PA Announcer:** Gord Breen. **Official Scorer:** Randy Fix.

**Stadium Name:** Ottawa Stadium. **Location:** Hwy. 417 to Vanier Parkway North, right on Coventry Road. **Standard Game Times:** 7:05 p.m.; Sat. and Sun. 2:05.

**Visiting Club Hotel:** Chimo Hotel, 1199 Joseph Cyr St., Ottawa, Ontario K1J 7T4. Telephone: (613) 744-1060.

## PAWTUCKET
## *RED SOX*

**Office Address:** One Columbus Ave., Pawtucket, RI 02860. **Mailing Address:** P.O. Box 2365, Pawtucket, RI 02861. **Telephone:** (401) 724-7300. **FAX:** (401) 724-2140.

**Affiliation (first year):** Boston Red Sox (1973). **Years in League:** 1973-.

**Team Colors:** Red, white and blue.

### Ownership, Management

**Operated by:** Pawtucket Red Sox Baseball Club, Inc.

**Principal Owner/Chairman:** Ben Mondor. **President:** Mike Tamburro.

**Vice President/General Manager:** Lou Schwechheimer. **Vice President/Treasurer:** Kathy Crowley. **Vice President/Sales and Marketing:** Michael Gwynn. **Vice President/Stadium Operations:** Mick Tedesco. **Vice President/Public Relations:** Bill Wanless. **Office Manager:** Kathy Davenport. **Director of Community Relations:** Greg McKinney. **Director of Ticket Sales:** Matt White. **Account Executives:** Ed Brock, Daryl Jasper, Rob Rice. **Director of Hospitality:** Kathy Walsh. **Clubhouse Managers:** Dave Johnson, Chris Parent.

### Field Staff

**Manager:** Buddy Bailey. **Coaches:** Luis Aguayo, John Cumberland (pitching).

**Trainer:** Kent Qualls.

### Game Information

**Radio Announcers:** Jack LeFaivre, Dave Shea. **No. of Games Broadcast:** Home-71, Away-71. **Flagship Station:** WARA 1320-AM.

**PA Announcer:** Jim Martin. **Official Scorer:** Unavailable.

**Stadium Name:** McCoy Stadium. **Location:** I-95 North to exit 28 (School Street); I-95 South to exit 2A (Newport Avenue). **Standard Game Times:** 7 p.m., Sun. 1.

**Visiting Club Hotel:** Comfort Inn, 2 George St., Pawtucket, RI 02860. Telephone: (401) 723-6700.

## RICHMOND
## *BRAVES*

**Office Address:** 3001 N. Boulevard, Richmond, VA 23230. **Mailing Address:** P.O. Box 6667, Richmond, VA 23230. **Telephone:** (804) 359-4444. **FAX:** (804) 359-0731.

**Affiliation (first year):** Atlanta Braves (1966). **Years in League:** 1884, 1915-17, 1954-64, 1966-.

**Team Colors:** Red and blue.

### Ownership, Management

**Operated by:** Atlanta National League Baseball, Inc.

**Principal Owner:** Ted Turner.

**General Manager:** Bruce Baldwin. **Assistant General Manager:** Ken Clary. **Office Manager:** Joanne Curnutt. **Receptionist:** Janet Harvey. **Stadium Operations Manager:** Dan Hoffman. **Field Maintenance Manager:** John Ferguson. **Group Sales Manager:** Rod Edmiston. **Assistant Group Sales Manager:** Todd Smeltzer. **Ticket Sales Manager:** Colleen Standiford. **Public Relations Manager:** John Atkinson. **Administrative Assistant:** Barbara Alvis. **Clubhouse Manager:** Steve Barden.

### Field Staff

**Manager:** Grady Little. **Coaches:** Glenn Hubbard, Bill Fischer (pitching).

**Trainer:** Jim Lovell.

### Game Information

**Radio Announcers:** Steve Stewart, Bill Roth. **No. of Games Broadcast:** Home-71, Away-71. **Flagship Station:** WRVA 910-AM.

**PA Announcer:** Mike Blacker. **Official Scorer:** Leonard Alley.

**Stadium Name:** The Diamond. **Location:** I-64 & I-95 junction, exit 78. **Standard Game Times:** 7 p.m.; Sun. 2.

**Visiting Club Hotel:** Holiday Inn I-64, 6531 W. Broad St., Richmond, VA 23230. Telephone: (804) 285-9951.

## ROCHESTER
## *RED WINGS*

**Office Address:** 500 Norton St., Rochester, NY 14621. **Telephone:** (716) 467-3000. **FAX:** (716) 467-6732.

**Affiliation (first year):** Baltimore Orioles (1961). **Years in League:** 1885-89, 1891-92, 1895-.

**Team Colors:** Red and black.

### Ownership, Management

**Operated by:** Rochester Community Baseball, Inc.

**Chairman of the Board:** Fred Strauss. **President:** Elliot Curwin. **Corporate Secreatry:** Naomi Silver.

**General Manager:** Dan Mason. **Controller:** Darlene Giardina. **Director of Stadium Operations:** Gene Buonomo. **Director of Media Relations/Broadcasting:** Glenn Geffner. **Director of Community Relations:** Chuck Hinkel. **Director of Promotions:** Steve Salluzzo. **Director of Group Sales:** Joe Steven Altobelli. **Director of Operations:** Will Rumbold. **Director of Merchandising:** Wendy Morrissette. **Ticket Office Manager:** Dave Welker. **Executive Secretary:** Pat Santillo. **Director of Concessions:** Greg Pries.

### Field Staff

**Manager:** Marv Foley. **Coaches:** Butch Davis, Claude Osteen (pitching).

**Trainer:** Kevin Harmon.

### Game Information

**Radio Announcer:** Glenn Geffner. **No. of Games Broadcast:** Home-71, Away-71. **Flagship Station:** WCMF 990-AM.

**PA Announcer:** Mike Schopp. **Official Scorer:** Len Lustik.

**Stadium Name:** Silver Stadium. **Location:** Two blocks south of Rt. 104, between Seneca and Clinton Avenues. **Standard Game Times:** 7:05 p.m., Sun. 2:05.

**Visiting Club Hotel:** Holiday Inn-Genesee Plaza, 120 E. Main St., Rochester, NY 14621. Telephone: (716) 546-6400.

## SCRANTON/W-B
## *RED BARONS*

**Office Address:** 235 Montage Mountain Rd., Moosic, PA 18507. **Mailing Address:** P.O. Box 3449, Scranton, PA 18505. **Telephone:** (717) 969-2255. **FAX:** (717) 963-6564.

**Affiliation (first year):** Philadelphia Phillies (1989). **Years in League:** 1989-.

**Team Colors:** Navy blue and cardinal.

### Ownership, Management

**Operated by:** Lackawanna County.

**Chairman of the Board:** Ted Burns.

**General Manager:** Bill Terlecky. **Assistant General Manager:** Rick Muntean. **Controller:** Tom Durkin. **Director of Public Relations:** Mike Cummings. **Head Groundskeeper:** Ray Nick. **Director of Ticket Sales:** Cathy Kacer. **Director of Group Sales:** Erin Muldoon. **Clubhouse Operations:** Frank Worsnick. **Office Manager:** Donna McDonald. **Administrative Assistants:** Kelly Byron, Karen Healey.

### Field Staff

**Manager:** Mike Quade. **Coaches:** Dave Cash, Jim Wright (pitching).

**Trainer:** Craig Strobel.

### Game Information

**Radio Announcer:** Kent Westling. **No. of Games Broadcast:** Home-71, Away-71. **Flagship Station:** WILK 980-AM.

**PA Announcer:** John Davies. **Official Scorer:** Robert McGoff.

**Stadium Name:** Lackawanna County Stadium. **Location:** I-81 to exit 51 (Davis Street). **Standard Game Times:** 7:30 p.m., Sun. 6.

**Visiting Club Hotel:** Lackawanna Station Hotel, 700 Lackawanna Ave., Scranton, PA 18503. Telephone: (717) 342-8300.

## SYRACUSE
## *CHIEFS*

**Office Address:** MacArthur Stadium, Syracuse, NY 13208. **Telephone:** (315) 474-7833. **FAX:** (315) 474-2658.

**Affiliation (first year):** Toronto Blue Jays (1978). **Years in League:** 1885-89, 1891-92, 1894-1901, 1918, 1920-27, 1934-55, 1961-.

**Team Colors:** Reflex blue and process blue.

### Ownership, Management

**Operated by:** Community Owned Baseball Club of Central New York, Inc.

**Chairman of the Board:** Richard Ryan. **President:** Donald Waful.

**Executive Vice President/General Manager:** Anthony "Tex" Simone. **Assistant General Manager:** John Simone. **Director of Business Operations:** John Eberl. **Director of Stadium Operations:** Paul Sechler. **Director of Sales and Marketing:** Lu Ann Wall. **Director of Ticket Sales:** Tom Van Schaack. **Director of Group Sales:** Vic Galucci. **Clubhouse Operations:** Elliott Degroot, Ted Phillips.

### Field Staff

**Manager:** Bob Didier. **Coaches:** Bill Monbouquette (pitching), Hector Torres.

**Trainer:** Steve McInerney.

### Game Information

**Radio Announcer:** Matt Vasgersian. **No. of Games Broadcast:** Home-71, Away-71. **Flagship Station:** WHEN 620-AM.

**PA Announcer:** Chris Cranozio. **Official Scorer:** Tom Leo.

**Stadium Name:** MacArthur Stadium. **Location:** Exit 22 (Hiawatha Blvd.) on westbound Route 81; Exit 7 (Court St.) on eastbound Route 690. **Standard Game Times:** 7 p.m., Sun. 6.

**Visiting Club Hotel:** Ramada Inn, 1308 Buckley Rd., North Syracuse, NY 13212. Telephone: (315) 457-8670.

## TOLEDO
## *MUD HENS*

**Office Address:** 2901 Key St., Maumee, OH 43537. **Mailing Address:** P.O. Box 6212, Toledo, OH 43614. **Telephone:** (419) 893-9483. **FAX:** (419) 893-5847.

**Affiliation (first year):** Detroit Tigers (1987). **Years in League:** 1889, 1965-.

**Team Colors:** Red, white and blue.

### Ownership, Management

**Operated by:** Toledo Mud Hens Baseball Club, Inc.

**Principal Owner:** Lucas County.

**President:** Edwin Bergsmark.

**General Manager:** Gene Cook. **Assistant General Manager/ Community Relations:** Jeff Condon. **Assistant General Manager/Media Relations:** Jim Konecny. **Assistant General Manager/Ticket Operations:** Ron Rado. **Marketing and Entertainment:** Scott Jeffer. **Marketing and Promotions:** Neil Neukam. **Business Manager:** Beth Keller. **Office Manager:** Carol Hamilton.

### Field Staff

**Manager:** Tom Runnells. **Coaches:** Rick Adair (pitching), Skeeter Barnes.

**Trainer:** Lon Pinhey.

### Game Information

**Radio Announcers:** Jim Weber, Frank Gilhooley. **No. of Games Broadcast:** Home-71, Away-71. **Flagship Station:** WMTR 96.1-FM.

**PA Announcer:** John Keller. **Official Scorer:** John Wagner.

**Stadium Name:** Ned Skeldon Stadium. **Location:** One mile east of Ohio Turnpike, exit 4 to Reynolds Road, north to Heatherdowns, right on Key Street; I-75 South to exit 201-A, right on Key Street. **Standard Game Times:** 7 p.m., Sun. 2.

**Visiting Club Hotel:** Ramada Inn, 2340 S. Reynolds Rd., Toledo, OH 43614. Telephone: (419) 865-1361.

# PACIFIC COAST LEAGUE

## Class AAA

Bill Cutler

**Mailing Address:** 2345 S. Alma School Road, Suite 110, Mesa, AZ 85210. **Telephone:** (602) 838-2171. **FAX:** (602) 838-2741.

**President/Secretary-Treasurer:** Bill Cutler. **Vice President:** Pat McKernan.

**Directors:** Joe Buzas (Salt Lake City), George Foster (Tacoma), Bob Goughan (Colorado Springs), Richard Holtzman (Tucson), Brent Imlach (Vancouver), Mel Kowalchuk (Edmonton), Pat McKernan (Albuquerque), Craig Pletenik (Phoenix), Russ Parker (Calgary), Hank Stickney (Las Vegas).

**Executive Committee:** Gary Arthur, George Foster, Bob Goughan.

**Office Secretaries:** Jeannie Bordes, Kathy Cutler.

**Years League Active:** 1903-1995.

**1995 Opening Date:** April 6. **Closing Date:** Sept. 4.

**No. of Games:** 144.

**Division Structure: Northern**—Calgary, Edmonton, Salt Lake City, Tacoma, Vancouver. **Southern**—Albuquerque, Colorado Springs, Las Vegas, Phoenix, Tucson.

**Playoff Format:** First-half division winners play second-half division winners in best-of-5 series. Division playoff winners meet in best-of-5 series for league championship.

**All-Star Game:** July 12 at Scranton/Wilkes-Barre (joint Triple-A game).

**Roster Limit:** 23 active, until midnight Aug. 10 when roster can be expanded to 25. **Player Eligibility Rule:** No restrictions.

**Brand of Baseball:** Rawlings.

**Statistician:** Howe Sportsdata International, Boston Fish Pier, West Bldg. #2—Suite 306, Boston MA 02210.

**Umpires:** Ron Barnes (El Cerrito, CA), Ted Barrett (Mesa, AZ), Ed Bean (Winter Haven, FL), Robert Brooks (Pleasanton, CA), Field Culbreth (Inman, SC), Kerwin Danley (Mesa, AZ), John Dezelan (Pittsburgh, PA), Ray DiMuro (Tucson, AZ), Mark Erramouspe (Rock Springs, WY), Mike Everitt (Phoenix, AZ), Martin Foster (Denver, CO), Brad Geaslin (Houston, TX), Jeff Nelson (Cottage Grove, MN), Tim Ronan (Anchorage, AK), Tim Vessey (Las Vegas, NV).

### 1994 Standings (Overall)

| Club (Affiliate) | W | L | Pct. | GB | '94 Manager |
|---|---|---|---|---|---|
| *#Albuquerque (Dodgers) | 83 | 56 | .597 | — | Rick Dempsey |
| Tucson (Astros) | 81 | 63 | .563 | 4½ | Rick Sweet |
| #Vancouver (Angels) | 77 | 65 | .542 | 7½ | Don Long |
| Salt Lake (Twins) | 74 | 70 | .514 | 11½ | Scott Ullger |
| #Colorado Springs (Rockies) | 70 | 69 | .504 | 13 | Brad Mills |
| Calgary (Mariners) | 71 | 72 | .497 | 14 | Steve Smith |
| Phoenix (Giants) | 70 | 72 | .493 | 14½ | Carlos Alfonso |
| Edmonton (Marlins) | 67 | 75 | .472 | 17½ | Sal Rende |
| Tacoma (Athletics) | 61 | 81 | .430 | 23½ | Casey Parsons |
| Las Vegas (Padres) | 56 | 87 | .392 | 29 | Russ Nixon |

*Won playoffs. #Won split-season pennant.

### Stadium Information

| | | Dimensions | | | | |
|---|---|---|---|---|---|---|
| Club | Stadium | LF | CF | RF | Capacity | '94 Att. |
| Albuquerque | Albuq. Sports | 360 | 410 | 340 | 10,510 | 376,272 |
| Calgary | Foothills | 345 | 400 | 345 | 8,000 | 297,981 |
| Colo. Springs | Sky Sox | 350 | 400 | 350 | 9,500 | 211,671 |
| Edmonton | Edmonton | 340 | 420 | 320 | 10,000 | 272,631 |
| Las Vegas | Cashman Field | 328 | 433 | 328 | 9,334 | 338,834 |
| Phoenix | Scottsdale | 360 | 430 | 340 | 10,200 | 315,859 |
| Salt Lake | Franklin Quest Field | 345 | 420 | 315 | 15,000 | 713,224 |
| Tacoma | Cheney | 325 | 425 | 325 | 10,000 | 347,719 |
| Tucson | Hi Corbett Field | 366 | 392 | 348 | 8,000 | 309,623 |
| Vancouver | Nat Bailey | 335 | 395 | 335 | 6,500 | 320,863 |

# ALBUQUERQUE
## *DUKES*

**Office Address:** 1601 Stadium Blvd. SE, Albuquerque, NM 87106. **Telephone:** (505) 243-1791. **FAX:** (505) 842-0561.

**Affiliation (first year):** Los Angeles Dodgers (1972). **Years in League:** 1972-.

**Team Colors:** Red and gold.

### Ownership, Management

**Operated by:** Albuquerque Professional Baseball, Inc.

**Principal Owner/Chairman of the Board:** Robert Lozinak.

**President/General Manager:** Pat McKernan. **Director of Media Relations:** David Sheriff. **Director of Ticket/Group Sales:** Duane Miller. **Director of Accounting:** Dawnene Shoup. **Director of Administration/ General Counsel:** Scott Jacobson. **Director of Sales:** James Guscott. **Concessions Manager:** Charles Ditzenberger. **Director of Marketing:** Glenn Kaiser. **Director of Merchandising:** Patrick McKernan. **Director of Stadium Operations:** Kelly Ledbetter.

### Field Staff

**Manager:** Rick Dempsey. **Coaches:** Burt Hooton (pitching), Dick McLaughlin.

**Trainer:** Stan Johnston.

### Game Information

**Radio Announcers:** Jim Lawwill, Mike Roberts. **No. of Games Broadcast:** Home-72, Away-72. **Flagship Station:** KOB 770-AM.

**PA Announcer:** David Sheriff. **Official Scorer:** Gary Herron.

**Stadium Name:** Albuquerque Sports Stadium. **Location:** I-25 to Stadium Blvd. exit, east on Stadium Blvd. **Standard Game Times:** 7 p.m., Sun. 1.

**Visiting Club Hotel:** Plaza Inn Albuquerque, 900 Medical Arts NE, Albuquerque, NM 87102. Telephone: (505) 243-5693.

# CALGARY
## *CANNONS*

**Office Address:** 2255 Crowchild Trail NW, Calgary, Alberta T2M 4M4. **Mailing Address:** P.O. Box 3690, Station B, Calgary, Alberta T2M 4M4. **Telephone:** (403) 284-1111. **FAX:** (403) 284-4343.

**Affiliation (first year):** Pittsburgh Pirates (1995). **Years in League:** 1985-.

**Team Colors:** Red, blue and white.

### Ownership, Management

**Operated by:** Braken Holdings Ltd.

**Principal Owners:** Russ Parker, Diane Parker, Brent Parker, Blake Parker, Darren Parker.

**Chairman of the Board/President:** Russ Parker.

**General Manager:** Gary Arthur. **Director of Accounting:** Chris Poffenroth. **Head Groundskeeper:** Gary Williams. **Director of Media/ Public Relations:** John Traub. **Director of Marketing/Promotions:** Karen Connellan. **Senior Account Representatives:** Mike Kaban, Darren Parker. **Director of Ticket Sales:** Greg Winthers. **Clubhouse Operations:** Blair McAusland. **Receptionist:** Christy Sabados.

### Field Staff

**Manager:** Bobby Meacham. **Coaches:** Wayne Garland (pitching), Ben Oglivie.

**Trainer:** Mike Sandoval.

### Game Information

**Radio Announcer:** Mark Stephen. **No. of Games Bradcast:** Home-23, Away-23. **Flagship Station:** CHQR 770-AM.

**PA Announcer:** Bill Clapham. **Official Scorers:** Darryl Haynes, Gus Collins.

**Stadium Name:** Foothills Stadium. **Location:** Trans Canada Highway to Crowchild Trail, north at intersection of 24th Avenue NW and Crowchild Trail. **Standard Game Times:** 7:05 p.m.; Sun. 1:35.

**Visiting Club Hotel:** Sandman Hotel, 888 7th Ave. SW, Calgary, Alberta T2P 3J3. Telephone: (403) 237-8626.

## COLORADO SPRINGS
## *SKY SOX*

**Office Address:** 4385 Tutt Blvd., Colorado Springs, CO 80922. **Telephone:** (719) 597-1449. **FAX:** (719) 597-2491.

**Affiliation (first year):** Colorado Rockies (1993). **Years in League:** 1988-.

**Team Colors:** Forest green, black and silver.

### Ownership, Management

**Operated by:** Colorado Springs Sky Sox, Inc.

**Principal Owners:** David G. Elmore, D.G. Elmore.

**President/General Manager:** Bob Goughan.

**Senior Vice President/Administration:** Sam Polizzi. **Senior Vice President/Finance:** Carrol Payne. **Vice President/Operations:** Dwight Hall. **Vice President/Marketing:** Rai Henninger. **Vice President/Stadium Operations:** Mark Leasure.

**Assistant General Manager/Public Relations:** Chris Costello. **Assistant General Manager/Corporate Development:** Chad Starbuck. **Assistant General Manager/Advertising:** Nick Sciarratta. **Director of Broadcast Operations:** Dan Karcher. **Director of Group Sales:** Brien Smith. **Director of Merchandising:** Robert Stein. **Clubhouse Operations:** Brian Ochsie, Murlin Whitten. **Director of Stadium Personnel:** John Montarone. **Marketing Representatives:** Josh Beser, Melissa Dudek, Chad Giddens, Chad Girard, Jim Hamel, Frank Scarola, Jeff Vernier. **Concessions:** Bernie Goughan, Don Giuliano.

### Field Staff

**Manager:** Brad Mills. **Coaches:** Frank Funk (pitching), Amos Otis.

**Trainer:** Keith Dugger.

### Game Information

**Radio Announcers:** Dick Chase, Dan Karcher. **No. of Games Bradcast:** Home-72, Away-72. **Flagship Stations:** KRDO 1240-AM, KKPC 1230-AM.

**PA Announcer:** Unavailable. **Official Scorers:** Greg Gandy, Marty Grantz.

**Stadium Name:** Sky Sox Stadium **Location:** I-25 South to Woodmen Road exit, east on Woodmen to Powers Blvd., right on Powers to Barnes Road. **Standard Game Times:** Mon.-Fri. (April-June 16) 6:35, (June 26-Sept.) 7:05; Sat. (April-June 17) 1:35, (June 24-Sept.) 7:05; Sun. 1:35.

**Visiting Club Hotel:** LeBaron Hotel, 314 W. Bijou St., Colorado Springs, CO 80905. Telephone: (719) 471-8680.

## EDMONTON
## *TRAPPERS*

**Office Address:** 10233 96th Ave., Edmonton, Alberta T5K 0A5. **Telephone:** (403) 429-2934. **FAX:** (403) 426-5640.

**Affiliation (first year):** Oakland Athletics (1995). **Years in League:** 1981-.

### Ownership, Management

**Principal Owner:** Peter Pocklington.

**President/General Manager:** Mel Kowalchuk. **Assistant General Manager:** Dennis Henke. **Director of Stadium Operations:** Richard Henke. **Media Communications Coordinator:** Colin MacPhail. **Director of Sales/Marketing:** Rob McGillis. **Senior Account Representatives:** Ken Charuk, Al Coates, Darin Kowalchuk, Gregg Pilling. **Director of Community Relations:** Lauri Holomis. **Director of Ticket Sales:** Barb Little. **Clubhouse Operations:** Quentin Warawa. **Office Manager:** Nancy Yeo.

### Field Staff

**Manager:** Gary Jones. **Coaches:** Orv Franchuk, Pete Richert (pitching).

**Trainer:** Walt Horn.

### Game Information

**Radio Announcer:** Al Coates. **No. of Games Broadcast:** Unavailable. **Flagship Station:** CHED 630-AM.

**PA Announcer/Official Scorer:** Al Coates.

**Stadium Name:** Edmonton Stadium. **Location:** 102nd Street and 96th Avenue. **Standard Game Times:** 7:05/7:35 p.m.; Sat. 7:05; Sun. 2:05.

**Visiting Club Hotel:** Edmonton Hilton, 10235 101st St., Edmonton, Alberta P5J 3E9. Telephone: (403) 428-7111.

## LAS VEGAS
### *STARS*

**Office Address:** 850 Las Vegas Blvd. N., Las Vegas, NV 89101. **Telephone:** (702) 386-7200. **FAX:** (702) 386-7214.

**Affiliation (first year):** San Diego Padres (1982). **Years in League:** 1982-.

**Team Colors:** Black, white, purple and teal.

#### Ownership, Management

**Operated by:** Las Vegas Stars Baseball Club.

**Principal Owners:** Hank Stickney, Ken Stickney.

**General Manager:** Don Logan. **Assistant General Manager:** Mark Grenier. **Controller:** Debbie Camama. **Director of Stadium Operations:** Nick Fitzenreider. **Head Groundskeeper:** Ron Shereda. **Director of Public Relations:** Eric Carrington. **Communications Director:** Bryan Dangerfield. **Director of Sales:** Steve Moser. **Senior Account Representative:** Scott Rikard. **Director of Community Relations:** Jennifer Arden. **Director of Promotions:** Tina Kunzer-Murphy. **Director of Ticket Sales:** Marie Schenk. **Director of Group Sales:** Lyndi Alongi. **Director of Special Projects:** Eric Dornack. **Clubhouse Operations:** Paul Minor. **Office Manager:** Mary McConnell.

#### Field Staff

**Manager:** Tim Flannery. **Coach:** Jon Matlack (pitching).

**Trainer:** Steve Sayles.

#### Game Information

**Radio Announcers:** Jon Sandler, Ken Korach. **No. of Games Broadcast:** Home-72, Away-72. **Flagship Station:** KORK 920-AM.

**PA Announcer:** Stan Harris. **Official Scorer:** Jim Gemma.

**Stadium Name:** Cashman Field. **Location:** Four blocks north of downtown on Las Vegas Blvd., or I-15 to Las Vegas Blvd. exit, north on Las Vegas Blvd. **Standard Game Times:** 7:05 p.m.; Sun. 2:05.

**Visiting Club Hotel:** Las Vegas Club Hotel and Casino, 18 E. Fremont St., Las Vegas, NV 89101. Telephone: (702) 385-1664.

## PHOENIX
### *FIREBIRDS*

**Office Address:** 7503 E. Osborn Rd., 2nd Floor, Scottsdale, AZ 85251. **Mailing Address:** P.O. Box 8528, Scottsdale, AZ 85252. **Telephone:** (602) 275-0500. **FAX:** (602) 990-8987.

**Affiliation (first year):** San Francisco Giants (1966). **Years in League:** 1958-59, 1966-.

**Team Colors:** Navy blue and red.

#### Ownership, Management

**Operated by:** Professional Baseball, Inc.

**Principal Owner:** Martin Stone. **President:** Larry Yount.

**General Manager:** Craig Pletenik. **Controller:** Mary Jo Balthasar. **Director of Stadium Operations:** Bob Linyard. **Head Groundskeeper:** Bill Murphy. **Director of Media/Public Relations:** Mike Muraco. **Director of Sales/Marketing:** Bill Gatlin. **Senior Account Representative:** Jim Bast. **Director of Promotions:** Tom Hecht. **Director of Ticket Sales:** Craig Bradley. **Clubhouse Operations:** Phil Garcia. **Office Manager:** Kristi Goldby. **Director of Sports Marketing:** Dan Wingold. **Public Relations Assistant:** Dave Fanucchi. **Administrative Assistants:** Chris Hatter, Mary LeBlanc, Brenda Morse.

#### Field Staff

**Manager:** Keith Bodie. **Coach:** Steve Cline (pitching).

**Trainer:** Bill Carpine.

#### Game Information

**Radio Announcer:** Russ Langer. **No. of Games Broadcast:** Home-72, Away-72. **Flagship Station:** KXAM 1310-AM.

**PA Announcer:** Bob Baker. **Official Scorer:** Dale Messmer.

**Stadium Name:** Scottsdale Stadium. **Location:** 202 Freeway East, exit on McDowell, right on McDowell, north on Scottsdale Road to Osborn, east to stadium. **Standard Game Times:** 7:05 p.m.; Sun. 6:05.

**Visiting Club Hotel:** Unavailable.

## SALT LAKE
*BUZZ*

**Office Address:** 77 West 1300 S., Salt Lake City, UT 84115. **Mailing Address:** P.O. Box 4108, Salt Lake City, UT 84110. **Telephone:** (801) 485-3800. **FAX:** (801) 485-6818.

**Affiliation (first year):** Minnesota Twins (1994). **Years in League:** 1915-25, 1958-65, 1970-84, 1994-.

**Team Colors:** Navy, gold and teal.

### Ownership, Management

**Operated by:** Buzas Baseball, Inc.

**Principal Owners:** Joe Buzas, Penny Buzas.

**President/Chairman of the Board:** Joe Buzas.

**Vice President/General Manager:** Tammy Felker-White. **Director of Marketing:** Steve Riley. **Director of Sales:** Rob White. **Business Manager:** Jackie Riley. **Media/Public Relations Manager:** Kent Haslam. **Clubhouse/Account Manager:** Rick Pollack. **Ticket Manager:** Jackie George. **Marketing Representative:** Brett Hullinger.

### Field Staff

**Manager:** Phil Roof. **Coaches:** Rick Anderson (pitching), Steve Liddle.

**Trainer:** Jim Kahmann.

### Game Information

**Radio Announcer:** Steve Klauke. **No. of Games Broadcast:** Home-72, Away-72. **Flagship Station:** KISN 570-AM.

**PA Announcers:** Dick Jacobson, Jeff Reeves. **Official Scorers:** Bruce Hilton, Howard Nakagama.

**Stadium Name:** Franklin Quest Field. **Location:** From I-15/I-80, east at 1300 South exit to corner of 1300 South and West Temple. **Standard Game Times:** 7 p.m.; Sun. (April-May) 2, (June-Sept.) 5.

**Visiting Club Hotel:** Red Lion Inn, 255 S. West Temple, Salt Lake City, UT 84101. Telephone: (801) 328-2000.

## TACOMA
*RAINIERS*

**Office Address:** 2502 S. Tyler, Tacoma, WA 98405. **Mailing Address:** P.O. Box 11087, Tacoma, WA 98411. **Telephone:** (206) 752-7707. **FAX:** (206) 752-7135.

**Affiliation (first year):** Seattle Mariners (1995). **Years in League:** 1904-05, 1960-.

**Team Colors:** Blue, teal and gray.

### Ownership, Management

**Operated by:** George's Pastime, Inc.

**Principal Owners:** George Foster, Sue Foster.

**Chairman:** George Foster.

**President/General Manager:** Dave Bean. **Director of Business Operations:** Tom Bordeaux. **Controller:** Maureen Mayo. **Director of Stadium Operations/Groundskeeper:** Bob Christofferson. **Director of Radio Broadcasting:** Bob Robertson. **Manager of Baseball Information/Communications:** Kevin Kalal. **Director of Sales/ Marketing, Group Sales:** Dave Carl. **Senior Account Representatives:** Mike Aceto, James Atterberry, Andrew Lee, Alan Rand, Ted Rich, Bryan Travis, John Zepp. **Director of Community Relations:** Scott Battishill. **Director of Promotions:** Mel Taylor. **Director of Ticket Sales:** Dan Graham. **Administrative Secretary:** Jan Plein. **Director of Merchandise:** Brendon Kensel. **Director of Food Services:** Bo Gottfried. **Administrative Assistant:** Tara Duncan.

### Field Staff

**Manager:** Steve Smith. **Coaches:** Jeff Andrews (pitching), Ken Griffey Sr.

**Trainer:** Randy Roetter.

### Game Information

**Radio Announcer:** Bob Robertson. **No. of Games Broadcast:** Home-72, Away-72. **Flagship Station:** Unavailable.

**PA Announcer:** Jeff Randall. **Official Scorer:** Darin Padur.

**Stadium Name:** Cheney Stadium. **Location:** From I-5, exit 132 (Highway 16 West) for two miles, 19th Avenue East exit to light, right for ½ mile. **Standard Game Times:** 7:05 p.m.; Sun. 1:35.

**Visiting Club Hotel:** Tacoma-Sheraton, 1320 Broadway, Tacoma, WA 98402. Telephone: (206) 572-3200.

## TUCSON
## *TOROS*

**Office Address:** 3400 E. Camino Campestre, Tucson, AZ 85716. **Mailing Address:** P.O. Box 27045, Tucson, AZ 85726. **Telephone:** (602) 325-2621. **FAX:** (602) 327-2371.

**Affiliation (first year):** Houston Astros (1980). **Years in League:** 1969-.

**Team Colors:** Red, black and yellow.

### Ownership, Management

**Operated by:** Tucson Toros, Inc.

**Principal Owner/President:** Richard Holtzman.

**Chairman of the Board:** John Henry.

**Vice President/General Manager:** Mike Feder. **Assistant General Manager:** Diane Ronstadt. **Director of Marketing and Public Relations:** Tammy Rohde. **Director of Group Sales:** Christy Garcia. **Director of Broadcasting:** Mike Minshall. **Director of Operations:** Doug Leary. **Business Manager:** Pattie Feder.

### Field Staff

**Manager:** Rick Sweet. **Coaches:** Don Reynolds, Brent Strom (pitching).

**Trainer:** Ron Porterfield.

### Game Information

**Radio Announcer:** Mike Minshall. **No. of Games Broadcast:** Home-72, Away-72. **Flagship Station:** KTKT 990-AM

**PA Announcer:** Bill Roemer. **Official Scorer:** Sean Fitzpatrick.

**Stadium Name:** Hi Corbett Field. **Location:** I-10 to Broadway exit, east to Randolph Way, south one mile. **Standard Games Times:** 7:30 p.m.; Mon.-Thur. (April-May) 7, Sun. (April-May) 6.

**Visiting Club Hotel:** Ramada Inn-Foothills, 6944 E. Tanque Verde, Tucson, AZ 85715. Telephone: (602) 886-9595.

## VANCOUVER
## *CANADIANS*

**Office Address:** 4601 Ontario St., Vancouver, B.C. V5V 3H4. **Telephone:** (604) 872-5232. **FAX:** (604) 872-1714.

**Affiliation (first year):** California Angels (1993). **Years in League:** 1956-62, 1965-69, 1978-.

**Team Colors:** Blue, white and red.

### Ownership, Management

**Operated by:** Japan Sports Systems

**Chairman of the Board:** Ray Perrault. **President:** John McHale.

**Vice President/General Manager:** Brent Imlach. **Manager of Stadium/Team Operations:** Bill Posthumus. **Manager of Marketing Services:** Ken Cooper. **Manager of Marketing Services/Souvenir Operations:** Torchy Pechet. **Manager of Accounting/Administration:** Harry Chan. **Manager of Media Services:** Steve Hoem. **Administrative Assistant:** Gisele Fisher.

### Field Staff

**Manager:** Don Long. **Coaches:** John Morris, Gary Ruby (pitching).

**Trainer:** Don McGann.

### Game Information

**Radio Announcer:** Unavailable. **No. of Games Broadcast:** Home-72. **Flagship Station:** CKMA 850-AM.

**PA Announcer:** Gerry Landa. **Official Scorer:** Tom Ruffin.

**Stadium Name:** Nat Bailey Stadium. **Location:** From downtown—Cambie Street Bridge, left on E. 33rd St., left on Clancy Loringer Way, right to stadium. From south—Highway 99 to Oak Street, right on 41st Ave., left on Ontario. **Standard Game Times:** 7:05 p.m.; Sun. 1:30.

**Visiting Club Hotel:** Coast Vancouver Airport Hotel, 1041 SW Marine Dr., Vancouver, B.C. V6P 6L6. Telephone: (604) 263-1555.

# EASTERN LEAGUE

## Class AA

John Levenda

**Office Address:** City Island, Harrisburg, PA 17101. **Mailing Address:** P.O. Box 60687, Harrisburg, PA 17106. **Telephone:** (717) 233-4909.

**President/Treasurer:** John Levenda.

**Vice Presidents:** Joe Buzas, Barry Gordon. **Secretary:** Joe Buzas.

**Directors:** Greg Agganis (Canton-Akron), Joe Buzas (Hardware City), Charles Eshbach (Portland), Barry Gordon (Norwich), Peter Kirk (Bowie), Ed Massey (New Haven), Steve Resnick (Harrisburg), Dick Stanley (Trenton), Craig Stein (Reading), Mike Urda (Binghamton).

**Years League Active:** 1923-.

**1995 Opening Date:** April 6. **Closing Date:** Sept. 5.

**No. of Games:** 142.

**Division Structure: North**—Binghamton, Hardware City, New Haven, Norwich, Portland. **South**—Bowie, Canton-Akron, Harrisburg, Reading, Trenton.

**Playoff Format:** First-half division winners play second-half division winners in best-of-5 series. Division playoff winners meet in best-of-5 series for league championship.

**All-Star Game:** July 10 at Shreveport, La. (joint Double-A game).

**Roster Limit:** 23 active, until midnight Aug. 10 when roster can be expanded to 24. **Player Eligibility Rule:** No restrictions.

**Brand of Baseball:** Rawlings ROM-EL.

**Statistician:** Howe Sportsdata International, Boston Fish Pier, West Bldg. #2—Suite 306, Boston MA 02210.

**Umpires:** Mark Facto (Ellicott City, MD), Greg Gibson (Franklin Furnace, OH), Brian Gilbert (Danville, IN), Sam Holbrook (Lexington, KY), Jeff Kowalczyk (Bloomington, IL), Scott Nance (Westminster, CO), Don Rea (Las Vegas, NV), Jim Reynolds (Wethersfield, CT), Mike Russell (Smethport, PA), Mitch Schwark (Melbourne, FL).

### 1994 Standings (Overall)

| Club (Affiliate) | W | L | Pct. | GB | '94 Manager |
|---|---|---|---|---|---|
| #Harrisburg (Expos) | 88 | 51 | .633 | — | David Jauss |
| Bowie (Orioles) | 84 | 58 | .592 | 5½ | Pete Mackanin |
| #*Binghamton (Mets) | 82 | 59 | .582 | 7 | John Tamargo |
| New Haven (Rockies) | 77 | 63 | .550 | 11½ | Paul Zuvella |
| Albany-Colonie (Yankees) | 71 | 70 | .504 | 18 | Bill Evers |
| Canton-Akron (Indians) | 69 | 73 | .486 | 20½ | Ted Kubiak |
| Portland (Marlins) | 60 | 81 | .426 | 29 | Carlos Tosca |
| New Britain (Red Sox) | 59 | 81 | .421 | 29½ | Jim Pankovits |
| Reading (Phillies) | 58 | 82 | .414 | 30½ | Bill Dancy |
| Trenton (Tigers) | 55 | 85 | .393 | 33½ | Tom Runnells |

#Won division pennant *Won playoffs

### Stadium Information

| Club | Stadium | Dimensions LF | CF | RF | Capacity | '94 Att. |
|---|---|---|---|---|---|---|
| Binghamton | Binghamton Municipal | 330 | 400 | 330 | 6,042 | 217,600 |
| Bowie | Prince George's | 309 | 405 | 309 | 10,000 | 293,665 |
| Canton-Akron | Thurman Munson | 330 | 400 | 330 | 5,700 | 255,002 |
| Harrisburg | RiverSide | 335 | 400 | 335 | 6,300 | 234,774 |
| Hardware City | Beehive Field | 325 | 400 | 325 | 4,700 | 129,696 |
| New Haven | Yale Field | 335 | 405 | 315 | 6,200 | 276,316 |
| Norwich | Unavailable | 309 | 405 | 309 | 6,000 | — |
| Portland | Hadlock Field | 315 | 400 | 325 | 6,000 | 375,197 |
| Reading | Municipal Memorial | 330 | 400 | 330 | 8,000 | 338,249 |
| Trenton | Mercer County | 330 | 407 | 330 | 6,439 | 318,252 |

Hardware City known as New Britain in 1994.
Norwich franchise operated in Albany-Colonie in 1994.

## BINGHAMTON
## *METS*

**Office Address:** 211 Henry St., Binghamton, NY 13901. **Mailing Address:** P.O. Box 598, Binghamton, NY 13902. **Telephone:** (607) 723-6387. **FAX:** (607) 723-7779.

**Affiliation (first year):** New York Mets (1992). **Years in League:** 1923-37, 1940-63, 1966-68, 1992-.

**Team Colors:** Blue and orange.

### Ownership, Management

**Operated by:** Binghamton Mets Baseball Club, Inc.

**Principal Owners:** David Maines, William Maines, George Scherer, Christopher Urda, Michael Urda.

**President:** Michael Urda.

**General Manager:** R.C. Reuteman. **Assistant General Manager:** Scott Brown. **Director of Business Operations:** Jeff Estes. **Head Groundskeeper:** Mike Williams. **Director of Marketing:** Meghan Molnar. **Director of Merchandise:** Jonathan Zale. **Clubhouse Operations:** Tony Cleary. **Bookkeeper:** Karen Micalizzi. **Administrative Assistants:** Dan Carpenter, Keith Flanders, Margaret Scarinzi, Sally Subik, Richard Tylicki, Steve Weydig.

### Field Staff

**Manager:** John Tamargo. **Coach:** Bill Latham (pitching).

**Trainer:** Michael Herbst.

### Game Information

**Radio Announcer:** Don Orsillo. **No. of Games Broadcast:** Home-71, Away-71. **Flagship Station:** WBNF 1290-AM.

**PA Announcer:** Roger Neal. **Official Scorer:** Steve Kraly.

**Stadium Name:** Binghamton Municipal. **Location:** I-81 to exit 4S (Binghamton), Rte. 11 exit to Henry Street. **Standard Game Times:** 7 p.m.; Sat. (April-June 17) 1:30, (June 18-Sept.) 7; Sun. 1:30.

**Visiting Club Hotel:** Holiday Inn Arena, 2-8 Hawley St., Binghamton, NY 13790. Telephone: (607) 722-1212.

## BOWIE
## *BAYSOX*

**Office Address:** 4101 NE Crain Hwy., Bowie, MD 20716. **Mailing Address:** P.O. Box 1661, Bowie, MD 20717. **Telephone:** (301) 805-6000. **FAX:** (301) 805-6008.

**Affiliation (first year):** Baltimore Orioles (1993). **Years In League:** 1993-.

**Team Colors:** Black, warm red and teal.

### Ownership, Management

**Operated by:** Maryland Baseball, LP.

**Principal Owners:** Peter Kirk, Pete Simmons, Hugh Schindel, Frank Perdue.

**Chairman of the Board:** Peter Kirk. **President:** Hugh Schindel.

**General Manager:** Keith Lupton. **Assistant General Manager:** Jon Danos. **Controller:** Matthew Ball. **Director of Stadium Operations:** Steve McCormick. **Head Groundskeeper:** Jimmy Juergens. **Director of Media/Public Relations:** Dave Collins. **Director of Community Relations:** Bud Freeman. **Director of Promotions:** Anna Lucente. **Director of Ticket Sales:** Kenny Peyton. **Director of Mini-Plan Sales:** Stanley Cohen. **Director of Group Sales:** Brenda Berger. **Director of Telemarketing:** Erick Royle. **Assistant Director of Telemarketing:** Mike Munter. **Director of Special Projects:** Jimmy Terrill. **Clubhouse Operations:** Kenny Slough, Dave Dolney. **Director of Food Service:** Patrick Carter. **Assistant Director of Food Service:** Jerry Bass. **Office Manager:** Margo Carpenter. **Receptionist:** Becci Velasco. **Accounting Staff:** Greg Hangemanole, Pat Kidd, Donna Parnell.

### Field Staff

**Manager:** Bob Miscik. **Coaches:** Julio Garcia, Chris Lein (pitching).

**Trainer:** Mitch Bibb.

### Game Information

**Radio Announcers:** Dave Collins, Jimmy Terrill. **No. of Games Broadcast:** Home-71; Away-71. **Flagship Station:** WMJS 92.7-FM.

**PA Announcer:** Bud Freeman. **Official Scorer:** Kenny Peyton.

**Stadium Name:** Prince George's Stadium. **Location:** From Washington—Capital Beltway to US 50 east, exit US 50 at US 301 south.

From Baltimore—I-695 to I-97 South to Rt. 3 (exit 7), Route 3 to US 50-301 interchange, stadium on left. **Standard Game Times:** 7:05 p.m., Sun. 2:05.

**Visiting Club Hotel:** Days Inn-Historic Annapolis, 2520 Riva Rd., Annapolis, MD 21401. Telephone: (410) 224-2800.

## CANTON-AKRON
## *INDIANS*

**Office Address:** 2501 Allen Ave. SE, Canton, OH 44707. **Telephone:** (216) 456-5100. **FAX:** (216) 456-5450.

**Affiliation (first year):** Cleveland Indians (1989). **Years in League:** 1989-.

**Team Colors:** Red, white and blue.

### Ownership, Management

**Operated by:** Canton Professional Baseball, Inc.

**Principal Owner/Chief Executive Officer:** Mike Agganis. **President:** Greg Agganis.

**General Manager:** Jeff Auman. **Director of Marketing/Promotions:** Vinny Maculaitis. **Director of Ticket Operations:** Drew Cooke. **Director of Player Facilities:** John Rinaldi. **Director of Finance:** Bob Larkins. **Director of Concessions:** Robin Holland. **Director of Group Sales:** Ed Goff. **Director of Merchandising/Group Sales Assistant:** Jason Kullman. **Director of Media Relations:** Scot Berggren.

### Field Staff

**Manager:** Ted Kubiak. **Coaches:** Greg Booker (pitching), Joe Mikulik.

**Trainer:** Dan DeVoe.

### Game Information

**Radio Announcers:** Unavailable. **No. of Games Broadcast:** Unavailable. **Flagship Station:** WNDQ 95.9-FM.

**Stadium Name:** Thurman Munson Memorial Stadium. **Location:** I-77 to exit 103 (Cleveland Ave.), left on Mills Ave., left on Allen Ave. **Standard Game Times:** 7:15 p.m.; Sat. (April) 1:35, (May-Sept.) 7:35; Sun. 1:35.

**Visiting Club Hotel:** Fairfield Inn, 5285 Broadmoor Circle NW, Canton, OH 44709. Telephone: (216) 493-7373.

## HARDWARE CITY
## *ROCK CATS*

**Office Address:** Beehive Field, Willowbrook Park Complex, New Britain, CT 06051. **Mailing Address:** P.O. Box 1718, New Britain, CT 06050. **Telephone:** (203) 224-8383. **FAX:** (203) 225-6267.

**Affiliation (first year):** Minnesota Twins (1995). **Years in League:** 1983-.

**Team Colors:** Red, white, black, gold and silver.

### Ownership, Management

**Operated by:** Buzas Enterprises, Inc.

**Principal Owner/Chairman:** Joe Buzas.

**President:** Dr. Hilary Buzas-Drammis.

**General Manager:** Gerald Berthiaume. **Assistant General Manager:** Steve Archibald. **Director of Stadium Operations:** Bill Sandillo. **Head Groundskeeper:** Dave Franczak. **Director of Media/Public Relations:** Chris Whalen. **Clubhouse Operations:** Greg Parker.

### Field Staff

**Manager:** Sal Butera. **Coach:** Jim Dwyer, Gorman Heimueller (pitching).

**Trainer:** Rick McWane.

### Game Information

**Radio Announcers:** Jim Lucas, Don Wardlow. **No. of Games Broadcast:** Home-71, Away-71. **Flagship Station:** WNEZ 910-AM.

**PA Announcer:** Unavailable. **Official Scorer:** Robert Kirschner.

**Stadium Name:** Beehive Field. **Location:** I-84 to 72 East (exit 35) to Ellis St. (exit 25), left at light, left on S. Main St., one mile on right. **Standard Game Times:** 7 p.m., Sun. 2.

**Visiting Club Hotel:** Ramada Hotel, 65 Columbus Blvd., New Britain, CT 06051. Telephone: (203) 224-9161.

# HARRISBURG
## *SENATORS*

**Office Address:** RiverSide Stadium, City Island, Harrisburg, PA 17101. **Mailing Address:** P.O. Box 15757, Harrisburg, PA 17105. **Telephone:** (717) 231-4444. **FAX:** (717) 231-4445.

**Affiliatiion (first year):** Montreal Expos (1991). **Years in League:** 1924-35, 1987-.

**Team Colors:** Black and red.

### Ownership, Management

**Operated by:** Pa. Baseball Club, L.P.

**Principal Owners:** Michael Leshner, Andrew Panico, Steven Resnick, Nancy Stein.

**President:** Steven Resnick.

**General Manager:** Todd Vander Woude. **Assistant General Managers:** Mark Clarke, Mark Mattern. **Director of Stadium Operations:** Anthony Fedullo. **Director of Public Relations:** Mark Mattern. **Director of Sales/Marketing:** Mark Clarke. **Director of Ticket Sales:** Karen Sambo. **Head Groundskeeper:** Tim Foreman. **Director of Group Sales:** Mark Sperandio. **Clubhouse Operations:** Steve Purvis. **Office Manager:** Marion Gaab. **Director of Broadcasting:** Brad Sparesus.

### Field Staff

**Manager:** Pat Kelly. **Coach:** Bo McLaughlin (pitching).

**Trainer:** Alex Ochoa.

### Game Information

**Radio Announcer:** Mark Mattern, Brad Sparesus. **No. of Games Broadcast:** Home-71, Away-71. **Flagship Station:** WKBO 1230-AM.

**PA Announcer:** Bob Morgan. **Official Scorer:** Skip Hutter.

**Stadium Name:** RiverSide Stadium. **Location:** I-83, exit 23 (Second Street) to Market Street, bridge to City Island. **Standard Game Times:** 7:05 p.m.; Sun. 1:05.

**Visiting Club Hotel:** Hilton Hotel and Towers, One N. Second St., Harrisburg, PA 17101. Telephone: (717) 233-6000.

# NEW HAVEN
## *RAVENS*

**Office Address:** 63 Grove St., New Haven, CT 06510. **Telephone:** (203) 782-3140. **FAX:** (203) 782-3150.

**Affiliation (first year):** Colorado Rockies (1994). **Years in League:** 1916-32, 1994-.

**Team Colors:** Teal and black.

### Ownership, Management

**Operated By:** New Haven Ravens Baseball, L.P.

**Principal Owner/President:** Edward Massey.

**General Manager:** Charles Dowd. **Assistant General Manager/ Operations, Concessions:** John Brandt. **Assistant General Manager/ Business:** Charles Leone. **Assistant General Manager/Public Relations:** Mary Lee Weber. **Director of Ticketing:** Joe Zajac. **Director of Group Sales:** Greg Rosen. **Director of Merchandise:** Tom McManus. **Director of Information/Publications:** Dave Brady. **Accounting Manager:** Tamara Nolin. **Director of Operations:** Chris Canetti. **Assistant Director of Merchandise/Group Sales:** Diana Kuen. **Administrative Assistant:** Lori McCarthy. **Assistant Director of Marketing:** Mark Tomey. **Head Groundskeeper:** Rick Capacellatro. **Home Clubhouse Manager:** Ian Bethune.

### Field Staff

**Manager:** Paul Zuvella. **Coaches:** Greg Gross, Chuck Estrada (pitching).

**Trainer:** Marc Gustafson.

### Game Information

**Radio Announcer:** Dave Brady. **No. of Games Broadcast:** Home-71, Away-71. **Flagship Station:** WAVZ 1300-AM.

**PA Announcer:** Glenn Dimenstein. **Official Scorer:** David Levine.

**Stadium Name:** Yale Field. **Location:** From I-95 East, exit 44; from I-95 West, exit 45; from I-91, exit 1 (downtown exit); from Merritt Parkway, exit 57. **Standard Game Times:** 7:05 p.m.; Sun. 2:05.

**Visiting Club Hotel:** Days Hotel, 490 Saw Mill Road, West Haven, CT 06516. Telephone: (203) 933-0344.

## NORWICH
## *NAVIGATORS*

**Office Address:** 14 Stott Ave., Norwich, CT 06360. **Mailing Address:** P.O. Box 6003, Yantic, CT 06389. **Telephone:** (203) 887-7962. **FAX:** (203) 886-5996.

**Affiliation (first year):** New York Yankees (1995). **Years in League:** 1995-.

**Team Colors:** Purple, green, yellow, brown, black and red.

### Ownership, Management

**Operated by:** Minor League Sports Enterprises, L.P.

**Principal Owners:** Barry Gordon, Hank Smith, Marc Klee, Robert Friedman, Neil Goldman.

**Chairman of the Board:** Barry Gordon. **President:** Hank Smith.

**General Manager:** George Brzezinski. **Assistant General Manager:** Matt Liscum. **Director of Finance/Merchandising:** Dennis Hannay. **Director of Media Relations/Broadcasting:** Shawn Holliday. **Director of Sales/Marketing:** Tom Hinsch. **Director of Ticket Sales:** Cathy Leet. **Director of Group Sales/Community Relations:** Russ Ruter. **Office Manager:** Leigh Crowe.

### Field Staff

**Manager:** Jimmy Johnson. **Coaches:** Tom Nieto, Juan Nieves (pitching).

**Trainer:** Greg Spratt.

### Game Information

**Radio Announcer:** Shawn Holliday. **No. of Games Broadcast:** Home-71, Away-71. **Flagship Station:** WVVE 102.3-FM.

**PA Announcer:** Unavailable. **Official Scorer:** Unavailable.

**Stadium Name:** Unavailable. **Location:** Unavailable. **Standard Game Times:** 7 p.m.; Sat. (April-May) 2, (June-Sept) 7; Sun. 2.

**Visiting Club Hotel:** Radisson Hotel of New London, 35 Governor Winthrop Blvd., New London, CT 06320. Telephone: (203) 443-7000.

## PORTLAND
## *SEA DOGS*

**Office Address:** 271 Park Ave., Portland, ME 04102. **Mailing Address:** P.O. Box 636, Portland, ME 04104. **Telephone:** (207) 874-9300. **FAX:** (207) 780-0317.

**Affiliation (first year):** Florida Marlins (1994). **Years in League:** 1994-.

**Team Colors:** Teal and white.

### Ownership, Management

**Operated By:** Portland, Maine Baseball, Inc.

**Principal Owner, Chairman of the Board:** Daniel Burke.

**President/General Manager:** Charles Eshbach. **Assistant General Manager:** John Kameisha. **Director of Business Operations:** James Heffley. **Director of Stadium Operations:** Michael Fagerson. **Head Groundskeeper:** Rick Anderson. **Director of Sales/Marketing:** Michael Gillogly. **Director of Ticket Sales:** Carol Doughty. **Director of Group Sales:** Bill Connelly. **Director of Special Projects:** Paul Orlando. **Director of Food Services:** Matthew Drivas. **Team Statistician:** Michael Beveridge.

### Field Staff

**Manager:** Carlos Tosca. **Coaches:** Rich Gale (pitching), Jeff Pentland.

**Trainer:** Mike McGowan.

### Game Information

**Radio Announcer:** Andy Young. **No. of Games Broadcast:** Home-71, Away-71. **Flagship Station:** WPOR 1490-AM.

**PA Announcer:** Dean Rogers. **Official Scorer:** Leroy Rand.

**Stadium Name:** Hadlock Field. **Location:** From south—I-295 to exit 5A, merge onto Congress Street, left at St. John Street, merge right onto Park Avenue; From north—I-295 to exit 6A, right on Park Avenue, ballpark on right. **Standard Game Times:** 7 p.m.; Sat.: 1, 7; Sun.: 1, 4.

**Visiting Club Hotel:** Eastland Plaza, 157 High St., Portland, ME 04101. Telephone: (207) 775-5411.

## READING
## *PHILLIES*

**Office Address:** Rt. 61 South/Centre Ave., Reading, PA 19605. **Mailing Address:** P.O. Box 15050, Reading, PA 19612. **Telephone:** (610) 375-8469. **FAX:** (610) 373-5868.

**Affiliation (first year):** Philadelphia Phillies (1967). **Years in League:** 1933-35, 1952-61, 1963-65, 1967-.

**Team Colors:** Red and white.

### Ownership, Management

**Operated By:** E & J Professional Baseball Club, Inc.

**Principal Owner/President:** Craig Stein.

**General Manager:** Chuck Domino. **Director of Sales and Marketing:** Todd Parnell. **Director of Food Service and Special Projects:** Andy Bortz. **Director of Media/Community Relations:** Mark Wallace. **Director of Group Sales and Tickets:** Scott Hunsicker.

**Director of Stadium Grounds:** Dan Douglas. **Director of Office Operations:** Denise Haage. **Group Sales Manager:** Howard Levy. **Ticket Manager:** Zach Conen.

### Field Staff

**Manager:** Bill Dancy. **Coach:** Bill Robinson.

**Trainer:** Brent Leiby.

### Game Information

**Radio Announcer:** Steve Degler. **No. of Games Broadcast:** Home-71, Away-71. **Flagship Station:** WRAW 1340-AM.

**PA Announcer:** Dave Bauman. **Official Scorer:** Ernie Adams.

**Stadium Name:** Reading Municipal Memorial Stadium. **Location:** From Pa. Turnpike, Rt. 222 North to 422 West to Rt. 61 South. From I-78, Rt. 61 South. **Standard Game Times:** 7:05; Sun. 1:05.

**Visiting Club Hotel:** Wellesley Inn, 910 Woodland Ave., Reading, PA 19610. Telephone: (610) 374-1500.

## TRENTON
## *THUNDER*

**Office Address:** 1 Thunder Rd., Trenton, NJ 08611. **Telephone:** (609) 394-3300. **FAX:** (609) 394-9666.

**Affiliation (first year):** Boston Red Sox (1995). **Years in League:** 1994-.

**Team Colors:** Kelly green, royal blue, yellow and black.

### Ownership, Management

**Operated by:** Garden State Baseball, LP.

**President:** Sam Plumeri.

**General Manager/Chief Operating Officer:** Wayne Hodes. **Assistant General Manager:** Brian Mahoney. **Director of Business Operations:** Todd Pae. **Director of Marketing/Merchandising:** Eric Lipsman. **Director of Media/Public Relations:** Tom McCarthy. **Director of Radio Broadcasting:** Nick Simonetta. **Director of Administration:** Christine King. **Director of Ticket Sales:** John Fierko. **Director of Group Sales:** Geoff Brown. **Director of Community Relations:** Rick Brenner. **Assistant Director of Merchandising:** Curtis Nelson. **Controller:** John Coletta. **Ticket Manager:** Phil Fagans. **Group Sales Manager:** Adam Palant. **Intern:** Chris Matthews. **Secretary:** Lisa Marino.

### Field Staff

**Manager:** Ken Macha. **Coach:** Al Nipper (pitching).

**Trainer:** Unavailable.

### Game Information

**Radio Announcers:** Nick Simonetta, Tom McCarthy. **No. of Games Broadcast:** Home-71, Away-71. **Flagship Station:** WTTM 920-AM.

**PA Announcer:** Brandon Hardison. **Official Scorers:** Jay Dunn, Andy Kaye.

**Stadium Name:** Mercer County Waterfront Park. **Location:** From New Jersey Turnpike, exit at 7A to Route 195 West. Exit at South Broad Street (exit 2), which will merge with US 206, continue on South Broad Street/US 206 for two miles, left at Lalor Street to Rt. 29, right at Delaware River. **Standard Game Times:** 7:05 p.m; Sat. (April) 1:35, (May-Sept.) 7:05; Sun. 1:35.

**Visiting Club Hotel:** Palmer Inn-Best Western, 3499 Rt. 1 South, Princeton, NJ 08540. Telephone: (609) 452-2500.

# SOUTHERN LEAGUE

## Class AA

**Mailing Address:** One Depot St., Suite 300, Marietta, GA 30060.

**Telephone:** (404) 428-4749. **FAX:** (404) 428-4849.

Arnold Fielkow

**President/Secretary-Treasuer:** Arnold Fielkow.

**Vice President:** Bill Hardekopf.

**Directors:** Dennis Bastien (Port City), Don Beaver (Knoxville), Peter Bragan Sr. (Jacksonville), Steve Bryant (Carolina), Steve DeSalvo (Greenville), Bill Hardekopf (Birmingham), David Hersh (Memphis), Richard Holtzman (Chattanooga), Connie Kowal/Mark McGuire (Orlando), Don Mincher (Huntsville).

**Vice President/Marketing, Media Relations:** Susan McCoy. **Executive Assistant:** Lori Webb.

**Years League Active:** 1964-.

**1995 Opening Date:** April 6. **Closing Date:** Sept. 4.

**No. of Games:** 144.

**Division Structure: East**—Carolina, Greenville, Jacksonville, Orlando, Port City. **West**—Birmingham, Chattanooga, Huntsville, Memphis, Nashville.

**Playoff Format:** First-half division winners play second-half division winners in best-of-5 series. Division playoff winners meet in best-of-5 series for league championship.

**All-Star Game:** July 10 at Shreveport, La. (joint Double-A game).

**Roster Limit:** 23 active, until midnight Aug. 10 when roster can be expanded to 24. **Player Eligibility Rule:** No restrictions.

**Brand of Baseball:** Rawlings.

**Statistician:** Howe Sportsdata International, Boston Fish Pier, West Bldg. #2—Suite 306, Boston MA 02210.

**Umpires:** Fred Cannon (Brookhaven, MS), Andy Fletcher (Memphis, TN), Matt Hughes (Las Vegas, NV), Chris Jarboe (Lutherville, MD), Ken Page (Phoenix, AZ), Chris Riba (New Richmond, WI), Paul Schrieber (Eugene, OR), Jeff Schrupp (Excelsior, MN), Tim Timmons (Columbus, OH), Bill Welke (Marshall, MI).

### 1994 Standings (Overall)

| Club (Affiliate) | W | L | Pct. | GB | '94 Manager |
|---|---|---|---|---|---|
| *#Huntsville (Athletics) | 81 | 57 | .587 | — | Gary Jones |
| Memphis (Royals) | 75 | 62 | .547 | 5½ | Ron Johnson |
| #Greenville (Braves) | 73 | 63 | .537 | 7 | Bruce Benedict |
| #Carolina (Pirates) | 74 | 66 | .529 | 8 | Bobby Meacham |
| Nashville (Twins) | 74 | 66 | .529 | 8 | Phil Roof |
| #Chattanooga (Reds) | 67 | 73 | .479 | 15 | Pat Kelly |
| Birmingham (White Sox) | 65 | 74 | .468 | 16½ | Terry Francona |
| Knoxville (Blue Jays) | 64 | 76 | .457 | 18 | Garth Iorg |
| Jacksonville (Mariners) | 60 | 77 | .438 | 20½ | Marc Hill |
| Orlando (Cubs) | 59 | 78 | .431 | 21½ | Dave Trembley |

*Won playoffs #Won split-season pennant

### Stadium Information

| | | Dimensions | | | | |
|---|---|---|---|---|---|---|
| Club | Stadium | LF | CF | RF | Capacity | '94 Att. |
| Birmingham | Hoover Metro. | 340 | 405 | 340 | 10,800 | 467,867 |
| Carolina | Five County | 330 | 400 | 330 | 6,000 | 319,279 |
| Chattanooga | Engel | 320 | 415 | 318 | 7,500 | 292,920 |
| Greenville | Greenville Muni. | 335 | 405 | 335 | 7,027 | 244,171 |
| Huntsville | Joe W. Davis | 345 | 405 | 330 | 10,200 | 297,801 |
| Jacksonville | Wolfson Park | 320 | 395 | 320 | 8,200 | 240,580 |
| Knoxville | Bill Meyer | 330 | 400 | 330 | 6,412 | 145,092 |
| Memphis | Tim McCarver* | 323 | 398 | 325 | 9.841 | 258,311 |
| Orlando | Tinker Field | 340 | 425 | 320 | 5,104 | 195,270 |
| Port City | Brooks Field | 340 | 380 | 340 | 4,000 | — |

Port City franchise operated in Nashville in 1994.

*Artificial turf infield

## BIRMINGHAM
## *BARONS*

**Office Address:** 100 Ben Chapman Dr., Birmingham, AL 35244. **Mailing Address:** P.O. Box 360007, Birmingham, AL 35236. **Telephone:** (205) 988-3200. **FAX:** (205) 988-9698.

**Affiliation (first year):** Chicago White Sox (1986). **Years in League:** 1964-65, 1967-75, 1981-.

**Team Colors:** Silver and black.

### Ownership, Management

**Operated by:** Birmingham Barons Baseball Club, Inc.

**Principal Owner:** Suntory International.

**President/General Manager:** Bill Hardekopf.

**Assistant General Manager:** Tony Ensor. **Director of Broadcasting:** Curt Bloom. **Director of Field Operations:** Anthony King. **Director of Group Sales:** Diane Godber. **Director of Media Relations:** Chris Pika. **Director of Public Relations:** Richard Flight. **Director of Stadium Operations/Merchandise:** Tim Wilding. **Assistant Director of Group Sales:** Jonathan Nelson. **Ticket Manager:** Joe Drake. **Office Manager:** Norma Rosebrough. **Accounting Clerk/Receptionist:** Kecia Arnold. **Clubhouse Manager:** Cory Sifford.

### Field Staff

**Manager:** Terry Francona. **Coaches:** Mike Barnett, Kirk Champion (pitching).

**Trainer:** Scott Johnson.

### Game Information

**Radio Announcer:** Curt Bloom. **No. of Games Broadcast:** Home-72, Away-72. **Flagship Station:** WAPI 1070-AM.

**PA Announcer:** Derek Scudder. **Official Scorer:** Bill Graham.

**Stadium Name:** Hoover Metropolitan Stadium. **Location:** I-459 to Hwy. 150 (exit 10) in Hoover. **Standard Game Times:** 7:10 p.m., Sun. 2.

**Visiting Club Hotel:** Riverchase Inn, 1800 Riverchase Dr., Hoover, AL 35244. Telephone: (205) 985-7500.

## CAROLINA
## *MUDCATS*

**Office Address:** 3501 N.C. Highway 39, Zebulon, NC 27597. **Mailing Address:** P.O. Drawer 1218, Zebulon, NC 27597. **Telephone:** (919) 269-2287. **FAX:** (919) 269-4910.

**Affiliation (first year):** Pittsburgh Pirates (1991). **Years in League:** 1991-.

**Team Colors:** Red, black and grey.

### Ownership, Management

**Operated by:** Carolina Mudcats Professional Baseball Club, Inc.

**Principal Owner/President:** Steve Bryant.

**General Manager:** Joe Kremer. **Director of Broadcasting:** Bob Licht. **Office Manager:** Jackie DiPrimo. **Sales Manager:** Duke Sanders. **Director of Concessions:** Johnny Gardner. **Director of Field Operations:** Bill Riggan. **Director of Ticket Operations:** Sandy Loughran. **Community Relations:** Kelly Edwards, Suzanne Jamieson. **Director of Promotions/Media Relations:** John Katz. **Director of Souvenirs:** Joe Chatman. **Director of Special Events:** Steve Sophis. **Account Executive:** Mark Reardon.

### Field Staff

**Manager:** Trent Jewett. **Coach:** Dave Rajsich (pitching), Don Werner.

**Trainer:** Sandy Krum.

### Game Information

**Radio Announcer:** Bob Licht. **No. of Games Broadcast:** Home-72, Away-72. **Flagship Station:** WYLT 850-AM.

**PA Announcer:** Duke Sanders. **Official Scorer:** Unavailable.

**Stadium Name:** Five County Stadium. **Location:** From Raleigh, I-64 East to 264 East, exit at Hwy. 39 in Zebulon. **Standard Game Times:** 7:35 p.m.; Sun. (April-May) 2:05, (June-Sept.) 6:05.

**Visiting Club Hotel:** Holiday Inn-North, 2815 Capital Blvd., Raleigh, NC 27604. Telephone: (919) 872-7666.

## CHATTANOOGA
## *LOOKOUTS*

**Office Address:** 1130 E. Third St., Chattanooga, TN 37401. **Mailing Address:** P.O. Box 11002, Chattanooga, TN 37401. **Telephone:** (615) 267-2208. **FAX:** (615) 267-4258.

**Affiliation (first year):** Cincinnati Reds (1988). **Years in League:** 1964-65, 1976-.

**Team Colors:** Red and white.

### Ownership, Management

**Operated by:** Engel Stadium Corporation.

**Principal Owner/Chairman of the Board:** Frank Burke.

**President/General Manager:** Bill Davidson. **Director of Promotions/Marketing:** Vicki Race. **Director of Sales:** Rich Mozingo. **Director of Media/Public Relations:** Dave Anderson. **Director of Administration:** Kathy Erickson. **Director of Broadcasting:** Larry Ward. **Director of Food/Beverage Sales:** Martin Ward. **Director of Community Relations/Ticket Sales:** Joann Ribar. **Director of Group Sales:** Hubert Conley. **Director of Stadium Operations:** Greg Grall. **Head Groundskeeper:** Mike White. **Administrative Assistant:** Dena Newberry.

### Field Staff

**Manager:** Dave Miley. **Coach:** Terry Abbott (pitching).

**Trainer:** Jim Knudtson.

### Game Information

**Radio Announcer:** Larry Ward. **No. of Games Broadcast:** Home-72, Away-72. **Flagship Station:** WSGC 101.9-FM.

**PA Announcer:** Mike Wolverton. **Official Scorer:** John Babb.

**Stadium Name:** Historic Engel Stadium. **Location:** I-24 to I-27 North to 4th St. exit, 1½ miles to ballpark. **Standard Game Times:** 7 p.m.; Wed. 12:30, Sun. 2.

**Visiting Club Hotel:** Days Inn Covention Centre, 1400 Mac Smith Rd., East Ridge, TN 37412. Telephone: (615) 894-0440.

## GREENVILLE
## *BRAVES*

**Office Address:** One Braves Ave., Greenville, SC 29607. **Mailing Address:** P.O. Box 16683, Greenville, SC 29606. **Telephone:** (803) 299-3456. **FAX:** (803) 277-7369.

**Affiliation (first year):** Atlanta Braves (1984). **Years in League:** 1984-.

**Team Colors:** Red, white and blue.

### Ownership, Management

**Operated by:** Atlanta National League Baseball Club, Inc.

**Principal Owner:** Ted Turner. **President:** Stan Kasten.

**General Manager:** Steve DeSalvo. **Assistant General Manager:** Mike Dunn. **Director of Stadium Operations:** Scott Scheidt. **Head Groundskeeper:** Matt Taylor. **Director of Media/Public Relations:** Matt Garvey. **Director of Sales/Marketing:** Sean O'Connor. **Director of Ticket Sales:** Jennifer Turner. **Director of Special Projects:** Jimmy Moore. **Director of Broadcasting:** Mark Hauser. **Ticket Manager:** Jim Bishop.

### Field Staff

**Manager:** Bruce Benedict. **Coaches:** Bruce Dal Canton (pitching), Randy Ingle.

**Trainer:** Dave Tomchek.

### Game Information

**Radio Announcers:** Mark Hauser, Doug Holliday. **No. of Games Broadcast:** Home-72, Away-72. **Flagship Station:** WBFM 98.1-FM.

**PA Announcer:** Chris Allen. **Official Scorer:** Jimmy Moore.

**Stadium Name:** Greenville Municipal Stadium. **Location:** I-85 to exit 46 (Mauldin Rd.), east 2 miles. **Standard Game Times:** 7:15 p.m, Sun. 4:15.

**Visiting Club Hotel:** Quality Inn, 50 Orchard Park Dr., Greenville, SC 29615. Telephone: (803) 297-9000.

## HUNTSVILLE
## *STARS*

**Office Address:** 3125 Leeman Ferry Rd., Huntsville, AL 35801. **Mailing Address:** P.O. Box

3125, Huntsville, AL 35804. **Telephone:** (205) 882-2562. **FAX:** (205) 880-0801.

**Affiliation (first year):** Oakland Athletics (1985). **Years In League:** 1985-.

**Team Colors:** Red and blue.

## Ownership, Management

**Operated by:** Huntsville Stars Baseball, LLC.

**General Manager:** Don Mincher. **Assistant General Manager:** Patrick Nichol. **Director of Operations/Stadium Personnel:** Whit Babcock. **Controller:** Pat Mincher. **Assistant Director of Operations:** Bryan Dingo. **Head Groundskeeper:** Tom McAfee. **Director of Media/Public Relations:** Steve Kornya. **Director of Group Sales:** Tim Harmon. **Ticket/Office Manager:** Kelly Watts.

## Field Staff

**Manager:** Dick Scott. **Coach:** Glenn Abbott (pitching).

**Trainer:** Dave Hollenback.

## Game Information

**Radio Announcer:** Steve Selby. **No. of Games Broadcast:** Home-72, Away-72. **Flagship Station:** WTKI 1450-AM.

**PA Announcer:** Chris Peace. **Official Scorer:** Larry Smith.

**Stadium Name:** Joe W. Davis Stadium. **Location:** I-65 to I-565 East, south on Memorial Parkway to Drake Ave. exit. **Standard Game Times:** 7:05 p.m.; Sun. (April-June) 2:05, (July-Sept.) 7:05.

**Visiting Club Hotel:** Unavailable.

# JACKSONVILLE
*SUNS*

**Office Address:** 1201 E. Duval St., Jacksonville, FL 32202. **Mailing Address:** P.O. Box 4756, Jacksonville, FL 32201. **Telephone:** (904) 358-2846. **FAX:** (904) 358-2845.

**Affiliation (first year):** Detroit Tigers (1995). **Years in League:** 1970-.

**Team Colors:** Red, royal blue and yellow.

## Ownership, Management

**Operated by:** Baseball Jax, Inc.

**Principal Owner/President:** Peter Bragan Sr.

**Vice President/General Manager:** Peter Bragan Jr. **Assistant General Manager:** Jay Grider. **Director of Stadium Operations:** Chris Browne. **Head Groundskeeper:** Mark Clay. **Director of Marketing:** Todd Budnick. **Director of Ticket Sales:** Amy Burdette. **Clubhouse Operations:** Pete Phillips, Larry Spears. **Office Manager:** Cathy Wiggins. **Director of Broadcasting:** Dan Vaughan. **Administrative Assistant:** Kevin Hyer. **Assistant to the President:** Jerry LeMoine.

## Field Staff

**Manager:** Bill Plummer. **Coaches:** Rich Bombard (pitching), Mark Meleski.

**Trainer:** Brian Goike.

## Game Information

**Radio Announcer:** Dan Vaughan. **No. of Games Broadcast:** Home-72, Away-72. **Flagship Station:** WZNZ 1460-AM.

**PA Announcer:** John Leard. **Official Scorer:** Nico Van Thyn.

**Stadium Name:** Wolfson Park. **Location:** I-95 to 20th St. East exit to downtown, right lane to Florida Ave., left at stop sign and follow signs. **Standard Game Times:** 7:35 p.m.; Sun. 3:35, 5:35.

**Visiting Club Hotels:** La Quinta Inn-Baymeadows, 8255 Dix Ellis Trail, Jacksonville, FL 32256. Telephone: (904) 731-9940.

# KNOXVILLE
*SMOKIES*

**Office Address:** 633 Jessamine St., Knoxville, TN 37917. **Telephone:** (615) 637-9494. **FAX:** (615) 523-9913.

**Affiliation (first year):** Toronto Blue Jays (1980). **Years in League:** 1964-67, 1972-.

**Team Colors:** Navy blue, silver, green and light blue.

## Ownership, Management

**Operated by:** Knoxville Smokies Baseball, Inc.

**Principal Owner/President:** Don Beaver.

**Vice President/General Manager:** Dan Rajkowski. **Assistant General**

**Manager:** Brian Cox. **Director of Stadium Operations:** Scott Saul. **Head Groundskeeper:** Kevin Zurcher. **Director of Media Relations/Broadcasting:** Garry Griffith. **Director of Sales/Marketing:** Mark Seaman. **Office Manager:** Jennifer Jones. **Intern:** Jay Campbell.

### Field Staff

**Manager:** Garth Iorg. **Coaches:** Mark Connor (pitching), Leroy Stanton. **Trainer:** Pat McMorran.

### Game Information

**Radio Announcer:** Garry Griffith. **No. of Games Broadcast:** Home-72, Away-72. **Flagship Station:** WXVO 98.7-FM.

**PA Announcer:** Unavailable. **Official Scorer:** Jack Tate.

**Stadium Name:** Bill Meyer Stadium. **Location:** I-40 to exit 388 (James White Parkway), right onto Summit Hill Drive, right on Central Ave., right on Willow Ave. **Standard Game Times:** 7:15 p.m., Sun. 5.

**Visiting Club Hotel:** Howard Johnson North, 118 Merchants Dr., Knoxville, TN 37912. Telephone: (615) 688-3141.

## MEMPHIS
## *CHICKS*

**Office Address:** 800 Home Run Lane, Memphis, TN 38104. **Telephone:** (901) 272-1687. **FAX:** (901) 278-3354.

**Affiliation (first year):** San Diego Padres (1995). **Years In League:** 1978-.

**Team Colors:** Blue, black and white.

### Ownership, Management

**Operated by:** Professional Sports and Entertainment of Tennessee, LP.

**Principal Owner/President:** David Hersh.

**General Manager:** Tom Ford. **Assistant General Manager:** Peter Thomas. **Controller:** Jeff Durbin. **Director of Stadium Operations/Groundskeeper:** Phil Goodwin. **Director of Community/Media Relations:** Jim Dominguez. **Director of Sales/Marketing:** Brian Grogg. **Senior Account Representative:** Stuart Rosenbaum. **Account Executives:** Kerry Krick, Lee Kushner, Jason Pawlowski. **Director of Ticket Sales:** Rene Harris. **Director of Group Sales:** Jarrod Coates. **Secretary:** Patty Haynes.

### Field Staff

**Manager:** Jerry Royster. **Coach:** Dean Treanor (pitching).

**Trainer:** George Poulis.

### Game Information

**Radio Announcer:** Tom Stocker. **No. of Games Broadcast:** Home-72, Away-72. **Flagship Station:** WREC 600-AM.

**PA Announcer:** Mark Bialek. **Official Scorer:** John Guinozzo.

**Stadium Name:** Tim McCarver Stadium. **Location:** I-240 South to Poplar Ave. West, left on Highland, right on Central, left on Early Maxwell. In State Fairgrounds complex next to Liberty Bowl. **Standard Game Times:** 7:15 p.m.; Sun. (April-May) 2:15, (June-Sept.) 6:15.

**Visiting Club Hotel:** Brownstone Hotel, 300 N. Second, Memphis, TN 38103. Telephone: (901) 525-2511.

## ORLANDO
## *CUBS*

**Office Address:** 287 S. Tampa Ave., Orlando, FL 32805. **Telephone:** (407) 245-2827. **FAX:** (407) 649-1637.

**Affiliation (first year):** Chicago Cubs (1993). **Years in League:** 1973-.

**Team Colors:** Royal blue, red, white and black.

### Ownership, Management

**Operated by:** Orlando Baseball Club, Inc.

**Principal Owner:** Chicago Cubs.

**Chairman of the Board:** Stanton Cook. **President:** Mark McGuire.

**General Manager:** Roger Wexelberg. **Assistant General Manager:** John Cody. **Head Groundskeeper:** Doug Lopas. **Director of Media Relations/Broadcasting:** Andrew Monaco. **Director of Sales:** Mike Roche. **Senior Account Representative:** Lisa Hughes. **Director of Marketing:** Andy Dunn. **Director of Ticket Sales:** Lynn Barnett. **Director of Novelties:** Mack Powell. **Director of Food Services:** Les Prather.

### Field Staff

**Manager:** Bruce Kimm. **Coaches:** Marty DeMerritt (pitching), Chris

Speier.

**Trainer:** Steve Melendez.

## Game Information

**Radio Announcer:** Andrew Monaco. **No. of Games Broadcast:** Home-72, Away-72. **Flagship Station:** WTLN 1520-AM.

**PA Announcer:** Tom Peters. **Official Scorers:** John Wilkening, Bill Smith.

**Stadium Name:** Tinker Field. **Location:** I-4 to East-West Expressway, west on East-West Expy. to Orange Blossom Trail exit, two blocks to stadium on right. **Standard Game Times:** 7 p.m.; Sun. (April-June) 2, (July-Sept.) 6.

**Visiting Club Hotel:** Ramada Orlando Central, 3200 West Colonial Dr., Orlando, FL 32808. Telephone: (407) 295-5270.

# PORT CITY (Wilmington) *ROOSTERS*

**Office Address:** Baseball Field House, 601 S. College Rd., Wilmington, NC 28403. **Mailing Address:** P.O. Box 7217, Wilmington, NC 28406. **Telephone:** (910) 350-7000. **FAX:** (910) 350-7098.

**Affiliation (first year):** Seattle Mariners (1995). **Years in League:** 1995.

## Ownership, Management

**Principal Owner:** Dennis Bastien.

**General Manager:** David Kotarba. **Assistant General Manager:** Stephen Staudigl. **Director of Stadium Operations:** James Murphy. **Head Groundskeeper:** Tommy Gaddy. **Concessions Manager:** Chad Woodard. **Director of Merchandising:** Damon Bartolo. **Director of Broadcasting:** David Kelly.

## Field Staff

**Manager:** Dave Myers. **Coaches:** Darrin Garner, Ron Romanick (pitching).

**Trainer:** Unavailable.

## Game Information

**Radio:** Unavailable.

**PA Announcer:** Unavailable. **Official Scorer:** Unavailable.

**Stadium Name:** Brooks Field. **Location:** From I-40 East, College Road South to UNC Wilmington, Brooks Field on campus. **Standard Game Times:** 7:05 p.m., Sun. 6:05.

**Visiting Club Hotel:** Unavailable.

# TEXAS LEAGUE

### Class AA

Tom Kayser

**Mailing Address:** 2442 Facet Oak, San Antonio, TX 78232. **Telephone:** (210) 545-5297. **FAX:** (210) 545-5298.

**President/Treasurer:** Tom Kayser.

**Vice President:** Miles Prentice. **Secretary:** Monty Hoppel.

**Directors:** Bob Beban (San Antonio), J. Con Maloney (Jackson), Taylor Moore (Shreveport), Jim Paul (El Paso), Miles Prentice (Midland), Joe Preseren (Tulsa), Steve Shaad (Wichita), Bill Valentine (Arkansas).

**Years League Active:** 1888-1890, 1892, 1895-1899, 1902-1942, 1946-.

**1995 Opening Date:** April 6. **Closing Date:** Aug. 31.

**No. of Games:** 136.

**Division Structure: East**—Arkansas, Jackson, Shreveport, Tulsa. **West**—El Paso, Midland, San Antonio, Wichita.

**Playoff Format:** First-half division winners play second-half division winners in best-of-5 series. Division playoff winners meet in best-of-7 series for league championship.

**1995 All-Star Game:** Two-game series vs. Mexican League at El Paso (June 11) and Torreon, Mexico (June 13); Joint Double-A all-star game at Shreveport (July 10).

**Roster Limit:** 23 active, until midnight Aug. 10 when roster can be expanded to 24. **Player Eligibility Rule:** No restrictions.

**Brand of Baseball:** Rawlings.

**Statistician:** Howe Sportsdata International, Boston Fish Pier, West Bldg. #2-Suite 306, Boston, MA 02210.

**Umpires:** Mike DiMuro (Tucson, AZ), Joel Fincher (Arlington, TX), Travis Katzenmeier (Liberal, KS), Ian Lamplugh (Victoria, B.C.), Bill Miller (Auburn, CA), Jeff Patterson (Imperial Beach, CA), Kraig Sanders (Little Rock, AR), Mike Stetson (Phoenix, AZ).

## 1994 Standings (Overall)

| Club (Affiliate) | W | L | Pct. | GB | '94 Manager |
|---|---|---|---|---|---|
| *#El Paso (Brewers) | 88 | 48 | .647 | — | Tim Ireland |
| #Jackson (Astros) | 74 | 61 | .548 | 13½ | Sal Butera |
| #Shreveport (Giants) | 73 | 63 | .537 | 15 | Ron Wotus |
| Arkansas (Cardinals) | 68 | 67 | .504 | 19½ | Chris Maloney |
| Tulsa (Rangers) | 63 | 73 | .463 | 25 | Stan Cliburn |
| San Antonio (Dodgers) | 62 | 74 | .456 | 26 | Tom Beyers |
| Midland (Angels) | 61 | 75 | .449 | 27 | Mario Mendoza |
| Wichita (Padres) | 54 | 82 | .397 | 34 | Keith Champion |

*Won playoffs. #Won split-season pennant

## Stadium Information

| | | Dimensions | | | | |
|---|---|---|---|---|---|---|
| Club | Stadium | LF | CF | RF | Capacity | '94 Att. |
| Arkansas | Ray Winder Field | 330 | 390 | 330 | 6,100 | 275,524 |
| El Paso | Cohen | 330 | 410 | 330 | 10,000 | 327,542 |
| Jackson | Smith-Wills | 330 | 400 | 330 | 5,200 | 148,647 |
| Midland | Christensen | 335 | 392 | 335 | 5,000 | 190,022 |
| San Antonio | Missions | 310 | 402 | 340 | 6,300 | 411,959 |
| Shreveport | Fair Grounds Field | 330 | 400 | 330 | 6,200 | 199,465 |
| Tulsa | Drillers | 335 | 390 | 340 | 10,813 | 344,764 |
| Wichita | Lawrence-Dumont* | 344 | 401 | 312 | 6,793 | 210,482 |

*Artificial turf infield

## ARKANSAS
*TRAVELERS*

**Office Address:** War Memorial Park, Little Rock, AR 72205. **Mailing Address:** P.O. Box 5599, Little Rock, AR 72215. **Telephone:** (501) 664-1555. **FAX:** (501) 664-1834.

**Affiliation (first year):** St. Louis Cardinals (1966). **Years in League:** 1966-.

**Team Colors:** Red, white and blue.

### Ownership, Management

**Operated by:** Arkansas Travelers Baseball Club, Inc.

**President:** Bert Parke.

**Executive Vice President/General Manager:** Bill Valentine. **Assistant General Manager/Corporate Sales, Public Relations:** Michael Beasley. **Assistant General Manager/Concessions, Operations:** John Evans. **Park Superintendent:** Greg Johnston. **Director of Stadium Operations:** J.P. Flynn. **Business Manager:** Leslie Wilson.

### Field Staff

**Manager:** Mike Ramsey. **Coaches:** Marty Mason (pitching), Jeff Shireman.

**Trainer:** Pete Fagan.

### Game Information

**Radio Announcer:** Bob Harrison. **No. of Games Broadcast:** Home-68. **Flagship Station:** KARN 920-AM.

**PA Announcer:** Unavailable. **Official Scorer:** George Schroeder.

**Stadium Name:** Ray Winder Field. **Location:** I-630 at Fair Park Blvd. exit. **Standard Game Times:** 7:30 p.m.

**Visiting Club Hotel:** Markham Inn, 5120 West Markham Ave., Little Rock, AR 72204. Telephone: (501) 666-0161.

## EL PASO
*DIABLOS*

**Office Address:** 9700 Gateway North Blvd., El Paso, TX 79924. **Mailing Address:** P.O. Drawer 4797, El Paso, TX 79914. **Telephone:** (915) 755-2000. **FAX:** (915) 757-0671.

**Affiliation (first year):** Milwaukee Brewers (1981). **Years in League:** 1962-70, 1972-.

### Ownership, Management

**Operated by:** El Paso Diablos, Inc.

**Principal Owner/President:** Jim Paul.

**Executive Vice President/General Manager:** Rick Parr. **Vice President/Associate General Manager:** Ken Schrom. **Vice President/ Business Manager:** Karen Paul. **Assistant General Manager:** Rob Sesich. **Director of Ticket Sales:** Becky Martin. **Director of Group Sales:** Beverly Mowad. **Assistant to the President:** Sharon Gaines. **Administrative Assistant:** Heather Smith. **Director of Broadcasting:** Matt Hicks. **Head Groundskeeper:** Alan Beshears. **Receptionist:** Mary Hill. **Account Executives:** Mark Brown, Rob Rixford.

### Field Staff

**Manager:** Tim Ireland. **Coaches:** Rob Derksen (pitching), Ken Phelps.

**Trainer:** Bryan Jaquette.

### Game Information

**Radio Announcers:** Matt Hicks, Bernie Ricono. **No. of Games Broadcast:** Home-68, Away-68. **Flagship Station:** KHEY 690-AM.

**PA Announcer:** Jeff Limberg. **Official Scorer:** Bernie Olivas.

**Stadium Name:** Cohen Stadium. **Location:** I-10 to US 54 North, Diana exit. **Standard Game Times:** 7 p.m., Sun. 6:30.

**Visiting Club Hotel:** Quality Inn, 6201 Gateway Blvd. West, El Paso, TX 79925. Telephone: (915) 778-6611.

## JACKSON
*GENERALS*

**Office Address:** 1200 Lakeland Dr., Jackson, MS 39216. **Mailing Address:** P.O. Box 4209,

Jackson, MS 39296. **Telephone:** (601) 981-4664. **FAX:** (601) 981-4669.

**Affiliation (first year):** Houston Astros (1991). **Years in League:** 1975-.

**Team Colors:** Royal blue, red and yellow.

### Ownership, Management

**Operated by:** Cowboy Maloney Supply Co., Inc.

**Principal Owners:** J. Con Maloney, Eddie Maloney.

**Chairman:** J. Con Maloney. **President:** Eddie Maloney.

**General Manager:** Bill Blackwell. **Assistant General Manager:** Adam Hathorn. **Director of Sales/Broadcasting:** Bill Walberg. **Director of Stadium Operations/Groundskeeper:** Joe Whipps. **Senior Account Representative:** Frank Williams. **Clubhouse Operations:** Duane McCain. **Office Manager:** Judy Blackwell.

### Field Staff

**Manager:** Tim Tolman. **Coach:** Charley Taylor (pitching).

**Trainer:** Mike Freer.

### Game Information

**Radio Announcer:** Bill Walberg. **No. of Games Broadcast:** Home-68, Away-68. **Flagship Station:** WJDS 620-AM.

**PA Announcer:** Glen Waddle. **Official Scorer:** Chan Hartzog.

**Stadium Name:** Smith-Wills Stadium. **Location:** I-55 to Lakeland Drive exit. **Standard Game Times:** 7 p.m.; Sun. (April-July) 2:30, (Aug.) 6.

**Visiting Club Hotel:** Quality Inn North, 4651 I-55 North, Jackson, MS 39206. Telephone: (601) 982-1044.

## MIDLAND
## *ANGELS*

**Office Address:** 4300 N. Lamesa Rd., Midland, TX 79705. **Mailing Address:** P.O. Box 51187, Midland, TX 79710. **Telephone:** (915) 683-4251. **FAX:** (915) 683-0994.

**Affiliation (first year):** California Angels (1985). **Years in League:** 1972-.

**Team Colors:** Red, blue and yellow.

### Ownership, Management

**Operated by:** Midland Sports, Inc.

**Principal Owners:** Miles Prentice, Bob Richmond.

**President:** Miles Prentice. **Executive Vice President:** Bob Richmond.

**General Manager:** Monty Hoppel. **Assistant General Manager:** Rick Carden. **Director of Business Operations:** Nancy Swallow. **Director of Concessions/Operations:** Jeff Corbett. **Head Groundskeeper:** Lee Velarde. **Director of Communications:** Scott Seator. **Director of Marketing:** Jeff VonHolle. **Director of Broadcasting:** Bob Hards. **Sales Manager:** Harold Fuller. **Office Manager:** Eloisa Robledo. **Administrative Assistant:** Christie Reaves. **Intern:** Miley Guzman.

### Field Staff

**Manager:** Mario Mendoza. **Coaches:** Jeff Barns, Kernan Ronan (pitching).

**Trainer:** Scott Sowell.

### Game Information

**Radio Announcer:** Bob Hards. **No. of Games Broadcast:** Home-68, Away-68. **Flagship Station:** KCRS 550-AM.

**PA Announcer:** Barry Sykes. **Official Scorer:** Bobby Dunn.

**Stadium Name:** Christensen Stadium. **Location:** Rankin Highway/Big Spring exit to Loop 250, exit right on Lamesa Road. **Standard Game Times:** 7 p.m.; Sun. 6.

**Visiting Club Hotel:** Midland Hilton, 117 W. Wall St., Midland, TX 79701. Telephone: (915) 683-6131.

## SAN ANTONIO
## *MISSIONS*

**Office Address:** 5757 Hwy. 90 W., San Antonio, TX 78227. **Telephone:** (210) 675-7275. **FAX:** (210) 670-0001.

**Affiliation (first year):** Los Angeles Dodgers (1977). **Years In League:** 1888, 1892, 1895-99, 1907-42, 1946-64, 1967-.

**Team Colors:** Metallic gold and black.

### Ownership, Management

**Operated by:** Elmore Sports Group.

**Principal Owner/President:** Dave Elmore.

**General Manager:** Burl Yarbrough. **Assistant General Manager:** David Oldham. **Director of Business Operations:** Marc Frey. **Director of Stadium Operations:** Jeff Long. **Head Groundskeeper:** Mike Pankey. **Director of Public Relations:** Wayne Witt. **Director of Marketing:** Dave Gasaway. **Director of Promotions:** Jere Hanks. **Director of Ticket Sales:** Jimi Olsen. **Director of Group Sales:** Jeff Windle. **Administrative Assistant:** Mario Garcia. **President, Diamond Concessions:** Doug Campbell.

### Field Staff

**Manager:** John Shelby. **Coaches:** Nate Oliver, Luis Tiant (pitching).
**Trainer:** Matt Wilson.

### Game Information

**Radio Announcer:** Roy Acuff, Brian Anderson. **No. of Games Broadcast:** Home-68, Away-68. **Flagship Station:** KKYX 680-AM.

**PA Announcer:** Stan Kelly. **Official Scorer:** Dennis Kunimura.

**Stadium Name:** Missions Stadium. **Location:** Hwy. 90 West at Callaghan. **Standard Game Times:** 7:05 p.m.; Sun. 6:05.

**Visiting Club Hotel:** Thrifty Inn, I-10 at Wurzbach, San Antonio, TX 78230. Telephone: (210) 696-0810.

## SHREVEPORT
## *CAPTAINS*

**Office Address:** 2901 Pershing Blvd., Shreveport, LA 71109. **Mailing Address:** P.O. Box 3448, Shreveport, LA 71133. **Telephone:** (318) 636-5555. **FAX:** (318) 636-5670.

**Affiliation (first year):** San Francisco Giants (1979). **Years in League:** 1895, 1908-10, 1915-32, 1938-42, 1946-57, 1968-.

**Team Colors:** Blue and red.

### Ownership, Management

**Operated by:** Shreveport Baseball, Inc.

**Principal Owner/President:** Taylor Moore. **Senior Vice President:** Charles Webb. **Vice President:** Loy Moore.

**General Manager:** Gilbert Little. **Assistant General Manager:** Terri Sipes. **Director of Stadium Operations:** Bill Johnson. **Head Groundskeeper:** Steve Bange. **Director of Media/Public Relations:** Dave Nitz. **Director of Group Sales:** Laura Robinson. **Clubhouse Operations:** J.J. Lewis. **Director of Food/Beverage:** Leroy Beasley. **Assistant Director of Food/Beverage:** Don Richardson. **Marketing Assistant:** Jerry Bagwell.

### Field Staff

**Manager:** Ron Wotus. **Coaches:** Frank Cacciatore, Joel Horlen (pitching).

**Trainer:** Ric Moreno.

### Game Information

**Radio Announcers:** Dave Nitz, Brady Body. **No. of Games Broadcast:** Home-68, Away-68. **Flagship Station:** KEEL 710-AM.

**PA Announcer:** Rick Stephenson. **Official Scorer:** Jim Dawson.

**Stadium Name:** Fair Grounds Field. **Location:** Hearne Ave. (US 171) exit off I-20, at Louisiana State Fairgrounds. **Standard Game Times:** April-May 7:05, June-Sept. 7:35; Sun. 6:05.

**Visiting Club Hotel:** Unavailable.

## TULSA
## *DRILLERS*

**Office Address:** 4802 E. 15th St., Tulsa, OK 74112. **Mailing Address:** P.O. Box 4448, Tulsa, OK 74159. **Telephone:** (918) 744-5998. **FAX:** (918) 747-3267.

**Affiliation (first year):** Texas Rangers (1977). **Years in League:** 1933-42, 1946-65, 1977-.

**Team Colors:** Red and white.

### Ownership, Management

**Operated by:** Tulsa Baseball, Inc.

**Principal Owner/President:** Went Hubbard.

**Executive Vice Presidents:** Chuck Lamson, Joe Preseren. **Head Groundskeeper:** Sam Clay. **Director of Public Relations:** Brian Carroll. **Director of Food/Beverage:** Chris Pound. **Director of Ticket Sales:** Tina Burney. **Director of Group Sales:** Paul Birutis. **Office Manager:** Debbie Jones. **Bookkeeper:** Cheryll Moore. **Assistant Director of Food/**

**Beverage:** Mike Melega. **Administrative Assistants:** Lance Sloan, Melanie Giles. **Assistant Groundskeeper:** Gary Shepherd.

### Field Staff

**Manager:** Bobby Jones. **Coach:** Jackson Todd (pitching).
**Trainer:** Tom Tisdale.

### Game Information

**Radio Announcer:** Bruce Howard. **No. of Games Broadcast:** Home-68, Road-68. **Flagship Station:** KAKC 1300-AM.

**PA Announcer:** Kirk McAnany. **Official Scorer:** John Klein.

**Stadium Name:** Drillers Stadium. **Location:** 3 miles north of I-44 and 1 ½ miles south of I-244 at 15th Street and Yale Avenue. **Standard Game Times:** 7:35 p.m.; Sun. (April-May) 2:05, (June-Aug.) 6:05.

**Visiting Club Hotel:** Ramada Hotel, 5000 E. Skelly Dr., Tulsa, OK 74135. Telephone: (918) 622-7000.

## WICHITA *WRANGLERS*

**Office Address:** 300 S. Sycamore, Wichita, KS 67213. **Mailing Address:** P.O. Box 1420, Wichita, KS 67201. **Telephone:** (316) 267-3372. **FAX:** (316) 267-3382.

**Affiliation (first year):** Kansas City Royals (1995). **Years in League:** 1987-.

**Team Colors:** Black, teal, red, purple and tan.

### Ownership, Management

**Operated by:** Wichita Baseball, Inc.

**Principal Owner:** Rich Products Corp.

**Chairman:** Robert Rich Sr. **President:** Robert Rich Jr. **Executive Vice President:** Melinda Rich. **Vice President/Rich Baseball Operations:** Mike Billoni. **Vice President/Stadium Services:** Jonathan Dandes. **Comptroller:** John Dougherty.

**Vice President/General Manager:** Steve Shaad. **Consultant to the General Manager:** Larry Davis. **Assistant General Manager/Baseball Operations:** Mark Schimming. **Assistant General Manager/Business Operations:** Brad Eldridge. **Assistant General Manager/National Baseball Congress:** Lance Deckinger. **Operations Manager:** Shawn Pfannenstiel. **Marketing Manager:** Kevin Gelbard. **Sales Manager:** Tom Davis. **Office Manager:** Kristen Winch. **Stadium Manager:** David Wagg. **Ticket Sales Coordinator:** Tim Lyons. **Account Executive:** Drew Swisher. **Broadcast Coordinator:** Dennis Higgins. **Publications Coordinator:** Chris Overholser. **Merchandise Coordinator:** Erik Jordan. **Ticket Sales Associate:** Chris Freshour. **Business Administration Assistant:** Josh Carroll. **Stadium Operations Assistant:** Mary Luce. **Public Relations Associate:** Trevor Vernon. **Marketing Associate:** Chris Erickson. **Business Associate:** Randy Shreiner. **Ticket Operations Associate:** Catherine Serrin. **Sales Associate:** Clint Thezan. **Assistant to the General Manager:** Greg Kalkwarf.

### Field Staff

**Manager:** Ron Johnson. **Coach:** Gary Lance (pitching), U.L. Washington.

**Trainer:** Frank Kyte.

### Game Information

**Radio Announcer:** Dennis Higgins. **No. of Games Broadcast:** Home-68, Away-68. **Flagship Station:** KFH 1330-AM.

**PA Announcer:** Jeff Couch. **Official Scorer:** Ted Woodward.

**Stadium Name:** Lawrence-Dumont Stadium. **Location:** I-135 to Kellogg Ave. West, north on Broadway, west on Lewis. **Standard Game Times:** 7:15 p.m.; Sun. (April-May) 2:15, (June-Aug.) 6:15.

**Visiting Club Hotel:** Ramada Hotel at Broadview Place, 400 W. Central, Wichita, KS 67202. Telephone: (316) 262-5000.

# CALIFORNIA LEAGUE

### Class A Advanced

Joe Gagliardi

**Office Address:** 2380 S. Bascom Ave., Ste. 200, Campbell, CA 95008. **Telephone:** (408) 369-8038. **FAX:** (408) 369-1409.

**President/Treasurer:** Joe Gagliardi.

**Vice Presidents:** Rick Smith, Bruce Bucz, Hank Stickney, Harry Stavrenos.

**Directors:** Fred Anderson (Modesto), Bobby Brett (High Desert), Bruce Bucz (Visalia), Mike Ellis (Riverside), Lowell Patton (Bakersfield), Dick Phelps (Stockton), Harry Stavrenos (San Jose), Hank Stickney (Rancho Cucamonga), Ken Stickney (Lake Elsinore), Donna Tuttle (San Bernardino).

**League Administrator:** Kathy Kelly.

**Years League Active:** 1941-1942, 1946-.

**1995 Opening Date:** April 6. **Closing Date:** Sept. 3.

**No. of Games:** 140.

**Division Structure: North**—Bakersfield, Modesto, San Jose, Stockton, Visalia. **South**—High Desert, Lake Elsinore, Rancho Cucamonga, Riverside, San Bernardino.

**Playoff Format:** First-half division winners play second-half division winners in best-of-3 series. Division playoff winners meet in best-of-5 series for league championship.

**All-Star Game:** June 20 at Lake Elsinore.

**Roster Limit:** 25 active. **Player Eligibility Rule:** No more than two players and one player-coach on active list may have more than six years experience.

**Brand of Baseball:** Rawlings ROM EL.

**Statistician:** Howe Sportsdata International, Boston Fish Pier, West Bldg. #2—Suite 306, Boston MA 02210; P.O. Box 5061, San Mateo, CA 94402.

## 1994 Standings (Overall)

| Club (Affiliate) | W | L | Pct. | GB | '94 Manager |
|---|---|---|---|---|---|
| #Modesto (Athletics) | 96 | 40 | .706 | — | Dick Scott |
| #Riverside (Mariners) | 87 | 49 | .640 | 9 | Dave Myers |
| *Rancho Cucamonga (Padres) | 77 | 59 | .566 | 19 | Tim Flannery |
| San Jose (Giants) | 74 | 62 | .544 | 22 | Dick Dietz |
| Bakersfield (Dodgers) | 69 | 67 | .507 | 27 | John Shelby |
| Central Valley (Rockies) | 65 | 71 | .478 | 31 | Bill Hayes |
| Lake Elsinore (Angels) | 65 | 71 | .478 | 31 | Mitch Seoane |
| Stockton (Brewers) | 54 | 82 | .397 | 42 | Lamar Johnson |
| San Bernardino (Co-op) | 48 | 88 | .353 | 48 | Greg Mahlberg |
| High Desert (Co-op) | 45 | 91 | .331 | 51 | Phil Hannon |

*Won playoffs #Won split-season pennant

## Stadium Information

| | | Dimensions | | | | |
|---|---|---|---|---|---|---|
| Club | Stadium | LF | CF | RF | Capacity | '94 Att. |
| Bakersfield | Sam Lynn | 328 | 354 | 328 | 3,200 | 141,505 |
| High Desert | Mavericks | 340 | 401 | 340 | 3,593 | 171,783 |
| Lake Elsinore | The Diamond | 330 | 400 | 310 | 8,066 | 357,123 |
| Modesto | Thurman Field | 345 | 410 | 355 | 2,500 | 109,314 |
| R. Cucamonga | R.C. Sports Complex | 330 | 400 | 330 | 4,600 | 386,633 |
| Riverside | Sports Center | 330 | 400 | 330 | 3,500 | 85,358 |
| San Bernardino | Fiscalini Field | 330 | 387 | 330 | 3,500 | 101,710 |
| San Jose | Municipal | 340 | 390 | 340 | 4,200 | 133,091 |
| Stockton | Hebert Field | 325 | 392 | 335 | 3,500 | 114,013 |
| Visalia | Recreation Park | 320 | 405 | 320 | 2,000 | 92,756 |

Visalia franchise was known as Central Valley in 1994

# BAKERSFIELD
## *BLAZE*

**Office Address:** 4009 Chester Ave., Bakersfield, CA 93301. **Mailing Address:** P.O. Box 10031, Bakersfield, CA 93389. **Telephone:** (805) 322-1363. **FAX:** (805) 322-6199.

**Affiliation:** Co-op. **Years In League:** 1941-42, 1946-75, 1978-79, 1982-.

**Team Colors:** Navy blue and red.

### Ownership, Management

**Principal Owner/President:** Lowell Patton.

**Vice President/General Manager:** Rick Smith. **Vice President/ Baseball Operations:** Jack Patton. **Assistant General Manager/Director of Stadium Operations:** Susan Wells. **Assistant General Manager/Director of Sales, Marketing:** Jim Gregovich. **Assistant General Manager/Director of Community Relations:** Stephanie Taylor. **Director of Ticket Sales:** Crickett Whitaker.

### Field Staff

**Manager:** Unavailable. **Coaches:** Unavailable.

**Trainer:** Unavailable.

### Game Information

**Radio Announcer:** Mark Roberts. **No. of Games Broadcast:** Home-70, Away-70. **Flagship Station:** Unavailable.

**PA Announcer:** Unavailable. **Official Scorer:** Dennis DeVos.

**Stadium Name:** Sam Lynn Ballpark. **Location:** Freeway 99 to California Ave. exit, east three miles to Chester Ave., left two miles to stadium. **Standard Game Times:** 7:15 p.m..

**Visiting Club Hotel:** Unavailable.

# HIGH DESERT
## *MAVERICKS*

**Office Address:** 12000 Stadium Way, Adelanto, CA 92301. **Telephone:** (619) 246-6287. **FAX:** (619) 246-3197.

**Affiliation (first year):** Baltimore Orioles (1995). **Years in League:** 1991-.

**Team Colors:** Red and black.

### Ownership, Management

**Operated by:** High Desert Mavericks, Inc.

**President:** Bobby Brett.

**General Manager:** Steve Pastorino. **Director of Stadium Operations:** Kurt Wise. **Director of Sales/Marketing:** Pete Thuresson. **Director of Public Relations:** Mike Lieberman. **Director of Concessions:** Michael Guarini. **Account Executive/Director of Merchandising:** Chris Westall. **Office Manager:** Tana Bertaux. **Head Groundskeeper:** Tino Gonzalez.

### Field Staff

**Manager:** Tim Blackwell. **Coaches:** Jeff Morris (pitching), Dave Stockstill.

**Trainer:** Dave Walker.

### Game Information

**Radio Announcer:** Chuck Valenches. **No. of Games Broadcast:** Home-70, Away-70. **Flagship Station:** K-STAR 1590-AM.

**PA Announcer:** Dan Hubbard. **Official Scorer:** Larry Ryser.

**Stadium Name:** Mavericks Stadium. **Location:** I-15 to Highway 395 to Adelanto Road. **Standard Game Times:** 7:05 p.m.; Sun. (April-May) 1:05, (June-Sept.) 5:05.

**Visiting Club Hotel:** Unavailable.

# LAKE ELSINORE
## *STORM*

**Office Address:** 500 Diamond Dr., Lake Elsinore, CA 92530. **Mailing Address:** P.O. Box 535, Lake Elsinore, CA 92530. **Telephone:** (909) 245-4487. **FAX:** (909) 245-0305.

**Affiliation (first year):** California Angels (1994). **Years in League:** 1994-.

**Team Colors:** Blue, silver and black.

## Ownership, Management

**Operated by:** Quantum Entertainment, Inc.

**Principal Owner/President:** Ken Stickney.

**General Manager:** Kevin Haughian. **Assistant General Manager/ Sales, Marketing, Public Relations:** David Louis. **National Sales Director:** Andy Schneeweiss. **Media/Public Relations Assistant:** Wayne Teats. **Regional Marketing Director:** Mark Ottinger. **Director of Ticket Operations:** Steve Lee. **Assistant Ticket Director:** Mike Rigano. **Director of Community Marketing:** George Stieren. **Group Sales Assistants:** Brent Boznanski, Kerry Fopma. **Director of Merchandising:** Tim Kastelic. **Director of Broadcasting:** Matt Devlin. **Special Events Coordinator:** Matthew Siroky. **Accounting Administrator:** Yvonne Hunneman. **Office Manager:** Jo Equila.

## Field Staff

**Manager:** Mitch Seoane. **Coaches:** Doug Davis, Howie Gershberg (pitching).

**Trainer:** Alan Russell.

## Game Information

**Radio Announcer:** Matt Devlin. **No. of Games Broadcast:** Home-71, Away-71. **Flagship Station:** KRTM 88.9-FM.

**PA Announcer:** Unavailable. **Official Scorer:** Unavailable.

**Stadium Name:** Lake Elsinore Diamond. **Location:** I-15 to Diamond Drive, west on Diamond to stadium. **Standard Game Times:** 7:05 p.m.; Sun. (April-June 4) 2:05 , (June 20-Sept.) 5:05.

**Visiting Club Hotel:** Lake View Inn, 31808 Casino Dr., Lake Elsinore, CA 92530. Telephone: (909) 674-9694.

# MODESTO
## *A's*

**Office Address:** 501 Neece Dr., Modesto, CA 95351. **Mailing Address:** P.O. Box 883, Modesto, CA 95353. **Telephone:** (209) 529-7368. **FAX:** (209) 529-7213.

**Affiliation (first year):** Oakland A's (1975). **Years in League:** 1946-64, 1966-.

**Team Colors:** Green and gold.

## Ownership, Management

**Operated by:** Modesto A's Baseball Club, Inc.

**Principal Owners:** Fred Anderson, Kevin McClatchy.

**Chairman of the Board:** Fred Anderson. **President:** Kevin McClatchy.

**General Manager:** Tim Marting. **Assistant General Manager/Public Relations:** David Gottfried. **Controller:** Bob Hernfeldt. **Director of Stadium Operations:** Jim Niskanen. **Head Groundskeeper:** Walter Woodley. **Director of Sales/Marketing:** David Meyerson. **Director of Community Relations/Ticket Sales:** Stephanie Platner.

## Field Staff

**Manager:** Casey Parsons. **Coach:** Rick Rodriguez (pitching).

**Trainer:** Rich Ramirez

## Game Information

**Radio Announcers:** Steve Patras, Marty Lanser. **No. of Games Broadcast:** Home-40, Away-40. **Flagship Station:** KFIV 1360-AM.

**PA Announcer:** Robert Chandler. **Official Scorer:** Robert Tennant.

**Stadium Name:** John Thurman Field. **Location:** Hwy. 99 to Tuolomne Blvd./B Street exit, one block west to Neece Dr., left ¼ mile to ballpark. **Standard Game Times:** 7:15 p.m.; Sun. (April-May) 1:15, (June-Aug.) 5:15.

**Visiting Club Hotels:** Vagabond Inn, 1525 McHenry Ave., Modesto, CA 95350. Telephone: (209) 521-6340; Red Lion Hotel, 1150 Ninth St., Modesto, CA 95354. Telephone: (209) 526-6000.

# RANCHO CUCAMONGA
## *QUAKES*

**Office Address:** 8408 Rochester Ave., Rancho Cucamonga, CA 91730. **Mailing Address:** P.O. Box 4139, Rancho Cucamonga, CA 91729. **Telephone:** (909) 481-5000. **FAX:** (909) 481-5005.

**Affiliation (first year):** San Diego Padres (1993). **Years In League:** 1993-.

**Team Colors:** Turquoise and white.

## Ownership, Management

**Operated by:** Valley Baseball Club, Inc.

**Principal Owners:** Hank Stickney, Mark Harmon, Bob Clark, Roy Englebrecht, Jack Cooley, Judith Hamilton.

**Board of Directors:** Hank Stickney, Lance Masters, Barry Axelrod, Bill Courtney, Roy Englebrecht.

**President/General Manager:** Hank Stickney.

**Executive Vice President:** Roy Englebrecht. **Vice President:** Scott Kelly. **Controller:** Jay Middleton. **Director of Operations:** Brent Mater. **Director of Special Events:** Diane Rinehart. **Ticket Sales Manager:** Jim Kiersnowski. **Group Sales Manager:** Michelle Van Elzakker. **Public Relations Manager:** Greg Scharlach. **Merchandise Manager:** Art Munda. **Senior Account Representative:** Rebecca Richardson. **Account Executive:** Brant Ringler. **Head Groundskeeper:** Rex Whitney. **Office Manager:** Janet Dube.

### Field Staff

**Manager:** Marty Barrett. **Coach:** Dave Smith (pitching).

**Trainer:** Jim Daniel.

### Game Information

**Radio Announcer:** Joe Castellano. **No. of Games Broadcast:** Home-70, Away-70. **Flagship Station:** KMNY 1600-AM.

**PA Announcer:** David Achord. **Official Scorer:** Larry Kavanaugh.

**Stadium Name:** The Epicenter. **Location:** I-10 to I-15 North, to Foothill Blvd., exit left to Rochester Ave., left to Stadium Way. **Standard Game Times:** 7:15 p.m.; Sun. (April-June 18) 1:15, (June 25-Sept.) 5:15.

**Visiting Club Hotel:** Best Western Heritage Inn, 8179 Spruce Ave., Rancho Cucamonga, CA 91730. Telephone: (909) 466-1111.

## RIVERSIDE
## *PILOTS*

**Office Address:** 1000 Blaine St., Riverside, CA 92507. **Mailing Address:** P.O. Box 56171, Riverside, CA 92517. **Telephone:** (909) 276-3352. **FAX:** (909) 276-4954.

**Affiliation (first year):** Seattle Mariners (1993). **Years in League:** 1941, 1988-90, 1993-.

**Team Colors:** Blue, teal and silver.

### Ownership, Management

**Operated by:** Clutch Play Baseball.

**Chairman:** Horn Chen. **President:** Mike Ellis.

**Vice President/General Manager:** Matt Ellis. **Assistant General Manager:** Kyle Fisher. **Director of Marketing:** Eileen Garcia. **Head Groundskeeper:** George Valencia.

### Field Staff

**Manager:** Terry Kennedy. **Coaches:** Juan Eichelberger (pitching), Tom LeVasseur.

**Trainer:** Robert Nodine.

### Game Information

**Radio:** Unavailable.

**PA Announcer:** Ed Vasquez. **Official Scorer:** Mike Hays.

**Stadium Name:** Riverside Sports Complex. **Location:** Blaine Street exit off Hwy. 60, north three blocks, stadium on right. **Standard Game Times:** 7:15 p.m.; Sun. 6.

**Visiting Club Hotel:** Unavailable.

## SAN BERNARDINO
## *SPIRIT*

**Office Address:** 1007 E. Highland Ave., San Bernardino, CA 92404. **Mailing Address:** P.O. Box 30780, San Bernardino, CA 92413. **Telephone:** (909) 881-1836. **FAX:** (909) 883-6279.

**Affiliation (first year):** Los Angeles Dodgers (1995). **Years in League:** 1941, 1987-.

**Team Colors:** Red, white and blue.

### Ownership, Management

**Operated by:** San Bernardino Spirit Baseball, Inc.

**Principal Owners:** David Elmore, Donna Tuttle.

**General Manager:** Jim Wehmeier. **Assistant General Manager:** Jason Watson. **Director of Business Operations:** Kathleen Hightower. **Director of Stadium Operations:** Matt Testrake. **Director of Media/Public Relations:** Rick Liebling. **Director of Sales/Marketing:** Charles Pickering. **Director of Merchandising:** Blake Inman. **Director of Ticket Sales:**

Steve Berry.

### Field Staff

**Manager:** Ron Roenicke. **Coaches:** Dino Ebel, Dennis Lewallyn (pitching).

**Trainer:** Mike Collins.

### Game Information

**Radio Announcer:** Mike Saeger. **No. of Games Broadcast:** Home-70, Away-70. **Flagship Station:** KMEN 1290-AM.

**PA Announcer:** Unavailable. **Official Scorer:** Unavailable.

**Stadium Name:** Fiscalini Field. **Location:** I-215 North to Highland Ave., east on Highland for 5 miles. **Standard Game Times:** 7 p.m.; Sun. (April-May) 2, (June-Aug.) 6.

**Visiting Club Hotel:** Radisson Hotel and Convention Center, 295 North E St., San Bernardino, CA 92401. Telephone: (909) 381-6181.

## SAN JOSE
## *GIANTS*

**Office Address:** 588 E. Alma Ave., San Jose, CA 95112. **Mailing Address:** P.O. Box 21727, San Jose, CA 95151. **Telephone:** (408) 297-1435. **FAX:** (408) 297-1453.

**Affiliation (first year):** San Francisco Giants (1988). **Years in League:** 1942, 1947-58, 1962-76, 1979-.

**Team Colors:** Orange and black.

### Ownership, Management

**Operated by:** Progress Sports Management.

**Principal Owners:** Winston Cox, Richard Beahrs.

**President:** Harry Stavrenos.

**General Manager:** Mark Wilson. **Assistant General Manager:** Buzz Hardy. **Director of Stadium Operations:** Rick Tracy. **Director of Sales:** Linda Pereira. **Director of Promotions:** Steve Fields.

### Field Staff

**Manager:** Carlos Lezcano. **Coaches:** Jim Davenport, Todd Oakes (pitching).

**Trainer:** Donna Papangellin.

### Game Information

**Radio Announcers:** Andre Polizzi, Steve Hilleary. **No. of Games Broadcast:** Home-20, Away-30. **Flagship Station:** KSJS 90.7-FM.

**PA Announcer:** Jim Chapman. **Official Scorers:** Ed Bautista, John Pletsch.

**Stadium Name:** Municipal Stadium. **Location:** From I-280—10th Street exit to Alma, left on Alma, stadium on right. From US 101—Tully Road exit to Senter, right on Senter, left on Alma, stadium on left. **Standard Game Times:** 7:15 p.m.; Sat. 5; Sun. (April-June) 1:30, (July-Aug.) 5.

**Visiting Club Hotel:** Gateway Inn, 2585 Seaboard Ave., San Jose, CA 95131. Telephone: (408) 435-8800.

## STOCKTON
## *PORTS*

**Office Address:** Billy Hebert Field, Sutter and Alpine Streets, Stockton, CA 95204. **Mailing Address:** P.O. Box 8550, Stockton, CA 95208. **Telephone:** (209) 944-5943. **FAX:** (209) 463-4937.

**Affiliation (first year):** Milwaukee Brewers (1978). **Years in League:** 1941, 1946-72, 1978-.

**Team Colors:** Blue and gold.

### Ownership, Management

**Operated by:** Joy in Mudville, Inc.

**Principal Owner:** Richard Phelps.

**General Manager:** Dan Chapman. **Assistant General Manager:** Alfred Spear. **Controller:** Margaret Womack. **Director of Stadium Operations:** Alan Fleming. **Director of Public Relations/Merchandising:** Jeff Curtis. **Office Manager:** Molly Rogers.

### Field Staff

**Manager:** Bob Mariano. **Coaches:** Gus Gil, Mark Littell (pitching).

**Trainer:** Richard Stark.

### Game Information

**Radio:** None.

**PA Announcer:** Johnny Milford. **Official Scorer:** Unavailable.

**Stadium Name:** Billy Hebert Field. **Location:** From I-5—March Lane exit east, south on Pacific Ave., east on Alpine Ave. From Hwy. 99—Wilson Way exit west to Alpine Ave, west on Alpine. **Standard Game Times:** 7:05 p.m.; Sun. 5.

**Visiting Club Hotel:** Stockton Inn, 4219 E. Waterloo Rd., Stockton, CA 95215. Telephone: (209) 931-3131.

# VISALIA
## *OAKS*

**Office Address:** 440 N. Giddings Ave., Visalia, CA 93291. **Mailing Address:** P.O. Box 48, Visalia, CA 93279. **Telephone:** (209) 625-0480. **FAX:** (209) 739-7732.

**Affiliation:** Independent. **Years in League:** 1946-62, 1968-75, 1977-.

**Team Colors:** Maroon, green and gold.

### Ownership, Management

**Operated by:** JSS/USA, Inc.

**Principal Owner/Chairman of the Board:** Keiichi Tsukamoto.

**President:** John McHale Sr. **Vice President:** Acey Kohrogi.

**Vice President/General Manager:** Bruce Bucz. **Assistant General Manager:** Bob Flanagan. **Assistant General Manager/Director of Stadium Operations:** Ken Nagata.

### Field Staff

**Manager:** Unavailable. **Coaches:** Unavailable.

**Trainer:** Unavailable.

### Game Information

**Radio:** None.

**PA Announcer/Official Scorer:** Harry Kargenian.

**Stadium Name:** Recreation Park. **Location:** US 99 to Hwy 198, east to Giddings Avenue, north one mile to ballpark. **Standard Game Times:** 7:05 p.m., Sun. 6:05.

**Visiting Club Hotel:** Thriftlodge, 4645 W. Mineral King Ave., Visalia, CA 93277. Telephone: (209) 732-5611.

# CAROLINA LEAGUE

## Class A Advanced

John Hopkins

**Office Address:** 1806 Pembroke Rd., Greensboro, NC 27408. **Mailing Address:** P.O. Box 9503, Greensboro, NC 27429. **Telephone:** (910) 691-9030. **FAX:** (910) 691-9070.

**President/Treasurer:** John Hopkins.

**Vice President:** Kelvin Bowles. **Executive Vice President:** Calvin Falwell. **Corporate Secretary:** Peter Kirk.

**Directors:** Don Beaver (Winston-Salem), Kelvin Bowles (Salem), Calvin Falwell (Lynchburg), Jim Goodmon (Durham), North Johnson (Kinston), Peter Kirk (Frederick), Matt Minker (Wilmington), Art Silber (Prince William).

**Years League Active:** 1945-.

**1995 Opening Date:** April 6. **Closing Date:** Sept. 2.

**No. of Games:** 140.

**Division Structure: Northern**—Frederick, Lynchburg, Prince William, Wilmington. **Southern**—Durham, Kinston, Salem, Winston-Salem.

**Playoff Format:** First-half division winners play second-half division winners in best-of-3 series. Division playoff winners meet in best-of-5 series for league championship.

**All-Star Game:** July 19 at Lynchburg.

**Roster Limit:** 25 active. **Player Eligibility Rule:** No age limit. No more than two players and one player-coach on active list may have more than six years experience.

**Brand of Baseball:** Rawlings.

**Statistician:** Howe Sportsdata International, Boston Fish Pier, West Bldg. #2—Suite 306, Boston MA 02210.

### 1994 Standings (Overall)

| Club (Affiliate) | W | L | Pct. | GB | '94 Manager |
|---|---|---|---|---|---|
| *#Wilmington (Royals) | 94 | 44 | .681 | — | Mike Jirschele |
| Frederick (Orioles) | 76 | 61 | .555 | 17½ | Mike O'Berry |
| Prince William (White Sox) | 71 | 65 | .522 | 22 | Dave Huppert |
| #Winston-Salem (Reds) | 67 | 70 | .489 | 26½ | Mark Berry |
| #Durham (Braves) | 66 | 70 | .485 | 27 | Matt West |
| Salem (Pirates) | 64 | 75 | .460 | 30½ | Trent Jewett |
| Kinston (Indians) | 60 | 78 | .435 | 34 | Dave Keller |
| Lynchburg (Red Sox) | 52 | 87 | .374 | 42½ | Mark Meleski |

*Won playoffs #Won split-season pennant

### Stadium Information

| | | Dimensions | | | | |
|---|---|---|---|---|---|---|
| Club | Stadium | LF | CF | RF | Capacity | '94 Att. |
| Durham | Athletic Park | 305 | 400 | 327 | 7,500 | 259,758 |
| Frederick | Grove | 325 | 400 | 325 | 5,400 | 344,563 |
| Kinston | Grainger | 335 | 390 | 335 | 4,100 | 122,557 |
| Lynchburg | City | 325 | 390 | 325 | 4,000 | 100,724 |
| Prince William | County | 315 | 400 | 315 | 6,000 | 210,401 |
| Salem | Salem Baseball | 316 | 408 | 302 | 5,000 | 153,575 |
| Wilmington | Frawley | 325 | 400 | 325 | 5,775 | 335,024 |
| Winston-Salem | Ernie Shore | 335 | 400 | 325 | 6,280 | 160,994 |

## DURHAM
*BULLS*

**Office Address:** 411 Blackwell St., Durham, NC 27701. **Mailing Address:** P.O. Box 507, Durham, NC 27702. **Telephone:** (919) 688-8211. **FAX:** (919) 688-4593.

**Affiliation (first year):** Atlanta Braves (1980). **Years in League:** 1945-1971, 1980-.

**Team Colors:** Royal blue and Texas tan.

### Ownership, Management

**Operated by:** Capitol Broadcasting Co., Inc.

**Principal Owner/President:** James Goodmon.

**Vice President/General Manager:** Peter Anlyan. **Director of Stadium Operations:** Bill Miller. **Stadium Operations Assistant:** Joe Bialek. **Director of Sales/Marketing:** Rod Meadows. **Director of Promotions:** Kevin Estrella. **Director of Ticket Sales:** Mike Snee. **Director of Group Sales:** Rodney Scott. **Office Manager:** Kecia Tillman. **Telemarketing Director:** Evan Saunderson. **Souvenir Managers:** Mike Davis, Anna Maynard. **Sales Assistant:** Jacqueline Jones. **Receptionist:** Dawn Phillips. **Group Sales Account Executive:** Valerie Parrish.

### Field Staff

**Manager:** Matt West. **Coaches:** Bill Slack (pitching), Brian Snitker.

**Trainer:** Jay Williams.

### Game Information

**Radio Announcer:** Steve Barnes. **No. of Games Broadcast:** Home-70, Away-70. **Flagship Station:** WDNC 620-AM.

**PA Announcer:** Unavailable. **Official Scorer:** Brent Belvin.

**Stadium Name:** New Durham Athletic Park. **Location:** From Raleigh—I-40 West to Hwy. 147 North, Roxboro Road exit to Willard, two blocks on Willard to stadium. From I-85—Gregson Street exit to downtown, left on Chapel Hill Street, right on Mangum Street. **Standard Game Times:** 7:30 p.m.; Sun. 6:05.

**Visiting Club Hotel:** Red Roof Inn, I-85 at Guess Road, Durham, NC 27705. Telephone: (919) 471-9882.

## FREDERICK
*KEYS*

**Office Address:** 6201 New Design Road., Frederick, MD 21701. **Mailing Address:** P.O. Box 3169, Frederick, MD 21705. **Telephone:** (301) 662-0013. **FAX:** (301) 662-0018.

**Affiliation (first year):** Baltimore Orioles (1989). **Years In League:** 1989-.

**Team Colors:** Black, orange, white and green.

### Ownership, Management

**Operated by:** Maryland Baseball Limited Partnership, Inc.

**Principal Owners:** Peter Kirk, Hugh Schindel, Frank Perdue, Pete Simmons.

**Chairman:** Peter Kirk. **President:** Hugh Schindel.

**General Manager:** Larry Martin. **Assistant General Manager:** Jim Halloran. **Director of Stadium Operations:** Dave Wisner. **Director of Public Relations:** Estelle Krieger. **Director of Promotions:** Steve Burton. **Director of Group Sales/Skybox Services:** Mark Thome. **Clubhouse Operations:** George Bell. **Office Manager:** Sharon Hoffman. **Director of Merchandise:** Pete Orth. **Director of Food Service Operations:** Jack Boehmer. **Director of Telemarketing:** Carolyn McDaniel. **Assistant Director of Telemarketing/Group Sales:** Gina Little. **Receptionist/Bookkeeper:** Laura Springer.

### Field Staff

**Manager:** Mike O'Berry. **Coaches:** Joe Durham, Larry McCall (pitching).

**Trainer:** Rudy Higgins.

### Game Information

**Radio Announcers:** Matt Hicks, Matt Noble. **No. of Games Broadcast:** Home-70, Away-70. **Flagship Station:** WQSI 820-AM.

**PA Announcer:** Jeff Wachter. **Official Scorer:** Bryan Hissey.

**Stadium Name:** Harry Grove Stadium. **Location:** On New Design Road, near intersection of I-70 and Route 355 (Market Street exit). **Standard Game Times:** 7:05 p.m.; Sun. (April-June) 2:05, (July-Aug.) 4:05.

**Visiting Club Hotel:** Comfort Inn, 420 Prospect Blvd., Frederick, MD 21701. Telephone: (301) 695-6200.

## KINSTON
### *INDIANS*

**Office Address:** 400 E. Grainger Ave., Kinston, NC 28501. **Mailing Address:** P.O. Box 3542, Kinston, NC 28502. **Telephone:** (919) 527-9111. **FAX:** (919) 527-2328.

**Affiliation (first year):** Cleveland Indians (1987). **Years in League:** 1956-57, 1962-74, 1978-.

**Team Colors:** Navy blue and red.

### Ownership, Management

**Operated by:** Slugger Partners, L.P.

**Principal Owners:** Cam McRae, North Johnson.

**Chairman:** Cam McRae. **President:** North Johnson. **Corporate Secretary:** Emily Ashburn.

**General Manager:** North Johnson. **Assistant General Manager:** David Echols. **Director of Publications/Advertising:** Kathy Mair.

### Field Staff

**Manager:** Gordy MacKenzie. **Coaches:** Tony Arnold (pitching), Dan Williams.

**Trainer:** Teddy Blackwell.

### Game Information

**Radio Announcer:** Bob McElligott. **No. of Games Broadcast:** Home-70, Away-70. **Flagship Station:** WELS 102.9-FM.

**PA Announcer:** Unavailable. **Official Scorer:** Karl Grant.

**Stadium Name:** Grainger Stadium. **Location:** ½ mile off Hwy. 11 and Route 70 Business. **Standard Game Times:** 7 p.m.; Sun. (April-June) 3, (July-Sept.) 7.

**Visiting Club Hotel:** Sheraton-Kinston, 1403 Richland Rd., Kinston, NC 28501. Telephone: (919) 523-1400.

## LYNCHBURG
### *HILL CATS*

**Office Address:** City Stadium, Fort Avenue and Wythe Road, Lynchburg, VA 24501. **Mailing Address:** P.O. Box 10213, Lynchburg, VA 24506. **Telephone:** (804) 528-1144. **FAX:** (804) 846-0768.

**Affiliation (first year):** Pittsburgh Pirates (1995). **Years in League:** 1966-.

**Team Colors:** Yellow, green and black.

### Ownership, Management

**Operated by:** Lynchburg Baseball Corp.

**President:** Calvin Falwell. **Vice President:** Rex Angel. **Treasurer:** Bill Hibbert. **Corporate Secretary:** Gene Gallagher.

**General Manager:** Paul Sunwall. **Assistant General Manager:** Ronnie Roberts. **Head Groundskeeper/Sales:** Darren Johnson. **Office Manager:** Karen East. **Concessions Manager:** Mike Byrd. **Director of Broadcasting/Sales:** John Miller. **Assistant Director of Broadcasting/Sales:** Anthony Marek.

### Field Staff

**Manager:** Marc Hill. **Coach:** Jim Bibby (pitching).

**Trainer:** Rod Lich.

### Game Information

**Radio Announcers:** John Miller, Anthony Marek. **No. of Games Broadcast:** Home-70, Away-70. **Flagship Station:** WLNI 105.9-FM.

**PA Announcer:** Chuck Young. **Official Scorers:** Malcolm Haley, Chuck Young.

**Stadium Name:** City Stadium. **Location:** U.S. 29 South to City Stadium exit; U.S. 29 North to Lynchburg College exit. **Standard Game Times:** 7:05 p.m.; Sun. (April-June) 2:05, (July-Sept.) 7:05.

**Visiting Club Hotel:** Best Western, 2815 Candlers Mountain Road, Lynchburg, VA 24502. Telephone: (804) 237-2986.

## PRINCE WILLIAM
## *CANNONS*

**Office Address:** 7 County Complex Ct., Woodbridge, VA 22193. **Mailing Address:** P.O. Box 2148, Woodbridge, VA 22193. **Telephone:** (703) 590-2311. **FAX:** (703) 590-5716.

**Affiliation (first year):** Chicago White Sox (1994). **Years in League:** 1978-.

**Team Colors:** Black, silver and white.

### Ownership, Management

**Operated by:** Prince William Professional Baseball Club, Inc.

**Principal Owner/President:** Art Silber.

**Vice President:** Pat Filippone. **Treasurer:** Lani Silber. **Corporate Secretary:** Seth Silber.

**Vice President/General Manager:** Pat Filippone. **Assistant General Manager:** Andy Ruge. **Director of Food Services:** Bob Kratky. **Direct Marketing Manager:** David John. **Director of Stadium Operations:** Matt Buckley. **Director of Community Relations:** Darran Miner. **Director of Broadcasting/Media Relations:** Jim Olson. **Operations Assistant:** Dave Hough. **Ticket Assistant:** Joe Mertinko.

### Field Staff

**Manager:** Dave Huppert. **Coaches:** Jaime Garcia (pitching), Jay Ward.

**Trainer:** Scott Takao.

### Game Information

**Radio Announcer:** Jim Olson. **No. of Games Broadcast:** Home-70; Away-70. **Flagship Station:** WAGE 1200-AM.

**PA Announcer:** Charles "Trip" Morgan. **Official Scorer:** John Oravec.

**Stadium Name:** Prince William County Stadium. **Location:** I-95 South to exit 160, left at second light, 6 miles on Old Bridge Rd.; I-95 North to exit 156, right on Hillendale Rd., left on Prince William Parkway, left at light. **Standard Game Times:** 7:30 p.m.; Sat. 7; Sun. 1:30.

**Visiting Club Hotel:** Days Inn-Potomac Mills, 14619 Potomac Mills Rd., Woodbridge, VA 22192. Telephone: (703) 494-4433.

## SALEM
## *AVALANCHE*

**Office Address:** 1004 Texas St., Salem, VA 24153. **Mailing Address:** P.O. Box 842, Salem, VA 24153. **Telephone:** (703) 389-3333. **FAX:** (703) 389-9710.

**Affiliation (first year):** Colorado Rockies (1995). **Years In League:** 1968-.

**Team Colors:** Purple, silver and black.

### Ownership, Management

**Operated by:** Salem Professional Baseball Club, Inc.

**Principal Owner/President:** Kelvin Bowles.

**General Manager:** Sam Lazzaro. **Assistant General Manager:** Dennis Robarge. **Director of Stadium Operations/Head Groundskeeper:** Stan Macko. **Director of Sales/Marketing:** Dave Shonk. **Director of Community Relations:** Lara Steward. **Director of Ticket Sales:** Mike Holdren. **Director of Group Sales:** Deron Marchant. **Director of Merchandising:** Sue Lazzaro.

### Field Staff

**Manager:** Bill Hayes. **Coach:** Billy Champion (pitching), Tony Torchia.

**Trainer:** Bill Borowski.

### Game Information

**Radio Announcer:** Unavailable. **No. of Games Broadcast:** Home-70, Away-70. **Flagship Station:** WROV 1240-AM.

**PA Announcer:** Craig Wright. **Official Scorer:** Brian Hoffman.

**Stadium Name:** Salem Baseball Stadium. **Location:** Salem Civic Center Complex exit off I-81 to Civic Center. **Standard Game Times:** 7 p.m.; Sun. (April-June) 3, (July-Sept.) 7.

**Visiting Club Hotel:** Days Inn-Airport, 8118 Plantation Rd., Roanoke, VA 24019. Telephone: (703) 366-0341.

## WILMINGTON
## *BLUE ROCKS*

**Office Address:** 801 S. Madison St., Wilmington, DE 19801. **Telephone:** (302) 888-2015. **FAX:** (302) 888-2032.

**Affiliation (first year):** Kansas City Royals (1993). **Years in League:** 1993-.

**Team Colors:** Blue and gold.

### Ownership, Management

**Operated by:** Wilmington Blue Rock, Inc.

**Principal Owner:** Matt Minker.

**Vice President/Baseball Administration:** Ken Shepard. **General Manager:** Chris Kemple. **Assistant General Manager/Director of Stadium Operations:** Dave Oster. **Director of Business Operations:** Craig Bailey. **Assistant Director of Stadium Operations:** Dac Carbone. **Director of Broadcasting/Media Relations:** Jim Rosenhaus. **Director of Sales/Marketing:** Christopher Hill. **Assistant Directors of Sales/ Marketing:** Christian Carlson, Jeff Tagliaferro. **Director of Merchandising:** Paul Siegwarth. **Director of Ticket Sales:** Andrew Layman. **Assistant Directors of Ticket Sales:** Dave Devaney, David Osborne. **Director of Group Sales:** Marla Chalfie. **Assistant Director of Group Sales:** Jim McNinch. **Office Manager:** Melody Hayes. **Directors of Food Services:** Mike Larkin, Brian Rappaport. **Merchandising Assistant:** Chris Parise. **Media/Comunity Relations Assistant:** Sam Nishi.

### Field Staff

**Manager:** John Mizerock. **Coaches:** Tom Burgmeier (pitching), Sixto Lezcano.

**Trainer:** John Finley.

### Game Information

**Radio Announcer:** Jim Rosenhaus. **No. of Games Broadcast:** Home-70, Away-70. **Flagship Station:** WJBR 1290-AM.

**PA Announcer:** John McAdams. **Official Scorers:** David Sannino, E.J. Casey.

**Stadium Name:** Daniel S. Frawley Stadium. **Location:** I-95 North to Maryland Ave. (Exit 6), right on South Madison to ballpark; I-95 South to Martin Luther King Blvd. (Exit 6), right on South Madison. **Game Times:** 7:05 p.m.; Sat: (April-May) 2:05, (June-Sept.) 7:05; Sun. 2:05.

**Visiting Club Hotel:** Holiday Inn Downtown, 700 King St., Wilmington, DE 19801. Telephone: (302) 655-0400.

## WINSTON-SALEM
## *WARTHOGS*

**Office Address:** 401 Deacon Blvd., Winston-Salem, NC 27105. **Mailing Address:** P.O. Box 4488, Winston-Salem, NC 27115. **Telephone:** (910) 759-2233. **FAX:** (910) 759-2042.

**Affiliation (first year):** Cincinnati Reds (1993). **Years in League:** 1945-.

### Ownership, Management

**Operated by:** Beaver Sports, Inc.

**Principal Owner/President:** Don Beaver.

**Vice President:** Marty Steele.

**General Manager:** Peter Fisch. **Assistant General Manager:** Matt Roy. **Director of Stadium Operations:** Doug Renner. **Head Groundskeeper:** Eddie Busque. **Director of Community Relations:** Marvin Julich. **Office Manager:** Stephanie Darr. **Director of Merchandising:** Kevin Craiglow. **Concessions Director:** David Martin.

### Field Staff

**Manager:** Mark Berry. **Coach:** Derek Botelho (pitching).

**Trainer:** Tom Spencer.

### Game Information

**Radio:** Unavailable.

**PA Announcer:** Unavailiable. **Official Scorers:** Peter Juran, James McClintock, Jay Payne.

**Stadium Name:** Ernie Shore Field. **Location:** I-40 business to Cherry St. exit, north through downtown to Deacon Blvd., right to park. **Standard Game Times:** 7:05 p.m.; Sun. (April-June) 2:05, (July-Sept.) 6:05.

**Visiting Club Hotels:** Holiday Inn-North, 3050 University Pkwy., Winston-Salem, NC 27105. Telephone: (910) 723-2911; Ramada Inn, 531 Akron Dr., Winston-Salem, NC 27105. Telephone: (910) 767-8240.

# FLORIDA STATE LEAGUE

### Class A Advanced

Chuck Murphy

**Street Address:** 103 E. Orange Ave., Daytona Beach, FL 32114. **Mailing Address:** P.O. Box 349, Daytona Beach, FL 32115. **Telephone:** (904) 252-7479. **FAX:** (904) 252-7495.

**President/Treasurer:** Chuck Murphy.

**Vice Presidents:** Ken Carson, Rob Rabenecker. **Corporate Secretary:** David Monaco.

**Directors:** Tim Bawmann (Kissimmee), Ken Carson (Dunedin), Tony Flores (St. Petersburg), Marvin Goldklang (Fort Myers), Woody Hicks (Lakeland), Jordan Kobritz (Daytona), Ken Lehner (Brevard County), Bill MacKay (Sarasota), Tim Murphy (Charlotte), Les Parker (Tampa), Rob Rabenecker (West Palm Beach), Tom Simmons (Vero Beach), John Timberlake (Clearwater), Ross Vecchio (St. Lucie).

**Years League Active:** 1919-1927, 1936-1941, 1946-.

**1995 Opening Date:** April 6. **Closing Date:** Sept. 3.

**No. of Games:** 140.

**Division Structure: West**—Charlotte, Clearwater, Dunedin, Fort Myers, Lakeland, St. Petersburg, Sarasota, Tampa. **East**—Brevard County, Daytona, Kissimmee, St. Lucie, Vero Beach, West Palm Beach.

**Playoff Format:** First-half division winners play second-half division winners in best-of-3 series. Division playoff winners meet in best-of-5 series for league championship.

**All-Star Game:** June 24 at Charlotte.

**Roster Limit:** 25. **Player Eligibility Rule:** No age limit. No more than two players and one player-coach may have more than six years experience.

**Brand of Baseball:** Rawlings.

**Statistician:** Howe Sportsdata International, Boston Fish Pier, West Bldg. #2-Suite 306, Boston, MA 02210.

## 1994 Standings (Overall)

| Club (Affiliate) | W | L | Pct. | GB | '94 Manager |
|---|---|---|---|---|---|
| *#Tampa (Yankees) | 80 | 52 | .606 | — | Jake Gibbs |
| #Brevard County (Marlins) | 78 | 61 | .561 | 5½ | Fredi Gonzalez |
| #West Palm Beach (Expos) | 71 | 60 | .542 | 8½ | Rob Leary |
| Clearwater (Phillies) | 72 | 62 | .537 | 9 | Don McCormack |
| St. Petersburg (Cardinals) | 74 | 65 | .532 | 9½ | Mike Ramsey |
| Fort Myers (Twins) | 71 | 63 | .530 | 10 | Steve Liddle |
| St. Lucie (Mets) | 71 | 65 | .522 | 11 | Rafael Landestoy |
| #Sarasota (Red Sox) | 69 | 64 | .519 | 11½ | DeMarlo Hale |
| Dunedin (Blue Jays) | 65 | 68 | .489 | 15½ | Jim Nettles |
| Lakeland (Tigers) | 63 | 68 | .481 | 16½ | G. Groninger/M. Wagner |
| Daytona (Cubs) | 61 | 73 | .455 | 20 | Ken Bolek |
| Vero Beach (Dodgers) | 60 | 75 | .444 | 21½ | Jon Debus |
| Charlotte (Rangers) | 60 | 76 | .441 | 22 | Tommy Thompson |
| Osceola (Astros) | 46 | 89 | .341 | 35½ | Tim Tolman |

*Won playoffs #Won split-season pennant

## Stadium Information

| | | Dimensions | | | | |
|---|---|---|---|---|---|---|
| Club | Stadium | LF | CF | RF | Cap. | '94 Att. |
| Brevard County | Space Coast | 340 | 404 | 340 | 8,100 | 144,688 |
| Charlotte | Charlotte County | 340 | 410 | 340 | 6,026 | 75,821 |
| Clearwater | Jack Russell Memorial | 340 | 410 | 340 | 6,926 | 82,494 |
| Daytona | Jackie Robinson Ballpark | 315 | 400 | 325 | 4,200 | 96,756 |
| Dunedin | Dunedin | 330 | 400 | 315 | 6,201 | 80,126 |
| Fort Myers | Lee County Sports | 330 | 405 | 330 | 7,500 | 95,688 |
| Kissimmee | Osceola County | 300 | 410 | 330 | 5,100 | 38,496 |
| Lakeland | Joker Marchant | 340 | 420 | 340 | 7,000 | 21,996 |
| St. Lucie | T.J. White | 338 | 410 | 338 | 7,400 | 67,999 |
| St. Petersburg | Al Lang | 330 | 400 | 330 | 7,004 | 108,283 |
| Sarasota | Ed Smith | 340 | 400 | 340 | 7,500 | 68,781 |
| Tampa | South Florida | 340 | 400 | 340 | 3,000 | 60,855 |
| Vero Beach | Holman | 340 | 400 | 340 | 6,474 | 68,903 |
| W. Palm Beach | Municipal | 330 | 405 | 330 | 4,200 | 72,097 |

Kissimmee known as Osceola in 1994

## BREVARD COUNTY
## *MANATEES*

**Office Address:** 5800 Stadium Pkwy., Melbourne, FL 32940. **Telephone:** (407) 633-9200. **FAX:** (407) 633-9210.

**Affiliation (first year):** Florida Marlins (1994). **Years in League:** 1994-.
**Team Colors:** Blue, black, orange and beige.

### Ownership, Management

**Operated by:** Florida Marlins, Inc.

**Principal Owner:** Wayne Huizenga. **President:** Don Smiley.

**General Manager:** Ken Lehner. **Assistant General Manager:** Russ Brandon. **President, Brevard Concessions:** Roy Lake. **Manager of Facility Operations:** Martin Becker. **Ticket Manager:** Maryruth Hughey. **Ticket Representative:** Dotty McGrady. **Bookkeeper:** Debbie Uher. **Administrative Assistants:** Jason Camp, David Wheat. **Head Groundskeeper:** Barney Lopas. **Executive Secretary:** Sara Shafer.

### Field Staff

**Manager:** Fredi Gonzalez. **Coaches:** Britt Burns (pitching), Jose Castro.

**Trainer:** Vinny Scavo.

### Game Information

**Radio:** None.

**PA Announcer:** Gary Henderson. **Official Scorer:** Ron Jernick.

**Stadium Name:** Space Coast Stadium. **Location:** I-95 South to Wickham Road (exit 73), west on Wickham to Lake Andrew Drive, right on St. Johns, right on Stadium Parkway; I-95 North to Fiske Blvd. (exit 74), south on Fiske to Stadium Parkway. **Standard Game Times:** 7:05 p.m., Sun. 1:35.

**Visiting Club Hotel:** Melbourne Hilton at Rialto, 200 Rialto Place, Melbourne, FL 32901. Telephone: (407) 768-0200.

## CHARLOTTE
## *RANGERS*

**Office Address:** 2300 El Jobean Rd., Port Charlotte, FL 33948. **Mailing Address:** P.O. Box 3609, Port Charlotte, FL 33949. **Telephone:** (813) 625-9500. **FAX:** (813) 624-5168.

**Affiliation (first year):** Texas Rangers (1987). **Years in League:** 1987-.
**Team Colors:** Red, blue and white.

### Ownership, Management

**Operated by:** Texas Rangers Baseball Club, Ltd.

**Principal Owners:** B/R Rangers Associates, Ltd. (George W. Bush, Rusty Rose). **President:** Tom Schieffer.

**General Manager:** Tim Murphy. **Assistant General Manager:** Ken Mallory. **Head Groundskeeper:** Tom Burns. **Director of Sales/Marketing:** Sean Doyle. **Office Manager:** Pam Munz. **Interns:** Mark Crowder, Phil Frye.

### Field Staff

**Manager:** Butch Wynegar. **Coach:** John Tudor (pitching).

**Trainer:** Guido Van Ryssegem.

### Game Information

**Radio:** None.

**PA Announcer:** Unavailable. **Official Scorer:** Peter Dulk.

**Stadium Name:** Charlotte County Stadium. **Location:** I-75 South to exit 32, follow Toledo Blade Blvd. west for seven miles to stop sign at SR 776, right on 776 for one mile. **Standard Game Times:** 7 p.m.; Sun. 6.

**Visiting Club Hotel:** Days Inn, 1941 Tamiami Trail, Murdock, FL 33948. Telephone: (813) 627-8900.

## CLEARWATER
## *PHILLIES*

**Office Address:** 800 Phillies Dr., Clearwater, FL 34615. **Mailing Address:** P.O. Box 10336, Clearwater, FL 34617. **Telephone:** (813) 441-8638. **FAX:** (813) 447-3924.

**Affiliation (first year):** Philadelphia Phillies (1985). **Years in League:** 1985-.
**Team Colors:** Red, white and blue.

### Ownership, Management

**Operated by:** The Philadelphia Phillies.

**Principal Owner/Chairman:** Bill Giles.

**General Manager:** Jim Herlihy. **Director of Business Operations:** Dianne Gonzalez. **Director of Stadium Operations:** Kent Harman. **Head Groundskeeper:** Opie Cheek. **Director of Sales/Marketing:** Toby O'Brien. **Director of Ticket Sales:** Jenna Bostic.

### Field Staff

**Manager:** Don McCormack. **Coaches:** Darold Knowles (pitching), Greg Legg.

**Trainer:** Clete Sigwart.

### Game Information

**Radio:** None.

**PA Announcer:** Don Guckian. **Official Scorer:** Unavailable.

**Stadium Name:** Jack Russell Memorial. **Location:** US Highway 19 north to Drew St., west to Greenwood Ave., north to Seminole St., right to park. **Standard Game Times:** 7 p.m., Sun. 5.

**Visiting Club Hotels:** Howard Johnson's, 20967 US 19 N., Clearwater, FL 34625. Telephone: (813) 799-1181; Holiday Inn, 21030 US 19 N., Clearwater, FL 34625. Telephone: (813) 797-8173.

## DAYTONA
## *CUBS*

**Office Address:** 105 E. Orange Ave., Daytona Beach, FL 32114. **Mailing Address:** P.O. Box 15080, Daytona Beach, FL 32115. **Telephone:** (904) 257-3172. **FAX:** (904) 257-3382.

**Affiliation (first year):** Chicago Cubs (1993). **Years in League:** 1920-24, 1928, 1936-41, 1946-73, 1977-87, 1993-.

**Team Colors:** Red, blue and black.

### Ownership, Management

**Operated by:** Florida Professional Sports, Inc.

**Principal Owner/President/General Manager:** Jordan Kobritz.

**Assistant General Manager:** Debbie Berg. **Director of Sales/Marketing:** Steve O'Donnell.

### Field Staff

**Manager:** Dave Trembley. **Coaches:** Gary Lucas (pitching), Richie Zisk.

**Trainer:** Jim O'Reilly.

### Game Information

**Radio:** None.

**PA Announcer:** Unavailable. **Official Scorer:** Lyle Fox.

**Stadium Name:** Jackie Robinson Ballpark. **Location:** I-95 to International Speedway Blvd. exit (Route 92), east to Beach St., south to Orange Ave., east to ballpark; A1A North or South to Orange Ave., west to ballpark. **Standard Game Times:** 7 p.m., Sun. 1.

**Visiting Club Hotels:** Best Western Mayan Inn, 103 S. Ocean Ave., Daytona Beach, FL 32118. Telephone: (904) 252-0584; Holiday Inn Oceanside, 905 S. Atlantic Ave., Daytona Beach, FL 32118. Telephone: (904) 255-5432.

## DUNEDIN
## *BLUE JAYS*

**Office Address:** Dunedin Stadium, 311 Douglas Ave., Dunedin, FL 34698. **Mailing Address:** P.O. Box 957, Dunedin, FL 34697. **Telephone:** (813) 733-9302. **FAX:** (813) 734-7661.

**Affiliation (first year):** Toronto Blue Jays (1987). **Years in League:** 1978-79, 1987-.

**Team Colors:** Light blue, dark blue and red.

### Ownership, Management

**Operated by:** Toronto Blue Jays.

**Director of Florida Operations:** Ken Carson.

**General Manager:** Gary Rigley. **Field Superintendent:** Eric Hansen. **Special Projects Coordinator:** Tricia Wyman. **Administrative Assistant/Concessions Manager:** Pat Smith. **Intern:** Greg Charlebois.

### Field Staff

**Manager:** Jim Nettles. **Coaches:** Rolando Pino, John Poloni (pitching). **Trainer:** Dennis Brogna.

## Game Information

**Radio:** None.

**PA Announcer:** Jim Henderson. **Official Scorer:** Bob Miller.

**Stadium Name:** Dunedin Stadium at Grant Field. **Location:** From North—US 19 to SR 580, west on 580 to Douglas Avenue, south on Douglas, ½ mile to stadium. From South—US 19 to Sunset Point Road, west on Sunset Point, north on Douglas Avenue. **Standard Game Times:** 7 p.m.; Sun. (April-May) 2, (June-Sept.) 6.

**Visiting Club Hotel:** Comfort Inn, 27988 US 19 N., Clearwater, FL 34621. Telephone: (813) 796-0135.

# FORT MYERS
## *MIRACLE*

**Office Address:** 14400 Six Mile Cypress Pkwy., Ft. Myers, FL 33912. **Telephone:** (813) 768-4210. **FAX:** (813) 768-4211.

**Affiliation:** Minnesota Twins (1993). **Years in League:** 1978-87, 1992-.

**Team Colors:** Navy blue and red.

## Ownership, Management

**Operated by:** Greater Miami Baseball Club, LP.

**Principal Owner:** Marvin Goldklang.

**President:** Mike Veeck.

**General Manager:** Mark Schuster. **Director of Marketing:** John Kuhn. **Director of Communications:** Lou Slack. **Director of Operations:** Patricia Edwards. **Head Groundskeeper:** Scott Swenson. **Senior Account Representative:** Linda McNabb. **Account Executive:** Derek Sharrer. **Office Manager:** Suzanne Reeves.

## Field Staff

**Manager:** Al Newman. **Coaches:** Jose Marzan, Rick Tomlin (pitching).

**Trainer:** Lanning Tucker.

## Game Information

**Radio Announcer:** Chris Faris. **No. of Games Broadcast:** Away-70. **Flagship Station:** WWCN 770-AM.

**PA Announcer:** Chris Faris. **Official Scorer:** Scott Pederson.

**Stadium Name:** Lee County Sports Complex. **Location:** Exit 21 off I-75, west on Daniels Parkway for 2 miles, left on Six Mile Cypress Parkway. **Standard Game Times:** 7:05 p.m.

**Visiting Club Hotel:** Wellesley Inn, 4400 Fort St. Extension, Fort Myers, FL 33912. Telephone: (813) 278-3949.

# KISSIMMEE
## *COBRAS*

**Office Address:** 1000 Bill Beck Blvd., Kissimmee, FL 34744. **Mailing Address:** P.O. Box 422229, Kissimmee, FL 34742. **Telephone:** (407) 933-5500. **FAX:** (407) 847-6237.

**Affiliation (first year):** Houston Astros (1985). **Years In League:** 1985-.

**Team Colors:** Navy, silver and dark green.

## Ownership, Management

**Operated by:** Houston Astros (McLane Group).

**Chairman:** Drayton McLane Jr.

**General Manager:** Tim Bawmann. **Assistant General Manager:** Tom Albano. **Controller:** Robert McBurnett. **Marketing Representative:** Holly Morgan. **Equipment Manager:** Jay Edmiston. **Office Manager:** Kathy Rogacki.

## Field Staff

**Manager:** Dave Engle. **Coaches:** Jack Billingham (pitching), Ivan DeJesus.

**Trainer:** Mike Ra.

## Game Information

**Radio:** None.

**PA Announcer:** Norm Allen. **Official Scorer:** Jeff Kuenzli.

**Stadium Name:** Osceola County Stadium. **Location:** Florida Turnpike exit 244, right on US 192, right on Bill Beck Blvd.; I-4 exit on 192 East, proceed 12 miles, stadium on left; 17-92 South to US 192, left for 3 miles. **Standard Game Times:** 7 p.m.; Sun. (April-May) 2, (June-Aug.) 6.

**Visiting Club Hotel:** Quality Inn, 2039 E. Irlo Bronson Hwy., Kissimmee, FL 34743. Telephone: (407) 846-7814.

## LAKELAND
### *TIGERS*

**Office Address:** 2125 North Lake Ave., Lakeland, FL 33805. **Mailing Address:** P.O. Box 90187, Lakeland, FL 33804. **Telephone:** (813) 688-7911. **FAX:** (813) 688-9589.

**Affiliation (first year):** Detroit Tigers (1960). **Years in League:** 1919-26, 1953-55, 1960, 1962-64, 1967-.

**Team Colors:** Navy blue and orange.

#### Ownership, Management

**Operated by:** Detroit Tigers, Inc.

**Principal Owners:** Mike Ilitch, Marion Ilitch.

**Chairman/President:** Mike Ilitch.

**General Manager:** Woody Hicks. **Assistant General Manager:** Tripp Norton. **Director of Public Relations/Sales, Marketing:** Kurt Luttermoser. **Director of Community Relations:** Patti Sarano. **Clubhouse Operations:** Dan Price. **Office Manager:** Becky Wright.

#### Field Staff

**Manager:** Dave Anderson. **Coaches:** Brian Allard (pitching), Tim Torricelli.

**Trainer:** Doug Teter.

#### Game Information

**Radio:** None.

**PA Announcer:** Wayne Koehler. **Official Scorer:** Sandy Shaw.

**Stadium Name:** Joker Marchant Stadium. **Location:** Exit 19 on I-4 to Lakeland Hills Blvd., left 1½ miles, stadium on left. **Standard Game Times:** 7 p.m.; Sun. (April-June) 2, (July-Sept.) 6.

**Visiting Club Hotel:** Unavailable.

## ST. LUCIE
### *METS*

**Office Address:** 525 NW Peacock Blvd., Port St. Lucie, FL 34986. **Telephone:** (407) 871-2100. **FAX:** (407) 878-9802.

**Affiliation (first year):** New York Mets (1988). **Years in League:** 1988-.

**Team Colors:** Blue and orange.

#### Ownership, Management

**Operated by:** New York Mets.

**General Manager:** Ross Vecchio. **Assistant General Manager:** Joel Scott. **Director of Media/Public Relations:** George McClelland. **Director of Ticket Sales:** Grace Benway. **Clubhouse Operations:** Carl Goodreau. **Office Manager:** Suzie Serna. **Administrative Assistants:** Curtis Brown, Jeff Higgins.

#### Field Staff

**Manager:** Rafael Landestoy. **Coach:** Randy Niemann (pitching).

**Trainer:** Larry Bennese.

#### Game Information

**Radio Announcer:** Andy Freed. **No. of Games Broadcast:** Home-70, Away-70. **Flagship Station:** WIRA 1400-AM.

**PA Announcer:** Phil Scott. **Official Scorer:** George McClelland.

**Stadium Name:** Thomas J. White Stadium. **Location:** Exit 63C (St. Lucie West Blvd.) off I-95, east ½ mile to NW Peacock, left on NW Peacock. **Standard Game Times:** 7 p.m., Sun. 2.

**Visiting Club Hotel:** Holiday Inn Port St. Lucie, 10120 S. Federal Hwy., Port St. Lucie, FL 34952. Telephone: (407) 337-2200.

## ST. PETERSBURG
### *CARDINALS*

**Office Address:** 180 2nd Ave. SE, St. Petersburg, FL 33701. **Mailing Address:** P.O. Box 12557, St. Petersburg, FL 33733. **Telephone:** (813) 822-3384. **FAX:** (813) 895-1556.

**Affiliation (first year):** St. Louis Cardinals (1966). **Years In League:** 1920-27, 1955-.

**Team Colors:** Red, navy blue and yellow.

## Ownership, Management

**Operated by:** Suncoast Baseball Club, Inc.

**Principal Owner/President:** Joel Schur.

**Vice President/General Manager:** Tony Flores. **Assistant General Manager:** Steven Cohen. **Director of Public Relations:** Andrew Needham. **Director of Promotions/Ticket Sales:** Robert Moreschi.

## Field Staff

**Manager:** Chris Maloney. **Coaches:** Rich Folkers (pitching), Johnny Lewis.

**Trainer:** Brad Bluestone.

## Game Information

**Radio:** None.

**PA Announcer:** Brian Warnock. **Official Scorer:** Larry Wiederecht.

**Stadium Name:** Al Lang Stadium. **Location:** I-275 to exit 9, to First Street South, left two blocks. **Standard Game Times:** 7:05 p.m.; Sun. 5.

**Visiting Club Hotel:** Heritage Holiday Inn, 234 3rd Ave. N., St. Petersburg, FL 33701. Telephone: (803) 822-4814.

# SARASOTA
*RED SOX*

**Office Address:** 2700 12th St., Sarasota, FL 34237. **Mailing Address:** P.O. Box 2816, Sarasota, FL 34230. **Telephone:** (813) 365-4460. **FAX:** (813) 365-4217.

**Affiliation (first year):** Boston Red Sox (1994). **Years in League:** 1966-67, 1969-.

**Team Colors:** Red and navy.

## Ownership, Management

**Operated by:** Boston Red Sox (Red Sox of Florida, Inc.)

**Director of Florida Operations:** Bill MacKay.

**General Manager:** Kevin Cummings. **Assistant General Manager:** Paul Taglieri. **Administrative Assistant:** Mark Tomko.

## Field Staff

**Manager:** Tommy Barrett. **Coach:** Jeff Gray (pitching).

**Trainer:** Unavailable.

## Game Information

**Radio Announcer:** Chuck Ellis. **No. of Games Broadcast:** Home-70. **Flagship Station:** Unavailable.

**PA Announcer:** Carl Webb. **Official Scorer:** Unavailable.

**Stadium Name:** Ed Smith Stadium. **Location:** I-75 to exit 39, 2 miles west to Tuttle Ave., right on Tuttle ½ mile to 12th St., stadium on left. **Standard Game Times:** 7 p.m.

**Visiting Club Hotel:** Wellesley Inn, 1803 N. Tamiami Trail, Sarasota, FL 34234. Telephone: (813) 366-5128.

# TAMPA
*YANKEES*

**Office Address:** 4202 E. Fowler Ave., Tampa, FL 33687. **Mailing Address:** P.O. Box 290698, Tampa, FL 33687. **Telephone:** (813) 632-9855. **FAX:** (813) 979-4752.

**Affiliation (first year):** New York Yankees (1994). **Years in League:** 1919-27, 1957-1988, 1994-.

**Team Colors:** Blue, white and red.

## Ownership, Management

**Operated by:** New York Yankees.

**Principal Owner:** George Steinbrenner.

**General Manager:** Scott Kelyman. **Assistant General Manager:** Sal Arena. **Director of Business Operations:** Chris Maragno. **Director of Sales/Marketing:** Peter Van Dyke. **Director of Advertising Sales:** Ricky Ware. **Receptionist/Secretary:** Barbara Mahovlich.

## Field Staff

**Manager:** Jake Gibbs. **Coaches:** Ken Dominguez, David Howard, Mark Shiflett (pitching).

**Trainer:** Tom Raynor.

## Game Information

**Radio:** None.

**PA Announcer:** Unavailable. **Official Scorer:** John Pizzio.

**Stadium Name:** Red McEwen Field. **Location:** From 275 North—east on Fowler Ave. (exit 34), left into Sundome entrance. From 75 North—west on Fowler Ave. (exit 54), right into Sundome entrance. **Standard Game**

Times: 7 p.m., Sun. 1.

**Visiting Club Hotel:** Colony Hotel, 820 E. Busch Blvd., Tampa, FL 33612. Telephone: (813) 933-4011.

# VERO BEACH
## *DODGERS*

**Office Address:** 4001 26th St., Vero Beach, FL 32960. **Mailing Address:** P.O. Box 2887, Vero Beach, FL 32961. **Telephone:** (407) 569-4900. **FAX:** (407) 567-0819.

**Affiliation (first year):** Los Angeles Dodgers (1980). **Years in League:** 1980-.

**Team Colors:** Blue and white.

### Ownership, Management

**Operated by:** Los Angeles Dodgers, Inc.

**President:** Peter O'Malley.

**General Manager:** Tom Simmons. **Assistant General Manager:** Jeff Maultsby. **Head Groundskeeper:** Ron Cummins. **Director of Ticket Sales:** Louise Boissy. **Clubhouse Operations:** John Ragley. **Administrative Assistants:** Matt Bennett, Bruce Gammell. **Secretary:** JoAnn Lane. **Secretary/Advertising:** Betty Rollins.

### Field Staff

**Manager:** Jon Debus. **Coaches:** Guy Conti (pitching), Tony Harris.

**Trainer:** Rob Giesecke.

### Game Information

**Radio Announcer:** Pete Michaud. **No. of Games Broadcast:** Home-70, Away-70. **Flagship Station:** WAXE 1370-AM.

**PA Announcer:** Dave Peterson. **Official Scorer:** Randy Phillips.

**Stadium Name:** Holman Stadium. **Location:** I-95 to Rt. 60 East, to 43rd Ave N., to 26th St., east one block; US 1 to Rt. 60 West, to 43rd Ave. N., to 26th St., east one block. **Standard Game Times:** 7 p.m..

**Visiting Club Hotel:** Vero Beach Inn, 4700 Hwy. A1A, Vero Beach, FL 32963. Telephone: (407) 231-1600.

# WEST PALM BEACH
## *EXPOS*

**Office Address:** 715 Hank Aaron Dr., West Palm Beach, FL 33401. **Mailing Address:** P.O. Box 3566, West Palm Beach, FL 33402. **Telephone:** (407) 684-6801. **FAX:** (407) 686-0221.

**Affiliation (first year):** Montreal Expos (1969). **Years in League:** 1955-56, 1965-.

**Team Colors:** Red, while and blue.

### Ownership, Management

**Operated by:** Montreal Expos Baseball.

**Chairman/President:** Claude Brochu.

**General Manager:** Rob Rabenecker. **Assistant General Manager/Business Operations, Communications:** Trina VanDerlip. **Assistant General Manager/Sales, Marketing:** Jared Kay. **Assistant General Manager/Stadium Operations, Merchandise:** Domenic Ruffa.

**Director of Stadium Operations/Head Groundskeeper:** Murray Cook. **Clubhouse Operations:** Mark Rego. **Office Manager:** Patricia Lobato.

### Field Staff

**Manager:** Gomer Hodge. **Coach:** Jeff Fischer (pitching).

**Trainer:** Unavailable.

### Game Information

**Radio:** None.

**PA Announcer:** Dick Sanford. **Official Scorer:** Unavailable.

**Stadium Name:** Municipal Stadium. **Location:** I-95 to exit 53, east ½ mile on Palm Beach Lakes Blvd. **Standard Game Times:** 7:05 p.m.; Sun. 5:05.

**Visiting Club Hotel:** Wellesley Inn, 1910 Palm Beach Lakes Blvd., West Palm Beach, FL 33409. Telephone: (407) 689-8540.

# MIDWEST LEAGUE

## Class A

George Spelius

**Office Address:** 1205 Cranston Rd., Beloit, WI 53511. **Mailing Address:** P.O. Box 936, Beloit, WI 53512. **Telephone:** (608) 364-1188. **FAX:** (608) 364-1913.

**President/Treasurer:** George H. Spelius.

**Directors:** John Baxter (South Bend), Lew Chamberlin (West Michigan), William Collins III (Battle Creek), Dennis Conerton (Beloit), Tom Dickson (Springfield), Richard Holtzman (Quad City), Wally Krouse (Cedar Rapids), Eric Margenau (Fort Wayne), Mark McGuire (Rockford), Rich Phelan (Clinton), Pete Vonachen (Peoria), Dave Walker (Burlington), Mike Woleben (Kane County), John Wollner (Wisconsin).

**Years League Active:** 1949-.

**1995 Opening Date:** April 7. **Closing Date:** Sept. 2.

**No. of Games:** 140.

**Division Structure: West**—Burlington, Cedar Rapids, Clinton, Peoria, Quad City, Springfield. **Central**—Beloit, Kane County, Rockford, Wisconsin. **East**—Battle Creek, Fort Wayne, South Bend, West Michigan.

**Playoff Format:** Eight teams qualify. First-half and second-half division champions, and two wild-card teams, play each other in best-of-3 series. Winners advance to best-of-3 semifinals (Western vs. Central; Eastern vs. wild card). Winners advance to best-of-5 series for league championship.

**All-Star Game:** June 20 at West Michigan.

**Roster Limit:** 25 active. **Player Eligibility Rule:** No age limit. No more than two players and one player-coach on active list may have more than five years experience.

**Brand of Baseball:** Rawlings ROM.

**Statistician:** Howe Sportsdata International, Boston Fish Pier, West Bldg. #2—Suite 306, Boston MA 02210.

### 1994 Standings (Overall)

| Club (Affiliate) | W | L | Pct. | GB | '94 Manager |
|---|---|---|---|---|---|
| #Rockford (Royals) | 89 | 50 | .640 | — | John Mizerock |
| *#Cedar Rapids (Angels) | 77 | 62 | .554 | 12 | Tom Lawless |
| Beloit (Brewers) | 76 | 64 | .543 | 13½ | Wayne Krenchicki |
| Appleton (Mariners) | 75 | 64 | .540 | 14 | Carlos Lezcano |
| West Michigan (Athletics) | 74 | 65 | .532 | 15 | Jim Colborn |
| South Bend (White Sox) | 72 | 67 | .518 | 17 | Mike Gellinger |
| Kane County (Marlins) | 71 | 68 | .511 | 18 | Lynn Jones |
| #Springfield (Padres) | 69 | 71 | .493 | 20½ | Ed Romero |
| Peoria (Cubs) | 68 | 70 | .493 | 20½ | Steve Roadcap |
| Fort Wayne (Twins) | 66 | 73 | .475 | 23 | Jim Dwyer |
| Madison (Cardinals) | 66 | 73 | .475 | 23 | Joe Cunningham |
| Quad City (Astros) | 57 | 81 | .413 | 31½ | Steve Dillard |
| Clinton (Giants) | 57 | 82 | .410 | 32 | Jack Mull |
| Burlington (Expos) | 55 | 82 | .401 | 33 | Lorenzo Bundy |

*Won playoffs #Won split-season pennant

### Stadium Information

| | | Dimensions | | | | |
|---|---|---|---|---|---|---|
| Club | Stadium | LF | CF | RF | Capacity | '94 Att. |
| Battle Creek | C.O. Brown | 325 | 400 | 330 | 6,200 | — |
| Beloit | Pohlman Field | 325 | 380 | 325 | 3,100 | 60,650 |
| Burlington | Community Field | 338 | 372 | 315 | 3,500 | 83,927 |
| Cedar Rapids | Veterans Memorial | 325 | 385 | 325 | 6,000 | 137,795 |
| Clinton | Riverview | 335 | 393 | 325 | 3,000 | 62,317 |
| Fort Wayne | Memorial | 335 | 405 | 335 | 6,300 | 266,670 |
| Kane County | Philip B. Elfstrom | 335 | 400 | 335 | 5,800 | 417,744 |
| Peoria | Pete Vonachen | 335 | 383 | 335 | 6,200 | 176,703 |
| Quad City | John O'Donnell | 340 | 390 | 340 | 5,500 | 260,471 |
| Rockford | Marinelli Field | 335 | 400 | 335 | 4,300 | 70,527 |
| South Bend | Coveleski Regional | 336 | 405 | 336 | 5,000 | 258,424 |
| Springfield | Robin Roberts | 320 | 415 | 320 | 5,000 | 54,218 |
| West Michigan | Old Kent Park | 327 | 402 | 327 | 8,429 | 475,212 |
| Wisconsin | Fox Cities | 330 | 400 | 330 | 6,500 | 76,281 |

Battle Creek franchise operated in Madison in 1994.
Wisconsin franchise was known as Appleton in 1994.

## BATTLE CREEK
*GOLDEN KAZOOS*

**Office Address:** 1392 Capital Ave. NE, Battle Creek, MI 49017. **Telephone:** (616) 660-2287. **FAX:** (616) 660-2288.

**Affiliation (first year):** Boston Red Sox (1995). **Years in League:** 1995-.

**Team Colors:** Green, cranberry and black.

### Ownership, Management

**Operated by:** American Baseball Capital, Inc.

**Principal Owners:** William Collins III, William Collins Jr., Tim Cullen, John Horshok, Lynn Urbanski.

**Chief Operating Officer:** Tim Cullen.

**Assistant General Manager:** Kevin Grzanka. **Director of Stadium Operations:** Steve Renard. **Head Groundskeeper:** Mel Lanford. **Director of Media/Public Relations:** Andy Milovich. **Director of Ticket Sales:** Tracy Thirion. **Director of Group Sales:** Jim Pool. **Director of Marketing:** Sara Weber. **Ticket Manager:** Pat Thomason. **Director of Regional Sales:** Trevor Glidden. **Administrative Assistant:** Jim Swinehart.

### Field Staff

**Manager:** DeMarlo Hale. **Coaches:** Darrell Evans, Rick Wise (pitching). **Trainer:** Brian Moore.

### Game Information

**Radio Announcers:** Ken Ervin, Terry Newton. **No. of Games Broadcast:** Home-70; Away-70. **Flagship Station:** WBCK 930-AM.

**PA Announcer:** Unavailable. **Official Scorer:** Unavailable.

**Stadium Name:** C.O. Brown Stadium. **Location:** I-94 to Hwy 194 (exit 98B) to Capital Ave NE, east to Bailey Park. **Standard Game Times:** 7:05 p.m., Sun. 2:05.

**Visiting Club Hotel:** Unavailable.

## BELOIT
*SNAPPERS*

**Office Address:** 2301 Skyline Dr., Beloit, WI 53511. **Mailing Address:** P.O. Box 855, Beloit, WI 53512. **Telephone:** (608) 362-2272. **FAX:** (608) 362-0418.

**Affiliation (first year):** Milwaukee Brewers (1982). **Years in League:** 1982-.

**Team Colors:** Navy blue and hunter green.

### Ownership, Management

**Operated by:** Beloit Professional Baseball Association.

**Chairman:** Howard Erickson. **President:** Dennis Conerton.

**General Manager:** Jeff Nelson. **Director of Broadcasting/Media Relations:** Brett Dolan. **Director of Sales/Marketing:** Bobby Stockhausen. **Director of Community Relations/Merchandising:** Tracie Nelson. **Head Groundskeeper:** John Sortedahl. **Clubhouse Operations:** Ari Oller.

### Field Staff

**Manager:** Dub Kilgo. **Coaches:** Mike Caldwell (pitching), Jon Pont.

**Trainer:** Jeff Paxson.

### Game Information

**Radio Announcer:** Brett Dolan. **No. of Games Broadcast:** Home-70; Away-70. **Flagship Stations:** WGEZ 1490-AM.

**PA Announcer:** Al Fagerli. **Official Scorer:** Dave Sennett.

**Stadium Name:** Pohlman Field. **Location:** I-90 to exit 81 west, right on Cranston Rd. **Standard Game Times:** April 6:30 p.m., May-Sept. 7; Sat. (April) 2, (May-Sept.) 7; Sun. 2

**Visiting Club Hotel:** Comfort Inn, 2786 Milwaukee Rd., Beloit, WI 53512. Telephone: (608) 362-2666.

## BURLINGTON
*BEES*

**Office Address:** 2712 Mt. Pleasant St., Burlington, IA 52601. **Mailing Address:** P.O. Box 824, Burlington, IA 52601. **Telephone:** (319) 754-5705. **FAX:** (319) 754-5882.

**Affiliation (first year):** San Francisco Giants (1995). **Years In League:** 1962-.

**Team Colors:** Black, blue and yellow.

## Ownership, Management

**Operated by:** Burlington Baseball, Inc.

**President:** David Walker.

**General Manager:** Ryan Richeal. **Assistant General Manager:** Karin Fullenkamp. **Director of Sales/Marketing:** Matt Harris. **Director of Ticket Sales:** Scott Mason. **Head Groundskeeper:** Unavailable.

## Field Staff

**Manager:** Mike Hart. **Coaches:** Mickey Brantley, Keith Comstock (pitching).

**Trainer:** Sy Katcher.

## Game Information

**Radio:** None.

**PA Announcer/Official Scorer:** Scott Mason.

**Stadium Name:** Community Field. **Location:** Hwy. 61 North to Mt. Pleasant St., east ¼ mile. **Standard Game Times:** 7 p.m.; Sat. (April-May) 4, (June-Aug.) 7; Sun. 4.

**Visiting Club Hotel:** Best Western-Pzazz, 3001 Winegard Dr., Burlington, IA 52601. Telephone: (319) 753-2223.

# CEDAR RAPIDS *KERNELS*

**Office Address:** 950 Rockford Rd. SW, Cedar Rapids, IA 52404. **Mailing Address:** P.O. Box 2001, Cedar Rapids, IA 52406. **Telephone:** (319) 363-3887. **FAX:** (319) 363-5631.

**Affiliation (first year):** California Angels (1993). **Years in League:** 1962-.

**Team Colors:** Navy blue, red and silver.

## Ownership, Management

**Operated by:** Cedar Rapids Baseball Club, Inc.

**President:** Wally Krouse.

**General Manager:** Jack Roeder. **Assistant General Manager:** Andrew Graykowski. **Head Groundskeeper:** Guy Curran. **Office Manager:** Nancy Cram.

## Field Staff

**Manager:** Tom Lawless. **Coaches:** Steve Renko (pitching), Charlie Romero.

Trainer: Jaime Macias.

## Game Information

**Radio Announcer:** John Doskow. **No. of Games Broadcast:** Home-70, Away-70. **Flagship Station:** KCRG 1600-AM.

**PA Announcer/Official Scorer:** Dale Brodt.

**Stadium Name:** Veterans Memorial Stadium. **Location:** I-380 to Wilson Ave., west to Rockford Rd., right to corner of 8th Ave. and 15th St. SW. **Standard Game Times:** 7 p.m.; Sun. 2.

**Visiting Club Hotels:** Village Inn, 100 F Ave. NW, Cedar Rapids, IA 52405. Telephone (319) 366-5323. Five Seasons Hotel, 350 1st Ave. NE, Cedar Rapids, IA 52401. Telephone: (319) 363-8161.

# CLINTON *LUMBER KINGS*

**Office Address:** 6th Ave. N. and 1st St., Clinton, IA 52732. **Mailing Address:** P.O. Box 1295, Clinton, IA 52733. **Telephone:** (319) 242-0727. **FAX:** (319) 242-1433.

**Affiliation (first year):** San Diego Padres (1995). **Years in League:** 1956-.

## Ownership, Management

**Operated by:** Clinton Baseball Club, Inc.

**President:** Rich Phelan.

**General Manager:** Leasa Brown. **Assistant General Manager:** Jim Van Sant. **Office Manager:** Kelly Ormsby.

## Field Staff

**Manager:** Ed Romero. **Coach:** Saul Soltero (pitching).

**Trainer:** Jason Haeussinger.

## Game Information

**Radio Announcer:** Unavailable. **No. of Games Broadcast:** Home-70, Away-70. **Flagship Station:** KCLN 97.7-FM.

**PA Announcer:** Unavailable. **Official Scorer:** Unavailable.

**Stadium Name:** Riverview Stadium. **Location:** Highway 30 East to 6th Avenue North, right on 6th, cross railroad tracks, stadium on right. **Standard Game Times:** 7:05 p.m., Sun. 5.

**Visiting Club Hotel:** Ramada Inn, 1522 Lincolnway Blvd., Clinton, IA 52732. Telephone: (319) 243-8841.

# FORT WAYNE *WIZARDS*

**Office Address:** 1616 E. Coliseum Blvd., Fort Wayne, IN 46805. **Telephone:** (219) 482-6400. **FAX:** (219) 471-4678.

**Affiliation (first year):** Minnesota Twins (1993). **Years in League:** 1993-.
**Team Colors:** Black, silver and blue.

## Ownership, Management

**Operated by:** United Baseball, Inc.
**Principal Owner:** Eric Margenau.

**General Manager:** Mike Tatoian. **Assistant General Manager:** Bret Staehling. **Director of Business Operations:** Jeff Hyde. **Director of Media/Public Relations:** Tom Nichols. **Director of Marketing:** Lesley Kellison. **Director of Corporate Sales:** Nina Zirille. **Director of Group Sales:** Amy Hill.

## Field Staff

**Manager:** Dan Rohn. **Coaches:** Jose Baez, Stu Cliburn (pitching).
**Trainer:** Brad Olson.

## Game Information

**Radio Announcer:** Tom Nichols. **No. of Games Broadcast:** Home-70, Away-70. **Flagship Station:** WQHK 1380-AM.

**PA Announcer:** Dan Knight. **Official Scorer:** Rich Tavierne.

**Stadium Name:** Memorial Stadium. **Location:** Exit 112A (Coldwater Road) off I-69 to Coliseum Blvd., east on Coliseum Blvd. to stadium. **Standard Game Times:** 7 p.m.; Sun. 2 or 6.

**Visiting Club Hotel:** Budgetel Inn, 1005 W. Washington Center Rd., Fort Wayne, IN 46805. Telephone: (219) 489-2220.

# KANE COUNTY *COUGARS*

**Office Address:** 34W002 Cherry Lane, Geneva, IL 60134. **Telephone:** (708) 232-8811. **FAX:** (708) 232-8815.

**Affiliation (first year):** Florida Marlins (1993). **Years In League:** 1991-.
**Team Colors:** Black, gold, green and white.

## Ownership, Management

**Operated by:** Cougars Baseball Partnership, Inc.
**Principal Owners:** Al Gordon, Mike Murtaugh, Mike Woldben.
**President:** Al Gordon.

**General Manager:** Bill Larsen. **Assistant General Manager:** Jeff Sedivy. **Business Manager:** Mary Almlie. **Director of Communications:** David Wills. **Director of Media Relations/Publications:** Marty Cusack. **Director of Merchandising:** Curtis Haug. **Director of Ticket Operations:** Burke Masters. **Director of Group Sales:** Shannon Schinzing. **Community Relations/Promotions:** Jeff Ney. **Assistant Director of Media Relations:** Paul Palian.**Head Groundskeeper:** Mike Clark. **Stadium/ Clubhouse Operations:** Mike Kurns.

## Field Staff

**Manager:** Lynn Jones. **Coaches:** Rod Allen, Brian Peterson (pitching).
**Trainer:** Pat Laverty.

## Game Information

**Radio Announcers:** David Wills, Mark Vasco, Bill Melton. **No. of Games Broadcast:** Home-70, Away-70. **Flagship Station:** WKKD 95.9-FM.

**PA Announcer:** Paul Palian. **Official Scorer:** Marty Cusack.

**Stadium Name:** Philip B. Elfstrom Stadium. **Location:** I-88 to Farnsworth Road North exit, 5 miles north to Cherry Lane, left to stadium. **Standard Game Times:** 7 p.m.; Sat. 5; Sun. 2.

**Visiting Club Hotel:** Travelodge, Naperville Road at East-West Tollway, Naperville, IL 60563. Telephone: (708) 505-0200.

## PEORIA
*CHIEFS*

**Office Address:** 1524 W. Nebraska Ave., Peoria, IL 61604. **Telephone:** (309) 688-1622. **FAX:** (309) 686-4516.

**Affiliation (first year):** St. Louis Cardinals (1995). **Years in League:** 1983-.

**Team Colors:** Navy blue and red.

### Ownership, Management

**Operated by:** Peoria Chiefs Community Baseball Club, LLC.

**President/General Manager:** Pete Vonachen Jr.

**Assistant General Manager:** Rocky Vonachen. **Director of Stadium Operations:** Tim Gorman. **Director of Broadcasting/Communications:** Bob Socci. **Director of Sales:** Dan Vonachen. **Senior Account Representative:** Ralph Rashid. **Director of Marketing/Promotions:** Greg Ayers. **Director of Group Sales:** Matt Fogerty. **Office Manager:** Barb Linberg. **Director of Merchandising:** Mark Vonachen.

### Field Staff

**Manager:** Roy Silver. **Coaches:** Ray Searage (pitching), Keith Smith.
**Trainer:** Bert Boyd.

### Game Information

**Radio Announcer:** Bob Socci. **No. of Games Broadcast:** Home-70, Away-70. **Flagship Station:** WOAM 1350-AM.

**PA Announcer:** Ed Hammond. **Official Scorer:** Phil Theobald.

**Stadium Name:** Pete Vonachen Stadium. **Location:** From I-74 East—exit 91 (from I-74 West, take exit 91B), left on North University, left on West Nebraska, left to ballpark. **Standard Game Times:** 7:05 p.m.; Sun. (April-May) 6:05, (June-Aug.) 2:05.

**Visiting Club Hotel:** Holiday Inn City Centre, 500 Hamilton Blvd., Peoria, IL 61602. Telephone: (309) 674-2500.

## QUAD CITY
*RIVER BANDITS*

**Office Address:** 209 S. Gaines St., Davenport, IA 52802. **Mailing Address:** P.O. Box 3496, Davenport, IA 52808. **Telephone:** (319) 324-2032. **FAX:** (319) 324-3109.

**Affiliation (first year):** Houston Astros (1993). **Years in League:** 1960-.

**Team Colors:** Red and black.

### Ownership, Management

**Operated by:** Quad City Professional Baseball Club, Inc.

**Principal Owner/Chairman:** Richard Holtzman.

**General Manager:** Dan Kable. **Assistant General Manager:** Chris Holvoet. **Director of Concessions:** Pat Daly. **Director of Stadium Operations:** Scott Morel. **Director of Marketing:** Mike Lizak. **Director of Community Relations:** Jeff Levy. **Director of Group Sales:** Andy Boyer.

### Field Staff

**Manager:** Jim Pankovits. **Coach:** Jim Hickey (pitching).
**Trainer:** Natan Lucero.

### Game Information

**Radio Announcer:** J.C. DeLass. **No. of Games Broadcast:** Home-70, Away-70. **Flagship Station:** KJOC 1170-AM.

**PA Announcer:** Unavailable. **Official Scorer:** Jim Tappa.

**Stadium Name:** John O'Donnell Stadium. **Location:** From I-74, south on SR 61 to corner of South Gaines St. and River Dr. **Standard Game Times:** 7 p.m.; Sun. (April-May) 2, (June-Sept.) 6.

**Visiting Club Hotel:** Riverview Inn, 227 LeClaire St., Davenport, IA 52801. Telephone: (319) 324-1921.

## ROCKFORD
*CUBBIES*

**Office Address:** 101 15th Ave., Rockford, IL 61104. **Mailing Address:** P.O. Box 6748, Rockford, IL 61125. **Telephone:** (815) 962-2827. **FAX:** (815) 961-2002.

**Affiliation (first year):** Chicago Cubs (1995). **Years in League:** 1988-.

**Team Colors:** Red and blue.

## Ownership, Management

**Operated By:** Chicago Cubs.

**President:** Mark McGuire.

**General Manager:** Michael Holmes. **Director of Ticket Operations:** Chris Gargani. **Director of Merchandising:** Pat Wilhelmi. **Director of Media/Public Relations:** Jeff Cummings. **Facility Supervisor:** Andy Williams. **Office Manager:** Tona Eisele.

## Field Staff

**Manager:** Steve Roadcap. **Coaches:** Steve Dillard, Alan Dunn (pitching).

**Trainer:** Greg Keuter.

## Game Information

**Radio Announcer:** Unavailable. **No. of Games Broadcast:** Home-70, Away 20. **Flagship Station:** WLUV 96.7-FM

**PA Announcer:** Lisa Fielding. **Official Scorer:** Dave Schultz.

**Stadium Name:** Marinelli Stadium. **Location:** I-90 West to US 20 West to Rt. 2, north on Main Street to 15th Ave., right across Rock River, to stadium. **Standard Game Times:** 7 p.m., Sun. 2.

**Visiting Club Hotel:** Howard Johnson, 3909 11th St., Rockford, IL 61109. Telephone: (815) 397-9000.

# SOUTH BEND
# *SILVER HAWKS*

**Office Address:** 501 W. South St., South Bend, IN 46601. **Mailing Address:** P.O. Box 4218, South Bend, IN 46634. **Telephone:** (219) 235-9988. **FAX:** (219) 235-9950.

**Affiliation (first year):** Chicago White Sox (1988). **Years in League:** 1988-.

**Team Colors:** Dark green, silver, gold and black.

## Ownership, Management

**Operated by:** Palisades Baseball, Ltd.

**Principal Owner:** Alan Levin. **President:** John Baxter.

**Vice President/General Manager:** John Tull. **Assistant General Manager:** Sean Willis. **Vice President/Sales, Marketing:** Rita Baxter. **Controller:** Andy Zmudzinski. **Director of Stadium Operations:** Al Bonowitz. **Head Groundskeeper:** Joel Reinebold. **Senior Account Representative:** Julie Magrane. **Director of Community Relations:** Traci Diehl. **Director of Ticket Sales:** Kim Vanderwall.

## Field Staff

**Manager:** Fred Kendall. **Coaches:** Mark Haley, Curt Hasler (pitching).

**Trainer:** Greg Barber.

## Game Information

**Radio Announcer:** Unavailable. **No. of Games Broadcast:** Home-70, Away-70. **Flagship Station:** WSBT 960-AM.

**PA Announcer:** Unavailable. **Official Scorer:** Forrest Miller.

**Stadium Name:** Stanley Coveleski Regional Stadium. **Location:** I-80/90 toll road to exit 77. Enter US 31-33 south to South Bend, to downtown (Main St.), to Western Ave., right on Western, left on Taylor. **Standard Game Times:** 7 p.m.; Sun. 2.

**Visiting Club Hotels:** University Park Inn, 52939 U.S. 31 North, South Bend, IN 46137. Telephone: (219) 272-1500.

# SULTANS OF
# *SPRINGFIELD*

**Office Address:** 1351 N. Grand Ave. E., Springfield, IL 62702. **Telephone:** (217) 544-7300. **FAX:** (217) 544-7388.

**Affiliation (first year):** Kansas City Royals (1995). **Years in League:** 1982-.

**Team Colors:** Purple, silver and black.

## Ownership, Management

**Operated by:** Take Me Out To The Ballgame, LLC.

**President:** Tom Dickson.

**General Manager:** Gillian Zucker. **Assistant General Manager:** Kevin Leuzinger. **Executive Director of Business Operations-Lansing:** Billy Johnson. **Director of Administration:** Amy Wolfe. **Head Groundskeeper:** Larry Rockford. **Office Manager-Lansing:** Robert Kurson.

## Field Staff

**Manager:** Brian Poldberg. **Coaches:** Mike Mason (pitching), Rafael Santana.

**Trainer:** Jeff Stevenson.

### Game Information

**Radio:** Unavailable.

**PA Announcer:** Unavailable. **Official Scorer:** Unavailable.

**Stadium Name:** Lanphier Park-Robin Roberts Stadium. **Location:** I-55 to Clearlake exit, right on 11th, right on North Grand. **Standard Game Times:** 7 p.m.; Sun. (April-June) 1, (July-Aug.) 6.

**Visiting Club Hotel:** Hilton of Springfield, 700 E. Adams St., Springfield, IL 62701. Telephone: (217) 789-1530.

## WEST MICHIGAN
## *WHITECAPS*

**Office Address:** 4500 W. River Dr., Comstock Park, MI 49321. **Mailing Address:** P.O. Box 428, Comstock Park, MI 49321. **Telephone:** (616) 784-4131. **FAX:** (616) 784-4911.

**Affiliation (first year):** Oakland Athletics (1994). **Years in League:** 1994-.

**Team Colors:** Aqua, yellow and black.

### Ownership, Management

**Operated by:** Whitecaps Professional Baseball Corp.

**Principal Owners:** Dennis Baxter, Lew Chamberlin.

**President:** Dennis Baxter. **Vice President/Managing Partner:** Lew Chamberlin.

**General Manager:** Scott Lane. **Director of Baseball Operations:** Jim Jarecki. **Director of Sales:** John Guthrie. **Director of Group Sales:** Greg Hill. **Media Relations/Merchandising:** Lori Clark. **Gameday Operations Manager:** Matt O'Brien. **Ticket Manager:** Bruce Radley. **Concessions Manager:** Mike Bezdek. **Community Relations Manager:** Erin Kauth. **Facility Maintenance Engineer:** Joe Eimer. **Head Groundskeeper:** Heather Nabozny. **Office Coordinator:** Ellen Chamberlin.

### Field Staff

**Manager:** Jim Colborn. **Coach:** Bert Bradley (pitching).

**Trainer:** Brian Thorson.

### Game Information

**Radio Announcers:** Rick Berkey, Rob Sanford. **No. of Games Broadcast:** Home-70, Away-70. **Flagship Station:** WOOD 1300-AM.

**PA Announcer:** Ric Campbell. **Official Scorer:** Unavailable.

**Stadium Name:** Old Kent Park. **Location:** US 131 North from Grand Rapids to West River Drive exit, through intersection to stadium. **Standard Game Times:** April-May 6:35 p.m., June-Aug. 7 ; Sat. (April-May) 2, (June-Sept) 7; Sun. 2.

**Visiting Club Hotel:** Radisson Hotel, 11 Monroe NW, Grand Rapids, MI 49503. Telephone: (616) 242-6000.

## WISCONSIN
## *TIMBER RATTLERS*

**Office Address:** 500 W. Franklin St., Appleton, WI 54911. **Mailing Address:** P.O. Box 464, Appleton, WI 54912. **Telephone:** (414) 733-4152. **FAX:** (414) 733-8032.

**Affiliation (first year):** Seattle Mariners (1993). **Years in League:** 1962-.

**Team Colors:** Bergundy, black, silver, gold and red.

### Ownership, Management

**Operated by:** Appleton Baseball Club, Inc.

**President:** John Wollner.

**General Manager:** Steve Malliet. **Assistant General Manager:** Mike Birling. **Director of Business Operations:** Jim Hyde. **Head Groundskeeper:** Gary Mayse. **Director of Media Relations:** Tim McCord. **Director of Public Relations:** Richelle Polello. **Director of Promotions:** David Frost. **Director of Ticket Sales:** Marti Wollner. **Director of Group Sales:** Angie Entwisle. **Office Manager:** Judy Wilhelm.

### Field Staff

**Manager:** Mike Goff. **Coach:** Delwyn Young.

**Trainer:** Allan Wirtala.

### Game Information

**Radio:** None.

**PA Announcer:** Unavailable. **Official Scorer:** Charlie Capper.

**Stadium Name:** Fox Cities Stadium. **Location:** Highway 41 to Wisconsin Ave. exit, west to Casaloma Drive, right on Casaloma, stadium ½ mile on right. **Standard Game Times:** 7 p.m., Sun. 1.

**Visiting Club Hotel:** Fairfield Inn, 132 Mall Dr., Appleton, WI 54915. Telephone: (414) 954-0202.

# SOUTH ATLANTIC LEAGUE

### Class A

John Moss

**Office Address:** 504 Crescent Hill, Kings Mountain, NC 28086. **Mailing Address:** P.O. Box 38, Kings Mountain, NC 28086. **Telephone:** (704) 739-3466. **FAX:** (704) 739-1974.

**President/Secretary-Treasurer:** John Moss.

**First Vice President:** Winston Blenckstone. **Second Vice President:** Bill Scripps.

**Directors:** Don Beaver (Hickory), Winston Blenckstone (Hagerstown), Charles Boggs (Charleston, WV), William Collins (Greensboro), Marvin Goldklang (Charleston, SC), Larry Hedrick (Piedmont), Richard Holtzman (Albany), Eric Margenau (Columbia), Ron McKee (Asheville), Chip Moore (Macon), Charles Morrow (Columbus), Charles Padgett (Fayetteville), Bill Scripps (Augusta), Ken Silver (Savannah).

**Years League Active:** 1948-1952, 1960-.

**1995 Opening Date:** April 6. **Closing Date:** Sept. 3.

**No. of Games:** 142.

**Division Structure: Northern**—Asheville, Charleston WV, Fayetteville, Greensboro, Hagerstown, Hickory, Piedmont. **Southern**—Albany, Augusta, Charleston SC, Columbia, Columbus, Macon, Savannah.

**Playoff Format:** First-half division winners play second-half division winners in best-of-3 division series. Division playoff winners meet in best-of-5 series for league championship.

**All-Star Game:** June 19 at Albany.

**Roster Limit:** 25 active. **Player Eligibility Rule:** No age limit. No more than two players and one player-coach on active list may have more than five years of experience.

**Brand of Baseball:** Rawlings.

**Statistician:** Howe Sportsdata International, Boston Fish Pier, West Bldg. #2—Suite 306, Boston MA 02210.

## 1994 Standings (Overall)

| Club (Affiliate) | W | L | Pct. | GB | '94 Manager |
|---|---|---|---|---|---|
| #Columbus (Indians) | 87 | 51 | .630 | — | Mike Young |
| #Hickory (White Sox) | 86 | 54 | .614 | 2 | Fred Kendall |
| *#Savannah (Cardinals) | 82 | 55 | .599 | 4½ | Luis Melendez |
| #Hagerstown (Blue Jays) | 80 | 56 | .588 | 6 | Omar Malave |
| Macon (Braves) | 73 | 64 | .533 | 13½ | Leon Roberts |
| Greensboro (Yankees) | 71 | 69 | .507 | 17 | Trey Hillman |
| Spartanburg (Phillies) | 67 | 72 | .482 | 20½ | Roy Majtyka |
| Charleston, W.Va. (Reds) | 65 | 75 | .464 | 23 | Tom Nieto |
| Albany (Orioles) | 63 | 74 | .460 | 23½ | Butch Wynegar |
| Fayetteville (Tigers) | 62 | 75 | .453 | 24½ | Dwight Lowry |
| Asheville (Rockies) | 60 | 73 | .451 | 24½ | Tony Torchia |
| Columbia (Mets) | 59 | 76 | .437 | 26½ | Ron Washington |
| Charleston, S.C. (Rangers) | 56 | 81 | .409 | 30½ | Walt Williams |
| Augusta (Pirates) | 50 | 86 | .368 | 36 | Scott Little |

*Won playoffs #Won split-season pennant

## Stadium Information

| | | Dimensions | | | | |
|---|---|---|---|---|---|---|
| Club | Stadium | LF | CF | RF | Capacity | '94 Att. |
| Albany | Polecat Park | 310 | 400 | 335 | 4,200 | 124,520 |
| Asheville | McCormick Field | 328 | 406 | 300 | 3,400 | 118,146 |
| Augusta | GreenJackets | 330 | 400 | 330 | 4,022 | 115,909 |
| Charleston, SC | College Park | 315 | 410 | 295 | 4,000 | 105,701 |
| Charleston, WV | Watt Powell Park | 340 | 406 | 330 | 6,800 | 103,985 |
| Columbia | Capital City | 330 | 395 | 330 | 6,000 | 146,676 |
| Columbus | Golden Park | 330 | 415 | 330 | 5,000 | 133,351 |
| Fayetteville | J.P. Riddle | 330 | 400 | 330 | 4,200 | 104,379 |
| Greensboro | War Memorial | 330 | 401 | 327 | 7,500 | 218,410 |
| Hagerstown | Municipal | 335 | 400 | 330 | 4,600 | 111,660 |
| Hickory | L.P. Frans | 330 | 401 | 330 | 5,100 | 270,880 |
| Macon | Luther Williams | 338 | 402 | 338 | 3,785 | 83,597 |
| Piedmont | Fieldcrest-Cannon | 330 | 400 | 310 | 4,700 | — |
| Savannah | Grayson | 290 | 400 | 310 | 8,500 | 111,143 |

Piedmont franchise operated in Spartanburg in 1994

## ALBANY
## *POLECATS*

**Office Address:** 1130 Ballpark Lane, Albany, GA 31705. **Mailing Address:** P.O. Box 50485, Albany, GA 31703. **Telephone:** (912) 435-6444. **FAX:** (912) 435-6618.

**Affiliation (first year):** Montreal Expos (1995). **Years in League:** 1992-.

**Team Colors:** Black, white and silver.

### Ownership, Management

**Operated by:** Albany Professional Baseball, Inc.

**Principal Owner:** Richard Holtzman.

**General Manager:** Mike Kardamis. **Director of Marketing:** Lorie Baran. **Director of Stadium Operations:** Eric Allman. **Director of Concessions:** Peter Laven. **Director of Group Sales:** Cherie Muza.

### Field Staff

**Manager:** Doug Sisson. **Coaches:** Stan Fansler (pitching), Angel Salazar.

**Trainer:** Lee Slagle.

### Game Information

**Radio Announcer:** Unavailable. **No. of Games Broadcast:** Home-71, Away-71. **Flagship Station:** WALG 1590-AM.

**PA Announcer:** Kurt Baker. **Official Scorer:** Paul McCorvey.

**Stadium Name:** Polecat Park. **Location:** Blaylock Street exit off US 19, north one mile, stadium on left. **Standard Game Times:** 7:05 p.m.; Sun. (first half) 2:05, (second half) 5:05.

**Visiting Club Hotel:** Holiday Inn Express, 911 E. Oglethorpe, Albany, GA 31701. Telephone: (912) 883-1650.

## ASHEVILLE
## *TOURISTS*

**Office Address:** 30 Buchanan St., Asheville, NC 28801. **Mailing Address:** P.O. Box 1556, Asheville, NC 28802. **Telephone:** (704) 258-0428. **FAX:** (704) 258-0320.

**Affiliation (first year):** Colorado Rockies (1994). **Years in League:** 1976-.

**Team Colors:** Navy blue, red and white.

### Ownership, Management

**Operated by:** Tourists Baseball, Inc.

**Principal Owner/President:** Peter Kern.

**General Manager:** Ron McKee. **Assistant General Manager:** R.J. Martino. **Director of Business Operations:** Carolyn McKee. **Senior Account Representative:** Terry Cole. **Concessions:** Jane Lentz.

### Field Staff

**Manager:** Bill McGuire. **Coaches:** Jack Lamabe (pitching), Joe Marchese.

**Trainer:** Bill Slosson.

### Game Information

**Radio:** None.

**PA Announcer:** Unavailable. **Official Scorer:** Unavailable.

**Stadium Name:** McCormick Field. **Location:** I-240 to Charlotte St. exit south, left on McCormick. **Standard Game Times:** 7 p.m.; Sun. 2.

**Visiting Club Hotel:** Days Inn/Holiday Inn Central, 201 Tunnel Rd., Asheville, NC 28805. Telephone: (704) 254-4311.

## AUGUSTA
## *GREENJACKETS*

**Office Address:** 78 Milledge Rd., Augusta, GA 30904. **Mailing Address:** P.O. Box 3746, Hill Station, Augusta, GA 30904. **Telephone:** (706) 736-7889. **FAX:** (706) 736-1122.

**Affiliation (first year):** Pittsburgh Pirates (1988). **Years in League:** 1988-.

**Team Colors:** Hunter green, purple, gold and azalea.

### Ownership, Management

**Operated by:** Scripps Baseball Group, Inc.

**Principal Owner/President:** Bill Scripps.

**General Manager:** Chris Scheuer. **Business Manager:** Nancy Crowe. **Director of Merchandising:** Harold Baker. **Sales Manager:** Marc Williamson. **Director of Media Relations/Operations:** Jim Wisler. **Director of Marketing:** Rik Duncan. **Concessions:** Steve Cain.

### Field Staff

**Manager:** Jeff Banister. **Coach:** Bruce Tanner (pitching).
**Trainer:** Todd Hoyt.

### Game Information

**Radio Announcers:** John Kelly, Charles McNeil. **No. of Games Broadcast:** Away-71. **Flagship Station:** WRDW 1480-AM.

**PA Announcer:** Tourye Hurst. **Official Scorer:** Frank Mercogliano.

**Stadium Name:** GreenJackets Stadium. **Location:** I-20 to Washington Rd., to Broad St., to Milledge Rd. **Standard Game Times:** 7 p.m; Wed. (April-May) 4; Sun. (April-May) 2:30.

**Visiting Club Hotel:** LaQuinta Inn, 3020 Washington Rd., Augusta, GA 30907. Telephone: (706) 733-2660.

## CHARLESTON *RIVERDOGS*

**Office Address:** 710 Rutledge Ave., Charleston, SC 29403. **Mailing Address:** P.O. Box 20849, Charleston, SC 29413. **Telephone:** (803) 723-7241. **FAX:** (803) 723-2641.

**Affiliation (first year):** Texas Rangers (1993). **Years in League:** 1973-78, 1980-.

**Team Colors:** Purple and teal.

### Ownership, Management

**Operated by:** South Carolina Baseball Club, LP.
**President:** Marvin Goldklang.

**General Manager:** Rob Dlugozima. **Assistant General Manager:** Stan Hughes. **Vice President/Sales:** Scott Skadan. **Director of Marketing/ Merchandise:** Mark Zeigler. **Director of Stadium Operations:** Curt VanDerzee. **Director of Promotions:** Carol Killough. **Director of Community Relations:** Alicia Kearney.

### Field Staff

**Manager:** Mike Berger. **Coach:** Brad Arnsberg (pitching).
**Trainer:** Mike Quinn.

### Game Information

**Radio Announcer:** Unavailable. **No. of Games Broadcast:** Home-71, Away-71. **Flagship Station:** WQSC 1340-AM.

**PA Announcer:** Gary Towles. **Official Scorer:** Unavailable.

**Stadium Name:** College Park. **Location:** I-26 East to exit 219-A (Rutledge Ave.), one mile to stadium. **Standard Game Times:** 7:30 p.m.; Sun. 5.

**Visiting Club Hotel:** Howard Johnson, 250 Spring St., Charleston, SC 29403. Telephone: (803) 722-4000.

## CHARLESTON *ALLEY CATS*

**Office Address:** 3403 MacCorkle Ave., Charleston, WV 25304. **Mailing Address:** P.O. Box 4669, Charleston, WV 25304. **Telephone:** (304) 344-2287. **FAX:** (304) 344-0083.

**Affiliation (first year):** Cincinnati Reds (1990). **Years in League:** 1987-.

**Team Colors:** Black, red and white.

### Ownership, Management

**Operated by:** Wheelers Baseball, LP.
**President:** Mike Paterno.

**General Manager:** Heath Brown. **Assistant General Manager:** Tim Bordner. **Director of Stadium Operations:** Will Gardner. **Director of Media Relations:** Allen Riffle. **Clubhouse Operations:** Eddy Lee.

### Field Staff

**Manager:** Razor Shines. **Coach:** Mack Jenkins (pitching).
**Trainer:** Billy Maxwell.

### Game Information

**Radio Announcer:** Allen Riffle. **No. of Games Broadcast:** Home-7, Away-71. **Flagship Station:** WBES 94.5-FM.

**PA Announcer:** Allen Riffle. **Official Scorer:** Fred Rutledge.

**Stadium Name:** Watt Powell Park. **Location:** I-64 East to 35th St. exit, stadium at bottom of hill; I-64 West to MacCorkle Ave., stadium three miles on left. **Standard Game Times:** 7:05 p.m.; Sun. 2:05.

**Visiting Club Hotel:** Travelodge of Dunbar, 1007 Dunbar Ave., Dunbar, WV 25064. Telephone: (304) 768-1000.

## COLUMBIA
### *BOMBERS*

**Office Address:** 301 S. Assembly St., Columbia, SC 29202. **Mailing Address:** P.O. Box 7845, Columbia, SC 29201. **Telephone:** (803) 256-4110. **FAX:** (803) 256-4338.

**Affiliation (first year):** New York Mets (1983). **Years in League:** 1960-61, 1983-.

**Team Colors:** Black and red.

### Ownership, Management

**Operated by:** United Baseball, Inc.

**Principal Owner/President:** Eric Margenau.

**General Manager:** Bill Shanahan. **Assistant General Manager:** Tim Swain. **Director of Stadium Operations:** Bob Hook. **Director of Media Relations:** Betty Morrah. **Director of Sales/Telemarketing:** Mark Lee. **Director of Promotions:** Jackie Scott. **Director of Group Sales:** Shirley Broughton. **Assistant Director of Telemarketing:** Mike Kozikowski.

### Field Staff

**Manager:** Howie Freiling. **Coach:** Ray Rippelmeyer (pitching).

**Trainer:** Jeff Weems.

### Game Information

**Radio Announcers:** Jim Powell. **No. of Games Broadcast:** Home-60, Away-20. **Flagship Station:** WVOC 560-AM.

**PA Announcer:** Mike Schell. **Official Scorer:** Julian Gibbons.

**Stadium Name:** Capital City Stadium. **Location:** I-26 to Columbia, right on South Assembly St., 4 miles on right. **Standard Game Times:** 7:05 p.m.; Sun. 6:05.

**Visiting Club Hotel:** Travelodge, 2210 Bush River Rd., Columbia, SC 29210. Telephone: (803) 798-9665.

## COLUMBUS
### *REDSTIXX*

**Office Address:** 100 Fourth St., Columbus, GA 31901. **Mailing Address:** P.O. Box 1886, Columbus, GA 31902. **Telephone:** (706) 571-8866. **FAX:** (706) 571-9107.

**Affiliation (first year):** Cleveland Indians (1991). **Years in League:** 1991-.

**Team Colors:** Red and navy.

### Ownership, Management

**Operated by:** Columbus Professional Baseball Club, Inc.

**Principal Owner/President:** Charles Morrow.

**Vice President/General Manager:** John Dittrich. **Director of Business Operations:** Lois Dittrich. **Director of Stadium Operations:** Jim Walker. **Director of Media Relations:** Sandi Karchmer. **Vice President/Sales, Marketing:** Rick Jacobson. **Director of Community Relations:** Carol Malone. **Director of Group Sales:** Dave Turner.

### Field Staff

**Manager:** Jeff Datz. **Coach:** Fred Gladding (pitching).

**Trainer:** Rick Jameyson.

### Game Information

**Radio Announcer:** Mark Littleton. **No. of Games Broadcast:** Home-71, Away-71. **Flagship Station:** WDAK 540-AM.

**PA Announcer:** Steve Thiele. **Official Scorer:** Kathy Gierer.

**Stadium Name:** Golden Park. **Location:** I-185 to exit 1 (Victory Drive N.), 8 miles to 4th St., stadium on left. **Standard Game Times:** 7:15 p.m.; Sun. 2:15.

**Visiting Club Hotel:** Holiday Inn Airport, 2800 Manchester Expy., Columbus, GA 31904. Telephone: (706) 324-0231.

## FAYETTEVILLE
### *GENERALS*

**Office Address:** 2823 Legion Rd., Fayetteville, NC 28306. **Mailing Address:** P.O Box 64939, Fayetteville, NC 28306. **Telephone:** (910) 424-6500. **FAX:** (910) 424-4325.

**Affiliation (first year):** Detroit Tigers (1987). **Years in League:** 1987-.

**Team Colors:** Navy blue and orange.

## Ownership, Management

**Operated by:** Fayetteville Baseball Club, Inc.

**Principal Owner/President:** Charles Padgett.

**General Manager:** Rick Furr. **Vice President/Sales, Marketing:** Dan McDonough. **Director of Business Operations:** Linda Bennett. **Director of Stadium Operations:** Chris Bertolli. **Director of Media/Public Relations:** Leisha Cowart. **Director of Community Relations:** Roger Worrell. **Director of Ticket Sales:** Mike Begley. **Director of Group Sales:** Darrell Rackley.

## Field Staff

**Manager:** Dwight Lowry. **Coaches:** Basilio Cabrera, Sid Monge (pitching).

**Trainer:** Matt Lewis.

## Game Information

**Radio Announcer:** Taylor Carr. **No. of Games Broadcast:** Home-71, Away-71. **Flagship Station:** WJSK 102.3-FM.

**PA Announcer:** Unavailable. **Official Scorer:** Sammy Batten.

**Stadium Name:** J.P. Riddle Stadium. **Location:** I-95 to exit 40 to 301 North, left on Owen Dr., left on Legion Rd. **Standard Game Times:** 7 p.m.; Sun. 5.

**Visiting Club Hotel:** Econo Lodge, 1952 Cedar Creek Rd., Fayetteville, NC 28306. Telephone: (910) 433-2100.

# GREENSBORO
# *BATS*

**Office Address:** 510 Yanceyville St., Greensboro, NC 27405. **Mailing Address:** P.O. Box 22093, Greensboro, NC 27420. **Telephone:** (910) 333-2287. **FAX:** (910) 273-7350.

**Affiliation (first year):** New York Yankees (1990). **Years in League:** 1979-.

**Team Colors:** Purple, turquoise, white, black and red.

## Ownership, Management

**Operated by:** Carolina Diamond Baseball Club, LP.

**Principal Owners:** William Collins, William Collins III, John Horshok, Donald Malan, Tim Cullen, Larry Trollinger.

**Chairman of the Board:** William Collins III. **Chief Operating Officer:** John Horshok.

**General Manager:** John Frey. **Director of Business Operations:** Vicki-Ann Moyer. **Director of Operations:** John Parisi. **Assistant Director of Operations:** John Tuders. **Director of Marketing/Public Relations:** Jerry Burkot. **Senior Account Executive:** Thomas Walter. **Director of Corporate Sales:** David Mulholland. **Director of Ticket Sales:** Mike Harris. **Director of Group Sales:** Jeff Morris. **Director of Merchandising:** Robin Morinsky. **Head Groundskeeper:** John Packer.

## Field Staff

**Manager:** Trey Hillman. **Coaches:** Pete Filson (pitching), Brian Milner.

**Trainer:** Chris DeLucia.

## Game Information

**Radio Announcer:** Bill Wardle. **No. of Games Broadcast:** Home-71, Away-71. **Flagship Station:** Unavailable.

**PA Announcer:** Gary Ross. **Official Scorer:** Ogi Overman.

**Stadium Name:** War Memorial Stadium. **Location:** I-40/I-85 to Elm-Eugene St. exit, north to Market St., east to Dudley, north to corner of Lindsay and Yanceyville Streets. **Standard Game Times:** 7:15 p.m.; Sun. 6:15.

**Visiting Club Hotel:** Travelodge, 2112 W. Meadowville Rd., Greensboro, NC 27403. Telephone: (910) 292-2020.

# HAGERSTOWN
# *SUNS*

**Office Address:** 274 E. Memorial Blvd., Hagerstown, MD 21740. **Mailing Address:** P.O. Box 230, Hagerstown, MD 21741. **Telephone:** (301) 791-6266. **FAX:** (301) 791-6066.

**Affiliation (first year):** Toronto Blue Jays (1993). **Years in League:** 1993-.

**Team Colors:** Blue and red.

## Ownership, Management

**Operated by:** Norwin Corp.

**Principal Owner/President/General Manager:** Winston Blenckstone.

**Assistant General Manager:** David Blenckstone. **Director of**

**Business Operations:** Carol Gehr. **Director of Stadium Operations:** Unavailable. **Head Groundskeeper:** Shawn Faith. **Director of Media/Public Relations:** Bill Berger. **Director of Community Relations:** Mike Krigbaum. **Director of Ticket Sales:** Les Seville. **Director of Special Projects:** Kim Bohle. **Clubhouse Operations:** Alec Aronow.

### Field Staff

**Manager:** Omar Malave. **Coaches:** Reggie Cleveland (pitching), Scott Miller.

**Trainer:** Doug Merrifield.

### Game Information

**Radio Announcer:** David Shinsky. **No. of Games Broadcast:** Home-71, Away-71. **Flagship Station:** WJEJ 1240-AM.

**PA Announcer:** Travis Medcalf. **Official Scorer:** Jan Marcus.

**Stadium Name:** Municipal Stadium. **Location:** Exit 32B from I-70, left on Cleveland; Exit 6 from I-81, right on Cleveland. **Standard Game Times:** 7:05 p.m.; Sun. 2:05.

**Visiting Club Hotel:** Ramada Inn Convention Center, 901 Dual Hwy., Hagerstown, MD 21740. Telephone: (301) 733-5100.

## HICKORY
## *CRAWDADS*

**Office Address:** 2500 Clement Blvd. NW, Hickory, NC 28601. **Mailing Address:** P.O. Box 1268, Hickory, NC 28603. **Telephone:** (704) 322-3000. **FAX:** (704) 322-6137.

**Affiliation (first year):** Chicago White Sox (1993). **Years in League:** 1952, 1960, 1993-.

**Team Colors:** Black, red and silver.

### Ownership, Management

**Operated by:** Hickory Baseball, Inc.

**President:** Don Beaver.

**Vice President/General Manager:** Marty Steele. **Assistant General Manager:** David Haas. **Director of Marketing/Media Relations:** Chris Gallas. **Director of Stadium Operations/Merchandising:** Nick Reese. **Director of Broadcasting:** Matt Swierad. **Director of Computer Operations:** Ed Shepherd. **Director of Ticket Operations:** Daron Montgomery. **Director of Community Relations:** Dale Coxe.

### Field Staff

**Manager:** Mike Rojas. **Coaches:** Bill Ballou (pitching), Dave Keller.

**Trainer:** Joe Geck.

### Game Information

**Radio Announcers:** Matt Swierad, Tim Grubbs. **No. of Games Broadcast:** Home-71, Road-71. **Flagship Station:** WMNC 92.1-FM.

**PA Announcer:** Tim Grubbs. **Official Scorers:** Jerry Burton, Tom Sparkman.

**Stadium Name:** L.P. Frans Stadium. **Location:** I-40 to Exit 123 (Lenoir North), 321 North to Clement Blvd., left for ¼-mile. **Standard Game Times:** 7 p.m.; Sun. (April-June) 2, (July-Sept.) 6.

**Visiting Club Hotel:** Red Roof Inn, 1184 Lenoir Rhyne Blvd., Hickory, NC 28602. Telephone: (704) 323-1500.

## MACON
## *BRAVES*

**Office Address:** Luther Williams Field, 7th Street, Macon, GA 31201. **Mailing Address:** P.O. Box 4525, Macon, GA 31208. **Telephone:** (912) 745-8943. **FAX:** (912) 743-5559.

**Affiliation (first year):** Atlanta Braves (1991). **Years in League:** 1962-63, 1980-87, 1991-.

**Team Colors:** Blue, red and gold.

### Ownership, Management

**Operated by:** Atlanta National League Baseball Club, Inc.

**Principal Owner:** Ted Turner. **League Director:** Chip Moore.

**General Manager:** Ed Holtz. **Office Manager:** Mary Holtz. **Director of Stadium Operations:** Terry Morgan. **Director of Sales/Marketing:** Jim Tessmer. **Head Groundskeeper:** George Stephens. **Director of Ticket Sales:** Ed Loomis. **Senior Account Representatives:** Brad Cork, Terry Morgan. **Concessions:** Pam Willett. **Security:** R.M. Willett.

### Field Staff

**Manager:** Nelson Norman. **Coaches:** Dave Hilton, Larry Jaster (pitching).

**Trainer:** Willy Johnson.

## Game Information

**Radio Announcers:** Brad Bibb, Bobby Pope. **No. of Games Broadcast:** Home-20. **Flagship Station:** WMAZ 940-AM.

**PA Announcers:** Jimmy Jones, Shannon Smallwood. **Official Scorer:** Kevin Colombe.

**Stadium Name:** Luther Williams Field. **Location:** Exit 4 off I-16. **Standard Game Times:** 7 p.m.; Sun. 2.

**Visiting Club Hotel:** Comfort Inn North, 2690 Riverside Dr., Macon, GA 31204. Telephone: (912) 746-8855.

# PIEDMONT
## *PHILLIES*

**Office Address:** 3080 Moose Rd., Kannapolis, NC 28081. **Mailing Address:** P.O. Box 322, Kannapolis, NC 28082. **Telephone:** (704) 932-3267. **FAX:** (704) 938-7040.

**Affiliation (first year):** Philadelphia Phillies (1995). **Years in League:** 1995-.

**Team Colors:** Red and blue.

## Ownership, Management

**Operated by:** Iredell Trading Co.

**Principal Owners:** Larry Hedrick, Sue Hedrick. **President:** Larry Hedrick.

**General Manager:** Jack Swallow. **Assistant General Manager:** Dan Zusman. **Director of Baseball/Ticket Operations:** Ken Fogel. **Director of Media Relations:** Mark Viniard. **Office Manager:** Robin Clay. **Sales Representatives:** Chip Dischinger, Barry Dyson, Eric Lowder. **Director of Field Operations:** Chad Casella.

## Field Staff

**Manager:** Roy Majtyka. **Coaches:** John Martin (pitching), Tony Scott.

**Trainer:** Troy Hoffert.

## Game Information

**Radio:** None.

**PA Announcer:** Unavailable. **Official Scorer:** Unavailable.

**Stadium Name:** Fieldcrest-Cannon Stadium. **Location:** I-85 South to exit 63, right on Lane St., right on China Grove St., right on Moose Rd. to stadium. I-85 North to exit 63, right on Lane St., left on Turkey Rd., left on Moose Rd. to stadium **Standard Game Times:** April-May 7:05 p.m., June-Sept. 7:35; Fri., Sat. 7:35; Sun. 2:05.

**Visiting Club Hotel:** Unavailable.

# SAVANNAH
## *CARDINALS*

**Office Address:** 1401 E. Victory Dr., Savannah, GA 31404. **Mailing Address:** P.O. Box 3783, Savannah, GA 31414. **Telephone:** (912) 351-9150. **FAX:** (912) 352-9722.

**Affiliation (first year):** St. Louis Cardinals (1984). **Years in League:** 1962, 1984-.

**Team Colors:** Red, white and navy blue.

## Ownership, Management

**Operated by:** Savannah Professional Baseball Club, Inc.

**Principal Owner/Chairman:** Ken Silver. **Vice President:** Ken Savin.

**General Manager:** Ric Sisler. **Assistant General Manager:** Mark Ruckwardt. **Head Groundskeeper:** Walter Reed. **Assistant General Manager/Public Relations:** Mitch Mann. **Director of Sales/Marketing:** Keith Croucher. **Office Manager:** Reba Rogers.

## Field Staff

**Manager:** Scott Melvin. **Coaches:** Mauricio Nunez, Dave Ricketts (pitching).

**Trainer:** Steve Proctor.

## Game Information

**Radio:** None.

**PA Announcer:** Hal Dutton. **Official Scorer:** Marcus Holland.

**Stadium Name:** Grayson Stadium. **Location:** I-16 to 37th St. exit, left on 37th, right on Abercorn St., left on Victory Dr., stadium two miles on right. **Standard Game Times:** 7:15 p.m; Sun. 2.

**Visiting Club Hotel:** Holiday Inn Midtown, 7100 Abercorn St., Savannah, GA 31406. Telephone: (912) 352-7100.

# NEW YORK-PENN LEAGUE

## Short Season Class A

**Mailing Address:** 1629 Oneida St., Utica, NY 13501. **Telephone:** (315) 733-8036. **FAX:** (315) 797-7403.

**President:** Bob Julian.

**Vice President:** Sam Nader. **Treasurer:** Clyde Smoll. **Secretary:** Mike Schell.

**Directors:** Mike Billoni (Jamestown), Bob Fowler (Utica), Barry Gordon (New Jersey), Alan Levin (Erie), Richard Murphy (Pittsfield), Sam Nader (Oneonta), Ray Pecor (Vermont), Leo Pinckney (Auburn), Brad Rogers (Batavia), Mike Schell (Watertown), Clyde Smoll (Elmira), Greg Sorbara (St. Catharines), Paul Velte (Williamsport), Skip Weisman (Hudson Valley).

**Executive Assistant:** Vonda Bonham.

**Years League Active:** 1939-.

**1995 Opening Date:** June 15. **Closing Date:** Sept. 1.

**No. of Games:** 76.

**Division Structure: McNamara**—Hudson Valley, New Jersey, Pittsfield, Vermont. **Pinckney**—Auburn, Elmira, Oneonta, Utica, Watertown, Williamsport. **Stedler**—Batavia, Erie, Jamestown, St. Catharines.

**Playoff Format:** Three division winners and a wild card will meet in best-of-3 semifinals. Winners meet in best-of-3 series for league championship.

**All-Star Game:** None.

**Roster Limit:** 25 active. **Player Eligibility Rule:** No more than two players who are 23 or older. No more than three players on active list may have four or more years of prior service.

**Brand of Baseball:** Rawlings.

**Statistician:** Howe Sportsdata International, Boston Fish Pier, West Bldg. #2—Suite 306, Boston MA 02210.

### 1994 Standings (Overall)

| Club (Affiliate) | W | L | Pct. | GB | '94 Manager |
|---|---|---|---|---|---|
| #Watertown (Indians) | 48 | 26 | .649 | — | Jeff Datz |
| Auburn (Astros) | 45 | 31 | .592 | 4 | Manny Acta |
| *#New Jersey (Cardinals) | 43 | 32 | .573 | 5½ | Roy Silver |
| #Jamestown (Tigers) | 42 | 32 | .568 | 6 | Dave Anderson |
| Vermont (Expos) | 42 | 33 | .560 | 6½ | Terry Kennedy |
| Batavia (Phillies) | 40 | 34 | .541 | 8 | Al LeBoeuf |
| Hudson Valley (Rangers) | 37 | 37 | .500 | 11 | Doug Sisson |
| Pittsfield (Mets) | 37 | 38 | .493 | 11½ | Howie Freiling |
| Utica (Red Sox) | 35 | 37 | .486 | 12 | Dave Holt |
| St. Catharines (Blue Jays) | 35 | 39 | .473 | 13 | J.J. Cannon |
| Elmira (Marlins) | 30 | 43 | .411 | 17½ | Jim Hendry |
| Welland (Pirates) | 30 | 44 | .405 | 18 | Jeff Banister |
| Oneonta (Yankees) | 30 | 45 | .400 | 18½ | Ken Dominguez |
| Williamsport (Cubs) | 26 | 49 | .347 | 22½ | Jerry Weinstein |

*Won playoffs #Won division title

### Stadium Information

| | | Dimensions | | | | |
|---|---|---|---|---|---|---|
| Club | Stadium | LF | CF | RF | Capacity | '94 Att. |
| Auburn | Falcon Park | 330 | 400 | 330 | 2,200 | 31,544 |
| Batavia | Dwyer | 325 | 400 | 325 | 2,500 | 41,502 |
| Elmira | Dunn Field | 325 | 386 | 325 | 5,000 | 60,464 |
| Erie | Unavailable | 312 | 400 | 328 | 6,000 | — |
| Hudson Valley | Dutchess | 325 | 400 | 325 | 4,300 | 138,116 |
| Jamestown | College | 335 | 410 | 353 | 3,324 | 49,706 |
| New Jersey | Skylands Park | 330 | 400 | 330 | 4,341 | 156,447 |
| Oneonta | Damaschke Field | 352 | 406 | 350 | 4,200 | 48,712 |
| Pittsfield | Wahconah Park | 334 | 374 | 333 | 4,200 | 59,122 |
| St. Catharines | Community Park | 310 | 400 | 310 | 3,000 | 31,539 |
| Utica | Donovan | 324 | 400 | 324 | 4,000 | 72,006 |
| Vermont | Centennial Field | 335 | 415 | 335 | 4,000 | 114,179 |
| Watertown | Duffy Fairgrounds | 330 | 410 | 330 | 3,269 | 57,089 |
| Williamsport | Bowman Field | 345 | 405 | 350 | 4,200 | 57,624 |

Erie franchise operated in Welland in 1994

## AUBURN
## *ASTROS*

**Office Address:** 108 N. Division St., Auburn, NY 13021. **Mailing Address:** Two South St., Auburn, NY 13021. **Telephone:** (315) 255-2489. **FAX:** (315) 255-2675.

**Affiliation (first year):** Houston Astros (1982). **Years in League:** 1958-80, 1982-.

### Ownership, Management

**Operated By:** Auburn Community Baseball, Inc.

**Chairman of the Board:** Ann Bunker.

**Vice President:** Leo Pinckney. **Treasurer:** Jim Hutchinson. **Corporate Secretary:** Andrew LaLonde.

**General Manager:** Shawn Smith. **Assistant General Manager:** Mark Harrington. **Director of Public Relations:** Unavailable. **Director of Ticket Sales:** Lynn Odrzywolski. **Director of Stadium Operations:** Unavailable. **Director of Facilities/Administrative Assistant:** Matthew King.

### Field Staff

**Manager:** Manny Acta. **Coach:** Don Alexander (pitching).

**Trainer:** Unavailable.

### Game Information

**Radio:** Unavailable.

**PA Announcer/Official Scorer:** Bob Coogan.

**Stadium Name:** Falcon Park. **Location:** One mile north of Rts. 5 and 20 on North Division Street. **Standard Game Times:** 7 p.m.; DH and Sun. 6.

**Visiting Club Hotel:** Unavailable.

## BATAVIA
## *CLIPPERS*

**Office Address:** Denio & Bank Streets, Batavia, NY 14021. **Mailing Address:** P.O. Box 802, Batavia, NY 14021. **Telephone:** (716) 343-7531. **FAX:** (716) 343-9372.

**Affiliation (first year):** Philadelphia Phillies (1988). **Years in League:** 1939-53, 1957-59, 1961-.

**Team Colors:** Blue and red.

### Ownership, Management

**Operated by:** Genesee County Professional Baseball, Inc.

**President:** Larry Roth.

**Vice President/General Manager:** Brad Rogers. **Assistant General Manager:** Julia Rogers. **Head Groundskeeper:** Dick Rogers. **Director of Sales/Marketing:** Kevin Witt. **Director of Ticket Sales:** Elanore Smith. **Clubhouse Operations:** Kevin Rogers.

### Field Staff

**Manager:** Al LeBoeuf. **Coaches:** Floyd Rayford, Ken Westray (pitching).

**Trainer:** Troy McIntosh.

### Game Information

**Radio Announcer:** Unavailable. **No. of Games Broadcast:** Home-16. **Flagship Station:** WBTA 1490-AM.

**PA Announcer/Official Scorer:** Wayne Fuller.

**Stadium Name:** Dwyer Stadium. **Location:** I-90 to exit 48, left on Rt. 98 South, left on Richmond Ave., left on Bank St. **Standard Game Times:** 7:05 p.m.

**Visiting Club Hotel:** Sheraton Inn & Convention Center, 8250 Park Rd., Batavia, NY 14020. Telephone: (716) 344-2100.

## ELMIRA
## *PIONEERS*

**Office Address:** 546 Luce St., Elmira, NY 14904. **Mailing Address:** P.O. Box 238, Elmira, NY 14902. **Telephone:** (607) 734-1811. **FAX:** (607) 734-4975.

**Affiliation (first year):** Florida Marlins (1993). **Years in League:** 1957-61, 1973-.

**Team Colors:** Blue, black and orange.

### Ownership, Management

**Operated by:** Diamond Action, Inc.

**Principal Owners:** Clyde Smoll, Charlene Smoll.
**President/General Manager:** Clyde Smoll.
**Director of Public Relations:** Marc Sanders. **Director of Sales/ Concessions:** Brian Lindsay. **Director of Finance/Administration:** Charlene Smoll.

### Field Staff

**Manager:** Paul Kirsch. **Coaches:** Bill Long (pitching), Steve McFarland.
**Trainer:** Tim Abraham.

### Game Information

**Radio Announcer:** Marc Sanders. **No. of Games Broadcast:** Home-5, Away-15. **Flagship Station:** Unavailable.

**PA Announcer:** Marc Sanders. **Official Scorer:** Mike Callahan.

**Stadium Name:** Dunn Field. **Location:** Rt. 17 to exit 56, left on Judson St., right on Water St., left on Maple Ave., left on Luce St. **Standard Game Times:** 7 p.m.; Sun. 2.

**Visiting Club Hotels:** Guthrie Inn, 255 Spring St., Sayre, PA 18840. Telephone: (717) 888-7711; Holiday Inn, East Water St., Elmira, NY 14901. Telephone: (607) 734-4211.

## ERIE
## *SEAWOLVES*

**Office Address:** 110 East 10th St., Erie, PA 16501. **Mailing Address:** P.O. Box 1776, Erie, PA 16507. **Telephone:** (814) 456-1300. **FAX:** (814) 456-7520.

**Affiliation (first year):** Pittsburgh Pirates (1995). **Years in League:** 1944-45, 1954-63, 1967, 1981-93, 1995.

**Team Colors:** Columbia blue, black, gold, red and grey.

### Ownership, Management

**Operated by:** Seawolves Partners.
**Principal Owners:** Alan Levin, Ken Silver.
**General Manager:** Erik Haag. **Assistant General Manager:** Brian Sloan. **Director of Sales/Promotions:** Keith Hallal.

### Field Staff

**Manager:** Scott Little. **Coach:** Larry Smith (pitching).
**Trainer:** Mark Mann.

### Game Information

**Radio:** Unavailable.

**PA Announcer:** Unavailable. **Official Scorer:** Unavailable.

**Stadium Name:** Unavailable. **Location:** US 79 North to East 12th St. exit, left on State St., right on 10th St. **Standard Game Times:** 7 p.m.; Sun. 2.

**Visiting Club Hotel:** Avalon Hotel, 16 West 10th St., Erie, PA 16501. Telephone: (814) 459-2220.

## HUDSON VALLEY
## *RENEGADES*

**Office Address:** 9D, North Road, Beacon, NY 12508. **Mailing Address:** P.O. Box 661, Fishkill, NY 12524. **Telephone:** (914) 838-0094. **FAX:** (914) 838-0014.

**Affiliation (first year):** Texas Rangers (1994). **Years in League:** 1994-.

**Team Colors:** Burgundy, green and black.

### Ownership, Management

**Operated by:** Keystone Professional Baseball Club, Inc.
**Principal Owner/Chairman of the Board:** Marvin Goldklang.
**President/General Manager:** Skip Weisman. **Assistant General Manager:** Kathy Lumbard-Cobb. **Director of Sales/Marketing:** Steve Gliner. **Director of Public Relations/Promotions:** Rick Zolzer. **Director of Ticket Operations:** Jessica Berry. **Coordinator/Customer Service:** Dottie Paponetti. **Office Manager:** Sharon Evans-Weisman. **Interns:** Mitchell Lotenberg, Chris Puzzuoli, Dennis Wansor.

### Field Staff

**Manager:** Bump Wills. **Coach:** Steve Foucault (pitching).
**Trainer:** Kevin Andrews.

### Game Information

**Radio Announcer:** Bill Rogan. **No. of Games Broadcast:** Home-38, Away-38. **Flagship Station:** WBNR 1260-AM.

**PA Announcer:** Rick Zolzer. **Official Scorer:** Bob Beretta.

**Stadium Name:** Dutchess Stadium. **Location:** From east—I-84 West to

Rt. 9D (exit 11), north ½ mile to stadium; From north, south and west—New York State Thruway to exit 17 in Newburgh, to I-84 East over Beacon-Newburgh Bridge to Rt. 9D (exit 11), north ½ mile to stadium. **Standard Game Times:** 7:15 p.m.; Sun. 1:35.

**Visiting Club Hotel:** Unavailable.

# JAMESTOWN
## *JAMMERS*

**Office Address:** 485 Falconer St., Jamestown, NY 14702. **Mailing Address:** P.O. Box 638, Jamestown, NY 14702. **Telephone:** (716) 664-0915. **FAX:** (716) 664-4175.

**Affiliation (first year):** Detroit Tigers (1994). **Years in League:** 1939-57, 1961-73, 1977-.

**Team Colors:** Red, silver and black.

### Ownership, Management

**Operated by:** Rich Products Corp.

**Principal Owners:** Robert Rich Jr., Melinda Rich.

**Chairman of the Board:** Robert Rich Sr.

**General Manager:** Shawn Reilly. **Assistant General Manager:** Christine Burgeson. **Head Groundskeeper:** Tom Casler. **Director of Public Relations/Group Sales:** Michael Ferguson.

### Field Staff

**Manager:** Bruce Fields. **Coach:** Juan Lopez.

**Trainer:** Mark Grosbeck.

### Game Information

**Radio:** None.

**PA Announcer:** Todd Peterson. **Official Scorer:** Jim Riggs.

**Stadium Name:** College Stadium. **Location:** Rt. 17 South to exit 12, right onto Rt. 60, left on Buffalo Street, left on Falconer Street. **Standard Game Times:** 7:05 p.m.

**Visiting Club Hotel:** Jamestown Holiday Inn, 150 W. Fourth St., Jamestown, NY 14701. Telephone: (716) 664-3400.

# NEW JERSEY
## *CARDINALS*

**Office Address:** 94 Championship Place, Skylands Park, Augusta, NJ 07822. **Mailing Address:** P.O. Box 117, Augusta, NJ 07822. **Telephone:** (201) 579-7500. **FAX:** (201) 579-7502.

**Affiliation (first year):** St. Louis Cardinals (1994). **Years in League:** 1994-.

**Team Colors:** Red, navy blue and gold.

### Ownership, Management

**Operated by:** Minor League Heroes, LP.

**Principal Owners:** Barry Gordon, Marc Klee.

**Chairman of the Board:** Barry Gordon. **President:** Marc Klee.

**Vice President/General Manager:** Tony Torre. **Director of Finance:** Warren Brown. **Head Groundskeeper:** Jerry Milan. **Director of Marketing:** Doug Stewart. **Director of Promotions:** Herm Sorcher. **Director of Ticketing:** Brian Eggers. **Director of Group Sales:** Bob Commentucci. **Office Manager:** Christine Sutton. **Director of Broadcasting:** Mike Curci. **Director of Advertising Sales:** John Levine. **Special Projects:** Kim Buckey.

### Field Staff

**Manager:** Luis Melendez. **Coaches:** Hub Kittle (pitching), Tim Redman.

**Trainer:** B.J. Maack.

### Game Information

**Radio Announcers:** Mike Curci, Phil Pepe. **No. of Games Broadcast:** Home-38, Away-10. **Flagship Station:** Unavailable.

**PA Announcer:** Unavailable. **Official Scorer:** Ken Hand.

**Stadium Name:** Skylands Park. **Location:** From I-80—exit 34B to Rt. 15 North to Rt. 565; From I-84—exit at Rt. 206 South to Rt. 565. **Standard Game Times:** 7 p.m.; Wed./Sun. 1; Sat. 5.

**Visiting Club Hotel:** Best Western Inn at Hunt's Landing, 900 Rts. 6 and 209, Matamoras, PA 18336. Telephone: (717) 491-2400.

## ONEONTA
## *YANKEES*

**Office Address:** 95 River St., Oneonta, NY 13820. **Telephone:** (607) 432-6326. **FAX:** (607) 432-1965.

**Affiliation (first year):** New York Yankees (1967). **Years in League:** 1966-.

**Team Colors:** Blue and white.

### Ownership, Management

**Operated by:** Oneonta Athletic Corp., Inc.

**Principal Owner/President:** Sam Nader.

**General Manager:** John Nader. **Assistant General Manager:** Bob Zeh. **Controller:** Sidney Levine. **Head Groundskeeper:** Ted Christman. **Director of Public Relations:** Suzanne Longo. **Director of Promotions:** Alice O'Conner. **Director of Special Projects:** Mark Nader.

### Field Staff

**Manager:** Rob Thomson. **Coaches:** Paul Faulk, Tom Filer (pitching), Terry Rupp.

**Trainer:** Carl Randolph.

### Game Information

**Radio:** None.

**PA Announcer:** Doug Decker. **Official Scorers:** David Bishop, Bob Whittemore.

**Stadium Name:** Damaschke Field. **Location:** Exit 15 off I-88. **Standard Game Times:** 7:15 p.m., Sun. 6.

**Visiting Club Hotel:** Town House Motor Inn, 318 Main St., Oneonta, NY 13820. Telephone: (607) 432-1313.

## PITTSFIELD
## *METS*

**Office Address:** 105 Wahconah St., Pittsfield, MA 01201. **Mailing Address:** P.O. Box 328, Pittsfield, MA 01202. **Telephone:** (413) 499-6387. **FAX:** (413) 443-7144.

**Affiliation (first year):** New York Mets (1989). **Years in League:** 1989-.

**Team Colors:** Royal blue and orange.

### Ownership, Management

**Operated by:** National Pastime Corporation.

**Principal Owners:** William Gladstone, Martin Barr, Alfred Roberts, John Burton, Stephen Siegel.

**President:** William Gladstone.

**General Manager:** Richard Murphy. **Assistant General Manager:** Richard Lenfest. **Director of Stadium Operations:** David Keane. **Director of Media/Public Relations:** Ethan Wilson. **Director of Ticket Sales:** Edward Forfa.

### Field Staff

**Manager:** Ron Gideon. **Coach:** Dave LaRoche (pitching).

**Trainer:** Unavailable.

### Game Information

**Radio:** Unavailable.

**PA Announcer:** David Curran. **Official Scorer:** Ethan Wilson.

**Stadium Name:** Wahconah Park. **Location:** Wahconah Street exit off Rt. 7 North. **Standard Game Times:** 7 p.m.; Sun. 1 or 6.

**Visiting Club Hotels:** Berkshire Hilton Inn, Berkshire Common, Pittsfield, MA 01201. Telephone: (413) 499-2000. Holiday Inn Berkshires, 40 Main St., North Adams, MA 01247. Telephone: (413) 663-6500.

## ST. CATHARINES
## *STOMPERS*

**Office Address:** 426 Merritt St., St. Catharines, Ontario L2P 1P3. **Telephone:** (905) 641-5297. **FAX:** (905) 641-3007.

**Affiliation (first year):** Toronto Blue Jays (1986). **Years in League:** 1986-.

**Team Colors:** Unavailable.

### Ownership, Management

**Operated by:** St. Catharines Baseball Club, Ltd.

**Principal Owners:** Home Innings, Inc.; Leadoff Investments, Ltd.; Ernie Whitt.

**President:** Greg Sorbara.

**General Manager:** John Belford. **Manager of Sales/Promotions:** Paul Pettipiece. **Secretary:** Eleanor Bowman.

### Field Staff

**Manager:** J.J. Cannon. **Coach:** Al Widmar (pitching).

**Trainer:** Scott Shannon.

### Game Information

**Radio:** None.

**PA Announcer:** Unavailable. **Official Scorer:** Unavailable.

**Stadium Name:** Community Park. **Location:** From east—Queen Elizabeth Expressway to Glendale exit, turn left then right on Merritt St., right on Seymour Ave.; From west—Queen Elizabeth Expressway to 406 North, left at Glendale Ave. exit, left on Merritt St., right on Seymour Ave. **Standard Game Times:** 7:05 p.m.; Sun: 2:05.

**Visiting Club Hotel:** Howard Johnson, 89 Meadowvale Drive, St. Catharines, Ontario L2N 3Z8. Telephone: (905) 934-5400.

## UTICA
## *BLUE SOX*

**Office Address:** 1700 Sunset Ave., Utica, NY 13502. **Mailing Address:** P.O. Box 751, Utica, NY 13503. **Telephone:** (315) 738-0999. **FAX:** (315) 738-0992.

**Affiliation (first year):** Boston Red Sox (1993). **Years in League:** 1977-.

**Team Colors:** Red, white and navy blue.

### Ownership, Management

**Operated by:** Utica Baseball Club, Ltd.

**Principal Owner/President:** Bob Fowler.

**General Manager:** Rob Fowler. **Director of Stadium Operations:** Chuck Fox. **Head Groundskeeper:** Butch Russo. **Clubhouse Operations:** Edward Jackson.

### Field Staff

**Manager:** Bob Geren. **Coach:** Bill Moloney (pitching).

**Trainer:** Bob Bill.

### Game Information

**Radio Announcer:** Bruce Markason. **No. of Games Broadcast:** Home-30; Away-6. **Flagship Station:** WIBX 950-AM.

**PA Announcer:** Rich Williams. **Official Scorer:** Tom Nowicki.

**Stadium Name:** Donovan Stadium. **Location:** New York State Thruway to exit 31 (Genesee Street), south to Burrstone Rd., right one block to stadium. **Standard Game Times:** 7 p.m.

**Visiting Club Hotel:** Howard Johnson Lodge, 302 N. Genesee St., Utica, NY 13502. Telephone: (315) 724-4141.

## VERMONT
## *EXPOS*

**Office Address:** 1 Main St., Winooski, VT 05404. **Telephone:** (802) 655-4200. **FAX:** (802) 655-5660.

**Affiliation (first year):** Montreal Expos (1994). **Years in League:** 1994-.

**Team Colors:** Red, white and blue.

### Ownership, Management

**Operated by:** Vermont Expos, Inc.

**Principal Owner/President:** Ray Pecor.

**General Manager:** Tom Racine. **Assistant General Manager:** Kyle Bostwick. **Director of Business Operations:** Mike Goglia. **Director of Stadium Operations:** Steve Bernard. **Head Groundskeeper:** Lee Keller. **Director of Sales/Marketing:** Chris Corley. **Director of Special Projects:** Jeff Edmond.

### Field Staff

**Manager:** Jim Gabella. **Coach:** Butch Hughes (pitching).

**Trainer:** Unavailable.

### Game Information

**Radio Announcer:** George Commo. **No. of Games Broadcast:** Home-20; Away-25. **Flagship Station:** WVMT AM-620.

**PA Announcer:** Rich Haskel. **Official Scorer:** Ev Smith.

**Stadium Name:** Centennial Field. **Location:** I-89 to exit 14W, right on East Ave for one mile, right at light. **Standard Game Times:** 7:05 p.m.; Sat.-Sun. 2:05.

**Visiting Club Hotel:** Econo Lodge, 1076 Williston Rd. South, Burlington, VT 05403. Telephone: (802) 863-1225.

# WATERTOWN *INDIANS*

**Office Address:** 900 Coffeen St., Watertown, NY 13601. **Mailing Address:** P.O. Box 802, Watertown, NY 13601. **Telephone:** (315) 788-8747. **FAX:** (315) 788-8841.

**Affiliation (first year):** Cleveland Indians (1989). **Years in League:** 1983-.

**Team Colors:** Red, white and blue.

## Ownership, Management

**Operated by:** Jefferson County Community Baseball.

**President:** Mike Schell.

**General Manager:** Jack Tracz. **Assistant General Manager:** Jeff Dumas. **Controller:** Jerry Gardner. **Head Groundskeeper:** Bill Nemergut. **Director of Public Relations:** Eric Valentine. **Director of Sales/ Marketing:** Jason Smorol. **Clubhouse Operations:** Fonzi Baker.

## Field Staff

**Manager:** Joel Skinner **Coaches:** Ken Rowe (pitching), Billy Williams.

**Trainer:** Nick Paparesta.

## Game Information

**Radio Announcer:** Roger Mirabito. **No. of Games Broadcast:** Unavailable. **Flagship Station:** WTNY 790-AM.

**PA Announcer:** Brian Hunsicker. **Official Scorer:** Dave Shampine.

**Stadium Name:** Alex T. Duffy Fairgrounds. **Location:** I-81 North to exit 46, right on Coffeen Street. **Standard Game Times:** 7 p.m, Sun. 6.

**Visiting Club Hotel:** Days Inn of Watertown, 1142 Arsenal St., Watertown, NY 13601. Telephone (315) 782-2700.

# WILLIAMSPORT *CUBS*

**Office Address:** Bowman Field, 100 W. 4th St., Williamsport, PA 17701. **Mailing Address:** P.O. Box 3173, Williamsport, PA 17701. **Telephone:** (717) 326-3389. **FAX:** (717) 326-3494.

**Affiliation (first year):** Chicago Cubs (1994). **Years in League:** 1923-37, 1968-72, 1994-.

**Team Colors:** Blue and red.

## Ownership, Management

**Operated by:** Geneva Cubs Baseball, Inc.

**Principal Owner/President:** Paul Velte.

**General Manager:** Doug Estes. **Director of Marketing/Public Relations:** Gabe Sinicropi. **Director of Stadium Operations:** Rick Warner. **Director of Box Office Operations:** Susan Smith. **Account Representatives:** Kim Kulp, Pat Petrozza.

## Field Staff

**Manager:** Oneri Fleita. **Coaches:** Mo Hill, Scott May (pitching).

**Trainer:** Dan Lovelace.

## Game Information

**Radio:** Unavailable.

**PA Announcer:** Unavailable. **Official Scorer:** Unavailable.

**Stadium Name:** Bowman Field. **Location:** From south—Rt. 15 to Maynard St., right on Maynard, left on 4th St. for one mile; From north—Rt. 15 to 4th St., left on 4th, ballpark on left. **Standard Game Times:** 7:05 p.m.

**Visiting Club Hotel:** Econolodge, 2401 E. Third St., Williamsport, PA 17701. Telephone: (717) 326-1501.

# NORTHWEST LEAGUE

## Short-Season Class A

**Office Address:** 5900 N. Granite Reef Rd. #105, Scottsdale, AZ 85250. **Mailing Address:** P.O. Box 4941, Scottsdale, AZ 85261. **Telephone:** (602) 483-8224. **FAX:** (602) 493-3450.

**President/Treasurer:** Bob Richmond.

**Vice President:** Bob Beban. **Corporate Secretary:** Melody Tucker.

**Directors:** Bob Bavasi (Everett), Bob Beban (Eugene), Bobby Brett (Spokane), Jack Cain (Portland), Dave Connell (Yakima), Fred Herrmann (Southern Oregon), Bill Pereira (Boise), Jerry Walker (Bellingham).

**Administrative Assistant:** Rob Richmond.

**Years League Active:** 1901-1922, 1937-1942, 1946-.

**1995 Opening Date:** June 15. **Closing Date:** Sept. 3.

**No. of Games:** 76.

**Division Structure: North**—Bellingham, Everett, Spokane, Yakima. **South**—Boise, Eugene, Portland, Southern Oregon.

**Playoff Format:** Division winners play best-of-3 series for league championship.

**All-Star Game:** None.

**Roster Limit:** 25 active. **Player Eligibility Rule:** No more than four players who are 23 or older. No more than three players on active list may have four or more years of prior service.

**Brand of Baseball:** Rawlings.

**Statistician:** Howe Sportsdata International, Boston Fish Pier, West Bldg. #2—Suite 306, Boston MA 02210.

### 1994 Standings (Overall)

| Club (Affiliate) | W | L | Pct. | GB | '94 Manager |
|---|---|---|---|---|---|
| #Yakima (Dodgers) | 49 | 27 | .645 | — | Joe Vavra |
| *#Boise (Angels) | 44 | 32 | .579 | 5 | Tom Kotchman |
| Bellingham (Mariners) | 42 | 34 | .553 | 7 | Mike Goff |
| Southern Oregon (Athletics) | 38 | 38 | .500 | 11 | Tom Dunton |
| Everett (Giants) | 37 | 39 | .487 | 12 | Mike Hart |
| Eugene (Royals) | 35 | 41 | .461 | 14 | Brian Poldberg |
| Spokane (Padres) | 30 | 46 | .395 | 19 | Tye Waller |
| Bend (Rockies) | 29 | 47 | .382 | 20 | Rudy Jaramillo |

*Won playoffs #Won division title

### Stadium Information

| | | Dimensions | | | | |
|---|---|---|---|---|---|---|
| Club | Stadium | LF | CF | RF | Capacity | '94 Att. |
| Bellingham | Joe Martin | 325 | 381 | 320 | 2,200 | 71,256 |
| Boise | Memorial | 335 | 405 | 335 | 4,500 | 156,950 |
| Eugene | Civic | 335 | 395 | 328 | 6,800 | 133,860 |
| Everett | Everett Memorial | 330 | 395 | 335 | 2,285 | 94,421 |
| Portland | Civic | 309 | 407 | 325 | 23,105 | — |
| Southern Oregon | Miles Field | 332 | 384 | 334 | 2,900 | 88,363 |
| Spokane | Seafirst | 335 | 398 | 335 | 7,101 | 156,092 |
| Yakima | Yakima County | 295 | 406 | 295 | 3,000 | 85,483 |

Portland franchise operated in Bend in 1994

## BELLINGHAM
## *GIANTS*

**Office Address:** 1316 King St., Bellingham, WA 98226. **Telephone:** (360) 671-6347. **FAX:** (360) 647-2254.

**Affiliation (first year):** San Francisco Giants (1995). **Years in League:** 1973-.

**Team Colors:** Orange and black.

### Ownership, Management

**Operated by:** Sports Enterprises, Inc.

**Principal Owners:** Jerry Walker, William Tucker.

**President/General Manager:** Jerry Walker.

**Assistant General Manager:** Michael Bruce. **Director of Stadium Operations:** Gregg Harlowe. **Head Groundskeeper:** Jim Bland. **Director of Sales/Marketing:** Ivan Walker. **Senior Account Representatives:** Mark Anderson, Seth Distler, Gregg Harlowe, Bruce Weed. **Director of Ticket/Group Sales:** Ken Troupe. **Director of Special Projects:** Robert Brazzel. **Clubhouse Operations:** Jason Stiles. **Concessions Managers:** Missy Bruce, Janet Walker.

### Field Staff

**Manager:** Glenn Tufts. **Coaches:** Juan Lopez, Elias Sosa (pitching).

**Trainer:** Ben Potenziano.

### Game Information

**Radio Announcers:** Rick Turner, Mark Scholten. **No. of Games Broadcast:** Home-18, Away-18. **Flagship Station:** KGMI 790-AM.

**PA Announcer:** Amy Mann. **Official Scorer:** Unavailable.

**Stadium Name:** Joe Martin Stadium. **Location:** I-5 exit #253, two blocks east to Orleans Street. **Standard Game Times:** 7:05 p.m.; Sun./holidays, 6:05.

**Visiting Club Hotel:** Best Western Lakeway Inn, 714 Lakeway Dr., Bellingham, WA 98226. Telephone: (360) 671-1011.

## BOISE
## *HAWKS*

**Office Address:** 5600 Glenwood St., Boise, ID 83714. **Telephone:** (208) 322-5000. **FAX:** (208) 322-7432.

**Affiliation (first year):** California Angels (1990). **Years in League:** 1975-76, 1978, 1985-.

**Team Colors:** Navy blue and scarlet red.

### Ownership, Management

**Operated by:** Diamond Sports, Inc.

**Principal Owner:** Bill Pereira. **President:** Peter Gray.

**Executive Vice President:** Cord Pereira.

**General Manager:** John Cunningham. **Controller:** Lee Ryan. **Director of Stadium Operations:** Tim Levenhagen. **Director of Media/Public Relations:** Jack Carnefix. **Director of Sales/Marketing:** Eric Trapp. **Director of Ticket Sales:** J.J. McLeod. **Ticket Account Executive:** Denise Jones. **Marketing Account Executive:** Greg Prado. **Creative Director:** Randy Rouse.

### Field Staff

**Manager:** Tom Kotchman. **Coaches:** Jim Bennett (pitching), Todd Claus.

**Trainer:** Unavailable.

### Game Information

**Radio Announcer:** Dave Hahn. **No. of Games Broadcast:** Home-38, Away-38. **Flagship Stations:** KTIK 1340-AM, KCID 107.1-FM.

**PA Announcer:** Greg Culver. **Official Scorer:** Andrew Swenson.

**Stadium Name:** Memorial Stadium. **Location:** Hwy. 84 to Cole Rd., south to Fairgrounds. **Standard Game Times:** 7:05 p.m.

**Visiting Club Hotel:** Ramada Inn, 1025 S. Capitol Blvd, Boise, ID 83706. Telephone: (208) 344-7971.

## EUGENE
## *EMERALDS*

**Office Address:** 2077 Willamette St., Eugene, OR 97405. **Mailing Address:** P.O. Box 5566,

Eugene, OR 97405. **Telephone:** (503) 342-5367. **FAX:** (503) 342-6089.

**Affiliation (first year):** Atlanta Braves (1995). **Years in League:** 1955-68, 1974-.

## Ownership, Management

**Operated by:** Eugene Baseball, Inc.

**Principal Owner/Chairman of the Board:** David Elmore.

**President/General Manager:** Bob Beban. **Assistant General Manager:** Todd Rahr. **Director of Marketing:** John Crenshaw. **Director of Public Relations:** Chris Metz. **Director of Ticket Sales:** Sean Jeffrey. **Clubhouse Operations:** Steve Martin.

## Field Staff

**Manager:** Paul Runge. **Coaches:** Wallace Johnson, Jerry Nyman (pitching).

**Trainer:** Mike Graus.

## Game Information

**Radio Announcer:** Dave Schultz. **No. of Games Broadcast:** Home-38, Away-38. **Flagship Station:** KPNW 1120-AM.

**PA Announcer:** Bryan Beban. **Official Scorer:** David Williford.

**Stadium Name:** Civic Stadium. **Location:** From I-5, Hwy. 126 to downtown, west to Pearl St., south to 20th. **Standard Game Times:** 7:05 p.m; Sun. 2 or 6.

**Visiting Club Hotel:** Eugene Motor Lodge, 476 E. Broadway, Eugene, OR 97401. Telephone: (503) 344-5233.

# EVERETT
## *AQUASOX*

**Office Address:** 2118 Broadway, Everett, WA 98201. **Mailing Address:** P.O. Box 7893, Everett, WA 98201. **Telephone:** (206) 258-3673. **FAX:** (206) 258-3675.

**Affiliation (first year):** Seattle Mariners (1995). **Years in League:** 1984-.

**Team Colors:** Navy blue, aqua blue, lime green and red.

## Ownership, Management

**Operated by:** Farm Club Sports, Inc.

**Principal Owners:** Robert Bavasi, Margaret Bavasi.

**President:** Bob Bavasi.

**General Manager:** Melody Tucker. **Assistant General Manager/Business, Stadium Operations:** Don Anderson. **Assistant General Manager/Concessions:** Robb Stanton. **Assistant General Manager/Promotions:** Aimee Bavasi. **Director of Media/Public Relations:** Mark Aucutt. **Director of Ticket Sales:** Lynda Dawson. **Administrative Aide:** Jim Averill. **Stadium Operations:** Gary Farwell. **Marketing Assistants:** Ron Coleman, Raul Rego.

## Field Staff

**Manager:** Orlando Gomez. **Coaches:** Roger Hansen (pitching), Bryan Price.

**Trainer:** Spyder Webb.

## Game Information

**Radio Announcer:** Mark Aucutt. **No. of Games Broadcast:** Home-38, Away-38. **Flagship Station:** KRKO 1380-AM.

**PA Announcer:** Tom Lafferty. **Official Scorer:** John Van Sandt.

**Stadium Name:** Everett Memorial Stadium. **Location:** Exit 192 off I-5 to corner of 39th and Broadway. **Game Times:** 7:05 p.m.; Sat-Sun. 6:05.

**Visiting Club Hotel:** Everett Pacific Hotel, 3105 Pine Ave., Everett, WA 98201. Telephone: (206) 339-3333.

# PORTLAND
## *ROCKIES*

**Office Address:** 1844 SW Morrison, Portland, OR 97205 **Mailing Address:** P.O. Box 998, Portland, OR 97207. **Telephone:** (503) 223-2837. **FAX:** (503) 223-2948.

**Affiliation (first year):** Colorado Rockies (1995). **Years in League:** 1973-77, 1995.

## Ownership, Management

**Operated by:** Portland Rockies, Inc.

**Principal Owners:** Jack Cain, Mary Cain.

**President:** Jack Cain.

**General Manager:** Mark Helminiak. **Director of Media/Public Relations:** Rich Burk. **Director of Sales/Marketing:** Tom Leip. **Senior Account Representatives:** John Garcia, Corey Kearsley, Mitch Mirsky,

Ken Ouderkirk, Katie Reeder, Kevin Robinson, Hank Sadouris, Jason Shepard, Melissa Sparks, Tom Strader. **Director of Merchandise:** Bob Cain.

### Field Staff

**Manager:** P.J. Carey. **Coaches:** Al Bleser, Stan Kyles (pitching). **Trainer:** Scott Gehret.

### Game Information

**Radio Announcer:** Rich Burk. **No. of Games Broadcast:** Home-38, Away-38. **Flagship Station:** KFXX 1520-AM.

**PA Announcer:** Unavailable. **Official Scorer:** Unavailable.

**Stadium Name:** Civic Stadium. **Location:** 1-405 South to Burnside exit, right on Morrison to stadium. **Standard Game Times:** 7:05 p.m.; Sun. 2:05.

**Visiting Club Hotel:** Red Lion Coliseum, 1225 N. Thunderbird Way, Portland, OR 97227. Telephone: (503) 235-8311.

## SOUTHERN OREGON
## *ATHLETICS*

**Office Address:** 1801 S. Pacific Hwy., Medford, OR 97501. **Mailing Address:** P.O. Box 1457, Medford, OR 97501. **Telephone:** (503) 770-5364. **FAX:** (503) 772-4466.

**Affiliation (first year):** Oakland Athletics (1979). **Years in League:** 1967-71, 1979-.

**Team Colors:** Green and yellow.

### Ownership, Management

**Operated by:** National Sports Organization, Inc.

**Principal Owners:** Fred Herrmann, Bud Kaufman, John LeCompte, Patsy Smullin, Dwain Cross.

**President/Chairman of the Board:** Fred Herrmann.

**General Manager:** William Courtney. **Assistant General Manager:** Dan Kilgras. **Director of Business Operations/Ticket Sales:** Suzanne Daniel. **Controller:** Lew Schwartz. **Head Groundskeeper:** Richard Steinmuller. **Director of Media/Public Relations:** Mike Staley. **Senior Account Representative:** Rocky Rocatelli. **Clubhouse Operations:** Chris Lessner. **Marketing and Promotions:** Nolan Robinson, Devon Smith.

### Field Staff

**Manager:** Tony DeFrancesco. **Coach:** Unavailable.
**Trainer:** Shane Borchert.

### Game Information

**Radio Announcer:** Jesse Johannesen. **No. of Games Broadcast:** Home-38, Away-38. **Flagship Station:** KRTA 610-AM.

**PA Announcer:** Unavailable. **Official Scorer:** B.G. Gould.

**Stadium Name:** Jackson & Perkins Gardens at Miles Field. **Location:** From exit 27 on I-5, west for ½ mile, left on South Pacific Hwy., south one mile, stadium on left. **Standard Game Times:** 7:05 p.m.; Sun. 6:05.

**Visiting Club Hotel:** Horizon Motor Inn, 1150 Barnett Rd., Medford, OR 97504. Telephone: (503) 779-5085.

## SPOKANE
## *INDIANS*

**Office Address:** 602 N. Havana, Spokane, WA 99202. **Mailing Address:** P.O. Box 4758, Spokane, WA 99202. **Telephone:** (509) 535-2922. **FAX:** (509) 534-5368.

**Affiliation (first year):** Kansas City Royals (1995). **Years in League:** 1972, 1983-.

**Team Colors:** Navy blue, red and white.

### Ownership, Management

**Operated by:** Longball, Inc.

**Principal Owners:** Bobby Brett, George Brett, Ken Brett, J.B. Brett.

**President:** Bobby Brett.

**General Manager:** Andrew Billig. **Assistant General Manager/Tickets:** Dave Cohen. **Assistant General Manager/Sponsorships:** Otto Klein. **Administrative Assistant:** Barbara Klante. **Controller:** Carol Dell. **Director of Stadium Operations:** Jim Fitzgerald. **Director of Media/Public Relations:** Todd Doolittle. **Account Executives:** Angelo Mazzella, Jeff Pilcher. **Assistant Director of Ticket Sales:** Ripper Hatch. **Director of Special Projects:** Dave Pier. **Merchandising:** Paul Barbeau. **Assistant Groundskeeper:** Larry Blumer.

### Field Staff

**Manager:** Al Pedrique. **Coaches:** Cliff Pastornicky, Theo Shaw (pitching).

**Trainer:** T.D. Forss.

### Game Information

**Radio Announcer:** Craig West. **No. of Games Broadcast:** Home-38, Away-38. **Flagship Station:** KGA 1510-AM.

**PA Announcer:** Jay Stewart. **Official Scorer:** Unavailable.

**Stadium Name:** Seafirst Stadium at Interstate Fairgrounds. **Location:** I-90 to Havana exit, follow directions to Interstate Fairgrounds. **Standard Game Times:** 7:05 p.m.; Sun. 6:05.

**Visiting Club Hotel:** Value Inns by Cavanaugh's, 1203 W. 5th Ave., Spokane, WA 99204. Telephone: (509) 624-4142.

## YAKIMA *BEARS*

**Office Address:** 810 W. Nob Hill Blvd., Yakima, WA 98902. **Mailing Address:** P.O. Box 483, Yakima, WA 98907. **Telephone:** (509) 457-5151. **FAX:** (509) 457-9909.

**Affiliation (first year):** Los Angeles Dodgers (1990). **Years in League:** 1955-66, 1990-.

**Team Colors:** Navy and gold.

### Ownership, Management

**Operated by:** Tradition Sports, Inc.

**Principal Owner/President:** Dave Connell.

**General Manager:** Bob Romero. **Assistant General Manager:** Eric Sesack. **Head Groundskeeper:** Mike Boekholder. **Director of Group Sales:** Ryan Connell. **Clubhouse Operations:** Craig Hyatt. **Office Manager:** Tammy Pettit.

### Field Staff

**Manager:** Joe Vavra. **Coaches:** Mark Brewer (pitching), Brett Magnusson.

**Trainer:** Jim Cranmer.

### Game Information

**Radio Announcer:** Larry Weir. **No. of Games Broadcast:** Home-38, Away-38. **Flagship Station:** KMWX 1460-AM.

**PA Announcer:** Mike Spencer. **Official Scorers:** Doug Evans, Gene Evans.

**Stadium Name:** Yakima County Stadium. **Location:** I-82 to Nob Hill Blvd. (exit 34), west on Nob Hill Blvd to 10th St., right on 10th, right on Pacific. **Standard Game Times:** 7:05 p.m.

**Visiting Club Hotel:** The Huntley Inn, 12 E. Valley Mall Blvd., Union Gap, WA 98903. Telephone: (509) 248-6924.

# APPALACHIAN LEAGUE

## Rookie Advanced Classification

**Mailing Address:** 20360 Carson Lane, Bristol, VA 24202. **Telephone:** (703) 669-3644. **FAX:** (703) 669-2618.

**President/Secretary-Treasurer:** Bill Halstead.

**Directors:** Chief Bender (Princeton), Rod Gilbreath (Danville), Mike Jorgensen (Johnson City), Steve Noworyta (Bristol), Steve Phillips (Kingsport), Jim Rantz (Elizabethton), Mark Shapiro (Burlington), Syd Thrift (Bluefield), Del Unser (Martinsville).

**Administrative Assistant:** Mary Halstead.

**Years League Active:** 1921-25, 1937-55, 1957-.

**1995 Opening Date:** June 19. **Closing Date:** Aug. 28.

**No. of Games:** 68.

**Division Structure: North**—Bluefield, Burlington, Danville, Martinsville, Princeton. **South**—Bristol, Elizabethton, Huntington, Johnson City, Kingsport.

**Playoff Format:** Division winners meet in best-of-3 series for league championship.

**All-Star Game:** None.

**Roster Limit:** 30 active. **Player Eligibility Rule:** No more than 12 players who are 21 or older, provided that no more than two of the 12 may be 23 or older.

**Brand of Baseball:** Rawlings.

**Statistician:** Howe Sportsdata International, Boston Fish Pier, West Bldg. #2—Suite 306, Boston MA 02210.

### 1994 Standings (Overall)

| Club (Affiliate) | W | L | Pct. | GB | '94 Manager |
|---|---|---|---|---|---|
| *#Princeton (Reds) | 41 | 25 | .621 | — | John Stearns |
| #Johnson City (Cardinals) | 42 | 26 | .618 | — | Steve Turco |
| Bluefield (Orioles) | 39 | 29 | .574 | 3 | Andy Etchebarren |
| Elizabethton (Twins) | 36 | 30 | .545 | 5 | Ray Smith |
| Kingsport (Mets) | 36 | 30 | .545 | 5 | Ron Gideon |
| Martinsville (Phillies) | 32 | 36 | .471 | 10 | Ramon Henderson |
| Bristol (Tigers) | 27 | 36 | .429 | 12½ | Kevin Bradshaw |
| Danville (Braves) | 28 | 39 | .418 | 13½ | Paul Runge |
| Huntington (Cubs) | 28 | 39 | .418 | 13½ | Steve Kolinsky |
| Burlington (Indians) | 23 | 42 | .354 | 17½ | Jim Gabella |

*Won playoffs #Won division title

### Stadium Information

| | | Dimensions | | | | |
|---|---|---|---|---|---|---|
| Club | Stadium | LF | CF | RF | Capacity | '94 Att. |
| Bluefield | Bowen Field | 335 | 365 | 335 | 3,000 | 39,169 |
| Bristol | DeVault Memorial | 325 | 400 | 310 | 1,500 | 23,929 |
| Burlington | Burlington Athletic | 335 | 410 | 335 | 3,500 | 48,329 |
| Danville | Dan Daniel Mem. Park | 330 | 400 | 330 | 3,000 | 70,862 |
| Elizabethton | Joe O'Brien Field | 335 | 407 | 320 | 1,500 | 20,009 |
| Huntington | St. Cloud Commons | 332 | 385 | 330 | 3,100 | 57,589 |
| Johnson City | Howard Johnson | 320 | 410 | 320 | 3,800 | 48,038 |
| Kingsport | Sports Complex | 330 | 410 | 330 | 2,500 | 34,124 |
| Martinsville | Hooker Field | 330 | 370 | 330 | 3,200 | 56,595 |
| Princeton | Hunnicutt Field | 330 | 396 | 330 | 1,537 | 39,426 |

## BLUEFIELD
## *ORIOLES*

**Mailing Address:** P.O. Box 356, Bluefield, WV 24701. **Telephone:** (703) 326-1326. **FAX:** (703) 326-1318.

**Affiliation (first year):** Baltimore Orioles (1957). **Years in League:** 1946-55, 1957-.

**Team Colors:** Orange, black and white.

### Ownership, Management

**Operated by:** Bluefield Baseball Club, Inc.

**Principal Owner:** City of Bluefield.

**President/Director of Business Operations:** George McGonagle.

**General Manager:** George Fanning. **Head Groundskeeper:** Alex Zachwieja. **Director of Public Relations:** Mike Judge. **Director of Community Relations:** Charles Peters. **Clubhouse Operations:** Dorion Cox.

### Field Staff

**Manager:** Andy Etchebarren. **Coach:** Charlie Puleo (pitching).

**Trainer:** Unavailable.

### Game Information

**Radio:** None.

**PA Announcer:** Bud Gallimore. **Official Scorer:** Mike Judge.

**Stadium Name:** Bowen Field. **Location:** Rt. 460 to West Gate Shopping Center, left at stop light, right at intersection, stadium on left. **Standard Game Times:** 7 p.m.; Sun. 6.

**Visiting Club Hotel:** Ramada Inn East River Mountain, 3175 E. Cumberland Rd., Bluefield, WV 24701. Telephone: (304) 325-5421.

## BRISTOL
## *WHITESOX*

**Office Address:** 1501 Euclid Ave., Bristol, VA 24201. **Mailing Address:** P.O. Box 1434, Bristol, VA 24203. **Telephone:** (703) 645-7275. **FAX:** (703) 645-7377.

**Affiliation (first year):** Chicago White Sox (1995). **Years in League:** 1921-25, 1940-55, 1969-.

**Team Colors:** Black, white and silver.

### Ownership, Management

**Operated by:** Bristol Baseball, Inc.

**Principal Owner:** Chicago White Sox.

**President:** Boyce Cox.

**General Manager:** Robert Childress.

### Field Staff

**Manager:** Unavailable. **Coach:** Mark Salas.

**Trainer:** Unavailable.

### Game Information

**Radio:** None.

**PA Announcer:** Jim Phillips. **Official Scorer:** Allen Shepherd.

**Stadium Name:** DeVault Memorial Stadium. **Location:** I-81 to Exit 3 onto Commonwealth Ave., right on Euclid Ave. for ½ mile. **Standard Game Times:** 7 p.m.

**Visiting Club Hotel:** Holiday Inn West, 2122 Euclid Ave., Bristol, VA 24201. Telephone: (703) 699-7171.

## BURLINGTON
## *INDIANS*

**Office Address:** 1450 Graham St., Burlington, NC 27215. **Mailing Address:** P.O. Box 1143, Burlington, NC 27216. **Telephone:** (910) 222-0223. **FAX:** (910) 226-2498.

**Affiliation (first year):** Cleveland Indians (1986). **Years in League:** 1986-.

**Team Colors:** Navy and red.

### Ownership, Management

**Operated by:** Burlington Baseball Club, Inc.

**Principal Owner:** Miles Wolff.

**Vice President:** Dan Moushon.

**General Manager:** Dean Gyorgy. **Assistant General Manager:** Josh

Gordon.

### Field Staff

**Manager:** Harry Spilman. **Coaches:** Minnie Mendoza, Dave Miller (pitching).

**Trainer:** Dave Lassiter.

### Game Information

**Radio Announcer:** Unavailable. **No. of Games Broadcast:** Home-34, Away-34. **Flagship Station:** WBBB 920-AM.

**PA Announcer:** Unavailable. **Official Scorer:** Richard Senzel.

**Stadium Name:** Burlington Athletic. **Location:** I-85/40 to exit 145, north on Rt. 100 (Maple Ave.) for 1½ miles, right on Mebane for 1½ miles, right on Beaumont, left on Graham. **Standard Game Times:** 7:05 p.m.

**Visiting Club Hotel:** Holiday Inn, 2444 Maple Ave., Burlington, NC 27215. Telephone: (910) 229-5203.

## DANVILLE
## *BRAVES*

**Office Address:** 302 River Park Dr., Danville, VA 24541. **Mailing Address:** P.O. Box 3637, Danville, VA 24543. **Telephone:** (804) 791-3346. **FAX:** (804) 791-3347.

**Affiliation (first year):** Atlanta Braves (1993). **Years in League:** 1993-.

**Team Colors:** Red, white and blue.

### Ownership, Management

**Operated by:** Danville Braves, Inc.

**Principal Owner/President:** Tim Cahill.

**General Manager:** Carper Cole. **Assistant General Manager:** Scott Rittenhouse. **Head Groundskeeper:** Ken Brinkley. **Office Manager:** Cheryl Nicoletti.

### Field Staff

**Manager:** Max Venable. **Coaches:** Angel Morris, Mark Ross (pitching).

**Trainer:** Unavailable.

### Game Information

**Radio:** Unavailable.

**PA Announcer:** Unavailable. **Official Scorer:** Stan Mitchell.

**Stadium Name:** Dan Daniel Memorial Park. **Location:** US 58 East to River Point Dr., right on River Park Dr. **Standard Game Times:** 7 p.m.

**Visiting Club Hotel:** Innkeeper, 3020 Riverside Dr., Danville, VA 24540. Telephone: (804) 799-1202.

## ELIZABETHTON
## *TWINS*

**Office Address:** Holly Lane, Elizabethton, TN 37643. **Mailing Address:** c/o City of Elizabethton, 136 S. Sycamore St., Elizabethton, TN 37643. **Telephone:** (615) 543-4395. **FAX:** (615) 542-1510 or 543-4395.

**Affiliation (first year):** Minnesota Twins (1974). **Years in League:** 1937-42, 1945-51, 1974-.

**Team Colors:** Red and navy blue.

### Ownership, Management

**Operated by:** City of Elizabethton.

**Principal Owner:** Minnesota Twins.

**President/General Manager:** Bill Crow.

**Head Groundskeeper:** Willie Church. **Clubhouse Operations:** David McQueen. **Office Manager:** Jane Crow.

### Field Staff

**Manager:** Unavailable. **Coaches:** Jim Shellenback (pitching), Ray Smith.

**Trainer:** Unavailable.

### Game Information

**Radio Announcer:** Frank Santore, Doug Jennett. **No. of Games Broadcast:** Home-34, Away-11. **Flagship Station:** WBEJ 1240-AM.

**PA Announcer:** Glen Hodge. **Official Scorer:** Bill Crow.

**Stadium Name:** Riverside Park/Joe O'Brien Field. **Location:** Highway 321 to Holly Lane. **Standard Game Times:** 7 p.m.

**Visiting Club Hotel:** Holiday Inn, 2406 N. Roan St., Johnson City, TN 37601. Telephone: (615) 282-2161.

# HUNTINGTON

**Office Address:** 1901 Jackson Ave., Huntington, WV 25704. **Mailing Address:** P.O. Box 7005, Huntington, WV 25775. **Telephone:** (304) 429-1700. **FAX:** (304) 429-1706.

**Affiliation:** Co-op. **Years in League:** 1990-.

**Team Colors:** Unavailable.

## Ownership, Management

**Operated by:** Huntington Professional Baseball.

**Principal Owners:** Ed Poppiti, Eugene Ferraro, Jim Amerian, Michael Arlia, William Adams.

**General Manager:** Andy Berg. **Assistant General Manager:** Brad Taylor. **Director of Media/Public Relations:** Betty Hoffman.

## Field Staff

**Manager:** Unavailable. **Coach:** Unavailable.

**Trainer:** Unavailable.

## Game Information

**Radio:** Unavailable.

**PA Announcer:** Unavailable. **Official Scorer:** Unavailable.

**Stadium Name:** St. Clouds Commons. **Location:** I-64 to Exit 6, exit at Madison Ave., left to 19th St., left to ballpark. **Standard Game Times:** 7:05 p.m.; Sun. 2:05.

**Visiting Club Hotel:** Unavailable.

# JOHNSON CITY
## *CARDINALS*

**Office Address:** 111 Legion St., Johnson City, TN 37605. **Mailing Address:** P.O. Box 568, Johnson City, TN 37605. **Telephone:** (615) 461-4850. **FAX:** (615) 461-4864.

**Affiliation (first year):** St. Louis Cardinals (1975). **Years in League:** 1921-24, 1937-55, 1957-61, 1964-.

**Team Colors:** Red, white and navy blue.

## Ownership, Management

**Operated By:** Johnson City Baseball, Inc.

**Principal Owner:** St. Louis Cardinals.

**Chairman of the Board:** Jack Chinouth. **President:** Lonnie Lowe.

**General Manager:** Rebecca Vaughn **Assistant General Manager:** Mary Lee Ingram. **Controller:** Ernest Cross. **Director of Stadium Operations:** Herb Ledford. **Head Groundskeeper:** Bill Foster. **Director of Sales/Marketing:** Julie Boggs. **Clubhouse Operations:** Carl Black.

## Field Staff

**Manager:** Steve Turco. **Coaches** Bo Milliken (pitching), Ramon Ortiz.

**Trainer:** Aaron Bruns.

## Game Information

**Radio Announcers:** Chip Kessler, Paul Overbay. **No. of Games Broadcast:** Home-8. **Flagship Station:** WJCW 910-AM.

**PA Announcer:** Mike Clark. **Official Scorer:** Jeremy Crawford.

**Stadium Name:** Howard Johnson Field. **Location:** I-81 to exit 181 (Market Street), left on Roan Street, left on Main Street to ballpark. **Standard Game Times:** 7 p.m., Sun. 3.

**Visiting Club Hotel:** Holiday Inn, 2406 N. Roan St., Johnson City, TN, 37605. Telephone: (615) 282-2161.

# KINGSPORT
## *METS*

**Office Address:** 433 East Center St., Kingsport, TN 37662. **Mailing Address:** P.O. Box 1128, Kingsport, TN 37662. **Telephone:** (615) 247-7181. **FAX:** (615) 247-2241.

**Affiliation (first year):** New York Mets (1980). **Years in League:** 1921-25, 1938-52, 1957, 1960-63, 1969-82, 1984-.

**Team Colors:** Orange and blue.

## Ownership, Management

**Operated by:** New York Mets.

**Chairman:** Nelson Doubleday. **President:** Fred Wilpon.

**General Manager:** Tom Throp.

## Field Staff

**Manager:** John Gibbons. **Coach:** Dave Jorn (pitching).
**Trainer:** Unavailable.

## Game Information

**Radio:** Unavailable.

**PA Announcer:** Unavailable. **Official Scorer:** Eddie Durham.

**Stadium Name:** Kingsport Sports Complex. **Location:** Exit 57 off I-81 to 181 North, West Stone Drive exit, left on West Stone Drive, right on Granby Road. **Standard Game Times:** 7 p.m.

**Visiting Club Hotel:** Holiday Inn, 700 Lynn Garden Dr., Kingsport, TN 37665. Telephone: (615) 247-3133.

# MARTINSVILLE *PHILLIES*

**Office Address:** Commonwealth Blvd. and Chatham Heights Rd., Martinsville, VA 24112. **Mailing Address:** P.O. Box 3614, Martinsville, VA 24115. **Telephone:** (703) 666-2000. **FAX:** (703) 666-2139.

**Affiliation (first year):** Philadelphia Phillies (1988). **Years in League:** 1988-.

**Team Colors:** Red, royal blue and white.

## Ownership, Management

**Operated by:** Martinsville Phillies Professional Baseball, Inc.

**President:** Tim Cahill.

**General Manager:** Lee McDaniel. **Assistant General Manager:** Troy Potthoff. **Head Groundskeeper:** Sam Pickurel. **Clubhouse Operations:** Troy Wells.

## Field Staff

**Manager:** Ramon Henderson. **Coaches:** Carlos Arroyo (pitching), Kelly Heath.

**Trainer:** Morgan Boyle.

## Game Information

**Radio:** None.

**PA Announcer:** Unavailable. **Official Scorer:** Unavailable.

**Stadium Name:** Hooker Field. **Location:** US 220 to Commonwealth Blvd., east for 3 miles; or US 58 to Chatham Heights Rd., north 2 blocks. **Standard Game Times:** 7 p.m.

**Visiting Club Hotel:** Dutch Inn, 633 Virginia Ave., Collinsville, VA 24078. Telephone: (703) 647-3721.

# PRINCETON *REDS*

**Office Address:** Hunnicutt Field, Bluefield-Princeton Rd., Princeton, WV 24740. **Mailing Address:** P.O. Box 5646, Princeton, WV 24740. **Telephone:** (304) 487-2000. **FAX:** (304) 425-6999.

**Affiliation (first year):** Cincinnati Reds (1991). **Years in League:** 1988-.

**Team Colors:** Red, black and white.

## Ownership, Management

**Operated by:** Princeton Baseball Association, Inc.

**Principal Owner:** Cincinnati Reds.

**President:** Dewey Russell.

**General Manager:** Jim Holland. **Director of Business Operations:** Linda Alvis. **Head Groundskeeper:** Frankie Bailey. **Administrative Assistants:** Jennifer Farmer, Paul Lambert.

## Field Staff

**Manager:** John Stearns. **Coach:** Brad Kelley (pitching).

**Trainer:** Dan Siegel.

## Game Information

**Radio:** None.

**PA Announcer:** Jared Hines. **Official Scorer:** Dick Daisey.

**Stadium Name:** Hunnicutt Field. **Location:** Exit 9 off I-77, US 460 west to Downtown exit, stadium located behind Mercer County Technical Education Center. **Standard Game Times:** 7 p.m.

**Visiting Club Hotel:** Days Inn of Princeton, I-77 & Rt. 460, Princeton, WV 24740. Telephone: (304) 425-8100.

# PIONEER LEAGUE

## Rookie Advanced Classification

**Office Address:** 812 W. 30th St., Spokane, WA 99203. **Mailing Address:** P.O. Box 2564, Spokane, WA 99220. **Telephone:** (509) 456-7615. **FAX:** (509) 456-0136.

**President/Secretary-Treasurer:** Jim McCurdy.

**Vice Presidents:** Michael Ellis, William Yuill.

**Directors:** David Baggott (Ogden), Michael Ellis (Lethbridge), Larry Geske (Great Falls), Kevin Greene (Idaho Falls), Richard Taylor (Butte), Bob Wilson (Billings), Bill Yuill (Medicine Hat).

**Years League Active:** 1939-1942, 1946-.

**1995 Opening Date:** June 17. **Closing Date:** Sept. 2.

**No. of Games:** 72.

**Division Structure: North**—Billings, Great Falls, Lethbridge, Medicine Hat. **South**—Butte, Helena, Idaho Falls, Ogden.

**Playoff Format:** First-half division winners play second-half division winners in best-of-3 series. Division playoff winners meet in best-of-5 series for league championship.

**All-Star Game:** None.

**Roster Limit:** 30 active. **Player Eligibility Rule:** No more than 17 players older than 21, provided that no more than two of the 17 are 23 or older. No player on active list may have more than three years of prior service.

**Brand of Baseball:** Rawlings.

**Statistician:** Howe Sportsdata International, Boston Fish Pier, West Bldg. #2—Suite 306, Boston MA 02210.

### 1994 Standings (Overall)

| Club (Affiliate) | W | L | Pct. | GB | '94 Manager |
|---|---|---|---|---|---|
| *#Billings (Reds) | 50 | 22 | .694 | — | Donnie Scott |
| #Helena (Brewers) | 44 | 28 | .611 | 6 | Dub Kilgo |
| Ogden (Independent) | 41 | 31 | .569 | 9 | Willie Ambos |
| Medicine Hat (Blue Jays) | 36 | 36 | .500 | 14 | Darren Balsley |
| Great Falls (Dodgers) | 34 | 38 | .472 | 16 | Ron Roenicke |
| Idaho Falls (Braves) | 30 | 42 | .417 | 20 | Max Venable |
| Lethbridge (Co-op) | 29 | 43 | .403 | 21 | Phillip Wellman |
| Butte (Co-op) | 24 | 48 | .333 | 26 | Bruce Crabbe |

*Won playoffs #Won division title

### Stadium Information

| | | Dimensions | | | | |
|---|---|---|---|---|---|---|
| Club | Stadium | LF | CF | RF | Capacity | '94 Att. |
| Billings | Cobb Field | 335 | 410 | 325 | 4,400 | 100,556 |
| Butte | Alumni Coliseum | 350 | 410 | 360 | 5,000 | 22,592 |
| Great Falls | Legion Park | 335 | 415 | 335 | 3,834 | 64,558 |
| Helena | Kindrick Field | 324 | 375 | 314 | 1,800 | 45,394 |
| Idaho Falls | McDermott Field | 350 | 400 | 340 | 2,800 | 53,180 |
| Lethbridge | Henderson | 330 | 400 | 330 | 2,750 | 42,970 |
| Medicine Hat | Athletic Park | 350 | 380 | 365 | 2,500 | 30,028 |
| Ogden | Simmons Field | 330 | 395 | 330 | 2,500 | 57,707 |

## BILLINGS
## *MUSTANGS*

**Office Address:** 901 North 27th St., Billings, MT 59103. **Mailing Address:** P.O. Box 1553, Billings, MT 59103. **Telephone:** (406) 252-1241. **FAX:** (406) 252-2968.

**Affiliation (first year):** Cincinnati Reds (1974). **Years in League:** 1948-63, 1969-.

### Ownership, Management

**Operated by:** Billings Pioneer Baseball Club.

**Chairman of the Board:** Ron May.

**President/General Manager:** Bob Wilson. **Assistant General Manager:** Gary Roller. **Head Groundskeeper:** Lowell Gorseth.

### Field Staff

**Manager:** Donnie Scott. **Coach:** Steve Oliverio (pitching).

**Trainer:** Unavailable.

### Game Information

**Radio Announcer:** Chris Degnan. **No. of Games Broadcast:** Home-36, Away-36. **Flagship Station:** KCTR 970-AM.

**PA Announcer:** Hank Cox. **Official Scorer:** Jack Skinner.

**Stadium Name:** Cobb Field. **Location:** I-90 to 27th Street exit, north to 9th Ave. **Standard Game Times:** 7 p.m.

**Visiting Club Hotel:** Rimrock Inn, 1203 N. 27th St., Billings, MT 59101. Telephone: (406) 252-7107.

## BUTTE
## *COPPER KINGS*

**Office Address:** P.O. Box 186, Butte, MT 59703. **Telephone:** (406) 723-8206. **FAX:** (406) 723-3376.

**Affiliation:** Independent. **Years in League:** 1978-85, 1987-.

### Ownership, Management

**Operated by:** Silverbow Baseball Inc.

**President:** Miles Wolff. **Vice President:** Rich Taylor.

**Vice President/General Manager:** Ted Tornow.

### Field Staff

**Manager:** Unavailable. **Coach:** Unavailable.

**Trainer:** Chris Tomashoff.

### Game Information

**Radio Announcer:** Unavailable. **No. of Games Broadcast:** Home-36, Away-36. **Flagship Station:** KXTL 1370-AM.

**PA Announcer:** Unavailable. **Official Scorer:** Unavailable.

**Stadium Name:** Alumni Coliseum. **Location:** I-90 to Montana Street exit, north to Park Street, west to stadium (Montana Tech campus). **Standard Game Times:** 7 p.m.

**Visiting Club Hotel:** Unavailable.

## GREAT FALLS
## *DODGERS*

**Office Address:** P.O. Box 1621, Great Falls, MT 59401. **Telephone:** (406) 452-5311. **FAX:** (406) 454-0811.

**Affiliation (first year):** Los Angeles Dodgers (1984). **Years in League:** 1948-63, 1969-.

### Ownership, Management

**Operated by:** Great Falls Baseball Club, Inc.

**President:** Larry Geske.

**General Manager:** Tom Seidler. **Assistant General Manager:** Patrick McCleary. **Head Groundskeeper:** Dick Pugh.

### Field Staff

**Manager:** John Shoemaker. **Coaches:** Edwin Correa (pitching), Mickey Hatcher.

**Trainer:** Ruben Barrera.

### Game Information

**Radio Announcer:** Gene Black. **No. of Games Broadcast:** Home-36,

Away-36. **Flagship Station:** KMSL 1450-AM.
**PA Announcer:** Tim Paul. **Official Scorer:** Al Audet.
**Stadium Name:** Legion Park. **Location:** 11 blocks east of Havre Highway on River Drive North. **Standard Game Times:** 7 p.m., Sun. 5.
**Visiting Club Hotel:** Mid-Town Motel, 526 2nd Ave. N., Great Falls, MT 59401. Telephone: (406) 453-2411.

# HELENA
## *BREWERS*

**Office Address:** P.O. Box 4606, Helena, MT 59604. **Telephone:** (406) 449-7616. **FAX:** (406) 449-6979.
**Affiliation (first year):** Milwaukee Brewers (1985). **Years in League:** 1978-.

### Ownership, Management
**Operated by:** Unavailable.
**Principal Owner, President:** Unavailable.
**General Manager:** Unavailable. **Acting GM:** Dave Endress.

### Field Staff
**Manager:** Alex Morales. **Coach:** Unavailable.
**Trainer:** Doug Michlovitz.

### Game Information
**Radio Announcer:** Unavailable. **No. of Games Broadcast:** Home-36, Away-36. **Flagship Station:** Unavailable.
**PA Announcer:** Unavailable. **Official Scorer:** Unavailable.
**Stadium Name:** Kindrick Legion Field. **Location:** Cedar Street exit off I-15, west to Main Street, left at Memorial Park. **Standard Game Times:** 7:05 p.m.; Sun. 5:05.
**Visiting Club Hotel:** Unavailable.

# IDAHO FALLS
## *BRAVES*

**Office Address:** 568 W. Elva, Idaho Falls, ID 83402. **Mailing Address:** P.O. Box 2183, Idaho Falls, ID 83403. **Telephone:** (208) 522-8363. **FAX:** (208) 522-9858.
**Affiliation (first year):** San Diego Padres (1995). **Years in League:** 1940-42, 1946-.

### Ownership, Management
**Operated by:** Elmore Sports Group.
**Principal Owner:** Dave Elmore.
**General Manager:** Kevin Greene. **Assistant General Manager:** Paul Fetz. **Assistant General Manager/Director of Public Relations:** David Sandler. **Director of Business Operations:** Diana Keller. **Director of Stadium Operations:** Craig Evans. **Director of Sales and Marketing/ Promotions:** Jeff Bertrand. **Director of Ticket Sales:** Josh Levi.

### Field Staff
**Manager:** Mike Basso. **Coaches:** Gary Roenicke, Scipio Spinks (pitching).
**Trainer:** Unavailable.

### Game Information
**Radio Announcers:** Jim Garshow, John Balginy. **No. of Games Broadcast:** Home-36. **Flagship Station:** KUPI 980-AM.
**PA Announcer:** Unavailable. **Official Scorer:** John Balginy.
**Stadium Name:** McDermott Field. **Location:** I-15 to W. Broadway exit, left onto Memorial Dr. to Mound Ave., right ¼ mile to stadium. **Standard Game Times:** 7:15 p.m., Sun. 5
**Visiting Club Hotel:** Motel West, 1540 W. Broadway, Idaho Falls, ID 83402. Telephone: (208) 522-1112.

# LETHBRIDGE
## *MOUNTIES*

**Office Address:** P.O. Box 1986, Lethbridge, Alberta T1J 4K5. **Telephone:** (403) 327-7975. **FAX:** (403) 327-8085.
**Affiliation:** Co-op. **Years in League:** 1975-83, 1992-.

### Ownership, Management
**Operated by:** Homeplate, Ltd.
**President:** Michael Ellis.

**Executive Vice President:** Keith Greer. **Vice Presidents:** Dave Davis, Matt Ellis, Lorenzo Gaglio, Anthony Pipitone, Michael Siegmund.

**General Manager:** Shawn Keba. **Assistant General Manager:** Eric Salpeter. **Director of Business Operations:** Wendy Kalkan. **Director of Marketing:** Mark Sluban. **Marketing Representative:** Mike Cowan.

### Field Staff

**Manager:** Unavailable. **Coaches:** Unavailable.

**Trainer:** Unavailable.

### Game Information

**Radio Announcer:** Unavailable. **No. of Games Broadcast:** Home-19, Away-15. **Flagship Station:** CJOC 1220-AM.

**PA Announcer:** Merv Caven. **Official Scorers:** Mary Dikawa, Dan Perry.

**Stadium Name:** Henderson Stadium. **Location:** Hwy. 314 to Mayor Magrath Dr. South, to North Parkside Dr. **Standard Game Times:** 7 p.m., Sun. 2.

**Visiting Club Hotel:** The Sandman Inn, 421 Mayor Magrath Dr. South, Lethbridge, Alberta T1V 3Y2. Telephone: (403) 328-1111.

## MEDICINE HAT
## *BLUE JAYS*

**Office Address:** P.O. Box 465, Medicine Hat, Alberta T1A 7G2. **Telephone:** (403) 526-0404. **FAX:** (403) 526-4000.

**Affiliation (first year):** Toronto Blue Jays (1978). **Years in League:** 1977-.

### Ownership, Management

**Principal Owners:** Bill Yuill, Chris McKenna.

**President:** Bill Yuill.

**General Manager:** Chris McKenna. **Administrative Assistant:** Raymonde Christensen.

### Field Staff

**Manager:** Darren Balsley. **Coaches:** Unavailable.

**Trainer:** Mike Wirtz.

### Game Information

**Radio Announcer:** Unavailable. **No. of Games Broadcast:** Home-10. **Flagship Station:** CHAT AM.

**PA Announcer:** Harv Speers. **Official Scorer:** Sheldon Jobb.

**Stadium Name:** Athletic Park. **Location:** First Street exit off Trans Canada Highway. **Standard Game Times:** 7 p.m., Sun. 2.

**Visiting Club Hotel:** Medicine Hat Inn, 530 4th St. SE, Medicine Hat, Alberta T1B 3T8. Telephone: (403) 526-1313.

## OGDEN
## *RAPTORS*

**Office Address:** 2404 Washington Blvd., Suite 312, Ogden, UT 84401. **Telephone:** (801) 393-2400. **FAX:** (801) 393-2473.

**Affiliation:** Independent. **Years in League:** 1939-42, 1946-55, 1966-74, 1994-.

### Ownership, Management

**Operated by:** Ogden Raptors Professional Baseball, Inc.

**Principal Owners:** Dave Baggott, Steve Buechele, John Lindquist, Jennifer Marshall, Ed Mattes, Jim O'Hara, Holly Preston, John Stein, Ron Yengich.

**Chairman/President:** Dave Baggott.

**General Managers:** Holly Preston, John Stein. **Head Groundskeeper:** Craig Holmes.

### Field Staff

**Manager:** Willie Ambos. **Coach:** Rich Morales.

**Trainer:** Unavailable.

### Game Information

**Radio Announcer:** Unavailable. **No. of Games Broadcast:** Home-36, Away-36. **Flagship Station:** KLO 910-AM.

**PA Announcer:** Dave Baggott. **Official Scorer:** John Stein.

**Stadium Name:** Serge Simmons Field. **Location:** I-15 North to 24th St. exit, right on "A" Ave., left on James Brown Dr. to Simmons Field. I-15 South to 21st St. exit, right on Lincoln, right on 24th St., left on "A" Ave, left on James Brown Dr. to Simmons Field. **Standard Game Times:** 7 p.m.

**Visiting Club Hotel:** Flying J Travel Plaza, 1206 W. 2100 St., South Ogden, UT, 84401. Telephone: (801) 393-8644.

# ARIZONA LEAGUE

### Rookie Classification

**Street Address:** 5900 N. Granite Reef, #105, Scottsdale, AZ 85250. **Mailing Address:** P.O. Box 4941, Scottsdale, AZ 85261. **Telephone:** (602) 483-8224. **FAX:** (602) 443-3450.

**President/Treasurer:** Bob Richmond.

**Vice President:** Tony Siegle. **Corporate Secretary:** Walt Palmer. **Administrative Assistant:** Rob Richmond.

**Years League Active:** 1988-.

**1995 Opening Date:** June 24. **Closing Date:** Aug. 31.

**No. of Games:** 56.

**All-Star Game:** None.

**Playoff Format:** None.

**Roster Limit:** 30 active. **Player Eligibility Rule:** No more than eight players 20 or older, and no more than two players 21 or older. At least 10 must be pitchers. No more than two years of prior service, excluding Rookie leagues outside the United States and Canada.

**Brand of Baseball:** Rawlings.

**Member Clubs (Managers):** Angels (Bruce Hines), Athletics (Juan Navarrete), Brewers (Ralph Dickenson), Mariners (Dave Brundage), Padres (Unavailable), Rockies (Jim Eppard).

**Division Structure:** None.

**Playing Sites: Angels**—Gene Autry Park, Mesa. **Athletics**—Papago Park Sports Complex, Phoenix. **Brewers**—Chandler Complex, Chandler. **Mariners**—Peoria Sports Complex, Peoria. **Padres**—Peoria Sports Complex, Peoria. **Rockies**—Fitch Park, Mesa.

**Statistician:** Howe Sportsdata International, Boston Fish Pier, West Bldg. #2—Suite 306, Boston MA 02210.

## 1994 Standings

| | W | L | Pct. | GB | '94 Manager |
|---|---|---|---|---|---|
| Cardinals | 34 | 22 | .607 | — | Scott Melvin |
| Athletics | 32 | 24 | .571 | 2 | Tony DeFrancesco |
| Brewers | 32 | 24 | .571 | 2 | Ralph Dickenson |
| Giants | 29 | 26 | .527 | 4½ | Alan Bannister |
| Padres | 28 | 27 | .509 | 5½ | Barry Moss |
| Angels | 23 | 32 | .418 | 10½ | Bill Lachemann |
| Rockies | 23 | 32 | .418 | 10½ | P.J. Carey |
| Mariners | 21 | 35 | .375 | 13 | Marty Martinez |

# GULF COAST LEAGUE

### Rookie Classification

**Mailing Address:** 1503 Clower Creek Dr., #H-262, Sarasota, FL 34231. **Telephone:** (813) 966-6407. **FAX:** (813) 966-6872.

**President:** Tom Saffell.

**Years League Active:** 1964-.

**1995 Opening Date:** June 19. **Closing Date:** Aug. 26.

**No. of Games:** 60.

**All-Star Game:** None.

**Playoff Format:** Four division winners meet in sudden-death playoff game. Winners advance to best-of-3 series for league championship.

**Roster Limit:** 30 active. **Player Eligibility Rule:** No more than eight players 20 or older, and no more than two players 21 or older. At least 10 must be pitchers. No more than two years of prior service, excluding Rookie leagues outside the U.S. and Canada.

**Brand of Baseball:** Rawlings

**Member Clubs (Managers): East**—Braves (Jim Saul), Expos (Rick Sofield), Marlins (Juan Bustabad), Mets (John Stephenson). **North**—Astros (Bobby Ramos), Blue Jays (Rocket Wheeler), Tigers (Kevin Bradshaw), Yankees (Rob Thomson). **Northwest**—Orioles (Geno Petralli), Pirates (Woody Huyke), Rangers (Chino Cadahia), White Sox (Mike Gellinger). **Southwest**—Cubs (Sandy Alomar Sr.), Red Sox (Felix Maldonado), Royals (Bob Herold), Twins (John Russell).

**Playing Sites: Astros**—Osceola County Stadium, Kissimmee. **Blue Jays**—Engelbert Complex/Grant Stadium, Dunedin. **Braves**—Municipal Stadium, West Palm Beach. **Cubs**—Red Sox Minor League complex, Fort Myers. **Expos**—Municipal Stadium, West Palm Beach. **Marlins**—Carl Barger Baseball Complex, Melbourne. **Mets**—St. Lucie County Sports Complex, Port St. Lucie. **Orioles**—Twin Lakes Park, Sarasota. **Pirates**—

Pirate City Complex, Bradenton. **Rangers**—Charlotte County Stadium, Port Charlotte. **Red Sox**—Red Sox Minor League complex, Fort Myers. **Royals**—Lee County Stadium, Fort Myers. **Tigers**—Tigertown, Lakeland. **Twins**—Lee County Stadium, Fort Myers. **Yankees**—Yankee Complex, Tampa. **White Sox**—Ed Smith Stadium/Complex, Sarasota.

**Statistician:** Howe Sportsdata International, Boston Fish Pier, West Bldg. #2, Suite 306, Boston, MA 02210.

## 1994 Standings

| | W | L | Pct. | GB | '94 Manager |
|---|---|---|---|---|---|
| #Royals | 47 | 12 | .797 | — | Bob Herold |
| *#Astros | 41 | 18 | .695 | 6 | Bobby Ramos |
| Red Sox | 40 | 20 | .667 | 7½ | Felix Maldonado |
| #Marlins | 38 | 21 | .644 | 9 | Juan Bustabad |
| Expos | 35 | 24 | .593 | 12 | Nelson Norman |
| Mets | 32 | 27 | .542 | 15 | Junior Roman |
| Rangers | 32 | 28 | .533 | 15½ | Chino Cadahia |
| Yankees | 26 | 32 | .448 | 20½ | Hector Lopez |
| Blue Jays | 26 | 34 | .433 | 21½ | Doug Ault |
| Cubs | 25 | 34 | .424 | 22 | Phil Bradley |
| Pirates | 25 | 35 | .417 | 22½ | Woody Huyke |
| Orioles | 23 | 36 | .390 | 24 | Oneri Fleita |
| Twins | 22 | 38 | .367 | 25½ | Jose Marzan |
| White Sox | 20 | 40 | .333 | 27½ | Mike Rojas |
| Braves | 13 | 46 | .220 | 34 | Jim Saul |

*Won playoffs #Won division title

# DOMINICAN SUMMER LEAGUE

### Rookie Classification

**Mailing Address:** c/o Banco del Progresso, Av. John F. Kennedy, No. 3, Santo Domingo, Dominican Republic.

**Telephone:** (809) 565-0714. **FAX:** (809) 565-0714.

**President:** Freddy Jana.

**Years League Active:** 1985-.

**1995 Opening Date:** June 1. **Closing Date:** Aug. 28.

**No. of Games:** 66-70.

**Roster Limit:** 30 active. **Player Eligibility Rule:** No more than eight players 20 or older, and no more than two players 21 or older. At least 10 must be pitchers. No more than two years of prior service, excluding Rookie leagues outside the U.S. and Canada.

**Member Clubs, 1995:** Unavailable. **Member Clubs, 1994: Santo Domingo Central Division:** Athletics, Blue Jays I, Cubs/Padres, Marlins, Royals/Rockies. **Santo Domingo East Division:** Blue Jays II, Dodgers I, Expos, Mariners, Tigers. **Santo Domingo West Division:** Cardinals/Phillies, Indians, Mets, Pirates, Yankees. **San Pedro de Macoris Division:** Angels, Astros/Brewers, Braves/Rangers, Dodgers II, Giants/Orioles, Toyo Carp (Japan).

# MINOR LEAGUE SCHEDULES

# CLASS AAA

## American Association

### Buffalo

**APRIL**
6-7-8-9........... Nashville
10-11 ........ New Orleans
12-13 ..... Oklahoma City
21-22............. Louisville
23-24......... Indianapolis

**MAY**
2-3-4 ..................... Iowa
5-6-7-8.............. Omaha
9-10 ............... Nashville
19-20-21-22 .......... N.O.
23-24-25-26... Okla. City
27-28-29......... Nashville

**JUNE**
7-8.................. Louisville
9-10-11 ...... Indianapolis
20-21-22............ Omaha
23-24-25-26........... Iowa

**JULY**
3-4-5-6........... Louisville
17-18-19 .... Indianapolis
20-21 ................ Omaha
22-23 .................... Iowa

**AUGUST**
1-2-3-4........... Louisville
5-6-7-8 ....... Indianapolis
18-19-20......... Nashville
22-23-34... New Orleans
25-26-27 Oklahoma City

### Indianapolis

**APRIL**
14-15-16......... Louisville
17-18-19-20 ....... Buffalo
26-27-28... New Orleans
29-30 ..... Oklahoma City

**MAY**
1 ............ Oklahoma City
9-10................ Louisville
12-13-14........... Omaha
15-16-17................ Iowa
30-31 ............. Nashville

**JUNE**
1 ..................... Nashville
2-3-4 ................. Buffalo
6..................... Louisville
12-13-14-15... Okla. City
16-17-18... New Orleans
27-28-29......... Nashville
30...................... Buffalo

**JULY**
1-2...................... Buffalo
7-8 ........................ Iowa
9-10.................. Omaha
15-16 ............. Nashville
24-25-26... New Orleans
27-28 ..... Oklahoma City

**AUGUST**
1-2 ................. Nashville
9-10-11-12......... Omaha
13-14-15-16.......... Iowa
17-18-19-20.... Louisville
28-29 ............. Nashville
30-31................. Buffalo

**SEPTEMBER**
1-2................. Louisville

### Iowa

**APRIL**
10-11......... Indianapolis
12-13............. Louisville
14-15................ Omaha
26-27-28 ........... Buffalo
29-30 ............. Nashville

**MAY**
1 ..................... Nashville
9-10 ......... New Orleans
18-19-20-21.... Louisville
22-23-24-25............ Indy
28-29 ................ Omaha

**JUNE**
8-9-10-11.......... Omaha
13-14-15......... Nashville
16-17-18-19 ....... Buffalo
27-28-29 Oklahoma City
30 ............ New Orleans

**JULY**
1-2 ........... New Orleans
13-14-15 Oklahoma City
16-17-18-19.......... N. O.
24-25-26 ......... Nashville
27-28................. Buffalo

**AUGUST**
4-5 ......... Oklahoma City
6-7-8......... New Orleans
17-18-19-20....... Omaha
22-23-24......... Louisville
25-26-27 .... Indianapolis

**SEPTEMBER**
1-2-3-4... Oklahoma City

### Louisville

**APRIL**
6-7-8-9 ....... Indianapolis
17-18-19-20.... Nashville
26-27-28 Oklahoma City
29-30 ........ New Orleans

**MAY**
1 .............. New Orleans
12-13-14................ Iowa
15-16-17........... Omaha
26-27-28-29........... Indy
30-31.................. Buffalo

**JUNE**
1......................... Buffalo
2-3-4 ............... Nashville
12-13-14-15.......... N.O.
16-17-18 Oklahoma City
27-28-29 ........... Buffalo
30 .................. Nashville

**JULY**
1-2 ................. Nashville
7-8-8.................. Omaha
9-10 ....................... Iowa
13-14-15-16 ....... Buffalo
24-25-26 Oklahoma City
27-28 ....... New Orleans
29-30......... Indianapolis

**AUGUST**
9-10-11-12............ Iowa
13-14-15........... Omaha
28-29................. Buffalo
30-31 ............. Nashville

**SEPTEMBER**
3-4............. Indianapolis

### Nashville

**APRIL**
10-11 ..... Oklahoma City
12-13 ........ New Orleans
14-15-16 ........... Buffalo
21-22......... Indianapolis
23-24 ............. Louisville

**MAY**
2-3-4................. Omaha
5-6-7-8.................. Iowa
19-20-21-22... Okla. City
23-24-25-26............N.O.

**JUNE**
5-6...................... Buffalo
7-8............. Indianapolis
9-10-11.......... Louisville
20-21-22............... Iowa
23-24-25-26....... Omaha

**JULY**
3-4-5-6 ....... Indianapolis
13-14.......... Indianapolis
17-18-19......... Louisville
20-21 ..................... Iowa
22-23 ................ Omaha
29-30-31 ............ Buffalo

**AUGUST**
3-4............. Indianapolis
5-6-7-8........... Louisville
22-23-24 Oklahoma City
25-26-27... New Orleans

**SEPTEMBER**
1-2-3-4 .............. Buffalo

### New Orleans

**APRIL**
14-15-15........ Okla. City
17-18-19-20........... Iowa

**MAY**
2-3-4 .......... Indianapolis
5-6-7-8............ Louisville
12-13-14 ............ Buffalo
15-16-17......... Nashville
27-28-29 Oklahoma City
30-31 ................ Omaha

**JUNE**
1-2 ..................... Omaha
3-4-5-6.................... Iowa
19-20-21......... Louisville
22-23-24-25............ Indy

**JULY**
3-4 ..................... Omaha
5-6 ......................... Iowa
7-8...................... Buffalo
9-10 ............... Nashville
20-21.......... Indianapolis
22-23 ............. Louisville
31 ...................... Omaha

**AUGUST**
1 ........................ Omaha
2-3 .......................... Iowa
10-11-12-13...... Buffalo
14-15-16-17...... Nashville
18-19-19-20... Okla. City
30-31 ..... Oklahoma City

**SEPTEMBER**
1-2-3-4.............. Omaha

### Oklahoma City

**APRIL**
6-7-8-9...... New Orleans
17-18-19-20....... Omaha
21-22-23-24........... Iowa

**MAY**
2-3-3.............. Louisville
5-6-7-8 ....... Indianapolis
12-13-14 ......... Nashville
15-16-17 ........... Buffalo
30-31 ..................... Iowa

**JUNE**
1-2 ......................... Iowa
3-4-5-6.............. Omaha
8-9-10-11.. New Orleans
19-20-21 .... Indianapolis
22-23-24-25.... Louisville

**JULY**
3-4 ......................... Iowa
5-6 ...................... Omaha
7-8 .................. Nashville
9-10.................... Buffalo
20-21 ............. Louisville
22-23......... Indianapolis
29-30 ........ New Orleans
31 .......................... Iowa

**AUGUST**

1 .......... Iowa
2-3 .......... Omaha
10-11-12-13 .... Nashville
14-15-16-17 ....... Buffalo
28-29 ........ New Orleans

### Omaha

**APRIL**

6-7-8-9 .......... Iowa
10-11 .......... Louisville
12-13 ......... Indianapolis
21-22-23-24 .......... N.O.
26-28 .......... Nashville
29-30 .......... Buffalo

**MAY**

1 .......... Buffalo
9-10 ....... Oklahoma City
18-19-20-21 .......... Indy
22-23-24-25 .... Louisville
26-27 .......... Iowa

**JUNE**

13-14-15 .......... Buffalo
16-17-18-18-19 .... Nash.
27-28-29 ... New Orleans
30 .......... Oklahoma City

**JULY**

1-2 ........ Oklahoma City
13-14-15 ... New Orleans
16-17-18-19 ... Okla. City
24-25-26 .......... Buffalo
27-28 .......... Nashville
29-30 .......... Iowa

**AUGUST**

4-5 .......... New Orleans
6-7-8 ...... Oklahoma City
22-23-24 .... Indianapolis
25-26-27 ......... Louisville
28-29-30-31 .......... Iowa

# International League

### Charlotte

**APRIL**

6-7-8-9 .......... Norfolk
17-18-19 ....... Rochester
21-22-23 ......... Syracuse
24-25-26-27 ....... Ottawa

**MAY**

3-4 .......... Richmond
5-6-7 .......... Pawtucket
8-9-10 .......... Toledo
23-24-25 .......... Toledo
26-27-28 ....... Richmond

**JUNE**

5-6 .......... Pawtucket
7-8-9 .......... Scranton
10-11-13 ....... Columbus
21-22 .......... Scranton
23-24-25 .......... Ottawa

**JULY**

3-4 .......... Norfolk
7-8-9-10 ........ Richmond
21-22-23 ....... Columbus
24-25-26 .......... Toledo
27-28-29-30 .. Rochester

**AUGUST**

11-12-13-14 ... Syracuse
15-16-17 .......... Norfolk
23-24 .......... Pawtucket
25-26-27 ....... Columbus

**SEPTEMBER**

1-2 .......... Scranton

### Columbus

**APRIL**

6-7-8-9 .......... Richmond
10-11-12 ....... Pawtucket
21-22-23 ......... Scranton
24-25-26 .......... Norfolk

**MAY**

5-6-7 .......... Syracuse
8-9-10 .......... Richmond
19-20-21 ......... Charlotte
22-23-24-25 .. Rochester

**JUNE**

1-2-3-4 .......... Norfolk
5-6-7-8-9 .......... Ottawa
17-18-19 ......... Charlotte
26-27-28 ....... Rochester
29-30 .......... Syracuse

**JULY**

1-2 .......... Syracuse
9-10 .......... Toledo
13-14-15-16 .. Pawtucket
17-18-19-20 .... Scranton
31 .......... Toledo

**AUGUST**

1 .......... Toledo
2-3-4 .......... Charlotte
5-6 .......... Norfolk
8-9-10 .......... Toledo
21-22 .......... Ottawa
23-24 .......... Richmond

**SEPTEMBER**

1-2 .......... Toledo

### Norfolk

**APRIL**

13-14-15-16 .. Rochester
17-18-19 ....... Columbus
28-29-30 ........ Charlotte

**MAY**

1-2-3-4 .......... Pawtucket
16-17-18 ......... Syracuse
19-20-21 .......... Toledo
25 .......... Richmond
26-27-28 ....... Columbus

**JUNE**

7-8-9 .......... Pawtucket
10-11-12-13 .... Scranton
19 .......... Richmond
20-21-22 .......... Ottawa
23-24-25 .......... Toledo

**JULY**

1-2 .......... Richmond
5-6 .......... Charlotte
7-8-9-10 .......... Ottawa
15-16 .......... Richmond
24-25-26 ....... Columbus
28-29-30 .......... Toledo
31 .......... Charlotte

**AUGUST**

1 .......... Charlotte
7-8-9-10 ......... Syracuse
11 .......... Richmond
18-19-20 .......... Scranton
21-22 .......... Charlotte
23-24-25 ....... Rochester

**SEPTEMBER**

1-2 .......... Richmond

### Ottawa

**APRIL**

14-15-16 ........ Charlotte
17-18-19-20 .. Pawtucket
28-29-30 ....... Richmond

**MAY**

2-3-4 .......... Columbus
5-6 .......... Scranton
12-13-14-15 ....... Norfolk
16-17-18 ....... Rochester
19-20-21 ....... Pawtucket
29-30-31 ......... Syracuse

**JUNE**

1-2-3-4 .......... Toledo
14-15-16 ....... Rochester
17-18-19 .......... Toledo
26-27-28 .......... Norfolk
30 .......... Scranton

**JULY**

1-2 .......... Scranton
13-14-15-16 .... Charlotte
17-18-19 ......... Syracuse
27-28-29-30 .. Richmond
31 .......... Scranton

**AUGUST**

1-2-3 .......... Scranton
11-12-13-14 .. Columbus
15-16-17 ....... Rochester
29-30-31 ......... Syracuse

**SEPTEMBER**

1-2 .......... Pawtucket

### Pawtucket

**APRIL**

14-15-16 .......... Toledo
24-25-26-27 .... Scranton
29-30 .......... Rochester

**MAY**

9-10-11 .......... Ottawa
12-13-14 ......... Charlotte
16-17-18 ....... Columbus
27-28 .......... Syracuse
29-30-31 ......... Scranton

**JUNE**

1-2-3-4 .......... Richmond
14-15-16 .......... Norfolk
17-18-19 ....... Rochester
23-24-25 ....... Richmond
29-30 .......... Charlotte

**JULY**

1-2 .......... Charlotte
3-4-5-6 .......... Columbus
20-21-22-23 .. Rochester
24-25-26 .......... Ottawa
27-28-29-30 ... Syracuse

**AUGUST**

7-8-9 .......... Ottawa
14-15-16-17 ....... Toledo
18-19-20 ......... Syracuse
21-22 .......... Scranton
28-29-30-31 ....... Norfolk

### Richmond

**APRIL**

14-15-16 ....... Columbus
17-18-19-20 ... Syracuse
21-22-23 .......... Ottawa

**MAY**

1-2 .......... Charlotte
5-6-7 .......... Toledo
19-20-21 ......... Syracuse
22-23 .......... Norfolk
29-30-31 ........ Columbus

**JUNE**

10-11-12-13 .. Pawtucket
14-15-16 ....... Columbus
17-18 .......... Norfolk
26-27-28 .......... Toledo
30 .......... Norfolk

**JULY**

3-4-5-6 .......... Ottawa
13-14 .......... Norfolk
18-19-19-20 .... Charlotte
21-22-23 .......... Toledo
24-25-26 ....... Rochester

**AUGUST**

4-5-6 .......... Scranton
7-8-9-10 ........ Rochester
12-13 .......... Norfolk
18-19-20 ......... Charlotte
25-26-27 ....... Pawtucket
28-29-30-31 .... Scranton

### Rochester

**APRIL**

6-7-8-9 .......... Scranton
10-11-12 .......... Ottawa
21-22-23 ....... Pawtucket
24-25-26-27 ....... Toledo

**MAY**
5-6-7-8 .............. Norfolk
12-13-14-15 .. Columbus
19-20-21 ......... Scranton
29-30-31 ......... Charlotte
**JUNE**
1 .................... Charlotte
3-4 .................. Syracuse
5-6-7-8-9 ....... Richmond
13 .................. Syracuse
21-22 ............ Richmond
24-25 ............ Syracuse
**JULY**
7-8 ................. Scranton
9-10 ............. Pawtucket
13-14 ............. Syracuse
17-18-19 ........... Norfolk
31 ................ Pawtucket
**AUGUST**
1-2-3 ............ Pawtucket
4-5-6 .................. Ottawa
11-12-13 ............ Toledo
18-19-20 ....... Columbus
21-22 ............ Syracuse
26-27-28 ........... Ottawa
29-30-31 ......... Charlotte

**Scranton/W-B**
**APRIL**
10-11-12 ........... Norfolk
14-15-16 ......... Syracuse
28-29-30 ............ Toledo
**MAY**
1 ........................ Toledo
2-3-4 ............ Rochester
7-8 .................... Ottawa
9-10 ............. Rochester
15-16-17-18 .. Richmond
23-24 ........... Pawtucket
25-26-27-28 ....... Ottawa
**JUNE**
2-3-4 .............. Charlotte
5-6 .................... Norfolk
16-17-18 ......... Syracuse
23-24-25 ....... Columbus
26-26-27-28 .......... Paw.
**JULY**
3-4-5-6 ......... Rochester
21-22-23 ........... Ottawa
24-25-26 ......... Syracuse
27-28-29-30 .. Columbus
**AUGUST**
7-8-9-10 ......... Charlotte
11-12-13 ....... Pawtucket
15-16-17 ....... Richmond
23-24-25 ............ Toledo
26-27 ................ Norfolk

**Syracuse**
**APRIL**
6-7-8-9 .............. Ottawa
10-11-12-13 .... Charlotte
25-26-27 ....... Richmond
28-29-30 ....... Columbus
**MAY**
1 ................... Columbus
9-10-11 .............. Norfolk
12-13-14 ......... Scranton
23-24 ................. Ottawa
25-26 ........... Pawtucket
**JUNE**
2 ................... Rochester
5-6-7-8-9 ........... Toledo
14-15 .............. Scranton
10-11-12 ....... Rochester
19-20 .............. Scranton
21-22 ........... Pawtucket
23 .................. Rochester
26-27-28 ......... Charlotte
**JULY**
7-8 ............... Pawtucket
9-10 ............... Scranton
15-16 ............ Rochester
20-21-22-23 ....... Norfolk
31 ................. Richmond
**AUGUST**
1-2-3 ............ Richmond
4-5-6 ............ Pawtucket
15-16-17 ....... Columbus
23-24-25 ........... Ottawa
26-27 .................. Toledo
**SEPTEMBER**
1-2 ............... Rochester

**Toledo**
**APRIL**
6-7-8-9 ......... Pawtucket
10-11-12 ....... Richmond
18-19-20 ......... Scranton
21-22-23 ........... Norfolk
**MAY**
2-3-4 .............. Syracuse
11-12-13-14 .. Richmond
15-16-17-18 .... Charlotte
26-27-28 ....... Rochester
29-30-31 ........... Norfolk
**JUNE**
10-11-12-13 ....... Ottawa
14-15-16 ......... Charlotte
20-21-22 ....... Columbus
29-30 ............ Rochester
**JULY**
1-2 ................ Rochester
3-4-5-6 ........... Syracuse
7-8 ................. Columbus
13-14-15-16 .... Scranton
17-18-19 ....... Pawtucket
**AUGUST**
2-3-4 .................. Norfolk
5-6 .................. Charlotte
18-19-20 ........... Ottawa
21-22 ............ Richmond
28-29-30-31 .. Columbus

# Pacific Coast League

**Albuquerque**
**APRIL**
6-7-8-9 ........... Salt Lake
11-12-13-14 .. Edmonton
24-25-26-27 . Vancouver
28-29-30 .. Colo. Springs
**MAY**
1 ............. Colo. Springs
11-12-13-14 . Las Vegas
15-16-17-18 ..... Phoenix
27-28-29-30 ...... Calgary
**JUNE**
1-2-3-4 ............ Tacoma
14-15-16-17 ....... Tucson
26-27-28-29 ....... Tucson
**JULY**
4-5-5-6 .......... Edmonton
7-8-8-9 ............. Phoenix
21-22-23-24 ..... Tacoma
25-26-27-28 .. Colo. Spr.
**AUGUST**
7-8-9-10 ........... Calgary
11-12-13-14 . Vancouver
15-16-17-18 ... Salt Lake
**SEPTEMBER**
1-2-3-4 ......... Las Vegas

**Calgary**
**APRIL**
20-21-22-23 ..... Phoenix
24-25-26-27 . Las Vegas
**MAY**
6-7-8-9 ............. Tacoma
15-16-17-18 ....... Tucson
19-20-21-22 . Vancouver
**JUNE**
1-2-3-4 ..... Colo. Springs
6-7-8-9 ........... Salt Lake
10-11-12-13 .. Edmonton
18-19-20-21 ........ Albuq.
23-24-24-25 ............ L.V.
30 ............ Colo. Springs
**JULY**
1-2-3 ........ Colo. Springs
4-5-5-6 ......... Vancouver
13-14-15-16 ........ Albuq.
25-26-27-28 ..... Phoenix
29-30-31 ......... Salt Lake
**AUGUST**
1 ..................... Salt Lake
15-16-17-18 .. Edmonton
19-20-21-22 ..... Tacoma
28-29-30-31 ....... Tucson

**Colo. Springs**
**APRIL**
6-7-8-9 .......... Edmonton
15-16-17-18 ..... Tacoma
20-21-22-23 ........ Albuq.
**MAY**
2-3-4-5 ......... Vancouver
6-7-8-9 ......... Las Vegas
23-24-25-26 ...... Calgary
**JUNE**
6-7-8-9 ............... Tucson
10-11-12-13 ... Salt Lake
14-15-16-17 ..... Phoenix
26-27-28-29 . Las Vegas
**JULY**
7-8-9-9 .......... Edmonton
17-18-19-20 ...... Calgary
21-22-23-24 . Vancouver
**AUGUST**
3-4-5-6 ............. Tacoma
7-8-9-10 ............. Tucson
11-12-13-14 ..... Phoenix
28-29-30-31 ........ Albuq.
**SEPTEMBER**
1-2-3-4 ........... Salt Lake

**Edmonton**
**APRIL**
16-17 .................Calgary
**MAY**
2-3-4-5 ............. Tacoma
11-12-13-14 ....... Tucson
15-16-17-18 .. Colo. Spr.
27-28-29-30 ..... Phoenix
**JUNE**
1-2-3-4 ........... Salt Lake
5-5 .................... Calgary
6-7-8-9 ...... Albuquerque
14-15-16-17 . Vancouver
26-27-28-29 ...... Calgary
30 ................. Vancouver
**JULY**
1-2-3 ........... Vancouver
13-14-15-16 ... Salt Lake
17-18-19-20 ........ Albuq.
21-22-23-24 ..... Phoenix
29-30-31 ....... Las Vegas
**AUGUST**
1 ................... Las Vegas
19-20-21-22 .. Colo. Spr.
24-25-26-27 ....... Tucson
28-29-30-31 ..... Tacoma

**Las Vegas**
**APRIL**
11-12-13-14 .. Colo. Spr.
15-16-17-18 ........ Albuq.
20-21-22-23 .. Edmonton
28-29-30 ...... Vancouver
**MAY**
1 ................... Vancouver
2-3-4-5 ............. Phoenix

15-16-17-18 ... Salt Lake
19-20-21-22 .. Edmonton
27-28-29-30 ..... Tacoma

**JUNE**

1-2-3-4............... Tucson
14-15-16-17...... Calgary
30............. Albuquerque

**JULY**

1-2-3 ......... Albuquerque
7-8-8-9.............. Tucson
21-22-23-24...... Calgary
25-26-27-28 ..... Tacoma

**AUGUST**

7-8-9-10........ Edmonton
11-12-13-14 ... Salt Lake
19-20-21-22 . Vancouver
24-25-26-27 .. Colo. Spr.
28-29-30-31 ..... Phoenix

## Phoenix

**APRIL**

6-7-8-9 ......... Las Vegas
11-12-13-14...... Calgary
24-25-26-27 .. Edmonton
28-29-30........... Tucson

**MAY**

1 ........................ Tucson
6-7-8-9...... Albuquerque
11-12-13-14 ... Salt Lake
19-20-21-22 .. Colo. Spr.

**JUNE**

1-2-3-4 ......... Vancouver
6-7-8-9 ............. Tacoma
22-23-24-25 .. Edmonton
26-27-27-28 ... Salt Lake

**JULY**

4-5-5-6 ......... Las Vegas
13-14-15-16 .. Colo. Spr.
17-18-19-20 . Vancouver

**AUGUST**

3-4-5-6.............. Calgary
7-8-9-10 ........... Tacoma
24-25-26-27 ........ Albuq.

**SEPTEMBER**

1-2-3-4............... Tucson

## Salt Lake

**APRIL**

10-12-13-14 . Vancouver
15-16-17-18 ..... Phoenix
28-29-30 ....... Edmonton

**MAY**

1.................... Edmonton
2-3-4-5............. Calgary
19-20-21-22....... Tucson
23-24-25-26 ........ Albuq.
27-28-29-30 .. Colo. Spr.

**JUNE**

14-16-17-17 ..... Tacoma
18-19-20-21 . Las Vegas

**JULY**

4-5-5-6..... Colo. Springs
7-8-9-10 ........... Tacoma
17-18-19-20 . Las Vegas
21-22-23-24....... Tucson
25-26-27-28 .. Edmonton

**AUGUST**

3-4-5-6...... Albuquerque
7-8-9-10....... Vancouver
19-20-21-22 ..... Phoenix
24-25-26-27...... Calgary

## Tacoma

**APRIL**

6-7-8-9 ......... Vancouver
11-12-13-14....... Tucson
24-25-26-27 ... Salt Lake
28-29-30 ........... Calgary

**MAY**

1........................ Calgary
11-12-13-14 .. Colo. Spr.
19-20-21-22 ........ Albuq.
23-24-25-26 .. Edmonton

**JUNE**

10-11-12-13 . Las Vegas
18-19-20-21 ..... Phoenix
22-23-24-25 .. Colo. Spr.
30 ................... Salt Lake

**JULY**

1-2-3............... Salt Lake
13-14-15-16 . Las Vegas
17-18-19-20....... Tucson
29-30-31 ... Albuquerque

**AUGUST**

1................ Albuquerque
11-12-13-14 .. Edmonton
15-16-17-18 ..... Phoenix
24-25-26-27 . Vancouver

**SEPTEMBER**

1-2-3-4 ............. Calgary

## Tucson

**APRIL**

6-7-8-9............. Calgary
20-21-22-23 ..... Tacoma
24-25-26-27 .. Colo. Spr.

**MAY**

2-3-4-5...... Albuquerque
6-7-8-9 ........... Salt Lake
23-24-25-26 . Las Vegas
27-28-29-30 . Vancouver

**JUNE**

10-11-12-13 ..... Phoenix
18-19-20-21 .. Edmonton
22-23-24-25 ... Salt Lake
30 ...................... Phoenix

**JULY**

1-2-3................. Phoenix
4-5-6-6 ............. Tacoma
13-14-15-16 . Vancouver
29-30-31 .. Colo. Springs

**AUGUST**

1 .............. Colo. Springs
3-4-5-6.......... Edmonton
11-12-13-14...... Calgary
15-16-17-18 . Las Vegas
19-20-21-22 ........ Albuq.

## Vancouver

**APRIL**

15-16-17-18....... Tucson
20-21-22-23 ... Salt Lake

**MAY**

6-7-8-10 ........ Edmonton
11-12-13-14...... Calgary
15-16-17-18 ..... Tacoma
23-24-25-26 ..... Phoenix

**JUNE**

6-7-8-9 ......... Las Vegas
10-11-12-13 ........ Albuq.
18-19-20-21 .. Colo. Spr.
22-23-24-25 ........ Albuq.
26-27-28-29 ..... Tacoma

**JULY**

7-8-9-9.............. Calgary
25-26-27-28....... Tucson
29-30-31........... Phoenix

**AUGUST**

1 ........................ Phoenix
3-4-5-6 ......... Las Vegas
15-16-17-18 .. Colo. Spr.
28-29-30-31 ... Salt Lake

**SEPTEMBER**

1-2-3-4 .......... Edmonton

# CLASS AA

## Eastern League

### Binghamton

**APRIL**
8-9 .................. Portland
10-11 .......... New Haven
14-15-16 .......... Reading
17-18-19 .......... Trenton
26-27 ........... Harrisburg

**MAY**
1-2-3................. Norwich
10-11 ............... Reading
12-13-14 ........... Canton
16-17-18..... New Haven
26-27-28. Hardware City

**JUNE**
5-6-7-8................. Bowie
16-17-18....... Harrisburg
23-24-25-26 ........... H.C.
27-28-29-30........... Port.

**JULY**
1-2-3.................... Bowie
12-13 ............... Trenton
14-15-16 .......... Portland
25-26 .......... New Haven
29-30................ Norwich
31 ...................... Canton

**AUGUST**
1-2-3................. Canton
4-5 .................... Trenton
13-14 .............. Reading
15-16-17-18 ..... Norwich
19-20........... Harrisburg
30-31...... Hardware City

**SEPTEMBER**
1-2 ............. New Haven

### Bowie

**APRIL**
6-7-8-9.............. Norwich
12-13............ Harrisburg
14-15-16 .......... Portland
26-27 ................ Trenton
28-29-30 .... Binghamton

**MAY**
1-2-3....... Hardware City
12-13-14 .......... Reading
22-23-24....... Harrisburg
25-26-27-28....... Canton
29-30-31 ........... Trenton

**JUNE**
12-13 ............... Reading
16-17-18............ Canton
19-20-21........... Norwich
23-24 ............... Reading

**JULY**
4-5 .................... Trenton
6-7-8-9.......... Harrisburg
17-18-19-20 .......... Bing.
21-22-23..... New Haven
25-26-27-28..... Portland

**AUGUST**
9-10 ................... Canton
11-12-13-14 New Haven
19-20-21-22 ........... H.C.
25-26 ................ Trenton
29-30 ............... Reading

### Canton-Akron

**APRIL**
10-11-12-13..... Portland
14-15-16 ................ H.C.
26-27 ............... Reading
28-29-30....... Harrisburg

**MAY**
1-2-3........... New Haven
16-17-18........... Norwich
19-20-21.............. Bowie
22-23-24 ........... Trenton

**JUNE**
2-3-4 ............... Portland
5-6-7-8 ................... H.C.
19-20-21 .............. Bing.
22-23-24-25 New Haven
27-28-29-30.. Harrisburg

**JULY**
4-5-6-7 ................. Bing.
12-13 .................. Bowie
14-15-16 .......... Reading
25-26-27-28 ..... Norwich
29-30 ........... Harrisburg

**AUGUST**
4-5-6-7 ............ Reading
15-16-17-18......... Bowie
19-20 ................ Trenton

**SEPTEMBER**
1-2-3-4 ............. Trenton

### Harrisburg

**APRIL**
6-7-8-9 .................. H.C.
10-11 .................. Bowie
14-15-16........... Norwich
21-22-23 .............. Bing.
24-25 ................ Canton

**MAY**
1-2-3 .............. Portland
16-17-18............... Bowie
19-20-21 ..... New Haven
27-28 ............... Trenton
29-30-31 ............ Canton

**JUNE**
2-3-4....... Hardware City
5-6 ............. New Haven
12-13......... Binghamton
14-15 ................ Canton
22-23-24-25 ..... Norwich

**JULY**
1-2-3 ............... Reading
19-20 .......... New Haven
21-22-23 .......... Trenton
27-28 .............. Reading
31 ..................... Trenton

**AUGUST**
1........................ Trenton
11-12.......... Binghamton
13-14 ................ Canton
15-16-17-18..... Portland
21-22 ............... Trenton
23-24-25-26..... Reading

**SEPTEMBER**
1-2-3-4................ Bowie

### Hardware City

**APRIL**
18-19-20............. Bowie
21-22-23..... New Haven
24-25 .............. Portland
26-27................ Norwich

**MAY**
5-6-7 ................ Trenton
8-9-10-11.......... Canton
12-13-14....... Harrisburg
19-20-21 .............. Bing.
23-24................. Norwich

**JUNE**
9-10-11 ................ Bing.
12-13.......... New Haven
16-17-18 .......... Reading
19-20-21 .......... Portland
27-28-29-30..... Reading

**JULY**
4-5............. New Haven
12-13 .............. Portland
17 .................... Norwich
21-22-23............ Canton
25-26-27-28...... Trenton
31 ........................ Bowie

**AUGUST**
1-2-3..................... Bowie
4-5 ............. New Haven
6-7-8-9.......... Harrisburg
13-14................ Norwich
25-26 .............. Portland
27-28-29 ............... Bing.

**SEPTEMBER**
1-2.................... Norwich

### New Haven

**APRIL**
6-7 .................. Reading
12-13........................ Bing.
14-15-16 ........... Trenton
17-18-19....... Harrisburg
26-27 .............. Portland

**MAY**
5-6-7 ................. Canton
8-9-10-11............. Bowie
12-13-14............. Norwich
22-23-24 .... Binghamton
29-30-31 .......... Reading

**JUNE**
2-3.................... Norwich
7-8.............. Harrisburg
9-10-11................ Bowie
16-17-18 .......... Portland
27-28-29-30 ...... Trenton

**JULY**
6-7......... Hardware City
12-13............... Norwich
14-15-16 ................ H.C.
17-18........... Harrisburg
27-28........ Binghamton
29-30 ...... Hardware City
31..................... Reading

**AUGUST**
1....................... Reading
2-3 .................. Portland
6-7.......................... Bing.
9-10.................. Norwich
23-24-25-26....... Canton
27-28 .............. Portland

**SEPTEMBER**
3-4 ......... Hardware City

### Norwich

**APRIL**
17-18-19 .......... Reading
21-22-23........... Canton
24-25 .......... New Haven
28-29-30 ......... Portland

**MAY**
5-6-7.................... Bowie
8-9-10-11 .......... Trenton
22 .......... Hardware City
25-26-27-28..... Reading
29-30-31 ............... Bing.

**JUNE**
4 ................ New Haven
7-8 .................. Portland
9-10-11 ............ Trenton
14-15 ......... New Haven
27-28-29-30......... Bowie

**JULY**
1-2-3....... Hardware City
8-9 ............. New Haven
14-15-16....... Harrisburg
18-19-20 ................ H.C.
31 .................... Portland

**AUGUST**
1...................... Portland
2-3-4-5.......... Harrisburg
11-12...... Hardware City
19-20 ............... Portland
21-22 .......... New Haven

23-24-25-26 .......... Bing.
27-28-29-30....... Canton

**SEPTEMBER**

3-4............. Binghamton

### Portland

**APRIL**

6-7............. Binghamton
18-19-20............ Canton
21-22-23............. Bowie

**MAY**

5-6-7 .......... Binghamton
8-9-10-11...... Harrisburg
12-13-14 ........... Trenton
22-23-24 .......... Reading
25-26-27-28 ........... N.H.
29-30-31 ................ H.C.

**JUNE**

9-10-11......... Harrisburg
12-13................ Norwich
14-15...... Hardware City
23-24-25-26...... Trenton

**JULY**

1-2-3........... New Haven
4-5-6-7.............. Norwich
8-9.......... Hardware City
17-18-19-20....... Canton
21-22-23........... Norwich

**AUGUST**

4-5-6-7................. Bowie
8-9............. Binghamton
21-22.......... Binghamton
23-24...... Hardware City
30-31 .......... New Haven

**SEPTEMBER**

1-2-3-4............. Reading

### Reading

**APRIL**

8-9 ............. New Haven
10-11-12-13 ..... Norwich
21-22-23 ........... Trenton
24-25.......... Binghamton
28-29-30 ............... H.C.

**MAY**

5-6-7............ Harrisburg
8-9.............. Binghamton
16-17-18.......... Portland
19-20-21.......... Norwich

**JUNE**

2-3-4.................... Bowie
5-6 ................... Portland
7-8 ..................... Trenton
9-10-11 ............. Canton
14-15.................. Bowie
19-20-21 ..... New Haven
25-26.................. Bowie

**JULY**

4-5 ............... Harrisburg
8-9 ..................... Canton
12-13............ Harrisburg
17-18 ................. Trenton
21-22-23 .... Binghamton
24-25............ Harrisburg
29-30 .............. Portland

**AUGUST**

9-10 ................... Trenton
11-12 .................. Canton
15-16-17-18 ........... H.C.
19-20 .......... New Haven
21-22 .................. Canton
27-28................... Bowie

### Trenton

**APRIL**

6-7-8-9.............. Canton
10-11-12-13 ........... H.C.
24-25 ..................... Bowie
28-29-30..... New Haven

**MAY**

1-2-3 ................ Reading
16-17-18 ................ H.C.
19-20-21 .......... Portland
25-26........... Harrisburg

**JUNE**

2-3-4 ......... Binghamton
5-6..................... Norwich
12-13 .................. Canton
14-15......... Binghamton
16-17-18........... Norwich
19-20-21....... Harrisburg

**JULY**

1-2-3................... Canton
6-7 .................... Reading
8-9............. Binghamton
14-15-16............. Bowie
19-20 ............... Reading
29-30 ................... Bowie

**AUGUST**

2-3 ...................... Reading
6-7...................... Norwich
11-12-13-14........... Port/
15-16-17-18 ........... N.H.
23-24 .................. Bowie
27-28-29-30.. Harrisburg

# Southern League



### Birmingham

**APRIL**

14-15-16-17.... Memphis
18-19-20-21...... Orlando
22-23-24-25......... Chatt.

**MAY**

4-5-6-7........... Huntsville
9-10 .......... Chattanooga
13-14-15-16 ....... Green.
17-18 ............. Knoxville
29-30-31 .......... Huntsville

**JUNE**

1 .................... Huntsville
2-3-4-5 .......... Greenville
7-8 .................. Knoxville
20-21-22-23... Huntsville
24-25-26-27.... Memphis
28-29-30 ... Chattanooga

**JULY**

1 .............. Chattanooga
12-13-14-15......... Chatt.
16-17-18-19........... Jax.
25-26-27-28 ......... Knox.
29-30-31 ......... Memphis

**AUGUST**

1 ..................... Memphis
13-14 ........ Chattanooga
16-17-18-19........... Wilm.
25-25-26-27..... Carolina

### Carolina

**APRIL**

6-7-8-9......... Wilmington
18-19-20-21............ Jax.

**MAY**

2-3 ............ Jacksonville
4-5-6-7.............. Orlando
18-18-19-20 ....... Green.
21-22-23-24 .......... Birm.
29-30-31 .......... Orlando

**JUNE**

1 ......................... Orlando
2-3 .................. Knoxville
15-16-17-18.......... Wilm.
20-21............. Greenville

**JULY**

2-3-4-5......... Wilmington
12-13-14-15... Huntsville
16-17-18-19.... Memphis
27-28-29-30-31....... Jax.

**AUGUST**

1................. Jacksonville
2-3-4-5.............. Orlando
11-12-13-14. Wilmington
18-19 ............. Knoxville
20-21-22-23......... Chatt.
30-31............ Greenville

**SEPTEMBER**

1-2-3-4 ........... Knoxville

### Chattanooga

**APRIL**

12-13 ............. Memphis
14-15-16-17..... Carolina
18-19-20-21... Huntsville
26-27-28-29 .......... Birm.

**MAY**

2-3 ................ Huntsville
11-12.......... Birmingham
15-16 ............. Knoxville
17-18-19-20. Wilmington
21-22 ............. Knoxville
27-28 ............. Knoxville

**JUNE**

2-3-4-5....... Jacksonville
7-8-9-10.......... Memphis
24-25-26-27...... Orlando

**JULY**

2-3-4-5 ....... Birmingham
16-17 ............. Knoxville
21-22-23-24 ... Geenville
29-30-31 ........ Huntsville

**AUGUST**

1 .................... Huntsville
2-3 .................. Memphis
9-10 ................ Huntsville
11-12.......... Birmingham
16-17-18-19 .. Greenville
28-29-30-31 . Birmington

**SEPTEMBER**

1-2-3-4............ Memphis

### Greenville

**APRIL**

14-15-16-17...... Orlando
18-19-20-21. Wilmington
30 .................... Memphis

**MAY**

1-2-3 ............... Memphis
4-5-6-7...... Chattanooga
11-12 ............. Knoxville
25-26-27-28..... Carolina
29-30-31 .... Jacksonville

**JUNE**

1................ Jacksonville
11-12-13-14 . Birminham
15-16 .............. Knoxville
22-23 ............... Carolina
24-25-26-27... Huntsville
28-29-30 ......... Knoxville

**JULY**

1...................... Knoxville
6-7-8-9........ Chattnooga
12-13-14-15............ Jax.
16-17 .................Orlando
29-30-31...... Wilmington

**AUGUST**

1 ................. Wilmington
6-7 ..................... Orlando
20-21-22-23 .......... Birm.
24-25-26-27.... Memphis
28-29 .............. Carolina

**SEPTEMBER**

1-2-3-4........... Huntsville

### Huntsville

**APRIL**

6-7-8-9...... Chattanooga
10-10-11-12 .......... Birm.
22-23-24-25.... Knoxville
26-27-28-29 .. Greenville

30 ............ Chattanooga

**MAY**

1 ............... Chattanooga
8-9-11-12 ......... Carolina
13-14-15-16. Wilmington
26-27-28 ......... Memphis

**JUNE**

7-8-9-10 ........ Greenville
11-12-13-14-15 .. Memp.
28-29-30 ......... Memphis

**JULY**

1 ..................... Memphis
6-7-8-9 ............ Knoxville
21-22-23-24 .......... Birm.
25-26-27-28 ......... Chatt.

**AUGUST**

2-3-4-5 .................. Birm.
7-8 ............ Chattanooga
13-14 .............. Memphis
16-17-18-19 ............ Jax.
20-21-22-23 ...... Orlando
28-29 .............. Memphis

## Jacksonville

**APRIL**

6-7-8-9 .......... Greenville
10-11-12-13 .... Knoxville
22-23-24-25 ..... Carolina
26-27-28-29 .......... Wilm.
30 ..................... Carolina

**MAY**

1 ....................... Carolina
9-10-11-12 ........ Orlando
18-19-20-21 .... Memphis
22-22-23-24 ... Huntsville
27-28 ................ Orlando

**JUNE**

9-10 .................. Orlando
11-12-13-14 ......... Chatt.
15-16-17-18 .......... Birm.
24-25-26-27 .......... Wilm.

**JULY**

2-3-4-5 .............. Orlando
6-7-8-9 ............. Carolina
21-22-23-24 .......... Wilm.
25-26 ................ Carolina

**AUGUST**

7-8-9-10 .......... Knoxville
11-12-13-14 .. Greenville
25-26-27-28 ...... Orlando

## Knoxville

**APRIL**

14-15-16-17 ... Huntsville
18-19-20-21 .... Memphis
30 ............... Birmingham

**MAY**

1-2-3 ........... Birmingham
4-5-6-7 ............ Memphis
9-10 .............. Greenville
13-14 ........ Chattanooga
19-20 .......... Birmingham
23-24-25-26 ......... Chatt.
29-30-31 ...... Wilmington

**JUNE**

1 ................. Wilmington
4-5 ................... Carolina
9-10 ........... Birmingham
11-12-13-14 .......... Wilm.
17-18 ............ Greenville
20-21-22-23 ............ Jax.
24-25-26-27 ..... Carolina

**JULY**

2-3-4-5 ...........Greenville
12-13-14-15 ...... Orlando
18-19 ........ Chattanooga
29-30-31 ........... Orlando

**AUGUST**

1 ....................... Orlando
2-3-4-5 ....... Jacksonville
16-17 ............... Carolina
24-25-26-27 ... Huntsville

## Memphis

**APRIL**

6-7-8-9 ....... Birmingham
10-11 ........ Chattanooga
22-23-24-25 .. Greenville
26-27-28-29 .... Knoxville

**MAY**

9-10-11-12 ... Wilmington
13-14-15-16 ..... Carolina
29-30-31 ... Chattanooga

**JUNE**

1 .............. Chattanooga
2-3-4-5-6 ........ Huntsville
16-17-18 ......... Huntsville
21-22-23 ... Chattanooga

**JULY**

2-3-4-5 ........... Huntsville
6-7-8-9 ......... Birmingham
21-22-23-24 .... Knoxville
25-26-27-28 .. Greenville

**AUGUST**

4-5-6 ......... Chattanooga
7-8-9-10 ..... Birmingham
11-12 ............. Huntsville
16-17-18-19 ...... Orlando
20-21-22-23 ............ Jax.
30-31 ............. Huntsville

## Orlando

**APRIL**

6-7-8-9 ........... Knoxville
10-11-12-13 .. Greenville
22-23-24-25. Wilmington
26-27-28-29 ..... Carolina

**MAY**

13-14-15-16 ............ Jax.
18-19-20-21 ... Huntsville
22-22-23-24 .... Memphis
25-26 ......... Jacksonville

**JUNE**

7-8 ............ Jacksonville
11-12-13-14 ..... Carolina
15-16-17-18 ......... Chatt.
28-29-30-30 ........... Jax.

**JULY**

1 ................ Jacksonville
6-7-8-9 ......... Wilmington
18-19 ............. Greenville
21-22-23-24 ..... Carolina
25-26-27-28 .......... Wilm.

**AUGUST**

9-10 .............. Greenville
11-12-13-14 .... Knoxville
29-30-31 .... Jacksonville

**SEPTEMBER**

1-3-3-4 ....... Birmingham

## Wilmington

**APRIL**

10-11-12-13 ..... Carolina
14-15-16-17 ............ Jax.
30 ..................... Orlando

**MAY**

1-2-3 ................. Orlando
4-5-6-7 ....... Jacksonville
21-22-23-24 .. Greenville
25-25-26-27 .......... Birm.

**JUNE**

2-3-4-5 ............. Orlando
7-8-9-10 ........... Carolina
20-21-22-23 ...... Orlando
28-29-30 .......... Carolina

**JULY**

1 ....................... Carolina
12-13-14-15 .... Memphis
16-17-18-19 ... Huntsville

**AUGUST**

2-3-4-5 .......... Greenville
7-8-9-10 ........... Carolina
21-21-22-23 .... Knoxville
24-25-26-27 ......... Chatt.
28-29-30-31 .... Knoxville

**SEPTEMBER**

1-2-3-4 ....... Jacksonville

# Texas League

## Arkansas

**APRIL**

6-7-8-8-10 ........ Jackson
11-12-13-14-15 .... Tulsa
21-22-22-24-25. Shreve.

**MAY**

8-9-10-11-12 ..... El Paso
13-13-15-16-17. Midland
30-31 ........... Shreveport

**JUNE**

1-2-3-3 ......... Shreveport
5-6-7-8-9-10 ......... Tulsa
27-28-29-30 ..... Jackson

**JULY**

1-1 .................... Jackson
11-12-13-14-15 ...... S.A.
16-17-18-19-20 . Wichita

**AUGUST**

1-2-3-4-5...... Shreveport
16-17-18-19-19 .... Tulsa
22-23-24-25-26 Jackson

## El Paso

**APRIL**

11-12-13-14-15 ...... S.A.
27-28-29-30 ...... Midland

**MAY**

1 ....................... Midland
2-3-4-5-6 ........... Wichita
19-20-21-22-23 ....... Ark.
24-25-26-27-28 .... Tulsa

**JUNE**

5-6-7-8-9-10 ...... Wichita
15-16-17-18-19-20 . Mid.
27-28-29-30 ............ S.A.

**JULY**

1-2 ............ San Antonio
11-12-13-14-15 Jackson
16-17-18-19-20. Shreve.

**AUGUST**

1-2-3-4-5 ........... Wichita
6-7-8-9-10 ......... Midland
22-23-24-25-26 ...... S.A.

## Jackson

**APRIL**

16-17-18-19-20 ....... Ark.
27-28-29-30. Shreveport

**MAY**

1 ................. Shreveport
2-3-4-5-6 .............. Tulsa
19-20-21-22-23 ...... S.A.
24-25-26-27-28 . Wichita

**JUNE**

15-16-17-18-19-20.. Ark.
21-22-23-24-25-26. Shreve.

**JULY**

3-4-5-6-7-8 ............Tulsa
21-22-23-24-25. El Paso
27-28-29-30-31. Midland

**AUGUST**

6-7-8-9-10.... Shreveport
11-12-13-14-15 ....... Ark.
27-28-29-30-31 .... Tulsa

## Midland

**APRIL**

16-17-18-19-20. El Paso
21-22-23-24-25 . Wichita

**MAY**

2-3-4-5-6.... San Antonio
19-20-21-22-23 .... Tulsa
24-25-26-27-28....... Ark.

**JUNE**

5-6-7-8-9-10 ........... S.A.
21-22-23-24-25-26 . E.P.
27-28-29-30....... Wichita

**JULY**

1-2 ..................... Wichita
11-12-13-14-15. Shreve.
16-17-18-19-20 Jackson

**AUGUST**

1-2-3-4-5.... San Antonio
11-12-13-14-15 . Wichita
16-17-18-19-20. El Paso

## San Antonio

**APRIL**

6-7-8-9-10......... Midland
21-22-23-24-25. El Paso
27-28-29-30....... Wichita

**MAY**

1 ........................ Wichita
8-9-10-11-12.... Jackson
13-14-15-16-17. Shreve.
30-31 ................ El Paso

**JUNE**

1-2-3-4 ............. El Paso
21-22-23-24-25-26. Wich.

**JULY**

3-4-5-6-7-8........ Midland
21-22-23-24-25....... Ark.
27-28-29-30-31 .... Tulsa

**AUGUST**

6-7-8-9-10.......... Wichita
11-12-13-14-15. El Paso
27-28-29-30-31. Midland

## Shreveport

**APRIL**

11-12-13-14-15 Jackson
16-17-18-19-20 .... Tulsa

**MAY**

2-3-4-5-6 ........ Arkansas
19-20-21-22-23 . Wichita
24-25-26-27-28 ...... S.A.

**JUNE**

5-6-7-8-9-10..... Jackson
15-16-17-18-19-20 Tulsa

**JULY**

3-4-5-6-7-8..... Arkansas
21-22-23-24-25. Midland
26-27-28-29-30. El Paso

**AUGUST**

11-12-13-14-15 .... Tulsa
16-17-18-19-20 Jackson
27-28-29-30-31....... Ark.

## Tulsa

**APRIL**

6-7-8-9-10.... Shreveport
21-22-23-24-25 Jackson
27-29-29-30 ... Arkansas

**MAY**

1 ..................... Arkansas
8-9-10-11-12..... Midland
13-14-15-16-17. El Paso
30-31 ................ Jackson

**JUNE**

1-2-3-4 ............. Jackson
21-22-23-24-25-26.. Ark.
27-28-29-30. Shreveport

**JULY**

1-2 .............. Shreveport
12-13-14-15-15 . Wichita
16-17-18-19-20 ...... S.A.

**AUGUST**

1-2-3-4-5.......... Jackson
6-7-8-9-10 ...... Arkansas
22-23-24-25-26. Shreve.

## Wichita

**APRIL**

6-7-8-9-10......... El Paso
11-12-13-14-15. Midland
16-17-18-19-20 ...... S.A.

**MAY**

8-9-10-11-12 Shreveport
13-14-15-16-17 Jackson
30-31 ................ Midland

**JUNE**

1-2-3-4.............. Midland
15-16-17-18-19-20 . S.A.

**JULY**

3-4-5-6-7-8........ El Paso
21-22-23-24-25 .... Tulsa
27-28-29-30-31 ....... Ark.

**AUGUST**

16-17-18-19-20 ...... S.A.
22-23-24-25-26. Midland
27-28-29-30-31 . El Paso

# CLASS A
## California League



### Bakersfield

**APRIL**
6-7 .................. Modesto
8-9-10............. San Jose
17-18-19.. Lake Elsinore
21-22-23........ San Bern.

**MAY**
4 ...................... Modesto
5-6-7........... High Desert
8-9-10-11 ........ Stockton
15-16-17-18..... Modesto
19-20-21 R. Cucamonga
30-31 .................. Visalia

**JUNE**
1 ......................... Visalia
2-3-4.............. San Jose
9-10-11........... Riverside
21-22.............. Stockton
23-24-25-26........ Visalia

**JULY**
1-2-3.............. San Jose
14-15-16.. Lake Elsinore
18-19-20.......... Modesto
25-26-27........ San Bern.
28-29-30..... High Desert
31 .................. San Jose

**AUGUST**
8-9-10.... R. Cucamonga
11-12-13......... Riverside
21-22-23-24 .... Stockton

**SEPTEMBER**
1-2-3 .................. Visalia

### High Desert

**APRIL**
14-15-16-17 ... Riverside
18-19-20......... San Jose
28-29-30........ San Bern.

**MAY**
1-2-3............ Bakersfield
12-13-14.. Lake Elsinore
19-20-21.......... Stockton
23-24 ................. Visalia

**JUNE**
2-3-4................ Modesto
5-6-7-8 .. R. Cucamonga
12-13-14-15 .. San Bern.
16-17-18......... Riverside
27-28-29 R. Cucamonga
30 ....................... Visalia

**JULY**
1-2-3 .................. Visalia
7-8-9-10.... Lake Elsinore
11-12-13...... Bakersfield
21-22-23......... San Jose
24-25-26 R. Cucamonga

**AUGUST**
8-9-10............. Stockton
11-12-13.. Lake Elsinore
15-16-17........ San Bern.
21-22-23......... Riverside

**SEPTEMBER**
1-2-3............... Modesto

### Lake Elsinore

**APRIL**
6-7.................. Stockton
8-9-10......... High Desert
11-12-13........ San Bern.
21-22-23 R. Cucamonga
28-29-30...... Bakersfield

**MAY**
1-2-3............... Modesto
15-16-17-18 ........... H.D.
19-20-21......... Riverside
25 ................. San Bern.
26-27-28-29 ... San Jose

**JUNE**
2-3-4...... R. Cucamonga
6-7-8 .................. Visalia
21-22-23..... High Desert
24-25............. San Jose
27 ................. San Bern.
30 ................. San Bern.

**JULY**
1-2..................San Bern.
11-12-13........ Riverside
17-18-19-20 .... R. Cuca.
28-29-30-31 .... Stockton

**AUGUST**
1-2-3............... Modesto
9-10.............. San Bern.
15-16-17...... Bakersfield
24-25-26-27 ... Riverside
29-30-31 ............ Visalia

### Modesto

**APRIL**
11-12-13...... Bakersfield
14-15-16.. Lake Elsinore
17 ...................... Visalia
21-22-23..... High Desert
24-25-26 ............ Visalia

**MAY**
5-6-7...... R. Cucamonga
9-10-11.......... San Bern.
22-23-24...... Bakersfield
26-27-28-29 ........ Stock.

**JUNE**
5-6-7-8........... Riverside
9-10-11........... Stockton
16-17-18......... San Jose
21-22 ................. Visalia
27-28-29-30 ...... Bakers.

**JULY**
1-2-3............... Stockton
10-11-12-13 ... San Jose
14-15-16..... High Desert
24-25............. Riverside
28-29-30........ San Bern.

**AUGUST**
7-8-9-10............ Visalia
18-19-20......... San Jose
21-22-23.. Lake Elsinore
25-26-27 R. Cucamonga

### R. Cucamonga

**APRIL**
6-7................ San Bern.
8-9-10............. Stockton
11-12-13..... High Desert
25-26-27...... Bakersfield
28-29-30.......... Modesto

**MAY**
1 ................... San Bern.
9-10-11.... Lake Elsinore
12-13-14-15 ... Riverside
23-24-25......... San Jose
26-27-28-29 .. San Bern.
30-31 ....... Lake Elsinore

**JUNE**
1 ............. Lake Elsinore
9-10-11 .............. Visalia
21-22-23......... San Jose
24-25-26........ San Bern.
30 ................... Riverside

**JULY**
1-2-3.............. Riverside
11-12-13............ Visalia
14-15-16.......... Stockton
21-22-23...... Bakersfield
31 .............. High Desert

**AUGUST**
1-2-3.......... High Desert
4-5-6-7..... Lake Elsinore
15-16.............. Riverside
18-19-20...... High Desert
29-30-31 .......... Modesto

### Riverside

**APRIL**
6-7............. High Desert
8-9-10........... San Bern.
11-12-13......... Stockton
21-22-23......... San Jose
24-25-26.. Lake Elsinore

**MAY**
5-6-7 .................. Visalia
8-9-10......... High Desert
22-23-24......... Lake Els.
26 .............. High Desert
27-28-29...... Bakersfield
30-31 .............. Modesto

**JUNE**
1 ...................... Modesto
12-13-14-15 .... R. Cuca.
21-22-23........ San Bern.
24-25-26..... High Desert

**JULY**
4-5-6........ Lake Elsinore
14-15-16 ............ Visalia
18-19-20......... San Jose
27 .............. High Desert
28-29-30.......... R. Cuca.

**AUGUST**
1-2-3.............. Stockton
4-5-6................ Modesto
14 ........... Lake Elsinore
18-19-20...... Bakersfield
28-29-30-31 .. San Bern.

**SEPTEMBER**
1-2-3...... R. Cucamonga

### San Bernardino

**APRIL**
14-15-16 R. Cucamonga
18-19-20......... Riverside
24-25-26......... San Jose

**MAY**
2-3-4 .................. Visalia
5-6-7-8..... Lake Elsinore
16-17-18......... Riverside
19-20-21.......... Modesto
22-23-24.......... Stockton

**JUNE**
6-7-8........... Bakersfield
9-10-11....... High Desert
16-17-18 R. Cucamonga
28-29....... Lake Elsinore

**JULY**
3 ............. Lake Elsinore
4-5-6........... High Desert
7-8-9-10 ......... Riverside
17-18-19.......... Stockton
21-22-23.......... Modesto

**AUGUST**
1-2-3.............. San Jose
4-5-6-7 ....... High Desert
11-12-13-14 .... R. Cuca.
18-19-20 ............ Visalia
25-26-27...... Bakersfield

**SEPTEMBER**
1-2-3........ Lake Elsinore

### San Jose

**APRIL**
11-12-13 ............ Visalia
14-15-16...... Bakersfield
27-28-29-30 .... Stockton

**MAY**
1-2-3.............. Riverside
12-13-14........ San Bern.

16-17-18 R. Cucamonga
19-20-21 ............ Visalia
30-31 .......... High Desert

**JUNE**

1 ................ High Desert
6-7-8 ............... Stockton
9-10-11-12 ............. L.E.
13-14-15.......... Modesto
28-29-30.......... Stockton

**JULY**

4-5-6 ............... Modesto
7-8-9 ........... Bakersfield
14-15-16........ San Bern.
24-25 ....... Lake Elsinore
26 .................. Modesto
27-28-29-30........ Visalia

**AUGUST**

8-9-10............ Riverside
11-12-13.......... Modesto
22-23-24 R. Cucamonga
25-26-27..... High Desert
28-29-30-31. Bakersfield

### Stockton

**APRIL**

14-15-16 ............ Visalia
18-19-20.......... Modesto
24-25-26..... High Desert

**MAY**

2-3-4...... R. Cucamonga
5-6-7.............. San Jose
12-13-14.......... Modesto
15-16-17-18........ Visalia
30-31 ........... San Bern.

**JUNE**

1 ................. San Bern.
2-3-4............... Riverside
13-14-15.. Lake Elsinore
16-17-17-18 .......Bakers.
23-24-25-26..... Modesto

**JULY**

4-5-6........... Bakersfield
7-8-9...... R. Cucamonga
11-12-13....... San Bern.
21-22-23......... Riverside
24-25-26 ............ Visalia

**AUGUST**

4-5-6........... Bakersfield
14-15-16-17 ... San Jose
18-19-20.. Lake Elsinore
28-29-30..... High Desert

**SEPTEMBER**

1-2-3.............. San Jose

### Visalia

**APRIL**

6-7.................. San Jose
8-9-10............. Modesto
18-19-20 R. Cucamonga
21-22-23......... Stockton
27 .............. High Desert
28-29-30........ Riverside

**MAY**

8-9-10-11 ....... San Jose
12-13-14...... Bakersfield
26 ............... Bakersfield
27-28-29..... High Desert

**JUNE**

2-3-4............. San Bern.
5 ..................... San Jose
13-14-15...... Bakersfield
16-17-18......... Lake Els.
27-28-29......... Riverside

**JULY**

4-5-6...... R. Cucamonga
7-8-9............... Modesto
17-18.......... High Desert
20 ................... Stockton
21-22-23......... Lake Els.

**AUGUST**

1-2-3........... Bakersfield
4-5-6.............. San Jose
11-12-13.......... Stockton
14-15-16-17..... Modesto
22-23-24........ San Bern.
25-26-27.......... Stockton

# Carolina League

### Durham

**APRIL**

6-7 ................ Lynchburg
11-12-13...... Wilmington
14-15-16......... Frederick
24-25-26-27 ........ Salem
28-29-30. Prince William

**MAY**

9-10-11 ......... Lynchburg
19-20-21............ Kinston
22-23 .... Winston-Salem
29-30-31...... Wilmington

**JUNE**

1-2-3-4........... Frederick
13-14-15 ............ Salem
16-17-18. Prince William
25-26 .... Winston-Salem
29-30 ............ Lynchburg

**JULY**

7-8-9................. Kinston
12-13-14.............. W.-S.
21-22-23-24. Wilmington
25-26-27......... Frederick

**AUGUST**

4-5-6 .................. Salem
7-8-9-10.. Prince William
18-19-20....... Lynchburg
21-22-23-24 ...... Kinston
31.......... Winston-Salem

**SEPTEMBER**

1-2 ........ Winston-Salem

### Frederick

**APRIL**

6-7-8-9 .............. Kinston
11-12-13.............. W.-S.
21-22-23........... Durham
24-25-26-27.. Lynchburg

**MAY**

5-6-7........... Wilmington
12-13-14. Prince William
15-16-17-18 ........ Salem
26-27-28............ Kinston
29-30-31.............. W.-S.

**JUNE**

9-10-11 ............ Durham
13-14-15....... Lynchburg
23-24-25-26. Wilmington

**JULY**

1-2-3....... Prince William
4-5-6 .................. Salem
10 ........... Prince William
21-22-23-24 ......... W.-S.
31 ..................... Durham

**AUGUST**

1-2-3................ Durham
4-5-6............. Lynchburg
15-16-17...... Wilmington
18-19-20............ Kinston
25-26-27 ............. Salem
28-29-30. Prince William

### Kinston

**APRIL**

11-12-13 ............. Salem
14-15-16....... Lynchburg
24-25-26-27. Wilmington
28-29-30................ W.-S.

**MAY**

9-10-11........... Frederick
12-13-14............ Durham
22-23-24-25 . Pr. William
29-30-31 ............ Salem

**JUNE**

1-2-3-4......... Lynchburg
13-14-15...... Wilmington
16-17-18................ W.-S.
27-28-29-30 ... Frederick

**JULY**

1-1-2-3............. Durham
12-13-14. Prince William
15-16-17.......... Frederick
21-22-23-24 ........ Salem
25-26-27....... Lynchburg

**AUGUST**

4-5-6............ Wilmington
7-8-9-10 Winston-Salem
15-16-17. Prince William
28-29-30........... Durham

### Lynchburg

**APRIL**

8-9 .................. Durham
17-18-19-20 . Pr. William
21-22-23............ Kinston

**MAY**

1-2-3-4........... Frederick
5-6-7 .................. Salem
15-16-17-18. Wilmington
19-20-21.............. W.-S.
24-25.................. Salem
26-27-28........... Durham

**JUNE**

5-6-7....... Prince William
9-10-11............. Kinston
20-21-22......... Frederick
23-24.................. Salem
27-28 ............... Durham

**JULY**

4-5-6........... Wilmington
7-8-9-10 Winston-Salem
15-16-17........... Durham
28-29-30. Prince William
31 ...................... Kinston

**AUGUST**

1-2-3................. Kinston
11-12-13......... Frederick
15-16-17 ............. Salem
25-26-27...... Wilmington
28-29-30............... W.-S.

### Prince William

**APRIL**

6-7-8-9 .................Salem
11-12-13........Lynchburg
21-22-23.......Wilmington
24-25-26-27 ..........W.-S.

**MAY**

5-6-7..................Kinston
15-16-17-18...... Durham
19-20-21......... Frederick
26-27-28 ............ Salem
29-30-31 ........ Lynchburg

**JUNE**

9-10-11........ Wilmington
13-14-15................ W.-S.
23-24-25-26 ...... Kinston

**JULY**

4-5-6................ Durham
7-8-9............... Frederick
15-16-17 ............. Salem
21-22-23-24.. Lynchburg

31 ................ Wilmington

**AUGUST**

1-2-3............ Wilmington
11-12-13.............. W.-S.
21-22-23-24 ... Frederick
25-26-27........... Durham
31 ..................... Kinston

**SEPTEMBER**

1-2..................... Kinston

### Salem

**APRIL**

14-15-16. Prince William
17-18-19-20 ...... Kinston
28-29-30......... Frederick

**MAY**

1-2-3-4............. Durham
9-10-11 . Winston-Salem
12-13-14...... Wilmington
22-23 ........... Lynchburg

**JUNE**

1-2-3-4.... Prince William
6-7-8................. Kinston
16-17-18......... Frederick
20-21-22........... Durham
25-26 ............ Lynchburg
27-28-29-30 ......... W.-S.

**JULY**

12-13-14....... Lynchburg
25-26-27. Prince William
28-29-30............ Kinston

**AUGUST**

7-8-9-10.......... Frederick
11-12-13........... Durham
18-19-20.............. W.-S.
21-22-23-24. Wilmington
28-29-30...... Wilmington
31 ................ Lynchburg

**SEPTEMBER**

1-2 ............... Lynchburg

### Wilmington

**APRIL**

14-15-16.............. W.-S.
17-18-19-20...... Durham
28-29-30....... Lynchburg

**MAY**

1-2-3-4 ............. Kinston
9-10-11 ... Prince William
19-20-21 ............ Salem
22-23-24-25 ... Frederick

**JUNE**

1-2-3-4 .. Winston-Salem
6-7-8................ Durham
16-17-18....... Lynchburg
20-21-22........... Kinston
27-28-29-30 . Pr. William

**JULY**

1-2-3 .................. Salem
7-8-9-10 .............. Salem
12-13-14......... Frederick
25-26-27.............. W.-S.
28-29-30........... Durham

**AUGUST**

7-8-9-10........ Lynchburg
11-12-13........... Kinston
18-19-20. Prince William
31 .................. Frederick

**SEPTEMBER**

1-2................. Frederick

### Winston-Salem

**APRIL**

6-7-8-9......... Wilmington
17-18-19-20 ... Frederick
21-22-23 ............ Salem

**MAY**

1-2-3-4.... Prince William
5-6-7................. Durham
12-13-14....... Lynchburg
15-16-17-18 ...... Kinston
24-25 ............... Durham
26-27-28...... Wilmington

**JUNE**

6-7-8.............. Frederick
9-10-11 .............. Salem
20-21-22. Prince William
23-24 ............... Durham

**JULY**

1-2-3............ Lynchburg
4-5-6................. Kinston
15-16-17...... Wilmington
28-29-30......... Frederick
31 ........................ Salem

**AUGUST**

1-2-3 ..................... Salem
4-5-6....... Prince William
15-16-17........... Durham
21-22-23-24.. Lynchburg
25-26-27............ Kinston

# Florida State League

### Brevard County

**APRIL**

6 ................. Vero Beach
8 ................. Vero Beach
10-11-12-13..... Dunedin
23-24-25-26 ....... Tampa
27 .................... St. Lucie

**MAY**

3-4 .... West Palm Beach
5-6-7-8......... Kissimmee
10-11 ............... Daytona
16-17 ............... Daytona
18 .................... St. Lucie
23-24-25-26.... Charlotte
30 ............... Vero Beach

**JUNE**

4-5-6-7......... Clearwater
8-9-10-11 ..... Fort Myers
15-16............... St. Lucie
17 ............... Vero Beach
26-27-28-29.... Sarasota
30..................... Daytona

**JULY**

1-2 .................. Daytona
4-5-6-7.. W. Palm Beach
14-15 ........... Kissimmee
25-26-27-28..... St. Pete.
29-30-31 ......... Lakeland

**AUGUST**

1 ..................... Lakeland
3 ...................... St. Lucie
5 ...................... St. Lucie
10-11-12..... Vero Beach
24 .............. Vero Beach
25 .................... St. Lucie
27-28 ........... Kissimmee
30..................... Daytona

**SEPTEMBER**

2 ...................... St. Lucie

### Charlotte

**APRIL**

7.................. Fort Myers
9................... Fort Myers
10-11 West Palm Beach
14-15...... St. Petersburg
16-17.................. Tampa
25-26 ............... Daytona
27-28 ........... Clearwater
30 .......... St. Petersburg

**MAY**

2.................... Fort Myers
4.................... Fort Myers
5 ...................... Lakeland
10-11 ............... Dunedin
12-13-14-15 Vero Beach
19-20 ............. Sarasota
21-22 ............. Lakeland
31 .................. Lakeland

**JUNE**

2-3 .................. Dunedin
8-9-10-11..... Kissimmee
13-14 ........... Clearwater
26-27-28-29 ....... Tampa

**JULY**

2-3 ............... Clearwater
14-15 ............... Dunedin
16-17-18-19 ........... B.C.
23-24 .............. Daytona
29-30 ............. Sarasota
31................. Fort Myers

**AUGUST**

1-2-3............ Fort Myers
6............. St. Petersburg
8-9.......... St. Petersburg
12-13 ............. Lakeland
17-18-19-20 .... St. Lucie
23-24 West Palm Beach
30-31 ............. Lakeland

**SEPTEMBER**

1-2 .................. Sarasota

### Clearwater

**APRIL**

6........................ Dunedin
8-9 .................... Dunedin
19 ........... St. Petersburg
21-22 .............. Charlotte
23-24-25-26.... Lakeland

**MAY**

1-2.......... St. Petersburg
4............. St. Petersburg
5-6-7-8 ............ St. Lucie
12-13 ............. Sarasota
14-15................. Tampa
17-18-19-20 ....... W.P.B.
21-22-23-24 Vero Beach
27........................ Tampa
30........................ Tampa

**JUNE**

8....................... Sarasota
9........................ Dunedin
11 ..................... Sarasota
17-18............ Fort Myers
19-20-21-22 ........... B.C.
26-27...... St. Petersburg
30 ................... Charlotte

**JULY**

1 ...................... Charlotte
8-9 ................... Sarasota
20-21-22-23. Kissimmee
25-26-27 .......... Dunedin
29-30-31 .......... Daytona

**AUGUST**

1........................ Daytona
8-9-10-11 ..... Fort Myers
13...................... Dunedin
19-20 .............. Lakeland
21-22.................... Tampa
23-24...... St. Petersburg
27-28 .............. Charlotte

### Daytona

**APRIL**

6 ................. Kissimmee
10-11-12-13 . Clearwater
14-15.............. St. Lucie
21-22.... Brevard County
23-24 ............. Charlotte

**MAY**

1-2-3-4............ Dunedin
5-6-7-8.. W. Palm Beach
14-15 ........... Kissimmee
27-28-29-30.... Lakeland

**JUNE**

4-5-6-7 ... St. Petersburg
13-14.... Brevard County
15-16 ......... Vero Beach

18-19-20.......... St. Lucie
26-27 ........... Kissimmee
29 ................ Kissimmee

**JULY**

3........... Brevard County
4-5-6-7........ Vero Beach
8-9........ Brevard County
21-22 ............. Charlotte
25-26-27-28 ....... Tampa

**AUGUST**

6-7-8-9.. W. Palm Beach
10-11-12.......... St. Lucie
21-22-23-24 . Fort Myers
25-26-27-28.... Sarasota
31 ......... Brevard County

**SEPTEMBER**

1-2 .............. Kissimmee

## Dunedin

**APRIL**

7.................. Clearwater
17-18 .............. Sarasota
20 ................... Lakeland
22........... St. Petersburg
23-24-25-26 Vero Beach
27........... St. Petersburg
29-30 ........... Clearwater

**MAY**

7-8 .................. Charlotte
17-18 .............. Sarasota
19-20............ Fort Myers
21-22-23-24 ....... W.P.B.
29-30...... St. Petersburg
31 ........................ Tampa

**JUNE**

1......................... Tampa
4-5-6-7 ............ St. Lucie
10................. Clearwater
14-15-16......... Lakeland
17-18-19-20 ....... Tampa

**JULY**

4.......................... Tampa
6-7 .................. Charlotte
8............. St. Petersburg
10........... St. Petersburg
18-19 ............. Sarasota
28................. Clearwater
29-30............ Fort Myers

**AUGUST**

2-3-4-5............. Daytona
6-7-8-9......... Kissimmee
12................. Clearwater
17-18-19-20 ........... B.C.
21-22 ............. Lakeland
24........................ Tampa
25-26 ............. Charlotte
30-31............ Fort Myers

**SEPTEMBER**

1-2 ............... Clearwater

## Fort Myers

**APRIL**

6 ..................... Charlotte
8 ..................... Charlotte
14-15.................. Tampa
16-17...... St. Petersburg
19-20-21-22. Kissimmee

**MAY**

1 ..................... Charlotte
3 ..................... Charlotte
8-9-10-11.... Vero Beach
12-13-14-15..... Dunedin
21-22 .............. Sarasota
23-24-25-26..... Daytona
29.................... Sarasota
31................. Clearwater

**JUNE**

1-2-3 ............ Clearwater
4-5 ................... Lakeland
13.................... Sarasota
19-20-21-22.... Sarasota
28-29...... St. Petersburg
30......................... Tampa

**JULY**

1-2-3 ................. Tampa

4-5 .............. Clearwater
8-9-10............. Charlotte
12-13 ............... Dunedin
14-15 .............. Lakeland
20-21-22-23 ........... B.C.
25-26-27-28 .... St. Lucie

**AUGUST**

4-5.......... St. Petersburg
14-15 ............... Lakeland
25-26-27-28 ....... W.P.B.

**SEPTEMBER**

3 ...................... Charlotte

## Kissimmee

**APRIL**

7-8-9 ................ Daytona
10-11-12. St. Petersburg
14-15-16-17 . Clearwater
26.................... Sarasota
27-28-29-30 ....... Tampa

**MAY**

1-2........ Brevard County
12-13.... Brevard County
17-18.......... Vero Beach
21 .................... St. Lucie
24 .................... St. Lucie
25-26-27-28..... Dunedin

**JUNE**

2-3 .................. Daytona
5 ................ Vero Beach
7 ................ Vero Beach
15-16-17-18 ....... W.P.B.
19-20-21-22.... Charlotte
28.................... Daytona
30.................... Sarasota

**JULY**

1...................... Sarasota
3...................... Sarasota
5............. St. Petersburg
9 ................ Vero Beach
10.................... Daytona
12-13.... Brevard County
16-17-18-19 . Fort Myers
25-26-27-28.... Lakeland
31 .................... St. Lucie

**AUGUST**

1 ...................... St. Lucie
4-5 .... West Palm Beach
10-11 West Palm Beach
21-22.... Brevard County
23-24............... St. Lucie
26 ............... Vero Beach
30-31 .......... Vero Beach

**SEPTEMBER**

3....................... Daytona

## Lakeland

**APRIL**

7.......................... Tampa
9.......................... Tampa
10-11-12-13 . Fort Myers
14-15-16-17 ........... B.C.
19.................... Dunedin
21-22 .............. Sarasota
27-28-29-30 Vero Beach

**MAY**

1...................... Sarasota
3-4 ............... Kissimmee
6 .......................Charlotte
19-20 ............ Kissimmee
24........... St. Petersburg
25-26 ........... Clearwater

**JUNE**

1 .................... Charlotte
2-3....................... Tampa
6-7 ................. Charlotte
9...................... Sarasota
10-11...... St. Petersburg
13..................... Dunedin
18........... St. Petersburg
21-22 ............... Dunedin
26-27............ Fort Myers
28-29 ........... Clearwater

**JULY**

4-5-6-7 ........... St. Lucie

12-13 ............. Charlotte
16-17-18-19..... Daytona
21-22-23-24 ....... W.P.B.

**AUGUST**

2-3......................... Tampa
6-7 ............... Clearwater
8-9 .................. Sarasota
10-11 .............. Charlotte
23-24 .............. Sarasota
26........... St. Petersburg
27-28 ............... Dunedin

**SEPTEMBER**

1 ............ St. Petersburg

## St. Lucie

**APRIL**

7 ....... West Palm Beach
9 ....... West Palm Beach
10-11-12-13.... Sarasota
17-18 ............... Daytona
19-20.... Brevard County
21 ............... Vero Beach
23-24-25-26 . Fort Myers
28-29.... Brevard County

**MAY**

9-10 ............ Kissimmee
12-13 ............... Daytona
14-15-16-17.... Lakeland
20 ............... Vero Beach
22-23 ........... Kissimmee
25 ..... West Palm Beach
27-28-29-30.... Charlotte

**JUNE**

10-11 .......... Vero Beach
13 ..... West Palm Beach
17..................... Daytona
26-27-28-29..... Dunedin
30........... St. Petersburg

**JULY**

1-2-3....... St. Petersburg
8-9-10 ................ W.P.B.
12-13-14-15. Clearwater
16-17-18-19 ....... Tampa
29-30 ........... Kissimmee

**AUGUST**

2........... Brevard County
4........... Brevard County
7-8 .............. Vero Beach
14-15-16 .......... Daytona
21-22 .......... Vero Beach
26......... Brevard County
31 ..... West Palm Beach

**SEPTEMBER**

1 ........... Brevard County

## St. Petersburg

**APRIL**

8-9 .................. Sarasota
13 ................ Kissimmee
20................. Clearwater
21..................... Dunedin
23-24-25-26 ....... W.P.B.
28..................... Dunedin
29 .................. Charlotte

**MAY**

3................... Clearwater
5-6............... Fort Myers
9.......................... Tampa
10-11 .......... Clearwater
12-13.................... Tampa
17-18........... Fort Myers
19-20-21-22 ........... B.C.
31 .................... St. Lucie

**JUNE**

1-2-3................ St. Lucie
8 ...................... Lakeland
9.......................... Tampa
15-16 ............. Charlotte
17 .................... Lakeland
19-20 ............... Lakeland
22......................... Tampa

**JULY**

4 ................. Kissimmee
6-7 ............... Kissimmee
9....................... Dunedin

12-13-14-15..... Daytona
16-17-18-19 Vero Beach
20........................ Tampa
24........................ Tampa

**AUGUST**

2-3 ................. Sarasota
7 ..................... Charlotte
10-11 ............... Dunedin
12-13........... Fort Myers
15-16 .............. Charlotte
17-18 .......... Clearwater
21-22 .............. Sarasota
25 .................... Lakeland
28........................ Tampa
30-31 .......... Clearwater

**SEPTEMBER**

2 ...................... Lakeland
3........................ Dunedin

## Sarasota

**APRIL**

6-7.......... St. Petersburg
14-15 .............. Dunedin
19-20 ............. Charlotte
23-24-25...... Kissimmee
27-28-29-30..... Daytona

**MAY**

2 ...................... Lakeland
7-8 .................. Lakeland
15-16...... St. Petersburg
23 .................... Lakeland
24-25-26 ............ Tampa
27-28........... Fort Myers
30................ Fort Myers
31 ......... Brevard County

**JUNE**

1-2-3..... Brevard County
10........................ Tampa
14................ Fort Myers
15-16 .......... Clearwater
17-18 ............. Charlotte

**JULY**

2 ................. Kissimmee
4-5 .................. Charlotte
6-7............... Fort Myers
10................. Clearwater
12-13-14-15 Vero Beach
16-17 ............... Dunedin
21-22-23-24 .... St. Lucie
25-26-27-28 ....... W.P.B.
31..................... Dunedin

**AUGUST**

1......................... Dunedin
4-5 ................... Lakeland
6-7............... Fort Myers
10-11................. Tampa
15-16 .......... Clearwater
17-18 ............... Lakeland
19-20...... St. Petersburg

**SEPTEMBER**

3................... Clearwater

## Tampa

**APRIL**

6 ...................... Lakeland
8 ...................... Lakeland
19-20-21-22 ....... W.P.B.

**MAY**

1-2-3-4 ........... St. Lucie
5-6 .................... Dunedin
8............ St. Petersburg
10-11 .............. Sarasota
17-18 ............... Charlotte
19-20-21-22..... Daytona
23........... St. Petersburg
28-29 .......... Clearwater

**JUNE**

4-5 ................. Charlotte
6-7................ Fort Myers
8......................... Dunedin
11....................... Dunedin
13-14...... St. Petersburg
15-16............ Fort Myers
21 .......... St. Petersburg

**JULY**

5......................... Dunedin
6-7 ............... Clearwater
8-9-10 ............. Lakeland
21-22...... St. Petersburg
29-30-31 ..... Vero Beach

**AUGUST**

1 ................ Vero Beach
4-5 .................. Charlotte
6-7-8-9 . Brevard County
12-13 .............. Sarasota
15-16 ............... Dunedin
17-18-19-20. Kissimmee
23....................... Dunedin
25-26 .......... Clearwater
27 .......... St. Petersburg
30-31 ............. Sarasota

**SEPTEMBER**

1-2................ Fort Myers
3 ...................... Lakeland

## Vero Beach

**APRIL**

7.......... Brevard County
9.......... Brevard County
10-11-12-13 ....... Tampa
19-20 .............. Daytona
22 .................... St. Lucie

**MAY**

1-2 .... West Palm Beach
3-4-5-6 ........... Sarasota
19 ..................... St. Lucie
25-26-27-27..... St. Pete.
29 ......... Brevard County
31..................... Daytona

**JUNE**

1........................ Daytona
2-3 .... West Palm Beach
4 ................. Kissimmee
6 ................. Kissimmee

8-9................... St. Lucie
13-14 ........... Kissimmee
18......... Brevard County
21-22 .............. Daytona
26-27-28-29 ....... W.P.B.
30 .................. Lakeland

**JULY**

1-2-3.............. Lakeland
8 .................. Kissimmee
10......... Brevard County
20-21-22-23..... Dunedin
25-26-27-28.... Charlotte

**AUGUST**

2-3-4-5......... Clearwater
6......................... St. Lucie
9......................... St. Lucie
13......... Brevard County
15-16 ........... Kissimmee
17-18-19-20 . Fort Myers
23......... Brevard County
25 ................ Kissimmee
27-28............... St. Lucie

**SEPTEMBER**

3.......... Brevard County

## W. Palm Beach

**APRIL**

6....................... St. Lucie
8....................... St. Lucie
12-13 ............. Charlotte
14-15-16-17 Vero Beach
27-28-29-30 . Fort Myers

**MAY**

10-11-12-13.... Lakeland
14-15.... Brevard County
26 .................... St. Lucie
27-28.... Brevard County
29-30-31 ...... Kissimmee

**JUNE**

1 ................. Kissimmee
4-5-6-7............ Sarasota
8-9-10-11.... Day. Beach
14 .................... St. Lucie
19-20.......... Vero Beach
21-22............... St. Lucie
30..................... Dunedin

**JULY**

1-2-3 ............... Dunedin
12-13-14-15 ....... Tampa
16-17-18-19 . Clearwater
29-30-31. St. Petersburg

**AUGUST**

1 ............ St. Petersburg
2-3 ............... Kissimmee
12-13 ............ Kissimmee
14-15.... Brevard County
17-18-19-20..... Daytona
21-22 ............. Charlotte
29-30............... St. Lucie

**SEPTEMBER**

1-2 ............. Vero Beach

# Midwest League

## Battle Creek

**APRIL**

9-10-11....... Fort Wayne
15-16......... W. Michigan
20-21-22-23 ....... Clinton
24-25-26-27 .. Quad City

**MAY**

6-7............ W. Michigan
9-10-11-12 Kane County
13-14-15-16 ......... Beloit
18 ............. W. Michigan
29-30.......... South Bend

**JUNE**

2 ................ Fort Wayne
5-6-7.......... South Bend
9-10-11-12 .... Burlington
18 ............... Fort Wayne
30 ............. W. Michigan

**JULY**

1 ............... W. Michigan
3-4-5-6 ......... Springfield
7-8-9-10 ............. Peoria
20-21 .......... Fort Wayne
24 ............... W. Michigan
27-28-29-30 .. Wisconsin
31 ................... Rockford

**AUGUST**

1-2-3 .............. Rockford
4-5............... South Bend
14-15......... W. Michigan
23-24......... South Bend
25-26-27-28... C. Rapids
29-30 .......... Fort Wayne
31 ............. South Bend

**SEPTEMBER**

2 ................ Fort Wayne

## Beloit

**APRIL**

7-8........... Kane County
11-12-13-14 .. Quad City
20 ............ Kane County
22-23 ............. Rockford
26-27-28 ....... Wisconsin
29.................... Rockford

**MAY**

3-4........... Kane County
19-20-21-22 .. Ft. Wayne
23-24-25-26 .... W. Mich.
27-28-29-30... C. Rapids

**JUNE**

1-2 ................ Wisconsin
5-6-7-7 ................ Peoria
13..................... Rockford
18..................... Rockford

22-23-24-25 ....... Clinton
27-28 ........ Kane County

**JULY**

3-4 .................. Rockford
7-8-9-10 ........ Burlington
12-13-14-15 South Bend
16-17-18-19 ... Battle Cr.

**AUGUST**

4-5 ............... Wisconsin
8-9-10-11 ..... Springfield
12-13 ........ Kane County
25-26-27 ....... Wisconsin
28-29-30 ......... Rockford
31 ............. Kane County

## Burlington

**APRIL**

7-8........... Cedar Rapids
11-12.................. Clinton
15-16-17-18 ......... Beloit
26-27....... Cedar Rapids
30 ................. Springfield

**MAY**

1 ................... Springfield
2-3-4-5........ South Bend
6-7................. Quad City
8-9 ...................... Peoria
15-16.................. Clinton
20 .................. Quad City
23-24 .................. Peoria

**JUNE**

1-2-3-4 ........... Rockford
13 ................. Springfield
14-15-16-17 .... W. Mich.
18 ................. Springfield
26-27-28-29 .. Ft. Wayne
30 .................. Quad City

**JULY**

3-4-5-6 .......... Wisconsin
14-15............. Quad City
20-21.............. Springfield
22-23....... Cedar Rapids
25........................ Peoria
28-29-30 ............ Clinton
31 ................. Springfield

**AUGUST**

1 ................... Springfield
4-5........... Cedar Rapids
8-9-10-11... Battle Creek
13-14-15 ............ Peoria
17-18-19-20... Kane Cty.

**SEPTEMBER**

1......................... Clinton

## Cedar Rapids

**APRIL**

9-10............... Burlington
11-12-13-14 .... Rockford
20-21............. Burlington
28-29-30......... Battle Cr.

**MAY**

1 ................ Battle Creek
2-3-4-5........ Fort Wayne
9.......................... Clinton
11-12 ................. Peoria
13-14.................. Clinton
16 .................. Quad City
17-18-19-20 ....... Spring.

**JUNE**

1 .................... Quad City
3-4 ...................... Peoria
9-10-11-12 Kane County
13 .................. Quad City
18 .................. Quad City
22-23-24-25 .... W. Mich.
30..................... Clinton

**JULY**

7-8-9-10 ........ Wisconsin
13 .................. Quad City
14-15-16-17 ........ Peoria
18-19............... Burlington
25-26.................. Clinton
31 .................. Quad City

**AUGUST**

1-2.................. Quad City
6-7................. Burlington
8-9-10-11.......... S. Bend
17-18-19-20 ......... Beloit
29-30-31....... Springfield

**SEPTEMBER**

1 .................. Springfield

## Clinton

**APRIL**

13-14............. Burlington
15-16-17-18 ........... K.C.
28-29-30..... South Bend

**MAY**

1 ................. South Bend
2-3-4-5....... W. Michigan
6-7-8....... Cedar Rapids
11-12............. Quad City
21-22............. Burlington
23-24.............. Quad City
27-28-29-30....... Spring.
31........................ Peoria

**JUNE**

1-2 ...................... Peoria
14-15-16-17 ......... Beloit
18......................... Peoria
26-27-28-29 ... Battle Cr.

**JULY**

1-2........... Cedar Rapids
12-13-14-15 ....... Spring.
18-19............. Quad City
20-21-22-23.... Rockford
27 ................. Burlington

**AUGUST**

4-5-6-7........ Fort Wayne
14-15............. Quad City
17-18-19-20.. Wisconsin
25-26-27-28........ Peoria
29-30-31 ....... Burlington

**SEPTEMBER**

2 ............. Cedar Rapids

## Fort Wayne

**APRIL**

7-8 ............. Battle Creek
13-14-15-16...... S. Bend
20-21-22-23 ........ Peoria
24-25-26-27 ....... Clinton

**MAY**

6 ................. South Bend
9-10-11-12...... Rockford
13-14-15-16 ........... K.C.
17 .............. Battle Creek
27 .......... West Michigan
29-30 ..... West Michigan

**JUNE**

1 ................ Battle Creek
5-6-7-8 .......... Burlington
9 ............ West Michigan
11 .......... West Michigan
13 .............. Battle Creek
30 ............... South Bend

**JULY**

1 ................. South Bend
3-4-5-6 .......... Quad City
7-8-9-10 ....... Springfield
22-23......... Battle Creek
25 ................ South Bend
27-28-29-30 ......... Beloit
31................... Wisconsin

**AUGUST**

1-2-3 ............. Wisconsin
11 .......... West Michigan
12-13......... Battle Creek
14-15.......... South Bend
20 .......... West Michigan
21-22-23-24.... C.Rapids
27-28 ..... West Michigan
31 .......... West Michigan

**SEPTEMBER**

1 ................ Battle Creek

## Kane County

**APRIL**

9-10.......................... Beloit
11-12-13-14........ Peoria
21 ......................... Beloit
22-23-24-25........... Burl.
28.................... Rockford

**MAY**

2 ........................... Beloit
5-6 .................... Rockford
17................. Wisconsin
19-20-21-22 .... W. Mich.
23-24-25-26...... S. Bend
27.................... Rockford
30.................... Rockford
31 ......................... Beloit

**JUNE**

1-2-3-4 ........ Springfield
7-8 ................ Wisconsin
13.................. Wisconsin
18.................. Wisconsin
22-23 ........... Wisconsin
29 ......................... Beloit
30.................... Rockford

**JULY**

1-2 .................. Rockford
3-4-5-6 .... Cedar Rapids
10.................... Rockford
12-13-14-15 ... Battle Cr.
16-17-18-19.. Ft. Wayne
20-21 ........... Wisconsin

**AUGUST**

4-5-6-7 .......... Quad City
8-9-10-11 ........... Clinton
14-15..................... Beloit
25..................... Rockford
30.................. Wisconsin

**SEPTEMBER**

1-2......................... Beloit

## Peoria

**APRIL**

7-8-9-10........ Wisconsin
15-16-17-18... C. Rapids
28-29-30 West Michigan

**MAY**

1 ........... West Michigan
3-4-5............. Quad City
13-14............. Burlington
16 ................. Springfield
17-18-19-20 ....... Clinton
21-22............ Springfield
25-26............. Burlington
30 .................. Quad City

**JUNE**

9-10-11-12...... Rockford
14-15-16-17 ... Battle Cr.
22-23-24-25.. Ft. Wayne
26-27-28-29...... S. Bend
30 ................ Springfield

**JULY**

1 .................. Springfield
12-13............ Burlington
18 ................. Springfield
20-21-22-23 ......... Beloit
24.................. Burlington
27-28-29-30... C. Rapids
31 ....................... Clinton

**AUGUST**

1-2-3 ................. Clinton
12................. Burlington
19-20............. Quad City
21-22-23-24 ........... K.C.
29-30............. Quad City

## Quad City

**APRIL**

15-16-17-18.......... Wisc.
28-29-30..... Fort Wayne

**MAY**

1 ................. Fort Wayne
2............................ Peoria
8-9............... Springfield
15 .......... Cedar Rapids
17-18-19 ................ Burl.
21-22....... Cedar Rapids
26-26.................. Clinton
27-28-29 ............. Peoria

**JUNE**

2............. Cedar Rapids

3-4........................ Clinton
5-6................ Springfield
9-10-11-12........ S. Bend
14-15-16-17... Kane Cty.
22-23-24-25 ... Battle Cr.
26-27-28-29 .... W. Mich.

**JULY**

1-2................ Burlington
12........... Cedar Rapids
16-17................ Clinton
20-21....... Cedar Rapids

**AUGUST**

3............. Cedar Rapids
8-9-10-11........ Rockford
12-13................. Clinton
17-18................... Peoria
21-22-23-24 ......... Beloit
25-26-27-28....... Spring.
31........................ Peoria

**SEPTEMBER**

1.......................... Peoria
2.................... Burlington

## Rockford

**APRIL**

7-8-9-9 .......... Quad City
15-16-17-18....... Spring.
24-25.................... Beloit
26-27 ........ Kane County
30-30.................... Beloit

**MAY**

7 .............. Kane County
18.......................... Beloit
19-20-21-22...... S. Bend
23-24-25-26 ... Battle Cr.
28-29........ Kane County
31................. Wisconsin

**JUNE**

5-6-7-8 .............. Clinton
14-15-16-17.. Wisconsin
22-23-24-25 .. Burlington
26......................... Beloit

**JULY**

5-6........................ Beloit
7-8-9......... Kane County
12-13-14-15.. Ft. Wayne
16-17-18-19 .... W. Mich.
24-25..................... Beloit

**AUGUST**

4-5-6-7............... Peoria
12-13-14-15... C. Rapids
21-22 ........... Wisconsin
26-27........ Kane County
31................. Wisconsin

**SEPTEMBER**

1-2 ............... Wisconsin

## South Bend

**APRIL**

9-10-11...... W. Michigan
12 ............... Fort Wayne
17-18......... Battle Creek
24-25-26-27........ Peoria

**MAY**

7 ................ Fort Wayne
9-10-11-12 ........... Beloit
13-14-15-16.......... Wisc.
18.................. Ft. Wayne
27-28......... Battle Creek

**JUNE**

3-4 .............. Fort Wayne
8 ................ Battle Creek
13 .......... West Michigan
14-15-16-17... C. Rapids
18 .......... West Michigan
22-23-24-25 . Springfield

**JULY**

2 ................ Fort Wayne
3-4-5-6 ............... Clinton
7-8-9-10 ........ Quad City
20-21-22.......... W. Mich.
26 ............... Fort Wayne
27-28-29-30.... Rockford
31 .................. Kane Cty.

**AUGUST**

1-2-3............. Kane Cty.
6-7 ............. Battle Creek
17-18-19..... Fort Wayne
20-21-22.... Battle Creek
25-26-27-28........... Burl.
29-30 ..... West Michigan

## Springfield

**APRIL**

7-8-9-10 ............ Clinton
11-12-13-14.......... Wisc.
20-21-22-23...... S. Bend
28-29............ Burlington

**MAY**

2-3-4-5....... Battle Creek
6-7 ...................... Peoria
11-12............ Burlington
13-14............. Quad City
15......................... Peoria
23-24-25-26... C. Rapids

**JUNE**

7-8................. Quad City
9-10-11-12 ........... Beloit
14-15-16-17.. Ft. Wayne
26-27-28-29... C. Rapids

**JULY**

2.......................... Peoria
16-17............ Burlington
19......................... Peoria
22-23-24-25... Kane Cty.
27-28-29-30 .. Quad City

**AUGUST**

2-3................ Burlington
4-5-6-7....... W. Michigan
17-18-19-20.... Rockford
21-22-23-24 ....... Clinton

**SEPTEMBER**

2........................ Peoria

## West Michigan

**APRIL**

7-8............. South Bend
12-13-14.... Battle Creek
17-18 .......... Fort Wayne
21-22-23-24 .. Quad City
24-25-26-27 . Springfield

**MAY**

9-10-11-12.... Wisconsin
13-14-15-16.... Rockford
17 .............. South Bend
28 ............... Fort Wayne

**JUNE**

1-2 ............. South Bend
3-4 ............ Battle Creek
5-6-7-8 .... Cedar Rapids
10 ............... Fort Wayne
12 ............... Fort Wayne

**JULY**

2 ............... Battle Creek
3-4-5-6 ................ Peoria
7-8-9-10 ............ Clinton
23 .............. South Bend
25 ............. Battle Creek
27-28-29-30... Kane Cty.
31 ......................... Beloit

**AUGUST**

1-2-3..................... Beloit
8-9-10......... Fort Wayne
12-13.......... South Bend
17-18-19.... Battle Creek
21-22-23-24 ........... Burl.
25-26 .......... Fort Wayne

**SEPTEMBER**

1-2 ............. South Bend

## Wisconsin

**APRIL**

20-21 .............. Rockford
22-23-24-25... C. Rapids
29-30........ Kane County

**MAY**

1 ............... Kane County
2-3-4 .............. Rockford
5-6-7..................... Beloit
19-20-21-22 ... Battle Cr.
23-24-25-26 .. Ft. Wayne
27-28-29-30 ........... Burl.

**JUNE**

3-4........................ Beloit
5-6........... Kane County
9-10-11-12 ......... Clinton
24-25-26................. K.C.
27-28-29 ......... Rockford
30 ........................ Beloit

**JULY**

1-2........................ Beloit
12-13-14-15 .... W. Mich.
16-17-18-19...... S. Bend
22-23-24-25 .. Quad City

**AUGUST**

6-7........................ Beloit
8-9-10-11 ............ Peoria
12-13-14-15....... Spring.
23-24 .............. Rockford
28-29....... Kane County

# South Atlantic League

## Albany

**APRIL**

6-7-8-9......... Char., WV
10-11-12-13........... Hag.
14-15............ Columbus
27-28-29-30 Fayetteville

**MAY**

1-2-3-4................ Macon
13-14............ Char., SC
17................. Columbus
18-19-20-21 ..... Augusta
22-23............. Columbia
24-25-26-27 .. Savannah

**JUNE**

6-7-8-9 .......... Piedmont
21-22............ Columbus
25-26............ Char., SC
29-30............ Savannah

**JULY**

1-2................ Savannah
9-10............... Columbus
12-13-14-15 ...... Hickory
16-17-18-19 ........ Gboro
27-28............ Columbus
29-30............... Augusta
31.................. Columbia

**AUGUST**

1-2-3 ............. Columbia
15-16-17-18.... Asheville
27-28................. Macon
29-30............ Char., SC
31..................... Augusta

**SEPTEMBER**

1....................... Augusta

## Asheville

**APRIL**

14-15.............. Piedmont
16-17.......... Hagerstown
18-19-20-21 ....... Albany
22-23-24-25 .. Columbus

**MAY**

5-6-7-8 ......... Savannah
15-16.......... Fayetteville
18-19................ Hickory
20-21-22-23.......... Hag.
28-29............... Hickory

**JUNE**
1-2-3-4.......... Char., SC
8-9.................... Hickory
10-11-12-13.. Char., WV
14-15-16-17 ........ Gboro
21-22............. Columbia
25-26 ........... Char., WV
29-30......... Greensboro
**JULY**
1-2............. Greensboro
3-4-5-6................ Macon
14-15............. Piedmont
25-26-27-28 Fayetteville
**AUGUST**
8-9................. Columbia
10-11-12-13 ..... Augusta
23-24............. Piedmont
29-30......... Hagerstown
31 ..................... Hickory
**SEPTEMBER**
1-2..................... Hickory

## Augusta
**APRIL**
10-11-12-13.... Asheville
14-15.................. Macon
22-23-24-25 ....Piedmont
29-30.............. Savannah
**MAY**
1-2-3-4.......... Char., WV
9-10-11-12 ......... Albany
16.................. Columbia
24-25........... Char., SC
**JUNE**
2-3-4-5 ....... Hagerstown
6..................... Columbia
8-9................ Savannah
10-11...............Columbia
14-15-16-17 .. Columbus
22 ....................... Macon
**JULY**
1-2-3-4 .......... Columbus
5-6................ Char., SC
7-8................. Savannah
12-13............. Savannah
16-17................... Macon
20-21-22-23 ... Columbia
24-25.................. Albany
27-28.................. Macon
**AUGUST**
2-3-4-5 ....... Greensboro
15-16-17-18 ...... Hickory
19-20-21-22 Fayetteville
25-26............ Char., SC

## Charleston, SC
**APRIL**
10-11-12-13 ........ Gboro
14-15-16-17 Fayetteville
**MAY**
5-6-7-8 ............... Albany
9-10-11-12.......... Macon
16-17............ Savannah
18-19............ Columbus
22-23............ Savannah
26-27............. Columbia
28-29-30-31 ......Augusta
**JUNE**
5-6-7 ............. Savannah
8-9................. Columbia
23-24................... Macon
29-30................. Hickory
**JULY**
1-2.................... Hickory
7-8................. Columbia
9-10.................. Augusta
20-21-22-23 ....... Albany
24-25-26-27 ... Piedmont
29-30................... Macon
**AUGUST**
2-3-4-5........... Asheville
15-16-17-18.. Char., WV
19-20-21-22 Hagerstown
23-24................ Augusta
31................... Columbus

**SEPTEMBER**
1-2-3 ............ Columbus

## Charleston, WV
**APRIL**
16-17................ Hickory
18-19-20-21... Char., SC
22-23-24-25 .. Savannah
**MAY**
5-6-7-8 ............ Piedmont
9-10-11-12 ..... Columbia
13-14........ Hagerstown
24-25-26-27 .... Asheville
28-29-30-30 ........ Gboro
**JUNE**
6-7............. Hagerstown
14-15-16-17 Fayetteville
21 .............. Hagerstown
27-28-29-30 ..... Augusta
**JULY**
7-8-9-10............. Macon
14-15.......... Fayetteville
16-17-18-19 .... Asheville
25-26-27-28 ...... Hickory
29-30............. Piedmont
**AUGUST**
2-3-4-5 ....... Hagerstown
6-7-8-9 ................ Albany
10-11-12-13 .. Columbus
27-28-29-30 ........ Gboro

## Columbia
**APRIL**
6-7-8-8.......... Char., SC
10-11-12-13 ... Piedmont
16-17............ Savannah
22-23-24-25 ........ Gboro
**MAY**
1-2-3-4.......... Char., SC
13-14 ............. Asheville
17.................... Augusta
20-21............ Columbus
28-29-30-31 ....... Albany
**JUNE**
1-2-3-4................ Macon
7...................... Augusta
12-13................ Augusta
17.................... Piedmont
23-24............ Savannah
25-26............ Columbus
27-28............ Savannah
30 ................... Piedmont
**JULY**
3-4-5-6 .............. Albany
12-13-14-15... Char., SC
16-17-18-19.......... Hag.
**AUGUST**
4-5................ Columbus
6-7 .................. Asheville
15-16-17-18 Fayetteville
19-20-21-22........ Macon
27-28................ Augusta
31 ................ Char., WV
**SEPTEMBER**
1-2-3 ............ Char., WV

## Columbus
**APRIL**
6-7-8-9 ....... Hagerstown
10-11-12-13.. Char., WV
16-17................... Albany
27-28-29-30 ... Columbia
**MAY**
1-2-3-4 ....... Fayetteville
13-14............... Augusta
16....................... Albany
22-23................ Augusta
**JUNE**
1-2-3-4 ......... Savannah
6-7-8-9................ Macon
10-11-12-13... Char., SC
23-24.................. Albany
27-28 ............Char., SC
29-30 ................. Macon

**JULY**
7-8...................... Albany
12-13-14-15 ........ Gboro
16-17-18-19 ...... Hickory
29-30............. Columbia
31 .................... Augusta
**AUGUST**
1 ........................ Augusta
2-3.................. Savannah
15-16-17-18 ... Piedmont
19-20-21-22 .... Asheville
25-26 ................. Macon
27-28............ Char., SC
29-30............. Columbia

## Fayetteville
**APRIL**
6-7-8 ................ Augusta
18-19-20-21 ... Columbia
22-23-24-25....... Macon
**MAY**
5-6............. Greensboro
9-10-11-12...... Asheville
20-21-22-23.. Char., WV
24-25............. Piedmont
26-27................ Hickory
**JUNE**
1-2................. Piedmont
6-7-8.......... Greensboro
10-11-12-13.......... Hag.
23-24............. Piedmont
25-26............... Hickory
**JULY**
1-2 ............... Char., WV
5-6................. Piedmont
7-8-9-10 .......... Asheville
12-13 ........... Char., WV
20-21-22-23 .. Columbus
31 ............... Hagerstown
**AUGUST**
1................ Hagerstown
6-7-8-9 .......... Savannah
10-11-12-13... Char., SC
23-24-25-26 ....... Albany
27-28................ Hickory
31 .............. Greensboro
**SEPTEMBER**
1 ................ Greensboro

## Greensboro
**APRIL**
14-15 ........... Char., WV
18-19-20-21 ..... Augusta
27-28-29-30.......... Hag.
**MAY**
1-2-3-4 ........... Asheville
7-8.............. Fayetteville
18-19.......... Fayetteville
20-21-22-23........ Macon
24-25-26-27 ...Columbus
**JUNE**
1-2-3-4 .............. Albany
9................. Fayetteville
10-11-12-13 ...... Hickory
21-22............. Piedmont
23-24 ............. Asheville
**JULY**
3-4-5-6......... Char., WV
7-8.................. Piedmont
20-21 ................ Hickory
25-26-27-28.......... Hag.
29-30.......... Fayetteville
31 .................. Piedmont
**AUGUST**
1..................... Piedmont
6-7-8-9........... Char., SC
10-11-12-13 .. Savannah
21-22................ Hickory
23-24-25-26 ....Columbia
**SEPTEMBER**
2-3.............. Fayetteville

## Hagerstown
**APRIL**
18-19-20-21 ...Savannah

22-23-24-25... Char., SC
**MAY**
1-2-3-4 ............Piedmont
5-6-7-8 .......... Columbia
9-10-11-12 . Greensboro
16-17-18-19.........Macon
28-29-30-31 Fayetteville
**JUNE**
8-9 ............... Char., WV
14-15-16-17 ...... Hickory
22 ................ Char., WV
23-24-25-26 ..... Augusta
27-28-29-30 Fayetteville
**JULY**
5-6-7-8............... Hickory
9-10........... Greensboro
20-21-22-23.... Asheville
**AUGUST**
6-7-8-9 .......... Columbus
10-11-12-13 ....... Albany
23-24-25-26.. Char., WV
27-28 ............. Asheville
31 .................. Piedmont
**SEPTEMBER**
1-2-3 ............. Piedmont

### Hickory
**APRIL**
6-7...................Piedmont
14-15...........Hagerstown
18-19-20-21 ...Columbus
22-23-24-25 ........Albany
27-28-29-30....Char., SC
**MAY**
5-6-7-8 ..............Augusta
11-12...............Piedmont
13-14...........Fayetteville
16-17..........Greensboro
24-25...........Hagerstown
30-31 ...............Asheville
**JUNE**
1-2-3-4...........Char., WV
6-7 ....................Asheville
21-22...........Fayetteville
23-24 ............Char., WV
27-28 ...............Asheville
**JULY**
3-4................Fayetteville
9-10.................Piedmont
22-23...........Greensboro
29-30...........Hagerstown
31 .................Char., WV
**AUGUST**
1 ....................Char., WV

2-3..................Piedmont
6-7-8-9................Macon
10-11-12-13 ....Columbia
19-20...........Greensboro
23-24-25-26 ...Savannah
29-30...........Fayetteville
**SEPTEMBER**
3.......................Asheville

### Macon
**APRIL**
6-7-8-9........... Asheville
10-11-12-13 ...... Hickory
16-17............... Augusta
18-19-20-21 ... Piedmont
27-28-29-30.. Char., WV
**MAY**
5-6-7-8 ......... Columbus
13-14............ Savannah
24-25............. Columbia
26-27............... Augusta
30-31............. Savannah
**JUNE**
10-11-12-13 ....... Albany
14-15-16-17... Char., SC
21 .................... Augusta
25-26............ Savannah
27-28................. Albany
**JULY**
1-2................. Columbia
12-13-14-15........... Hag.
18-19............... Augusta
20-21............ Savannah
24-25............. Columbia
31 ................ Char., SC
**AUGUST**
1 .................. Char., SC
2-3-4-5 .........Fayetteville
15-16-17-18 ........ Gboro
23-24............ Columbus
29-30............... Augusta
**SEPTEMBER**
2-3..................... Albany

### Piedmont
**APRIL**
8-9.................. Hickory
16-17......... Greensboro
27-28-29-30.... Asheville
**MAY**
9-10................. Hickory
13-14......... Greensboro
16-17-18-19.. Char., WV
20-21-22-23 ...... Hickory
26-27..........Hagerstown

28-29-30-31 .. Columbus
**JUNE**
3-4.............. Fayetteville
14-15-16 ........ Columbia
25-26-27-28 ........ Gboro
29 ................... Columbia
**JULY**
1-2-3-4 ....... Hagerstown
12-13 ............. Asheville
16-17-18-19 Fayetteville
20-21-22-23...Char., WV
**AUGUST**
4-5..................... Hickory
6-7-8-9 ............ Augusta
11-12-13-14........ Macon
19-20-21-22 ....... Albany
25-26 ............. Asheville
27-28-29-30 .. Savannah

### Savannah
**APRIL**
6-7-8-9 ....... Greensboro
10-11-12-13 Fayetteville
14-15............. Columbia
27-28............... Augusta
**MAY**
1-2-3-4.............. Hickory
9-10-11-12 .... Columbus
18-19............. Columbia
20-21 ............ Char., SC
28-29 ................. Macon
**JUNE**
10-11-12-13 ... Piedmont
14-15-16-17 ....... Albany
21-22 ............ Char., SC
27-28............. Columbia
**JULY**
3-4 ................ Char., SC
5-6................ Columbus
9-10............... Columbia
14-15............... Augusta
16-17-18........ Char., SC
22-23 .................. Macon
24-25............ Columbus
29-30-31 ......... Asheville
**AUGUST**
1...................... Asheville
4-5...................... Albany
15-16-17-18........ Hager.
19-20-21-22.. Char., WV
31 ....................... Macon
**SEPTEMBER**
1 ......................... Macon
2-3................... Augusta

# Short Season Class A
## New York-Penn League

### Auburn
**JUNE**
21 ................ Watertown
23-24 ......... Williamsport
27-28.............. Vermont
30 ........................ Elmira
**JULY**
1-2......... Hudson Valley
3.................. Watertown
5-6 ......................... Erie
7.................. Watertown
9-10............ Jamestown
13 ........................ Elmira
18 .......................... Utica
20-21 .......... New Jersey
24-25 ......... Williamsport
26-27.............. Oneonta
29 ...................... Batavia
31 ........................ Elmira
**AUGUST**
2............................ Utica
5.................. Watertown

6......................... Elmira
9.................. Watertown
10-11 .............. Pittsfield
12.......................... Utica
16-17.............. Oneonta
21-22...... St. Catharines
27.......................... Utica
30...................... Batavia
**SEPTEMBER**
1................... Watertown

### Batavia
**JUNE**
19 .......... St. Catharines
21 ............... Jamestown
23-24 ...................... Erie
27 .......... St. Catharines
29-30 .............. Pittsfield
**JULY**
2................. Jamestown
4 ............ St. Catharines
9.......................... Elmira

12-13 ........ Williamsport
14-15 ............... Oneonta
17 ................ Jamestown
18-19 .......... New Jersey
21 ................ Jamestown
24 .......... St. Catharines
26-27 ...................... Erie
28 ...................... Auburn
**AUGUST**
5 ............ St. Catharines
6-7.......... Hudson Valley
8-9 .................. Vermont
10-11 ...................... Erie
13............... Jamestown
14-15.......................... Utica
16-17........... Watertown
24.......................... Elmira
27.............. Jamestown
29 ...................... Auburn
**SEPTEMBER**
1 ............ St. Catharines

## Elmira

**JUNE**

15-16 ..... Erie
19-20 ..... Watertown
25-26 ..... Utica
27-28 ..... Hudson Valley
29 ..... Auburn

**JULY**

4 ..... Williamsport
5-6 ..... Jamestown
7 ..... Oneonta
10 ..... Batavia
12 ..... Auburn
16-17 ..... Vermont
19 ..... Oneonta
20 ..... Williamsport
28-29 ..... New Jersey
30 ..... Auburn

**AUGUST**

2 ..... Williamsport
4-5 ..... Pittsfield
7 ..... Auburn
8 ..... Williamsport
14-15 ..... St. Catharines
16-17 ..... Utica
22 ..... Williamsport
23 ..... Batavia
25-26 ..... Watertown
27 ..... Oneonta
29 ..... Oneonta
31 ..... Williamsport

## Erie

**JUNE**

20 ..... Jamestown
21-22 ..... St. Catharines
25-26 ..... Batavia
28 ..... Jamestown
29-30 ..... Hudson Valley

**JULY**

1-2 ..... St. Catharines
3 ..... Jamestown
12-13 ..... Utica
14-15 ..... Watertown
18-19 ..... Vermont
22-23 ..... Batavia
25 ..... Jamestown

**AUGUST**

4-5 ..... New Jersey
6-7 ..... Oneonta
8-9 ..... Pittsfield
15 ..... Jamestown
16-17 ..... Williamsport
18-19 ..... Auburn
20-21 ..... Elmira
25-26 ..... Batavia
29-30 ..... St. Catharines

**SEPTEMBER**

1 ..... Jamestown

## Hudson Valley

**JUNE**

15 ..... New Jersey
17-18 ..... Pittsfield
19-20 ..... Vermont
23-24 ..... Utica
25-26 ..... Auburn

**JULY**

4 ..... New Jersey
7-8 ..... Jamestown
9-10 ..... St. Catharines
14-15 ..... Vermont
16-17 ..... Williamsport
24-25 ..... Oneonta
26-27 ..... Watertown
30-31 ..... Erie

**AUGUST**

1-2 ..... Batavia
12-13 ..... Elmira
18 ..... New Jersey
21-22 ..... Pittsfield
23 ..... New Jersey
25 ..... New Jersey
27-28 ..... Pittsfield
29-30 ..... Vermont
31 ..... New Jersey

## Jamestown

**JUNE**

15-16 ..... Williamsport
17-18 ..... Auburn
19 ..... Erie
22 ..... Batavia
23-24 ..... St. Catharines
27 ..... Erie
29-30 ..... Vermont

**JULY**

1 ..... Batavia
4 ..... Erie
12-13 ..... Watertown
14-15 ..... Elmira
16 ..... Batavia
18-19 ..... Hudson Valley
20 ..... Batavia
22-23 ..... St. Catharines
24 ..... Erie
26-27 ..... New Jersey

**AUGUST**

4-5 ..... Oneonta
6-7 ..... Pittsfield
8-9 ..... Utica
12 ..... Batavia
14 ..... Erie
16-17 ..... St. Catharines
28 ..... Batavia
31 ..... Erie

## New Jersey

**JUNE**

16 ..... Hudson Valley
17-18 ..... Vermont
19-20 ..... Pittsfield
23-24 ..... Elmira
25-26 ..... Williamsport

**JULY**

3 ..... Hudson Valley
5-6 ..... Vermont
7-8 ..... Erie
9-10 ..... Utica
12-13 ..... Pittsfield
22-23 ..... Auburn
24-25 ..... Watertown
30-31 ..... Jamestown

**AUGUST**

1-2 ..... St. Catharines
8-9 ..... Oneonta
14-15 ..... Pittsfield
17 ..... Hudson Valley
21-22 ..... Batavia
24 ..... Hudson Valley
26 ..... Hudson Valley
27-28 ..... Vermont

**SEPTEMBER**

1 ..... Hudson Valley

## Oneonta

**JUNE**

15 ..... Utica
17-18 ..... Batavia
20 ..... Utica
25-26 ..... Pittsfield
27-28 ..... New Jersey

**JULY**

4 ..... Utica
5-6 ..... Watertown
8 ..... Elmira
9-10 ..... Williamsport
16-17 ..... Auburn
18 ..... Elmira
20-21 ..... Vermont
22-23 ..... Watertown
28-29 ..... St. Catharines
30-31 ..... Williamsport

**AUGUST**

10-11 ..... Hudson Valley
14-15 ..... Auburn
19-20 ..... Jamestown
22 ..... Utica
23-24 ..... Erie
26 ..... Utica
28 ..... Elmira
30 ..... Elmira
31 ..... Utica

## Pittsfield

**JUNE**

15-16 ..... Vermont
21-22 ..... New Jersey
23-24 ..... Watertown

**JULY**

1-2 ..... Oneonta
3-4 ..... Vermont
5-6 ..... Hudson Valley
7-8 ..... Batavia
14-15 ..... New Jersey
22-23 ..... Elmira
24-25 ..... Utica
28-29 ..... Hudson Valley
30-31 ..... St. Catharines

**AUGUST**

1-2 ..... Jamestown
12-13 ..... Erie
16-17 ..... Vermont
19-20 ..... Hudson Valley
23-24 ..... Auburn
25-26 ..... Williamsport
29-30 ..... New Jersey

## St. Catharines

**JUNE**

15-16 ..... Auburn
17-18 ..... Elmira
20 ..... Batavia
25-26 ..... Jamestown
28 ..... Batavia
29-30 ..... New Jersey

**JULY**

3 ..... Batavia
12-13 ..... Oneonta
14-15 ..... Utica
16-17 ..... Erie
18-19 ..... Pittsfield
20-21 ..... Erie
25 ..... Batavia
26-27 ..... Williamsport

**AUGUST**

4 ..... Batavia
6-7 ..... Vermont
8-9 ..... Hudson Valley
10-11 ..... Jamestown
18-19 ..... Watertown
25-26 ..... Jamestown
27-28 ..... Erie
31 ..... Batavia

## Utica

**JUNE**

16 ..... Oneonta
17-18 ..... Erie
19 ..... Oneonta
21-22 ..... Elmira
27 ..... Watertown

**JULY**

1-2 ..... Vermont
3 ..... Oneonta
5-6 ..... Batavia
7-8 ..... Williamsport
16-17 ..... New Jersey
19 ..... Auburn
20-21 ..... Pittsfield
26-27 ..... Elmira
28-29 ..... Jamestown
30 ..... Watertown

**AUGUST**

3 ..... Auburn
4-5 ..... Hudson Valley
10-11 ..... Williamsport
13 ..... Auburn
18 ..... Oneonta
21 ..... Watertown
23-24 ..... St. Catharines
25 ..... Oneonta
28 ..... Auburn
30 ..... Watertown

**SEPTEMBER**

1 ..... Oneonta

### Vermont
**JUNE**
21-22 Hudson Valley
23-24 Oneonta
25-26 Watertown
**JULY**
7-8 St. Catharines
9-10 Pittsfield
12-13 Hudson Valley
22-23 Utica
24-25 Elmira
26-27 Pittsfield
30-31 Batavia
**AUGUST**
1-2 Erie
10-11-12-13 New Jersey
14-15 Hudson Valley
19-20 New Jersey
21-22 Jamestown
23-24 Williamsport
25-26 Auburn
31 Pittsfield
**SEPTEMBER**
1 Pittsfield

### Watertown
**JUNE**
15-16 Batavia
17-18 Williamsport
22 Auburn
28 Utica
29-30 Oneonta
**JULY**
1-2 Elmira
4 Auburn
8 Auburn
9-10 Erie
16-17 Pittsfield
18-19 Williamsport
20-21 Hudson Valley
28-29 Vermont
31 Utica
**AUGUST**
2-3 Oneonta
4 Auburn
6-7 New Jersey
8 Auburn
10-11 Elmira
12-13 St. Catharines
20 Utica
23-24 Jamestown
29 Utica
31 Auburn

### Williamsport
**JUNE**
19-20 Auburn
21-22 Oneonta
27-28 Pittsfield
29-30 Utica
**JULY**
1-2 New Jersey
3 Elmira
5-6 St. Catharines
14-15 Auburn
21 Elmira
22-23 Hudson Valley
28-29 Erie
**AUGUST**
1 Elmira
4-5 Vermont
6-7 Utica
9 Elmira
12-13 Oneonta
14-15 Watertown
18 Elmira
19-20 Batavia
27-28 Watertown
29-30 Jamestown
**SEPTEMBER**
1 Elmira

# Northwest League

### Bellingham
**JUNE**
16-18 Everett
22-23-24-25-26 Portland
**JULY**
3-4-5 Yakima
9-10-11-12-13 Eugene
20-21-22-23 Spokane
29-30-31 S. Oregon
**AUGUST**
1-2 S. Oregon
9-10-11 Yakima
18-19-20-21-22 Boise
29-30 Spokane
31 Everett
**SEPTEMBER**
1-2-3 Everett

### Boise
**JUNE**
17-18 S. Oregon
19-20-21 Eugene
28-29-30 Bellingham
**JULY**
1-2 Bellingham
9-10-11-12-13 Yakima
20-21-22-23 S. Oregon
29-30-31 Spokane
**AUGUST**
1-2 Spokane
8-9-10-11 Portland
12-13-14-15-16 Everett
28-29-30 Eugene
**SEPTEMBER**
2-3 Portland

### Eugene
**JUNE**
17-18 Portland
22-23-24-25-26 Spokane
**JULY**
3-4-5-6-7-8 Boise
14-15-16-17-18 Everett
24-25-26-27-28 Bell.
**AUGUST**
3-4-5-6 S. Oregon
12-13-14-15-16 Yakima
24-25-26-27 Portland
31 S. Oregon
**SEPTEMBER**
1 S. Oregon

### Everett
**JUNE**
15-17 Bellingham
22-23-24-25-26 Boise
**JULY**
3-4-5 Spokane
9-10-11-12-13 S. Ore.
20-21-22-23 Yakima
29-30-31 Eugene
**AUGUST**
1-2 Eugene
4-5 Bellingham
9-10-11 Spokane
18-19-20-21-22 Portland
24-25 Yakima
26-27 Bellingham

### Portland
**JUNE**
15-16 Eugene
19-20-21 S. Oregon
28-29-30 Everett
**JULY**
1-2 Everett
9-10-11-12-13 Spokane
17-18 Yakima
20-21-22-23 Eugene
29-30-31 Yakima
**AUGUST**
4-5-6-7 Boise
12-13-14-15-16 Bell.
28-29-30 S. Oregon
31 Boise
**SEPTEMBER**
1 Boise

### So. Oregon
**JUNE**
15-16 Boise
22-23-24-25-26 Yakima
**JULY**
3-4-5-6-7-8 Portland
14-15-16-17-18 Bell.
24-25-26-27-28 Everett
**AUGUST**
8-9-10-11 Eugene
12-13-14-15-16 Spo.
24-25-26-27 Boise
**SEPTEMBER**
2-3 Eugene

### Spokane
**JUNE**
17-18 Yakima
19-20-21 Everett
28-29-30 S. Oregon
**JULY**
1-2 S. Oregon
6-7-8 Bellingham
14-15-16-17-18 Boise
24-25-26-27-28 Port.
**AUGUST**
4-5 Yakima
6-7-8 Everett
18-19-20-21-22 Eugene
23-24-25 Bellingham
31 Yakima
**SEPTEMBER**
1 Yakima

### Yakima
**JUNE**
15-16 Spokane
19-20-21 Bellingham
28-29-30 Eugene
**JULY**
1-2 Eugene
6-7-8 Everett
14-15-16 Portland
24-25-26-27-28 Boise
**AUGUST**
1-2 Portland
6-7-8 Bellingham
18-19-20-21-22 S.O.
26-27 Spokane
28-29-30 Everett
**SEPTEMBER**
2-3 Spokane

# ROOKIE LEAGUES

## Appalachian League

### Bluefield

**JUNE**
19-20............ Burlington
25-26.......... Martinsville
27-28............. Princeton

**JULY**
3-4 .............. Huntington
5-6-7................ Danville
16-17............. Kingsport
18-19 ........ Johnson City
20-21 ......... Elizabethton
28 ............. Elizabethton
29-30.................. Bristol
31 ................ Burlington

**AUGUST**
1-2................ Burlington
9-10-11........ Martinsville
12-13-14 ........ Princeton
22-23-24 ...... Huntington
25-26 ............... Danville

### Bristol

**JUNE**
19-20 .......... Huntington
23-24 ........ Johnson City
25-26 ......... Elizabethton
27-28............ Burlington

**JULY**
3 .............. Johnson City
5-6-7 ............. Kingsport
12-13................ Danville
14-15.......... Martinsville
22-23-24.......... Bluefield
26-27............. Princeton
31................ Huntington

**AUGUST**
1-2 .............. Huntington
6 ............... Johnson City
8 ............... Johnson City
9-10-11...... Elizabethton
16-17-18 ....... Burlington
25-26............. Kingsport

### Burlington

**JUNE**
21-22............. Princeton
24 ................ Martinsville
25-26 ............... Danville
29-30.................. Bristol

**JULY**
3-4.............. Martinsville
8-9-10............. Bluefield
16-17 .......... Huntington
18-19............. Kingsport
26-27-28... Johnson City
29-30 ......... Elizabethton

**AUGUST**
3-4-5 ............. Princeton
12-13-14............... Bristol
19-20-21 .......... Danville
22-23.......... Martinsville
27-28 ............... Bluefield

### Danville

**JUNE**
21-22 ............... Bluefield
27-28.......... Martinsville

**JULY**
1-2................ Burlington
3-4................. Princeton
8-9-10........ Elizabethton
16-17.................. Bristol
18-19 ........... Huntington
26-27-28 ........ Kingsport
29-30 ........ Johnson City

**AUGUST**
3-4-5................ Bluefield
6..................... Princeton
9-10-11 ......... Burlington
12-13-14...... Martinsville
23-24............. Princeton
27-28 ........ Elizabethton

### Elizabethton

**JUNE**
19-20 ............... Danville
23-24............. Kingsport
27-28........ Johnson City

**JULY**
1-2....................... Bristol
5-6-7 ............ Huntington
12-13.......... Martinsville
14-15.............. Princeton
22-23-24 ....... Burlington
26-27 .............. Bluefield
31 .................... Danville

**AUGUST**
1-2 .................. Danville
6-7-8 .............. Kingsport
12-13-14........ John. City
19-20-21............. Bristol
25-26 ........... Huntington

### Huntington

**JUNE**
21-22 ......... Elizabethton
23-24 ............... Bluefield
29-30............. Kingsport

**JULY**
1-2 ........... Johnson City
8-9-10.................. Bristol
12-13............ Burlington
14-15 ............... Danville
20-21 .......... Martinsville
22-23-24 ........ Princeton

**AUGUST**
3-4-5.......... Elizabethton
6-7-8................ Bluefield
16-17-18 ........ Kingsport
19-20-21 ... Johnson City
27-28................... Bristol

### Johnson City

**JUNE**
19-20............. Kingsport
25-26 .......... Huntington
29-30 ......... Elizabethton

**JULY**
4 ......................... Bristol
5-6-7........... Martinsville
14-15 ............... Bluefield
16-17............. Princeton
20-21............ Burlington
22-23-24.......... Danville
31 ................... Kingsport

**AUGUST**
1-2................. Kingsport
7......................... Bristol
9-10-11 ........ Huntington
16-17-18.... Elizabethton
22-23-24............. Bristol
25-26.......... Martinsville

### Kingsport

**JUNE**
21-22.................. Bristol
27-28 .......... Huntington

**JULY**
1-2.................. Princeton
3-4 ............ Elizabethton
8-9-10....... Johnson City
12-13 ............... Bluefield
14-15............ Burlington
20-21 ................ Danville
22-23-24...... Martinsville

**AUGUST**
3-4-5................... Bristol
9-10-11 .......... Princeton
12-13-14 ...... Huntington
22-23-24.... Elizabethton
27-28........ Johnson City

### Martinsville

**JUNE**
21-22........ Johnson City
23................. Burlington
29-30 ............... Danville

**JULY**
1-2 .................. Bluefield
8-9-10 ............ Princeton
16-17......... Elizabethton
18-19................... Bristol
26-27-28 ...... Huntington
29-30............. Kingsport

**AUGUST**
3-4-5......... Johnson City
6-7-8 ............ Burlington
16-17-18........... Danville
19-20-21 .......... Bluefield
24................. Burlington
27-28............. Princeton

### Princeton

**JUNE**
19-20........... Martinsville
23-24 ............... Danville
25-26..............Kingsport
29-30 ............... Bluefield

**JULY**
5-6-7 ............ Burlington
12-13........ Johnson City
18-19 ......... Elizabethton
20-21.................. Bristol
28 ....................... Bristol
29-30 .......... Huntington
31 ............... Martinsville

**AUGUST**
1-2.............. Martinsville
7-8 .................... Danville
16-17-18.......... Bluefield
19-20-21 ........ Kingsport
22 ...................... Danville
25-26............ Burlington

# Pioneer League

## Billings

**JUNE**

17-18 .......... Great Falls
19-20 ....... Medicine Hat
26-27-28 ..... Great Falls

**JULY**

4-5-6 ........... Lethbridge
12-13-14 .............. Butte
15-16-17 ........... Helena
26-27-28... Medicine Hat
31 ............... Great Falls

**AUGUST**

1-2 ............... Great Falls
3-4 ............... Lethbridge
8-9-10 .......... Idaho Falls
11-12-13 ............ Ogden
22-23-24 ....... Lethbridge
31 ........... Medicine Hat

**SEPTEMBER**

1-2 ........... Medicine Hat

## Butte

**JUNE**

17-18 ................ Helena
24-25 .......... Idaho Falls
26-27-28 ............ Ogden

**JULY**

1-2-3 ........... Idaho Falls
7 ......................... Helena
9-10 .................... Ogden
19-20-21 ........... Billings
22-23-24 ..... Great Falls
30-31 ................ Helena

**AUGUST**

2-3-4 ................... Ogden
8-9-10 ........... Lethbridge
11-12-13... Medicine Hat
22-23-24 ...... Idaho Falls
25 ....................... Helena
30-31 ................ Helena

## Great Falls

**JUNE**

21-22-23 ........... Billings
24-25 ........... Lethbridge

**JULY**

2-3 ..................... Billings
4-5-6 ......... Medicine Hat
12-13-14 ........... Helena
15-16-17 .............. Butte
26-27-28 ....... Lethbridge

**AUGUST**

3-4 ........... Medicine Hat
8-9-10 ................ Ogden
11-12-13 ...... Idaho Falls
22-23-24... Medicine Hat
25-26-27 ........... Billings
30 ................ Lethbridge

**SEPTEMBER**

1-2 ............... Lethbridge

## Helena

**JUNE**

19-20 ................. Ogden
21-22-23 ...... Idaho Falls
29-30 .................. Butte

**JULY**

1-2-3 ................... Ogden
8 ........................... Butte
9-10 ............ Idaho Falls
19-20-21 ...... Great Falls
22-23-24 ........... Billings
31 ......................... Butte

**AUGUST**

1 ........................... Butte
2-3-4 ........... Idaho Falls
8-9-10 ....... Medicine Hat
11-12-13 ....... Lethbridge
22-23-24 ............ Ogden
26 ......................... Butte

**SEPTEMBER**

1-2 ....................... Butte

## Idaho Falls

**JUNE**

17-18 ................. Ogden
19-20 .................. Butte
26-27-28 ........... Helena

**JULY**

4-5-6 .................... Butte
7-8 ...................... Ogden
12-13-14 ....... Lethbridge
15-16-17... Medicine Hat
26-27-28 ........... Helena
31 ....................... Ogden

**AUGUST**

1 ......................... Ogden
5-6 ...................... Helena
15-16-17 ........... Billings
18-19-20 ...... Great Falls
25-26 ................. Ogden
27-28-29 .............. Butte

## Lethbridge

**JUNE**

17-18 ....... Medicine Hat
19-20 .......... Great Falls
26-27-28... Medicine Hat
29-30 ................ Billings

**JULY**

1 ......................... Billings
7-8-9-10 ....... Great Falls
19-20-21 ...... Idaho Falls
22-23-24 ............ Ogden
29-30 ................ Billings

**AUGUST**

2 .............. Medicine Hat
5-6 .............. Great Falls
15-16-17 .............. Butte
18-19-20 ........... Helena
25-26 ........ Medicine Hat
28-29-30 ............Billings

## Medicine Hat

**JUNE**

21-22-23....... Lethbridge
24-25 ................ Billings
29-30 .......... Great Falls

**JULY**

1 ................. Great Falls
2-3 ................ Lethbridge
7-8-9-10 ............ Billings
19-20-21 ............ Ogden
22-23-24 ...... Idaho Falls
29-30 .......... Great Falls
31 ................ Lethbridge

**AUGUST**

1 ................... Lethbridge
5-6 ..................... Billings
15-16-17 ........... Helena
18-19-20 .............. Butte
27 ................ Lethbridge
28-29-30 ...... Great Falls

## Ogden

**JUNE**

21-22-23 .............. Butte
24-25 ................ Helena
29-30 .......... Idaho Falls

**JULY**

4-5-6 ................. Helena
12-13-14... Medicine Hat
15-16-17....... Lethbridge
26-27-28 .............. Butte
29-30 .......... Idaho Falls

**AUGUST**

5-6 ........................ Butte
15-16-17 ...... Great Falls
18-19-20 ........... Billings
27-28-29 ........... Helena
30-31 .......... Idaho Falls

**SEPTEMBER**

1-2 .............. Idaho Falls

# INDEPENDENT LEAGUES

## Foreign Leagues

## Winter Leagues

# INDEPENDENT LEAGUES

## ATLANTIC COAST LEAGUE

**Office Address:** P.O. Box 1384, Gastonia, NC 28053. **Telephone:** (704) 864-4487. **FAX:** (704) 864-5580.

**President:** Patrick Gaffney. **Vice President:** James Schuetz.

**Years League Active:** First year.

**Member Clubs:** Florence (S.C.), Gastonia (N.C.), Greenwood (S.C.), Spartanburg (S.C.)

**1995 Opening Date:** June 12. **Closing Date:** Aug. 31.

**No. of Games, Regular Season:** 76.

**Roster Limit:** 23.

## FRONTIER LEAGUE

**Mailing Address:** P.O. Box 2662, Zanesville, OH 43702. **Telephone:** (614) 452-7400. **FAX:** (614) 452-2999.

**President:** Bruce Engel. **Vice President:** Steve Sturgill. **Treasurer:** Bob Wolfe. **Corporate Secretary:** Jim LeCrone.

**Board of Directors:** John Cate (Richmond), Chris Hanners (Chillicothe), Jim Nelson (Ohio Valley), Tom Sullivan (Evansville).

**Executive Director:** Bill Lee. **Administrative Assistant:** Kathy Lee.

**Years League Active:** 1993-.

**1995 Opening Date:** June 15. **Closing Date:** Aug. 28.

**No. of Games:** 70. **All-Star Game:** July 25 at Johnstown, PA.

**Playoff Format:** Top four teams meet in best-of-3 semifinal series. Winners meet in best-of-3 series for league championship.

**Roster Limit:** 24.

**Brand of Baseball:** Wilson.

**Statistician:** Howe Sportsdata International, Boston Fish Pier, West Bldg. #2—Suite 306, Boston MA 02210.

### CHILLICOTHE PAINTS

**Office Address:** 59 N. Paint St., Chillicothe, OH 45601. **Telephone:** (614) 773-8326. **FAX:** (614) 773-8338.

**Principal Owner/President:** Chris Hanners.

**General Manager:** Shirley Bandy. **Chief Operating Officer:** Robert Kalb. **Director of Stadium Operations:** Tony Bandy. **Head Groundskeeper:** Jess Griffith. **Director of Media/Public Relations:** Bryan Wickline. **Director of Community Relations:** Harry Chenault. **Director of Promotions:** Heidi Simpson. **Director of Special Projects:** Ken Wilson. **Clubhouse Operations:** Butch Atteberry.

**Manager/Director of Baseball Operations:** Roger Hanners. **Coaches:** Tom Monroe, Jeff Noble.

**Stadium Name:** V.A. Memorial Stadium.

### EVANSVILLE OTTERS

**Office Address:** 1701 North Main St., Evansville, IN 47711. **Telephone:** (812) 435-8686. **FAX:** (812) 435-8688.

**President:** Tom Sullivan.

**General Manager:** Jim Miller. **Assistant General Manager:** Pam Miller. **Director of Stadium Operations:** Matt Vollman. **Senior Account Representative:** Mike Skvara.

**Director of Scouting/Player Development:** Charlie Sullivan.

**Manager:** Boots Day.

**Stadium Name:** Bosse Field.

### JOHNSTOWN STEAL

**Office Address:** 211 Main St., Johnstown, PA 15901. **Telephone:** (814) 536-8326. **FAX:** (814) 539-0056.

**Principal Owners:** Bruce Engel, Thomas Begel, Tom Lindemuth.

**General Manager:** Mark McCulloch. **Assistant General Manager/ Office Manager:** Joanne Wilson. **Sales Executive/Promotions:** Brian Vuletich. **Director of Media Relations:** Keith Rummell.

**Manager:** Mal Fichman. **Coaches:** Keith Lytle, Wayne Rosenthal.

**Stadium Name:** Johnstown Point Stadium.

### NEWARK BUFFALOS

**Office Address:** 31 N. Fourth St., Newark, OH 43055. **Telephone:** (614) 349-9866. **FAX:** (614) 349-9758.

**Principal Owners:** Jim LeCrone, Ted Gerber, Jack Sherman.

**General Manager:** Robert Jones. **Head Groundskeeper:** Donny Swonger. **Secretary:** Alyce Cummings. **Account Representatives:** Bruce Bennett, Frank Jinks.

**Manager:** John Pacella. **Coach:** Jerry Wieber.

**Stadium Name:** Don Edward Park.

### OHIO VALLEY REDCOATS

**Mailing Address:** P.O. Box 1583, Parkersburg, WV 26102. **Telephone:** (304) 422-0426. **FAX:** (304) 485-7510.

**Owner/General Manager:** Jim Nelson.

**Manager:** Greg Tagert. **Coach:** Tom Sutaris.

**Stadium Name:** Bennett Stump Field.

### PORTSMOUTH EXPLORERS

**Office Address:** 1020 7th St., Portsmouth, OH 45662. **Telephone:** (614) 353-7647. **FAX:** (614) 353-5824.

**President/General Manager:** Steve Sturgill. **Vice President:** Brian Noble.

**Manager:** Unavailable.

**Stadium Name:** Branch Rickey Park.

### RICHMOND ROOSTERS

**Mailing Address:** P.O. Box 2447, Richmond, IN 47375. **Telephone:** (317) 935-7529. **FAX:** (317) 962-7047.

**President:** John Cate.

**Vice President/Director of Sales, Marketing and Promotions:** Gary Kitchel. **Director of Player Personnel:** Tom Cooper. **Administrative Assistant:** Darlene Hileman.

**Manager:** Unavailable.

**Stadium Name:** Don McBride Stadium.

### ZANESVILLE GREYS

**Mailing Address:** P.O. Box 5076, Zanesville, OH 43702. **Telephone:** (614) 454-7397. **FAX:** (614) 454-8601.

**President/General Manager:** Bob Wolfe. **Assistant General Manager:** Brent Pine. **Director of Stadium Operations:** Paul Singer. **Director of Sales/Marketing:** William Mohler. **Clubhouse Operations:** John Bonifield. **Office Manager:** Joan Benincasa.

**Manager:** Eric Welch.

**Stadium Name:** Zanesville Municipal Stadium.

## GOLDEN STATE LEAGUE

**Mailing Address:** 10216 Cozycroft Ave., Chatsworth, CA 91311. **Telephone:** (818) 349-1592. **FAX:** (818) 886-7224.

**President:** Bob Weinstein.

**Years League Active:** First year.

**Member Clubs, Division Structure: North**—Central Coast Condors (Paso Robles), Merced, Sierra Nevada Miners (Chico). **South**—Antelope Valley Ravens (Palmdale), Coachella Valley Desertdawgs (Indio), Imperial Valley Brahmas (Brawley).

**1995 Opening Date:** May 10. **Closing Date:** Oct. 2.

**No. of Games, Regular Season:** 132.

**Playoff Format:** First-half division winners meet second-half winners in best-of-3 series. Winners meet in best-of-5 series for league championship.

## MID-AMERICA LEAGUE

**Mailing Address:** 1915 Scott St., Lafayette, IN 47904. **Telephone:** (317) 449-0565. **FAX:** (317) 447-8116.

**President:** Jim Gonzales.

**Years League Active:** First year.

**Member Clubs:** Anderson (Ind.), Lafayette (Ind.), Lake County (Ind.), Kokomo (Ind.).

**1995 Opening Date:** June 13. **Closing Date:** Aug. 28.

**No. of Games, Regular Season:** 60.

## MID-SOUTH BASEBALL LEAGUE

**Mailing Address:** P.O. Box 578, Booneville, MS 38829. **Telephone:** (601) 462-5906, ext. 24.

**President:** Richard Grottanelli.

**Years League Active:** First year.

**Member Clubs:** Clarksville (Ohio), Greenville (Miss.), Joplin (Mo.), Meridian (Miss.), Owensboro (Ky.), Paducah (Ky.), Pine Bluff (Ark.), Springfield (Mo.).

**No. of Games, Regular season:** 90.

**Roster Limit:** 19.

## NORTH ATLANTIC BASEBALL LEAGUE

**Office Address:** 823-C North Highway, Southampton, NY 11968. **Telephone:** (516) 287-0557. **FAX:** (516) 283-2252.

**President:** Edward Broidy. **Vice President:** Jerry Kissel. **Administrative Assistants:** Ken Boglia, Bob Nasso, Mary Reilly.

**Years League Active:** First year.

**Member Clubs:** Nashua (N.H.), Newark (N.Y.), Niagara Falls (N.Y.), Quebec City (Quebec), Wayne (N.J.), Welland (Ontario).

**1995 Opening Date:** July 1. **Closing Date:** Sept. 3.

**No. of Games, Regular Season:** 60.

**Roster Limit:** 22.

## NORTHEAST BASEBALL LEAGUE

**Office Address:** 48 Mamaroneck Ave., Suite 30, White Plains, NY 10601. **Telephone:** (914) 683-5200. **FAX:** (914) 683-0484.

**President:** Denise Byrd.

**Years League Active:** 1995-.

**1995 Opening Date:** June 16. **Closing Date:** Aug. 31.

**No. of Games, Regular Season:** 70.

**Playoff Format:** Second- and third-place teams meet in sudden-death semifinal. Winner meets first-place team in best-of-3 series for league championship.

**Roster Limit:** 22.

### ALBANY DIAMOND DOGS

**Office Address:** Watervliet-Shaker Road, Heritage Park, Albany, NY 12211. **Telephone:** (518) 869-9234. **FAX:** (518) 869-5291.

**President:** Tom Sullivan. **General Manager:** Rip Rowan. **Assistant General Manager:** John Thomas.

**Manager:** Doc Edwards.

### GLENS FALLS BOBCATS

**Office Address:** East Field Dix Ave., Glens Falls, NY 12801. **Telephone:** (518) 743-9720. **FAX:** (518) 743-9721.

**President:** Vic Walker. **Assistant General Manager:** Paul Sirbono.

**General Manager/Manager:** Dave LaPoint.

### NEWBURGH NIGHT HAWKS

**Office Address:** 35 Washington Ave., Newburgh, NY 12550. **Telephone:** (914) 565-3230.

**Principal Owner:** Bill Cummings. **Director of Business Operations:** Jody Jankowski.

**Manager:** Ron Leflore.

### SULLIVAN MOUNTAIN LIONS

**Office Address:** 292 Broadway, Monticello, NY 12701. **Telephone:** (914) 791-5500.

**President:** Jay Acton. **General Manager:** Pete Jameson.

**Manager:** Howie Bedell.

### TORRINGTON LANDSHARKS

**Mailing Address:** P.O. Box 1402, Torrington, CT 06790. **Telephone:** (516) 741-2763. **FAX:** (516) 741-2713.

**President:** Jeffrey Kunion. **Assistant General Manager:** Grant Griesser.

**Manager:** Dan Shwam.

### YONKERS HOOT OWLS

**Office Address:** 48 Mamaroneck Ave., White Plains, NY 10601. **Telephone:** (914) 683-5200.

**Owner:** Adele Leone. **Executive Vice President:** Richard Monaco. **General Manager:** Unavailable.

**Manager:** Unavailable.

## NORTHERN LEAGUE

**Office Address:** 524 S. Duke St., Durham, NC 27701. **Mailing Address:** P.O. Box 1282, Durham, NC 27702. **Telephone:** (919) 956-8150. **FAX:** (919) 683-2693.

**President/Commissioner:** Miles Wolff. **Executive Director:** Dan Moushon. **Corporate Secretary:** David Kemp.

**Director of Baseball Operations:** Nick Belmonte, 860 NE 173rd Terrace, Miami, FL 33162. Telephone: (305) 651-1493.

**Board of Directors:** Marvin Goldklang (St. Paul), Sam Katz (Winnipeg), Ricky May (Thunder Bay), Bill Pereira (Sioux City), Harry Stavrenos (Sioux Falls), Jim Wadley (Duluth-Superior).

**Years League Active:** 1965-71, 1993-.

**1995 Opening Date:** June 2. **Closing Date:** Sept. 4.

**No. of Games, Regular Season:** 84.

**Playoff Format:** First-half winner meets second-half winner in best-of-5 series for league championship.

**Roster Limit:** 22.

**Brand of Baseball:** Rawlings ROM.

**Statistician:** Howe Sportsdata International, Boston Fish Pier, West Bldg. #2—Suite 306, Boston MA 02210.

### 1994 Standings (Overall)

| Club | W | L | Pct. | GB | '94 Manager |
|---|---|---|---|---|---|
| #Sioux City | 52 | 28 | .650 | — | Ed Nottle |
| Sioux Falls | 47 | 33 | .472 | 5 | Frank Verdi |
| St. Paul | 43 | 36 | .544 | 9½ | Tim Blackwell |
| *#Winnipeg | 43 | 37 | .538 | 10 | Doug Simunic |
| Thunder Bay | 35 | 45 | .438 | 17 | Dan Shwam |
| Duluth-Superior | 19 | 60 | .241 | 32½ | Howie Bedell |

*Won playoffs #Won split-season title

## DULUTH-SUPERIOR DUKES

**Office Address:** Holiday Center, 207 W. Superior St., Duluth, MN 55802. **Mailing Address:** P.O. Box 205, Duluth, MN 55801. **Telephone:** (218) 727-4525. **FAX:** (218) 727-4533.

### Ownership, Management

**Operated By:** Dukes Baseball, Inc.

**Chief Executive Officer/President:** Jim Wadley.

**General Manager:** Frank Gahl. **Director of Media Relations:** Bob Gustafson. **Account Representative:** Peg Puhl. **Director of Community Relations:** Elizabeth Garber. **Head Groundskeeper:** Ray Adameak. **Office Manager:** Suzi Gahl.

**Director of Baseball Operations:** Tom Romenesko.

**Manager:** Tommy Thompson.

### Game Information

**Radio Announcers:** Mark Fleischer, Ray Higgins. **No. of Games Broadcast:** Home-42, Away-42. **Flagship Station:** WDSM 710-AM.

**Stadium Name:** Wade Stadium. **Location:** I-35 to 40th Ave. exit, 5 blocks west to Grand Ave., left to 35th Ave., left at Superior Street. **Standard Game Times:** 7:05 p.m., Sat. 2:05.

## ST. PAUL SAINTS

**Office Address:** 1771 Energy Park Dr., St. Paul, MN 55108. **Telephone:** (612) 644-6659. **FAX:** (612) 644-1627.

### Ownership, Management

**Principal Owners:** Marvin Goldklang, Mike Veeck, Bill Murray, Van Schley.

**Chairman:** Marvin Goldklang. **President:** Mike Veeck.

**General Manager:** Bill Fanning. **Director of Operations:** Tom Whaley. **Stadium Operations:** Bob Klepperich. **Head Groundskeeper:** Constance Rudolf. **Director of Media Relations:** Dave Wright. **Director of Community Relations:** Annie Huidekoper. **Director of Group Sales:** Peter Orme. **Ticket Manager:** Barbara Gorrie. **Director of Merchandise:** Bill Fisher. **Director of Advertising Sales:** Dan Craighead. **Clubhouse Operations:** Brent Proulx.

**Director, Player Procurement:** Van Schley.

**Manager:** Marty Scott. **Coach:** Wayne Terwilliger.

### Game Information

**Radio Announcer:** Dave Wright. **No. of Games Broadcast:** Home-42, Away-42. **Flagship Station:** KLBB 1400-AM.

**Stadium Name:** Midway Stadium. **Location:** I-94, north on Snelling Ave. to Energy Park Drive, west ½ mile to stadium. **Standard Game Times:** 7:05 p.m., Sun. 2:05.

## SIOUX CITY EXPLORERS

**Office Address:** 3400 Line Dr., Sioux City, IA 51106. **Telephone:** (712) 277-9467. **FAX:** (712) 277-9406.

### Ownership, Management

**President:** Bill Pereira.

**General Manager:** Tim Utrup. **Director of Operations:** Andrew Wheeler. **Director of Ticket Sales:** Jim Frye. **Director of Marketing:** Jim Frevola. **Marketing Account Executive:** Dennis Burbank. **Director of Ticketing:** Bret Beer. **Ticketing Account Executive:** Marty Millard. **Director of Merchandising:** Time Kelly. **Controller:** Roger Finch.

**Baseball Operations Director:** Ed Nottle.

**Manager:** Unavailable.

### Game Information

**Radio Announcer:** Jim Frevola. **No. of Games Broadcast:** Home-42, Away-42. **Flagship Station:** KSCG 1360-AM.

**Stadium Name:** Lewis and Clark Park. **Location:** I-29 to exit 143, east 4 blocks, left at US 75 to ballpark. **Standard Game Times:** 7:05 p.m., Sun. 2:05.

## SIOUX FALLS CANARIES

**Office Address:** 119 Main St., Sioux Falls, SD 57102. **Mailing Address:** P.O. Box 84412, Sioux Falls, SD 57118. **Telephone:** (605) 333-0179. **FAX:** (605) 333-0139.

### Ownership, Management

**President:** Harry Stavrenos.

**General Manager:** Gary Weckwerth. **Assistant General Manager:** Travis Lee. **Director of Ticket Sales:** Becky Moen. **Clubhouse Operations:** Larry McKenney. **Director of Food/Beverage:** George Stavrenos.

**Manager:** Frank Verdi. **Coach:** Bob Beattie.

### Game Information

**Radio Announcer:** Brian Burkett. **No. of Games Broadcast:** Home-42, Away-42. **Flagship Station:** KWSN 1230-AM.

**Stadium Name:** Sioux Falls Stadium. **Location:** I-29 to Russell Street exit, right on West Avenue. **Standard Game Times:** 7:05 p.m., Sun. 2:05.

## THUNDER BAY WHISKEY JACKS

**Office Address:** 425 Winnipeg Ave., Thunder Bay, Ontario P7B 6B7.

**Mailing Address:** P.O. Box 864, Thunder Bay, Ontario P7C 4X7. **Telephone:** (807) 344-5225. **FAX:** (807) 343-4611.

### Ownership, Management

**President:** Ricky May.

**General Manager:** Joe Easton. **Assistant General Manager:** Rye Pothakos. **Director of Merchandise/Finance:** Angela Carl.

**Manager:** Doug Ault.

### Game Information

**Radio:** None.

**Stadium Name:** Port Arthur Stadium. **Location:** Highway 61 North, right onto Harbour Expressway, left on Memorial Ave, ballpark one mile north on left. **Standard Game Times:** 7:05 p.m., Sun. 1:05.

## WINNIPEG GOLDEYES

**Office Address:** 1430 Maroons Road, Winnipeg, Manitoba R3G 0L5. **Telephone:** (204) 982-2273. **FAX:** (204) 982-2274.

### Ownership, Management

**President:** Sam Katz.

**General Manager:** John Hindle. **Director of Business Operations:** Andrew Collier. **Director of Media/Public Relations:** Peter Young. **Director of Marketing:** Kevin Moore. **Senior Account Representatives:** Tim Kennedy, Jeremy Fever. **Director of Sales:** Val Overwater. **Director of Group Sales:** Kevin East. **Office Manager:** Barb McTavish. **Receptionist:** Carleigh Hemminger.

**Manager:** Doug Simunic.

### Game Information

**Radio Announcer:** Peter Young. **No. of Games Broadcast:** Home-42, Away-42. **Flagship Station:** CKRC 630-AM

**Stadium Name:** Winnipeg Stadium. **Location:** Pembina Highway to Rt. 155, left to Rt. 90, right to Ness Avenue, right to St. James Street, left to stadium. **Standard Game Times:** 7:05 p.m., Sun. 1:05.

## 1995 Northern League Schedule

### Duluth

**JUNE**

6-7-8 ......... Sioux Falls
13-14-15 .... Sioux City
16-17-18 Thunder Bay
26-27-28 ........ St. Paul
30 ................ Winnipeg

**JULY**

1-2 .............. Winnipeg
14-15-16 .... Sioux City
17-18-19...... Winnipeg
28-29 ..... Thunder Bay

**AUGUST**

4-5-6 ............. St. Paul
8-9-10 ........ Sioux City
18-19-20 ........ St. Paul
21-22-23 Thunder Bay
27 .......... Thunder Bay
30-31 ........ Sioux Falls

**SEPTEMBER**

1 ............... Sioux Falls
2-3-4........... Winnipeg

### St. Paul

**JUNE**

9-10-11............ Duluth
17-18-19 .... Sioux City
20-21-22 .......... Duluth
30 ............. Sioux Falls

**JULY**

1-2 ............ Sioux Falls
3-4-5........... Winnipeg
14-15-16 ... Sioux Falls
17-18-19 Thunder Bay
24-25-26 .......... Duluth
28-29-30...... Winnipeg

**AUGUST**

8-9-10 .... Thunder Bay
11-12-13..... Sioux City
21-22-23 .... Sioux City
30-31 ..... Thunder Bay

**SEPTEMBER**

1 ........... Thunder Bay
2-3-4 ......... Sioux Falls

### Sioux City

**JUNE**

6-7-8 ............. St. Paul
9-10-11 .. Thunder Bay
20-21-22...... Winnipeg
23-24-25 .......... Duluth

**JULY**

4-5-6 ......... Sioux Falls
7-8-9 .............. St. Paul
17-18-19 ... Sioux Falls
25-26-27 ... Sioux Falls

**AUGUST**

1-2-3 .............. St. Paul
4-5-6........... Winnipeg
14-15-16 .......... Duluth
24-25-26 .......... Duluth
30-31 .......... Winnipeg

**SEPTEMBER**

1 .................. Winnipeg
2-3-4 ...... Thunder Bay

### Sioux Falls

**JUNE**

2-3-4 .......... Sioux City
9-10-11 ........ Winnipeg
13-14-15........ St. Paul
23-24-25...... Winnipeg
27-28-29 Thunder Bay

**JULY**

7-8-9 ...... Thunder Bay
10-11-12........... Duluth
21-22-23 ........ St. Paul
28-29-30 .... Sioux City

**AUGUST**

1-2-3 ................ Duluth
11-12-13 Thunder Bay
14-15-16...... Winnipeg
24-25-26........ St. Paul
27-28-29 .... Sioux City

### Thunder Bay

**JUNE**

2-3-4 ................ Duluth
12-13-14...... Winnipeg
19-20-21 ... Sioux Falls
23-24-25 ........ St. Paul
30 ............... Sioux City

**JULY**

1-2.............. Sioux City
4-5-6 ................ Duluth
11-12-13..... Sioux City
21-22-23 .... Sioux City
25-26-27...... Winnipeg
30..................... Duluth

**AUGUST**

4-5-6 ......... Sioux Falls
15-16-17 ........ St. Paul
18-19-20 ... Sioux Falls
24-25-26...... Winnipeg
28-29 ............... Duluth

### Winnipeg

**JUNE**

2-3-4 ............. St. Paul
6-7-8 ...... Thunder Bay
16-17-18 ... Sioux Falls
27-28-29 .... Sioux City

**JULY**

7-8-9 ................ Duluth
10-11-12 ........ St. Paul
14-15-16 Thunder Bay
21-22-23 .......... Duluth

**AUGUST**

1-2-3 ...... Thunder Bay
7-8-9 ......... Sioux Falls
11-12-13........... Duluth
18-19-20 .... Sioux City
21-22-23 ... Sioux Falls
27-28-29 ........ St. Paul

## PRAIRIE LEAGUE

**Office Address:** 451 Ball Way, Saskatoon, Saskatchewan S7K 6E6. **Telephone:** (306) 934-5599. **FAX:** (306) 934-2112.

**Coordinator/Secretary:** David Ferguson.

**Years League Active:** First year.

**Member Clubs:** Aberdeen (S.D.), Brandon (Manitoba), Minot (N.D.), Moose Jaw (Sask.), Regina (Sask.) Cyclones, Saskatoon (Sask.) Riot.

**1995 Opening Date:** June 9. **Closing Date:** Sept. 4.

**No. of Games, Regular Season:** 72.

**Roster Limit:** 20.

## TEXAS-LOUISIANA LEAGUE

**Mailing Address:** 13455 Noel Road, Suite 1650, Dallas, TX 75240. **Telephone:** (214) 991-3332. **FAX:** (214) 991-8887.

**President:** Byron Pierce.

**Executive Vice President/Chief Financial Officer:** Doug Theodore. **Director of Baseball Operations:** Jack Lazorko. **Director of Merchandising:** Sheryl Kolb. **Administrative Assistant:** Penny Farthing.

**Years League Active:** 1994-.

**1995 Opening Date:** May 19. **Closing Date:** Sept. 4.

**No. of Games, Regular Season:** 96.

**Playoff Format:** First-half division winners play second-half winners in sudden-death series. Division playoff winners meet in best-of-5 series for league championship.

**Roster Limit:** 22.

**Brand of Baseball:** Worth.

**Statistician:** Howe Sportsdata International, Boston Fish Pier, West Bldg. #2, Suite 306, Boston, MA 02210.

### ABILENE PRAIRIE DOGS

**Mailing Address:** 401 Cypress, Suite 420, Abilene, TX 79601. **Telephone:** (915) 673-7364. **FAX:** (915) 677-3294.

**General Manager:** Byron Pierce. **Assistant General Manager:** Kyle Scharhag. **Director of Promotions/Media Relations:** Bruce Unrue.

**Manager:** Charley Kerfeld.

**Stadium Name:** Crutcher-Scott Field.

### ALEXANDRIA ACES

**Office Address:** One Babe Ruth Dr., Alexandria, LA 71301. **Mailing Address:** P.O. Box 6005, Alexandria, LA 71307. **Telephone:** (318) 473-2237. **FAX:** (318) 473-2229.

**General Manager:** Craig Brasfield. **Assistant General Manager:** Bart Greenberger. **Director of Stadium Operations:** Jodie White. **Head Groundskeeper:** John Hickman. **Director of Media/Public Relations:** Lyn Rollins.

**Manager:** Stan Cliburn.

**Stadium Name:** Bringhurst Field.

### AMARILLO DILLAS

**Mailing Address:** P.O. Box 31241, Amarillo, TX 79120. **Telephone:** (806) 342-3455. **FAX:** (806) 374-2269.

**General Manager:** Cliff Dochterman. **Assistant General Manager/ Sales, Marketing:** Jim Peterson. **Assistant General Manager/ Concessions, Merchandise:** Virginia Rogich. **Assistant General Manager/ Stadium Operations:** David Baur. **Ticket Manager:** Jerel Beaty. **Media Relations Director:** Barry Burns.

**Manager:** Ross Grimsley.

**Stadium Name:** Potter County Memorial Stadium.

### CORPUS CHRISTI BARRACUDAS

**Office Address:** 3062 Oso Dr., Corpus Christi, TX 78415. **Mailing Address:** P.O. Box 271129, Corpus Christi, TX 78427. **Telephone:** (512) 857-2722. **FAX:** (512) 857-6469.

**General Manager:** Michael Schiff. **Assistant General Manager:** Jason Bogle. **Director of Stadium Operations:** Wayne Mueller. **Director of Public Relations/Broadcasting:** David Schultz.

**Manager:** Mark Wasinger.

**Stadium Name:** Cabaniss Field.

### LAREDO APACHES

**Mailing Address:** P.O. Box 1965, Laredo, TX 78044. **Telephone:** (210) 712-2255. **FAX:** (210) 712-0018.

**General Manager:** Derek Leistra.

**Manager:** Jose Cruz.

**Stadium Name:** West Martin Stadium.

### LUBBOCK

**Mailing Address:** P.O. Box 2608, Lubbock, TX 79408. **Telephone:** Unavailable.

**General Manager:** Jason Bogle.

**Manager:** Unavailable.

**Stadium Name:** Dan Law Field.

## MOBILE BAYSHARKS

**Mailing Address:** P.O. Box 81214, Mobile, AL 36689. **Telephone:** (334) 342-7427. **FAX:** (334) 342-4701.

**General Manager:** Matthew Riley. **Assistant General Manager/ Operations:** Gary Saunders. **Assistant General Manager/Public Relations:** Elmer LeSuer. **Director of Office Operations/Tickets:** Monica Cooper. **Merchandising/Corporate Sales:** Roxann Fry.

**Manager:** Butch Hobson.

**Stadium Name:** Stanky Field.

## PUEBLO BIGHORNS

**Mailing Address:** 2200 Bonforte Blvd., Pueblo, CO 81001. **Telephone:** (719) 549-2444. **FAX:** (719) 549-2570.

**President:** Doug Theodore.

**General Manager:** Fred Palmerino. **Business Operations Manager:** Rose Golini. **Office Manager:** Lisa Vicars.

**Manager:** Jim Essian.

**Stadium Name:** Rawlings Field.

## RIO GRANDE VALLEY WHITEWINGS

**Mailing Address:** P.O. Box 530007, Harlingen, TX 78553. **Telephone:** (210) 412-9464. **FAX:** (210) 412-9479.

**General Manager:** Brian Borchardt. **Assistant General Manager/ Operations:** Beto Elizondo. **Assistant General Manager/Marketing:** Mark O'Brien. **Office Manager:** Marilyn Farley.

**Manager:** Alan Ashby.

**Stadium Name:** Harlingen Field.

## TYLER WILDCATTERS

**Mailing Address:** P.O. Box 7807, Tyler, TX 75711. **Telephone:** (903) 597-9453. **FAX:** (903) 597-6464.

**General Manager:** Joe Scrivner. **Assistant General Manager:** David Burke. **Director of Group Sales/Office Manager:** Amber Scrivner. **Group**

**Manager:** Wayne Krenchicki.

**Stadium Name:** Mike Carter Field.

# WESTERN LEAGUE

**Office Address:** 4800 SW MacAdam, Suite 100, Portland, OR 97201. **Telephone:** (503) 221-1189. **FAX:** (503) 221-1902.

**President:** Bruce Engel. **Vice President of Development:** Gary Thomsen. **Secretary/Treasurer:** Kenneth Wright. **Administrative Coordinator:** Andreen Quinlan. **Director of Player Development:** Mal Fichman. **Umpire in Chief:** Joe Yonto.

**Years League Active:** 1995-.

**Member Clubs, Division Structure: North**—Bend, Grays Harbor, Surrey, Tri-Cities. **South**—Long Beach, Palm Springs, Salinas, Sonoma County.

**1995 Opening Date:** May 19. **Closing Date:** Sept. 3.

**No. of Games, Regular Season:** 90.

**All-Star Game:** July 11 (site unavailable).

**Playoff Format:** First and second-half division winners meet in best-of-3 semifinal. Winners meet in best-of-5 series for league championship.

**Roster Limit:** 20-24.

## BEND BANDITS

**Mailing Address:** P.O. Box 1027, Bend, OR 97709. **Telephone:** (503) 383-1983. **FAX:** (503) 383-2004

**President/General Manager:** Ed Zschau. **Director of Business Operations:** Shauna Basile. **Director of Stadium Operations:** Doug Russell. **Director of Marketing/Community Relations:** Laura Fitzpatrick. **Senior Account Representatives:** Cory O'Donnell, Bob Fitzsimmons. **Director of Ticket Sales:** Michael Curto. **Director of Merchandising:** Chip Miller. **Director of Facilities:** Vince Genna.

**Manager:** Al Gallagher. **Coach:** Dennis Burtt.

**Stadium Name:** Vince Genna Stadium.

## GRAYS HARBOR GULLS

**Mailing Address:** 1017 S. Boone St., Aberdeen WA 98520. **Telephone:** (360) 532-4488. **FAX:** (360) 532-4122.

**President:** Jim Wilson.

**General Manager:** Patrick Brown. **Director of Business Operations:** Megan Haile. **Director of Sales/Marketing:** Sandy Ralls. **Director of Merchandising:** Ted Scott.

**Manager:** Nate Colbert. **Coaches:** Brad Ross, Champ Summers.

**Stadium Name:** Olympic Stadium.

## LONG BEACH BARRACUDA

**Office Address:** 249 E. Ocean Blvd., Suite 1020, Long Beach, CA 90802. **Telephone:** (310) 436-2525. **FAX:** (310) 436-4992.

**Chairman:** Jim Agate. **President:** Chris Gibbs. **Senior Vice President:** Patrick Elster.

**General Manager:** Paula Pyers. **Director of Marketing:** Robert Brennfleck. **Senior Account Representatives:** Bill Chapin, Eirik Prosser, Dennis O'Connor. **Director of Community Relations:** Glenn Marshall.

**Manager:** Jeff Burroughs.
**Stadium Name:** 49er Field.

## PALM SPRINGS SUNS

**Office Address:** 1901 E. Baristo, Palm Springs, CA 92262. **Telephone:** (619) 323-7867. **FAX:** (619) 323-8649.

**Chairman:** Paul Scheibe. **President:** Don DiCarlo.

**General Manager:** Al Campanis. **Director of Business Operations/ Ticket Sales:** Darryl Dunn. **Director of Stadium Operations:** Anthony DiCarlo. **Director of Media/Public Relations:** Larry Hausner. **Director of Sales/Marketing:** Dennis Brown. **Senior Account Representatives:** Carlos Barbosa, Brian Bennett, Derek Dehdashtian, Rudy Morales, Pat Richert. **Director of Community Relations:** Al Stone. **Office Manager:** Alice Holly.

**Manager:** Bill Sudakis. **Coach:** John Verhoeven.
**Stadium Name:** Suns Stadium.

## SALINAS PEPPERS

**Mailing Address:** 1398 Northridge Mall, Salinas, CA 93906. **Telephone:** (408) 449-9100. **FAX:** (408) 449-4610 .

**President:** Bruce Engel.

**General Manager:** Keith Blanchard. **Assistant General Managers:** Andrea D'on Peterson, Bill Ritz. **Senior Account Representatives:** Dan Bohon, Gary Hackett, Chris Huntington, Jeff Ritz. **Director of Community Relations:** Eddie Jurak. **Director of Group Sales:** Dan Bohon. **Office Manager:** Vera Blanchard.

**Manager:** Eddie Jurak.
**Stadium Name:** Salinas Municipal Stadium.

## SONOMA COUNTY CRUSHERS

**Mailing Address:** 5900 Labath Ave., Rohnert Park, CA 94928. **Telephone:** (707) 588-8300. **FAX:** (707) 588-8721.

**President, General Manager:** Robert Fletcher. **Director of Operations:** Lynne Saunders. **Head Groundskeeper:** Dolf Hes. **Director of Sales/Marketing:** Leianne Messina. **Director of Community Relations:** Warren Hopkins. **Director of Promotions/Ticket Sales:** Kevin Wolski. **Office Manager:** Joan Hopkins.

**Manager:** Paul Deese.
**Stadium Name:** Rohnert Park Stadium.

## SURREY GLACIERS

**Mailing Address:** Unit 101-17702 56th Ave., Surrey, B.C. V3S 1C7. **Telephone:** (604) 576-7840. **FAX:** (604) 576-7850.

**President/General Manager:** Stu Kehoe. **Director of Sales/ Marketing:** John Marshall. **Director of Special Projects:** Frank Rudd. **Clubhouse Operations:** Jeff Kehoe. **Office Manager/Accountant:** Sue Goldsmith.

**Director of Baseball Operations/Manager:** Dick Phillips.
**Stadium Name:** Stetson Bowl.

## TRI-CITY POSSE

**Mailing Address:** P.O. Box 1324, Pasco, WA 99301. **Telephone:** (509) 545-6111. **FAX:** (509) 545-6036.

**Principal Owner:** Kenneth Wright.

**General Manager:** Suzan Bond. **Assistant General Manager:** Sean Kelly. **Head Groundskeeper:** Bruce Schnabel. **Director of Ticket Sales:** Rob Ellsworth.

**Manager:** Tom Trebelhorn.
**Stadium Name:** Unavailable.

# COLORADO SILVER BULLETS

**(Women's Professional Baseball)**

**Mailing Address:** 1575 Sheridan Rd. NE, Atlanta, GA 30324. **Telephone:** (404) 636-8200. **FAX:** (404) 636-0530.

**Operated By:** Hope-Beckham, Inc.
**Principal Owners:** Paul Beckham, Bob Hope.
**Chairman of the Board:** Paul Beckham. **President:** Bob Hope.

**Vice President of Finance:** Randal Greene. **Director of Baseball Operations:** Tommy Jones. **Director of Public Relations:** Debra Larson. **Director of Business Operations:** Kevin Lewis. **Events Coordinator:** John Niekro. **Administrator:** Molly Leonard.

**Manager:** Phil Niekro. **Coaches:** Bruce Crabbe, Johnny Grubb, Joe Niekro (pitching).

**1995 Opening Date:** May 7. **Closing Date:** Sept. 10.
**No. of Games, Regular Season:** 50.
**Roster Limit:** 20.

## MEDITERRANEAN BASEBALL LEAGUE

**Mailing Address:** 1575 Sheridan Road NE, Atlanta, GA 30324. **Telephone:** (404) 636-8200. **FAX:** (404) 636-0530.

**Director of Operations:** Joe Bailey.

# MEXICAN LEAGUE

## Class AAA

**NOTE:** The Mexican League is a member of the National Association of Professional Baseball Leagues and has AAA classification. However, its member clubs operate largely independent of Major League Baseball, and for that reason the league is listed in the international and winter league section.

**Mailing Address:** Angel Pola #16, Col. Periodista, Mexico, D.F. CP 11220. **Telephone:** 011-525-557-10-07 or 011-525-557-14-08. **FAX:** 011-525-395-24-54.

**President:** Pedro Treto Cisneròs.

**Vice President:** Roberto Mansur Galan.

**Assistant to the President/Public Relations:** Nestor Alva Brito. **Treasurer:** Salvador Velazquez Andrade. **Secretaries:** Socorro Becerra Campos, Irene Garcia.

**Years League Active:** 1955-.

**1995 Opening Date:** March 29. **Closing Date:** July 23.

**No. of Games, Regular Season:** 116.

**Division Structure: South**—Campeche, Mexico City Red Devils, Mexico City Tigers, Minatitlan, Puebla, Tabasco, Veracruz, Yucatan; **North**—Aguascalientes, Jalisco, Laredo, Monclova, Monterrey, Reynosa, Saltillo, Union Laguna.

**Playoff Format:** Three-tier playoffs involving top four teams in each zone. Winners in each zone play a best-of-7 series for league championship.

**All-Star Series vs. Texas League:** June 11 at El Paso; June 13 at Torreon (Union Laguna).

**Roster Limit:** 25. **Roster Limit, Imports:** 4.

**Brand of Baseball:** Rawlings.

**Statistician:** Ana Luisa Perea Talarico, Angel Pola #16, Col. Periodista, CP 11220 Mexico, D.F.

### 1994 Standings

| North | W | L | Pct. | GB |
|---|---|---|---|---|
| Monterrey Sultans | 79 | 51 | .608 | — |
| Saltillo | 76 | 53 | .589 | 2½ |
| Monterrey Ind. | 74 | 54 | .578 | 4 |
| Union Laguna | 72 | 57 | .558 | 6½ |
| Monclova | 69 | 62 | .527 | 11½ |
| Laredo | 64 | 67 | .489 | 15½ |
| Jalisco | 51 | 77 | .398 | 27 |
| Aguascalientes | 48 | 82 | .369 | 31 |

| South | W | L | Pct. | GB |
|---|---|---|---|---|
| *M.C. Reds | 82 | 45 | .646 | — |
| Veracruz | 64 | 56 | .533 | 14½ |
| Yucatan | 66 | 58 | .532 | 14½ |
| Campeche | 64 | 57 | .529 | 15 |
| M.C. Tigers | 61 | 66 | .480 | 21 |
| Tabasco | 59 | 67 | .468 | 22½ |
| Minatitlan | 57 | 71 | .445 | 25½ |
| Puebla | 33 | 96 | .256 | 50 |

*Won playoffs

### AGUASCALIENTES RAILROADMEN

**Office Address:** Av. Adolfo Lopez Mateos Ote. #407, Despacho 306, Colonia Centro, Aguascalientes, Aguascalientes. **Telephone:** (49) 15-80-33 or 18-77-78. **FAX:** (49) 15-24-79.

**President:** Oscar Lomelin Ibarra. **General Manager:** Ernesto Rios.

**Field Manager:** Jose Guerrero.

### CAMPECHE PIRATES

**Office Address:** Unidad Deportiva 20 de Noviembre, Local 4, Campeche, Campeche. **Telephone:** (981) 6-38-07. **FAX:** (981) 6-60-71.

**Working Agreement:** Florida Marlins.

**President:** Gustavo Ortiz Avila. **General Manager:** Maria del Socorro Morales Martinez.

**Field Manager:** Javier Martinez Marquez.

### JALISCO COWBOYS

**Office Address:** Mexicaltzingo No. 1987, Int. 201, Sector Juarez, Guadalajara, Jalisco, CP 44100. **Telephone:** (36) 26-60-66 or 26-77-22.

**President:** Guillermo Cosio Gaona. **General Manager:** Armando Navarro Pena.

**Manager:** Fernando Villaescusa.

### LAREDO OWLS

**Office Address:** Porfirio Diaz No. 2210, Colonia Viveros, Nuevo Laredo, Tamaulipas, CP 88230. **Telephone:** (87) 19-12-35. **FAX:** (87) 19-12-36.

**President:** Manuel Canales Escamilla. **General Manager:** Samuel Lozano Medina.

**Manager:** Andres Mora.

### MEXICO CITY RED DEVILS

**Office Address:** Av. Cuauhtemoc #451-101 or 102, Col. Piedad

Narvarte, Mexico, D.F., CP 03020. **Telephone:** (5) 639-87-22 or 639-87-22.

**President:** Roberto Mansur Galan. **General Manager:** Pedro Mayorquin Aguilar.

**Manager:** Marco Antonio Vazquez.

## MEXICO CITY TIGERS

**Office Address:** Tuxpan No. 45-A Sto. PISO, Col. Roma Sur, Mexico, D.F., CP 06070. **Telephone:** (5) 584-02-49 or 584-02-16. **FAX:** (5) 564-48-75.

**Working Agreement:** Atlanta Braves.

**President:** Carlos Peralta. **General Manager:** Alfonso Lopez.

**Field Manager:** Dan Firova.

## MINATITLAN OILERS

**Office Address:** Merida y Justo Sierra, Minatitlan, Veracruz, CP 96790. **Telephone:** (22) 4-02-08.

**President:** Guillermo Alvarado Rocha. **General Manager:** Felipe Rodriguez Garcia.

**Manager:** Unavailable.

## MONCLOVA STEELERS

**Office Address:** Venustiano Carranza No. 221, Oriente Altos, Monclova, Coahuila, CP 25700. **Telephone:** (86) 33-74-33. **FAX:** (86) 33-88-97.

**President:** Alonso Ancira Gonzalez. **General Manager:** Miguel Sotelo.

**Manager:** Gerardo Gutierrez.

## MONTERREY SULTANS

**Office Address:** Av. Manuel L. Barragan S/N, Estadio Monterrey AP 870, Monterrey, Nuevo Leon, CP 64460. **Telephone:** (83) 51-80-22 or 51-02-09. **FAX:** (83) 51-94-67.

**President:** Jose Maiz Garcia. **General Manager:** Roberto Magdaleno Ramirez.

**Manager:** Joel Serna.

## PUEBLA PARROTS

**Office Address:** Estadio Hermanos Serdan, Unidad Deportiva CP 72220, Puebla, Puebla. **Telephone:** (22) 22-21-16. **FAX:** (22) 22-21-17.

**President:** Rafeal Moreno Valle. **General Manager:** Tomas Herrera Olachea.

**Manager:** Francisco Estrada.

## REYNOSA BRONCOS

**Office Address:** Carretera A Monterrey, Parque Adolfo Lopez Mateos, Reynosa, Tamaulipas. **Telephone:** (89) 24-17-50 or 24-26-95.

**Working Agreement:** Los Angeles Dodgers.

**President:** Eduardo Trevino. **General Manager:** Rogelio Treto Cisneros.

**Manager:** Aurelio Rodriguez.

## SALTILLO SARAPE MAKERS

**Office Address:** Hidalgo Norte No. 2492, Col. Republica Ote. Saltillo, Coahuila, CP 25280. **Telephone:** (84) 16-97-55. **FAX:** (84) 16-94-55.

**President:** Javier Cabello Siller. **General Manager:** Victor Favela Lopez.

**Manager:** Roberto Castellon.

## TABASCO OLMECAS

**Office Address:** Explanada de la Cd. Deportiva, Estadio de Beisbol Centenario, del 27 de Febrero, Villahermosa, Tabasco, CP 86100. **Telephone:** (93) 15-08-36. **FAX:** (93) 15-32-37.

**President:** Diego Rosique Palavicini. **General Manager:** Manuel Granier.

**Manager:** Juan Navarrete.

## UNION LAGUNA COTTON PICKERS

**Office Address:** Calle Juan Gutemberg S/N, Estadio de la Revolucion, Torreon, Coahuila, Mexico, CP 27000. **Telephone:** (17) 17-43-35. **FAX:** (17) 18-55-15.

**President:** Jorge Duenez Zurita. **General Manager:** Guillermo Garibay Fernandez.

**Field Manager:** Francisco Galindo Canales.

## VERACRUZ EAGLES

**Office Address:** Nuevo Parque Deportivo Veracruzano, Av. Jacarandas S/N Fracc. Virginia, Boca Del Rio, Veracruz, CP 94294. **Telephone:** (29) 35-53-63. **FAX:** (29) 35-50-65.

**President:** Vicente Perez Avella. **General Manager:** Manuel Cortes Conde.

**Manager:** Jorge Tellaeche.

## YUCATAN LIONS

**Office Address:** Calle 50 #406-B, Col. Jesus Carranza, Merida, Yucatan, CP 97000. **Telephone:** (99) 26-30-22 or 26-34-19. **FAX:** (99) 26-36-31.

**President:** Ricardo Ricalde Duran. **General Manager:** Jose Rivera Ancona.

**Manager:** Carlos Paz.

# JAPANESE LEAGUES

**Mailing Address:** Imperial Tower, 7F, 1-1-1 Uchisaiwai-cho, Chiyoda-ku, Tokyo 100, Japan. **Telephone:** 011-03-3502-0022. **FAX:** 011-03-3502-0140.

**Commissioner:** Ichiro Yoshikuni.

**Executive Secretary:** Yoshiaki Kanai. **Assistant Director of International Affairs:** Nobuhisa "Noby" Ito.

**Japan Series:** Best-of-7 series between Central and Pacific League champions, begins Oct. 21 at home of Pacific League club.

**All-Star Series:** July 25 at Yokohama, July 26 at Hiroshima.

**Roster Limit:** 70 per organization. Major league club is permitted to register 28 players at a time, though only 25 may be available for each game. **Roster Limit, Imports:** 3.

## PACIFIC LEAGUE

**Mailing Address:** Asahi Bldg. 9F, 6-6-7 Ginza, Chuo-ku, Tokyo 104. **Telephone:** 03-3573-1551. **FAX:** 03-3572-5843.

**President:** Kazuo Harano. **Secretary General:** Shigeru Murata.

**Years League Active:** 1950-.

**1995 Opening Date:** April 1. **Closing Date:** Sept. 24.

**No. of Games, Regular Season:** 130. **Playoff Format:** None.

### 1994 Standings, 1995 Stadiums

| Club | W | L | T | Pct. | GB | Stadium | Cap. |
|---|---|---|---|---|---|---|---|
| Seibu Lions | 76 | 52 | 2 | .594 | — | Seibu Lions | 37,008 |
| Orix Blue Wave | 68 | 59 | 3 | .535 | 7½ | Kobe Green | 35,000 |
| Kintetsu Buffaloes | 68 | 59 | 3 | .535 | 7½ | Fujiidera | 32,000 |
| Fukuoka Daiei Hawks | 69 | 60 | 1 | .535 | 7½ | Fukuoka Dome | 48,000 |
| Chiba Lotte Marines | 55 | 73 | 2 | .430 | 21 | Chiba Marine | 30,000 |
| Nippon Ham Fighters | 46 | 79 | 5 | .368 | 28½ | Toyko Dome | 56,000 |

### CHIBA LOTTE MARINES

**Mailing Address:** WBG Marive West 25F, 2-6 Nakase, Mihama-ku, Chiba-shi, Chiba-ken 261-71. **Telephone:** 043-297-2101. **FAX:** 043-297-2181.

**General Manager:** Tatsuro Hirooka. **Field Manager:** Bobby Valentine. **Coach:** Tom Robson. **Farm Team Manager**: Lenn Sakata.

**1995 Foreign Players:** Julio Franco, Eric Hillman, Pete Incaviglia.

### FUKUOKA DAIEI HAWKS

**Mailing Address:** Fukuoka Dome 6F, 2-2-2 Jigyohama, Chuo-ku, Fukuoka 810. **Telephone:** 092-844-1189. **FAX:** 092-844-4600.

**President:** Rikuo Nemoto. **General Manager:** Ryuzo Setoyama.

**Field Manager:** Sadaharu Oh.

**1995 Foreign Players:** Kevin Mitchell, Kevin Reimer, Bobby Thigpen.

### KINTETSU BUFFALOES

**Mailing Address:** Kintetsu Namba Bldg. 7F, 4-1-15 Namba, Chuo-ku, Osaka 542. **Telephone:** 06-644-5557. **FAX:** 06-641-7422.

**President, General Manager:** Yasuo Maeda.

**Field Manager:** Keishi Suzuki.

**1995 Foreign Players:** Kevin Mitchell, Ralph Bryant, Dennis Powell.

### NIPPON HAM FIGHTERS

**Mailing Address:** Roppongi Denki Bldg. 6F, 6-1-20 Roppongi, Minato-ku, Tokyo 106. **Telephone:** 03-3403-9131. **FAX:** 03-3403-9143.

**President:** Saburo Mochida. **General Manager:** Takeshi Kojima.

**Field Manager:** Toshiharu Ueda.

**1995 Foreign Players:** Rob Ducey, Kip Gross, Tim McIntosh.

### ORIX BLUE WAVE

**Mailing Address:** Kanri Center, 2F, Midoridai, Suma-ku, Kobe 654-01. **Telephone:** 078-795-1001. **FAX:** 078-795-1005.

**President:** Toshio Saruwatari. **General Manager:** Shigeyoshi "Steve" Ino.

**Field Manager:** Akira Ogi.

**1995 Foreign Players:** Doug Jennings, Troy Neel.

### SEIBU LIONS

**Mailing Address:** Seibu Lions Stadium, 2135 Kami-Yamaguchi, Tokorozawa-shi, Saitama-ken 359. **Telephone:** 0429-24-1155. **FAX:** 0429-28-1919.

**President:** Iwao Misugi. **General Manager:** Kenji Ono.

**Field Manager:** Osamu Higashio.

**1995 Foreign Players:** Orestes Destrade, Darrin Jackson, Taigen Kaku (Taiwan).

## CENTRAL LEAGUE

**Mailing Address:** Asahi Bldg. 3F, 6-6-7 Ginza, Chuo-ku, Tokyo 104. **Telephone:** 03-3572-1673. **FAX:** 03-3571-4545.

**President:** Hiromori Kawashima.

**Secretary General:** Ryoichi Shibusawa. **Planning Department:** Masaaki Nagino.

**Years League Active:** 1950-.

**1995 Opening Date:** April 7. **Closing Date:** Oct. 1.

**No. of Games, Regular Season:** 130. **Playoff Format:** None.

### 1994 Standings, 1995 Stadiums

| Club | W | L | T | Pct. | GB | Stadium | Cap. |
|---|---|---|---|---|---|---|---|
| Yomiuri Giants | 70 | 60 | 0 | .538 | — | Tokyo Dome | 56,000 |
| Chunichi Dragons | 69 | 61 | 0 | .531 | 1 | Nagoya | 35,000 |
| Hiroshima Carp | 66 | 64 | 0 | .508 | 4 | Hiroshima | 32,000 |
| Yakult Swallows | 62 | 68 | 0 | .477 | 8 | Meiji Jingu | 48,000 |
| Hanshin Tigers | 62 | 68 | 0 | .477 | 8 | Koshien | 55,000 |
| Yokohama BayStars | 61 | 69 | 0 | .469 | 9 | Yokohama | 30,000 |

### CHUNICHI DRAGONS

**Mailing Address:** Chunichi Bldg. 9F, 4-1-1 Sakae, Naka-ku, Nagoya 460. **Telephone:** 052-252-5226. **FAX:** 052-251-8649.

**President:** Satoru Nakayama. **General Manager:** Hiroo Ito.

**Field Manager:** Morimichi Takagi.

**1995 Foreign Players:** Mel Hall, Rich Monteleone, Alonzo Powell.

### HANSHIN TIGERS

**Mailing Address:** 1-47 Koshien-cho, Nishinomiya-shi, Hyogo-ken 663. **Telephone:** 0798-46-1515. **FAX:** 0798-40-0934.

**President:** Kazuhiko Miyoshi. **General Manager:** Kuniaki "James" Sawada.

**Field Manager:** Katsuhiro Nakamura.

**1995 Foreign Players:** Scott Coolbaugh, Glenn Davis, Tateo Kakuri (Taiwan).

### HIROSHIMA TOYO CARP

**Mailing Address:** 5-25 Motomachi, Naka-ku, Hiroshima 730. **Telephone:** 082-221-2040. **FAX:** 082-228-5013.

**General Manager:** Chitomi Takahashi.

**Field Manager:** Toshiyuki Mimura.

**1995 Foreign Players:** Luis Medina, Robinson Perez, Felix Ramirez.

### YAKULT SWALLOWS

**Mailing Address:** Yakult Bldg. 7F, 1-1-19 Higashi Shimbashi, Minato-ku, Tokyo 105. **Telephone:** 03-3574-0671. **FAX:** 03-3574-6764.

**President:** Kiyoto Sakai. **General Manager:** Itaru Taguchi.

**Field Manager:** Katsuya Nomura.

**1995 Foreign Players:** Terry Bross, Hensley Meulens, Tom O'Malley.

### YOKOHAMA BAYSTARS

**Mailing Address:** Nihon Seimei Yokohama Hon-machi Bldg., 6F, 2-22 Hon-machi, Naka-ku, Yokohama 231. **Telephone:** 045-681-0811. **FAX:** 045-661-2500.

**President:** Takashi Ohori. **General Manager:** Terumoto Wako.

**Field Manager:** Akihito Kondo.

**1995 Foreign Players:** Glenn Braggs, Bobby Rose, Jeff Schwarz.

### YOMIURI GIANTS

**Mailing Address:** Takebashi 3-3 Bldg., 3-3 Kanda Nishiki-cho, Chiyoda-ku, Tokyo 101. **Telephone:** 03-3295-7711. **FAX:** 03-3295-7731.

**General Manager:** Teruhiko Hoshina.

**Field Manager:** Shigeo Nagashima.

**1995 Foreign Players:** Jack Howell, Jimmy Jones, Shane Mack.

# FOREIGN LEAGUES

## CHINESE PROFESSIONAL BASEBALL LEAGUE

**(Taiwan)**

**Mailing Address:** 14F, No. 126, Sec. 4, Nanking E. Road, Taipei, Taiwan. **Telephone:** 886-2-577-6992. **FAX:** 886-2-577-2606.

**Commissioner:** C.K. Chen. **Secretary-General:** Daniel Tu.

**Years League Active:** 1990-

**No. of Games, Regular Season:** 90.

### 1994 Standings

| Club | W | L | T | Pct. | GB |
|---|---|---|---|---|---|
| Brother Elephants* | 64 | 24 | 2 | .727 | — |
| President Lions | 48 | 38 | 4 | .558 | 15 |
| China Times Eagles | 46 | 43 | 1 | .517 | 18½ |
| Mercury Tigers | 40 | 47 | 3 | .460 | 23½ |
| Weichuan Dragons | 36 | 52 | 2 | .409 | 28 |
| Jungo Bears | 29 | 59 | 2 | .330 | 35 |

*Won first- and second-half titles

### BROTHER ELEPHANTS

**Mailing Address:** No. 255, Nanking E. Road, Sec. 3, Taipei, Taiwan. **Telephone:** 886-2-712-3456. **FAX:** 886-2-717-2258.

**General Manager:** Juei-ho Hung.

### CHINA TIMES EAGLES

**Mailing Address:** No. 240, Hoping W. Road, Taipei, Taiwan. **Telephone:** 886-2-308-7111, ext. 8119. **FAX:** 886-2-306-3481.

**General Manager:** Sam Wen.

### JUNGO BEARS

**Mailing Address:** 19F, No. 337, Taya Road, Taichung, Taiwan. **Telephone:** 886-4-297-3736. **FAX:** 886-4-295-1277.

**General Manager:** Chen Yi-ping.

### MERCURY TIGERS

**Mailing Address:** 2F, No. 140, Chungking N. Road, Sec. 4, Taipei, Taiwan. **Telephone:** 886-2-816-4700. **FAX:** 886-2-816-1896.

**President:** Vincent Mao.

### PRESIDENT LIONS

**Mailing Address:** No. 25, Hsinghua Street, Tainan, Taiwan. **Telephone:** 886-6-228-8959. **FAX:** 886-6-228-8983.

**President:** Jiun-nan Kuo.

### WEICHUAN DRAGONS

**Mailing Address:** No. 125, Sungkiang Road, Taipei, Taiwan. **Telephone:** 886-2-507-8221, ext. 587. **FAX:** 886-2-507-7470.

**Vice General Manager:** George Chao.

## KOREAN BASEBALL ORGANIZATION

**(South Korea)**

**Mailing Address:** 946-16 DoKok-Dong, Kangnam-Ku, Seoul, South Korea. **Telephone:** 011-82-2-557-7700. **FAX:** 011-82-2-557-7800.

**Commissioner:** Sang Hoon Lee.

**Years League Active:** 1982-

**No. of Games, Regular Season:** 140.

**Member Clubs:** Bing Gu Ray Eagles (Taejon), Hac Hac Tigers (Kwangju), LG Twins (Seoul), Lotte Giants (Pusan), OB Bears (Seoul), Pacific Giants (Inchon), Sam Sung Lions (Taegu), Ssang-Bang Wool Raiders (Cheonchu).

## ITALIAN BASEBALL FEDERATION

**(Italy)**

**Mailing Address:** Viale Tiziano, 74, 00196, Rome, Italy. **Telephone:** 011-39-6-368-58130. **FAX:** 011-39-6-368-58201.

**President:** Aldo Notari. **Secretary General:** Dino Rossi.

## ROYAL DUTCH BASEBALL FEDERATION

**(Holland)**

**Mailing Address:** Post Bus 60, NL-2080 AB, Sant Poort, Zuid, Holland. **Telephone:** 31-23-390-244. **FAX:** 31-23-385-922.

**President:** Henk den Duijn.

# WINTER BASEBALL

## CARIBBEAN BASEBALL CONFEDERATION

**Mailing Address:** Frank Felix Miranda No. 1, Naco, P.O. Box 21070 y 21416, Santo Domingo, Dominican Republic. **Telephone:** (809) 562-4737 or 562-4715. **FAX:** (809) 565-4654.

**Commissioner:** Juan Fco. Puello Herrera (Dominican Republic).

**Member Leagues:** Dominican Republic, Mexican Pacific, Puerto Rican, Venezuelan.

**1996 Caribbean World Series:** Feb. 3-8 at Santo Domingo, Dominican Republic.

## DOMINICAN LEAGUE

**Mailing Address:** Estadio Quisqueya, Santo Domingo, Dominican Republic. **Telephone:** (809) 567-6371. **FAX:** (809) 567-5720.

**President:** Dr. Leonardo Matos. **Vice President:** Marcos Rodriguez.

**Years League Active:** 1951-.

**1994-95 Opening Date:** Oct. 28, 1994. **1994-95 Closing Date:** Dec. 30, 1994.

**No. of Regular Season Games:** 48.

**Playoff Format:** Top four teams meet in an 18-game round-robin tournament. Top two finishers meet in a best-of-7 series for league championship. Winner advances to Caribbean World Series.

**Roster Limit:** 30. **Roster Limit, Imports:** 7.

### AGUILAS

**Mailing Address:** Estadio Cibao, Santiago, Dom. Rep. **Telephone:** (809) 575-4310.

**Primary Working Agreement:** None.

**President:** Ricardo Hernandez. **General Manager:** Winston Llenas. **1994-95 Manager:** Miguel Dilone.

### AZUCAREROS

**Mailing Address:** Estadio Francisco Micheli, La Romana, Dom. Rep. **Telephone:** (809) 556-4955.

**Primary Working Agreement:** Los Angeles Dodgers.

**President:** Arturo Gil Baez. **General Manager:** Ralph Avila. **1994-95 Manager:** Art Howe.

### ESCOGIDO LIONS

**Mailing Address:** P.O. Box 1287, Santo Domingo, Dom. Rep. **Telephone:** (809) 565-1910. **FAX:** (809) 567-7643.

**Primary Working Agreement:** None.

**President:** Daniel Aquino. **1994-95 Managers:** Luis Pujols, Tim Johnson.

### ESTRELLAS

**Mailing Address:** Estadio Tetello Vargas, San Pedro de Macoris, Dom. Rep. **Telephone:** (809) 566-9171.

**Primary Working Agreement:** None.

**President/General Manager:** Manuel Antun. **1994-95 Manager:** Nelson Norman.

### LICEY TIGERS

**Mailing Address:** Estadio Quisqueya, Santo Domingo, Dom. Rep. **Telephone:** (809) 567-3090. **FAX:** (809) 542-7714.

**Primary Working Agreement:** Oakland Athletics.

**President:** Tancredo Aybar Castellanos. **General Manager:** Ramon Naranjo. **Director of Public Relations:** Bienvenido Rojas. **1994-95 Managers:** Casey Parsons, Elvio Jimenez.

## MEXICAN PACIFIC LEAGUE

**Mailing Address:** Pesqueria No. 301-R, Navojoa, Sonora, Mexico. **Telephone:** (52-642) 2-3100. **FAX:** (52-642) 2-7250.

**President:** Dr. Arturo Leon Lerma. **General Manager:** Obiel Denis.

**Years League Active:** 1958-.

**1994-95 Opening Date:** Oct. 25, 1994. **Closing Date:** Dec. 30, 1994.

**No. of Regular Season Games:** 58.

**Playoff Format:** Six teams advance to best-of-7 quarterfinals. Three winners and losing team with best regular-season record play advance to best-of-7 semifinals. Winners meet in best-of-7 series for league championship. Winner advances to Caribbean World Series.

**Roster Limit:** 25. **Roster Limit, Imports:** 7.

### CULIACAN TOMATOGROWERS

**Mailing Address:** Av. A. Obregon 348 Sur, CP 80000, Culiacan,

Sinaloa, Mexico. **Telephone:** (67) 52-04-48. **FAX:** (67) 12-24-46.

**Primary Working Agreement:** San Francisco Giants.

**President:** Juan Manuel Ley Lopez. **General Manager:** Jaime Blancarte. **1994-95 Manager:** Marco Antonio Vazquez.

### GUASAVE COTTONEERS

**Mailing Address:** Ave. Obregon #43, Guasave, Sinaloa, Mexico. **Telephone:** (68) 72-14-31. **FAX:** (68) 72-14-31.

**Primary Working Agreement:** California Angels.

**President:** Reynaldo Valencia Amador. **General Manager:** Narciso Orona de los Palos. **1994-95 Manager:** Mario Mendoza.

### HERMOSILLO ORANGEGROWERS

**Mailing Address:** Nayarti 130, Local 4, Hermosillo, Sonora, Mexico. **Telephone:** (62) 14-07-80. **FAX:** (62) 15-57-31.

**Primary Working Agreement:** None.

**President:** Enrique Mazon. **General Manager:** Marco Antonio Manzo. **1994-95 Manager:** Marv Foley.

### LOS MOCHIS SUGARCANE GROWERS

**Mailing Address:** Angel Flores #473 Sur, Los Mochis, Sinaloa, Mexico CP 81200. **Telephone:** (68) 18-25-05. **FAX:** (68) 15-00-45.

**Primary Working Agreement:** None.

**President:** Mario Lopez Valdez. **General Manager:** Antonio Castro. **1994-95 Manager:** Aurelio Rodriguez.

### MAZATLAN DEER

**Mailing Address:** Estadio Teodoro Mariscal, Apartado Postal 488, Mazatlan, Sinaloa, Mexico. **Telephone:** (69) 83-30-12. **FAX:** (69) 83-71-89.

**Primary Working Agreement:** None.

**President:** Hermilo Diaz Bringas. **General Manager:** Miguel Angel Ahumada. **1994-95 Manager:** Ozzie Virgil.

### MEXICALI EAGLES

**Mailing Address:** Calzada Ex-Avacion, Mexicali, Baja California. **Telephone:** (65) 67-00-40. **FAX:** (65) 67-00-95.

**Primary Working Agreement:** Los Angeles Dodgers.

**President:** Mario Hernandez. **General Manager:** Juanita Perez. **1994-95 Manager:** Raul Cano.

### NAVOJOA MAYOS

**Mailing Address:** Allende #208, Novojoa, Sonora, Mexico. **Telephone:** (64) 22-14-33. **FAX:** (64) 22-89-97.

**Primary Working Agreement:** Montreal Expos.

**President:** Victor Cuevas Garibay. **General Manager:** Lauro Villalobos. **1994-95 Managers:** Dave Machemer, Jose Bojorquez.

### OBREGON YAQUIS

**Mailing Address:** Yucatan y Nayarit #294, Edifico C, Dpto. #11, Ciudad Obregon, Sonora, Mexico. **Telephone:** (64) 14-11-56. **FAX:** (64) 14-11-56.

**Primary Working Agreement:** None.

**President:** Luis Felipe Garcia de Leon. **General Manager:** Rodolfo Espinoza. **1994-95 Manager:** Francisco Estrada.

## PUERTO RICAN LEAGUE

**Mailing Address:** P.O. Box 1852, Hato Rey, PR 00919. **Telephone:** (809) 765-6285 or 765-7285. **FAX:** (809) 767-3028.

**President:** Santiago Soler Favale. **Executive Director/Administrator:** Benny Agosto.

**Years League Active:** 1938-.

**1994-95 Opening Date:** Nov. 2, 1994. **1994-95 Closing Date:** Jan. 8, 1995.

**No. of Regular Season Games:** 54.

**Playoff Format:** Top four teams meet in a 12-game round robin tournament. Top two finishers meet in a best-of-9 series for league championship. Winner advances to Caribbean World Series.

**Roster Limit:** 26. **Roster Limit, Imports:** 4. Up to six more may be used to replace native players who are injured or are major leaguers who elect not to play.

### ARECIBO WOLVES

**Mailing Address:** P.O. Box 1633, Arecibo, PR 00613. **Telephone:** (809) 880-1800. **FAX:** (809) 880-1800.

**Primary Working Agreement:** Cincinnati Reds.

**President:** Josue Vega. **General Manager:** Jose "Che" Conde. **1994-95 Managers:** Dave Miley, Pat Kelly.

### CAGUAS CRIOLLOS

**Mailing Address:** P.O. Box 1415, Caguas, PR 00726. **Telephone:** (809) 743-0545. **FAX:** (809) 258-2222.

**Primary Working Agreement:** Boston Red Sox.

**Owner/President:** Enrique Hernandez. **General Manager:** Felix Millan. **1994-95 Managers:** Mike Easler, Felix Millan.

### MAYAGUEZ INDIANS

**Mailing Address:** Ave. Zamora No. 6, Urb. Villa Lydia, Aguadilla, PR

00603. **Telephone:** (809) 834-1111. **FAX:** (809) 834-7480.
**Primary Working Agreement:** San Diego Padres.
**President/General Manager:** Luis Mendez. **1994-95 Manager:** Tom Gamboa.

### PONCE LIONS

**Mailing Address:** Box 7444, Ponce, PR 00732. **Telephone:** (809) 848-4717 or 843-8487. **FAX:** 843-0990.
**Primary Working Agreement:** None.
**President/General Manager:** Jose Santiago. **1994-95 Manager:** Sandy Alomar Sr.

### SAN JUAN SENATORS

**Mailing Address:** P.O. Box 366246, San Juan, PR 00936. **Telephone:** (809) 754-1300. **FAX:** (809) 763-2217.
**Primary Working Agreement:** None.
**President:** Benjamin Rivera. **General Manager:** Ramon Aviles. **1994-95 Manager:** Luis Melendez.

### SANTURCE CRABBERS

**Mailing Address:** P.O. Box 1077, Hato Rey, PR 00919. **Telephone:** (809) 274-0240 or 274-0241. **FAX:** (809) 765-0410.
**President:** Reinaldo Paniagua Diaz. **General Manager:** Frankie Thon. **1994-95 Manager:** Max Oliveras.

## VENEZUELAN LEAGUE

**Mailing Address:** Avenida Sorbona, Edif. Marta-2do. Piso, No. 25, Colinas de Bello Monte, Caracas, Venezuela. **Telephone:** (011-58-2) 751-2079 or 751-1891. **FAX:** (011-58-2) 751-0891.
**President:** Carlos Cordido. **Vice President:** Jaime Benitez. **Vice President/General Manager:** Domingo Alvarez.
**Years League Active:** 1946-.
**Division Structure: East**—Caracas, La Guaira, Magallanes, Oriente. **West**—Aragua, Cabimas, Lara, Zulia.
**1994-95 Opening Date:** Oct. 15, 1994. **1994-95 Closing Date:** Dec. 30, 1994.
**No. of Regular Season Games:** 60.
**Playoff Format:** Top four teams meet in a 12-game round-robin series. Top two finishers meet in a best-of-7 series for league championship. Winner advances to Caribbean World Series.
**Roster Limit:** 25. **Roster Limit, Imports:** 7.

### ARAGUA TIGERS

**Mailing Address:** Estadio Jose Perez Colmenares, Barrio la Demoncracia Maracay-Edo, Aragua, Venezuela. **Telephone:** (58-43) 54-4632. **FAX:** (58-43) 54-4134.
**Primary Working Agreement:** Atlanta Braves.
**President:** Homero Diaz Osuna. **General Manager:** Carlos Isava. **1994-95 Manager:** Grady Little.

### CABIMAS OILERS

**Mailing Address:** Avenida 11 (Veritos), Edificio 95.5, Piso 3, Maracaibo, Edo., Zulia, Venezuela. **Telephone:** (58-14) 61-9589 or (58-64) 51-3746. FAX (58-64) 51-3746.
**Primary Working Agreement:** Milwaukee Brewers.
**President:** Andres Finol. **General Manager:** Enrique Finol. **1994-95 Manager:** Duffy Dyer.

### CARACAS LIONS

**Mailing Address:** Avenida Francisco de Miranda, Centro Segueros Piso 4, La Paz, Oficina Norte 42-C, Caracas, Venezuela. **Telephone:** (58-22) 38-7733. **FAX:** (58-22) 38-0691.
**Primary Working Agreement:** Los Angeles Dodgers.
**President:** Pablo Morales. **Vice President/General Manger:** Oscar Prieto. **1994-95 Managers:** Phil Regan, Pompeyo Davalillo.

### La GUAIRA TIBURONES

**Mailing Address:** Urbanizacion Miramar-Maiguetia, La Guaira, Venezuela. **Telephone:** (58-31) 25-5-79. **FAX:** (58-31) 23-1-16.
**Primary Working Agreement:** Kansas City Royals.
**President/General Manager:** Pedro Padron Panza. **1994-95 Manager:** Luis Salazar.

### LARA CARDINALS

**Mailing Address:** Av. Rotaria, Estadio Barquisimeto, Barquisimeto, Venezuela 3001. **Telephone:** (58-51) 42-31-32 or 42-45-43. **FAX:** (58-51) 42-19-21.
**Primary Working Agreement:** Toronto Blue Jays.
**President:** Adolfo Alvarez. **General Manager:** Humberto Oropeza. **1994-95 Manager:** Mel Queen.

### MAGALLANES NAVIGATORS

**Mailing Address:** Centro Comercial Caribbean Plaza, Modulo 8, Planta Alta-Local 173, Valencia, Cara Bobo, Venezuela. **Telephone:** (58-41) 24-

09-80 or 24-03-21. **FAX:** (58-41) 24-07-05.

**Primary Working Agreement:** Houston Astros.

**President/General Manager:** Alfredo Guadarrama. **1994-95 Manager:** Dave Hudgens.

### ORIENTE CARIBBEANS

**Mailing Address:** Ave. Stadium, Centro Comercial Novocentro 2do Piso, Local 2-4, Puerto la Cruz, Edo. Anzoategui, Venezuela. **Telephone:** (58-81) 66-25-36. **FAX:** (58-81) 66-70-54.

**Primary Working Agreement:** Chicago White Sox.

**President:** Pablo Ruggieri. **General Manager:** Luis Aponte. **1994-95 Manager:** Fred Kendall.

### ZULIA EAGLES

**Mailing Address:** Ave. 8 (Santa Rita), Edificio las Carolinas Mezanina, Local M-10, Maracaibo, Zulia, Venezuela. **Telephone:** (58-61) 99-98-34 or 97-98-35. **FAX:** (58-61) 98-02-10.

**Primary Working Agreement:** Chicago Cubs/Detroit Tigers.

**President:** Lucas Rincon. **General Manager:** Ruperto Machado Silva. **1994-95 Manager:** Ruben Amaro.

# OTHER WINTER LEAGUES

## ARIZONA FALL LEAGUE

**Mailing Address:** 10201 S. 51st St., Suite 230, Phoenix, AZ 85044. **Telephone:** (602) 496-6700. **FAX:** (602) 496-6384.

**Executive Vice President:** Steve Cobb. **Director of Baseball Operations:** Dan O'Brien. **Administrative Assistant:** Joan McGrath.

**Years League Active:** 1992-.

**Division Structure: North**—Peoria, Scottsdale, Sun Cities. **South**—Chandler, Mesa, Tempe.

**1994 Opening Date:** Oct. 6. **1994 Closing Date:** Nov. 30.

**No. of Regular Season Games:** 51.

**Playoff Format:** Division champions meet in best-of-3 series for league championship.

**Roster Limit:** 28. One foreign player permitted per club, but none from Puerto Rico, Dominican Republic or Venezuela.

### CHANDLER DIAMONDBACKS

**Mailing Address:** Compadre Stadium, 4001 S. Alma School Road, Chandler, AZ 85248.

**Working Agreement:** Florida Marlins, Milwaukee Brewers, Minnesota Twins, Pittsburgh Pirates. **1994 Manager:** Lamar Johnson (Brewers).

### MESA SAGUAROS

**Mailing Address:** HoHoKam Park, 1235 N. Center St., Mesa, AZ 85201.

**Working Agreement:** Atlanta Braves, Chicago Cubs, Houston Astros, Montreal Expos. **1994 Manager:** Jerry Manuel (Expos).

### PEORIA JAVELINAS

**Mailing Address:** Peoria Complex, 16101 N. 83rd Ave, Peoria, AZ 85382.

**Working Agreement:** Cincinnati Reds, New York Yankees, Oakland Athletics, Philadelphia Phillies, Seattle Mariners. **1994 Manager:** John Stearns (Reds).

### SCOTTSDALE SCORPIONS

**Mailing Address:** Scottsdale Stadium, 7402 E. Osborne, Scottsdale, AZ 85251.

**Working Agreement:** Baltimore Orioles, Boston Red Sox, Chicago White Sox, Kansas City Royals, San Francisco Giants. **1994 Manager:** Terry Francona (White Sox).

### SUN CITIES SOLAR SOX

**Mailing Address:** Peoria Complex, 16101 N. 83rd Ave, Peoria, AZ 85382.

**Working Agreement:** Cleveland Indians, Colorado Rockies, New York Mets, San Diego Padres, Toronto Blue Jays. **1994 Manager:** Brian Graham (Indians).

### TEMPE RAFTERS

**Mailing Address:** Tempe Diablo Stadium, 2200 W. Alameda, Tempe, AZ 85282.

**Working Agreement:** California Angels, Detroit Tigers, Los Angeles Dodgers, St. Louis Cardinals, Texas Rangers. **1994 Manager:** Ken Macha (Angels).

## AUSTRALIAN BASEBALL LEAGUE

**Mailing Address:** Level 4, 120 Clarence St., Sydney, New South Wales, 2000 Australia. **Telephone:** (011-61-2) 299-4766. **FAX:** (011-61-2) 299-4769.

**General Manager:** Stefan Kamasz. **Administrative Assistant:** Jane Taylor. **Media Director:** Jerry Caraccioli. **Umpire Controller:** Geoff Robertson.

## ADELAIDE GIANTS

**Mailing Address:** Unit 4, 83-85 Fullarton Rd., Kent Town, SA 5067 Australia. **Telephone:** (8) 364-3977. **FAX:** (8) 364-1730.

**Primary Working Agreement:** Los Angeles Dodgers.

**General Manager:** Brian Dutton. **1994-95 Manager:** Tony Harris.

## BRISBANE BANDITS

**Mailing Address:** 30 Macrossan St., Brisbane, Queensland 4000 Australia. **Telephone:** (7) 832-4688. **FAX:** (7) 832-2065.

**Primary Working Agreement:** Milwaukee Brewers.

**General Manager:** Tom Nicholson. **1994-95 Manager:** Dan Radison.

## CANBERRA BUSHRANGERS

**Mailing Address:** Suite 3, North Bourne Chambers, 54 North Bourne Ave., Canberra City, ACT 2601, Australia. **Telephone:** (6) 248-6110. **FAX:** (6) 248-6150.

**Primary Working Agreement:** New York Yankees.

**Owner:** Bruce Portner. **1994-95 Manager:** Rob Thomson.

## EAST COAST COUGARS

**Mailing Address:** Beenleigh Tavern, 15 Distillery Rd., Beenleigh, Queensland 4207 Australia. **Telephone:** (7) 287-4666. **FAX:** (7) 807-7262.

**Primary Working Agreement:** California Angels.

**General Manager:** Glen Partridge. **1994-95 Manager:** Tom Lawless.

## HUNTER EAGLES

**Mailing Address:** Office 2, Level 1, 50 Flushcombe Rd., Blacktown, New South Wales 2148 Australia. **Telephone:** (2) 831-8431. **FAX:** (2) 831-8430.

**Primary Working Agreement:** Montreal Expos.

**General Manager:** John Boyton. **1994-95 Manager:** Gomer Hodge.

## MELBOURNE MONARCHS

**Mailing Address:** P.O. Box 462, Footscray West, Victoria, Australia 3012. **Telephone:** (61-3) 689-3100. **FAX:** (61-3) 689-8094.

**Primary Working Agreement:** New York Mets.

**President:** Dennis Calimberti. **General Manager:** Phil Allen. **1994-95 Manager:** Jon Deeble.

## MELBOURNE REDS

**Mailing Address:** 28 Miles St., Mulgrave, 3170, Victoria, Australia. **Telephone:** (61-3) 561-9495. **FAX:** (61-3) 561-9510.

**Primary Working Agreement:** Atlanta Braves.

**President/General Manager:** Tony Peek. **1994-95 Manager:** Paul Runge.

## PERTH HEAT

**Mailing Address:** P.O. Box 844, South Perth, Western Australia 6151 Australia. **Telephone:** (61-9) 474-2199. **FAX:** (61-9) 474-3061.

**Primary Working Agreement:** Baltimore Orioles.

**General Manager:** Michael Palmer. **1994-95 Manager:** Tony Adamson.

## SYDNEY BLUES

**Mailing Address:** P.O. Box 2479, Nth Parramatta, New South Wales 2151 Australia. **Telephone:** (02) 890-2755. **FAX:** (02) 890-2225.

**Primary Working Agreement:** Toronto Blue Jays.

**President:** Ian Maurice. **General Manager:** Unavailable. **1994-95 Manager:** Rocket Wheeler.

# HAWAII WINTER BASEBALL

**Mailing Address:** 1210 Auahi St., Suite 231, Honolulu, HI 96814. **Telephone:** (808) 592-2255. **FAX:** (808) 592-2260.

**President:** Frank Kudo.

## HILO STARS

**Mailing Address:** P.O. Box 1051, Hilo, HI 96720. **Telephone:** (808) 969-9033. **FAX:** (808) 961-6053.

**President:** Bob Berg. **General Manager:** Clyde Nekoba. **1994 Manager:** Mark Wasinger.

## HONOLULU SHARKS

**Mailing Address:** Suite 231, 1210 Auahi St., Honolulu, HI 96814. **Telephone:** (808) 592-2255.

**General Manager:** Carl Iwasaki. **1994 Manager:** Tom Kotchman.

## KAUAI EMERALDS

**Mailing Address:** 3113 Kuhio Highway, Kauai, HI 96766. **Telephone:** (808) 245-6123. **FAX:** (808) 245-4199.

**General Manager:** Jim Koishigawa. **1994 Manager:** Trent Jewett.

## MAUI STINGRAYS

**Mailing Address:** P.O. Box 1193, Wailuku, HI 96793. **Telephone:** (808) 242-2950. **FAX:** (808) 244-1059.

**President:** Bob Berg. **General Manager:** Lane Fujii. **1994 Manager:** Gene Glynn.

# COLLEGE BASEBALL

## High School Baseball

## Amateur Baseball

## Youth Baseball

# COLLEGE BASEBALL

## NATIONAL COLLEGIATE ATHLETIC ASSOCIATION

**Mailing Address:** 6201 College Blvd., Overland Park, KS 66211. **Telephone:** (913) 339-1906. **FAX:** (913) 339-0026.

**Executive Director:** Cedric Dempsey. **Director of Championships:** Dennis Poppe. **College World Series Contact:** Jim Wright. **Statistics Contact:** John Painter. **Chairman, Baseball Committee:** Ron Maestri (University of New Orleans).

**1996 National Convention:** Jan. 6-10 at Dallas, TX.

### 1995 Championship Tournaments

**NCAA Division I**

**College World Series**............................................ Omaha, NE, June 2-10.
**Regionals**.................................... campus sites, May 25-28 or May 26-29.
**Play-ins**................................................................ campus sites, May 19-21.

**NCAA Division II**

**World Series** .......................................... Montgomery, AL, May 27-June 3.

**NCAA Division III**

**World Series**......................................................... Salem, VA, May 25-30.

## NATIONAL ASSOCIATION OF INTERCOLLEGIATE ATHLETICS

**Mailing Address:** 6120 S. Yale Ave., Ste. 1450, Tulsa, OK 74136. **Telephone:** (918) 494-8828. **FAX:** (918) 494-8841.

**Chief Executive Officer:** Dr. James Chasteen. **Baseball Administrator:** Duane DaPron.

### 1995 Championship Tournament

**NAIA World Series** .................................... Sioux City, IA, May 26-June 1.

## NATIONAL JUNIOR COLLEGE ATHLETIC ASSOCIATION

**Mailing Address:** P.O. Box 7305, Colorado Springs, CO 80933. **Telephone:** (719) 590-9788. **FAX:** (719) 590-7324.

**Executive Director:** George Killian. **Division I Baseball Tournament Director:** Sam Suplizio. **Division II Tournament Director:** John Daigle. **Division III Tournament Director:** William Reemtsen.

### 1995 Championship Tournaments

**Division I**

**Junior College World Series**........... Grand Junction, CO, May 27-June 2.

**Division II**

**World Series** .................................................... Millington, TN, May 20-26.

**Division III**

**World Series**......................................................... Batavia, NY, May 20-26.

## COMMUNITY COLLEGE LEAGUE OF CALIFORNIA

**Mailing Address:** 2017 O St., Sacramento, CA 95814. **Telephone:** (916) 444-1600. **FAX:** (916) 444-2954.

**Commissioner of Athletics:** Walter Rilliet. **Associate Commissioner of Athletics:** Pamela Walker.

**Director, Junior College Athletic Bureau:** Fred Baer. **Telephone:** (415) 345-4114. **FAX:** (415) 593-5973.

### 1995 Championship Tournament

**State Championships**..............................Fresno City College, May 27-29.

## AMERICAN BASEBALL COACHES ASSOCIATION

**Office Address:** 108 S. University Ave., Suite 3, Mt. Pleasant, MI 48858. **Telephone:** (517) 775-3300. **FAX:** (517) 775-3600.

**Executive Director:** Dave Keilitz. **Assistant to the Executive Director:** Karen Duncan. **Office Manager:** Pad McNeel. **President:** Carroll Land (Point Loma Nazarene, Calif., College).

**1996 National Convention:** Jan. 4-7 at Nashville, TN.

# NCAA DIVISION I CONFERENCES

## ATLANTIC COAST CONFERENCE

**Mailing Address:** P.O. Drawer ACC, Greensboro, NC 27419. **Telephone:** (910) 854-8787. **FAX:** (910) 854-8797.

**Baseball Members:** Clemson, Duke, Florida State, Georgia Tech, Maryland, North Carolina, North Carolina State, Virginia, Wake Forest.

**Director of Media Relations:** Brian Morrison.

**1995 Tournament:** Nine teams, double-elimination. May 16-21 at Greenville, S.C.

## ATLANTIC 10 CONFERENCE

**Mailing Address:** 101 Interchange Plaza, Suite 202, Cranbury, NJ 08512. **Telephone:** (609) 860-9100. **FAX:** (609) 860-0142.

**Baseball Members:** Duquesne, George Washington, Massachusetts, Rhode Island, Rutgers, St. Bonaventure, St. Joseph's, Temple, West Virginia.

**Director of Communications:** Ray Cella.

**1995 Tournament:** Four teams, double-elimination. May 12-14 at Boyertown, Pa.

## BIG EAST CONFERENCE

**Mailing Address:** 56 Exchange Terrace, Providence, RI 02903. **Telephone:** (401) 272-9108. **FAX:** (401) 751-8540.

**Baseball Members:** Boston College, Connecticut, Georgetown, Pittsburgh, Providence, St. John's, Seton Hall, Villanova.

**Director of Service Bureau:** Joe Gomes.

**1995 Tournament:** Four teams, double-elimination. May 16-19 at regular-season champion.

## BIG EIGHT CONFERENCE

**Mailing Address:** 104 W. Ninth St., Suite 408, Kansas City, MO 64105. **Telephone:** (816) 471-5088. **FAX:** (816) 471-4601.

**Baseball Members:** Iowa State, Kansas, Kansas State, Missouri, Nebraska, Oklahoma, Oklahoma State.

**Service Bureau Director:** Jeff Bollig.

**1995 Tournament:** Six teams, double-elimination. May 18-21 at Oklahoma City, Okla.

## BIG SOUTH CONFERENCE

**Mailing Address:** 1551 21st Ave. N., Suite 11, Myrtle Beach, SC 29577. **Telephone:** (803) 448-9998. **FAX:** (803) 626-7167.

**Baseball Members:** Charleston Southern, Coastal Carolina, Liberty, Maryland-Baltimore County, UNC Asheville, UNC Greensboro, Radford, Towson State, Winthrop.

**Assistant Public Relations Director:** Mike Shank.

**1995 Tournament:** None.

## BIG TEN CONFERENCE

**Mailing Address:** 1500 W. Higgins Rd., Park Ridge, IL 60068. **Telephone:** (708) 696-1010. **FAX:** (708) 696-1110.

**Baseball Members:** Illinois, Indiana, Iowa, Michigan, Michigan State, Minnesota, Northwestern, Ohio State, Penn State, Purdue.

**Print Communications Intern:** Roderick Drew.

**1995 Tournament:** Four teams, double-elimination. May 18-21 at regular-season champion.

## BIG WEST CONFERENCE

**Mailing Address:** 2 Corporate Park, Suite 206, Irvine, CA 92714. **Telephone:** (714) 261-2525. **FAX:** (714) 261-2528.

**Baseball Members:** UC Santa Barbara, Cal State Fullerton, Long Beach State, Nevada, Nevada-Las Vegas, New Mexico State, Pacific, San Jose State.

**Information Director:** Dennis Bickmeier.

**1995 Tournament:** Four teams, double-elimination. May 12-14 at Blair Field, Long Beach.

## COLONIAL ATHLETIC ASSOCIATION

**Mailing Address:** 8625 Patterson Ave., Richmond, VA 23229. **Telephone:** (804) 754-1616. **FAX:** (804) 754-1830.

**Baseball Members:** East Carolina, George Mason, James Madison, UNC Wilmington, Old Dominion, Richmond, William & Mary.

**Assistant Commissioner:** Tripp Sheppard.

**1995 Tournament:** Seven teams, double-elimination. May 17-20 at Kinston, N.C.

## GREAT MIDWEST CONFERENCE

**Mailing Address:** 35 E. Wacker Dr., Suite 650, Chicago, IL 60601. **Telephone:** (312) 553-0483. **FAX:** (312) 553-0495.

**Baseball Members:** Alabama-Birmingham, Cincinnati, Dayton, Memphis, Saint Louis.

**Communications Assistant:** Russ Anderson.

**1995 Tournament:** Five teams, double-elimination. May 18-21 at St. Louis.

## IVY LEAGUE

**Mailing Address:** 120 Alexander St., Princeton, NJ 08544. **Telephone:** (609) 258-6426. **FAX:** (609) 258-1690.

**Baseball Members: Rolfe**—Brown, Dartmouth, Harvard, Yale. **Gehrig**—Columbia, Cornell, Pennsylvania, Princeton.

**Associate Director:** Chuck Yrigoyen.

**1995 Tournament:** Best-of-3 series between division champions. May 6-7 at Rolfe Division champion.

## METRO CONFERENCE

**Mailing Address:** Two Ravinia Drive, Suite 210, Atlanta, GA 30346. **Telephone:** (404) 395-6444. **FAX:** (404) 395-6423.

**Baseball Members:** Louisville, UNC Charlotte, South Florida, Southern Mississippi, Tulane, Virginia Commonwealth, Virginia Tech.

**Assistant Commissioner:** Jamie Kimbrough. **Director of Communications:** Katrina Ross.

**1995 Tournament:** Seven teams, double-elimination. May 17-21 at Charlotte, NC.

## METRO ATLANTIC ATHLETIC CONFERENCE

**Mailing Address:** 1090 Amboy Ave., Edison, NJ 08837. **Telephone:** (908) 225-0202. **FAX:** (908) 225-5440.

**Baseball Members: North**—Canisius, LeMoyne, Niagara, Siena. **South**—Fairfield, Iona, Manhattan, St. Peter's.

**Director of Public Relations:** Jay Cavallo.

**1995 Tournament:** Four teams, double-elimination. May 12-14 at Albany, N.Y.

## MID-AMERICAN CONFERENCE

**Mailing Address:** Four SeaGate, Suite 102, Toledo, OH 43604. **Telephone:** (419) 249-7177. **FAX:** (419) 249-7199.

**Baseball Members:** Akron, Ball State, Bowling Green State, Central Michigan, Eastern Michigan, Kent, Miami (Ohio), Ohio, Toledo, Western Michigan.

**Director of Communications:** Sue Wagner.

**1995 Tournament:** Four teams, double-elimination. May 18-20 at regular-season champion.

## MID-CONTINENT CONFERENCE

**Mailing Address:** 40 Shuman Blvd., Suite 118, Naperville, IL 60563. **Telephone:** (708) 416-7560. **FAX:** (708) 416-7564.

**Baseball Members: East**—Central Connecticut State, C.W. Post, New York Tech, Pace, Troy State, Youngstown State. **West**—Chicago State, Eastern Illinois, Northeastern Illinois, Valparaiso, Western Illinois.

**Assistant Commissioner:** Tom Lessig.

**1995 Tournament:** Four teams, double-elimination. May 12-14 at regular-season champion.

## MID-EASTERN ATHLETIC CONFERENCE

**Mailing Address:** 102 N. Elm St., Suite 401, Greensboro, NC 27420. **Telephone:** (910) 275-9961. **FAX:** (910) 275-9964.

**Baseball Members: North**—Coppin State, Delaware State, Howard, Maryland-Eastern Shore. **South**—Bethune-Cookman, Florida A&M, North Carolina A&T State.

**Director of Service Bureau:** Larry Barber.

**1995 Tournament:** Seven teams, double-elimination. April 19-22 at Tallahassee, Fla.

## MIDWESTERN COLLEGIATE CONFERENCE

**Mailing Address:** 201 S. Capitol Ave., Suite 500, Indianapolis, IN 46225. **Telephone:** (317) 237-5625. **FAX:** (317) 237-5620.

**Baseball Members: East**—Cleveland State, Detroit Mercy, LaSalle, Wright State, Xavier. **West**—Butler, Illinois-Chicago, Northern Illinois, Notre Dame, Wisconsin-Milwaukee.

**Director of Communications:** Will Hancock.

**1995 Tournament:** Six teams, double-elimination. May 13-17 at South Bend, Ind.

## MISSOURI VALLEY CONFERENCE

**Mailing Address:** 1000 St. Louis Station, Suite 333, St. Louis, MO 63103. **Telephone:** (314) 421-0339. **FAX:** (314) 421-3505.

**Baseball Members:** Bradley, Creighton, Evansville, Illinois State, Indiana State, Northern Iowa, Southern Illinois, Southwest Missouri State, Wichita State.

**Assistant Commissioner, Communications:** Jack Watkins.

**1995 Tournament:** Six teams, double-elimination. May 17-20 at Springfield, Ill.

## NORTH ATLANTIC CONFERENCE

**Mailing Address:** P.O. Box 69, Orono, ME 04473. **Telephone:** (207) 866-2383. **FAX:** (207) 866-7524.

**Baseball Members:** Boston University, Delaware, Drexel, Hartford, Hofstra, Maine, New Hampshire, Northeastern, Vermont.

**Staff Associate:** Len Harlow.

**1995 Tournament:** Six teams, double-elimination. May 12-15 at regular-season champion.

## NORTHEAST CONFERENCE

**Mailing Address:** 900 Route 9, Woodbridge, NJ 07095. **Telephone:** (908) 636-9119. **FAX:** (908) 636-6496.

**Baseball Members:** Fairleigh Dickinson, Long Island, Marist, Monmouth, Mount St. Mary's, Rider, St. Francis (N.Y.), Wagner.

**Publicity Director:** David Siroty.

**1995 Tournament:** Four teams, double-elimination. May 12-14 at Ewing, N.J.

## OHIO VALLEY CONFERENCE

**Mailing Address:** 278 Franklin Road, Suite 103, Brentwood, TN 37027. **Telephone:** (615) 371-1698. **FAX:** (615) 371-1788.

**Baseball Members:** Austin Peay State, Eastern Kentucky, Middle Tennessee State, Morehead State, Murray State, Southeast Missouri State, Tennessee-Martin, Tennessee Tech.

**Information Director:** Rob Washburn.

**1995 Tournament:** Four teams, double-elimination. May 13-15 at regular-season champion.

## PACIFIC-10 CONFERENCE

**Mailing Address:** 800 S. Broadway, Suite 400, Walnut Creek, CA 94596. **Telephone:** (510) 932-4411. **FAX:** (510) 932-4601.

**Baseball Members: North**—Gonzaga, Oregon State, Portland, Portland State, Washington, Washington State. **South**—Arizona, Arizona State, California, UCLA, Southern California, Stanford.

**Public Relations Intern:** Cara Gamberdella.

**1995 Tournament:** Best-of-3 series between division champions. May 18-20 at Southern Division champion.

## PATRIOT LEAGUE

**Mailing Address:** 3897 Adler Place, Bethlehem, PA 18017. **Telephone:** (610) 691-2414. **FAX:** (610) 691-8414.

**Baseball Members:** Army, Bucknell, Fordham, Holy Cross, Lafayette, Lehigh, Navy.

**Assistant Director, Media Relations:** Suzanne Bourque.

**1995 Tournament:** None.

## SOUTHEASTERN CONFERENCE

**Mailing Address:** 2201 Civic Center Blvd., Birmingham, AL 35203. **Telephone:** (205) 458-3000. **FAX:** (205) 458-3030.

**Baseball Members: East**—Florida, Georgia, Kentucky, South Carolina, Tennessee, Vanderbilt. **West**—Alabama, Arkansas, Auburn, Louisiana State, Mississippi, Mississippi State.

**Associate Director of Media Services:** Glenn Thackston.

**1995 Tournaments: East**—Six teams, double-elimination. May 18-21 at Knoxville, TN. **West**—Six teams, double-elimination. May 18-21 at Starkville, MS.

## SOUTHERN CONFERENCE

**Mailing Address:** One West Pack Square, Suite 1508, Asheville, NC 28801. **Telephone:** (704) 255-7872. **FAX:** (704) 251-5006.

**Baseball Members:** Appalachian State, The Citadel, Davidson, East Tennessee State, Furman, Georgia Southern, Marshall, Virginia Military Institute, Western Carolina.

**Media Relations Assistant:** Deana Monahan.

**1995 Tournament:** Eight teams, double-elimination. April 27-30 at Charleston, S.C.

## SOUTHLAND CONFERENCE

**Mailing Address:** 1309 W. 15th St., Suite 303, Plano, TX 75075. **Telephone:** (214) 424-4833. **FAX:** (214) 424-4099.

**Baseball Members:** McNeese State, Nicholls State, Northeast Louisiana, Northwestern State, Sam Houston State, Southwest Texas State, Stephen F. Austin State, Texas-Arlington, Texas-San Antonio.

**Director of Media Relations:** Tammy Broz.

**1995 Tournament:** Four teams, double-elimination. May 13-16 at Shreveport, La.

## SOUTHWEST CONFERENCE

**Mailing Address:** P.O. Box 569420, Dallas, TX 75356. **Telephone:** (214) 920-1729. **FAX:** (214) 920-1758.

**Baseball Members:** Baylor, Houston, Rice, Texas, Texas A&M, Texas Christian, Texas Tech.

**Director of Media Relations:** Bo Carter.

**1995 Tournament:** Four teams, double-elimination. May 18-21 at College Station, Texas.

## SOUTHWESTERN ATHLETIC CONFERENCE

**Mailing Address:** Louisiana Superdome, 1500 Sugar Bowl Drive, New Orleans, LA 70112. **Telephone:** (504) 523-7574. **FAX:** (504) 523-7513.

**Baseball Members: East**—Alabama State, Alcorn State, Jackson

State, Mississippi Valley State. **West**—Grambling State, Prairie View A&M, Southern, Texas Southern.

**Director of Publicity:** Lonza Hardy.

**1995 Tournament:** Four teams, double-elimination. April 28-May 1 at Natchez, Miss.

### SUN BELT CONFERENCE

**Mailing Address:** One Galleria Blvd., Suite 2115, Metairie, LA 70001. **Telephone:** (504) 834-6600. **FAX:** (504) 834-6806.

**Baseball Members:** Arkansas-Little Rock, Arkansas State, Jacksonville, Lamar, Louisiana Tech, New Orleans, South Alabama, Southwestern Louisiana, Texas-Pan American, Western Kentucky.

**Associate Director of Communications:** Paul Dauphin.

**1995 Tournament:** Six teams, double-elimination. May 17-20 at regular-season champion.

### TRANSAMERICA ATHLETIC CONFERENCE

**Mailing Address:** 3370 Vineville Ave., Suite 108-B, Macon, GA 31204. **Telephone:** (912) 474-3394. **FAX:** (912) 474-4272.

**Baseball Members:** Campbell, Centenary, Central Florida, Charleston, Florida Atlantic, Florida International, Georgia State, Mercer, Samford, Southeastern Louisiana, Stetson.

**Sports Information Director:** Tom Snyder.

**1995 Tournament:** Four teams, double-elimination. May 11-13 at regular-season champion.

### WEST COAST CONFERENCE

**Mailing Address:** 400 Oyster Point Blvd., Suite 221, South San Francisco, CA 94080. **Telephone:** (415) 873-8622. **FAX:** (415) 873-7846.

**Baseball Members:** Loyola Marymount, Pepperdine, Saint Mary's, San Diego, San Francisco, Santa Clara.

**Assistant Commissioner:** Don Ott.

**1995 Tournament:** None.

### WESTERN ATHLETIC CONFERENCE

**Mailing Address:** 14 W. Dry Creek Circle, Littleton, CO 80120. **Telephone:** (303) 795-1962. **FAX:** (303) 795-1960.

**Baseball Members: East**—Air Force, Brigham Young, Grand Canyon, New Mexico, Utah, Wyoming. **West**—Cal. Poly San Luis Obispo, Cal State Northridge, Fresno State, Hawaii, Sacramento State, San Diego State.

**Associate Commissioner:** Jeff Hurd.

**1995 Tournament:** Best-of-3 series between division champions. May 18-20 at Wastern Division champion.

## NCAA DIVISION II CONFERENCES

(Select Conferences Only)

### CALIFORNIA COLLEGIATE ATHLETIC ASSOCIATION

**Mailing Address:** 40 Via di Roma Walk, Long Beach, CA 90803. **Telephone:** (310) 985-4065. **FAX:** (310) 985-8067.

**Baseball Members:** Cal Poly Pomona, UC Riverside, Cal State Dominguez Hills, Cal State Los Angeles, Cal State San Bernardino,

**Publicity Director:** Grayle Howlett.

**1995 Tournament:** None.

### GULF SOUTH CONFERENCE

**Mailing Address:** 4 Office Park Circle, Suite 218, Birmingham, AL 35223. **Telephone:** (205) 870-9750. **FAX:** (205) 870-4723.

**Baseball Members: West**—Central Arkansas, Delta State, Henderson State, Livingston, Mississippi College. **East**—Lincoln Memorial, North Alabama, Valdosta State, West Florida, West Georgia.

**Publicity Director:** Tom Bonerbo.

**1995 Tournament:** April 28-30 at Eastern Division champion.

### PEACH BELT ATHLETIC CONFERENCE

**Mailing Address:** P.O. Box 204290, Augusta, GA 30917. **Telephone:** (706) 860-8499. **FAX:** (706) 650-8113.

**Baseball Members:** Armstrong State, Augusta, Columbus, Francis Marion, Georgia College, Kennesaw State, Pembroke State, South Carolina-Aiken, South Carolina-Spartanburg

**Publicity Director:** Torye Hurst.

**1995 Tournament:** May 6, 11-13 at Augusta, GA.

### SUNSHINE STATE CONFERENCE

**Mailing Address:** 7061 Grand National Dr., Suite 138, Orlando, FL 32819. **Telephone:** (407) 248-8460. **FAX:** (407) 248-8325.

**Baseball Members:** Barry, Eckerd, Florida Southern, Florida Tech, North Florida, Rollins, St. Leo, Tampa.

**Publicity Director:** Walter Riddle.

**1995 Tournament:** None.

# NCAA Division I Teams

**AIR FORCE ACADEMY** Falcons
**Conference:** Western Athletic/East.
**Mailing Address:** Building 2169, Room 100D, Colorado Springs, CO 80840.
**Head Coach:** Eric Campbell. **Telephone:** (719) 472-2057.
**SID:** Dave Toller. **Telephone:** (719) 472-2313. **FAX:** (719) 472-3798.

**AKRON** Zips
**Conference:** Mid-American.
**Mailing Address:** JAR Arena, Carroll Street, Akron, OH 44325.
**Head Coach:** Dave Fross. **Telephone:** (216) 972-7277.
**SID:** Tom Liggett. **Telephone:** (216) 972-7468. **FAX:** (216) 374-8844.

**ALABAMA** Crimson Tide
**Conference:** Southeastern/West.
**Mailing Address:** P.O. Box K, Tuscaloosa, AL 35487.
**Head Coach:** Jim Wells. **Telephone:** (205) 346-6171.
**SID:** Barry Allen. **Telephone:** (205) 348-6084. **FAX:** (205) 348-8841.

**ALABAMA-BIRMINGHAM** Blazers
**Conference:** Great Midwest.
**Mailing Address:** 617 13th St. S., Birmingham, AL 35294.
**Head Coach:** Pete Rancont. **Telephone:** (205) 934-5181.
**SID:** Reid Adair. **Telephone:** (205) 934-0722. **FAX:** (205) 934-7505.

**ALABAMA STATE** Hornets
**Conference:** Southwestern Athletic/East.
**Mailing Address:** P.O. Box 271, Montgomery, AL 36101.
**Head Coach:** Larry Watkins. **Telephone:** (205) 293-4228.
**SID:** Peter Forest. **Telephone:** (205) 293-4511. **FAX:** (205) 262-2971.

**ALCORN STATE** Braves
**Conference:** Southwestern Athletic/East.
**Mailing Address:** P.O. Box 510, Lorman, MS 39096.
**Head Coach:** Willie McGowan. **Telephone:** (601) 877-6279.
**SID:** Derick Hackett. **Telephone:** (601) 877-6466. **FAX:** (601) 877-3821.

**APPALACHIAN STATE** Mountaineers
**Conference:** Southern.
**Mailing Address:** Broome-Kirk Gymnasium, Boone, NC 28608.
**Head Coach:** Jim Morris. **Telephone:** (704) 262-6097.
**SID:** Rick Covington. **Telephone:** (704) 262-2268. **FAX:** (704) 262-6106.

**ARIZONA** Wildcats
**Conference:** Pacific-10/South.
**Mailing Address:** 229 McKale Center, Tucson, AZ 85721.
**Head Coach:** Jerry Kindall. **Telephone:** (602) 621-4102.
**SID:** Stacee Manske. **Telephone:** (602) 621-4163. **FAX:** (602) 621-2681.

**ARIZONA STATE** Sun Devils
**Conference:** Pacific-10/South.
**Mailing Address:** P.O. Box 872505, Tempe, AZ 85287.
**Head Coach:** Pat Murphy. **Telephone:** (602) 965-6085.
**SID:** Paul Kirk. **Telephone:** (602) 965-6592. **FAX:** (602) 965-5408.

**ARKANSAS** Razorbacks
**Conference:** Southeastern/West
**Mailing Address:** Broyles Athletic Complex, Fayetteville, AR 72701.
**Head Coach:** Norm DeBriyn. **Telephone:** (501) 575-3655.
**SID:** Jeff Muir. **Telephone:** (501) 575-2751. **FAX:** (501) 575-7481.

**ARKANSAS-LITTLE ROCK** Trojans
**Conference:** Sun Belt.
**Mailing Address:** 2801 South University, Little Rock, AR 72204.
**Head Coach:** Gary Hogan. **Telephone:** (501) 663-8095.
**SID:** Warren Miller. **Telephone:** (501) 569-3306. **FAX:** (501) 569-3030.

**ARKANSAS STATE** Indians
**Conference:** Sun Belt.
**Mailing Address:** P.O. Box 1000, State University, AR 72467.
**Head Coach:** Bill Bethea. **Telephone:** (501) 972-2700.
**SID:** James Barr. **Telephone:** (501) 972-2541. **FAX:** (501) 972-3367.

**ARMY** Cadets
**Conference:** Patriot.
**Mailing Address:** Howard Road, Building 639, West Point, NY 10996.
**Head Coach:** Dan Roberts. **Telephone:** (914) 938-3712.
**SID:** Bob Beretta. **Telephone:** (914) 938-3303. **FAX:** (914) 446-2556.

**AUBURN** Tigers
**Conference:** Southeastern/West.
**Mailing Address:** P.O. Box 351, Auburn University, AL 36831.
**Head Coach:** Hal Baird. **Telephone:** (205) 844-9767.
**SID:** Scott Stricklin. **Telephone:** (205) 844-9800. **FAX:** (205) 844-9807.

**AUSTIN PEAY STATE** Governors
**Conference:** Ohio Valley.
**Mailing Address:** P.O. Box 4515, Clarksville, TN 37044.
**Head Coach:** Gary McClure. **Telephone:** (615) 648-6266.
**SID:** Cris Belvin. **Telephone:** (615) 648-7561. **FAX:** (615) 648-7562.

**BALL STATE** Cardinals
**Conference:** Mid-American.

**Mailing Address:** 2000 University Ave., Muncie, IN 47306.
**Head Coach:** Pat Quinn. **Telephone:** (317) 285-8907.
**SID:** Bob Moore. **Telephone:** (317) 285-8242. **FAX:** (317) 285-8929.

### BAYLOR Bears

**Conference:** Southwest.
**Mailing Address:** 3031 Dutton Ave., Waco, TX 76711.
**Head Coach:** Steve Smith. **Telephone:** (817) 755-3029.
**SID:** Tommy Newsom. **Telephone:** (817) 755-3066. **FAX:** (817) 755-1369.

### BETHUNE-COOKMAN Wildcats

**Conference:** Mid-Eastern Athletic.
**Mailing Address:** 640 Second Ave., Daytona Beach, FL 32115.
**Head Coach:** Brian Rhees. **Telephone:** (904) 255-1401, ext. 349.
**SID:** Earl Kitchings. **Telephone:** (904) 255-1401, ext. 263. **FAX:** (904) 253-4231.

### BOSTON COLLEGE Eagles

**Conference:** Big East.
**Mailing Address:** 321 Conte Forum, Chestnut Hill, MA 02167.
**Head Coach:** Rich Maloney. **Telephone:** (617) 552-3092.
**SID:** Dick Kelley. **Telephone:** (617) 552-3004. **FAX:** (617) 552-4903.

### BOSTON UNIVERSITY Terriers

**Conference:** North Atlantic.
**Mailing Address:** 285 Babcock St., Boston, MA 02215.
**Head Coach:** Bill Mahoney. **Telephone:** (617) 353-5409.
**SID:** Dan Furlong. **Telephone:** (617) 353-2872. **FAX:** (617) 353-5286.

### BOWLING GREEN STATE Falcons

**Conference:** Mid-American.
**Mailing Address:** Perry Stadium, Bowling Green, OH 43403.
**Head Coach:** Danny Schmitz. **Telephone:** (419) 372-7065.
**SID:** Mark Kunstmann. **Telephone:** (419) 372-7076. **FAX:** (419) 372-6015.

### BRADLEY Braves

**Conference:** Missouri Valley.
**Mailing Address:** 1501 W. Bradley Ave., Peoria, IL 61625.
**Head Coach:** Dewey Kalmer. **Telephone:** (309) 677-2684.
**SID:** John Young. **Telephone:** (309) 677-2687. **FAX:** (309) 677-2665.

### BRIGHAM YOUNG Cougars

**Conference:** Western Athletic/East.
**Mailing Address:** 30 SFH, Provo, UT 84602.
**Head Coach:** Gary Pullins. **Telephone:** (801) 378-5049.
**SID:** Ralph Zobell. **Telephone:** (801) 378-4911. **FAX:** (801) 378-3520.

### BROWN Bears

**Conference:** Ivy League/Rolfe.
**Mailing Address:** Box 1932, Providence, RI 02912.
**Head Coach:** Bill Almon. **Telephone:** (401) 863-3090.
**SID:** Marybeth Bird. **Telephone:** (401) 863-2219. **FAX:** (401) 863-1436.

### BUCKNELL Bison

**Conference:** Patriot.
**Mailing Address:** Davis Gym, Lewisburg, PA 17837.
**Head Coach:** Gene Depew. **Telephone:** (717) 524-3301.
**SID:** Bob Behler. **Telephone:** (717) 524-1227. **FAX:** (717) 524-1660.

### BUTLER Bulldogs

**Conference:** Midwestern Collegiate.
**Mailing Address:** 4600 Sunset Ave., Indianapolis, IN 46208.
**Head Coach:** Steve Farley. **Telephone:** (317) 283-9375.
**SID:** Jim McGrath. **Telephone:** (317) 283-9671. **FAX:** (317) 283-9808.

### C.W. POST Pioneers

**Conference:** Mid-Continent/East.
**Mailing Address:** Northern Boulevard, Brookville, NY 11548.
**Head Coach:** Dick Vining. **Telephone:** (516) 299-2289.
**SID:** Jeremy Kniffin. **Telephone:** (516) 299-2675. **FAX:** (516) 626-0150.

### CALIFORNIA Golden Bears

**Conference:** Pacific-10/South.
**Mailing Address:** 210 Memorial Stadium, Berkeley, CA 94720.
**Head Coach:** Bob Milano. **Telephone:** (510) 643-6006.
**SID:** Scott Ball. **Telephone:** (510) 642-5363. **FAX:** (510) 643-7778.

### UCLA Bruins

**Conference:** Pacific-10/South.
**Mailing Address:** 405 Hilgard Ave., Los Angeles, CA 90024.
**Head Coach:** Gary Adams. **Telephone:** (310) 477-8702.
**SIDs:** John Dolak, Jeff Blank. **Telephone:** (310) 206-6831. **FAX:** (310) 825-8664.

### UC SANTA BARBARA Gauchos

**Conference:** Big West.
**Mailing Address:** Robertson Gym, 302B, Santa Barbara, CA 93106.
**Head Coach:** Bob Brontsema. **Telephone:** (805) 893-3690.
**SID:** Ted Cummins. **Telephone:** (805) 893-8603. **FAX:** (805) 893-4537.

### CAL POLY SAN LUIS OBISPO Mustangs

**Conference:** Western Athletic/West.
**Mailing Address:** One Grand Ave., San Luis Obispo, CA 93407.
**Head Coach:** Ritch Price. **Telephone:** (805) 756-1201.
**SID:** Eric McDowell. **Telephone:** (805) 756-6531. **FAX:** (805) 756-2650.

**CAL STATE FULLERTON** Titans
**Conference:** Big West.
**Mailing Address:** 800 N. State College Blvd., PE 133C, Fullerton, CA 92634.
**Head Coach:** Augie Garrido. **Telephone:** (714) 773-3789.
**SID:** Jason Pommier. **Telephone:** (714) 773-3970. **FAX:** (714) 773-3141.

**CAL STATE NORTHRIDGE** Matadors
**Conference:** Western Athletic/West.
**Mailing Address:** 18111 Nordhoff St., Northridge, CA 91330.
**Head Coach:** Bill Kernen. **Telephone:** (818) 885-3233.
**SID:** Barry Smith. **Telephone:** (818) 885-3243. **FAX:** (818) 885-4762.

**CAMPBELL** Camels
**Conference:** TransAmerica Athletic.
**Mailing Address:** 215 Pope St., Buies Creek, NC 27506.
**Head Coach:** John Daurity. **Telephone:** (910) 893-1354.
**SID:** Derek Smolik. **Telephone:** (910) 893-1331. **FAX:** (910) 893-1330.

**CANISIUS** Golden Griffins
**Conference:** Metro Atlantic/North
**Mailing Address:** 2001 Main St., Buffalo, NY 14208.
**Head Coach:** Don Colpoys. **Telephone:** (716) 858-7030.
**SID:** John Maddock. **Telephone:** (716) 888-2977. **FAX:** (716) 888-2980.

**CENTENARY** Gents
**Conference:** TransAmerica Athletic.
**Mailing Address:** Box 41188, Shreveport, LA 71134.
**Head Coach:** Wayne Rathbun. **Telephone:** (318) 869-5095.
**SID:** Jeff Conrad. **Telephone:** (318) 869-5092. **FAX:** (318) 869-5145.

**CENTRAL CONNECTICUT STATE** Blue Devils
**Conference:** Mid-Continent/East.
**Mailing Address:** Kaiser Hall, 1615 Stanley St., New Britain, CT 06050.
**Head Coach:** George Redman. **Telephone:** (203) 832-3074.
**SID:** Brent Rutkowski. **Telephone:** (203) 832-3058. **FAX:** (203) 832-3084.

**CENTRAL FLORIDA** Golden Knights
**Conference:** TransAmerica Athletic.
**Mailing Address:** Building 39, Room 109, Orlando, FL 32816.
**Head Coach:** Jay Bergman. **Telephone:** (407) 823-0140.
**SID:** Steve Nelson. **Telephone:** (407) 823-2729. **FAX:** (407) 823-5266.

**CENTRAL MICHIGAN** Chippewas
**Conference:** Mid-American.
**Mailing Address:** 108 West Hall, Mt. Pleasant, MI 48858.
**Head Coach:** Dean Kreiner. **Telephone:** (517) 774-6670.
**SID:** Fred Stabley Jr. **Telephone:** (517) 774-3277. **FAX:** (517) 774-7324.

**CHAPMAN** Panthers
**Conference:** Independent.
**Mailing Address:** 333 N. Glassell, Orange, CA 92666.
**Head Coach:** Rex Peters. **Telephone:** (714) 997-6662.
**SID:** Jim Moore. **Telephone:** (714) 997-6691. **FAX:** (714) 532-6010.

**CHARLESTON** Cougars
**Conference:** TransAmerica Athletic.
**Mailing Address:** 26 George St., Charleston, SC 29424.
**Head Coach:** Ralph Ciabattari. **Telephone:** (803) 953-5916.
**SID:** Tony Ciuffo. **Telephone:** (803) 953-5465. **FAX:** (803) 953-6534.

**CHARLESTON SOUTHERN** Buccaneers
**Conference:** Big South.
**Mailing Address:** P.O. Box 10087, Charleston, SC 29411.
**Head Coach:** Randy Mazey. **Telephone:** (803) 863-7591.
**SID:** Mike Hoffman. **Telephone:** (803) 863-7688. **FAX:** (803) 863-7676.

**CHICAGO STATE** Cougars
**Conference:** Mid-Continent/West.
**Mailing Address:** 9500 South King Drive, Chicago, IL 60628.
**Head Coach:** Kevin McCray. **Telephone:** (312) 995-3655.
**SID:** David Vandewalle. **Telephone:** (312) 995-2217. **FAX:** (312) 995-3659.

**CINCINNATI** Bearcats
**Conference:** Great Midwest.
**Mailing Address:** Mail Location 21, Cincinnati, OH 45221.
**Head Coach:** Bruce Gordon. **Telephone:** (513) 556-0566.
**SID:** Alyson Footer. **Telephone:** (513) 556-5191. **FAX:** (513) 556-0619.

**THE CITADEL** Bulldogs
**Conference:** Southern.
**Mailing Address:** P.O. Box 7, Citadel Station, Charleston, SC 29409.
**Head Coach:** Fred Jordan. **Telephone:** (803) 953-5070.
**SID:** Brian Kuhlmann. **Telephone:** (803) 953-5120. **FAX:** (803) 953-5058.

**CLEMSON** Tigers
**Conference:** Atlantic Coast.
**Mailing Address:** P.O. Box 31, Clemson, SC 29633.
**Head Coach:** Jack Leggett. **Telephone:** (803) 656-1947.
**SID:** Bob Bradley, Chris Metzler. **Telephone:** (803) 656-2114. **FAX:** (803) 656-0299.

**CLEVELAND STATE** Vikings
**Conference:** Midwestern Collegiate/East.
**Mailing Address:** CSU Convocation Center, 2000 Prospect, Cleveland, OH 44115.

**Head Coach:** Kevin Rhomberg. **Telephone:** (216) 687-4822.
**SID:** Dave Trebisky. **Telephone:** (216) 687-4818. **FAX:** (216) 523-7257.

### COASTAL CAROLINA Chanticleers

**Conference:** Big South.
**Mailing Address:** P.O. Box 1954, Conway, SC 29527.
**Head Coach:** John Vrooman. **Telephone:** (803) 349-2932.
**SID:** Kevin Hadsell. **Telephone:** (803) 349-2809. **FAX:** (803) 349-2819.

### COLGATE Red Raiders

**Conference:** Patriot.
**Mailing Address:** 13 Oak St., Hamilton, NY 13346.
**Head Coach:** Mike Doherty. **Telephone:** (315) 824-7574.
**SID:** Jeff Fanter. **Telephone:** (315) 824-7566. **FAX:** (315) 824-7977.

### COLUMBIA Lions

**Conference:** Ivy League/Gehrig.
**Mailing Address:** Dodge Fitness Center, 116th Street and Broadway, New York, NY 10027.
**Head Coach:** Paul Fernandes. **Telephone:** (212) 854-2543.
**SID:** Bill Steinman. **Telephone:** (212) 854-2534. **FAX:** (212) 854-8168.

### CONNECTICUT Huskies

**Conference:** Big East.
**Mailing Address:** U-78, 2095 Hillside Rd., Storrs, CT 06269.
**Head Coach:** Andy Baylock. **Telephone:** (203) 486-2458.
**SID:** Kyle Muncy. **Telephone:** (203) 486-3531. **FAX:** (203) 486-5085.

### COPPIN STATE Eagles

**Conference:** Mid-Eastern Athletic.
**Mailing Address:** 2500 W. North Ave., Baltimore, MD 21216.
**Head Coach:** Jason Booker. **Telephone:** (410) 383-5686.
**SID:** David Popham. **Telephone:** (410) 383-5642. **FAX:** (410) 669-6154.

### CORNELL Big Red

**Conference:** Ivy League/Rolfe.
**Mailing Address:** P.O. Box 729, Ithaca, NY 14851.
**Head Coach:** Tom Ford. **Telephone:** (607) 255-6604.
**SID:** Dave Wohlhueter. **Telephone:** (607) 255-3753. **FAX:** (607) 255-9791.

### CREIGHTON Blue Jays

**Conference:** Missouri Valley.
**Mailing Address:** Vinardi Athletic Center, 2500 Burt St., Omaha, NE 68178.
**Head Coach:** Jack Dahm. **Telephone:** (402) 280-2720.
**SID:** Vince Lodl. **Telephone:** (402) 280-5544. **FAX:** (402) 280-2495.

### DARTMOUTH Big Green

**Conference:** Ivy League/Rolfe.
**Mailing Address:** 6083 Alumni Gym, Hanover, NH 03755.
**Head Coach:** Bob Whalen. **Telephone:** (603) 646-2477.
**SID:** Matt Jennings. **Telephone:** (603) 646-2468. **FAX:** (603) 646-1286.

### DAVIDSON Wildcats

**Conference:** Southern.
**Mailing Address:** P.O. Box 1750, Davidson, NC 28036.
**Head Coach:** Dick Cooke. **Telephone:** (704) 892-2368.
**SID:** Emil Parker. **Telephone:** (704) 892-2374. **FAX:** (704) 892-2636.

### DAYTON Flyers

**Conference:** Great Midwest.
**Mailing Address:** Box 1220, 300 College Park, Dayton, OH 45469.
**Head Coach:** Chris Sorrell. **Telephone:** (513) 229-4456.
**SID:** Bill Behrns. **Telephone:** (513) 229-4460. **FAX:** (513) 229-4461.

### DELAWARE Fightin' Blue Hens

**Conference:** North Atlantic.
**Mailing Address:** Bob Carpenter Center, Newark, DE 19716.
**Head Coach:** Bob Hannah. **Telephone:** (302) 831-8596.
**SID:** Michael Hirschman. **Telephone:** (302) 831-2186. **FAX:** (302) 831-8653.

### DELAWARE STATE Hornets

**Conference:** Mid-Eastern Athletic.
**Mailing Address:** 1200 N. Dupont Highway, Dover, DE 19901.
**Head Coach:** Harry Van Sant. **Telephone:** (302) 739-4928.
**SID:** Dennis Jones. **Telephone:** (302) 739-4926. **FAX:** (302) 739-5241.

### DETROIT MERCY Titans

**Conference:** Midwestern Collegiate/East.
**Mailing Address:** 4001 W. McNichols Road, Detroit, MI 48219.
**Head Coach:** Bob Miller. **Telephone:** (313) 993-1725.
**SID:** Ken Lasky. **Telephone:** (313) 993-1745. **FAX:** (313) 993-1765.

### DREXEL Dragons

**Conference:** North Atlantic.
**Mailing Address:** 32nd and Chestnut Streets, Building 14-312, Philadelphia, PA 19104.
**Head Coach:** Don Maines. **Telephone:** (215) 590-8931.
**SID:** Scott Lowe. **Telephone:** (215) 590-8946. **FAX:** (215) 590-8068.

### DUKE Blue Devils

**Conference:** Atlantic Coast.
**Mailing Address:** 115 Cameron Indoor Stadium, Durham, NC 27706.
**Head Coach:** Steve Traylor. **Telephone:** (919) 684-2358.
**SID:** Tom Kosempa. **Telephone:** (919) 684-2633. **FAX:** (919) 684-2489.

**DUQUESNE** Dukes

**Conference:** Atlantic-10.
**Mailing Address:** A.J. Palumbo Center, Pittsburgh, PA 15282.
**Head Coach:** Mike Wilson. **Telephone:** (412) 396-5245.
**SID:** George Nieman. **Telephone:** (412) 396-5376. **FAX:** (412) 396-6210.

**EAST CAROLINA** Pirates

**Conference:** Colonial Athletic.
**Mailing Address:** Third Floor, Sports Medicine Building, Greenville, NC 27858.
**Head Coach:** Gary Overton. **Telephone:** (919) 328-4604.
**SID:** John Gilger. **Telephone:** (919) 328-4522. **FAX:** (919) 328-4528.

**EAST TENNESSEE STATE** Buccaneers

**Conference:** Southern.
**Mailing Address:** P.O. Box 70641, Johnson City, TN 37614.
**Head Coach:** Ken Campbell. **Telephone:** (615) 929-4496.
**SID:** Keith Tunnell. **Telephone:** (615) 929-5612. **FAX:** (615) 929-6138.

**EASTERN ILLINOIS** Panthers

**Conference:** Mid-Continent/West.
**Mailing Address:** Lantz Gym, Charleston, IL 61920.
**Head Coach:** Jim Schmitz. **Telephone:** (217) 581-2522.
**SID:** Dave Kidwell. **Telephone:** (217) 581-6408. **FAX:** (217) 581-6408.

**EASTERN KENTUCKY** Colonels

**Conference:** Ohio Valley.
**Mailing Address:** 205 Begley Building, Kit Carson Dr., Richmond, KY 40475.
**Head Coach:** Jim Ward. **Telephone:** (606) 622-2128.
**SID:** Karl Park. **Telephone:** (606) 622-1253. **FAX:** (606) 622-1230.

**EASTERN MICHIGAN** Eagles

**Conference:** Mid-American.
**Mailing Address:** 200 Bowen Fieldhouse, Ypsilanti, MI 48197.
**Head Coach:** Roger Coryell. **Telephone:** (313) 487-0315.
**SID:** Emily Griffin. **Telephone:** (313) 487-0317. **FAX:** (313) 485-3840.

**EVANSVILLE** Purple Aces

**Conference:** Missouri Valley
**Mailing Address:** 1800 Lincoln Ave., Evansville, IN 47722.
**Head Coach:** Jim Brownlee. **Telephone:** (812) 479-2059.
**SID:** Jay Jameson. **Telephone:** (812) 479-2059. **FAX:** (812) 479-2199.

**FAIRFIELD** Stags

**Conference:** Metro Atlantic/South.
**Mailing Address:** North Benson Road, Fairfield, CT 06430.
**Head Coach:** John Slosar. **Telephone:** (203) 254-4000, ext. 2605.
**SID:** Christopher Tetro. **Telephone:** (203) 254-4000, ext. 2877. **FAX:** (203) 254-4117.

**FAIRLEIGH DICKINSON** Knights

**Conference:** Northeast.
**Mailing Address:** Temple Avenue, Rothman Center, Hackensack, NJ 07601.
**Head Coach:** Dennis Sasso. **Telephone:** (201) 692-2245.
**SID:** Carmine Faccenda. **Telephone:** (201) 692-2149. **FAX:** (201) 692-9361.

**FLORIDA** Gators

**Conference:** Southeastern/East.
**Mailing Address:** Box 14485, Gainesville, FL 32604.
**Head Coach:** Andy Lopez. **Telephone:** (904) 375-4683, ext. 4400.
**SID:** Steve McClain. **Telephone:** (904) 375-4683, ext. 6100. **FAX:** (904) 375-4809.

**FLORIDA A&M** Rattlers

**Conference:** Mid-Eastern Athletic.
**Mailing Address:** Room 204-D, Gaither Athletic Center, Tallahassee, FL 32307.
**Head Coach:** Joe Durant. **Telephone:** (904) 599-3202.
**SID:** Alvin Hollins Jr. **Telephone:** (904) 599-3200. **FAX:** (904) 599-3206.

**FLORIDA ATLANTIC** Owls

**Conference:** TransAmerica Athletic.
**Mailing Address:** 500 NW 20th St., Boca Raton, FL 33431.
**Head Coach:** Kevin Cooney. **Telephone:** (407) 367-3956.
**SID:** Katrina McCormick. **Telephone:** (407) 367-3163. **FAX:** (407) 367-3963.

**FLORIDA INTERNATIONAL** Golden Panthers

**Conference:** TransAmerica Athletic.
**Mailing Address:** University Park Campus, Miami, FL 33199.
**Head Coach:** Danny Price. **Telephone:** (305) 348-3166.
**SID:** Stuart Davidson. **Telephone:** (305) 348-2084. **FAX:** (305) 348-2963.

**FLORIDA STATE** Seminoles

**Conference:** Atlantic Coast.
**Mailing Address:** P.O. Drawer 2195, Tallahassee, FL 32316.
**Head Coach:** Mike Martin. **Telephone:** (904) 644-1073.
**SID:** Bob Burda. **Telephone:** (904) 644-1077. **FAX:** (904) 644-3820.

**FORDHAM** Rams

**Conference:** Patriot.
**Mailing Address:** 441 East Fordham Road, Bronx, NY 10458.
**Head Coach:** Dan Gallagher. **Telephone:** (718) 817-4292.
**SID:** Bill Holtz. **Telephone:** (718) 817-4240. **FAX:** (718) 817-4244.

**FRESNO STATE** Bulldogs

**Conference:** Western Athletic/West.
**Mailing Address:** Room 153, 5305 N. Campus Drive, Fresno, CA 93740.
**Head Coach:** Bob Bennett. **Telephone:** (209) 278-2178.
**SID:** Josh Lehman. **Telephone:** (209) 278-2509. **FAX:** (209) 278-4689.

**FURMAN** Paladins

**Conference:** Southern.
**Mailing Address:** 3300 Poinsett Highway, Greenville, SC 29613.
**Head Coach:** Ron Smith. **Telephone:** (803) 294-2146.
**SID:** Rob Olterman. **Telephone:** (803) 294-2061. **FAX:** (803) 294-3061.

**GEORGE MASON** Patriots

**Conference:** Colonial Athletic.
**Mailing Address:** 4400 University Dr., Fairfax, VA 22030.
**Head Coach:** Bill Brown. **Telephone:** (703) 993-3282.
**SID:** Ben Trittipoe. **Telephone:** (703) 993-3263. **FAX:** (703) 993-3259.

**GEORGE WASHINGTON** Colonials

**Conference:** Atlantic-10.
**Mailing Address:** 600 22nd St. NW, Washington, DC 20052.
**Head Coach:** Jay Murphy. **Telephone:** (202) 994-0327.
**SID:** Betsy Barrett. **Telephone:** (202) 994-8604. **FAX:** (202) 994-2713.

**GEORGETOWN** Hoyas

**Conference:** Big East.
**Mailing Address:** 37th & O Streets NW, Washington, DC 20057.
**Head Coach:** Kirk Mason. **Telephone:** (202) 687-2462.
**SID:** Bill Hurd. **Telephone:** (202) 687-2491. **FAX:** (202) 687-2491.

**GEORGIA** Bulldogs

**Conference:** Southeastern/East.
**Mailing Address:** P.O. Box 1472, Athens, GA 30613.
**Head Coach:** Steve Webber. **Telephone:** (706) 542-7971.
**SID:** Christopher Lakos. **Telephone:** (706) 542-1621. **FAX:** (706) 542-7993.

**GEORGIA SOUTHERN** Eagles

**Conference:** Southern.
**Mailing Address:** Landrum Box 8085, Statesboro, GA 30460.
**Head Coach:** Jack Stallings. **Telephone:** (912) 681-5187.
**SID:** Matt Rogers. **Telephone:** (912) 681-5239. **FAX:** (912) 681-0046.

**GEORGIA STATE** Panthers

**Conference:** TransAmerica Athletic.
**Mailing Address:** University Plaza, Atlanta, GA 30303.
**Head Coach:** Mike Hurst. **Telephone:** (404) 651-1198.
**SID:** Peter O'Reilly. **Telephone:** (404) 651-2071. **FAX:** (404) 651-3204.

**GEORGIA TECH** Yellow Jackets

**Conference:** Atlantic Coast.
**Mailing Address:** 150 Bobby Dodd Way NW, Atlanta, GA 30332.
**Head Coach:** Danny Hall. **Telephone:** (404) 894-5471.
**SID:** Mike Stamus. **Telephone:** (404) 894-5445. **FAX:** (404) 853-2674.

**GONZAGA** Bulldogs

**Conference:** Pacific-10/North.
**Mailing Address:** E. 502 Boone Ave., Spokane, WA 99258.
**Head Coach:** Steve Hertz. **Telephone:** (509) 328-4220, ext. 4226.
**SID:** Oliver Pierce. **Telephone:** (509) 328-4220, ext. 6373. **FAX:** (509) 484-2830.

**GRAMBLING STATE** Tigers

**Conference:** Southwestern Athletic/West.
**Mailing Address:** P.O. Box N, Grambling, LA 71245.
**Head Coach:** Wilbert Ellis. **Telephone:** (318) 274-2218.
**SID:** Kim Spears. **Telephone:** (318) 274-2479. **FAX:** (318) 274-2761.

**GRAND CANYON** Antelopes

**Conference:** Western Athletic/East.
**Mailing Address:** 3300 W. Camelback Road, Phoenix, AZ 85061.
**Head Coach:** Gil Stafford. **Telephone:** (602) 589-2805.
**SID:** Deron Filip. **Telephone:** (602) 589-2795. **FAX:** (602) 589-2529.

**HARTFORD** Hawks

**Conference:** North Atlantic.
**Mailing Address:** 200 Bloomfield Ave., West Hartford, CT 06117.
**Head Coach:** Jim Bretz. **Telephone:** (203) 768-4656.
**SID:** James Keener. **Telephone:** (203) 768-4620. **FAX:** (203) 768-4068.

**HARVARD** Crimson

**Conference:** Ivy League/Rolfe.
**Mailing Address:** Department of Athletics, 60 John F. Kennedy St., Cambridge, MA 02138.
**Head Coach:** Leigh Hogan. **Telephone:** (617) 495-2629.
**SID:** Buffy Gifford. **Telephone:** (617) 495-2206. **FAX:** (617) 495-2130.

**HAWAII** Rainbows

**Conference:** Western Athletic/West.
**Mailing Address:** 1337 Lower Campus Road, Honolulu, HI 96822.
**Head Coach:** Les Murakami. **Telephone:** (808) 956-6247.
**SID:** Markus Owens. **Telephone:** (808) 956-7523. **FAX:** (808) 956-4470.

**HAWAII-HILO** Vulcans

**Conference:** Independent.

**Mailing Address:** 200 W. Kawili St., Hilo, HI 96720.
**Head Coach:** Joey Estrella. **Telephone:** (808) 933-3700.
**SID:** Kelly Leong. **Telephone:** (808) 933-3543. **FAX:** (808) 933-3711.

### **HOFSTRA** Flying Dutchmen

**Conference:** North Atlantic.
**Mailing Address:** 1000 Hempstead Turnpike, PFC 240, Hempstead, NY 11550.
**Head Coach:** Rich Martin. **Telephone:** (516) 463-5065.
**SID:** Jim Sheehan. **Telephone:** (516) 463-6764. **FAX:** (516) 463-5033.

### **HOLY CROSS** Crusaders

**Conference:** Patriot.
**Mailing Address:** One College Street, Worcester, MA 01610.
**Head Coach:** Jack Whalen. **Telephone:** (508) 793-3628.
**SID:** Tracy King. **Telephone:** (508) 793-2583. **FAX:** (508) 793-2309.

### **HOUSTON** Cougars

**Conference:** Southwest.
**Mailing Address:** Room 155, 3855 Holman, Houston, TX 77204.
**Head Coach:** Rayner Noble. **Telephone:** (713) 743-9396.
**SID:** Patti Warner. **Telephone:** (713) 743-9409. **FAX:** (713) 743-9411.

### **HOWARD** Bison

**Conference:** Mid-Eastern Athletic.
**Mailing Address:** 511 Gresham Place NW, Washington, DC 20059.
**Head Coach:** Chuck Hinton. **Telephone:** (202) 806-5162.
**SID:** Edward Hill. **Telephone:** (202) 806-7182. **FAX:** (202) 806-9090.

### **ILLINOIS** Fighting Illini

**Conference:** Big Ten.
**Mailing Address:** Assembly Hall, Room 115, 1800 S. First St., Champaign, IL 61820.
**Head Coach:** Itch Jones. **Telephone:** (217) 333-8605.
**SID:** Kent Brown. **Telephone:** (217) 333-1391. **FAX:** (217) 333-5540.

### **ILLINOIS-CHICAGO** Flames

**Conference:** Midwestern Collegiate/West.
**Mailing Address:** Box 4348, Chicago, IL 60680.
**Head Coach:** Dean Refakes. **Telephone:** (312) 996-8645.
**SID:** Anne Schoenherr. **Telephone:** (312) 996-5880. **FAX:** (312) 996-5882.

### **ILLINOIS STATE** Redbirds

**Conference:** Missouri Valley.
**Mailing Address:** 123 Horton Field House, Normal, IL 61761.
**Head Coach:** Jeff Stewart. **Telephone:** (309) 438-5151.
**SID:** Jamie Hall. **Telephone:** (309) 438-3825. **FAX:** (309) 438-5634.

### **INDIANA** Hoosiers

**Conference:** Big Ten.
**Mailing Address:** 17th & Fee Lane, Assembly Hall, Bloomington, IN 47405.
**Head Coach:** Bob Morgan. **Telephone:** (812) 855-1680.
**SID:** Todd Starowitz. **Telephone:** (812) 855-9399. **FAX:** (812) 855-2754.

### **INDIANA STATE** Sycamores

**Conference:** Missouri Valley.
**Mailing Address:** Room 118, Indiana State Arena, Terre Haute, IN 47809.
**Head Coach:** Bob Warn. **Telephone:** (812) 237-4051.
**SID:** Tom James. **Telephone:** (812) 237-4160. **FAX:** (812) 237-4157.

### **IONA** Gaels

**Conference:** Metro Atlantic/South.
**Mailing Address:** Mulcahy Center, 715 North Ave., New Rochelle, NY 10801.
**Head Coach:** Al Zoccolillo. **Telephone:** (914) 633-2319.
**SID:** Bob Walsh. **Telephone:** (914) 633-2057. **FAX:** (914) 633-2072.

### **IOWA** Hawkeyes

**Conference:** Big Ten.
**Mailing Address:** 340 Carver-Hawkeye Arena, Iowa City, IA 52242.
**Head Coach:** Duane Banks. **Telephone:** (319) 335-9389.
**SID:** Erik Snider. **Telephone:** (319) 335-9411. **FAX:** (319) 335-9411.

### **IOWA STATE** Cyclones

**Conference:** Big Eight.
**Mailing Address:** Olsen Annex, 1802 S. Fourth St., Ames, IA 50011.
**Head Coach:** Bob Randall. **Telephone:** (515) 294-4132.
**SID:** Erin Davison. **Telephone:** (515) 294-4132. **FAX:** (515) 294-0558.

### **JACKSON STATE** Tigers

**Conference:** Southwestern Athletic/East.
**Mailing Address:** 1325 West Lynch St., Jackson, MS 39217.
**Head Coach:** Robert Braddy. **Telephone:** (601) 968-2425.
**SID:** Samuel Jefferson. **Telephone:** (601) 968-2273. **FAX:** (601) 968-2000.

### **JACKSONVILLE** Dolphins

**Conference:** Sun Belt.
**Mailing Address:** 2800 University Blvd. N., Jacksonville, FL 32211.
**Head Coach:** Terry Alexander. **Telephone:** (904) 744-3950, ext. 7412.
**SID:** Richard Paige. **Telephone:** (904) 745-7402. **FAX:** (904) 743-0067.

### **JAMES MADISON** Dukes

**Conference:** Colonial Athletic.
**Mailing Address:** South Main, Harrisonburg, VA 22807.
**Head Coach:** Kevin Anderson. **Telephone:** (703) 568-6467.

**SID:** Curt Dudley. **Telephone:** (703) 568-6154. **FAX:** (703) 568-3703.

**KANSAS** Jayhawks

**Conference:** Big Eight.
**Mailing Address:** 202 Allen Fieldhouse, Lawrence, KS 66045.
**Head Coach:** Dave Bingham. **Telephone:** (913) 864-7907.
**SID:** Chris Padgett. **Telephone:** (913) 864-3417. **FAX:** (913) 864-7944.

**KANSAS STATE** Wildcats

**Conference:** Big Eight.
**Mailing Address:** Suite 144, Bramlage Coliseum, 1800 College Ave., Manhattan, KS 66502.
**Head Coach:** Mike Clark. **Telephone:** (913) 532-5723.
**SID:** Dan Ballou. **Telephone:** (913) 532-6735. **FAX:** (913) 532-6093.

**KENT** Golden Flashes

**Conference:** Mid-American.
**Mailing Address:** P.O. Box 5190, 154 Memorial Gym, Kent, OH 44242.
**Head Coach:** Rick Rembielak. **Telephone:** (216) 672-3696.
**SID:** Greg Seiler. **Telephone:** (216) 672-2110. **FAX:** (216) 672-2112.

**KENTUCKY** Wildcats

**Conference:** Southeastern/East.
**Mailing Address:** Room 23, Memorial Coliseum, Lexington, KY 40506.
**Head Coach:** Keith Madison. **Telephone:** (606) 257-6500.
**SID:** Laura Boswell. **Telephone:** (606) 257-3838. **FAX:** (606) 323-4310.

**LAFAYETTE** Leopards

**Conference:** Patriot.
**Mailing Address:** Room 17, Watson Hall, High Street, Easton, PA 18042.
**Head Coach:** Greg Vogel. **Telephone:** (610) 250-5476.
**SID:** Dave Walters. **Telephone:** (610) 250-5122. **FAX:** (610) 250-5127.

**LAMAR** Cardinals

**Conference:** Sun Belt.
**Mailing Address:** Box 10066, LU Station, Beaumont, TX 77710.
**Head Coach:** Jim Gilligan. **Telephone:** (409) 880-8315.
**SID:** Tim McMurray. **Telephone:** (409) 880-2323. **FAX:** (409) 880-2338.

**LA SALLE** Explorers

**Conference:** Midwestern Collegiate/East.
**Mailing Address:** 1900 W. Olney Ave., Box 805, Philadelphia, PA 19141.
**Head Coach:** Gene McDonnell. **Telephone:** (215) 951-1516.
**SID:** Howard Pachasa. **Telephone:** (215) 951-1513. **FAX:** (215) 951-1694.

**LEHIGH** Engineers

**Conference:** Patriot.
**Mailing Address:** Taylor Gym, 641 Taylor St., Bethlehem, PA 18015.
**Head Coach:** Tom Morgan. **Telephone:** (610) 758-4315.
**SID:** Glenn Hofmann. **Telephone:** (610) 758-3174. **FAX:** (610) 758-4407.

**LE MOYNE** Dolphins

**Conference:** Metro Atlantic/North.
**Mailing Address:** Springfield Road, Syracuse, NY 13214.
**Head Coach:** Dick Rockwell. **Telephone:** (315) 445-4450.
**SID:** Jay Whipple. **Telephone:** (315) 445-4412. **FAX:** (315) 445-4678.

**LIBERTY** Flames

**Conference:** Big South.
**Mailing Address:** Box 20000, Lynchburg, VA 24506.
**Head Coach:** Johnny Hunton. **Telephone:** (804) 582-2100.
**SID:** James Vernon. **Telephone:** (804) 582-2292. **FAX:** (804) 582-2076.

**LONG BEACH STATE** 49ers

**Conference:** Big West.
**Mailing Address:** 1250 Bellflower Blvd., Long Beach, CA 90840.
**Head Coach:** Dave Snow. **Telephone:** (310) 985-4661.
**SID:** Thom Simmons. **Telephone:** (310) 985-7978. **FAX:** (310) 985-8197.

**LONG ISLAND** Blackbirds

**Conference:** Northeast.
**Mailing Address:** University Plaza, Brooklyn, NY 11201.
**Head Coach:** Frank Giannone. **Telephone:** (718) 488-1538.
**SID:** Bob Gesslein. **Telephone:** (718) 488-1420. **FAX:** (718) 243-0766.

**LOUISIANA STATE** Tigers

**Conference:** Southeastern/West.
**Mailing Address:** P.O. Box 25095, Baton Rouge, LA 70894.
**Head Coach:** Skip Bertman. **Telephone:** (504) 388-4148.
**SID:** Bill Franques. **Telephone:** (504) 388-8226. **FAX:** (504) 388-1861.

**LOUISIANA TECH** Bulldogs

**Conference:** Sun Belt.
**Mailing Address:** P.O. Box 3166, Ruston, LA 71272.
**Head Coach:** Mike Kane. **Telephone:** (318) 257-4111.
**SID:** Hank Largin. **Telephone:** (318) 257-3144. **FAX:** (318) 257-3757.

**LOUISVILLE** Cardinals

**Conference:** Metro.
**Mailing Address:** Floyd & Brandeis Streets, Louisville, KY 40292.
**Head Coach:** Gene Baker. **Telephone:** (502) 852-0103.
**SID:** Nancy Smith. **Telephone:** (502) 852-6581. **FAX:** (502) 852-7401.

**LOYOLA MARYMOUNT** Lions

**Conference:** West Coast.

**Mailing Address:** Loyola Blvd. @ W. 80th, Los Angeles, CA 90045.
**Head Coach:** Jody Robinson. **Telephone:** (310) 338-2765.
**SID:** Bruce Meyers. **Telephone:** (310) 338-7643. **FAX:** (310) 338-2703.

### **MAINE** Black Bears

**Conference:** North Atlantic.
**Mailing Address:** 186 Memorial Gym, Orono, ME 04469.
**Head Coach:** John Winkin. **Telephone:** (207) 581-1096.
**SID:** Joe Roberts. **Telephone:** (207) 581-3596. **FAX:** (207) 581-3297.

### **MANHATTAN** Jaspers

**Conference:** Metro Atlantic/South.
**Mailing Address:** Manhattan College Parkway, Riverdale, NY 10471.
**Head Coach:** Gary Puccio. **Telephone:** (718) 920-0486.
**SID:** Jeff Bernstein. **Telephone:** (718) 920-0228. **FAX:** (718) 543-8802.

### **MARIST** Red Foxes

**Conference:** Northeast.
**Mailing Address:** McCann Center, North Road, Poughkeepsie, NY 12601.
**Head Coach:** Art Smith. **Telephone:** (914) 575-3000, ext. 2570.
**SID:** Dann Sullivan. **Telephone:** (914) 575-3000, ext. 2322. **FAX:** (914) 471-0466.

### **MARSHALL** Thundering Herd

**Conference:** Southern.
**Mailing Address:** P.O. Box 1360, Huntington, WV 25715.
**Head Coach:** Howard McCann. **Telephone:** (304) 696-5277.
**SID:** John Winters. **Telephone:** (304) 696-5275. **FAX:** (304) 696-2325.

### **MARYLAND** Terrapins

**Conference:** Atlantic Coast.
**Mailing Address:** P.O. Box 295, College Park, MD 20741.
**Head Coach:** Tom Bradley. **Telephone:** (301) 314-5904.
**SID:** Unavailable. **Telephone:** (301) 314-7062. **FAX:** (301) 314-9094.

### **MARYLAND-BALTIMORE COUNTY** Retrievers

**Conference:** Big South.
**Mailing Address:** 5401 Wilkens Ave., Baltimore, MD 21228.
**Head Coach:** John Jancuska. **Telephone:** (410) 455-2239.
**SID:** Jerry Milani. **Telephone:** (410) 455-2639. **FAX:** (410) 455-3994.

### **MARYLAND-EASTERN SHORE** Hawks

**Conference:** Mid-Eastern Athletic.
**Mailing Address:** Tawes Gymnasium, Backbone Road, Princess Anne, MD 21853.
**Head Coach:** Kaye Pinhey. **Telephone:** (410) 651-6539.
**SID:** Bradford Evans. **Telephone:** (410) 651-6499. **FAX:** (410) 651-6499.

### **MASSACHUSETTS** Minutemen

**Conference:** Atlantic-10.
**Mailing Address:** 255A Boyden Building, Commonwealth Avenue, Amherst, MA 01003.
**Head Coach:** Mike Stone. **Telephone:** (413) 545-3120.
**SID:** Charlie Bare. **Telephone:** (413) 545-2439. **FAX:** (413) 545-1556.

### **McNEESE STATE** Cowboys

**Conference:** Southland.
**Mailing Address:** P.O. Box 92735, Lake Charles, LA 70609.
**Head Coach:** Jim Ricklefsen. **Telephone:** (318) 475-5484.
**SID:** Louis Bonnette. **Telephone:** (318) 475-5207. **FAX:** (318) 475-5202.

### **MEMPHIS** Tigers

**Conference:** Great Midwest.
**Mailing Address:** 205 Athletic Office Building, 570 Normal, Memphis, TN 38152.
**Head Coach:** Jeff Hopkins. **Telephone:** (901) 678-2452.
**SID:** Rob Stallins. **Telephone:** (901) 678-2337. **FAX:** (901) 678-4134.

### **MERCER** Bears

**Conference:** TransAmerica Athletic.
**Mailing Address:** 1400 Coleman Ave., Macon, GA 31207.
**Head Coach:** Barry Myers. **Telephone:** (912) 752-2738.
**SID:** Kevin Coulombe. **Telephone:** (912) 752-2994. **FAX:** (912) 752-2061.

### **MIAMI** Hurricanes

**Conference:** Independent.
**Mailing Address:** Box 248167, Coral Gables, FL 33124.
**Head Coach:** Jim Morris. **Telephone:** (305) 284-4171.
**SID:** Dan Happoldt. **Telephone:** (305) 284-3244. **FAX:** (305) 284-2807.

### **MIAMI** Redskins

**Conference:** Mid-American.
**Mailing Address:** 230 Millett Hall, Oxford, OH 45056.
**Head Coach:** Jon Pavlisko. **Telephone:** (513) 529-6631.
**SID:** Michael Harris. **Telephone:** (513) 529-4327. **FAX:** (513) 529-6729.

### **MICHIGAN** Wolverines

**Conference:** Big Ten.
**Mailing Address:** 1000 S. State St., Ann Arbor, MI 48109.
**Head Coach:** Bill Freehan. **Telephone:** (313) 747-4550.
**SID:** Jim Schneider. **Telephone:** (313) 763-1381. **FAX:** (313) 747-1188.

### **MICHIGAN STATE** Spartans

**Conference:** Big Ten.

**Mailing Address:** 116 Linton Hall, East Lansing, MI 48824.
**Head Coach:** Tom Smith. **Telephone:** (517) 355-3419.
**SID:** Roman Uschak. **Telephone:** (517) 355-2771. **FAX:** (517) 353-9636.

### MIDDLE TENNESSEE STATE Blue Raiders

**Conference:** Ohio Valley.
**Mailing Address:** MTSU Box 20, Murfreesboro, TN 37132.
**Head Coach:** Steve Peterson. **Telephone:** (502) 898-2984.
**SID:** Dan Cotton. **Telephone:** (502) 898-2450. **FAX:** (502) 898-5626.

### MINNESOTA Golden Gophers

**Conference:** Big Ten.
**Mailing Address:** 516 15th Ave. SE, Bierman Building, Room 208, Minneapolis, MN 55455.
**Head Coach:** John Anderson. **Telephone:** (612) 625-1060.
**SID:** Marc Ryan. **Telephone:** (612) 625-4090. **FAX:** (612) 625-0359.

### MISSISSIPPI Rebels

**Conference:** Southeastern/West.
**Mailing Address:** P.O. Box 217, University, MS 38677.
**Head Coach:** Don Kessinger. **Telephone:** (601) 232-7538.
**SID:** J.D. Hamilton. **Telephone:** (601) 232-7522. **FAX:** (601) 232-7006.

### MISSISSIPPI STATE Bulldogs

**Conference:** Southeastern/West.
**Mailing Address:** P.O. Box 5308, Mississippi State, MS 39762.
**Head Coach:** Ron Polk. **Telephone:** (601) 325-2805.
**SID:** Jason Cook. **Telephone:** (601) 325-2703. **FAX:** (601) 325-2563.

### MISSISSIPPI VALLEY STATE Delta Devils

**Conference:** Southwestern Athletic/East.
**Mailing Address:** P.O. Box 743, Itta Bena, MS 38941.
**Head Coach:** Cleotha Wilson. **Telephone:** (601) 254-3398.
**SID:** Charles Prophet. **Telephone:** (601) 254-3552. **FAX:** (601) 254-6641.

### MISSOURI Tigers

**Conference:** Big Eight.
**Mailing Address:** Hearnes Center, Columbia, MO 65211.
**Head Coach:** Tim Jamieson. **Telephone:** (314) 882-0731.
**SID:** Steve Wujek. **Telephone:** (314) 882-3241. **FAX:** (314) 882-4720.

### MONMOUTH Hawks

**Conference:** Northeast.
**Mailing Address:** Cedar Avenue, West Long Branch, NJ 07764.
**Head Coach:** Dean Ehehalt. **Telephone:** (908) 571-3415.
**SID:** Chris Risden. **Telephone:** (908) 571-3415. **FAX:** (908) 571-3535.

### MOREHEAD STATE Eagles

**Conference:** Ohio Valley.
**Mailing Address:** UPO 1023, Morehead, KY 40351.
**Head Coach:** Frank Spaniol. **Telephone:** (606) 783-2881.
**SID:** Randy Stacy. **Telephone:** (606) 783-2500. **FAX:** (606) 783-2550.

### MOUNT ST. MARY'S Mountaineers

**Conference:** Northeast.
**Mailing Address:** Route 15, Emmitsburg, MD 21727.
**Head Coach:** Ray Ruffing. **Telephone:** (301) 447-5296.
**SID:** Eric Kloiber. **Telephone:** (301) 447-5384. **FAX:** (301) 447-5300.

### MURRAY STATE Racers

**Conference:** Ohio Valley.
**Mailing Address:** Room 211, Stewart Stadium, Murray, KY 42071.
**Head Coach:** Mike Thieke. **Telephone:** (502) 762-4892.
**SID:** Bryan Morgan. **Telephone:** (502) 762-4270. **FAX:** (502) 762-6814.

### NAVY Midshipmen

**Conference:** Patriot.
**Mailing Address:** Ricketts Hall, 566 Brownson Road, Annapolis, MD 21402.
**Head Coach:** Bob MacDonald. **Telephone:** (410) 293-2831.
**SID:** Scott Strasemeier. **Telephone:** (410) 268-6226. **FAX:** (410) 269-6779.

### NEBRASKA Cornhuskers

**Conference:** Big Eight.
**Mailing Address:** 116 South Stadium, Lincoln, NE 68588.
**Head Coach:** John Sanders. **Telephone:** (402) 472-2269.
**SID:** George Mauzy. **Telephone:** (402) 472-2263. **FAX:** (402) 472-2005.

### NEVADA Wolf Pack

**Conference:** Big West.
**Mailing Address:** Mail Stop 232, Reno, NV 89557.
**Head Coach:** Gary Powers. **Telephone:** (702) 784-6900.
**SID:** Mike May. **Telephone:** (702) 784-4600. **FAX:** (702) 784-4386.

### NEVADA-LAS VEGAS Rebels

**Conference:** Big West.
**Mailing Address:** 4505 Maryland Parkway, Las Vegas, NV 89154.
**Head Coach:** Fred Dallimore. **Telephone:** (702) 895-3499.
**SID:** Jim Gemma. **Telephone:** (702) 895-3995. **FAX:** (702) 895-0989.

### NEW HAMPSHIRE Wildcats

**Conference:** North Atlantic.
**Mailing Address:** 224 Field House, Durham, NH 03824.
**Head Coach:** Chris Serino. **Telephone:** (603) 862-3905.
**SID:** John Sudsbury. **Telephone:** (603) 862-3906. **FAX:** 603 862-3839.

**NEW MEXICO** Lobos
**Conference:** Western Athletic/East.
**Mailing Address:** South Campus, Albuquerque, NM 87131.
**Head Coach:** Rich Alday. **Telephone:** (505) 277-5121.
**SID:** Jim Shelton. **Telephone:** (505) 277-6970. **FAX:** (505) 277-0142.

**NEW MEXICO STATE** Aggies
**Conference:** Big West.
**Mailing Address:** Box 3145, Las Cruces, NM 88003.
**Head Coach:** Elliot Avent. **Telephone:** (505) 646-5813.
**SID:** Steve Shutt. **Telephone:** (505) 646-3929. **FAX:** (505) 646-2425.

**NEW ORLEANS** Privateers
**Conference:** Sun Belt.
**Mailing Address:** Lakefront Arena, New Orleans, LA 70148.
**Head Coach:** Tom Schwaner. **Telephone:** (504) 286-7021.
**SID:** Ed Cassiere. **Telephone:** (504) 286-6284. **FAX:** (504) 286-7240.

**NEW YORK TECH** Bears
**Conference:** Mid-Continent/East.
**Mailing Address:** Northern Boulevard, Old Westbury, NY 11568.
**Head Coach:** Bob Hirschfield. **Telephone:** (516) 686-7513.
**SID:** Tom Riordan. **Telephone:** (516) 686-7626. **FAX:** (516) 626-0750.

**NIAGARA** Purple Eagles
**Conference:** Metro Atlantic/North.
**Mailing Address:** O'Shea Hall, Niagara University, NY 14109.
**Head Coach:** Jim Mauro. **Telephone:** (716) 286-8588.
**SID:** Mark Vandergrift. **Telephone:** (716) 286-8586. **FAX:** (716) 286-8581.

**NICHOLLS STATE** Colonels
**Conference:** Southland.
**Mailing Address:** P.O. Box 2032, Thibodaux, LA 70310.
**Head Coach:** Mike Knight. **Telephone:** (504) 448-4795.
**SID:** Ron Mears. **Telephone:** (504) 448-4282. **FAX:** (504) 448-4924.

**NORTH CAROLINA** Tar Heels
**Conference:** Atlantic Coast.
**Mailing Address:** P.O. Box 2126, Chapel Hill, NC 27514.
**Head Coach:** Mike Roberts. **Telephone:** (919) 962-2351.
**SID:** Sheri West. **Telephone:** (919) 962-2123. **FAX:** (919) 962-0612.

**UNC ASHEVILLE** Bulldogs
**Conference:** Big South.
**Mailing Address:** One University Heights, Asheville, NC 28804.
**Head Coach:** Bill Hillier. **Telephone:** (704) 251-6920.
**SID:** Mike Gone. **Telephone:** (704) 251-6923. **FAX:** (704) 251-6388.

**UNC CHARLOTTE** 49ers
**Conference:** Metro.
**Mailing Address:** Highway 49, Charlotte, NC 28223.
**Head Coach:** Loren Hibbs. **Telephone:** (704) 547-3935.
**SID:** James McCoy. **Telephone:** (704) 547-4937. **FAX:** (704) 547-4918.

**UNC GREENSBORO** Spartans
**Conference:** Big South.
**Mailing Address:** 337 HHP Building, Greensboro, NC 27412.
**Head Coach:** Mike Gaski. **Telephone:** (910) 334-3247.
**SID:** Jill Herskovitz. **Telephone:** (910) 334-5615. **FAX:** (910) 334-3182.

**UNC WILMINGTON** Seahawks
**Conference:** Colonial Athletic.
**Mailing Address:** 601 S. College Road, Wilmington, NC 28403.
**Head Coach:** Mark Scalf. **Telephone:** (910) 395-3570.
**SID:** Joe Browning. **Telephone:** (910) 395-3236. **FAX:** (910) 395-3686.

**NORTH CAROLINA A&T** Aggies
**Conference:** Mid-Eastern Athletic.
**Mailing Address:** 108 Memorial Union, Greensboro, NC 27411.
**Head Coach:** Richard Watkins. **Telephone:** (910) 334-7712.
**SID:** Charles Mooney. **Telephone:** (910) 334-7141. **FAX:** (910) 334-7181.

**NORTH CAROLINA STATE** Wolfpack
**Conference:** Atlantic Coast.
**Mailing Address:** P.O. Box 8501, Raleigh, NC 27695.
**Head Coach:** Ray Tanner. **Telephone:** (919) 515-3612.
**SID:** Bruce Winkworth. **Telephone:** (919) 515-2102. **FAX:** (919) 515-2898.

**NORTHEAST LOUISIANA** Indians
**Conference:** Southland.
**Mailing Address:** 308 Stadium Drive, Monroe, LA 71209.
**Head Coach:** Smoke Laval. **Telephone:** (318) 342-5395.
**SID:** Troy Mitchell. **Telephone:** (318) 342-5462. **FAX:** (318) 342-5464.

**NORTHEASTERN** Huskies
**Conference:** North Atlantic.
**Mailing Address:** 360 Huntington Ave., Boston, MA 02115.
**Head Coach:** Neil McPhee. **Telephone:** (617) 373-3657.
**SID:** Jack Grinold. **Telephone:** (617) 373-2691. **FAX:** (617) 373-3152.

**NORTHEASTERN ILLINOIS** Golden Eagles
**Conference:** Mid-Continent/West.
**Mailing Address:** 5500 N. St. Louis Ave., Chicago, IL 60625.
**Head Coach:** Jim Hawrysko. **Telephone:** (312) 794-2884.

**SID:** Mark Johnson. **Telephone:** (312) 794-6241. **FAX:** (312) 794-6244.

### NORTHERN ILLINOIS Huskies

**Conference:** Midwestern Collegiate/West.
**Mailing Address:** 112 Evans Field House, Dekalb, IL 60115.
**Head Coach:** Spanky McFarland. **Telephone:** (815) 753-0147.
**SID:** Kari Brackett. **Telephone:** (815) 753-1706. **FAX:** (815) 753-9540.

### NORTHERN IOWA Panthers

**Conference:** Missouri Valley.
**Mailing Address:** 23rd and College, Cedar Falls, IA 50614.
**Head Coach:** Dave Schrage. **Telephone:** (319) 273-6323.
**SID:** Matt Gruhn. **Telephone:** (319) 273-6354. **FAX:** (319) 273-3602.

### NORTHWESTERN Wildcats

**Conference:** Big Ten.
**Mailing Address:** 1501 Central St., Evanston, IL 60208.
**Head Coach:** Paul Stevens. **Telephone:** (708) 491-4652.
**SID:** Mark Simpson. **Telephone:** (708) 491-8806. **FAX:** (708) 491-8818.

### NORTHWESTERN STATE Demons

**Conference:** Southland.
**Mailing Address:** 112 Prather Coliseum, Natchitoches, LA 71497.
**Head Coach:** Dave Van Horn. **Telephone:** (318) 357-4139.
**SID:** Daucy Crizer. **Telephone:** (318) 357-6467. **FAX:** (318) 357-4515.

### NOTRE DAME Fighting Irish

**Conference:** Midwestern Collegiate/West.
**Mailing Address:** Joyce Center, Notre Dame, IN 46556.
**Head Coach:** Paul Mainieri. **Telephone:** (219) 631-8466.
**SID:** Ken Horn. **Telephone:** (219) 631-7516. **FAX:** (219) 631-7941.

### OHIO Bobcats

**Conference:** Mid-American.
**Mailing Address:** 105 Convocation Center, Athens, OH 45701.
**Head Coach:** Joe Carbone. **Telephone:** (614) 593-1180.
**SID:** Ken Dewey. **Telephone:** (614) 593-1298. **FAX:** (614) 593-2420.

### OHIO STATE Buckeyes

**Conference:** Big Ten.
**Mailing Address:** 124 St. John Arena, 410 Woody Hayes Drive, Columbus, OH 43210.
**Head Coach:** Bob Todd. **Telephone:** (614) 292-1075.
**SID:** Bob Goldring, Bryan Ramsey. **Telephone:** (614) 292-6861. **FAX:** (614) 292-8547.

### OKLAHOMA Sooners

**Conference:** Big Eight.
**Mailing Address:** Memorial Stadium, Norman, OK 73019.
**Head Coach:** Larry Cochell. **Telephone:** (405) 325-8354.
**SID:** Mike Treps. **Telephone:** (405) 325-8225. **FAX:** (405) 325-8374.

### OKLAHOMA STATE Cowboys

**Conference:** Big Eight.
**Mailing Address:** 202 Gallagher-Iba Arena, Stillwater, OK 74078.
**Head Coach:** Gary Ward. **Telephone:** (405) 744-5849.
**SID:** Michael Noteware. **Telephone:** (405) 744-5749. **FAX:** (405) 744-7754.

### OLD DOMINION Monarchs

**Conference:** Colonial Athletic.
**Mailing Address:** Building 136, Athletic Administration, Norfolk, VA 23529.
**Head Coach:** Tony Guzzo. **Telephone:** (804) 683-4360.
**SID:** Carol Hudson. **Telephone:** (804) 683-3372. **FAX:** (804) 683-3119.

### ORAL ROBERTS Golden Eagles

**Conference:** Independent.
**Mailing Address:** 7777 S. Lewis, Tulsa, OK 74171.
**Head Coach:** Allan Barker. **Telephone:** (918) 495-7130.
**SID:** Scott Vallery. **Telephone:** (918) 495-7102. **FAX:** (918) 495-7123.

### OREGON STATE Beavers

**Conference:** Pacific-10/North.
**Mailing Address:** 209 Gill Coliseum, Corvallis, OR 97331.
**Head Coach:** Pat Casey. **Telephone:** (503) 737-2825.
**SID:** Steve Fenk. **Telephone:** (503) 737-3720. **FAX:** (503) 737-3072.

### PACE Setters

**Conference:** Mid-Continent/East.
**Mailing Address:** 861 Bedford Road, New York, NY 10570.
**Head Coach:** Fred Calaicone. **Telephone:** (914) 773-3411.
**SID:** John Balkam. **Telephone:** (914) 773-3411. **FAX:** (914) 773-3491.

### PACIFIC Boxers

**Conference:** Big West.
**Mailing Address:** 3601 Pacific Ave., Stockton, CA 95211.
**Head Coach:** Quincey Noble. **Telephone:** (209) 946-2709.
**SID:** Kevin Messenger. **Telephone:** (209) 946-2479. **FAX:** (209) 946-2757.

### PENNSYLVANIA Quakers

**Conference:** Ivy League/Gehrig.
**Mailing Address:** Weightman Hall South, 235 S. 33rd St., Philadelphia, PA 19104.
**Head Coach:** Bob Seddon. **Telephone:** (215) 898-6282.
**SID:** Chris Beckett. **Telephone:** (215) 898-6128. **FAX:** (215) 898-1747.

**PENN STATE** Nittany Lions

**Conference:** Big Ten.
**Mailing Address:** 234 Recreation Building, University Park, PA 16802.
**Head Coach:** Joe Hindelang. **Telephone:** (814) 863-0237.
**SID:** Jeff Brewer. **Telephone:** (814) 865-1757. **FAX:** (814) 863-3165.

**PEPPERDINE** Waves

**Conference:** West Coast.
**Mailing Address:** 24255 Pacific Coast Highway, Malibu, CA 90263.
**Head Coach:** Pat Harrison. **Telephone:** (310) 456-4199.
**SID:** Mike Zapolski. **Telephone:** (310) 456-4333. **FAX:** (310) 456-4322.

**PITTSBURGH** Panthers

**Conference:** Big East.
**Mailing Address:** P.O. Box 7436, Pittsburgh, PA 15213.
**Head Coach:** Mark Jackson. **Telephone:** (412) 648-8208.
**SID:** Harry Ennis. **Telephone:** (412) 648-8240. **FAX:** 648-8248.

**PORTLAND** Pilots

**Conference:** Pacific 10/North
**Mailing Address:** 5000 N. Willamette Blvd., Portland, OR 97203.
**Head Coach:** Terry Pollreisz. **Telephone:** (503) 283-7117.
**SID:** Kevin Toon. **Telephone:** (503) 283-7439. **FAX:** (503) 283-7242.

**PORTLAND STATE** Vikings

**Conference:** Pacific-10/North.
**Mailing Address:** P.O. Box 751, Portland, OR 97207.
**Head Coach:** Dave Dangler. **Telephone:** (503) 725-3852.
**SID:** Larry Sellers. **Telephone:** (503) 725-2525. **FAX:** (503) 725-5610.

**PRAIRIE VIEW A&M** Panthers

**Conference:** Southwestern Athletic/West.
**Mailing Address:** P.O. Box 97, Prairie View, TX 77446.
**Head Coach:** John Tankersley. **Telephone:** (409) 857-4290.
**SID:** Harlan Robinson. **Telephone:** (409) 857-2114. **FAX:** (409) 857-2408.

**PRINCETON** Tigers

**Conference:** Ivy League/Gehrig.
**Mailing Address:** P.O. Box 71, Room Nine, Jadwin Gym, Princeton, NJ 08544.
**Head Coach:** Tom O'Connell. **Telephone:** (609) 258-5059.
**SID:** Laura Stange. **Telephone:** (609) 258-3568. **FAX:** (609) 258-4477.

**PROVIDENCE** Friars

**Conference:** Big East.
**Mailing Address:** River Avenue, Providence, RI 02918.
**Head Coach:** Paul Kostacopoulos. **Telephone:** (401) 865-2273.
**SID:** Tim Connor. **Telephone:** (401) 865-2272. **FAX:** (401) 865-2583.

**PURDUE** Boilermakers

**Conference:** Big Ten.
**Mailing Address:** 1790 Mackey Arena, West Lafayette, IN 47907.
**Head Coach:** Steve Green. **Telephone:** (317) 494-3998.
**SID:** Brad Hainje. **Telephone:** (317) 494-6235. **FAX:** (317) 494-5447.

**RADFORD** Highlanders

**Conference:** Big South.
**Mailing Address:** P.O. Box 6916, Radford, VA 24142.
**Head Coach:** Lew Kent. **Telephone:** (703) 831-5881.
**SID:** Mike Ashley. **Telephone:** (703) 831-5211. **FAX:** (703) 831-5036.

**RHODE ISLAND** Rams

**Conference:** Atlantic-10.
**Mailing Address:** 207 Keaney Gymnasium, Kingston, RI 02881.
**Head Coach:** Frank Leoni. **Telephone:** (401) 792-4550.
**SID:** Jim Brunswick. **Telephone:** (401) 792-2409. **FAX:** (401) 792-5354.

**RICE** Owls

**Conference:** Southwest.
**Mailing Address:** P.O. Box 1892, Houston, TX 77251.
**Head Coach:** Wayne Graham. **Telephone:** (713) 527-6022.
**SID:** Mark Sanders. **Telephone:** (713) 527-4034. **FAX:** (713) 527-6019.

**RICHMOND** Spiders

**Conference:** Colonial Athletic.
**Mailing Address:** Robins Center, Richmond, VA 23173.
**Head Coach:** Ron Atkins. **Telephone:** (804) 289-8391.
**SID:** Phil Stanton. **Telephone:** (804) 289-8320. **FAX:** (804) 289-8820.

**RIDER** Broncs

**Conference:** Northeast.
**Mailing Address:** 2083 Lawrenceville Road, Lawrenceville, NJ 08648.
**Head Coach:** Sonny Pittaro. **Telephone:** (609) 896-5054.
**SID:** Bud Focht. **Telephone:** (609) 896-5138. **FAX:** (609) 896-0341.

**RUTGERS** Scarlet Knights

**Conference:** Atlantic-10.
**Mailing Address:** Louis Brown Athletic Center, P.O. Box 1149, Piscataway, NJ 08855.
**Head Coach:** Fred Hill. **Telephone:** (908) 445-3063.
**SID:** Scott Novak. **Telephone:** (908) 445-4200. **FAX:** (908) 445-3063.

**SACRAMENTO STATE** Hornets

**Conference:** Western Athletic/West.
**Mailing Address:** 6000 J St., Sacramento, CA 95819.
**Head Coach:** John Smith. **Telephone:** (916) 278-7225.
**SID:** John Kerr, Craig Lawson. **Telephone:** (916) 278-6896. **FAX:** (916) 278-5429.

**ST. BONAVENTURE** Bonnies

**Conference:** Atlantic-10.
**Mailing Address:** Department of Athletics, St. Bonaventure, NY 14778.
**Head Coach:** Larry Sudbrook. **Telephone:** (716) 375-2641.
**SID:** Jim Englehardt. **Telephone:** (716) 375-2319. **FAX:** (716) 375-2383.

**ST. FRANCIS** Terriers

**Conference:** Northeast.
**Mailing Address:** 180 Remsen St., Brooklyn, NY 11201.
**Head Coach:** Frank Del George. **Telephone:** (718) 522-2300, ext. 365.
**SID:** Jim Hoffman. **Telephone:** (718) 522-2300, ext. 885. **FAX:** (718) 797-2140.

**ST. JOHN'S** Red Storm

**Conference:** Big East.
**Mailing Address:** Grand Central & Utopia Parkways, Jamaica, NY 11439.
**Head Coach:** Joe Russo. **Telephone:** (718) 990-6148.
**SID:** Chris DeLorenzo. **Telephone:** (718) 990-6367. **FAX:** (718) 969-8468.

**ST. JOSEPH'S** Hawks

**Conference:** Atlantic-10.
**Mailing Address:** 5600 City Ave., Philadelphia, PA 19131.
**Head Coach:** Chris Loschiavo. **Telephone:** (610) 660-1718.
**SID:** Ken Krsolovic. **Telephone:** (610) 660-1704. **FAX:** (610) 660-1724.

**SAINT LOUIS** Billikens

**Conference:** Great Midwest.
**Mailing Address:** Room 39, DeBourg Hall, 221 N. Grand Blvd., St. Louis, MO 63103.
**Head Coach:** Bob Hughes. **Telephone:** (314) 977-3172.
**SID:** Russ Brightman. **Telephone:** (314) 977-3981. **FAX:** (314) 977-3178.

**ST. MARY'S** Gaels

**Conference:** West Coast.
**Mailing Address:** P.O. Box 5100, Moraga, CA 94575.
**Head Coach:** Don Jamerson. **Telephone:** (510) 631-4400.
**SID:** Scott Leykam-Hampton. **Telephone:** (510) 631-4402. **FAX:** (510) 631-4405.

**ST. PETER'S** Peacocks

**Conference:** Metro Atlantic/South.
**Mailing Address:** 2641 Kennedy Blvd., Jersey City, NJ 07306.
**Head Coach:** Bruce Sabatini. **Telephone:** (201) 915-9459.
**SID:** Tim Camp. **Telephone:** (201) 915-9101. **FAX:** (201) 915-9102.

**SAM HOUSTON STATE** Bearkats

**Conference:** Southland.
**Mailing Address:** P.O. Box 2268, Huntsville, TX 77341.
**Head Coach:** John Skeeters. **Telephone:** (409) 294-1731.
**SID:** Paul Ridings. **Telephone:** (409) 294-1764. **FAX:** (409) 294-3538.

**SAMFORD** Bulldogs

**Conference:** TransAmerica Athletic.
**Mailing Address:** 800 Lakeshore Drive, Birmingham, AL 35229.
**Head Coach:** Tommy Walker. **Telephone:** (205) 870-2134.
**SID:** Riley Adair. **Telephone:** (205) 870-2799. **FAX:** (205) 870-2654.

**SAN DIEGO** Toreros

**Conference:** West Coast.
**Mailing Address:** Alcala Park, San Diego, CA 92110.
**Head Coach:** John Cunningham. **Telephone:** (619) 260-8894.
**SID:** Daniel Jankowski. **Telephone:** (619) 260-4745. **FAX:** (619) 292-0388.

**SAN DIEGO STATE** Aztecs

**Conference:** Western Athletic/West.
**Mailing Address:** Dept of Athletics, SDSU, San Diego, CA 92182.
**Head Coach:** Jim Dietz. **Telephone:** (619) 594-6889.
**SID:** Dave Kuhn. **Telephone:** (619) 594-5547. **FAX:** (619) 582-6541.

**SAN FRANCISCO** Dons

**Conference:** West Coast.
**Mailing Address:** 2130 Fulton St., San Francisco, CA 94117.
**Head Coach:** Rich Hill. **Telephone:** (415) 666-2934.
**SID:** Pete LaFleur. **Telephone:** (415) 666-6161. **FAX:** (415) 666-2929.

**SAN JOSE STATE** Spartans

**Conference:** Big West.
**Mailing Address:** One Washington Square, San Jose, CA 95192.
**Head Coach:** Sam Piraro. **Telephone:** (408) 924-1254.
**SID:** Phil Simon. **Telephone:** (408) 924-1217. **FAX:** (408) 924-1291.

**SANTA CLARA** Broncos

**Conference:** West Coast.
**Mailing Address:** Toso Pavillion, Santa Clara, CA 95053.
**Head Coach:** John Oldham. **Telephone:** (408) 554-4680.
**SID:** Jim Young. **Telephone:** (408) 554-4661. **FAX:** (408) 554-6942.

### **SETON HALL** Pirates

**Conference:** Big East.1
**Mailing Address:** 400 S. Orange Ave., South Orange, NJ 07079.
**Head Coach:** Mike Sheppard. **Telephone:** (201) 761-9557.
**SID:** Sean Morrison. **Telephone:** (201) 761-9493. **FAX:** (201) 761-9061.

### **SIENA** Saints

**Conference:** Metro Atlantic/North.
**Mailing Address:** 515 Loudon Road, Loudonville, NY 12211.
**Head Coach:** Tony Rossi. **Telephone:** (518) 783-5044.
**SID:** Chris Caporale. **Telephone:** (518) 783-2411. **FAX:** (518) 783-2992.

### **SOUTH ALABAMA** Jaguars

**Conference:** Sun Belt.
**Mailing Address:** 1107 HPELS Building, Mobile, AL 36688.
**Head Coach:** Steve Kittrell. **Telephone:** (334) 460-6876.
**SID:** Fred Huff. **Telephone:** (334) 460-7035. **FAX:** (334) 460-7297.

### **SOUTH CAROLINA** Gamecocks

**Conference:** Southeastern/East.
**Mailing Address:** Rosewood Drive, Columbia, SC 29208.
**Head Coach:** June Raines. **Telephone:** (803) 777-3829.
**SID:** Tom Price. **Telephone:** (803) 777-0298. **FAX:** (803) 777-2967.

### **SOUTH FLORIDA** Bulls

**Conference:** Metro.
**Mailing Address:** 4202 E. Fowler Ave., Tampa, FL 33620.
**Head Coach:** Eddie Cardieri. **Telephone:** (813) 974-3105.
**SID:** Jack Heilig. **Telephone:** (813) 974-4092. **FAX:** (813) 974-5328.

### **SOUTHEAST MISSOURI STATE** Indians

**Conference:** Ohio Valley.
**Mailing Address:** One University Plaza, Cape Girardeau, MO 63701.
**Head Coach:** Mark Hogan. **Telephone:** (314) 651-2645.
**SID:** Bryan McGowan. **Telephone:** (314) 651-2294. **FAX:** (314) 651-2810.

### **SOUTHEASTERN LOUISIANA** Lions

**Conference:** TransAmerica Athletic.
**Mailing Address:** P.O. Drawer 880, SLU Station, Hammond, LA 70402.
**Head Coach:** Greg Marten. **Telephone:** (504) 549-2253.
**SID:** Jack Duggan. **Telephone:** (504) 549-3774. **FAX:** (504) 549-3495.

### **SOUTHERN** Jaguars

**Conference:** Southwestern Athletic/West.
**Mailing Address:** P.O. Box 9942, Baton Rouge, LA 70813.
**Head Coach:** Roger Cador. **Telephone:** (504) 771-2513.
**SID:** Rodney Lockett. **Telephone:** (504) 771-4142. **FAX:** (504) 771-4400.

### **SOUTHERN CALIFORNIA** Trojans

**Conference:** Pacific-10/South.
**Mailing Address:** HER-103, University Park, Los Angeles, CA 90089.
**Head Coach:** Mike Gillespie. **Telephone:** (213) 740-8444.
**SID:** Nancy Mazmanian. **Telephone:** (213) 740-8480. **FAX:** (213) 740-7584.

### **SOUTHERN ILLINOIS** Salukis

**Conference:** Missouri Valley.
**Mailing Address:** SIU Arena, Carbondale, IL 62901.
**Head Coach:** Dan Callahan. **Telephone:** (618) 453-2802.
**SID:** Gene Green. **Telephone:** (618) 453-7236. **FAX:** (618) 453-2648.

### **SOUTHERN MISSISSIPPI** Golden Eagles

**Conference:** Metro.
**Mailing Address:** Southern Station, Box 5161, Hattiesburg, MS 39406.
**Head Coach:** Hill Denson. **Telephone:** (601) 266-5017.
**SID:** Stephen Ivy. **Telephone:** (601) 266-4503. **FAX:** (601) 266-4507.

### **SOUTHERN UTAH** Thunderbirds

**Conference:** Independent.
**Mailing Address:** 350 W. Center St., Cedar City, UT 84720.
**Head Coach:** Jeff Scholzen. **Telephone:** (801) 586-7932.
**SID:** Neil Gardner. **Telephone:** (801) 586-7753. **FAX:** (801) 865-8077.

### **SOUTHWEST MISSOURI STATE** Bears

**Conference:** Missouri Valley.
**Mailing Address:** 901 S. National, Springfield, MO 65804.
**Head Coach:** Keith Guttin. **Telephone:** (417) 836-5242.
**SID:** Jon Martin, Mark Stillwell. **Telephone:** (417) 836-5402. **FAX:** (417) 836-4868.

### **SOUTHWEST TEXAS STATE** Bobcats

**Conference:** Southland.
**Mailing Address:** 136 Jowers Center, San Marcos, TX 78666.
**Head Coach:** Howard Bushong. **Telephone:** (512) 245-3586.
**SID:** Corey Bobo. **Telephone:** (512) 245-2966. **FAX:** (512) 245-2967.

### **SOUTHWESTERN LOUISIANA** Ragin' Cajuns

**Conference:** Sun Belt.
**Mailing Address:** 201 Reinhardt Drive, Lafayette, LA 70506.
**Head Coach:** Tony Robichaux. **Telephone:** (318) 482-6189.
**SID:** Charlie Cavell. **Telephone:** (318) 482-6331. **FAX:** (318) 482-6649.

### **STANFORD** Cardinal

**Conference:** Pacific-10/South.
**Mailing Address:** Department of Athletics, Stanford, CA 94305.

**Head Coach:** Mark Marquess. **Telephone:** (415) 723-4528.
**SID:** Scott McConnell. **Telephone:** (415) 723-4418. **FAX:** (415) 725-2957.

### STEPHEN F. AUSTIN Lumberjacks

**Conference:** Southland.
**Mailing Address:** P.O. Box 13010, Nacogdoches, TX 75962.
**Head Coach:** Rick Zamora. **Telephone:** (409) 468-4350.
**SID:** Ross Johnson. **Telephone:** (409) 468-2606. **FAX:** (409) 468-4593.

### STETSON Hatters

**Conference:** TransAmerica Athletic.
**Mailing Address:** Campus Box 8317, DeLand, FL 32720.
**Head Coach:** Pete Dunn. **Telephone:** (904) 822-8106.
**SID:** Tom McClellan. **Telephone:** (904) 822-8131. **FAX:** (904) 822-8132.

### TEMPLE Owls

**Conference:** Atlantic-10.
**Mailing Address:** McGonigle Hall 101, Philadelphia, PA 19122.
**Head Coach:** Skip Wilson. **Telephone:** (215) 204-7447.
**SID:** Kevin Kaufman. **Telephone:** (215) 204-7446. **FAX:** (215) 204-7499.

### TENNESSEE Volunteers

**Conference:** Southeastern/East.
**Mailing Address:** P.O. Box 47, Knoxville, TN 37901.
**Head Coach:** Rod Delmonico. **Telephone:** (615) 974-1223.
**SID:** Mike Cawood. **Telephone:** (615) 974-1212. **FAX:** (615) 974-1269.

### TENNESSEE-MARTIN Pacers

**Conference:** Ohio Valley.
**Mailing Address:** 304 Administration, Martin, TN 38238.
**Head Coach:** Vernon Prather. **Telephone:** (901) 587-7660.
**SID:** Lee Wilmot. **Telephone:** (901) 587-7632. **FAX:** (901) 587-7624.

### TENNESSEE TECH Golden Eagles

**Conference:** Ohio Valley.
**Mailing Address:** Department of Athletics, P.O. Box 5057, Cookeville, TN 38501.
**Head Coach:** David Mays. **Telephone:** (615) 372-3925.
**SID:** Rob Schabert. **Telephone:** (615) 372-3088. **FAX:** (615) 372-6139.

### TEXAS Longhorns

**Conference:** Southwest.
**Mailing Address:** P.O. Box 7399, Austin, TX 78713.
**Head Coach:** Cliff Gustafson. **Telephone:** (512) 471-5732.
**SID:** Amy Stabley. **Telephone:** (512) 471-6039. **FAX:** (512) 471-6040.

### TEXAS-ARLINGTON Mavericks

**Conference:** Southland
**Mailing Address:** P.O. Box 19079, Arlington, TX 76019.
**Head Coach:** Butch McBroom. **Telephone:** (817) 273-2261.
**SID:** Steve Weller. **Telephone:** (817) 273-2239. **FAX:** (817) 273-2254

### TEXAS-PAN AMERICAN Broncos

**Conference:** Sun Belt.
**Mailing Address:** 1201 W. University Drive, Edinburg, TX 78539.
**Head Coach:** Al Ogletree. **Telephone:** (210) 381-2234.
**SID:** Mark Vinson. **Telephone:** (210) 381-2240. **FAX:** (210) 381-2398.

### TEXAS-SAN ANTONIO Roadrunners

**Conference:** Southland.
**Mailing Address:** 6900 Loop 1604 West, San Antonio, TX 78249.
**Head Coach:** Jimmy Shankle. **Telephone:** (210) 691-4805.
**SID:** Rick Nixon. **Telephone:** (210) 691-4551. **FAX:** (210) 691-4569.

### TEXAS A&M Aggies

**Conference:** Southwest.
**Mailing Address:** Joe Routt Boulevard, College Station, TX 77843.
**Head Coach:** Mark Johnson. **Telephone:** (409) 845-9534.
**SID:** Alan Cannon. **Telephone:** (409) 845-5725. **FAX:** (409) 845-0564.

### TEXAS CHRISTIAN Horned Frogs

**Conference:** Southwest.
**Mailing Address:** P.O.Box 32924, Fort Worth, TX 76129.
**Head Coach:** Lance Brown. **Telephone:** (817) 921-7985.
**SID:** Trey Carmichael. **Telephone:** (817) 921-7969. **FAX:** (817) 921-7964.

### TEXAS SOUTHERN Tigers

**Conference:** Southwestern Athletic/West.
**Mailing Address:** 3100 Cleburne St., Houston, TX 77004.
**Head Coach:** Candy Robinson. **Telephone:** (713) 527-7993.
**SID:** Andre Smith. **Telephone:** (713) 527-7270. **FAX:** (713) 639-1045.

### TEXAS TECH Red Raiders

**Conference:** Southwest.
**Mailing Address:** P.O. Box 43021, Lubbock, TX 79409.
**Head Coach:** Larry Hays. **Telephone:** (806) 742-3355.
**SID:** Kelly Robinson. **Telephone:** (806) 742-2770. **FAX:** 806 742-1970.

### TOLEDO Rockets

**Conference:** Mid-American.
**Mailing Address:** 2801 W. Bancroft St., Toledo, OH 43606.
**Head Coach:** Joe Kruzel. **Telephone:** (419) 537-2526.
**SID:** Jeff Hoffman. **Telephone:** (419) 537-3791. **FAX:** (419) 537-3795.

### TOWSON STATE Tigers

**Conference:** Big South.

**Mailing Address:** Towson Center, Towson, MD 21204.
**Head Coach:** Mike Gottlieb. **Telephone:** (410) 830-3775.
**SID:** Dan O'Connell. **Telephone:** (410) 830-2232. **FAX:** (410) 830-3861.

### **TROY STATE** Trojans

**Conference:** Mid-Continent/East.
**Mailing Address:** Davis Field House, Troy State University, Troy, AL 36082.
**Head Coach:** John Mayotte. **Telephone:** (334) 670-3480.
**SID:** Mike Fuller. **Telephone:** (334) 670-3480. **FAX:** (334) 670-3278.

### **TULANE** Green Wave

**Conference:** Metro.
**Mailing Address:** James W. Wilson Jr. Center, New Orleans, LA 70118.
**Head Coach:** Rick Jones. **Telephone:** (504) 862-8239.
**SID:** Scott Spencer. **Telephone:** (504) 865-5506. **FAX:** (504) 865-5512.

### **UTAH** Utes

**Conference:** Western Athletic/East.
**Mailing Address:** John Huntsman Center, Salt Lake City, UT 84112.
**Head Coach:** Steve Gillespie. **Telephone:** (801) 581-5323.
**SID:** Mickelle Marston. **Telephone:** (801) 581-3511. **FAX:** (801) 581-4358.

### **VALPARAISO** Crusaders

**Conference:** Mid-Continent/West.
**Mailing Address:** Recreation Center, Valparaiso, IN 46383.
**Head Coach:** Paul Twenge. **Telephone:** (219) 464-5239.
**SID:** Bill Rogers. **Telephone:** (219) 464-5232. **FAX:** (219) 464-5762.

### **VANDERBILT** Commodores

**Conference:** Southeastern/East.
**Mailing Address:** Box 120158, 2601 Jess Neely Drive, Nashville, TN 37212.
**Head Coach:** Roy Mewbourne. **Telephone:** (615) 322-4122.
**SID:** Mark Bechtel. **Telephone:** (615) 322-4121. **FAX:** (615) 343-7064.

### **VERMONT** Catamounts

**Conference:** North Atlantic.
**Mailing Address:** 86 S. Williams St., Burlington, VT 05401.
**Head Coach:** Bill Currier. **Telephone:** (802) 656-7701.
**SID:** Paul Stanfield. **Telephone:** (802) 656-1109. **FAX:** (802) 656-8328.

### **VILLANOVA** Wildcats

**Conference:** Big East.
**Mailing Address:** Lancaster & Ithan Avenues, Villanova, PA 19085.
**Head Coach:** George Bennett. **Telephone:** (610) 519-4529.
**SID:** Dean Kenefick. **Telephone:** (610) 519-4120. **FAX:** (610) 519-7323.

### **VIRGINIA** Cavaliers

**Conference:** Atlantic Coast.
**Mailing Address:** P.O. Box 3785, University Hall, Charlottesville, VA 22903.
**Head Coach:** Dennis Womack. **Telephone:** (804) 982-5775.
**SID:** Tom Sullivan. **Telephone:** (804) 982-5500. **FAX:** (804) 982-5525.

### **VIRGINIA COMMONWEALTH** Rams

**Conference:** Metro.
**Mailing Address:** 819 W. Franklin St., Richmond, VA 23284.
**Head Coach:** Paul Keyes. **Telephone:** (804) 828-4820.
**SID:** Mark Halstead. **Telephone:** (804) 828-7000. **FAX:** (804) 828-9428.

### **VIRGINIA MILITARY INSTITUTE** Keydets

**Conference:** Southern.
**Mailing Address:** Cameron Hall, Lexington, VA 24450.
**Head Coach:** Scott Gines. **Telephone:** (703) 464-7609.
**SID:** Pete Lefresne. **Telephone:** (703) 464-7253. **FAX:** (703) 464-7583.

### **VIRGINIA TECH** Hokies

**Conference:** Metro.
**Mailing Address:** 364 Jamerson Center, Blacksburg, VA 24061.
**Head Coach:** Chuck Hartman. **Telephone:** (703) 231-6417.
**SID:** Dave Smith. **Telephone:** (703) 231-6726. **FAX:** (703) 231-6984.

### **WAGNER** Seahawks

**Conference:** Northeast.
**Mailing Address:** 631 Howard Ave., Staten Island, NY 10301.
**Head Coach:** Rich Vitaliano. **Telephone:** (718) 390-3165.
**SID:** Tushar Saxena. **Telephone:** (718) 390-3227. **FAX:** (718) 390-3347.

### **WAKE FOREST** Demon Deacons

**Conference:** Atlantic Coast.
**Mailing Address:** P.O. Box 7426, Winston-Salem, NC 27109.
**Head Coach:** George Greer. **Telephone:** (910) 759-7891.
**SID:** Dan Zacharias. **Telephone:** (910) 759-5640. **FAX:** (910) 759-5140.

### **WASHINGTON** Huskies

**Conference:** Pacific-10/North.
**Mailing Address:** 202 Graves Building, Seattle, WA 98195.
**Head Coach:** Ken Knutson. **Telephone:** (206) 543-9365.
**SID:** Jeff Bechthold. **Telephone:** (206) 543-2230. **FAX:** (206) 543-5000.

### **WASHINGTON STATE** Cougars

**Conference:** Pacific-10/North.
**Mailing Address:** M-8 Bohler Gym, Pullman, WA 99164.
**Head Coach:** Steve Farrington. **Telephone:** (509) 335-0211.
**SID:** Rod Commons. **Telephone:** (509) 335-0269. **FAX:** (509) 335-0267.

**WEST CHESTER** Rams

**Conference:** Independent.
**Mailing Address:** Room 8, Hollinger Fieldhouse, West Chester, PA 19383.
**Head Coach:** Carl Giuranna. **Telephone:** (610) 436-2152.
**SID:** Tom DiCamillo. **Telephone:** (610) 436-3316. **FAX:** (610) 436-2966.

**WEST VIRGINIA** Mountaineers

**Conference:** Atlantic-10.
**Mailing Address:** Box 877, Morgantown, WV 26507.
**Head Coach:** Greg Van Zant. **Telephone:** (304) 293-2308.
**SID:** John Antonik. **Telephone:** (304) 293-2821. **FAX:** (304) 293-4105.

**WESTERN CAROLINA** Catamounts

**Conference:** Southern.
**Mailing Address:** 2517 Ramsey Center, Cullowhee, NC 28723.
**Head Coach:** Keith LeClair. **Telephone:** (704) 227-7338.
**SID:** Steve White. **Telephone:** (704) 227-7171. **FAX:** (704) 227-7688.

**WESTERN ILLINOIS** Leathernecks

**Conference:** Mid-Continent.
**Mailing Address:** Western Hall 213, Macomb, IL 61455.
**Head Coach:** Dick Pawlow. **Telephone:** (309) 298-1521.
**SID:** Doug Smiley. **Telephone:** (309) 298-1133. **FAX:** (309) 298-3366.

**WESTERN KENTUCKY** Hilltoppers

**Conference:** Sun Belt.
**Mailing Address:** Wetherby Administration Building, 1526 Russellville Road, Bowling Green, KY 42101.
**Head Coach:** Joel Murrie. **Telephone:** (502) 745-6078.
**SID:** Sally Krauss. **Telephone:** (502) 745-4298. **FAX:** (502) 745-3444.

**WESTERN MICHIGAN** Broncos

**Conference:** Mid-American.
**Mailing Address:** B-205 Ellsworth Hall, Kalamazoo, MI 49008.
**Head Coach:** Fred Decker. **Telephone:** (616) 387-8149.
**SID:** John Beatty. **Telephone:** (616) 387-4138. **FAX:** (616) 387-4139.

**WICHITA STATE** Shockers

**Conference:** Missouri Valley.
**Mailing Address:** Campus Box 18, Wichita, KS 67208.
**Head Coach:** Gene Stephenson. **Telephone:** (316) 689-3636.
**SID:** Larry Rankin. **Telephone:** (316) 689-3265. **FAX:** (316) 689-3336.

**WILLIAM & MARY** Tribe

**Conference:** Colonial Athletic.
**Mailing Address:** P.O. Box 399, Williamsburg, VA 23187.
**Head Coach:** Jim Farr. **Telephone:** (804) 221-3399.
**SID:** David Johnson, Mike Lynch. **Telephone:** (804) 221-3344. **FAX:** (804) 221-3412.

**WINTHROP** Eagles

**Conference:** Big South.
**Mailing Address:** Winthrop Coliseum, Rock Hill, SC 29733.
**Head Coach:** Joe Hudak. **Telephone:** (803) 323-2129.
**SID:** Jack Frost. **Telephone:** (803) 323-2129. **FAX:** (803) 323-2433.

**WISCONSIN-MILWAUKEE** Panthers

**Conference:** Midwestern Collegiate/West.
**Mailing Address:** P.O. Box 413, Milwaukee, WI 53201.
**Head Coach:** Jerry Augustine. **Telephone:** (414) 229-5670.
**SID:** Rocco Gasparro. **Telephone:** (414) 229-4593. **FAX:** (414) 229-6759.

**WRIGHT STATE** Raiders

**Conference:** Midwestern Collegiate/East.
**Mailing Address:** P.O. Box 516, Dayton, OH 45435.
**Head Coach:** Ron Nischwitz. **Telephone:** (513) 873-2771.
**SID:** Jeff Lightner. **Telephone:** (513) 873-2771. **FAX:** (513) 873-2368.

**WYOMING** Cowboys

**Conference:** Western Athletic.
**Mailing Address:** Box 3414, Laramie, WY 82071.
**Head Coach:** Dave Taylor. (307) 766-2340.
**SID:** Steve Weakland. **Telephone:** (307) 766-2256. **FAX:** (307) 766-2346.

**XAVIER** Muskateers

**Conference:** Midwestern Collegiate/East.
**Mailing Address:** 3800 Victory Parkway, Cincinnati, OH 45207.
**Head Coach:** John Morrey. **Telephone:** (513) 745-3413.
**SID:** Courtney Morrison. **Telephone:** (513) 745-3416. **FAX:** (513) 745-2825.

**YALE** Bulldogs

**Conference:** Ivy League/Rolfe.
**Mailing Address:** 402-A Yale Station, New Haven, CT 06520.
**Head Coach:** John Stuper. **Telephone:** (203) 432-7422.
**SID:** Steve Conn. **Telephone:** (203) 432-1455. **FAX:** (203) 432-1454.

**YOUNGSTOWN STATE** Penguins

**Conference:** Mid-Continent/East.
**Mailing Address:** 410 Wick Ave., Stambaugh Stadium 2006, Youngstown, OH 44555.
**Head Coach:** Dan Kubacki. **Telephone:** (216) 742-3485.
**SID:** Greg Gulas. **Telephone:** (216) 742-3192. **FAX:** (216) 742-3191.

# HIGH SCHOOL BASEBALL

## NATIONAL FEDERATION OF STATE HIGH SCHOOL ASSOCIATIONS

**Office Address:** 11724 NW Plaza Circle, Kansas City, MO 64195. **Mailing Address:** P.O. Box 20626, Kansas City, MO 64195. **Telephone:** (816) 464-5400. **FAX:** (816) 464-5571.

**Executive Director:** Robert Kanaby. **Associate Director:** Fritz McGinness. **Assistant Director/Baseball Rules Editor:** Brad Rumble. **Director of Public Relations:** Bruce Howard.

## NATIONAL HIGH SCHOOL BASEBALL COACHES ASSOCIATION

**Mailing Address:** P.O. Box 12354, Omaha, NE 68112. **Telephone:** (402) 457-1962. **FAX:** Same.

**Executive Director:** Jerry Miles. **Administrative Assistant:** Elaine Miles. **President:** Iran Novick (Placentia, CA).

**1995 National Convention:** Dec. 1-3 at Anaheim, CA.

# NATIONAL SHOWCASE EVENTS

**(For High School Players)**

## AREA CODE GAMES

**Mailing Address:** P.O. Box 213, Santa Rosa, CA 95402. **Telephone:** (707) 525-0498. **FAX:** (707) 525-0214.

**President, Goodwill Series, Inc.:** Bob Williams.

**1995 Area Code Games:** Aug. 14-19, Blair Field, Long Beach, CA.

## TEAM ONE NATIONAL SHOWCASE

**Mailing Address:** 10999 Reed Hartman Hwy., Cincinnati, OH 45242. **Telephone:** (513) 791-6070. **FAX:** (513) 793-8614.

**President, Team One Sports Marketing:** Jeff Spelman.

**1995 Team One National Showcase:** June 22-25, Crosley Field, Blue Ash, OH. **Regional Showcases:** July 7-9, New Orleans, LA (Tulane University); July 21-23, City Stadium, Lynchburg, VA; Aug. 11-13, Lexington, KY (University of Kentucky).

## NATIONAL AMATEUR ALL-STAR BASEBALL TOURNAMENT

**Mailing Address:** 343 West Erie, Ste. 430, Chicago, IL 60610. **Telephone:** (800) 622-2877. **FAX:** (312) 642-2607.

**Operated by:** Amateur All-Star Baseball, Inc.

**Chairman:** Alan Cox. **President:** Ron Berryman. **Executive Director:** Steve Timothy.

**Associate Members:** American Amateur Baseball Congress, Babe Ruth Baseball, Dixie Baseball, PONY Baseball, National Amateur Baseball Federation.

**1995 Tournament:** June 20-24, Bosse Field, Evansville, IN.

# AMATEUR BASEBALL

## U.S. OLYMPIC COMMITTEE

**Mailing Address:** One Olympic Plaza, Colorado Springs, CO 80909. **Telephone:** (719) 632-5551. **FAX:** (719) 578-4654.

**President:** Dr. Leroy Walker. **Interim Executive Director:** John Krimsky Jr.. **Director of Public Relations:** Mike Moran.

## INTERNATIONAL BASEBALL ASSOCIATION

**Mailing Address:** Avenue de Mon-Repos 24, Case Postale 131, 1000 Lausanne 5, Switzerland. **Telephone:** 41-21-311-1863. **FAX:** 41-21-311-1864.

**President:** Aldo Notari (Italy). **Secretary General:** Richard Case. **Executive Director:** Miquel Ortin.

### 1995 Events

**Pan American Games:** March 11-27 at Mar Del Plata, Argentina.

**President's Cup:** April 28-May 7 at Buenos Aires, Argentina.

**IBA World Baseball Week in Asia:** Tokyo, May 19-June 1; Seoul, South Korea, June 2-7; Taiwan, June 8-13.

**European Championships:** July 7-16 at Haarlem, Netherlands.

**AA Youth World Championships:** July 22-Aug. 6 at Londrina, Brazil.

**World Children's Baseball Fair:** Aug. 2-8 at Gifu City, Japan.

**America's Challenge Cup:** Aug. 2-13 at Edmonton, Alberta.

**AAA Youth World Championships:** Aug. 11-20, Cape Cod/Boston, MA.

**Asian Championships:** Sept. 17-25 at Kurashiki City, Japan.

**Intercontinental Cup:** Oct. 21-Nov. 6 at Havana, Cuba.

## USA BASEBALL

**Mailing Address, Corporate Headquarters:** 2160 Greenwood Ave., Trenton, NJ 08609. **Telephone:** (609) 586-2381. **FAX:** (609) 587-1818.

**Mailing Address, Training Base:** 4880 Navy Road, Millington, TN 38053. **Telephone:** (901) 872-8326. **FAX:** (901) 872-0313

**Chairman of the Board:** Cliff Lothery. **President:** Mark Marquess. **Executive Vice President:** Neil Lantz. **Secretary:** Tom Hicks. **Treasurer:** Gale Montgomery.

**Executive Director/Chief Executive Officer:** Richard Case. **Deputy Director:** Wanda Rutledge. **Associate Director/USA Team General Manager:** Mike Fiore.

**Controller:** Barbara Case. **Operations Director:** Pam Case.

**Special Projects Manager:** Paul Seiler. **Marketing and Licensing Director:** Derek Bradley. **Media Relations Director:** George Doig. **Administrative Coordinator:** Chris Kelleher.

**National Members:** Amateur Athletic Union, American Amateur Baseball Congress; American Baseball Coaches Association; American Legion Baseball; Dixie Baseball; Little League Baseball; National Amateur Baseball Federation; National Baseball Congress; National Collegiate Athletic Association; National Association of Intercollegiate Athletics; National Junior College Athletic Association; National Federation of State High School Athletic Associations; Police Athletic League; PONY Baseball, Inc.; YMCA of the USA.

### 1995 Events

**Pan American Games:** March 11-27 at Mar Del Plata, Argentina.

**U.S. Olympic Festival:** July 18-26 at Colorado Springs, CO.

**World Junior Championships** (17-18): Aug. 11-20 at Cape Cod/ Boston, MA.

**Intercontinental Cup:** Oct. 21-Nov. 6 at Havana, Cuba.

**USA Baseball Fall Trials:** Oct. 29-Nov. 7 at Homestead, Fla.

## BASEBALL CANADA

**Mailing Address:** 1600 James Naismith Dr., Gloucester, Ontario K1B 5N4. **Telephone:** (613) 748-5606. **FAX:** (613) 748-5767.

**Executive Director:** Duncan Grant.

## NATIONAL BASEBALL CONGRESS

**Mailing Address:** P.O. Box 1420, Wichita, KS 67201. **Telephone:** (316) 267-3372. **FAX:** (316) 267-3382.

**President:** Bob Rich Jr. **Executive Vice President:** Melinda Rich.

**Vice President/General Manager:** Steve Shaad. **Assistant General Manager:** Lance Deckinger. **NBC National Commissioner:** Larry Davis. **Director of Administration:** Dian Overaker. **Marketing and Public Relations Coordinator:** Chris Overholser. **Stadium Manager:** Mark Schimming. **Business Manager:** Brad Eldridge.

**1995 NBC World Series:** Aug. 1-15, Lawrence-Dumont Stadium, Wichita, KS.

**Year Founded:** 1931.

# SUMMER COLLEGE LEAGUES

## ALASKA LEAGUE

**Mailing Address:** 1625 Old Steese Highway, Fairbanks, AK 99701. **Telephone:** (907) 452-1991. **FAX:** (907) 277-4316.

**Commissioner:** Ralph Seekins. **Publicity Director:** Don Dennis.

**Years League Active:** 1974-.

**1995 Opening Date:** June 6. **Closing Date:** Aug. 7.

**No. of Games, Regular Season:** 55.

**All-Star Game:** None. **Playoff Format:** None.

**Roster Limit:** 21, plus exemption for Alaska residents.

### ALASKA GOLDPANNERS

**Mailing Address:** P.O. Box 71154, Fairbanks, AK 99707. **Telephone:** (907) 451-0095. **FAX:** (907) 452-8209.

**President:** Bill Stroecker. **General Manager:** Don Dennis. **Head Coach:** Stacy Parker (Orange Coast, Calif. CC). **Assistant Coach:** Jeff Scholzen (Southern Utah).

### ANCHORAGE BUCS

**Mailing Address:** P.O. Box 24-0061, Anchorage, AK 99524. **Telephone:** (907) 274-2827. **FAX:** (907) 277-4316.

**President:** Pat Kennedy. **General Manager:** Dennis Mattingly. **Head Coach:** Bo Hall. **Assistant Coach:** Marco O'Brian.

### HAWAII ISLAND MOVERS

**Mailing Address:** P.O. Box 17865, Honolulu, HI 96817. **Telephone:** (808) 848-5203. **FAX:** (808) 841-2321.

**President/General Manager:** Donald Takaki. **Head Coach:** Tom Gushiken (Kansas State). **Assistant Coach:** Chad Konishi (California).

### OAKLAND OAKS

**Mailing Address:** 50 Sandringham Rd., Piedmont, CA 94611. **Telephone:** 510-530-2727. **FAX:** 510-530-2729.

**General Manager:** Bob Epstein. **Head Coach:** Dave Lawn (California).

## ALASKA CENTRAL LEAGUE

**Mailing Address:** 800 Harbor Circle, Anchorage, AK 99515. **Telephone:** (907) 345-9205. **FAX:** (907) 345-9206.

**President:** Lou Sinnett. **Executive Director:** Jack Slama.

**1995 Opening Date:** June 5. **Closing Date:** July 31.

**No. of Games, Regular Season:** 42.

**All-Star Game:** None.

**Playoff Format:** None. Regular-season champion advances to National Baseball Congress World Series.

**Roster Limit:** 25.

### ANCHORAGE GLACIER PILOTS

**Mailing Address:** P.O. Box 100895, Anchorage, AK 99510. **Telephone:** (907) 274-3627. **FAX:** (907) 274-3628.

**General Manager:** Lou Sinnett. **Head Coach:** Kevin Smallcomb.

### MAT-SU MINERS

**Mailing Address:** HC 04 Box 9480, Palmer, AK 99645. **Telephone:** (907) 745-6401. **FAX:** (907) 745-7275.

**President:** Vikki Christianson. **General Manager:** Stan Zaborac Jr. **Head Coach:** Unavailable.

### PENINSULA OILERS

**Mailing Address:** P.O. Box 318, Kenai, AK 99611. **Telephone:** (907) 283-7133. **FAX:** (907) 283-3390.

**President:** Raymond Measles. **Baseball Operations Manager:** Coral Seymour. **Head Coach:** Sonny Golloway (Oklahoma). **Assistant Coach:** Robert Miller (Riverside, Calif., JC).

## ARIZONA COLLEGIATE LEAGUE

**Mailing Address:** 6223 E Calle Redonda, Scottsdale, AZ 85251. **Telephone:** (602) 990-2404. **FAX:** Same.

**Commissioner/President:** Tom Krawczyk. **Vice President:** Fred Board. **Administation Assistants:** Jim Brand, Todd Curson, Cliff Tait.

**Years League Active:** 1989-

**Member Clubs:** Glendale Angels, Mesa Yankees, Peoria Royals, Phoenix Athletics, Scottsdale Braves, Tempe Giants.

**1995 Opening Date:** June 5.**1995 Closing Date:** July 30.

**No. of Games, Regular Season:** 40.

**Playoff Format:** All teams qualify for playoffs. Top two teams receive first-round byes. All series best-of-3.

**Roster Limit:** 22.

## ATLANTIC COLLEGIATE LEAGUE

**Mailing Address:** 130 Colony Ave., Park Ridge, NJ 07656. **Telephone:** (201) 391-9376. **FAX:** (201) 391-9276.

**Commissioner:** John Belson. **President:** Bob Pertsas. **Executive Vice President:** Tom Bonekemper.

**Member Clubs, Divisions: Kaiser**—Brooklyn Clippers, Nassau Collegians, New York Generals. **Wolff**—Jersey Pilots, Scranton/Wilkes-Barre Twins, Sussex Colonels. **Unnamed**—Delaware Gulls, Quakertown Blazers, West Deptford.

**1995 Opening Date:** June 1. **Closing Date:** Aug. 14.

**No. of Games, Regular Season:** 36.

**All-Star Games:** July 10 at Scranton/Wilkes-Barre; July 17 at Sussex.

**Playoff Format:** Three division winners and second-place team with best record meet in best-of-3 semifinals. Winners meet in best-of-3 series for league championship.

**Roster Limit:** 21.

## CAPE COD LEAGUE

**Mailing Address:** P.O. Box 164, South Harwich, MA 02661. **Telephone:** (508) 432-1774. **FAX:** (508) 432-9766.

**Commissioner:** Fred Ebbett.

**President:** Judy Scarafile. Mailing Address: 449 Braggs Lane, Barnstable Village, MA 02630. Telephone: (508) 362-3036.

**Vice Presidents:** James Higgins, Don Tullie.

**Publicity Director:** Missy Alaimo. **Telephone:** (508) 975-2405.

**Years League Active:** 1885-.

**Member Clubs, Division Structure: East**—Brewster, Chatham, Harwich, Orleans, Yarmouth-Dennis. **West**—Bourne, Cotuit, Falmouth, Hyannis, Wareham.

**1995 Opening Date:** June 9. **1995 Closing Date:** August 10.

**No. of Games, Regular Season:** 44.

**All-Star Game:** July 22 at Falmouth.

**Playoff Format:** Top two teams in each division meet in best-of-3 semifinals. Winners meet in best-of-3 series for league championship.

**Roster Limit:** 23.

### BOURNE BRAVES

**Mailing Address:** 314 Gifford Ave., Falmouth, MA 02553. **Telephone:** (508) 540-4700. **FAX:** (508) 457-7948.

**President:** Robert Corradi. **General Manager:** Dennis Butts. **Head Coach:** Bob Stead. **Assistant Coach:** Earl Mattheson.

### BREWSTER WHITECAPS

**Mailing Address:** P.O. Box 1319, Brewster, MA 02631. **Telephone:** (617) 720-7870. **FAX:** (617) 720-7877.

**President:** Robert Riedl. **General Managers:** Howard Wayne, Sol Yas. **Head Coach:** Steve Rousey (Long Beach State). **Assistant Coach:** Mike Kirby (Cal State Fullerton).

### CHATHAM A's

**Mailing Address:** 61 Whidah Dr., East Harwich, MA 02645. **Telephone:** (508) 945-4014.

**General Manager:** Jeff McGuire. **Head Coach:** John Schiffner (Providence College).

### COTUIT KETTLEERS

**Mailing Address:** P.O. Box 411, Cotuit, MA 02635. **Telephone:** (508) 888-2336. **FAX:** (508) 888-8134.

**President/General Manager:** Richard Sadowski. **Head Coach:** Mike Coutts (Maine).

### FALMOUTH COMMODORES

**Mailing Address:** 33 Winter Green Rd., Mashpee, MA 02649. **Telephone:** (508) 548-5800. **FAX:** (508) 540-3835.

**President:** Bob Weiss. **General Manager:** Chuck Sturtevant. **Head Coach:** Harvey Shapiro (Bowdoin, Me., College). **Assistant Coach:** Dick Schoonover (Ohio State).

### HARWICH MARINERS

**Mailing Address:** 2 Concord Drive, Harwich, MA 02645. **Telephone:** (508) 432-2124.

**President:** Mary Henderson. **General Manager:** John Ferreira. **Head Coach:** Bruce Peddie (Mansfield, Pa.). **Assistant Coach:** Tom Bell.

### HYANNIS METS

**Mailing Address:** P.O. Box 852, Hyannis, MA 02601. **Telephone:** (508) 428-2705.

**President:** David Sauro. **General Manager:** Jim Lynch. **Head Coach:** Steve Mrowka (Georgia College). **Assistant Coach:** Jim Stone (Blair Academy).

### ORLEANS CARDINALS

**Mailing Address:** P.O. Box 504, Orleans, MA 02653. **Telephone:** (508) 255-0793.

**President:** Jeff Rueland. **General Manager:** Joseph Rossetti. **Head Coach:** Rolando Casanova (Florida International). **Assistant Coach:** Tony Casas (Lynn, Mass., College).

### WAREHAM GATEMEN

**Mailing Address:** 27 Mattapoisett Neck Road, Mattapoisett, MA 02739. **Telephone:** (508) 758-6579. **FAX:** (508) 758-2112.

**President:** John Wylde.

**General Manager:** Jim Hubbard. **Head Coach:** Don Reed. **Assistant Coach:** Joe Walsh (Suffolk, Mass.).

### YARMOUTH-DENNIS RED SOX

**Mailing Address:** 51 Nautical Lane, South Yarmouth, MA 02664. **Telephone:** (508) 394-0604.

**President:** Gary Ellis. **General Manager:** Jim Hagemeister. **Head Coach:** John Barlowe (Vanderbilt). **Assistant Coach:** Juan Ranero (Rowan, N.J., College).

## CENTRAL ILLINOIS COLLEGIATE LEAGUE

**Mailing Address:** R.R. 13, Box 369, Bloomington, IL 61704. **Telephone:** (309) 828-4429. **FAX:** Same.

**President:** Duffy Bass. **Commissioner:** Mike Woods. **Administrative Assistant:** Tom Lamonica. **Publicity Director:** Jim Bowers.

**Years League Active:** 1963-.

**Member Clubs:** Champaign County Colts, Danville Dans, Decatur Blues, Springfield Rifles, Twin City Stars.

**1995 Opening Date:** June 6. **Closing Date:** July 31.

**No. of Games, Regular Season:** 40.

**All-Star Game:** None.

**Playoff Format:** All five teams, double-elimination tournament.

**Roster Limit:** 23.

## GREAT LAKES LEAGUE

**Mailing Address:** P.O. Box 1121, Bowling Green, OH 43402. **Telephone:** (419) 354-5556. **FAX:** (419) 352-3898.

**Commissioner:** Ray Neill. **President:** Barry Ruben. **Vice President:** Larry Bialorucki. **Treasurer:** Ron Miller. **Publicity Director:** Bartt Davis.

**Years League Active:** 1986-.

**Member Clubs, Division Structure: North**—Euclid, Lima, Motor City, Sandusky, Toledo. **South**—Central Ohio, Columbus, Dayton, Grand Lake, Springfield.

**1995 Opening Date:** June 10. **Closing Date:** Aug. 7.

**No. of Games, Regular Season:** 40.

**All-Star Game:** July 15 at Lima, Ohio.

**Playoff Format:** Top two teams in each division meet in best-of-5 series. Winners meet in best-of-5 series for league championship.

**Roster Limit:** 25.

### CENTRAL OHIO

**Mailing Address:** 809 Vernon Rd., Columbus, OH 43209. **Telephone:** (614) 236-8141. **FAX:** (614) 231-0212.

**President:** Tom Hochanadel. **General Manager:** Wendell Kessler. **Head Coach:** Ron Golden (Ohio State).

### COLUMBUS ALL-AMERICANS

**Mailing Address:** 4507 Dirham Lane, Hilliard, OH 43026. **Telephone:** (614) 876-6108. **FAX:** (614) 529-6015.

**President:** Jery DiCuccio. **General Manager:** Rodney Garnett. **Head Coach:** Roger Ingles (Ohio Wesleyan).

### DAYTON

**Mailing Address:** 11546 Steck Rd., Brookville, OH 45309. **Telephone:** (513) 833-2326. **FAX:** (513) 833-5248.

**General Manager/Head Coach:** Fred Scherman.

### EUCLID

**Mailing Address:** 22700 Shore Center Dr., Euclid, OH 44123. **Telephone:** (216) 261-7400. **FAX:** (216) 289-1635.

**President/General Manager:** Ed Carpenter. **Head Coach:** Howie Krause (Cleveland State). **Assistant Coach:** Joe Charboneau.

### GRAND LAKE MARINERS

**Mailing Address:** P.O. Box 203, Celina, OH 45822. **Telephone:** (419) 678-5496.

**President/General Manager:** Denny Dysert. **Head Coach:** Tom Brunswick. **Assistant Coaches:** Lou Brunswick, Mark Brunswick, Jeff Parker (Earlham, Ind., College).

### LIMA LOCOS

**Mailing Address:** 3700 S. Dixie Highway, Lima, OH 45806. **Telephone:** (419) 991-4701. **FAX:** (419) 999-4586.

**General Manager:** Barry Ruben. **Head Coach:** Dave Martin.

### MOTOR CITY PRIDE

**Mailing Address:** 1113 Forestdale, Royal Oak, MI 48067. **Telephone:** (313) 399-7611. **FAX:** None.

**President:** Tim Whitney. **General Manager/Head Coach:** Dave Jennings.

### SANDUSKY BAY STARS

**Mailing Address:** P.O. Box 2145, Sandusky, OH 44870. **Telephone:** (419) 626-8702. **FAX:** Same.

**President:** Joe Castello. **General Manager:** Ray Neill. **Head Coach:** Chuck Meyer (Ashland, Ohio, U.). **Assistant Coach:** Chris Cullen (Ashland).

### SPRINGFIELD ELECTROS

**Mailing Address:** P.O. Box 282, Enon, OH 45323. **Telephone:** (513) 323-0072. **FAX:** (513) 298-0268.

**President/General Manager:** Brian Miller. **Head Coach:** Bill Mote.

### SYLVANIA SOX

**Mailing Address:** P.O. Box 501, Sylvania, OH 43560. **Telephone:** (419) 691-0200. **FAX:** (419) 698-8998.

**President:** Barry Soskin. **Head Coach:** Unavailable.

## JAYHAWK LEAGUE

**Mailing Address:** 5 Adams Place, Halstead, KS 67056. **Telephone:** (316) 755-2361. **FAX:** (316) 755-1285.

**Commissioner:** Bob Considine. **President:** Don Carlile. **Vice President:** Jerry Colborn. **Publicity Director:** Pat Chambers.

**Years League Active:** 1976-.

**Member Clubs, Division Structure: East**—Nevada (Mo.) Griffons, Red Oak (Iowa) Red Sox, St. Joseph (Mo.) Cardinals, Topeka (Kan.) Capitals. **West**—Elkhart (Kan.) Dusters, Hays (Kan.) Larks, Liberal (Kan.) Bee Jays, Wichita (Kan.) Broncos.

**1995 Opening Date:** June 1. **Closing Date:** July 23.

**No. of Games, Regular Season:** 48.

**All-Star Game:** None.

**Playoff Format:** Division winners meet in best-of-3 series for league championship.

**Roster Limit:** 25.

## NEW ENGLAND COLLEGIATE LEAGUE

**Mailing Address:** 57 Steuben St., Meriden, CT 06451. **Telephone:** (203) 238-4111. **FAX:** Same.

**President:** Joel Cooney. **Executive Vice President:** Joseph Consentino. **Commissioner:** George Foster.

**Years League Active:** 1994-.

**Member Clubs:** Bristol NightHawks, Central Massachusetts, Danbury Westerners, Eastern Tides, Middletown Giants, Waterbury Barons.

**1995 Opening Date:** June 3. **Closing Date:** July 31.

**No. of Games, Regular Season:** 40.

**All-Star Game:** At Norwich, Conn. (date unavailable).

**Playoff Format:** First half winner plays second half winner in best-of-5 series for league championship.

**Roster Limit:** 21.

## NORTHEASTERN COLLEGIATE LEAGUE

**Mailing Address:** 26 Clearview Place, Binghamton, NY 13901. **Telephone:** (607) 648-5276. **FAX:** (607) 648-4668.

**Commissioner:** Ed Daub. **Chairman of the Board:** Bob Ballizzi. **Statistician:** Richard Cuykendall.

**Years League Active:** 1979-.

**Member Clubs:** Cohocton Red Wings, Cortland Apples, Geneva Knights, Hornell Dodgers, Ithaca Lakers, Schenectady Mohawks, Utica-Rome Indians.

**1995 Opening Date:** June 7. **Closing Date:** July 31.

**No. of Games, Regular Season:** 42.

**All-Star Game:** None.

**Playoff Format:** Top five teams, double-elimination tournament.

**Roster Limit:** 24.

## NORTHWOODS LEAGUE

**Mailing Address:** P.O. Box 1234, Highland City, FL 33846. **Telephone:** (813) 644-4022.

**President:** George MacDonald Jr. **Vice Presidents:** Dick Radatz Jr., William McKee, John Wendel.

**Years League Active:** 1994-.

**Member Clubs:** Dubuque (Iowa) Mud Puppies, Kenosha (Wis.) Kroakers, Manitowoc (Wis.) Skunks, Rochester (Minn.) Honkers, Waterloo Iowa), Wausau (Wis.) Woodchucks.

**1995 Opening Date:** June 9. **Closing Date:** Aug. 10.

**No. of Games, Regular Season:** 60.

**All-Star Game:** July 22 at Wausau, Wis.

**Playoff Format:** First half winner plays second half winner in best-of-3 series for league championship.

**Roster Limit:** 20.

# PACIFIC INTERNATIONAL LEAGUE

**Mailing Address:** P.O. Box 1257, Coupeville, WA 98239. **Telephone:** (206) 678-6181. **FAX:** (206) 678-6181.

**President:** Steve Konek. **Secretary-Treasurer:** Steve Potter.

**Member Clubs:** Bellevue (Wash.), Coquitlam (B.C.) Athletics, Everett (Wash.) Merchants, Grand Forks (B.C.) Rattlers, Hermiston (Ore.) Sox, Kelowna (B.C.) Grizzlies, Seattle Performance Radiator Studs, Portland Taylor Electric, Tacoma Timbers, West Seattle Classics.

# SAN DIEGO COLLEGIATE LEAGUE

**Mailing Address:** 948 Jasmine Court, Carlsbad, CA 92009. **Telephone:** (619) 438-0347.

**Commissioner:** Gerald Clements. **Vice President:** John Verdusco. **Administrative Assistant:** Alan Caldwell. **Publicity Director:** Dave Kuhn.

**Years League Active:** 1984-.

**Member Clubs, Division Structure: National**—Beach City Cubs, El Cajon Padres, North County Mets. **American**—East County Angels, San Diego Royals, South Bay Indians.

**1995 Opening Date:** June 2. **Closing Date:** Aug. 6.

**No. of Games, Regular Season:** 32.

**All-Star Game:** None.

**Playoff Format:** Division winners meet in best-of-3 series for league championship.

**Roster Limit:** 21.

# SHENANDOAH VALLEY LEAGUE

**Mailing Address:** P.O. Box 2246, Staunton, VA 24401. **Telephone:** (703) 886-1748. **FAX:** (703) 885-7612.

**Commissioner/President:** David Biery. **Executive Vice President:** James Weissenborn. **Vice President/Public Relations:** Curtiss Dudley.

**1995 Opening Date:** June 2. **Closing Date:** July 24.

**No. of Games, Regular Season:** 40.

**Playoff Format:** Top four teams meet in best-of-5 semifinal series. Winners meet in best-of-5 series for league championship.

**Roster Limit:** 25.

### FRONT ROYAL CARDINALS

**Mailing Address:** P.O. Box 1296, Front Royal, VA 22630. **Telephone:** (703) 636-9606. **FAX:** Same.

**President/General Manager:** Darryl Windham. **Head Coach:** Todd Held.

### HARRISONBURG TURKS

**Mailing Address:** 1489 S. Main St., Harrisonburg, VA 22801. **Telephone:** (703) 434-5919.

**President/General Manager:** Bob Wease. **Head Coach:** Victor Solis (Oklahoma City). **Assistant Coach:** Jeff Ludwig.

### NEW MARKET REBELS

**Mailing Address:** P.O. Box 902, New Market, VA 22844. **Telephone:** (703) 740-8569. **FAX:** (703) 740-4186.

**President:** Allen Johnson. **Vice President:** James Weissenborn. **General Manager:** Thomas Linski. **Head Coach:** Fritz Hamburg (New Mexico State). **Assistant Coach:** Mel Morris (Broadway, Va., HS).

### STAUNTON BRAVES

**Mailing Address:** P.O. Box 621, Staunton, VA 24402. **Telephone:** (703) 886-0987. **FAX:** (703) 886-7760.

**President:** Garland Eutslev. **General Manager:** Tom Chrisman. **Head Coach:** Mike Bocock (Chowan, N.C., JC). **Assistant Coach:** Steve Flack (Chowan, N.C., JC).

### WAYNESBORO GENERALS

**Mailing Address:** P.O. Box 243, Waynesboro, VA 22980. **Telephone:** (703) 943-6868. **FAX:** (703) 943-9645.

**President/General Manager:** Warren Shand. **Head Coach:** Jim Nietopski (Presbyterian,S.C., College).

### WINCHESTER ROYALS

**Mailing Address:** 228 S. Pleasant Valley Road, Winchester, VA 22601. **Telephone:** (703) 662-4466. **FAX:** (703) 662-2627.

**President/General Manager:** Donald Jones. **Head Coach:** Karl Kuhn (Charleston Southern).

# YOUTH BASEBALL

## ALL AMERICAN AMATEUR BASEBALL ASSOCIATION

**Mailing Address:** 340 Walker Dr., Zanesville, OH 43701. **Telephone:** (614) 453-7349.

**President:** George Arcurio Jr. **Executive Director:** Tom Checkush.

**Year Founded:** 1944.

**1995 National Tournament** (21 and under): Aug. 12-19 at Johnstown, PA.

## AMATEUR ATHLETIC UNION

**Mailing Address:** AAU House, 3400 W. 86th St., Indianapolis, IN 46268. **Telephone:** (317) 872-2900. **FAX:** (317) 875-0548.

## AMERICAN AMATEUR BASEBALL CONGRESS

**National Headquarters:** 118-19 Redfield Plaza, P.O. Box 467, Marshall, MI 49068. **Telephone:** (616) 781-2002. **FAX:** (616) 781-2060.

**President:** Joe Cooper.

**Year Founded:** 1935.

**Age Classifications, World Series**

**Roberto Clemente** (8 and under) ................ Jonesboro, GA, Aug. 3-6.
**Willie Mays** (10 and under) ................ Rex, GA, Aug. 3-6.
**Pee Wee Reese** (12 and under) ................ Toa Baja, PR, Aug. 8-13.
**Sandy Koufax** (14 and under) ................ Jersey City, NJ, Aug. 10-13.
**Mickey Mantle** (16 and under) ................ Unavailable, Aug. 10-13.
**Connie Mack** (18 and under) ................ Farmington, NM, Aug. 11-18.
**Stan Musial** (unlimited) ................ Battle Creek, MI, Aug. 17-21.

## AMERICAN LEGION BASEBALL

**National Headquarters:** National Americanism Commission, P.O. Box 1055, Indianapolis, IN 46206. **Telephone:** (317) 630-1213.

**Program Coordinator:** Jim Quinlan.

**Year Founded:** 1926.

**1995 World Series** (19 and under): Aug. 25-29 at Fargo, ND.

## BABE RUTH BASEBALL

**International Headquarters:** 1770 Brunswick Pike, P.O. Box 5000, Trenton, NJ 08638. **Telephone:** (609) 695-1434. **FAX:** (609) 695-2505.

**President/Chief Executive Officer:** Ronald Tellefsen.

**Year Founded:** 1951.

**Age Classifications, World Series**

**Bambino** (11-12) ................ Abbeville, LA, Aug. 12-19.
**13-Prep** ................ Kinston, NC, Aug. 19-26.
**13-15** ................ Millville, NJ, Aug. 19-26.
**16** ................ Jamestown, NY, Aug. 19-26.
**16-18** ................ Trail, British Columbia, Aug. 19-26.

## CONTINENTAL AMATEUR BASEBALL ASSOCIATION

**Mailing Address:** 82 University St., Westerville, OH 43081. **Telephone:** (614) 882-1361. **FAX:** (614) 899-2103.

**President:** Carl Williams. **Executive Director:** Roger Tremaine.

**Year Founded:** 1984.

## DIXIE BASEBALL, INC.

**Mailing Address:** P.O. Box 222, Lookout Mountain, TN 37350. **Telephone:** (615) 821-6811.

**Executive Director:** Nick Senter.

**Commissioner, Dixie Boys/Majors:** Jimmy Brown. **Commissioner, Dixie Youth:** Gale Montgomery.

**Year Founded:** 1956.

**Age Classifications, World Series**

**Dixie Youth** (12 and under) ................ Lexington, SC, Aug. 14-19.
**Dixie Boys** (13-14) ................ Troy, AL, Aug. 4-11.
**Dixie Pre-Majors** (15-16) ................ Mauldin, SC, Aug. 4-11.
**Dixie Majors** (15-18) ................ Sebring, FL, Aug. 4-11.

## HAP DUMONT YOUTH BASEBALL

**Mailing Address:** 1325 Westlink, Wichita, KS 67212. **Telephone:** (316) 721-1779. **FAX:** (316) 721-8054.

**National Chairman:** Jerry Crowell.

**Year Founded:** 1978.

## LITTLE LEAGUE BASEBALL, INC.

**International Headquarters:** P.O. Box 3485, Williamsport, PA 17701. **Telephone:** (717) 326-1921. **FAX:** (717) 326-1074.

**Chairman:** Dr. Luke LaPorta. **Vice Chairman:** James Whittington. **Chief Executive Officer:** Dr. Creighton Hale. **President:** Steve Keener.

**Director of Communications:** Dennis Sullivan. **Director of Special**

**Projects:** Scott Rosenberg.
**Year Founded:** 1939.

**Age Classifications, World Series**

**Little League** (11-12) .......... Williamsport, PA, Aug. 21-26.
**Junior League** (13) .......... Taylor, MI, Aug. 14-19.
**Senior League** (13-15) .......... Kissimmee, FL, Aug. 13-19.
**Big League** (16-18) .......... Ft. Lauderdale, FL, Aug. 11-19.

## NATIONAL AMATEUR BASEBALL FEDERATION

**Mailing Address:** P.O. Box 705, Bowie, MD 20718. **Telephone:** (301) 262-5005. **FAX:** Same.

**Executive Director:** Charles Blackburn.

**Year Founded:** 1914.

**Age Classifications, World Series**

**Freshman** (12 and under) .......... Sylvania, OH, July 20-23.
**Sophomore** (14 and under) .......... Miamisburg, OH, July 28-31.
**Junior** (16 and under) .......... Northville, MI, Aug. 3-6.
**Senior** (18 and under) .......... Marietta, GA, Aug. 12-15.
**High School** (high school students) .......... Fort Campbell, KY, Aug. 4-7.
**College** (22 and under) .......... Cincinnati, OH, Aug. 10-13.
**Major** (unlimited) .......... Louisville, KY, Aug. 17-20.
**Renaissance** (30 and over) .......... Boyertown, PA, Sept. 1-4.

## NATIONAL ASSOCIATION OF POLICE ATHLETICS LEAGUES

**Mailing Address:** 200 Castlewood Dr., Suite 400, North Palm Beach, FL 33408. **Telephone:** (407) 844-1823. **FAX:** (407) 863-6120.

**Executive Director:** Joseph Johnson. **Director of Marketing and Member Services:** Sally Cunningham. **Director of Sports Development and Education:** Tina Lux.

**Year Founded:** 1944

**Age Classifications, World Series**

**16 and Under** .......... Indianapolis, IN, Aug. 6-11

## NATIONAL JUNIOR BASEBALL LEAGUE

**Mailing Address:** P.O. Box 1021, East Northport, NY 11731. **Telephone, FAX:** (516) 757-6675.

**President:** Nick Nappy.

**Year Founded:** 1989.

**Age Classifications, World Series**

**12 and under** .......... Long Island, NY, Aug. 13-20.
**14 and under** .......... Long Island, NY, Aug. 13-20.
**16 and under** .......... Long Island, NY, Aug. 13-20.
**18 and under** .......... Long Island, NY, Aug. 13-20.

## PONY BASEBALL, INC.

**National Headquarters:** P.O. Box 225, Washington, PA 15301. **Telephone:** (412) 225-1060. **FAX:** (412) 225-9852.

**President:** Abraham Key.

**Year Founded:** 1951.

**Age Classifications, World Series**

**Shetland** (5-6) .......... No National Tournament.
**Pinto** (7-8) .......... No National Tournament.
**Mustang** (9-10) .......... Irving, TX, Aug. 9-12.
**Bronco** (11-12) .......... Monterey, CA, Aug. 10-15.
**Pony** (13-14) .......... Washington, PA, Aug. 12-19.
**Colt** (15-16) .......... Lafayette, IN, Aug. 8-15.
**Palomino** (17-18) .......... Greensboro, NC, Aug. 9-13.

## REVIVING BASEBALL IN INNERCITIES (RBI)

**Mailing Address:** 350 Park Ave., New York, NY 10022. **Telephone:** (212) 339-7800.

**Founder/Chairman:** John Young. **Administrator:** Kathy Francis.

**Year Founded:** 1989.

## U.S. AMATEUR BASEBALL ASSOCIATION

**Mailing Address:** 7101 Lake Ballinger Way, Edmonds, WA 98020. **Telephone:** (206) 776-7130.

**Director:** Al Rutledge.

**Year Founded:** 1969.

**Age Classifications, World Series**

**11 and under** .......... Salem, OR, Aug. 11-20.
**12 and under** .......... Aurora, CO, Aug. 11-20.
**13 and under** .......... White Rock, B.C., Aug. 11-19.
**14 and under** .......... Vacaville, CA, Aug. 11-19.
**15 and under** .......... Magna, UT, Aug. 4-12.
**16 and under** .......... Aurora, CO, Aug. 5-13.
**17 and under** .......... Canby, OR, Aug. 11-20.
**18 and under** .......... Hoquiam, WA, July 29-Aug. 6.
**19 and under** .......... Fresno, CA, July 14-23.
**Tournament of Champions** .......... Sumner, WA, Aug. 6-13.

# SERVICE DIRECTORY

# SERVICE DIRECTORY

## APPAREL

**A. J. Advertising**
201-236-2300
Fax: 201-236-2303

**Amapro Sporting Goods, Inc.**
718-204-7282/800-426-2776
Fax: 718-204-2512

**Bike Athletic**
615-546-4703
Fax: 615-549-7988

**Champion Products**
910-519-6637
Fax: 910-519-7909

**DeLong**
515-236-3106/800-733-5664
Fax: 515-236-4891

**Minor Leagues, Major Dreams**
P.O. Box 6098
Anaheim, CA 92816
714-758-1700/800-345-2421
Fax: 714-758-8006

**Native Sun Sportswear**
813-528-2111/800-777-5800
Fax: 813-528-8441

**Rawlings Sporting Goods**
314-349-3500/800-729-7770
Fax: 314-349-3576

**Rolin USA**
212-465-8206
Fax: 212-465-8207

**Russell Athletic**
205-329-5089
Fax: 205-329-4640

**Sahara Sportswear**
915-833-1145/800-669-5646
Fax: 915-833-4190

**Starter Sportswear, Inc.**
203-781-4000/800-967-8271
Fax: 203-781-5096

## ATHLETIC TRAINING

**Cripps First Aid & Med. Supply**
314-567-9908
Fax: 314-567-6706

**Micro Bio-Medics, Inc.**
904-363-1396/800-345-9883
Fax: 904-363-1496

**Saleen Sportnet**
800-382-5399
Fax: 714-581-5400

**Sports Health**
A Division of School Health Corp.
865 Muirfield Dr.
Hanover Park, IL 60103
800-323-1305

**U.S.A. Products, Inc.**
913-888-5755
Fax: 913-492-3314

## AUDIO/MUSIC PRODUCTIONS SOUND EFFECTS

**John Rosenfelder/Ear Bender**
213-857-5815
Fax: 213-857-6615

**Stanley Sound Productions**
Bill Heald/Baseball Blips
#6 Supplee Place
Belleair, FL 34616
813-442-4971

**Sound Creations**
21 Royal Oak Road
Lawrenceville, NJ 08648
800-541-5444/609-882-5222
Fax: 609-584-0001

## AUDIO/VIDEO

**Exceptional Player**
1031 Union Street
Shelbyville, TN 37160
800-642-4698 (8-5 cst.)

**Hit Doctor**
P.O. Box 1199
Voorhees, NJ 08043
800-644-8362

**John Rosenfelder/Ear Bender**
365 S. Cochran Avenue
Los Angeles, CA 90036-3317
213-857-5815
Fax: 213-857-6615

## BAGS

**ATEC**
800-755-5100
Fax: 702-352-2822

**Diamond Sports**
310-598-9717
Fax: 310-598-0906

**Gerry Cosby & Company**
212-563-6464
Fax: 212-967-0876

**KR Industries, Inc.**
708-863-1200
Fax: 708-222-1400

## BASEBALL CARDS

**Cuban Baseball Cards**
Grosnor Sportscards
800-268-9066

**Fleer**
609-231-6200

**Minford's Minors**
2901 Squirrel Creek Road
Newland, NC 28657
704-733-1145

**Topps**
718-768-8900

**Upper Deck**
619-929-6500

## BASEBALLS

**Baden Sports, Inc.**
206-925-0500
Fax: 206-925-0570

**Rawlings Sporting Goods**
314-349-3500/800-729-7770

**Wilson Sporting Goods, Co.**
800-628-1188

## BASES

**ATEC**
702-352-2800/800-755-5100
Fax: 702-352-2822

**Diamond Sports**
310-598-9717
Fax: 310-598-0906

**Hollywood Bases, Inc.**
4831 Sky Way Drive
Marysville, CA 95901
800-421-2243
Fax: 916-741-9355

**Markwort Sporting Goods Co.**
314-652-3757
Fax: 314-652-6241

## BATS

**Glomar Enterprises**
116 W. Walnut Ave.
Fullerton, CA 92632
714-871-5956
Fax: 714-871-5958

**Easton Sports, Inc.**
415-347-3900/800-347-3901

**Heavy Hitter Industries, Inc.**
619-749-7833
Fax: 619-749-7829

**Hillerich & Bradsby Co.**
800-282-2287

**Irwin Sports/Cooper Baseball**
416-533-3521
416-533-0715

**Kissimmee Sticks**
2551 Princess Way
Kissimmee, FL 34746
407-396-4085
Fax: 407-396-2411

**Markwort Sporting Goods Co.**
314-652-3757
Fax: 314-652-6241

**Winning Edge Sports**
P.O. Box 602
Winnetka, IL 60093
800-438-2228

**Worth Sports Company**
800-423-3714
Fax: 615-454-9164

## BATTING CAGES

**ATEC**
10 Greg Street
Sparks, NV 89431
800-755-5100
Fax: 702-352-2822

**C & H Baseball**
801 7th Ave. West
Bradenton, FL 34205
800-248-5192
813-748-0012

**The Jugs Company**
800-547-6843

**Saleen Sportnet**
800-382-5399
Fax: 714-581-5400

## CAMPS/SCHOOLS

**Doyle Baseball**
813-293-8994/800-443-5536

**Hollywood Legends**
(310) 281-7354

**Lock Haven Univ. Baseball Camp**
Akeley Hall, LHU
Lock Haven, PA 17745
717-893-2500
Fax: 717-893-2774

**Mickey Owen Baseball School, Inc.**
P.O. Box 88
Miller, MO 65707
417-882-2799/800-999-8369
Fax: 417-889-6978

## CAPS/HEADWEAR

**American Baseball Cap, Inc.**
800-345-8211
Fax: 215-565-8413

**Great White Headwear**
P.O. Box 1423
Kernersville, NC 27285
800-304-7504
Fax: 910-996-5184

**Markwort Sporting Goods Co.**
314-652-3757

**Minor Leagues, Major Dreams**
P.O. Box 6098
Anaheim, CA 92816
714-758-1700/800-345-2421
Fax: 714-758-8006

**New Era Cap Company**
8061 Erie Road, Box 208
Derby, NY 14047-0208
800-989-0445
Fax: 716-549-5424

**Pro-line Cap Company**
8224 White Settlement Road
Fort Worth, TX 76108
817-246-4931
Fax: 817-367-1585

**Roman Company**
508-583-5515/800-288-5515

## CATCHING EQUIPMENT

**All-Star/Ampac Enterprises, Inc.**
800-777-3810
Fax: 508-425-4068

**Diamond Sports**
310-598-9717
Fax: 310-598-0906

**Easton Sports, Inc.**
800-347-3901

**Irwin Sports/Cooper Baseball**
416-533-3521
416-533-0715

**Markwort Sporting Goods Co.**
314-652-3757
Fax: 314-652-6241

**Rawlings Sporting Goods**
800-729-7770
Fax: 314-349-3576

**Wilson Sporting Goods Co.**
800-628-1188
Fax: 312-714-4595

## COLLECTIBLE PROTECTION

**BallQube, Inc.**
P.O. Box 631414
Nacogdoches, TX 75963-1414
800-543-1470
Fax: 409-569-9710

**Swing Frame**
10 Buckminster Road
Rockville Centre, NY 11570
516-678-7772
Fax: 516-678-0907

## COMPUTER SOFTWARE/ TICKET & SPONSORSHIP SALES

**Teamwork Enterprises/SEAT**
708-513-7753

## CONSULTING/ TICKET SALES SEMINAR

**Teamwork Enterprises**
Jack Mielke
708-513-7753

## EQUIPMENT/PROTECTION

**Tuff Toe, Inc.**
1571 S. Sunkist St. # E
Anaheim, CA 92806
800-888-0802
Fax: 714-935-2838

## ENTERTAINMENT

**Bleacher Preacher/Jerry Pritikin**
7847 W. Church St.
Morton Grove, IL 60053
708-965-8138

**The Blues Bros. Act of LaCrosse**
608-796-0796
Fax: 608-791-1021

**Famous Chicken**
619-278-1987
Fax: 619-278-1991

**Morganna The Kissing Bandit**
P.O. Box 20281
Columbus, OH 43220
614-457-9563

**John Rosenfelder/Ear Bender**
213-857-5815
Fax: 213-857-6615

**Jeff Scanlan/Sports Magic**
410 S. Albert Street
Mt. Prospect, IL 60056
708-342-TEAM (8326)

**The World's Greatest Traveling BB Show, Formerly Billy Bird & Co.**
P.O. Box 36061
Louisville, KY 40233
502-458-4020
Fax: 502-458-0867

## FIELD WALL PADDING/ PROTECTION

**Promats, Inc.**
P.O. Box 508
Fort Collins, CO 80522
800-678-6287
Fax: 303-482-7740

## FIREWORKS

**Melrose Pyrotechnics, Inc.**
803-286-7262/800-771-7976

## FOOD SERVICE

**Anton Argires, Inc.**
312-226-7805/800-837-0100
Fax: 312-226-5154

**ARA Leisure Services, Inc.**
215-238-3445/800-999-8989
Fax: 215-238-4099

**Carolina Fine Snacks/Peanuts**
3718 Alliance Drive
Greensboro, NC 27407
910-852-1900
Fax: 910-852-1901

**DiGiovanni's Food Service**
6700 Clark Road
Sarasota, FL 34241
813-925-2179

**FUNacho**
513-874-8485/800-386-2246
Fax: 513-874-8668

**Houston's Peanuts**
P.O. Box 160
Dublin, NC 28332
800-334-8383
Fax: 910-862-8076

**Mobile Merchandising Concepts**
P.O. Box 33
263 Providence Road
South Grafton, MA 01560-0033
508-839-9765
Fax: 508-839-9763

**The Peanut Roaster, Inc.**
P.O. Box 5037
Cary, NC 27512
919-469-1676
Fax: 919-467-7444

**Peanut Processors, Inc.**
910-862-3126/800-334-8383
Fax: 910-862-8076

**Slush Puppie, Corp.**
513-244-2400/800-543-0860
Fax: 513-251-3458

**Vinnie's Hot Soft Pretzels**
P.O. Box 59
Durham, NC 27702
919-477-3715/800395-4977
Fax: 919-477-3093

**Volume Services**
803-597-8331
Fax: 803-597-8218

## GIFT ITEMS

**Heavy Hitter Industries, Inc.**
619-749-7833
Fax: 619-749-7829

**Schneidereit, Inc.**
4070 Nelson Ave, Ste G
Concord, CA 94520
510-609-2170
Fax: 510-609-2176

## GLOVE CARE/REPAIR

**Brucker Glove Company**
6949A La Tijera Blvd.
Los Angeles, CA 90045
213-776-1340/800-733-4719

**Damon Carr Enterprises**
470-555 Wingfield Road North
Susanville, CA 96130-5768
800-742-5358

**Henry's Glove Repair**
719 Moody Street
Waltham, MA 02154-5005
617-891-0621

## GLOVES

**Diamond Sports**
310-598-9717
Fax: 310-598-0906

**Easton Sports, Inc.**
800-347-3901

**Glovesmith, Inc.**
20 Village Plaza
Arnold, MO 63010
314-467-3905
Fax: 314-467-6509

**Henry's Glove Repair**
719 Moody Street
Waltham, MA 02154-5005
617-891-0621

**Hillerich & Bradsby Co.**
800-282-2287

**Irwin Sports/Cooper Baseball**
416-533-3521
416-533-0715

**Kissimmee Sticks**
2551 Princess Way
Kissimmee, FL 34746
407-396-4085
Fax: 407-396-2411

**Markwort Sporting Goods Co.**
314-652-3757
Fax: 314-652-6241

**Mizuno Sports**
800-966-1299/800-966-1234

**Rawlings Sporting Goods**
314-349-3500/800-729-7770

**Rolin USA**
470 7th Ave., 4th Floor
New York, NY 10018
212-465-8206
Fax: 212-465-8207

**SSK America**
301-549-2762
Fax: 301-549-2904

**Worth Sports Company**
800-423-3714
Fax: 615-454-9164

**Zett Equipment**
800-277-7933

## GRAPHIC DESIGN

**Low And Inside Creative Serv.**
P.O. Box 290228
Minneapolis, MN 55429
612-797-0777
Fax: 612-797-7441

## INFIELD RAINCOVERS

**Covermaster, Inc.**
800-387-5808
Fax: 416-742-6837

## LIGHTING

**Universal Sports Lighting, Inc.**
Box 218, 116 N. Kickapoo
Lincoln, IL 62656
217-732-3200
Fax: 217-735-4442

## MASCOT COSTUMES

**Teamwork Enterprises**
708-513-7753

## MERCHANDISING

**Mobile Merchandising Concepts**
P.O. Box 33
263 Providence Road
South Grafton, MA 01560-0033
508-839-9765
Fax: 508-839-9763

## NETTING/POSTS

**ATEC Grand Slam USA**
800-755-5100
Fax: 702-352-2822

**C & H Baseball**
800-248-5192
Fax: 813-748-0012

**Covermaster Inc.**
800-387-5808
Fax: 416-742-6837

**Miller Net & Twine**
901-744-3804/800-423-6603

**National Batting Cages, Inc.**
503-357-6615/800-547-8800
Fax: 503-628-3871

**Saleen Sportnet**
800-382-5399
Fax: 714-581-5400

## ON DECK CIRCLES

**Reed Rubber Company**
5425 Manchester Ave.
St. Louis, MO 63110
800-325-9698
Fax: 314-645-5272

## PITCHING MACHINES

**Acupitch**
818-718-1087
Fax: 818-718-1062

**ATEC**
10 Greg Street
Sparks, NV 89431
800-755-5100
Fax: 702-352-2822

**BATA Baseball Machines**
619-744-3878/800-762-2282

**Hollywood Bases, Inc.**
800-421-2243
Fax: 916-741-9355

**The Jugs Company**
11885 SW Herman Rd.
Tualatin, OR 97062
800-547-6843
Fax: 503-691-1100

**Little Pop Fly, Inc.**
108 Live Oak Court
Willow Park, TX 76087
817-441-8717

**Master Pitching Machine, Inc.**
800-878-8228
Fax: 816-452-7581

## PLACEMENT/SCOUTING

**Premier Baseball Scouting Bureau**
P.O. Box 2657
Corinth, MS 38834
601-462-5906 (Ext. 32)

## PLAYING FIELD PRODUCTS

**Alpine's Precision Grading**
5313 Brookeville Road
Gaithersburg, MD 20882
301-963-8833
Fax: 301-963-7901

**Balsam Corporation/Astroturf**
314-997-8200/800-358-8553
Fax: 314-997-6071

**Beacon Ballfields:**
Div: LoDe Star L.L.C.
Box 45557
Madison, WI 53744
800-747-5985
Fax: 608-274-6072

**C & H Baseball**
800-248-5192
Fax: 813-748-0012

**Covermaster, Inc.**
100 Westmore Drive, 11-D
Rexdale, Ontario M9V 5C3
800-387-5808
Fax: 416-742-6837

**Diamond-Dry**
800-962-2068
Fax: 217-735-4442

**Hollywood Bases, Inc.**
4831 Sky Way Drive
Marysville, CA 95901
800-421-2243
Fax: 916-741-9355

**Partac Peat Corporation**
Kelsey Park
Great Meadows, NJ 07838
908-637-4191/800-247-BEAM
Fax: 908-637-8421

**Promats, Inc.**
P.O. Box 508
Fort Collins, CO 80522
800-678-6287
Fax: 303-482-7740

**Saleen Sportnet**
800-382-5399
714-581-5400

**Southern Turf Nurseries**
800-448-8069
Fax: 404-448-6832

**Stabilizer, Inc.**
4832 E. Indian School Rd.
Phoenix, AZ 85018
602-952-8009/800-336-2468
Fax: 602-852-0718

## PRINTING

**Inkwell Promotions**
908-536-2822
Fax: 908-972-2547

**Insta Graphic Systems**
310-404-3000
Fax: 310-404-3010

**Low And Inside Creative Serv.**
P.O. Box 290228
Minneapolis, MN 55429
612-797-0777
Fax: 612-797-7441

**Multi-Ad Services**
1720 W. Detweiller Drive
Peoria, IL 61615
800-447-1950 (Ext. 399)
Fax: 309-692-5444

**Sports Print**
800-966-6845
Fax: 404-525-7733

**Trademark Printing**
345 Shoreway Road
San Carlos, CA 94070
415-592-9130
Fax: 415-592-2776

## PROFESSIONAL SERVICES

**American Specialty**
Underwriters Insurance
617-938-6300
Fax: 617-938-0996

**Baseball Opportunities**
P.O. Box 4941
Scottsdale, AZ 85261-4941
602-483-8224

**L. D. Astorino & Associates Ltd.**
227 Fort Pitt Blvd.
Pittsburg, PA 15222
412-765-1700
Fax: 412-765-1711

**Resnick, Amsterdam, Leshner P.C.**
7 East Skippack Pike, Suite 275
Ambler, PA 19002
215-628-8080
Fax: 215-628-4752

**S.R.O. Partners**
503-297-2392
Fax: 503-291-7909

**Thomas E. Wood, Inc./K & K**
219-459-5604/800-648-6404
Fax: 219-459-5940

## PROMOTIONAL ITEMS

**American Promotions of IL**
P.O. Box 8792
Waukegan, IL 60079
708-956-0615
Fax: 708-290-9883

**Farm Team America**
203-323-1646
Fax: 203-323-1653

**Imprinted Products Corp.**
800-544-5646
Fax: 619-268-5801

**Preferred Specialties**
17 MacDade Blvd.
Collingdale, PA 19023
610-534-4112
Fax: 610-534-4113

**USA Products**
913-888-5755
Fax: 913-492-3314

## PUBLICATIONS

**Baseball Parent**
4437 Kingston Pike #2204BA
Knoxville, TN 37919-5226
615-523-1274
Fax: 615-673-8926

**Baseball Fanzine Directory**
612-797-0777
Fax: 612-797-7441

**Braunstein's Met & Yankee Minor League Reporter**
117 West 74th St. #4C
New York, NY 10023
212-258-0226
Fax: 212-307-9518

**Low And Inside**
P.O. Box 290228
Minneapolis, MN 55429
612-797-0777
Fax: 612-797-7441

**The Thinking Pitcher**
P.O. Box 14595
Bradenton, FL 34280-4595
813-795-0356
Fax: 813-795-0356

## PUBLICITY/ SPORTS MARKETING

**Wirz & Associates**
326 West Main Street
Milford, CT 06460
203-874-7085
Fax: 203-874-7205

## RADAR EQUIPMENT

**ATEC**
10 Greg Street
Sparks, NV 89431
800-755-5100
Fax: 702-352-2822

**The Jugs Company**
11885 SW Herman Road
Tualatin, OR 97062
800-547-6843
Fax: 503-691-1100

**Radar Sales**
612-557-6654
Fax: 612-550-04541

**Tru-Pitch**
813-573-9701
Fax: 813-572-4487

## SCOREBOARDS

**Daktronics, Inc.**
331 32nd Avenue
Brookings, SD 57006
800-843-9878
Fax: 605-697-4700

**Fairtron Corporation**
515-265-5305/800-247-0265
Fax: 515-265-3364

**Nevco Scoreboard Company**
301 East Harris Avenue
Greenville, IL 62246
618-664-0360/800-851-4040
Fax: 618-664-0398

**Spectrum Scoreboards**
10048 Easthaven
Houston, TX 77075
800-392-5050
Fax: 713-944-1290

## SCOUTING/TEAM TRAVEL

**Diamond Travel**
151 N. Delaware St., Suite 140
Indianapolis, IN 46204
800-269-6150
Fax: 317-267-0261

## STADIUM ARCHITECTS

**Ellerbe Becket, Inc.**
605 West 47th Street
Kansas City, MO 64112
816-561-4443
Fax: 816-561-2863

**HNTB Sports Architecture**
1201 Walnut, Suite 700
Kansas City, MO 64106
816-472-1201
Fax: 816-472-4060

**HOK Sports Facilities Group**
323 W. 8th St., Suite 700
Kansas City, MO 64105
816-221-1576
Fax: 816-221-5816

**L. D. Astorino & Associates Ltd.**
227 Fort Pitt Blvd.
Pittsburg, PA 15222
412-765-1700
Fax: 412-765-1711

**Lehrer McGovern Bovis**
212-576-8717
Fax: 212-532-1763

**Lescher & Mahoney, Inc.**
1509 West Swann Ave., Suite 240
Tampa, FL 33606
813-254-9811
Fax: 813-254-4230

**Thursday Architects**
312-271-7781
Fax: 312-275-1858

## STADIUM SEATING

**American Desk Mfg. Co.**
817-773-1776/800-433-3142
Fax: 817-773-7370

**American Seating Company**
616-732-6895
Fax: 616-732-6446

**Caddy Products**
7667 Cahill Road
Minneapolis, MN 55439-2749
612-828-0030/800-845-0591
Fax: 612-829-0166

**Contour Seats, Inc.**
610-395-5144/800-247-4509
Fax: 610-398-7099

**Dant Clayton Corporation**
502-634-3626/800-626-2177
Fax: 502-637-9983

**KR Industries, Inc.**
708-863-1200
Fax: 708-222-1400

**Southern Bleacher Company**
P.O. Box One
Graham, TX 76450
817-549-0733/800-433-0912
Fax: 817-549-1365

**Sturdisteel Company**
P.O. Box 2655
Waco, Tx 76702
800-433-3116
Fax: 817-666-4472

## TICKETS

**Celebrity Ticket**
908-220-0330
Fax: 908-754-5726

**EASY Computer Systems**
P.O. Box AA
Branson, MO 65615
417-335-3279
Fax: 417-335-5246

**Globe Ticket and Label Co.**
404-762-9711/800-523-5968
Fax: 404-762-9260

**Hill Arts & Entertainment Systems**
37 SoundView Rd.
Guilford, CT 06437
203-453-1718
Fax: 203-458-2465

**National Ticket Co.**
800-829-0829
Fax: 800-829-0888

**Quick Tick International**
800-231-6144
Fax: 713-690-6662

**Select Ticketing Systems**
800-333-8448
Fax: 315-471-2715

**Ticket Craft, Inc.**
800-645-4944
Fax: 516-826-0163

**TicketStop, Inc.**
206-641-9657
Fax: 206-641-8151

**Weldon, Williams & Lick, Inc.**
501-783-4113
Fax: 501-783-7050

## TRAVEL

**Broach Sports Tours**
P.O. Box 470976
Charlotte, NC 28247
704-366-6345
Fax: 704-362-2151

**Jay Buckley Tours**
P.O. Box 213
La Crosse, WI 54602-0213
608-788-9200

## UNIFORMS

**DeLong**
515-236-3106
Fax: 515-236-4891

**Markwort Sporting Goods Co.**
314-652-3757
Fax: 314-652-6241

**Rawlings Sporting Goods**
800-729-7770
Fax: 314-349-3576

**Rolin USA**
212-465-8206
Fax: 212-465-8207

**Russell Athletic**
205-329-5089
Fax: 205-329-4640

**Wilson Sporting Goods Co.**
800-628-1188
Fax: 312-714-4595

**Worth Sports Company**
800-423-3714
Fax: 615-454-9164

# 1995 DIRECTORY INDEX

## MAJOR LEAGUE TEAMS

### American League



### National League



## MINOR LEAGUE TEAMS

| | | | | |
|---|---|---|---|---|
| 110 | Colorado Springs | PCL | 719-597-1449 | 719-597-2491 |
| 159 | Columbia | SAL | 803-256-4110 | 803-256-4338 |
| 159 | Columbus, GA | SAL | 706-571-8866 | 706-571-9107 |
| 103 | Columbus, OH | IL | 614-462-5250 | 614-462-3271 |
| 177 | Danville | Appy | 804-791-3346 | 804-791-3347 |
| 144 | Daytona | FSL | 904-257-3172 | 904-257-3382 |
| 144 | Dunedin | FSL | 813-733-9302 | 813-734-7661 |
| 138 | Durham | Carolina | 919-688-8211 | 919-688-4593 |
| 110 | Edmonton | PCL | 403-429-2934 | 403-426-5640 |
| 177 | Elizabethton | Appy | 615-543-4395 | 615-543-4395 |
| 127 | El Paso | Texas | 915-755-2000 | 915-757-0671 |
| 164 | Elmira | NYP | 607-734-1811 | 607-734-4975 |
| 165 | Erie | NYP | 814-456-1300 | 814-456-7520 |
| 171 | Eugene | Northwest | 503-342-5367 | 503-342-6089 |
| 172 | Everett | Northwest | 206-258-3673 | 206-258-3675 |
| 159 | Fayetteville | SAL | 910-424-6500 | 910-424-4325 |
| 145 | Fort Myers | FSL | 813-768-4210 | 813-768-4211 |
| 152 | Fort Wayne | Midwest | 219-482-6400 | 219-471-4678 |
| 138 | Frederick | Carolina | 301-662-0013 | 301-662-0018 |
| 181 | Great Falls | Pioneer | 406-452-5311 | 406-454-0811 |
| 160 | Greensboro | SAL | 910-333-2287 | 910-273-7350 |
| 122 | Greenville | Southern | 803-299-3456 | 803-277-7369 |
| 160 | Hagerstown | SAL | 301-791-6266 | 301-791-6066 |
| 116 | Hardware City | Eastern | 203-224-8383 | 203-225-6267 |
| 117 | Harrisburg | Eastern | 717-231-4444 | 717-231-4445 |
| 182 | Helena | Pioneer | 406-449-7616 | 406-449-6979 |
| 161 | Hickory | SAL | 704-322-3000 | 704-322-6137 |
| 132 | High Desert | Cal | 619-246-6287 | 619-246-3197 |
| 165 | Hudson Valley | NYP | 914-838-0094 | 914-838-0014 |
| 178 | Huntington | Appy | 304-429-1700 | 304-429-1706 |
| 122 | Huntsville | Southern | 205-882-2562 | 205-880-0801 |
| 182 | Idaho Falls | Pioneer | 208-522-8363 | 208-522-9858 |
| 98 | Indianapolis | Am. Assoc. | 317-269-3545 | 317-269-3541 |
| 99 | Iowa | Am. Assoc. | 515-243-6111 | 515-243-5152 |
| 127 | Jackson | Texas | 601-981-4664 | 601-981-4669 |
| 123 | Jacksonville | Southern | 904-358-2846 | 904-358-2845 |
| 166 | Jamestown | NYP | 716-664-0915 | 716-664-4175 |
| 178 | Johnson City | Appy | 615-461-4850 | 615-461-4864 |
| 152 | Kane County | Midwest | 708-232-8811 | 708-232-8815 |
| 178 | Kingsport | Appy | 615-247-7181 | 615-247-2241 |
| 139 | Kinston | Carolina | 919-527-9111 | 919-527-2328 |
| 145 | Kissimmee | FSL | 407-933-5500 | 407-847-6237 |
| 123 | Knoxville | Southern | 615-637-9494 | 615-523-9913 |
| 132 | Lake Elsinore | Cal | 909-245-4487 | 909-245-0305 |
| 146 | Lakeland | FSL | 813-688-7911 | 813-688-9589 |
| 111 | Las Vegas | PCL | 702-386-7200 | 702-386-7214 |
| 182 | Lethbridge | Pioneer | 403-327-7975 | 403-327-8085 |
| 99 | Louisville | Am. Assoc. | 502-367-9121 | 502-368-5120 |
| 139 | Lynchburg | Carolina | 804-528-1144 | 804-846-0768 |
| 161 | Macon | SAL | 912-745-8943 | 912-743-5559 |
| 179 | Martinsville | Appy | 703-666-2000 | 703-666-2139 |
| 183 | Medicine Hat | Pioneer | 403-526-0404 | 403-526-4000 |
| 124 | Memphis | Southern | 901-272-1687 | 901-278-3354 |
| 128 | Midland | Texas | 915-683-4251 | 915-683-0994 |
| 133 | Modesto | Cal | 209-529-7368 | 209-529-7213 |
| 100 | Nashville | Am. Assoc. | 615-242-4371 | 615-256-5684 |
| 117 | New Haven | Eastern | 203-782-3140 | 203-782-3150 |
| 166 | New Jersey | NYP | 201-579-7500 | 201-579-7502 |
| 100 | New Orleans | Am. Assoc. | 504-282-6777 | 504-282-9821 |
| 104 | Norfolk | IL | 804-622-2222 | 804-624-9090 |
| 118 | Norwich | Eastern | 203-887-7962 | 203-886-5996 |
| 183 | Ogden | Pioneer | 801-393-2400 | 801-393-2473 |
| 101 | Oklahoma City | Am. Assoc. | 405-946-8989 | 405-942-4198 |
| 101 | Omaha | Am. Assoc. | 402-734-2550 | 402-734-7166 |
| 167 | Oneonta | NYP | 607-432-6326 | 607-432-1965 |
| 124 | Orlando | Southern | 407-245-2827 | 407-649-1637 |
| 104 | Ottawa | IL | 613-747-5969 | 613-747-0003 |
| 105 | Pawtucket | IL | 401-724-7300 | 401-724-2140 |
| 153 | Peoria | Midwest | 309-688-1622 | 309-686-4516 |
| 111 | Phoenix | PCL | 602-275-0500 | 602-990-8987 |
| 162 | Piedmont | SAL | 704-932-3267 | 704-938-7040 |
| 167 | Pittsfield | NYP | 413-499-6387 | 413-443-7144 |
| 125 | Port City | Southern | 910-350-7000 | 910-350-7098 |
| 118 | Portland, ME | Eastern | 207-874-9300 | 207-780-0317 |
| 172 | Portland, OR | Northwest | 503-223-2837 | 503-223-2948 |
| 140 | Prince William | Carolina | 703-590-2311 | 703-590-5716 |
| 179 | Princeton | Appy | 304-487-2000 | 304-425-6999 |
| 153 | Quad City | Midwest | 319-324-2032 | 319-324-3109 |
| 133 | Rancho Cucamonga | Cal | 909-481-5000 | 909-481-5005 |
| 119 | Reading | Eastern | 610-375-8469 | 610-373-5868 |

| | | | | |
|---|---|---|---|---|
| 105 | Richmond | IL | 804-359-4444 | 804-359-0731 |
| 134 | Riverside | Cal | 909-276-3352 | 909-276-4954 |
| 106 | Rochester | IL | 716-467-3000 | 716-467-6732 |
| 153 | Rockford | Midwest | 815-962-2827 | 815-961-2002 |
| 167 | St. Catharines | NYP | 905-641-5297 | 905-641-3007 |
| 146 | St. Lucie | FSL | 407-871-2100 | 407-878-9802 |
| 146 | St. Petersburg | FSL | 813-822-3384 | 813-895-1556 |
| 140 | Salem | Carolina | 703-389-3333 | 703-389-9710 |
| 112 | Salt Lake | PCL | 801-485-3800 | 801-485-6818 |
| 128 | San Antonio | Texas | 210-675-7275 | 210-670-0001 |
| 134 | San Bernardino | Cal | 909-881-1836 | 909-883-6279 |
| 135 | San Jose | Cal | 408-297-1435 | 408-297-1453 |
| 147 | Sarasota | FSL | 813-365-4460 | 813-365-4217 |
| 162 | Savannah | SAL | 912-351-9150 | 912-352-9722 |
| 106 | Scranton/W-B | IL | 717-969-2255 | 717-963-6564 |
| 129 | Shreveport | Texas | 318-636-5555 | 318-636-5670 |
| 154 | South Bend | Midwest | 219-235-9988 | 219-235-9950 |
| 173 | Southern Oregon | Northwest | 503-770-5364 | 503-772-4466 |
| 173 | Spokane | Northwest | 509-535-2922 | 509-534-5368 |
| 154 | Springfield | Midwest | 217-544-7300 | 217-544-7388 |
| 135 | Stockton | Cal | 209-944-5943 | 209-463-4937 |
| 107 | Syracuse | IL | 315-474-7833 | 315-474-2658 |
| 112 | Tacoma | PCL | 206-752-7707 | 206-752-7135 |
| 147 | Tampa | FSL | 813-632-9855 | 813-979-4752 |
| 107 | Toledo | IL | 419-893-9483 | 419-893-5847 |
| 119 | Trenton | Eastern | 609-394-3300 | 609-394-9666 |
| 113 | Tucson | PCL | 602-325-2621 | 602-327-2371 |
| 129 | Tulsa | Texas | 918-744-5998 | 918-747-3267 |
| 168 | Utica | NYP | 315-738-0999 | 315-738-0992 |
| 113 | Vancouver | PCL | 604-872-5232 | 604-872-1714 |
| 168 | Vermont | NYP | 802-655-4200 | 802-655-5660 |
| 148 | Vero Beach | FSL | 407-569-4900 | 407-567-0819 |
| 136 | Visalia | Cal | 209-625-0480 | 209-739-7732 |
| 169 | Watertown | NYP | 315-788-8747 | 315-788-8841 |
| 155 | West Michigan | Midwest | 616-784-4131 | 616-784-4911 |
| 148 | West Palm Beach | FSL | 407-684-6801 | 407-686-0221 |
| 130 | Wichita | Texas | 316-267-3372 | 316-267-3382 |
| 169 | Williamsport | NYP | 717-326-3389 | 717-326-3494 |
| 141 | Wilmington | Carolina | 302-888-2015 | 302-888-2032 |
| 141 | Winston-Salem | Carolina | 910-759-2233 | 910-759-2042 |
| 155 | Wisconsin | Midwest | 414-733-4152 | 414-733-8032 |
| 174 | Yakima | Northwest | 509-457-5151 | 509-457-9909 |

Phone and FAX numbers for minor league offices can be found on page 96.

## OTHER ORGANIZATIONS

| Page | Organization | Phone | FAX |
|---|---|---|---|
| 258 | AAABA | 614-453-7349 | — |
| 258 | AABC | 616-781-2002 | 616-781-2060 |
| 92 | ABC-TV | 212-456-7777 | — |
| 228 | ABCA | 517-775-3300 | 517-775-3600 |
| 253 | Alaska Central League | 907-345-9205 | 907-345-9206 |
| 253 | Alaska League | 907-452-1991 | 907-277-4316 |
| 15 | American League | 212-339-7600 | 212-593-7138 |
| 258 | American Legion Baseball | 317-630-1213 | — |
| 251 | Area Code Games | 707-525-0498 | 707-525-0214 |
| 225 | Arizona Fall League | 602-496-6700 | 602-496-6384 |
| 253 | Arizona Collegiate League | 602-990-2404 | — |
| 92 | Associated Press | 212-621-1630 | 212-621-1639 |
| 90 | Assoc. of Prof. BB Players of America | 714-892-9900 | 714-897-0233 |
| 253 | Atlantic Collegiate League | 201-391-9376 | 201-391-9276 |
| 225 | Australian Baseball League | 612-299-4766 | 612-299-4769 |
| 258 | Babe Ruth Baseball | 609-695-1434 | 609-695-2505 |
| 90 | Baseball Assistance Team | 212-339-7884 | 212-888-8632 |
| 93 | Baseball Business Journal | 804-824-3942 | 804-824-3942 |
| 252 | Baseball Canada | 613-748-5606 | 613-748-5767 |
| 90 | Baseball Chapel | 201-838-8111 | 201-838-1145 |
| 93 | Baseball Digest | 708-491-6440 | 708-491-0867 |
| 89 | Baseball Network | 212-977-7300 | 212-977-7977 |
| 90 | Baseball Trade Show | 813-823-4050 | 813-821-5819 |
| 92 | Baseball Writers Assoc. of America | 516-981-7938 | — |
| 92 | Canadian Press | 416-594-2154 | — |
| 92 | CTV | 416-595-4100 | 416-595-5998 |
| 254 | Cape Cod League | 508-432-1774 | 508-432-9766 |
| 222 | Caribbean Baseball Confederation | 809-562-4737 | 809-565-4654 |
| 92 | CBS Radio | 212-975-4321 | 212-975-3515 |
| 255 | Central Illinois Collegiate League | 309-828-4429 | 309-828-4429 |
| 93 | Collegiate Baseball | 602-623-4530 | 602-624-5501 |
| 216 | Colorado Silver Bullets | 404-636-8200 | 404-636-0530 |
| 228 | CC League of California | 916-444-1600 | 916-444-2954 |

| | | | |
|---|---|---|---|
| 258 | Continental Amateur BB Assoc. | 614-882-1361 | 614-899-2103 |
| 258 | Dixie Baseball, Inc. | 615-821-6811 | — |
| 222 | Dominican League | 809-567-6371 | 809-567-5720 |
| 91 | Elias Sports Bureau | 212-869-1530 | 212-354-0980 |
| 92 | ESPN Radio | 203-585-2661 | 203-589-5523 |
| 91 | ESPN TV | 203-585-2000 | 203-585-2422 |
| 209 | Frontier League | 614-452-7400 | 614-452-2999 |
| 255 | Great Lakes League | 419-354-5556 | 419-352-3898 |
| 90 | Hall of Fame | 607-547-7200 | 607-547-2044 |
| 226 | Hawaii Winter Baseball | 808-592-2255 | 808-592-2260 |
| 91 | Howe Sportsdata International | 617-951-0070 | 617-737-9960 |
| 252 | International Baseball Assoc. | 41-21-311-1863 | 41-21-311-1864 |
| 93 | International Baseball Rundown | 708-668-8341 | 708-668-2148 |
| 219 | Japanese Baseball | 03-3502-0022 | 03-3502-0140 |
| 256 | Jayhawk League | 316-755-2361 | 316-755-1285 |
| 258 | Little League Baseball, Inc. | 717-326-1921 | 717-326-1074 |
| 13 | MLB International | 212-977-7301 | 212-977-7309 |
| 90 | MLB Players Alumni Association | 813-822-3399 | 813-822-6300 |
| 13 | MLB Player Relations Comm. | 212-339-7400 | 212-371-2242 |
| 89 | MLB Productions | 201-807-0888 | 201-807-0272 |
| 13 | MLB Properties | 212-339-7900 | 212-339-7628 |
| 89 | MLB Umpire Dev. Program | 813-823-1286 | 813-823-7212 |
| 89 | Major Leage Players Assoc. | 212-826-0808 | 212-752-3649 |
| 89 | Major League Scouting Bureau | 714-458-7600 | 714-458-9454 |
| 89 | Major League Umpires Assoc. | 215-979-3200 | — |
| 217 | Mexican League | 525-557-1007 | 525-395-2454 |
| 222 | Mexican Pacific League | 52-642-2-3100 | 52-642-2-7250 |
| 259 | National Amateur Baseball Fed. | 301-262-5005 | 301-262-5005 |
| 92 | National Assoc. of Baseball Writers and Broadcasters | 813-823-4050 | 813-821-5819 |
| 228 | NAIA | 918-494-8828 | 918-494-8841 |
| 252 | National Baseball Congress | 316-267-3372 | 316-267-3382 |
| 91 | NBC-TV | 212-664-4444 | 212-664-6365 |
| 228 | NCAA | 913-339-1906 | 913-339-0026 |
| 259 | Nat'l Assoc. of Police Ath. Leagues | 407-844-1823 | 407-863-6120 |
| 92 | Nat'l Collegiate BB Writers Assoc. | 904-375-4683 | 904-375-4809 |
| 251 | Nat'l Fed. of State HS Associations | 816-464-5400 | 816-464-5571 |
| 251 | Nat'l HS Baseball Coaches Assoc. | 402-457-1962 | 402-457-1962 |
| 228 | NJCAA | 719-590-9788 | 719-590-7324 |
| 45 | National League | 212-339-7700 | 212-935-5069 |
| 256 | New England Collegiate League | 203-238-4111 | 203-238-4111 |
| 211 | Northeast Baseball League | 914-683-5200 | 914-683-0484 |
| 256 | Northeastern Collegiate League | 607-648-5276 | 607-648-4668 |
| 211 | Northern League | 919-956-8150 | 919-683-2693 |
| 256 | Northwoods League | 813-644-4022 | — |
| 13 | Office of the Commissioner | 212-339-7800 | 212-355-0007 |
| 257 | Pacific International League | 206-678-6181 | 206-678-6181 |
| 259 | Pony Baseball, Inc. | 412-225-1060 | 412-225-9852 |
| 90 | Professional Baseball Employment Opportunities | 800-842-5618 | 704-668-4762 |
| 223 | Puerto Rican League | 809-765-6285 | 809-767-3028 |
| 259 | RBI | 212-339-7800 | — |
| 91 | SABR | 216-575-0500 | 216-575-0502 |
| 257 | San Diego Collegiate League | 619-438-0347 | — |
| 257 | Shenandoah Valley League | 703-886-1748 | 703-885-7612 |
| 93 | The Sporting News | 314-997-7111 | 314-993-7723 |
| 93 | Sports Illustrated | 212-522-1212 | 212-522-0610 |
| 92 | The Sports Network | 416-494-1212 | 416-490-7010 |
| 92 | SportsTicker | 201-309-1200 | 201-860-9742 |
| 93 | Spring Training Baseball Yearbook | 919-967-2420 | 919-967-6294 |
| 91 | STATS, Inc. | 708-676-3322 | 708-676-0821 |
| 93 | Street and Smith's Baseball | 212-880-8698 | 212-880-4347 |
| 251 | Team One National Showcase | 513-791-6070 | 513-793-8614 |
| 214 | Texas-Louisiana League | 214-991-3332 | 214-991-8887 |
| 259 | US Amateur Baseball Assoc. | 206-776-7130 | — |
| 252 | USA Baseball | 609-586-2381 | 609-587-1818 |
| 252 | US Olympic Committee | 719-632-5551 | 719-578-4654 |
| 93 | USA Today | 703-276-3762 | 703-558-3988 |
| 93 | USA Today Baseball Weekly | 703-558-5630 | 703-558-4678 |
| 224 | Venezuelan League | 582-751-2079 | 582-751-0891 |
| 215 | Western League | 503-221-1189 | 503-221-1902 |
| 92 | WGN TV | 312-528-2311 | — |
| 92 | WTBS TV | 404-827-1700 | 404-827-1593 |
| 92 | WWOR TV | 201-330-2246 | 201-330-3844 |